Paul Revere's midnight ride is a legendary American history—yet it has been largely ignored by scholars, and left to patriotic writers and debunkers. Now one of the foremost American historians offers the first serious study of this event—what led to it, what really happened, what followed—uncovering a truth more remarkable than the many myths it has inspired.

In *Paul Revere's Ride*, David Hackett Fischer has created an exciting narrative that offers new insight into the coming of the American Revolution. From research in British and American archives, the author unravels a plot that no novelist would dare invent—a true story of high drama and deep suspense, of old-fashioned heroes and unvarnished villains, of a beautiful American spy who betrayed her aristocratic British husband, of violent mobs and marching armies, of brave men dying on their doorsteps, of high courage, desperate fear, and the destiny of nations.

The narrative is constructed around two thematic lines. One story centers on the American patriot Paul Revere; the other, on British General Thomas Gage. Both were men of high principle who played larger roles than recent historiography has recognized. Thomas Gage was not the Tory tyrant of patriot legend, but an English Whig who believed in liberty and the rule of law. In 1774 and 1775, General Gage's advice shaped the fatal choices of British leaders, and his actions guided the course of American events. Paul Revere was more than a "simple artizan," as his most recent biographer described him fifty years ago. The author presents new evidence that revolutionary Boston was a world of many circles—more complex than we have known. Paul Revere and his friend Joseph Warren ranged more widely through those circles than any other leaders. They became the linchpins of the Whig movement.

On April 18th, 1775, Paul Revere played that role in a manner that has never been told before. He and William Dawes were not the only midnight riders to carry the Lexington alarm. This first careful study of that event finds evidence of more than sixty men and women who were abroad that night on the same mission. The more we learn about them, the more interesting Paul Revere's role becomes. More than any other figure, he organized that activity and set it in motion.

That night, Paul Revere had many other adventures. He was captured by a British patrol, and was freed in time to rescue Hancock and Adams (twice) and save the secret papers of the Revolution. At sunrise he was present on Lexington Green when the first shots were fired, in what General John Galvin describes as "one of the least known of all American battles." Drawing on extensive new research, Fischer finds evidence that this conflict was very different from the spontaneous rising of patriot legend. The New England militia were elaborately organized and actively led. On the morning of April

# Paul Revere's Ride

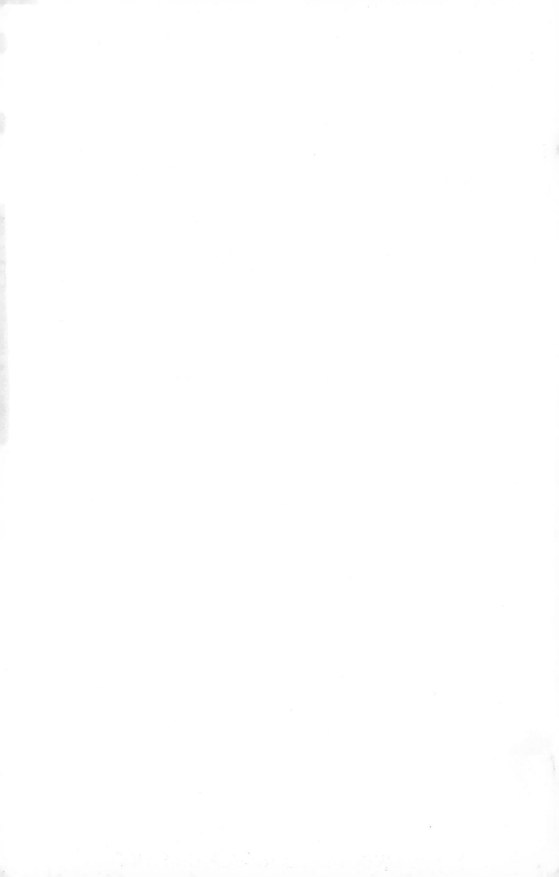

# PAUL REVERE'S RIDE

DAVID HACKETT FISCHER

New York   Oxford
OXFORD UNIVERSITY PRESS
1994

Oxford University Press

Oxford   New York   Toronto
Delhi   Bombay   Calcutta   Madras   Karachi
Kuala Lumpur   Singapore   Hong Kong   Tokyo
Nairobi   Dar es Salaam   Cape Town
Melbourne   Auckland   Madrid

and associated companies in
Berlin   Ibadan

Published by Oxford University Press, Inc.
200 Madison Avenue, New York, New York 10016

Oxford is a registered trademark of Oxford University Press

Library of Congress Cataloging-in-Publication Data
Fischer, David Hackett, 1935–
Paul Revere's Ride
David Hackett Fischer.
p.   cm.
Includes bibliographical references (p.) and index.
ISBN 0–19–508847–6
1. Revere, Paul, 1735–1818.
2. Massachusetts—History—Revolution, 1775–1783.
3. Lexington, Battle of, 1775.
4. Concord, Battle of, 1775.
I. Title.
F69.R43F57   1994
973.3'311'092—dc20   93–25739

4 6 8 9 7 5 3
Printed in the United States of America
on acid-free paper

*For Susie, with love*

# CONTENTS

# MAPS

# ILLUSTRATIONS

# INTRODUCTION

### ❧ Paul Revere Remounted

> Paul Revere?
> Ain't he the Yankee who had to go for help?"
> —old Texas joke

OUR BRITISH FRIENDS had never heard of him. "Paul Revere?" one asked incredulously, as we led him captive along Boston's Freedom Trail, "a midnight ride? . . . captured by *us?*"

Our visitor was a man of learning. We were as surprised by his ignorance, as he was by the story itself. In our mutual astonishment we discovered the enduring strength of national cultures in the modern world.

Nearly everyone who has been raised in the United States knows of Paul Revere. The saga of the midnight ride is one of many shared memories that make Americans one people, diverse as we may be. Even in these days of national amnesia the story of Paul Revere's ride is firmly embedded in American folklore. His name is so familiar that it has become a general noun in American speech. During the Presidential election of 1992, a Republican journalist ambiguously described a defeated Democratic candidate as "an economic Paul Revere." Whether that phrase was intended to mean a heroic messenger of alarm, or a messenger who failed to reach his destination, was not immediately clear.[1]

Ambiguity is an important part of the legend of Paul Revere, and a key to its continuing vitality. The story has been told so many different ways that when Americans repeat it to their children, they are not certain which parts of the tale are true, or if any part of it actually happened. They are also divided in how they feel about it. A curious paradox of American culture is the persistence of two parties who might be called the Filiopietists and Iconoclasts. Both have been strongly attracted to the legend of Paul Revere, for opposite reasons. Filiopietists love to celebrate the midnight ride. Iconoclasts delight in debunking it.

Together, these two parties have produced a large literature on an inexhaustible subject—poetry in abundance, fiction, oratory, essays, humor, criticism, and popular biography. One of the earliest films on American history was Thomas Edison's "Midnight Ride of Paul Revere" in 1914. American composers have given us several musical versions of the event—a march, a suite, and even an operetta. American artists have created many imaginative paintings and prints. American scientists have contributed monographs on the meteorology, astronomy, and geology of Paul Revere's ride. The most imaginative works are the many children's books the story has inspired. The most bizarre are the fables concocted by cynical Boston journalists every April 18, in their annual search for a new angle on an old story.

But one genre is strangely missing from this list. Professional historians have shown so little interest in the subject that in two centuries no scholar has published a full-scale history of Paul Revere's ride. During the 1970s, the event disappeared so completely from academic scholarship that several leading college textbooks in American history made no reference to it at all. One of them could barely bring itself to mention the battles of Lexington and Concord.[2]

The cause of this neglect is complex. One factor is a mutual antipathy that has long existed between professional history and popular memory. Another of more recent vintage is a broad prejudice in American universities against patriotic events of every kind, especially since the troubled years of Vietnam and Watergate. A third and fourth are the popular movements called multiculturalism and political correctness. As this volume goes to press, the only creature less fashionable in academe than the stereotypical "dead white male," is a dead white male on horseback.

Perhaps the most powerful factor, among professional historians at least, is an abiding hostility against what is contemptuously called *histoire événimentielle* in general. As long ago as 1925, the antiquarian scholar Allen French fairly complained that "modern history burrows so deeply into causes that it scarcely has room for events."[3] His judgment applies even more forcefully today. Path-breaking scholarship in the 20th century has dealt mainly with social structures, intellectual systems, and material processes. Much has been gained by this enlargement of the historian's task, but something important has been lost. An entire generation of academic historiography has tended to lose sense of the causal power of particular actions and contingent events.

An important key here is the idea of contingency—not in the sense of chance, but rather of "something that may or may not happen," as one dictionary defines it. An organizing assumption of this work is that contingency is central to any historical process, and vital to the success of our narrative strategies about the past.

This is not to raise again ill-framed counterfactual questions about what might have happened in the past. It is rather to study historical events as a series of real choices that living people actually made. Only by reconstructing that sort of contingency (in this very particular sense) can we hope to know "what it was like" to have been there; and only through that understanding can we create a narrative tension in the stories we tell about the past.[4]

To that end, this inquiry studies the coming of the American Revolution as a series of contingent happenings, shaped by the choices of individual actors within the context of large cultural processes. It centers on two actors in particular. One of them is Paul Revere. Historians have not placed him in the forefront of America's revolutionary movement. He held no high offices, wrote none of the great papers, joined few of the large deliberative assemblies, commanded no army, and did not advertise his acts. But in another way he was a figure of very high importance. The historical Paul Revere was much more than merely a midnight messenger. He was also an organizer of collective effort in the American Revolution. During the pivotal period from the Fall of 1774 to the Spring of 1775, he had an uncanny genius for being at the center of events. His actions made a difference, most of all in mobilizing the acts of many others. The old Texas canard that remembers Paul Revere as the "Yankee who had to go for help," when shorn of its pejoratives, is closer to the mark than the mythical image of the solitary rider. His genius was to promote collective action in the cause of freedom—a paradox that lies closer to the heart of the American experience than the legendary historical loners we love to celebrate.[5]

The other leading actor in this story is General Thomas Gage, commander in chief of British forces in America and the last Royal

Governor of Massachusetts. General Gage has rarely been remembered with sympathy or respect on either side of the water. He was not a great commander, to say the least. But he was a man of high principle and integrity who personified the British cause in both its strength and weakness. In the disasters that befell him, Thomas Gage was truly a tragic figure, a good and decent man who was undone by his virtues. During the critical years of 1774 and 1775, he also played a larger role than has been recognized by scholars of the American Revolution. It was his advice that shaped the fatal choices of leading British ministers, and his actions that guided the course of American events. Without Thomas Gage there might well have been no Coercive Acts, no midnight ride, and no fighting at Lexington and Concord.

One purpose of this book is to study that series of events as a sequence of choices by Paul Revere, General Gage and many other leaders. Another purpose is to look again at the cultures within which those choices were made. In that respect, Paul Revere's ride offers a special opportunity. It was part of a larger event, vividly remembered by people who were alive in 1775 as the Lexington Alarm.

Most readers of this book have lived through similar happenings in the 20th century. We tend to remember them with rare clarity. To take the most familiar example, many of us can recollect precisely what we were doing on the afternoon of November 22, 1963, when we learned that President John F. Kennedy had been shot. Many other events in American history have had that strange mnemonic power. This historian is just old enough to share the same sort of memory about an earlier afternoon, on December 7, 1941. More than fifty years afterward, I can still see the dappled sunlight of that warm December afternoon, and still feel the emotions, and hear the words, and recall even trivial details of the place where my family first heard the news of the Japanese attack upon Pearl Harbor.

It was much the same for Americans who heard the Lexington Alarm in 1775. They also would long remember how that news reached them, and what was happening around them. Many of their recollections were set down on paper immediately after the event. Others were recorded later, or passed down more doubtfully as grandfathers' tales. These accounts survive in larger numbers than for any other event in early American history. Taken together, they are a window into the world of Paul Revere and Thomas Gage.

When we look through that window, we may see many things. In particular we can observe the cultures that produced these men, and the values that framed their attitudes and acts. From a distance, the principles of Paul Revere and Thomas Gage appear similar to one another, and not very different from those we hold today. Some of the important words they used were superficially the same—words such as "liberty," "law," "justice," and what even General Gage himself celebrated as "the common rights of mankind."

But when we penetrate the meaning of those words, we discover that the values of Paul Revere and Thomas Gage were in fact very far apart, and profoundly different from our own beliefs. Paul Revere's idea of liberty was not the same as our modern conception of individual autonomy and personal entitlement. It was not a form of "classical Republicanism," or "English Opposition Ideology," or "Lockean Liberalism," or any of the learned anachronisms that scholars have invented to explain a way of thought that is alien to their own world.

Paul Revere's ideas of liberty were not primarily learned from books, or framed in terms of what he was against. He believed deeply in New England's inherited tradition of ordered freedom, which gave heavy weight to collective rights and individual responsibilities—more so than is given by our modern calculus of individual rights and collective responsibilities.[6]

In 1775, Paul Revere's New England notions of ordered freedom were challenged by another libertarian tradition that had recently developed in the English-speaking world—one that was personified in General Thomas Gage. Its conception of liberty was more elitist and hierarchical than those of Paul Revere, but also more open and tolerant, and no less deeply believed. The American Revolution arose from a collision of libertarian systems. The conflict between them led to a new birth of freedom that would be more open and expansive than either had been, or wished it to be. To explore the cultural dimensions of that struggle is another purpose of this book.

We shall begin by meeting our two protagonists, Paul Revere and Thomas Gage. Then we shall follow them through eight months from September 1, 1774, to April 19, 1775—the period of the powder alarms, the Concord mission, the midnight ride, the march of the Regulars, the muster of the Massachusetts farmers, the climactic battles of Lexington and Concord, and the bloody aftermath.

To reconstruct that sequence of happenings, the best and only instrument is narrative. Whatever one might think of Paul Revere's ride as myth and symbol, most people will agree it is a wonderful story. Edmund Morgan observes that the midnight ride is one of the rare historical events that respect the Aristotelian unities of time and place and action. For dramatic intensity few fictional contrivances can hope to match it.

This book seeks to tell that story. Its purpose is to return to the primary sources, to study what actually happened, to put Paul Revere on his horse again, to take the midnight ride seriously as an historical event, to suspend fashionable attitudes of disbelief toward an authentic American hero, and to move beyond the prevailing posture of contempt for a major British leader. Most of all, it is to study both Paul Revere and Thomas Gage with sympathy and genuine respect.

To do those things is to discover that we have much to learn from these half-remembered men—a set of truths that our generation has lost or forgotten. In their different ways, they knew that to be free is to choose. The history of a free people is a history of hard choices. In that respect, when Paul Revere alarmed the Massachusetts countryside, he was carrying a message for us.

Paul Revere's Ride

Paul Revere
A portrait by John Singleton Copley, circa 1770
(Museum of Fine Arts, Boston)

# PAUL REVERE'S AMERICA

∾ The Patriot Rider's Road to Revolution

> Town born! Turn out!
>
> —Boston street cry, 1770

I N OUR MIND'S EYE we tend to see Paul Revere at a distance, mounted on horseback, galloping through the dark of night. Often we see him in silhouette. His head is turned away from us, and his features are hidden beneath a large cocked hat. Sometimes even his body is lost in the billowing folds of an old fashioned riding coat. The image is familiar, but strangely indistinct.

Those who actually knew Paul Revere remembered him in a very different way, as a distinctive individual of strong character and vibrant personality. We might meet the man of their acquaintance in a portrait by his fellow townsman John Singleton Copley. The canvas introduces us to Paul Revere at about the age of thirty-five, *circa* 1770. The painter has caught him in an unbuttoned moment, sitting in his shirtsleeves, concentrating on his work. Scattered before him are the specialized tools of an 18th-century silversmith: two etching burins, a steel engraving needle, and a hammering pillow beneath his arm. With one hand he holds an unfinished silver teapot of elegant proportions. With the other he rubs his chin as he contemplates the completion of his work.

The portrait is the image of an artisan, but no ordinary artisan. His shirt is plain and simple, but it is handsomely cut from fine linen. His open vest is relaxed and practical, but it is tailored in bottle-green velvet and its buttons are solid gold. His work table is functional and unadorned, but its top is walnut or perhaps mahogany, and it is polished to a mirror finish. He is a mechanic in the 18th-century sense of a man who makes things with his hands, but no ordinary things. From raw lumps of metal he creates immortal works of art.

The man himself is of middling height, neither tall nor short. He is strong and stocky, with broad shoulders, a thick neck, muscular arms and powerful wrists. In his middle thirties, he is beginning to put on weight. The face is round and fleshy, but there is a sense of seriousness in his high forehead and strength in his prominent chin. His dark hair is neatly dressed in the austere, old-fashioned style that gave his English Puritan ancestors the name of Roundheads, but his features have a sensual air that calls to mind his French forebears. The eyes are deep chestnut brown, and their high-arched brows give the face a permanently quizzical expression. The gaze is clear and very direct. It is the searching look of an intelligent observer who sees much and misses little; the steady look of an independent man.

On its surface the painting creates an image of simplicity. But as we begin to study it, the surfaces turn into mirrors and what seems at first sight to be a simple likeness becomes a reflective composition of surprising complexity. The polished table picks up the image of the workman. The gleaming teapot mirrors the gifted fingers that made it. We look more closely, and discover that the silver bowl reflects a bright rectangular window that opens outward on the town of Boston. The artisan looks distantly toward that window and his community in a "reflective" mood, even as he himself is reflected in his work. As we stand before the painting, its glossy surface begins to reflect us as well. It throws back at us the lights and shadows of our own world.

To learn more about Paul Revere is to discover that the artist has brilliantly captured his subject in that complex web of reflections. This 18th-century Boston silversmith was very much a product of his time and place. For all of his Huguenot origins, Paul Revere was a New England Yankee to the very bottom of his Boston riding boots. If we can see him in Copley's painting, we can also hear him speak in the eccentric way he spelled his words. His spelling tells us that Paul Revere talked with a harsh, nasal New England twang. His strong Yankee accent derived from a family of East Anglian dialects that came to Boston in the 17th century, and can still be faintly heard today.

When Paul Revere's friends wrote in defense of their cherished charter rights, they spelled "charter" as *chattaer,* with two *t*'s and one *r*, and probably pronounced it with no *r* at all. All his life Paul Revere spelled "get" as *git*. His mother's maiden name of Hitchborn was written *Hitchbon* in the town of Boston, which was pronounced *Bast'n*. His friends wrote *mash* for "marsh" and *want* for "weren't," *hull* for "whole" and *foller* for "follow," *sarve* for "serve" and *acummin* for "coming." They favored biblical cadences such as *"we there abode"* and homely expressions such as *"something wet and misty."* This was the folk-speech of an Anglo-American culture that was already six generations old by 1775, and deeply rooted in Paul Revere's New England.[1]

But in another way, the provincial ring of Paul Revere's Yankee speech could mislead us. Just as in the surfaces and subtle depths of Copley's painting, there was more to this man than met the ear. His simple New England twang belied a remarkable complexity of character and culture—the complexity of the nation that he helped to create. Paul Revere was half French and half English, and always entirely American. He was second-generation American on one side, and old-stock American on the other, and cherished both beginnings. He was the product of a Puritan City on a Hill and a lusty, brawling Atlantic seaport, both in the same American town. He thought of himself as an artisan and a gentleman without the slightest sense of contradiction—a new American attitude toward class. He was a man on the make, consumed with personal ambition; and yet he was devoted to his community. He believed passionately in the rule of law, but he assaulted his own kinsman, and did not hesitate to take the law into his own hands. He helped to start a revolution, but his purpose was to resist change and to preserve the values of the past. He was Tocqueville's American archetype, the "venturous conservative," consumed with restless energy and much attracted to risk, but never questioning the great ideas in which he always believed. His ideas were a classic example of what Gunnar Myrdal has called the American creed: "conservative in fundamental principles . . . but the principles conserved are liberal, and some, indeed, are radical."

His temperament was as American as his ideas. Like many of his countrymen he was a moralist and also something of a hedonist—a man who sought the path of virtue but enjoyed the pleasures of the world. He suffered deeply from the slings of fortune, and yet he remained an incurable American optimist, even an optimistic fatalist. His complex identities were a source of happiness and fulfillment to him—not of frustration or despair.

Paul Revere was many things and one thing, quintessentially American.

The story of this American life begins 3000 miles away, on the small island of Guernsey in the English Channel. The year was 1715. Peace had recently returned to Europe after a long war, and the sea lanes were open again. On the isle of Guernsey, a small French lad named Apollos Rivoire, twelve years old, was taken by his uncle to the harbor of St. Peter Port. He was put aboard a ship, and sent alone to make his fortune in America.

Like so many immigrants who came before and after him, this child was a religious refugee. He was from a family of French Huguenots, and had been born in the parish of Sainte-Foy-la-Grande, thirty-eight miles east of Bordeaux in the valley of the Gironde. That region had been a hotbed of French Calvinism until the cruel Catholic persecutions of Louis XIV. Some of the Calvinist Rivoire family were forcibly converted to the Roman Church. Others fled abroad—among them young Apollos Rivoire, who was sent to his uncle Simon Rivoire in Guernsey, and later bound as an apprentice to an elderly silversmith in Calvinist New England, where many Huguenots were finding sanctuary.[2]

Apollos Rivoire sailed to Boston on November 15, 1715, six days before his thirteenth birthday. He entered the shop of a gifted Yankee artisan, and showed a rare talent in his craft. As more of his work has come to light, experts have studied it with growing respect. A small token of his skill is a set of tiny sleeve buttons that survives today in an American museum. Their delicate tactile beauty has a grace and refinement and sensuality that set them apart from the often austere art of Puritan New England. They are among the finest gold work that was done in British America.[3]

In 1722, his master died. Apollos Rivoire bought his freedom from the estate for forty pounds, and set himself up as a goldsmith in Boston. It was not easy to get started. At least three times he was in court for debts he could not pay.[4] Another problem was his name, which did not roll easily off Yankee tongues. After it was mangled into Reviere, Reveire, Reverie, and even Rwoire, the young immigrant changed it to Revere, "merely on account that the bumpkins pronounce it easier," his son later explained. Paul Revere was a self-made name for a self-made man, in the bright new world of British America.[5]

Like many another French Huguenot, this young immigrant

These artifacts testify to the extraordinary skill and creativity of Apollos Rivoire, the father and teacher of Paul Revere. The small sleeve buttons (made circa 1730) are among the finest surviving gold work ever done in British America. Their delicate floral pattern and swirling leaf border are common design motifs of the period, but their deceptively simple shape and proportions are very distinctive, and exceptionally difficult to manufacture. The various elements are brought together in a design that combines vitality and symmetry with high success. In the same manner, the silver tankard above (made by Apollos Rivoire circa 1750) develops the conventional designs of English craftsmanship with a distinctive flair that was unique to its gifted maker. The result is an extraordinary synthesis of refinement and strength. (Courtesy of the Yale University Art Gallery and the Henry Francis Dupont Winterthur Museum).

moved freely among New England Puritans who shared his Calvinist faith. But the two cultures were not the same, as Apollos
Rivoire discovered when the first Christmas came. French Huguenots celebrated the joy of Christ's birth with a sensuous feast
that shocked the conscience of New England. Puritans sternly forbade Christmas revels, which they regarded as pagan indulgence,
and proscribed even the word Christmas because they believed
that every day belonged to Christ. In 1699, Boston magistrate
Samuel Sewall reprimanded a townsman for "partaking with the
French Church on the 25 [of] December on account of its being
Christmas-day, as they abusively call it."[6]

Despite these differences, or perhaps because of them,
Huguenots and Puritans intermarried at a rapid rate. Of all
French weddings in Boston before 1750, no fewer than 88 percent
were to an English spouse. One of these mixed marriages was that
of Apollos Rivoire. In 1729 he married a Yankee girl named Deborah Hitchborn and became part of her large family, which supplied the other side of Paul Revere's inheritance.[7]

The history of the Boston Hitchborns is a classic American
saga. The founder was Deborah's great-grandfather, David Hitchborn, who came to New England from old Boston in Lincolnshire
during the Puritan Great Migration. He appears to have been a
servant of humble rank and restless disposition. For some unknown offence, a stern Puritan magistrate sentenced him to wear
an iron collar "till the court please, and serve his master."[8]

The second generation of Hitchborns left servitude behind
and became their own masters—still very poor, but proud and
independent. The third generation were people of modest property and standing; among them was Thomas Hitchborn, proprietor of Hitchborn wharf and owner of a lucrative liquor license
that allowed him to sell Yankee rum to seamen and artisans on the
waterfront. The fourth generation were solid and respectable Boston burghers; they included Thomas Hitchborn's daughter Deborah (1704–77), a godfearing Yankee girl who married the gifted
Huguenot goldsmith Apollos Rivoire, owned the Puritan Covenant in Boston's New Brick Church, and raised her children in the
old New England way. The fifth generation began with her eldest
surviving son, the patriot Paul Revere, who was baptized in Boston
on December 22, 1734.[9]

Paul Revere grew up among the Hitchborn family—he had
no other in America. His playmates were his nine Hitchborn
cousins. When the time came to baptize his own children, all were

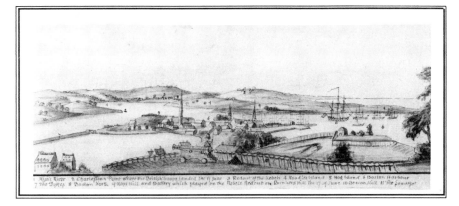

Boston in 1775
A view of the North End from Beacon Hill. The large warship in the harbor is
HMS *Somerset,* and the highest steeple is the Old North Church. Ink and water-
color drawing. (Library of Congress)

given Hitchborn family names except the patronymic Paul. He
never learned to speak his father's language. In 1786 he wrote, "I
can neither read nor write French, so as to take the proper meaning." But he cherished the emblems of his French heritage—a
silver seal from the old country, a few precious papers, and the
stories that his father told him. In a mysterious way, something of
the spirit of France entered deep into his soul—a delight in pleasures of the senses, an ebullient passion for life, an *elan* in the way
he lived it, and an indefinable air that set him apart from his
Yankee neighbors.[10]

At the same time, he became a Yankee too. His mind and
character were shaped by the established institutions of New
England—family, school, church, and the town itself. Probably he
learned his letters in a kitchen school where ancient Puritan dames
kept order with their pudding sticks, and little Yankee children
learned to recite the alphabet as if it were a prayer. At about the
age of seven, he was sent to Boston's North Writing School, famous for its stern Calvinist pedagogues who specialized in purging
the old Adam from obstreperous youth. Their methods were
harsh, but highly effective. Paul Revere gained a discipline of
thought without losing his curiosity about the world. His teachers
made him a lifelong learner; all his life it was said that he "loved his
books."[11]

In a larger sense, the town of Boston became his school, and
the waterfront served as his playground. An engraving he later

made of Boston's North Battery shows three boys splashing in the
harbor near his childhood home. One of them might have been
young Paul Revere.[12] The Boston of his youth was very different
from the city that stands on the same spot today—closer in some
ways to a medieval village than to the modern metropolis of steel
and glass. In 1735, Boston was a tight little town of 15,000 inhabitants, crowded onto a narrow hill-covered peninsula that sometimes became an island at high tide. From a distance the skyline of
the town was dominated by its steeples. Boston had fourteen
churches in 1735, all but three of them Calvinist. Despite complaints of spiritual declension by the town's Congregational ministers, the founding vision of St. Matthew's "City on a Hill" was still
strong a century after its founding. Such was the rigor and austerity of this Puritan community that Samuel Adams called it a
"Christian Sparta."[13]

The town was not welcoming to strangers. From the mainland
it could be entered only through a narrow gate across the slender
isthmus called Boston Neck, or by ferry from Charlestown. On
Boston Neck the first structure that greeted a traveler was a large
and well-used gallows. In Charlestown, the road to the ferry led
past a rusted iron cage that held the rotting bones of Mark, an
African slave who had poisoned his master. The slave's accomplice
had been burned at the stake.

But there was also another side of Boston. This City on a Hill
was a busy seaport. No part of the town was more than a few blocks
from salt water. The housefronts echoed to the cry of oystermen
with bags of bivalves on their shoulders, shouting "Oise, buy-ni-
oise: here's oise!" Lobstermen pushed their barrows, "always
painted red within and blue without," calling "Lob, buy Lob!" as
they went along the streets.[14] On the waterfront the boys of Boston darted to and fro beneath bowsprits and mooring lines, while
fishermen unloaded their catch and artisans toiled at their maritime trades. Seamen in short jackets strolled from one tavern to
the next, and prostitutes beckoned from alleys and doorways. "No
town of its size could turn out more whores than this town could,"
one 18th-century visitor marveled. All this was part of the education of Paul Revere.[15]

Inside Boston's North End where Paul Revere lived most of
his life, visitors found themselves in a maze of crooked streets and
close-built brick and wooden houses, with weather-blackened clapboards and heavy forbidding doors. The inhabitants were closely
related by blood and marriage, intensely suspicious of strangers,

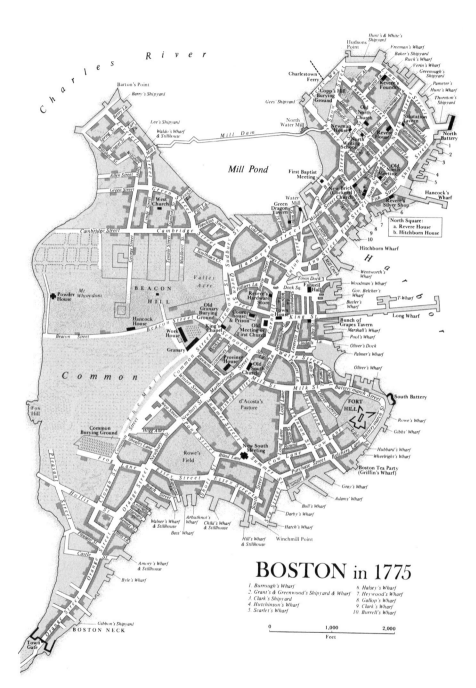

# BOSTON in 1775

1. Burrough's Wharf
2. Grant's & Greenwood's Shipyard & Wharf
3. Clark's Shipyard
4. Hutchinson's Wharf
5. Scarlet's Wharf
6. Halsey's Wharf
7. Heywood's Wharf
8. Gallop's Wharf
9. Clark's Wharf
10. Burrell's Wharf

0    1,000    2,000
Feet

Charles River

Barton's Point
Barry's Shipyard
Lee's Shipyard
Waldo's Wharf & Stillhouse
Mill Dam

Mill Pond

Charlestown Ferry
Hudsons Point
Hunt's & White's Shipyard
Freeman's Wharf
Baker's Shipyard
Ruck's Wharf
Verin's Wharf
Greenough's Shipyard
Pameter's
Hunt's Wharf
Thornton's Shipyard

Gees' Shipyard
North Water Mill

Copp's Hill Burying Ground
Revere's Foundry
Old North Church
Newman House
North Writing School
Salutation Tavern
North Battery

First Baptist Meeting
Water Mill
Green Dragon Tavern
New Brick (Cockerel) Church
Old North Meeting
Revere's Silver Shop

North Square:
a. Revere House
b. Hitchborn House

Hancock's Wharf

Hitchborn Wharf

West Church
Barry La.
Spring St.
Allen Street
Green Street

Cambridge Street

George Street
BEACON HILL
Mt Whoredom
Powder House
Hancock House
Work House
Granary

Beacon Street

Common

Fox Hill

Common Burying Ground

Valley Acre

Old Granary Burying Ground
Court house & Prison
King's Chapel
Old Meeting or First Church

Province House
Old South Church

d'Acosta's Pasture

Revere's Hardware Store

Town Dock
Dock Sq.
Faneuil

Wentworth's Wharf
Woodman's Wharf
Gov. Belcher's Wharf
Butler's Wharf

T-Wharf

Long Wharf

King St.

Bunch of Grapes Tavern
Marshall's Wharf
Pool's Wharf
Oliver's Dock
Palmer's Wharf

Oliver's Wharf

FORT HILL
South Battery

Rowe's Wharf
Gibbs' Wharf

Hubbard's Wharf
Wheelright's Wharf

Boston Tea Party (Griffin's Wharf)

New South Meeting

Rowe's Field

Gray's Wharf

Adams' Wharf

Bull's Wharf
Darby's Wharf
Hatch's Wharf

Walner's Wharf & Stillhouse
Arbuthnot's Wharf
Child's Wharf & Stillhouse
Bass' Wharf

Hill's Wharf & Stillhouse
Winchmill Point

Amory's Wharf & Stillhouse
Byle's Wharf

Gibbon's Shipyard
BOSTON NECK
Town Gate

Harbor

and firmly set in their ancestral ways. In time of danger, an ancient cry would ring through the streets: "Town born! Turn out!"[16]

Even as a child, Paul Revere entered into Boston habits. Near his house was a handsome brick church, variously called Christ Church, North Church, or the Eight Bell Church, after its carillon of English bells. One bell was inscribed "We are the first ring of bells cast for the British Empire in North America AR Ano 1744."[17] The great bells fascinated the boys of the North End. In their early teens, Paul Revere and his friends founded a bell ringers' association. They sent a petition to the Rector, proposing that "if we can have liberty from the wardens of Dr. Cuttler's church, we will attend there once a week on evenings to ring the bells for two hours."

That document tells us many things about Paul Revere and his road to revolution. These boys of Boston drew up a solemn covenant, and instituted a government among themselves very much like Boston's town meeting. They agreed that "we will choose a moderator every three months whose business shall be to give out the changes and other business as shall be agreed by a majority of votes then present . . . all differences to be decided by a majority of voices." Membership was restricted as narrowly as in a New England church or town. The boys decided that "none shall be admitted a Member of this society without a unanimous vote." They also covenanted not to demean themselves by Roman Catholic corruptions, and promised to work for their rewards: "No member," they voted, "shall begg money of any person."[18]

This simple document, drawn up by Boston boys barely in their teens, summarizes many of the founding principles of New England: the sacred covenant and the rule of law, self-government and majority vote, fundamental rights and free association, private responsibility and public duty, the gospel of service and the ethic of work, and a powerful idea of community.

Another of those principles was the doctrine of the calling. Paul Revere was taught that every Christian had two callings—a special calling to work in one's vocation, and a general calling to do Christ's work in the world. The great Boston divine Cotton Mather explained this idea in a homely metaphor that would have been instantly clear to any boy who lived near Boston's waterfront. Getting to Heaven, said Cotton Mather, was like rowing a boat with two oars: pull on one oar alone, and the boat will spin in circles.

All his life, Paul Revere pulled on both oars. He became an apprentice to his father and mastered the special calling of "gold-

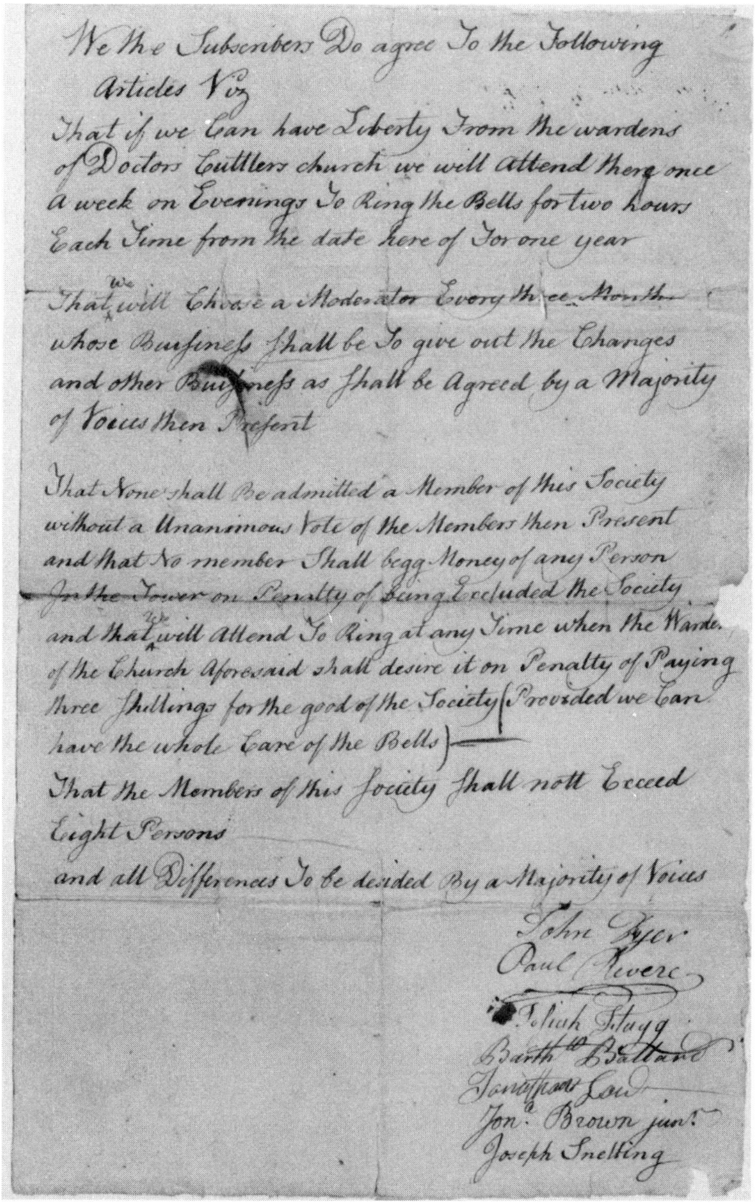

We the Subscribers Do agree To the following
Articles Viz

That if we Can have Liberty From the wardens
of Doctors Cuttlers church we will attend there once
a week on Evenings To Ring the Bells for two hours
Each Time from the date here of For one year

That we will Chuse a Moderator Every three Months
whose Business Shall be To give out the Changes
and other Business as Shall be Agreed by a Majority
of Voices then Present

That None shall Be admitted a Member of this Society
without a Unanimous Vote of the Members then Present
and that No member Shall begg Money of any Person
In the Tower on Penalty of being Excluded the Society
and that we will Attend To Ring at any Time when the Wardens
of the Church Aforesaid shall desire it on Penalty of Paying
three Shillings for the good of the Society (Provided we Can
have the whole Care of the Bells)———

That the Members of this Society Shall nott Exceed
Eight Persons

and all Differences To be decided By a Majority of Voices

John Dyer
Paul Revere
Josiah Flagg
Barth'd Ballard
Jonathan Law
Jon'a Brown jun'r
Joseph Snelling

Bell Ringers' Agreement, circa 1750
This covenant was signed by seven boys of Boston, including Paul Revere at about
the age of fifteen. It is in the possession of the Old North Church.

smith," working sometimes in that precious metal, but more often in silver, and later in copper and brass as well. When his father died in 1754, Paul Revere took over the business at the age of nineteen and became the main support of his family.[19] He worked hard, survived difficult times, and gradually became affluent, though never rich. He was known in town as a man who knew the value of money. Even his most intimate relationships were cast in terms of cash accounts. He looked faithfully after his widowed mother, but charged her room and board in his own home. This was the custom in Boston, where everyone was expected to pay his way.[20]

Paul Revere applied his artisan's skills to many profitable tasks. He made frames for miniature portraits by John Singleton Copley. He studied the difficult art of copper-plate engraving, and did many illustrations for Boston printers. As a sideline he learned a method of "setting false teeth," and advertised that "persons so unfortunate as to lose their Fore-Teeth by Accident, and other-ways, to their great detriment not only in looks but speaking may have them replaced with artificial ones . . . by PAUL REVERE Goldsmith."[21]

But his major employment before the Revolution was as a silversmith. Much of his business in this thrifty Yankee town consisted of mending and repair work. In 1763, he billed Peter Jenkins for "making a fellow to your buckle." His account books were filled with similar charges for "mending bruises" or patching holes in silver vessels.[22] Many of Boston's leading Whigs were his customers. He sold a freemason's medal to James Graham; a new brandy cock to Sam Adams who had worn out his old one; and a bosom pin to the beautiful Mrs. Perez Morton, whose portrait by Gilbert Stuart is one of the glories of American art.[23] At the same time, he also supplied the extravagant tastes of the new Imperial elite. In 1764, he charged Andrew Oliver, Junior, son of Boston's much hated Imperial Stamp Officer, for "making a sugar dish out of an Ostrich egg."[24]

Paul Revere also made small items of gold, but most of all he was known for his silver. The products of his shop are interesting in many ways, not least for what they reveal about the personality of their maker. His best work was executed to a high standard— the more difficult the piece, the greater the skill that it displayed. But the silver that came from Paul Revere's shop also showed a highly distinctive pattern of minor flaws. Experts observe that his silver-soldering was not good, his interior finish was sometimes slovenly, and his engraving was often slightly off-center. Paul Revere was never at his best in matters of routine, and tended to become more than a little careless in tedious and boring operations. But he had a brilliant eye for form, a genius for invention, and a restless energy that expressed itself in the animation of his work. Two centuries later, his pieces are cherished equally for the touchmark of their maker and the vitality of his art.[25]

At the same time that Paul Revere worked at his special vocation, he also served his general calling as a Christian and churchgoer, citizen and townsman, husband and father. In August 1757 he married his first wife, Sarah Orne. Little is known about this union. The first baby arrived eight months after the wedding—a common occurrence in mid-18th-century New England, where as many as one-third of the brides in Yankee towns were pregnant on their wedding day. Eight children were born in swift succession.[26] Sarah died in 1773, worn out by her many deliveries. Paul Revere buried her in Boston's bleak Old Granary Burying Ground beneath a grim old-fashioned Puritan grave marker with a hideous death's head and crossbones, which were meant to remind survivors of their own mortality.[27]

Five months later Paul Revere married Rachel Walker, a lively young woman of good family, eleven years his junior. According to family tradition they met in the street near his shop. It was a love match. Paul Revere wrote poetry to his wife—"the fair one who is closest to my heart." A draft of one love poem survives incongruously on the back of a bill for "mending a spoon." Rachel returned his affection. She was a woman of strength and sunny disposition, deeply religious and devoted to her growing family. Eight more children were born of this union, which by all accounts was happy and complete.[28]

But in another way this family was deeply troubled. The dark shadow of death loomed constantly over it. Of Paul Revere's eleven brothers and sisters, five died in childhood and two as young adults. Among his sixteen children, five were buried as infants and five more in early adulthood. He was only nineteen when his father died, and forty-two when he lost his mother. Many of these deaths came suddenly, with shattering force. The children died mostly of "fevers" that struck without warning. Whenever his babies took sick, Paul Revere was overcome by an agony of fear for his "little lambs," as he called them. Their numbers did not diminish the depth of his anxiety. Even his ebullient spirits were utterly crushed and broken by their death.[29]

In Paul Revere's time, many people suffered in the same way. Their repeated losses gave rise to a fatalism that is entirely foreign to our thoughts. Rachel once wrote to her husband, "Pray keep up your spirits and trust yourself and us in the hands of a good God who will take care of us. Tis all my dependence, for vain is the help of man."[30]

Most people were fatalists in that era, but their fatalism took different forms. The Calvinist creed of New England taught that the "natural man" was impotent in the world, but with God's Grace he became the instrument of irresistible will and omnipotent force. This paradox of instrumental fatalism was a powerful source of energy and purpose in New England. It also became a spiritual force of profound importance in Paul Revere's career.[31]

On the Puritan Sabbath, he went faithfully to church. All his life Paul Revere belonged to Boston's New Brick Church, often called the "Cockerel" after the plumed bird that adorned its steeple vane. His children were baptized there, as he himself had been. It was said that he attended church "as regularly as the Sabbath came."[32]

On weekdays he served his community. Like Benjamin Franklin, another Boston-born descendant of Puritan artisans, Paul Revere became highly skilled at the practical art of getting things done. When Boston imported its first streetlights in 1774, Paul Revere was asked to serve on the committee that made the arrangements. When the Boston market required regulation, Paul Revere was appointed its clerk. After the Revolution, in a time of epidemics he was chosen health officer of Boston, and coroner of Suffolk County. When a major fire ravaged the old wooden town, he helped to found the Massachusetts Mutual Fire Insurance Company, and his name was the first to appear on its charter of incorporation. As poverty became a growing problem in the new republic, he called the meeting that organized the Massachusetts Charitable Mechanic Association, and was elected its first president. When the community of Boston was shattered by the most sensational murder trial of his generation, Paul Revere was chosen foreman of the jury.[33]

With all of these activities he gained a rank that is not easily translated into the conventional language of social stratification. Several of his modern biographers have misunderstood him as a "simple artizan," which certainly he was not.[34] Paul Revere formed a class identity of high complexity—a new American attitude that did not fit easily into European categories. All his life Paul Revere

The immigrant Apollos Rivoire changed his name, but kept his French identity, and engraved an elegant coat of arms on his bookplate. His American son Paul Revere thought of himself as both an artisan and a gentleman, and laughed even at his own pretensions—a new American attitude toward class. With self-deprecating humor, he modified the family arms on his bookplate to include a jolly British lion, a jaunty Gallic cock, and the militant American motto, *Pugna pro Patria.* Both bookplates are in the American Antiquarian Society.

associated actively with other artisans and mechanics and was happy to be one of them. When he had his portrait painted by Copley he appeared in the dress of a successful artisan.[35] At the same time he also considered himself a gentleman, and laid claim to an old French coat of arms that was proudly engraved on his bookplates. This was not merely a self-conceit. A commission from the governor in 1756 addressed him as "Paul Revere, Gentleman." In 1774, Boston's town meeting also recognized him in the same way. On his midnight ride he dressed as a gentleman, and even his British captors ceremoniously saluted him as one of their own rank, before threatening to blow out his brains. One officer pointed his pistol and said in the manner of one gentleman to another, "May I crave your name, sir?"[36]

Paul Revere's idea of a gentleman was distinctively American, and very different from its European usage. Once he defined a gentleman as a man who "respects his own credit." Later in life, when dealing with the trustees of an academy who had failed to pay for one of his bells, Paul Revere wrote scathingly, "Are any of the Trustees Gentlemen, or are they persons who care nothing for

In 1773 Paul Revere married Rachel Walker, his second wife. He wrote her love poems on the back of his shop accounts, and in 1784–85 had this miniature painted on ivory, probably by Joseph Dunkerly. It is set in a handsome gold frame that her husband probably made himself. Paul Revere had sixteen children (eight by Rachel) and at least 52 grandchildren. (Museum of Fine Arts, Boston)

This house stood on Boston's North Square nearly a century before Paul Revere bought it in 1770. He lived here until 1780, later moving to a three-story brick mansion at Charter and Hanover streets. In the summer, the Revere family kept a country cottage at Cantondale. But always he will be associated mainly with the house where he was living in 1775. This early postcard captures the busy street life of Boston's North End from Paul Revere's era to our own time. (Paul Revere Memorial Association)

character?"[37] The status of a gentleman for Paul Revere was a social rank and a moral condition that could be attained by self-respecting men in any occupation. European writers understood the idea of a "bourgeois gentilhomme" as a contradiction in terms, but in the new world of British America these two ranks comfortably coexisted, and Paul Revere was one of the first to personify their union. In his own mind he was an artisan, a businessman, and a gentleman altogether.[38]

He was also an associating sort of man. When he died, a newspaper reported that his body was followed to the grave by "troops of friends." In Boston he had many boon companions. He kept a small boat on the waterfront and a riding horse in his own barn next to his house in Boston, and he liked to fish and shoot, and ride for recreation across the Massachusetts countryside. He knew the inside of many taverns in the town, and enjoyed a game of cards or backgammon, and signed a petition to permit a playhouse in a town that had banned actors for two centuries.[39]

Among his many friends, Paul Revere was known for candor and directness, even to a fault. He was in the habit of speaking his mind; and when words failed him, sometimes he used his fists. In 1761, at the age of thirty-six, he came to blows with Thomas Fosdick, a hatter who had married one of Paul Revere's many Hitchborn cousins. Nobody remembers what the quarrel was about. Something that Thomas Fosdick said or did so infuriated Paul Revere that he attacked his kinsman.

New England did not tolerate that sort of violence. Paul Revere was hauled into Boston's Court of Common Pleas, where a stern New England judge found him guilty of "assaulting and beating" his kinsman, ordered him to pay a fine, and made him give bond for his good behavior. But the fine was only six shillings, eight pence; and one of Paul Revere's bondsmen was the brother of the victim. Whatever the facts, both the judge and at least one member of the Fosdick family appear to have felt that Thomas Fosdick got what he deserved. The incident did not lower Paul Revere's standing in the town.[40]

He was a gregarious man, always a great joiner. In 1755 he joined the militia as a lieutenant of artillery, and served in an expedition against Crown Point during the French and Indian War.[41] After he returned in 1760, he became an active Mason, and in 1770 was elected master of his lodge. Freemasonry was deeply important to Paul Revere. All his life he kept its creed of enlightened Christianity, fraternity, harmony, reason, and community service. Often he was to be found at the Green Dragon Tavern, one of the grandest hostelries in Boston, which his lodge bought for its Masonic Hall.[42]

Another of his haunts was a tavern called the Salutation, after its signboard that showed two gentlemen deferring elaborately to one another. Here Paul Revere was invited to join the North Caucus Club, a political organization—one of three in Boston, founded by Sam Adams's father as a way of controlling the politics of the town. The North Caucus was a gathering of artisans and ship's captains who exchanged delegates with the other Caucuses and settled on slates of candidates before town meetings.[43]

Paul Revere was also invited to join the Long Room Club, which met above a printing shop in Dassett Alley, where Benjamin Edes and John Gill published the *Boston Gazette*. This secret society was an inner sanctum of the Whig movement in Boston—smaller and more select than the North Caucus. Its seventeen members included the most eminent of Boston's leading Whigs. Most had been to Harvard College. Nearly all were lawyers, physicians, ministers, magistrates, and men of independent means. Paul Revere was the only "mechanic."[44] The printing shop of Benjamin Edes below the Long Room Club became a favorite meeting place for Boston Whigs. In the Fall of 1772, John Adams happened by Edes's office. Inside he found James Otis, "his eyes, fishy and fiery and acting wildly as ever he did." Standing beside him was Paul Revere.[45]

Another political rendezvous was a tavern called Cromwell's Head, whose owner Joshua Brackett was a friend and associate of Paul Revere. Its signboard, which was meant to symbolize the Puritan origins of Boston Whiggery, hung so low over the door that everyone who entered was compelled to bow before the Old Protector. Paul Revere was one of the few men who was comfortable in all of these places. Each of them became an important part of Boston's revolutionary movement.[46]

In 1765, the town of Boston was not flourishing. Its population had scarcely increased in fifty years. Business conditions were poor. Many artisans and merchants fell into debt during this difficult period, including Paul Revere himself, who was temporarily short of cash. In 1765, an attempt was made to attach his property for a debt of ten pounds. He managed to settle out of court, and was lucky to stay afloat in a world depression.

This was the moment when Britain's Parliament, itself hard pressed, unwisely decided to levy taxes on its colonies. America

The Sons of Liberty or Rescinders' Bowl was made by Paul Revere for the subscribers whose names appear around the rim. It commemorated the ninety-two Massachusetts legislators who defied the King's command to rescind a Circular Letter that summoned all the colonies to resist the Townshend Acts. The bowl is embellished with liberty poles, liberty caps, Magna Carta, the English Bill of Rights, and John Wilkes' polemic, No. 45 North Briton. The inscription condemns "the insolent Menaces of Villains in Power." (Museum of Fine Arts, Boston)

instantly resisted, and in the summer of 1765 Paul Revere joined a new association that called itself the Sons of Liberty. In the manner of Freemasonry, its members exchanged cryptic signs and passwords, and wore special insignia that might have been made by Paul Revere—a silver medal with a Liberty Tree and the words "Sons of Liberty" engraved on its face.[47]

The Sons of Liberty took a leading part in Boston's campaign against the Stamp Act. When Parliament at last repealed the hated tax, Paul Revere helped to organize a public celebration on Boston Common. He engraved a design for a large paper obelisk, illuminated by 280 lamps and covered with symbols of liberty and defiance.[48]

That moment of triumph was short-lived. In 1767, desperate British ministers tried again to tax America, in a new set of measures called the Townshend Acts. The legislature of Massachusetts responded with a Circular Letter to its sister colonies, urging all to resist as one. British leaders were so outraged that the King himself ordered the Massachusetts Circular Letter to be rescinded. The legislature refused by a vote of 92 to 17. Paul Revere was commissioned by the Sons of Liberty to make a silver punch bowl commemorating the "Glorious 92." The "Rescinders' Bowl" became a cherished icon of the American freedom.[49]

While the Massachusetts legislature acted and resolved against the Townshend duties, Paul Revere organized resistance in another way. The taxes were to be enforced by new customs officers. Many were corrupt and rapacious placemen. When these hated men appeared in Boston, the Sons of Liberty turned out on moonless nights with blackened faces and white nightcaps pulled low around their heads. More than a few customs commissioners fled for their lives. On one occasion a Boston merchant noted in his diary, "Two commissioners were very much abused yesterday when they came out from the Publick dinner at Concert Hall. . . . Paul Revere and several others were the principal Actors."[50]

The British government answered Boston's defiance with a massive show of force. On September 30, 1768, a British fleet sailed into Boston harbor, and anchored in a great ring around the waterfront, their decks cleared for action and cannon trained on the town. Paul Revere watched with mounting anger as two regiments of Regulars landed on Long Wharf with weapons loaded, and marched into the heart of his community. Afterward he went back to his shop, got out a sheet of copper, and made an engraving of that "insolent parade," as he called it.[51]

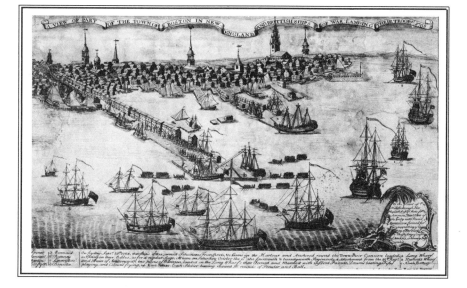

Immediately after the Boston Massacre in 1770, Paul Revere reissued this print of an event that had happened two years before. It represents the landing of the Regulars with loaded weapons, while ships of the Royal Navy trained their guns on the town. He wished to portray a tyrannical government in the act making war upon its own people. The town of Boston, with its many exaggerated steeples and wharves is meant to appear pious, industrious and entirely innocent. (American Antiquarian Society)

The coming of the Regulars increased the violence in Boston. The soldiers were sometimes the aggressors, but more often they were the victims of assaults by angry townsmen. Finally on the cold winter night of March 5, 1770, the soldiers fired back at their tormentors. Six people were killed. The ancestral cry of "Town born! Turn out!" echoed once again through narrow streets, and Boston came close to revolution.[52] Paul Revere did another engraving of a drawing by Henry Pelham titled "Fruits of Arbitrary Power, or The Bloody Massacre Perpetrated in King Street." The print helped to create an image of British tyranny and American innocence that still shapes our memory of the event.[53]

Revere and his fellow Whigs did not hesitate to use violence to promote their ends, but they did so in a very careful way. The Boston Massacre threatened to alienate moderates from their cause. Instantly they took counter measures. They made certain that the British soldiers received a fair trial and Paul Revere helped to supply the evidence. In 1771 they prudently organized a movement in town meeting to build a more secure powder magazine

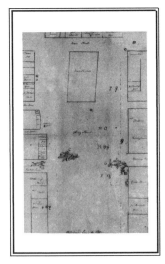

The best known of Paul Revere's engravings was his print of the Boston Massacre (1770). Like most of his projects, many people had a hand in it. The drawing was by Henry Pelham (who was not happy that Revere beat him to the market). It was printed by Benjamin Edes, colored by Christian Remick, and widely copied in America and Europe. Of the many impressions that survive, half are in original frames that were also made by Paul Revere. (American Antiquarian Society)

For the trials that followed, he drew another pen-and-ink diagram of the Massacre, showing more accurately than the print the positions of the soldiers and the townspeople who were killed. (Boston Public Library)

away from the docks and in a safer part of town. The petition was signed by John Hancock, Sam Adams, and Paul Revere.[54]

The Boston Massacre was accompanied by other acts of violence which the Whig leaders channeled toward their own ends. Paul Revere was increasingly prominent in this effort. In 1770 a frightened customs officer fired into a mob that had gathered before his house, and killed a boy named Christopher Seider.[55] The town made the child into a martyr. On the anniversary of his death a huge crowd gathered in a silent demonstration. The chosen place was the home of Paul Revere, which was specially illuminated for the occasion. Every window in his house showed a brightly lighted scene—on one side the Boston Massacre; on the other, the ghost of the murdered boy; in the center an allegorical female figure of America with a liberty cap on her head, grinding a British grenadier beneath her heel. The *Boston Gazette* reported, "In the evening, there was a very striking exhibition at the dwelling house of Mr. Paul Revere, fronting old North Square . . . the spectators, which amounted to many thousands, were struck with solemn silence and their faces covered with melancholy gloom."[56]

After the Boston Massacre, Parliament retreated yet again. The Regulars were withdrawn from Boston, and the Townshend duties were repealed, except for a symbolic tax on tea so small that British ministers believed even Boston might be willing to swallow it. It was a fatal miscalculation. When the tea ships reached America in 1773, the response was an explosion of anger throughout the colonies. Boston was not the first American town to refuse the tea, or the most violent, but it acted with its usual panache. Paul Revere and his mechanics staged a brilliant piece of political theater. They covered their faces with lamp black and red ochre, dressed themselves as Indians (the symbol of American freedom in the 18th century), and emptied the East Indian tea chests into Boston harbor. The Tea Party was organized in a highly sophisticated way. The men were divided into different groups, and told the names only of their own section commanders—a classic example of cellular organization that would be used in other movements of a very different nature.[57] Immediately afterward a Boston street ballad called "The Rallying of the Tea Party" identified only two leaders by name: Dr. Joseph Warren and "bold" Paul Revere:

> Rally Mohawks! Bring out your axes,
> And tell King George we'll pay no taxes
> On his foreign tea . . .

Our Warren's there, and bold Revere
With hands to do and words to cheer
For Liberty and laws.

These men carefully controlled their acts of violence in defense of
what they called "Liberty and laws." Even as they hurled the tea
into Boston harbor, they replaced a broken lock to demonstrate
that their quarrel was not against property or order. One man who
stole a small amount of tea for his own use was made to run the
gauntlet, and his coat was nailed to the whipping post. Those
symbolic gestures were lost on British leaders.[58]

After the Tea Party, Boston took the lead in creating a network of committees and congresses throughout the colonies. Here
again Paul Revere played a prominent role. On December 17 1773,
he had made one of the first of many revolutionary rides. Boston's
town meeting issued a formal justification of the Tea Party, and
appointed a committee of leading citizens to visit towns throughout New England. It asked Paul Revere to travel on the same
errand to the Whigs of New York and Philadelphia. From late
1773 to 1775, he made at least five journeys to those cities. Each
trip was a major expedition on 18th-century highways. Sometimes
he rode his own large gray saddle horse. On one occasion he
traveled in a small carriage.[59]

As great events followed rapidly, he was on the road again and
again. Parliament responded to the Tea Party with statutes that
closed the port of Boston, abrogated the charter of Massachusetts,
curtailed most town meetings, created a new system of courts in
the colony, and authorized Imperial officers to send Americans to
Britain for trial. London called these punitive measures Coercive
Laws; America knew them as the Intolerable Acts. When news of
their passage reached Boston in early 1774, Paul Revere made a
ride to New York and Philadelphia, to help concert methods of
resistance.[60]

In the summer, representatives from towns in Suffolk
County, met together, and agreed to a set of resolutions drafted by
Dr. Joseph Warren. These "Suffolk Resolves" proclaimed the Intolerable Acts to be unconstitutional and recommended sanctions
against Britain. They also urged the people of Massachusetts to
form their own government, and prepare to fight in its defense.

After the vote, Paul Revere saddled his horse and carried the
Suffolk Resolves to Philadelphia. His mission was urgent. The
Continental Congress was in session and waiting for news from
New England. Revere left Boston on September 11, 1774, and

reached Philadelphia on September 16, nearly 350 miles on rough and winding 18th-century roads in the unprecedented time of five days. The next day, Congress agreed to a ringing endorsement of the Suffolk Resolves—a decisive step on the road to revolution. Paul Revere started home again on September 18, and was in Boston on the 23rd, with news that greatly encouraged resistance in New England. He had only a few days with his new bride. Then he was off again to visit leaders in New York and Philadelphia on September 29, and was back by October 19. Perhaps a bit saddle-sore, he traveled in a sulky.[61]

There were other short trips in New England. These journeys were reported in the Gazettes, and noticed with alarm by Imperial leaders. In January, 1775, when Paul Revere rode from Boston to a gathering of Whigs in Exeter, New Hampshire, Royal Governor John Wentworth wrote, "Paul Revere went express thither yesterday noon. It portends a storm rather than peace."[62]

For two years, Paul Revere became the Mercury of the American Revolution. Often he was called a "messenger," "courier," or "express," which understated his role. A Tory writer described him grandly as "Paul Revere, silversmith, ambassador from the Committee of Correspondence in Boston to the Congress in Philadelphia," which exaggerated his function.[63] He was less than an ambassador, but more than merely a messenger. His importance as a leader had grown steadily with the revolutionary movement.

Other men were more prominent in the public eye—Sam Adams, John Hancock and Joseph Warren. But none was truly in charge. There were no controlling figures in Boston's revolutionary movement, which was an open alliance of many different groups.[64] Here was the source of Paul Revere's importance. He knew everyone and moved in many different circles. In Boston this great joiner helped to link one group to another, and was supremely good at getting things done.

An indicator of his importance, and a clue to the much-misunderstood structure of the revolutionary movement, may be found in a comparison of seven groups of Boston Whigs (Appendix D). Altogether they included 255 men. The great majority (82%) were on only one list. Nobody appeared on all seven of them, or even six. Two men, and only two, were on as many as five. One was Joseph Warren. The other was Paul Revere.

The revolutionary movement in Boston was not small, tightly controlled, and hierarchical. It was large, open, diverse, complex and pluralistic, a world of many circles. Paul Revere and Joseph

Warren moved in more of these circles than any of the other Boston leaders. This gave them their special roles as linchpins of the revolutionary movement. They were not the people who pulled the strings (nobody did that), but they became leading communicators, coordinators and organizers of collective effort in the cause of freedom.[65]

There was a limit to how high Paul Revere could rise in public life. He never had a classical education, and could not write the great papers or deliver the polished speeches. Another Whig leader, Dr. Thomas Young, wrote condescendingly of Revere, "No man of his rank and opportunities in life deserves better of the community," a biting Boston phrase that suggested something of the social constraints in his world.[66] After independence, Revere sometimes complained that he was not promoted to high public office. But behind the scenes, and among his many friends, Paul Revere became a major leader by 1774, more so than is recognized by academic historians, who understandably tend to be more interested in talkers and writers. Paul Revere was an actor and a doer. His leading role came to him because he was a man who other men could trust to keep his word and get things done, and also because he was deeply committed to the common cause of liberty.

Paul Revere did not think of that cause as we do today—not as the beginning of a new era. He regarded British Imperial measures as "newfangled" innovations, and believed that he was defending the inherited folk rights of New England: its ancient custom of self-government, its sacred idea of the covenant, and its traditional way of life.[67]

We misunderstand Paul Revere's revolutionary thinking if we identify it with our modern ideas of individual freedom and tolerance that later spread through the world. Bostonians had very different attitudes in 1775. Samuel Adams often spoke of what he called the "publick liberty," or the "liberty of America," or sometimes the "liberty of Boston." Their idea of liberty was both a corporate and an individual possession. It had a double meaning in New England, akin to the Puritan idea of a special and general calling and Cotton Mather's two oars. It referred not only to the autonomy of each person's rights, but also to the integrity of the group, and especially to the responsibility of a people to regulate their own affairs. We remember the individual rights and forget the collective responsibilities. We tend to interpret Thomas Jefferson's ambiguous reference to the "pursuit of happiness" as an individual quest, but in 1774 Paul Revere's town meeting spoke of "social happiness" as its goal."[68]

Also distinctive to this culture was its idea of equality. The motto of Boston's Sons of Liberty was "Equality Before the Law." They did not believe in equality of possessions, or even equality of esteem, but they thought that all people had an equal right to be judged according to their worth. Paul Revere's business associate Nathaniel Ames wrote:

> All men are by Nature equal
> But differ greatly in the sequel.[69]

For Paul Revere and "town-born" Boston these principles did not derive from abstract premises, but from tradition and historical experience. In America it has always been so. Milan Kundera has recently reminded us that "the struggle against power is the struggle of memory against forgetting." This was Paul Revere's road to revolution. It was also his message for our time.[70]

# GENERAL GAGE'S DILEMMA

∾ The Agony of an Imperial Whig

An Englishman is the unfittest person on earth
to argue another Englishman into slavery.

—Edmund Burke, 1775

O N THE HOT SUMMER AFTERNOON of August 27, 1774,
while Paul Revere was preparing for yet another ride to
Philadelphia, a senior British officer sat at his desk in
Danvers, Massachusetts, seething with anger and frustration.
Lieutenant-General the Honourable Thomas Gage was commander in chief of British forces in the New World. Mighty powers
were his to command. A single stroke of his fine quill pen could
start regiments marching from the Arctic to the Antipodes. The
merest nod of his powdered head could cause fortresses to rise on
the far frontier, and make roads appear in the trackless wilderness.
In the late summer of 1774, General Thomas Gage was the most
powerful man in North America.

And yet as he toiled over his endless correspondence in a
borrowed country mansion on this sweltering August day, his letters overflowed with impotent rage. The source of his frustration
was a political office that he had recently been given. In addition to
his military duties, the King had appointed him Royal Governor of
Massachusetts, with orders to reduce that restless province to obedience and peace. Parliament had armed him for that task with
special powers such as no Royal Governor had possessed before.
For months he had tried to act with firmness and restraint, but the

people of New England had stubbornly set all his efforts at defiance.

Thomas Gage thought of himself as a fair-minded and moderate man, a friend of liberty and a defender of what he was pleased to call the "common rights of mankind." He rather liked Americans—at least, some Americans. He had married an American, and loved her dearly—his beautiful, headstrong Margaret. But even his wife was being difficult these days. She was away from him for long periods, and when they were together she lectured him about liberty and justice in that self-righteous American way.[1]

What was it, he wondered, about these impossible people? Was it something in the soil, or the American air? General Gage reminded himself that most of these infuriating provincials were British too—blood of his blood, flesh of his own freeborn nation. They had been allowed more liberties than any people on the face of the globe, yet they complained that he was trying to enslave them. They were taxed more lightly than the subjects of any European state, but refused even the trivial sums that Parliament had levied upon them. They professed loyalty to their rightful Sovereign, but tarred and feathered his Royal officers, and burned His Majesty's ships to the water's edge.

Now, on top of every other outrage, General Gage had just been told that some of these New England people were making threats against his own person. His Captain of Engineers John Montresor, an able but irritating officer, had informed him that he was no longer safe in the country and must move to Boston, under the guns of the British garrison.[2]

Boston! Thomas Gage had come to hate that town. A few months later he would write, "I wish this cursed place was burned."[3] Of all the Yankee race, General Gage believed that Bostonians were the worst. In 1770 he had written, "America is a mere bully, from one end to the other, and the Bostonians by far the greatest bullies."[4] Many British soldiers shared that same opinion. Gage's able subordinate, Lord Percy, had arrived in the New World thinking well of America. A few weeks among the Bostonians had changed his mind, and persuaded him that they were "a set of sly, artful, hypocritical rascals, cruel, and cowards."[5] One of the most sly and artful of them all, in the opinion of these angry men, was a Boston silversmith who had become so familiar to them that he was identified in General Gage's correspondence merely by his initials: *"P:--- R:---."*[6]

In origins and attitudes, Thomas Gage and Paul Revere were as far apart as two self-styled gentlemen could be, and still remain within the English-speaking world of the 18th century. Gage was the older of the two, having been born about the year 1720. He was the younger son of an aristocratic Anglo-Catholic family with its seat at Firle Place, Sussex, in the south of England.[7]

For many generations, Thomas Gage's ancestors had shown a genius for embracing the great lost causes of British history. As early as 1215, several Sussex Gages were said to have backed King John against Magna Carta. When the Reformation came to England they sided with the Catholic party, and one of them became the jailor of the Protestant Princess Elizabeth, England's future Queen.[8] During the English Civil War, the Gages rallied to the Royalist cause of Charles I and suffered a heavy defeat. In the Glorious Revolution of 1688, they stood with James II and were defeated yet again. When the house of Hanover inherited the throne the Gages became Jacobites, stubbornly faithful to the hopeless cause of a Catholic King over the water. Through many generations, the Gages of Firle had remained steadfast to the cause of hierarchy, authority, and the Roman Catholic Church.[9]

In 1715, that pattern suddenly changed. Sir William Gage, the seventh baronet, decided to convert from Catholicism to the Protestant Church of England. According to the Anglo-Catholic poet Alexander Pope who knew him well, he did so not from high principle but because he wished to "have the use of horses, forbidden to all those who refused to take the oath of allegiance to the Church." Whatever the reason, the Gages outwardly joined England's Protestant establishment, while some of them inwardly retained their Catholic faith.[10]

The property of the Anglican convert Sir William Gage was inherited by our general's father, Thomas Gage of Sherburne, who appears to have been a corrupt and dissolute man, not highly esteemed by some who knew him. One acquaintance described him as "a petulant, silly, busy, meddling, profligate fellow." He spent much of his time at London's gaming tables, while his beautiful wife became so notorious for her promiscuity that one fashionable Augustan rake offered to pay his debts "when Lady Gage grows chaste."[11]

The Gages may not have been an admirable couple, but London found them amusing, and they were well connected at Court. In 1720, for no apparent merit, Thomas Gage of Sherburne was raised to the peerage as the first Viscount Gage. This improbable pair became the parents of our General Thomas Gage. He was their second son.

Young Tom Gage, like his fictional contemporary Tom Jones whom he resembled in some respects, was raised on an idyllic West Country estate called Highmeadow in Gloucestershire. At about the age of nine he was sent to the Westminster School, and studied there for eight years. Away from home, he grew into a person very different from his parents—disciplined and hardworking, cautious and serious, not clever or witty, but upright, solid, and well-meaning.

The English education of Thomas Gage made a striking contrast with the American schooling of Boston boys such as Paul Revere. Both of them learned English as their mother tongue, but they were trained to speak in different dialects. When they came to their great dispute over the Massachusetts Charter, Paul Revere pronounced it *chaa-taa*. Thomas Gage said *chawh-tawh*. Behind that superficial distinction of speech lay two profoundly different English-speaking cultures. Thomas Gage's dialect had only recently developed as the linguistic property of Britain's narrow ruling class. Its fluted tones and mellow cadences were the exclusive emblems of a small elite who claimed to rule the English-speaking world by right of birth and breeding.[12]

The dialect of England's governing class was the outward expression of a culture as idiosyncratic as the folkways of New England. Thomas Gage and Paul Revere were both taught to cherish English law and liberties, but they understood that common heritage in very different ways. For Thomas Gage, the rule of law meant the absolute supremacy of that many-headed sovereign, the King-in-Parliament. For Paul Revere it meant the right of a free-born people to be governed by laws of its own making. Both were highly principled men, but their principles were worlds apart. The ideas they shared in common were the ethical foundation-stones of English-speaking society. Their differences were what the American Revolution was about.

Neither Thomas Gage nor Paul Revere was a man of learning. They did not attend college or university. While in their teens, both were required to make their own way in the world, but they did so in different ways. Where Paul Revere followed a calling, Thomas Gage found a career. The future British general had been born to aristocratic privilege, but he was disqualified by the order of his birth from inheriting the landed wealth on which it rested. Like many younger sons of aristocratic families, he was sent into

the army. A King's commission was purchased for him at an early
age in Cholmondeley's Regiment of Foot.

Thomas Gage liked the army. He found pleasure in its pageantry, and comfort in its discipline. In combat he proved his
courage many times on what his contemporaries called the field of
honor. But he was a soldier who learned to hate war, with very
good reason. It was his fate to witness the worst that 18th-century
warfare could do. As a junior officer, he was present at the British
defeat at Fontenoy (May 11, 1745), one of the bloodiest conflicts in
the 18th century. This was the battle that began as if it were a ball,
when a British Guardsman stepped forward, swept off his hat, and
bowed gallantly to the French Guards only fifty yards away. According to a more doubtful tradition that officer also courteously
invited the enemy to take first shot: *"Que Messieurs les enemis tirent
les premiers."* The battle of Fontenoy ended with 30,000 men fallen
on a Flanders field, in scenes of horror and brutality beyond description.[13]

A year later Thomas Gage was in Scotland for another epic
slaughter. This time he was on the winning side at the battle of
Culloden (April 27, 1746) which broke the power of the Highland
clans and left Drumossie Moor carpeted with corpses of kilted
warriors. In later years Thomas Gage and his contemporaries liked
to call themselves "Old Cullodeners."

After Culloden, Gage returned to Flanders. A period of
peacetime soldiering followed, on the staff of the Earl of Albe-
marle, father of an old school friend. Then, in 1755, he was posted
to America with General Edward Braddock. It was Gage who commanded the vanguard on Braddock's expedition against the
French in the Ohio Valley. On July 9, 1755, that ill-fated force
marched blindly into a forest ambush and was nearly annihilated.
As always, Gage conducted himself bravely in combat. Wounded
himself, he improvised a rear guard that allowed the escape of a
few survivors, including George Washington.[14]

In the French and Indian War that followed, Thomas Gage
was authorized to raise a new type of regiment, called the 80th
Foot, or Gage's Light Armed Infantry, and modeled after the
American Rangers. He recruited men of independent spirit,
dressed them in brown camouflage coats with black buttons, and
hoped to train them in new tactics for forest fighting. Instead, he
was ordered to lead the light infantry against the ramparts of Fort
Ticonderoga, in a headlong frontal assault on a strongly fortified
position. With high courage Gage and his men charged directly

into an impenetrable *abattis* of fallen timber that had been cunningly prepared to entrap them. The result was yet another glorious disaster for British arms. As Gage's light infantry struggled with desperate bravery to break through that trap, they were caught in a deadly crossfire. Bodies in brown and red coats were left in grotesque postures, suspended from a tangle of dead branches on that killing ground. More than 1600 men fell. Once again Gage himself was among the many wounded.[15]

After each defeat Thomas Gage was promoted. In 1759, he became a brigadier and was given command of a major British expedition in the conquest of Canada. His orders were to march from Lake Ontario and capture Montreal while James Wolfe attacked the fortress of Quebec. Wolfe's campaign succeeded brilliantly. Gage was unable to get started. His mission ended in a fiasco that was thankfully lost in the shadow of the triumph at Quebec.

When the other generals went home Gage remained in America, and was promoted yet again—this time to the rank of major-general and the office of commander in chief for British America. Never fortunate in war, Gage was more successful as a peacetime soldier. He was known for discipline and strict economy, which won approval from his superiors in London. King George III thought highly of him. Gage's high office was due in part to Royal favor.

A portrait by John Singleton Copley shows Gage in the uniform of a British general, *circa* 1768-69. He was a handsome man, with delicate, fine-boned features. But even in middle life he looked ten years older than his true age. His hair was sparse and gray, and his skin appeared as pale and dry as a piece of old parchment. His eyes were very tired—the sad, haunted, world-weary eyes of an old soldier who had seen too much of death and suffering, and lost too many comrades to the cruelty of war. His expression suggested an air that the battle-worn proconsuls of an earlier empire had called the *tedium vitae,* a weariness of life itself.[16]

By temperament and principle this British proconsul was a cautious and conservative man, with an infinite capacity for taking pains. His conservatism grew stronger as his responsibilities increased. It was reinforced in middle age when he became a man of property. While commander in chief, he married a beautiful American heiress, Margaret Kemble of New Brunswick, New Jersey, and acquired a large family. He also made a fortune of his own

General Thomas Gage, a
portrait by John Single-
ton Copley, circa 1769.
The painting was "univer-
sally acknowledg'd" to be
"a most striking likeness"
in the words of Captain
John Small on Gage's
staff. (Yale University Art
Gallery)

by windfalls that came from his offices. Through friends in high
places he acquired 18,000 acres in New York's Oneida County, and
a large tract of Canadian land that is now Gagetown, New
Brunswick. He also bought a plantation on the West Indian island
of Montserrat that brought him an income of 600 pounds a year.[17]

By 1774, General Gage had acquired a strong stake in America and the Empire. He wanted very much to keep the peace. He
worked faithfully to support the authority of King and Parliament,
while seeking to conciliate the Americans. Even his enemies regarded him as decent, able and full of good intentions. One called
him "a good and wise man . . . surrounded with difficulties."[18]

Like Paul Revere, General Gage was also respected as a man
of honor and integrity. As a young lieutenant his nickname in the
army had been "Honest Tom."[19] Unlike many of his family, he
made his peace with England's Protestant establishment, and
whole-heartedly embraced its principles as his own. His politics
were firmly within the English Whig tradition. He believed deeply
in the British Constitution and the rule of law. In America, Gage
always insisted that his troops were bound by "constitutional laws,"
and permitted them to "do nothing but what is strictly legal," even

Margaret Kemble Gage, a portrait by John Singleton Copley, circa 1771. "Beyond compare the best Lady's portrait I ever drew," the artist himself wrote with pride. (Timken Gallery of Art, San Diego, California)

in the face of heavy provocation.[20] He recognized an obligation to respect what he called "the common rights of mankind." But at the same time he also saw the need for strict authority and decisive action, if the empire was to be preserved.[21]

Here was General Gage's dilemma. On the one hand, he wrote that "the strictest orders have been given, to treat the inhabitants on all occasions, with leniety, moderation and justice; that they shall . . . be permitted to enjoy unmolested the common rights of mankind."[22] On the other hand, he declared that, "lenient measures, and the cautious and legal exertion of the coercive powers of government, have served only to render them more daring and licentious."[23]

Edmund Burke summarized General Gage's dilemma in a sentence. "An Englishman," Burke observed in Parliament, "is the unfittest person on earth to argue another Englishman into slavery."[24]

The outbreak of the Imperial quarrel over the Stamp Act in 1765 took Gage completely by surprise. He had no idea what to do, and wrote home to a minister in London, "I must confess to you,

Sir, that during these commotions in North-America, I have never been more at a loss how to act."[25]

As resistance grew into mob violence, Gage began to think that the trouble arose not from the mobs themselves, but from colonial elites who set the rioters in motion. In company with others of his rank, he believed that the "lower orders," or the "inferior people," as he described the vast majority of humanity, were of no political importance.

After the Stamp Act Riots he wrote, "The plan of the people of property, is to raise the lower class to prevent the execution of the Law . . . The lawyers are the source from which these clamors have flowed . . . merchants in general, assembly men, magistrates, &c have been united in this plan of riots, and without the influence and instigation of these the inferior people would have been quiet . . . The sailors who are the only people who may be properly stiled Mob, are entirely at the command of the Merchants who employ them."[26]

Further, Gage persuaded himself that of all the colonial elites, a few designing men in Boston were the ringleaders. He believed that some of these leaders were quite mad, and in the case of James Otis he was correct. Others he took to be merely corrupt, and he succeeded in buying the allegiance of Dr. Benjamin Church, who became Gage's secret agent while sitting at the inner councils of the revolutionary movement. But when Gage tried to bribe Samuel Adams and other Whig leaders, he discovered the limits of that idea.

Where bribery failed, Gage tried a show of force. It was he who recommended in 1768 that two regiments of British infantry should be sent to Boston to "overawe" the inhabitants. Other British leaders wanted to keep the troops at Castle William in Boston harbor, so as not to inflame the people. Gage urged that the troops be landed in the town itself and be quartered among the population—the act that outraged Paul Revere and many Bostonians. Further, Gage unwisely chose for that difficult assignment the 29th Foot, a regiment notorious for poor discipline, hot-tempered officers, and repeated violent clashes with civilians in Canada and New York. It would be soldiers of the 29th who fired without orders in the incident that Paul Revere called the Bloody Massacre. Had Gage chosen another unit, the course of events might have been very different.[27]

After the Massacre, the British regiments were withdrawn from the town, much against Gage's wishes. He agreed that the

29th Foot should be sent away, but thought that other troops should remain.[28] He was appalled by the irresolution of other British leaders. When he was overruled, he wrote angrily to his superiors in London, "You have yielded by bits, and in such a manner, as it appeared that every thing was constrained, and extorted from you: such a conduct could not fail to encourage people here to commit every extravagance to gain their ends, and on demand has risen upon another."[29]

But Gage himself began to take another view of the American problem. He decided that his first impression was wrong—that the trouble did not rise from corrupt elites alone, but from a deeper root that was embedded in American conditions and institutions, and specifically in the growth of what he called democracy. As early as 1772, he wrote to his superiors in London, "Democracy is too prevalent in America, and claims the greatest attention to prevent its increase."[30]

A large part of the problem, he was convinced, arose from the vast abundance of cheap land in America. Gage observed that "the people themselves have gradually retired from the Coast," and "are, already, almost out of the reach of Law and Government." In 1770 he told his superiors in London that it was "the interest of Great Britain to confine the Colonists on this side of the back-country." By restricting American settlement to the Atlantic coast, he believed that the material base of American "democracy" might be undercut.[31]

The second part of General Gage's policy was root and branch reform of American institutions, especially in New England. Like many members of Britain's ruling elite, he deeply disapproved of the folkways of New England. Town meetings in particular, which the Whigs of Boston regarded as the palladium of their liberty, appeared to Thomas Gage as instruments of "democraticall despotism." The British general advised London to abolish town meetings altogether and replace them with oligarchic British borough governments.[32]

The laws and covenants that New Englanders perceived as the ark of their ancestral rights were seen by Gage to be merely a bizarre form of litigious anarchy. New England, he wrote, was a "country, where every man studies law, and interprets the laws to suit his purposes." Gage proposed to limit access to law, and shift trials in political cases to England.[33]

The austere system of Calvinist faith and Puritan morals that lay at the heart of the New England Way was despised by Gage as a

structure of organized hypocrisy. "They have a particular manner
in perverting and turning everything to their own purposes," he
wrote. Gage proposed to restrain the Congregational churches of
New England, and to strengthen the Anglican establishment in
America.[34]

The Puritan ethic of work and calling that Paul Revere served
all his life had no meaning to Thomas Gage, and was condemned
by him as a fraud and a humbug. "The protection of Britain has
made them opulent," Gage wrote in one of his more memorable
prophecies: "Were they cast off and declared aliens, they must
become a poor and needy people." He proposed to keep America
in a condition of commercial dependency on Britain. "When all
connection, upheld by commerce, with the mother country, shall
cease, it may be suspected that an independency of her government will soon follow."[35]

Gage urged his superiors in London to act decisively on these
assumptions. As early as 1770, he advised the King and his ministers to enact a set of coercive laws— specifically, to punish Boston
for its violence, to abrogate the charter of Massachusetts, and to
abolish town meetings in New England. On September 8, 1770, he
wrote:

> I hope that Boston will be called to strict account, and I think it must be
> plain to every man that no peace will ever be established in that province,
> till the King nominates his council, and appoints the magistrates, and that
> all town-meetings are absolutely abolished; whilst those meetings exist the
> people will be kept in a perpetual heat.[36]

Parliament was not ready for such strong measures when this
advice was written. But three years later, the Boston Tea Party
convinced the rulers of the Empire that General Gage had been
correct.

At that critical moment Gage happened to be in London. He
had returned on leave to England in June 1773. It was his first visit
home since he had sailed to America with the Braddock expedition
nearly twenty years earlier. He wrote to a friend that London
seemed as strange to him as Constantinople, or "any other city I
had never seen." He was appalled by its corruption, and by the
incompetence of the government. "This is a strange place," he
wrote, "I have much business with many people and can never find
them. Many have business with me, and are hunting me whilst I
am seeking others, so that it is a perpetual hunt."[37]

He was still in England, rusticating at his childhood home of
Highmeadow in Gloucestershire, when news of the Boston Tea

Party arrived in February 1774. King George III summoned him to an audience, and was much impressed by Gage's forthright suggestions. The King instructed his ministers to "hear his ideas as to the mode of compelling Boston to submit to whatever may be thought necessary."[38]

The King's chief minister, Lord North, did as he was told. In 1774, Parliament enacted a set of Coercive Acts that were modeled on General Gage's ideas. The port of Boston was closed. The structure of government of Massachusetts was modified much as Gage requested. Most town meetings were curtailed. Trials for political offences were transferred from the colonies to England. To enforce this new policy, Gage himself was ordered back to America as commander in chief and governor of Massachusetts.[39]

When Gage arrived in Boston, the town received him politely, and even gave him a public dinner in Fanueil Hall. "They are making a good deal of ceremony with me," he wrote, "much less ceremony and more obedience to the laws would please me better."[40] But when he began to enforce the Coercive Acts (which Americans called the Intolerable Acts), relations rapidly cooled. In 1774, Gage published a proclamation forbidding most town meetings except by permission, and sent troops to stop a town meeting in Salem. The stubborn Salemites responded by barring the doors of their town house and going on with their meeting. The Regulars, under orders not to use force, retreated in bewilderment.[41]

Gage himself tried to suspend town meetings in Boston, with no better success. He summoned the selectmen before him and forbade them to convene a town meeting that had just been announced. The Boston leaders solemnly explained to him that they had "called no meeting," but that "a former meeting had only adjourned themselves." As always, Gage was scrupulous to act within the law. He was baffled by the legalistic arguments of the Boston leaders. Tory Lieutenant-Governor Andrew Oliver wrote that Gage was "a gentleman of an amiable character, and of an open honest mind; too honest to deal with men who from their cradles had been educated in the wily arts of chicane." Town meetings continued in Boston.[42]

Some of his subordinates were less scrupulous about their methods, with explosive results. In 1774, a Yankee sailor named Samuel Dyer was caught trying to persuade soldiers of the King's Own to desert. The regimental commander, Lt. Col. George Maddison, asked Admiral John Montagu to impress Dyer into the Royal Navy and "carry him to England." This was done, but Dyer gained his liberty in England. He returned to America a free man, full of rage against his persecutors. In Boston, he went looking for Colonel Maddison, found two other British officers in the street, and instantly attacked, attempting to assassinate one of them with his own sword. New England Whigs were appalled by Dyer's violence, which threatened the moral standing of their cause. They arranged his capture, and a Massachusetts court ordered him confined as a lunatic. But the people of New England were deeply shocked that Colonel Maddison and Admiral Montagu had ordered a man to be pressed and deprived of his freedom for a political act. It confirmed their worst suspicions of Imperial power.[43]

Under the terms of the Coercive Acts, Gage nominated Royal judges to the Massachusetts bench—a major break with precedent. He chose men mostly for strong Loyalist principles. So hostile was the population that juries refused to serve, and many of the new judges refused to sit on the bench, in fear of their lives. A member of one of the first juries to defy him was Paul Revere.[44]

As governor, Gage also tried to restrain the Congregational clergy of New England. The ministers asked him to proclaim a day of Fasting and Prayer, an old New England custom in troubled times. Gage refused, explaining candidly, "I saw no cause for an extraordinary day of humiliation, which was only to give an opportunity for sedition to flow from the Pulpits." The clergy went ahead without him, and another bond of union was broken.[45]

In the face of growing anger throughout New England, Gage advised his superiors to stand firm and yield nothing. He told them that the time for "conciliating, moderation, reasoning is over. Nothing can be done but by forcible means." But still he hoped to avoid bloodshed. "I mean my Lord," he wrote home to London, "to avoid any bloody crisis as long as possible, unless forced into it by themselves, which may happen."[46]

Gage did not believe that the troubles in Massachusetts would spread throughout America. He knew about Paul Revere's rides to New York and Philadelphia, and was well informed about meetings of the Continental Congress.[47] But the British general regarded Congress as a "motley crew," and did not imagine that it could ever act together. He had no fear that the contagion of revolution would seriously infect the southern plantations or the western backcountry. These colonies might "talk very high," he assured London, "but they can do nothing. Their numerous slaves in the bowels of their country, and the Indians at their backs, will always keep them quiet." [48]

This soldier who hated war did not wish to use force against the Americans, except as the last resort. His purpose was to remove from Yankee hands the means of violent resistance until a time when cooler heads would prevail. To that end, General Gage proposed to disarm New England by a series of small surgical operations--meticulously planned, secretly mounted, and carried forward with careful economy of force. His object was not to provoke a war but to prevent one.[49]

New England's Whig leaders were vulnerable to such a strategy. Many weapons were in the hands of the people, but not enough for long struggle against the King's troops, and there was no easy source of resupply. Few firearms were manufactured in New England; gunpowder had to be imported from abroad. This gave General Gage his opportunity. While still in his summer house at Danvers, he began to plan a series of missions against the arsenals and powderhouses of New England, designed to remove as many munitions as possible—enough to make it impossible for the people of that region to make a determined stand against him.[50]

The plan had one major weakness. It could only succeed by surprise. The people of New England were jealous of their liberties, including their liberty to keep and bear arms. If they learned in advance of General Gage's intentions, his strategy for stopping the movement toward war could start one instead. The British commander knew that the Whigs of Boston had been organizing against him, and were attempting to penetrate his designs. Prominent among them was a leader whose incessant activities were particularly dangerous to their scheme—the busy Boston silversmith named Paul Revere.

# FIRST STROKES

### ∾ Thomas Gage, Paul Revere, and the Powder Alarms

> A check anywhere wou'd be fatal, and the first stroke
> will decide a great deal."
>
> —Thomas Gage, Sept. 2, 1774[1]

EARLY IN THE MORNING of September 1, 1774, General Gage set his plan in motion. His first step was to seize the largest stock of gunpowder in New England. It was stored in a magazine called the Provincial Powder House, high on a remote hill, six miles northwest of Boston. Many towns kept their munitions there, as did the Province of Massachusetts itself.

During the summer of 1774, the towns had quietly withdrawn their supplies from the Powder House, leaving only the provincial reserve. Loyalists called this supply the King's powder. Most people in Massachusetts believed that it belonged to them.

General Gage was told of the withdrawals by William Brattle, a much-hated Cambridge Tory. The British commander resolved to remove the remaining gunpowder before it disappeared into the countryside. As governor of Massachusetts he had the authority to take that step. He kept carefully within the letter of the law.[2]

The mission was planned in high secrecy. To lead it, Gage selected one of his most able officers, Lieutenant-Colonel George Maddison, commander of the 4th (King's Own) Foot. Maddison was given 260 picked men, "draughted from the several regiments" in the garrison. For quick surprise and ease of transport, Gage availed himself of the Royal Navy's command of coastal waters, and decided to strike suddenly from the sea, using longboats borrowed from ships in Boston harbor.

At 4:30 in the morning of September 1, 1774, while the unsuspecting town was still asleep, Colonel Maddison's men crept out of their quarters and marched quietly to Long Wharf, where the navy was waiting with a flotilla of thirteen longboats, bobbing gently on the morning tide. The soldiers climbed awkwardly into the boats, and within minutes the coxswains pushed off, rowing across Boston harbor to the Mystic River.[3]

The soldiers came ashore at a landing place called Temple's Farm, and marched quickly to the Powder House on Quarry Hill about a mile away. The sheriff of Middlesex County, Colonel David Phips, gave them the keys to the building, a windowless stone tower with one of Benjamin Franklin's new lightning rods rising from the center of its shingled roof. No lanterns could be lighted in the building for fear of explosion, and the morning was still very dark. The soldiers waited for the light to improve, then brought out the gunpowder. All 250 half-barrels were carried to the boats and delivered to Boston. As the sun rose over Quarry Hill, a small detachment marched on to Cambridge, and brought away two brass field pieces that belonged to the Province. By noon the munitions were deposited in Castle William, and the men were back in their barracks.[4]

General Gage was very pleased. His staff had planned the mission perfectly, and Colonel Maddison had executed it without a

The Massachusetts Provincial Powder House still stands today at Powderhouse Square, Somerville, Massachusetts. The removal of munitions by the 64th Foot on Sept. 1, 1774, triggered the great New England Powder Alarm. (James Hunnewell, *History of Charlestown* (Boston, 1888))

hitch. The largest supply of gunpowder in Massachusetts had been secured at a stroke, without a shot fired. It was a model operation in all respects, save one. The British commander had completely misunderstood the temper of New England.

The people were caught entirely by surprise. Through the day, reports began to fly across the countryside. It was rumored that the Province had been "robbed of its powder," that the Regulars were marching, that war had begun, that six people were killed, that the King's ships were bombarding Boston. None of this was true, but many people gave way to a wild panic that would long be remembered in New England as the Powder Alarm.[5]

All that day church bells tolled in the towns. At dusk great fire-beacons that had warned of war against the French were set alight, burning brightly across the open countryside. As far away as Connecticut, the militia began to march toward Boston. That night, a young traveler named McNeil happened to be on the road from the Connecticut Valley to Boston. He stopped at a tavern in Shrewsbury, about halfway in between. About midnight he was awakened by loud voices and a violent knocking at the door. He heard someone tell the landlord that "the powder was taken." Within fifteen minutes, fifty men had gathered at the tavern, "equipping themselves and sending off posts to the neighboring towns." He remembered that "the men set off as fast as they were equipped."

Early the next morning, September 2, 1774, McNeil set out for Boston. Afterward he wrote that "he never saw such a scene before. All along [the road] were armed men rushing forward— some on foot, some on horseback. At every house women and children [were] making cartridges, running bullets, making wallets [pouches of food], baking biscuits, crying and bemoaning and at the same time animating their husbands and sons to fight for their liberties, though not knowing whether they should ever see them again. . . . They left scarcely half a dozen men in a town, unless old and decrepit, and in one town the landlord told him that himself was the only man left."[6]

Ezra Stiles, a Congregationalist clergyman with a passion for statistics, estimated that "perhaps more than one third the effective men in all New England took arms and were on actual march for Boston." Another observer reported that 20,000 men marched from the Connecticut Valley alone, "in one body armed and equipped," and were halfway to Boston before they were called back.[7]

William Brattle's letter to General Gage somehow fell into Whig hands and was given to the newspapers. When the people of New England discovered what had happened, anxiety and fear gave way to unbridled fury. The rage of an entire region fell on a few Tories who happened to be within reach. Whig leaders who had been trying to awaken a spirit of resistance suddenly found themselves trying, in Joseph Warren's words, "to prevent the people from coming to immediate acts of violence."[8]

On the morning of September 2, a huge crowd of 4,000 angry men gathered on Cambridge Common, mostly farmers from the towns between Sudbury and Boston. Whig leaders persuaded them to leave their firearms in Watertown. Armed only with wooden cudgels, they marched to "Tory Row" in Cambridge, and gathered around William Brattle's mansion. This elegant house had been his family's seat through four generations. Its gardens and private mall extended all the way to the Charles River. The property itself was protected by Whig leaders, but Brattle was forced to flee for his life, and took refuge at Castle William in Boston harbor. He sent a pathetic letter to the newspapers: "My banishment from my house, the place of my nativity," he wrote, "my house being searched though I am informed it was without damage, grieves me deeply . . . I am extremely sorry for what has taken place; I hope I may be forgiven." But he was not forgiven. William Brattle was never allowed to go home again. He was a fugitive for the rest of his days.

The mob went on to visit Colonel David Phips, the Tory sheriff who had delivered the keys of the powderhouse, and compelled him to swear in writing that he would never enforce the Coercive Acts and would recall every writ issued "under the new establishment." Another inhabitant of Tory Row, Thomas Oliver, was made to resign his seat on Gage's new Royal Council. He wrote on a slip of paper, "My house at Cambridge being surrounded by about four thousand people, in compliance with their command I sign my name."[9]

It was a fiercely hot day, and tempers rose with the thermometer. The crowd moved to the house of Tory barrister Jonathan Sewall, and things got out of hand. Someone inside the Sewall mansion fired a pistol. An unruly mob of boys and servants smashed the windows and threatened to pull down the entire building. While Whig leaders held the crowd at bay, Jonathan Sewall fled to Boston. A few months later he left the country, never to return. Printed papers were nailed to the doors of Sewall's fellow lawyers, threatening death to any member of the Bar who appeared in the new courts created by the Coercive Acts.[10]

Some of the mob, who were mounted, came upon Customs Commissioner Benjamin Hallowell in his opulent "post-chaise," escorted by a servant in livery. A countryman came up to him and cried, "Damn you, how do you like us now, you Tory son of a bitch?" Hallowell took his servant's horse and galloped toward Boston with a pistol in his hand, pursued by a howling mob of infuriated Yankees, said to number 160 mounted men and horses. Behind the thundering mob galloped three frantic Whig leaders, hoping to prevent bloodshed. As Hallowell approached the British sentries at Boston Neck, his horse collapsed. With the mob in full cry close behind him he sprinted to the safety of the British lines.

When the danger of violence passed, Boston Whigs rejoiced in the dramatic turn of events and spread the news to other colonies. Paul Revere, unable to travel himself, dispatched riders bearing his personal letters to leaders in other colonies. To his good friend John Lamb, a leading Whig in New York, Revere wrote triumphantly,

> Dear Sir,
>     I embrace this oppertunity to inform you, that we are in Spirits, tho' in a garrison; the Spirit of Liberty never was higher than at present, the troops have the horrors amazingly. By reason of some late movements of our friends in the Country, our new fangled Councellors are resigning their places every day; our Justices of the courts, who now hold their commissions during the pleasure of his Majesty, or the Governor, cannot git a jury to act with them, in short the Tories are giving way everywhere in our Province.[11]

It is interesting to observe that Paul Revere's thinking centered on "the Spirit of Liberty," at a time when Thomas Gage thought mainly about material aspects of the problem. While Imperial leaders were laboring to remove the physical means of resistance, New England Whigs were promoting the spiritual will to resist. The two parties to this great conflict were not merely thinking different things; they were thinking differently.

General Gage was amazed by the rising of the countryside against him, and astounded by the anger he had awakened in New England. Instantly his mood changed, and suddenly he turned very cautious. His staff had already been planning another mission to seize munitions in Worcester, forty miles inland. This second strike was postponed, and later abandoned altogether.

The British commander began to think defensively. He or-

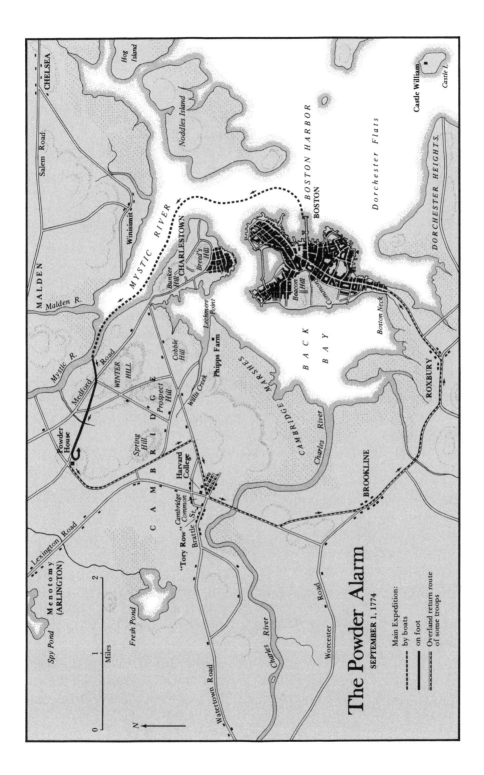

# The Powder Alarm

### SEPTEMBER 1, 1774

**Main Expedition:**
---- by boats
—— on foot
---- Overland return route
of some troops

CHELSEA

Salem Road

Hog Island

Noddles Island

MYSTIC RIVER

Winisimit

MALDEN

Malden R.

BOSTON HARBOR

Dorchester Flats

Castle William

Castle I.

DORCHESTER HEIGHTS.

BOSTON

Beacon Hill

Bunker Hill

CHARLESTOWN

Breed's Hill

Lechmere Point

Cobble Hill

Phipps Farm

Willis Creek

Prospect Hill

WINTER HILL

Medford

Road

Mystic R.

Powder House

Spring Hill

CAMBRIDGE

Harvard College

Cambridge Common

"Tory Row"

Brattle St.

MARSHES

BACK BAY

Charles River

Boston Neck

ROXBURY

BROOKLINE

Worcester Road

Charles River

Watertown Road

Fresh Pond

Spy Pond

Menotomy (ARLINGTON)

Lexington Road

N

0   1   2
Miles

**Thursday, September 1, 1774.**

ANY One, and every One of the BAR that shall presume, after this Day, to appear in Court, or otherwise, to do any Business with the Judges, shall assuredly suffer the Pains of Death.

After the powder alarm, this hastily printed handbill was tacked on the doors of Massachusetts lawyers, of whom many were Tories. (Public Record Office)

dered the town of Boston to be closed and fortified. Heavy cannon were emplaced on Roxbury Neck, in fear that the "country people" might storm the town. The inhabitants were ordered to surrender their weapons, lest they rise against the garrison. Stocks of powder and arms in the possession of merchants were forcibly purchased by the Crown.[12]

As commander in chief for America, Gage did what he could to concentrate his forces in Boston. But by late October he had only 3000 Regulars in the town, not nearly enough to control a province that had mustered ten times as many men against him in a single day. The first hints of winter were beginning to be felt in the crisp New England air, and the season for campaigning was nearly at an end.[13]

General Gage began to send home dispatches that differed very much from his strong advice of the past five years. In the weeks after the Powder Alarm, he informed London that "the whole country was in arms and in motion." He reported that "from present appearances there is no prospect of putting the late acts in force, but by first making a conquest of the New-England provinces."[14]

In November Gage went further, and urged that the Coercive Acts (which he himself had proposed) should be suspended until more troops could be sent to Boston. This idea caused consternation in London. The King himself angrily rejected Gage's advice as "the most absurd that can be suggested."[15]

At the same time, Gage begged his superiors for massive reinforcement. To Barrington he wrote, "If you think ten thousand men sufficient, send twenty; if one million is thought enough, give two; you save both blood and treasure in the end."[16]

In London those numbers were thought to be absurd, even hysterical. At the moment when Gage was asking for 20,000 reinforcements, only 12,000 regular infantry existed in all of Britain.[17] The King's ministers replied that "such a force cannot be collected without augmenting our army to a war establishment." Gage was sent a battalion of 400 Marines, and told to get on with the job.[18]

Meanwhile, the Whig leaders of New England were gathering their own resources with greater success. A convention met in Worcester on September 21, 1774, and urged town meetings to organize special companies of minutemen, so that one-third of the militia would be in constant readiness to march. It recommended that a system of alarms and express riders be organized throughout the colony. In October, the former legislature of Massachusetts met in defiance of Governor Gage, and declared itself to be the First Provincial Congress. It created a Committee of Safety and a Committee of Supplies, modeled after the institutions of England's Puritan Revolution and armed with executive powers.

The people of New England vowed never again to be taken by surprise. In Boston, Paul Revere went instantly to work on that particular problem. His chosen instrument was a favorite device in Boston: the voluntary association. Many years later he recalled that "in the Fall of 1774 and Winter of 1775 I was one of upwards of thirty, chiefly mechanics, who formed ourselves into a committee for the purpose of watching the movements of the British soldiers, and gaining every intelligence of the movements of the Tories. We held our meetings at the Green Dragon Tavern."[19]

Paul Revere himself was the leader of this clandestine organization. Its activities were shrouded in the deepest secrecy. He wrote, "We were so careful that our meetings should be kept secret, that every time we met, every person swore upon the Bible that he would not discover any of our transactions but to Messrs Hancock, Adams, Doctors Warren, Church and one or two more."[20]

Despite these precautions, General Gage quickly learned about this secret society. His source was Dr. Benjamin Church, who sat in the highest councils of the Whig movement, and betrayed it for money. The Whigs of Boston were soon painfully aware that Gage knew what they were doing. Many years later, Paul Revere remembered that "a gentleman who had connections with the Tory party, but was a Whig at heart, acquainted me that our meetings were discovered, and mentioned the identical words that were spoken among us the night before." Paul Revere's mechanics were unable to discover who was betraying them, and began to suspect one another. All the while they continued to report their activities to Dr. Benjamin Church, never imagining that Church himself was the traitor.[21]

Even as General Gage knew what Paul Revere and his friends were doing, he made no attempt to stop them. Perhaps he saw no reason to try, as long as Doctor Church was keeping him so well informed. Without interference, the Boston mechanics met at the Green Dragon Tavern, and organized themselves into regular watches. "We frequently took turns, two by two," Revere remembered, "to watch the soldiers by patrolling the streets all night."[22]

In our mind's eye, we might see them in the pale glow of Boston's new street lights, patrolling the icy streets on long winter nights, their hands tucked under arms for warmth, and the collars of their short mechanics' jackets turned high against the bitter Boston wind. All the while General Gage's officers watched the watchmen through frosted window panes, then gathered around white oak fires in cozy winter quarters, and laughed knowingly into their steaming mugs of mulled Madeira.

Early in December, 1774, the British command recovered its nerve, and decided to strike again. An Order in Council prohibited the export of arms and ammunition to America, and ordered Imperial officials to stop "the importation thereof into any part of North America," and to secure the munitions that were already in the colonies. Particularly at risk was a large supply of gunpowder, cannon, and small arms in New Hampshire. It was kept at Fort William and Mary, near the entrance to Portsmouth harbor, fifty miles north of Boston. The ramshackle fortress was garrisoned only by six invalid British soldiers, and vulnerable to attack.

This time the Whigs of New England were on their guard. Paul Revere's clandestine network functioned with high efficiency, and caught wind of the new British policy. Once again, Revere himself played a pivotal role. With various reports in hand, he and his friends decided to warn the people of New Hampshire that a large British expedition was ordered to Fort William and Mary, and possibly underway.[23]

The date was December 12, 1774. British warships were indeed at sea along the coast of New England in severe winter

The Green Dragon Tavern was a massive brick building on the west side of Union Street. Modeled on another Green Dragon Tavern in Bishopsgate, London, it was operating in Boston as early as 1712, and became a center of revolutionary activity. The building was bought by Revere's Masonic Lodge, hence the square and compass in the corner. The vehicle is a one-horse chaise such as Paul Revere himself used on at least one of his revolutionary rides. This ink and watercolor drawing by John Johnson in 1773 is in the American Antiquarian Society.

weather, and were thought to be heading for New Hampshire. Among them was *HMS Somerset,* a ship of the line with a large force of British Marines on board. In the latitude of Portsmouth, she met a fierce snowstorm that churned the coastal waters of New England into a seamen's hell. A gale howled through her rigging, and foaming torrents of green water cascaded from her plunging bows. She was forced to heave to, her sails "close-reefed and banded," with hand pumps "constantly going throughout the ship," to keep her from sinking.[24]

Admiral Graves wrote later, "This sort of storm is so severe it cannot be looked against, and by the snow freezing as fast as it falls, baffles all resistance—for the blocks become choked, the tackle encrusted, the ropes and sails quite congealed, and the whole ship freezes upon whatever part it falls and soon covers the forepart of a ship with ice." One may imagine the misery of her crew as they worked the frozen sails against the gale that was blowing in their faces. They had to "pour boiling water upon the tacks and sheets and with clubs and bats beat off the ice, before the cordage can be rendered flexible."[25]

Meanwhile, early in the morning of December 13, Paul Revere saddled his horse and hurried north to warn the people of Portsmouth. It proved to be one of his most difficult rides. Winter had come early to New Hampshire in 1774. The snow was deep on the ground by Thanksgiving Day, November 24. Another snow fell on December 9, and turned the highways into morasses of mud and slush. Then, in a typical New England sequence, the weather turned bitter cold. The thick slush froze in rough furrows on the rutted roads.[26]

It was the sort of day when weatherwise Yankee travelers bided their time by tavern hearths. But Paul Revere could not wait for the weather. Determined to win his race against the Regulars, he mounted his horse and rode sixty miles from Boston to Portsmouth, under dark December skies. A piercing west wind howled across the dangerous highway, and chilled him to the bone.

Revere reached Portsmouth on the afternoon of December 13, 1774, and went straight to the waterfront house of Whig merchant Samuel Cutts. Portsmouth's Committee of Correspondence quickly convened, and Revere reported his news. He told the Portsmouth Whigs that two regiments of Regulars were coming to seize the powder at Fort William and Mary. Further, he warned them that the King had issued an Order in Council prohibiting export of munitions to the colonies, and that new supplies would not be easy to obtain.[27]

While the Whigs of Portsmouth were pondering this news, a Tory townsman reported Paul Revere's arrival to New Hampshire's Royal Governor John Wentworth, a man of energy and decision. Wentworth instantly alerted the small garrison at the fort, and dispatched an express rider to General Gage and Admiral Graves with an urgent request for help.[28]

In fact, Paul Revere's intelligence was not entirely correct. No British expedition had yet sailed for Portsmouth. HMS *Somerset* was merely in passage from Britain to America, and her Marines were part of the battalion promised to General Gage. But when Wentworth's message arrived in Boston, Admiral Graves ordered a small sloop, HMS *Canceaux,* to depart immediately for Portsmouth with another detachment of Marines on board. A larger

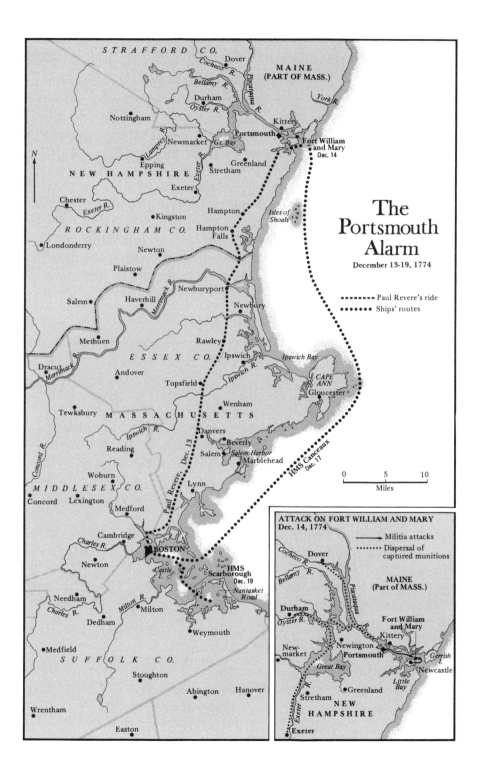

N

STRAFFORD CO.
Cocheco R.
Dover
MAINE
(PART OF MASS.)
Bellamy R.
Durham
York R.
Oyster R.
Kittery
Nottingham
Portsmouth
Lamprey R.
Newmarket
Gt. Bay
Fort William
and Mary
Dec. 14
Epping
Greenland
NEW HAMPSHIRE
Stretham
Exeter R.
Chester
Exeter
Kingston
Hampton
Isles of
Shoals
ROCKINGHAM CO.
Hampton
Falls
Londonderry
Newton
Plaistow
Merrimack R.
Salem
Haverhill
Newburyport
Methuen
Newbury

The
Portsmouth
Alarm

December 13-19, 1774

••••••• Paul Revere's ride
••••••• Ships' routes

Rawley
ESSEX CO.
Ipswich
Ipswich Bay
Dracut
Merrimack
Andover
Ipswich R.
Topsfield
CAPE
ANN
Gloucester
Tewksbury
MASSACHUSETTS
Wenham
Ipswich R.
Reading
Danvers
Beverly
Salem
Salem Harbor
Marblehead
Woburn
Lynn
HMS Cerceaux
Dec. 17
MIDDLESEX CO.
Concord
Lexington
Medford

0      5      10
Miles

Charles R.
Cambridge
Newton
BOSTON
Castle
I.
HMS
Scarborough
Dec. 19
Needham
Milton R.
Milton
Nantasket
Road
Charles R.
Dedham
Medfield
Weymouth
SUFFOLK CO.
Stoughton
Wrentham
Abington
Hanover
Easton

ATTACK ON FORT WILLIAM AND MARY
Dec. 14, 1774
⟶ Militia attacks
••••••• Dispersal of
captured munitions
Cocheco R.
Dover
Bellamy R.
MAINE
(Part of MASS.)
Durham
Piscataqua
Oyster R.
Fort William
and Mary
New-
market
Newington
Kittery
Portsmouth
Gerrish
I.
Great Bay
Newcastle
Little
Bay
Stretham
Greenland
NEW
Exeter
HAMPSHIRE
Exeter

frigate, HMS *Scarborough*, was ordered to follow as soon as she could get under way.

Meanwhile, the New Hampshire men were acting quickly on the information that Paul Revere had brought them. Early on the morning of December 14, a fife and drum paraded through the streets of Portsmouth. By noon, 400 militiamen mustered in the town. They collected a fleet of small boats, and prepared to assault the fort. At about 3 o'clock in the afternoon the attack began, under cover of a snow storm. Some of the New Hampshire men marched overland to the fort. Others approached it by sea, paddling down the Piscataqua River in the eery silence of the falling snow, as clouds of white flakes swirled around them.[29]

The garrison of British invalids saw them coming through the snow, and prepared to resist. The attackers demanded the surrender of the fort. Captain Cochran told them "on their peril not to enter. They replied they would." The British garrison, outnumbered 400 to 6, bravely hoisted the King's colors, manned the ramparts and managed to fire three four-pounders before the New Hampshire men swarmed over the walls from every side. Even then, the gallant British garrison continued fighting with small arms until they were overpowered by weight of numbers. The fort commander, Captain Cochran, surrendered his sword but was allowed to keep it. The New Hampshire men gave three cheers, and then to the horror of the garrison hauled down the King's colors. Captain Cochran drew his sword that had just been returned to him, and was wounded and "pinioned" by the New Hampshiremen. Another of the British Regulars bravely tried to stop them. A Yankee snapped a pistol in the soldier's face, then knocked him down with the butt end of it. These were truly the first blows of the American Revolution, four months before the battles of Lexington and Concord.[30]

The New Hampshiremen took possession of the fort and broke open the magazine. They carried away more than 100 barrels of gunpowder by boat to the town of Durham, and then by cart to hiding places in the interior.[31]

While the fight was going on, couriers were spreading Paul Revere's message through the country towns of New Hampshire. By morning, more than a thousand men marched on Portsmouth. It was reported that "the men who came down are those of the best property and note in the province." They returned to the fort and took away a supply of muskets and sixteen cannon, leaving about twenty heavy pieces behind.[32]

The British reinforcements were too late. HMS *Canceaux* did not sail from Boston until December 17. She had a favoring wind, and managed to reach Portsmouth without incident. But when she arrived, a cunning Yankee pilot conned her into shallow water at high tide, and the British warship found herself helplessly "benipped" behind a shoal, unable to move for days. Admiral Graves, a rough unpolished sea officer with a furious temper, was reduced to a state of apoplectic rage.

HMS *Scarborough* was unable to get under way until December 19. As she left harbor the fickle Boston wind veered from the west to the northeast, and the weather turned so threatening that she was forced to anchor in Nantasket Road south of Boston until the wind changed. The storm-beaten frigate did not arrive in Portsmouth until a week after the attack on the fort. The New Hampshiremen had long since released their prisoners and melted away into the countryside. Paul Revere trotted back to Boston, his mission completed. The British commander of the expedition came ashore to find an infuriated Royal governor, a defeated garrison, a looted fort, and a hostile population.[33]

For General Gage, the Portsmouth Alarm was a heavy defeat. The people of New Hampshire had been needlessly provoked to commit an overt act of armed rebellion. They had attacked the King's troops, seized a large supply of powder, and carried it beyond the reach of British arms. Other towns throughout New England had acted in the same way. In Newport, Providence, and New London, cannon and munitions had been removed from forts and hidden in the interior.[34]

The British leaders had no doubt as to the identity of the man who had brought about their humiliation. They attributed their defeat directly to Paul Revere. In New Hampshire, Governor Wentworth wrote that the trouble began with "Mr. Revere and the dispatch he brought with him, before which all was perfectly quiet and peaceable in the place."[35]

Paul Revere's role was well known to British leaders in Boston. Within a few days of the event, Lord Percy wrote home, "Tuesday last Mr. Paul Revere (a person who is employed by the Committee of Correspondence, here, as a messenger) arrived at Portsmouth with a letter from the committee here to those of that place, on receipt of which, circular letters were wrote to all the neighboring towns; and an armed body of 400 or 500 men marched the next day into the town of Portsmouth."[36]

Many British officers wondered why General Gage did not

arrest a man who so openly defied him. Some would cheerfully have clapped him in irons, and left him to rot in a damp dungeon at Castle William in Boston harbor. But Thomas Gage believed strictly in the rule of law. The Whig leaders, Revere among them, were allowed to remain at liberty while frustrated British soldiers cursed their commander and their Yankee tormentors in equal measure. Even Gage's lieutenant Lord Percy, outwardly loyal to his chief, wrote privately, "The general's great lenity and moderation serve only to make them more daring and insolent."[37]

In February, Gage's staff began to plan another stroke. A large supply of munitions was thought to be accumulating in the seaport town of Salem, the "shire town" for Essex County in the northeast corner of Massachusetts. Reports reached the British commander that many old ships' cannon were being converted into field pieces at a Salem forge, and that eight new brass guns had been imported from abroad. General Gage decided to go after them.[38]

Command of the mission was given to Lieutenant Colonel Alexander Leslie, an able and experienced officer, known for his moderation and restraint. Loyalist Ann Hulton described Leslie as "amiable and good . . . of a noble Scotch family but distinguished more by his humanity and affability." Here was a man that Gage could trust.

Again the British commander in chief moved with his habitual caution and secrecy. Thomas Hutchinson Junior wrote of this expedition, "The general is so very secret in all his motions that his aide de camp knew nothing of this till it was put in execution."[39] Elaborate precautions were taken to prevent detection by Paul Revere and his mechanics. For security, the mission was assigned to the 64th Foot, quartered on Castle Island in the harbor. These men were ordered to travel by sea directly from the island in the dark of night, so that nobody would see them depart.[40]

Once again, Paul Revere got wind of the impending expedition before it sailed. The information came to him in a roundabout way, perhaps from the Colony's secretary, Thomas Flucker, who worked in Province House with General Gage. Flucker may have passed on the news to his Whig son-in-law, bookseller Henry Knox, who relayed it to Paul Revere.[41]

Revere appears to have been informed only that something was stirring in the harbor. His mechanics' network went instantly into operation. The day before the expedition was to depart, three

Had General Gage been less Whiggish in his respect for the rule of law, Paul Revere might have worn these handcuffs and leg irons, which were later recovered from the wreck of HMS *Somerset* on Cape Cod and are at the Pilgrim Monument and Provincetown Museum.

men rowed out to Castle Island to find out "what was acting," to use Revere's favorite phrase. As they approached the island, the British soldiers were waiting, and the Boston men were arrested for trespass. One wonders if the report from Gage's headquarters may have been leaked to Revere deliberately, as bait for a trap. In any case, the mechanics were caught, and held on the island from Saturday afternoon until Monday morning, "lest we should send an express to our brethren at Marblehead and Salem."[42]

While Paul Revere's mechanics were kept prisoner, the British troops of the 64th Foot got off without detection, 240 strong. A little after midnight, February 26, 1775, their transport sailed north across Massachusetts Bay on a course for Marblehead. They reached their destination about nine o'clock in the morning of February 27, and dropped anchor by a secluded beach in Homan's Cove on Marblehead Neck. Colonel Leslie kept his soldiers hidden in the hold. Only a few crewmen were visible on deck.[43]

It was a quiet Sunday in Marblehead, and the countryside was silent and peaceful. The Regulars waited patiently until the people of Marblehead went to their meetinghouses for their afternoon sermon. Then, between two and three o'clock in the afternoon, Leslie ordered his men into action. His Regulars swarmed out of the ship's hold, landed ashore, and quickly formed on a road near the beach.[44]

Colonel Leslie gave the order to advance, and the long red

column went swinging into its march toward Salem, five miles away. The Regulars were confident that nothing could stand in their way, and decided to announce their presence. The fifes and drums of the 64th Foot suddenly shattered the stillness of the Sabbath with a raucous rendition of Yankee Doodle.

The landing of the soldiers had already been observed by several men of Marblehead, who sprinted to their meetinghouse and sounded the alarm. Whig leader Major John Pedrick decided to warn Salem, but he could get there only by the road the Regulars had taken. Major Pedrick mounted his horse, and rode slowly past the Regulars, politely saluting Colonel Leslie, whom he had met before. Leslie returned the salute, and ordered his regiment to "file to the right and left and give Major Pedrick the pass."

When out of sight Pedrick put spurs to his horse, and galloped on to Salem. He went to the home of Colonel David Mason, who ran into the meetinghouse, where the congregation had gathered for the afternoon service, and shouted as he came down the aisle, "The Regulars are coming after the guns and are now near Malloon's Mills!"

Bells began to ring and drums beat "to arms" throughout the town. The people poured out of their churches and ran to save the guns. Baptists and Congregationalists forgot their differences and joined in a common effort. Even Quaker David Boyce hitched up his team and helped to haul away the heavy cannon. Some weapons were taken to an oak woodlot and hidden under the leaves. Others were carried to a remote part of town called Orne's Point.[45]

Meanwhile, the British troops were on the march. To delay them a party of townsmen hurried to a bridge between Salem and Marblehead and frantically ripped up some of the planking to delay the Regulars. Colonel Leslie's column was forced to halt while a party of soldiers repaired the structure. The Salem men won a few precious moments for the teams who were removing the cannon. But the Regulars soon improvised a surface over the bridge and crossed into Salem center, where they halted for a moment in Town House Square.

The townspeople watched as several of their Tory neighbors came forward. One was seen "whispering in the Colonel's ear." Then the British column started off at a quick-march, straight toward the cannon, with a large crowd of Salem men and boys walking beside them.

In their path was a drawbridge over an arm of the sea called

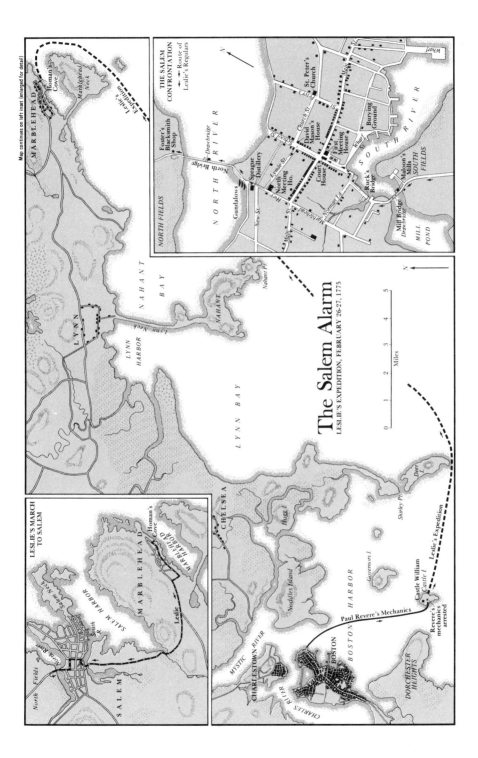

Map continues on left inset (enlarged for detail)

MARBLEHEAD

Homan's
Cove

Marblehead Neck

Leslie's
Expedition

Map continues on left inset (enlarged for detail)

THE SALEM
CONFRONTATION

—— Route of
Leslie's Regulars

N

St. Peter's
Church

Church St.

Foster's
Blacksmith
Shop

David
Mason's
House

NORTH RIVER

Drawbridge

North Bridge

Sprague
Distillery

Gundalows

New St.

NORTH FIELDS

Court
House

First
Meeting
House

North Meeting Ho.

Burying
Ground

Wharf

Ruck's
Bridge

Maloon's
Mills

SOUTH
FIELDS

Mill Bridge
Drawbridge

MILL
POND

SOUTH RIVER

Wharf

N A H A N T

B A Y

NAHANT

Nahant Pt.

L Y N N   B A Y

LYNN
HARBOR

Lynn Neck

LYNN

# The Salem Alarm
LESLIE'S EXPEDITION, FEBRUARY 26-27, 1775

N

Miles

0   1   2   3   4   5

CHELSEA

Hogg I.

Shirley Pt.

Deer

Leslie's Expedition

LESLIE'S MARCH
TO SALEM

Homan's
Cove

MARBLEHEAD

Salem Neck

SALEM HARBOR

South R.
Harbor

Leslie

North Fields

SALEM

MARBLEHEAD
HARBOR

Noddles Island

Governors I.

BOSTON HARBOR

Castle William
Castle I.

Leslie's Expedition

MYSTIC RIVER

CHARLESTOWN RIVER

BOSTON

CHARLES RIVER

Paul Revere's Mechanics

Revere's
mechanics
arrested

DORCHESTER
HEIGHTS

North River. Just as the soldiers approached it, the men of Salem raised the drawbridge from the north side. There was no other way across. The troops were forced to halt at the bridge.

Colonel Leslie hurried forward, and demanded to know why the men of Salem dared to obstruct the King's highway. They replied that the road belonged to them. The British commander "stamped and swore and ordered the bridge to be lowered at once," threatening to open fire if he was not obeyed. Militia captain John Felt warned him, "You had better be damned than fire! You have no right to fire without further orders! If you fire you'll all be dead men."

The crowd began to grow. Several Salem men sat provocatively on the raised edge of the open drawbridge, dangling their feet and shouting defiantly at the Regulars, "Soldiers! Red Jackets! Lobster Coats! Cowards! Damnation to Your Government!"

While the Salem men gathered at the head of the British column, the Marblehead Regiment was mustering behind its rear. These Marblehead men were a special breed. Many were cod fishermen—rugged, weatherbeaten, hard-handed seamen who earned their living in open boats on the dangerous waters of the North Atlantic. Some were veterans of the French wars. They were as stubborn and independent as their Boston cousins, and feared no mortal power on this earth—least of all the red-coated Regulars who had invaded their town. The men of Marblehead moved into strong positions along the Salem Road, and prepared to fight.[46]

It was a sharp wintry New England day. As the Regulars stood waiting in their ranks, some began to shiver in the damp cold. The men of Salem taunted them. One shouted across the river, "I should think you were all fiddlers, you shake so!"[47]

In the river near the bridge were three large sailing scows called "gundalows" in the old New England dialect. Colonel Leslie noticed the boats and ordered his troops to seize them. The Salem men moved more quickly. They jumped into the boats and smashed their bottoms to keep the Regulars from using them. The soldiers ran to stop them, threatening to use their bayonets. A Salem man named Joseph Whicher, the foreman of a distillery, rose up before them and defiantly tore open his shirt, daring the troops to attack. An infuriated British soldier lunged forward and "pricked" the American's naked chest with his bayonet.[48]

The mood of the crowd began to change. They closed in around the soldiers, who pushed them back with bayonets. Suddenly, a man dressed in black moved through the throng toward

Colonel Leslie, and spoke to him in a voice that demanded to be heard:

"I desire you do not fire on these innocent people."

"Who are you?" said Colonel Leslie.

"I am Thomas Barnard, a minister of the gospel, and my mission is peace," the clergyman replied. The two men, one in black and the other in red, began to talk. The hour was growing late—five o'clock in the evening. The winter sun was going down, and wind was cruel in the damp salt air.

Colonel Leslie had reason to be concerned, not merely for the success of his mission, but the safety of his force. Whig leader Benjamin Daland (today remembered as the Paul Revere of Salem) had galloped to Danvers with the news of the Regulars. Now he was back again, and many others with him. By five o'clock militia were streaming into Salem from as far as Amesbury, twenty-five miles to the north.

As more men poured into the town, the Salem minister proposed to the British colonel a cunning Yankee compromise—the bridge would be lowered if the Regulars promised on their honor to march only to the forge about 100 yards beyond. If they found no cannon they were to turn around and go back to their ships. Colonel Leslie was willing to accept those terms, knowing that he could accomplish nothing more at that late hour. The people of Salem were happy to agree, knowing that the cannon were safely removed.

The drawbridge came creaking down. The British soldiers marched solemnly across it, found nothing, and turned to march back again. As they started their retreat, a window flew open in a house by the road, and a young Salem woman named Sarah Tarrant thrust out her head. "Go home," she screamed at the Regulars, "and tell your master he sent you on a fool's errand, and has broken the peace of our Sabbath." She added contemptuously, "Do you think we were born in the woods, to be frightened by owls?" An frustrated Regular raised his firelock and took aim at her head. Sarah Tarrant said defiantly, "Fire, if you have the courage, but I doubt it."[49]

The British troops returned ignominiously to their ship, fifes and drums playing with empty bravado. They were escorted by a vast crowd of men from Salem and Danvers and many other towns. As the column crossed into Marblehead, and the men of that community also came out of their positions and joined the procession, marching in mock-cadence beside the British troops.

As the Regulars boarded their transport and sailed away, American militiamen converged on Salem from many towns in Essex County—from Danvers and Marblehead, Beverly and Lynn End, Reading and Stoneham. When they learned that the Regulars had left empty-handed, many shared a sense of triumph that made the Imperial cause seem not evil but absurd. An American journalist commented, "It is regretted that an officer of Colonel Leslie's worth should be obliged, in obedience to his orders, to come upon so pitiful an errand." Even Loyalists were appalled by what had happened. Thomas Hutchinson wrote, "It is very uncertain whether he succeeded in the errand he went upon."[50]

General Gage confessed in his candid way that the mission had been a "mistake." Worse than merely a defeat, it was received by both sides as a disgrace to British arms. Something was happening in these alarms that meant more trouble for the Imperial cause than the loss of a few cannon. When Joseph Whicher exposed his naked breast to a British bayonet, and Sarah Tarrant dared a Regular to fire "if you have the courage," a new spirit was rising in Massachusetts. Each side tested the other's resolve in these encounters. One side repeatedly failed that test.[51]

Why it did so is a question of much importance in our story. Had General Gage been the tyrant that many New England Whigs believed him to be, the outcome might have been very different. But Thomas Gage was an English gentleman who believed in decency, moderation, liberty, and the rule of law. Here again was the agony of an old English Whig: he could not crush American resistance to British government without betraying the values which he believed that government to represent.

On the other side, Paul Revere and the Whigs of New England faced no such dilemma. Their values were consistent with their interests and their acts. That inner harmony became their outward strength.

# MOUNTING TENSIONS

## ✎ Inevitability as an Act of Choice

> On both sides large preparations are making . . .
> bloodshed and desolation seem inevitable."
>
> —Robert Auchmuty to Thomas Hutchinson,
> March 3, 1775, Hutchinson papers, BL

> It is certain both sides were ripe for it, and a single
> blow would have occasioned the commencement of
> hostilities."
>
> —Lt. Frederick Mackenzie, Royal Welch
> Fusiliers, Boston, March 6, 1775

As SPRING APPROACHED in 1775, the atmosphere in Boston grew heavy with foreboding. "Things now every day begin to grow more and more serious," Lord Percy wrote home on April 8. It was one of the few facts on which everyone could agree. Here was a curious phenomenon, rarely studied by historians of war, and yet always part of its antecedents. On both sides, men acquiesced in a growing sense that conflict was inevitable. Many adopted this idea of inevitability, as an act of choice. That expanding attitude rapidly became the father of the fact.[1]

The wretched weather did not help. A dreary season of mud and flood and drizzle that New England dignifies by the name of spring literally created a climate of despair. One British soldier wrote home that even springtime in New England was "cold and disagreeable, a kind of second winter."[2]

After many months of frost, Boston larders were empty, and food was increasingly scarce. The price of fresh provisions rose so high in the crowded town that General Gage was forced to put his army on salt rations. One of his officers wrote privately, "Tommy

65

feels no affection for his army, and is more attached to a paltry œconomy."[3]

Even the drinking water went foul. The 43rd Foot reported that the water in its reservoirs "smells so excessively strong that many of the men drop down in fits while they are pumping."[4] The health of the garrison was not good. A "malignant spotted fever" (perhaps typhus) broke out among the Royal Irish. They were quarantined on a transport in the harbor. The "throat distemper" (possibly diphtheria) spread through the garrison, killing General Gage's confidential secretary and many others. Sam Adams reported to his friends in Virginia, "The army has been sickly through the winter and continue so. Many have died. Many have deserted. Many I believe intend to desert."[5]

The British infantry were kept busy drilling on the Common and shooting at floating marks in Boston harbor. Twice a day they were ordered to stand parade in rigid formation, and made to endure spit-and-polish inspections while gangs of ragged apprentices shouted insults from a safe distance. The men were increasingly bored, angry, and hungry—a recipe for disaster in any army.

The common British soldier has rarely received his due in histories of the American Revolution. Many people regarded them as rough, unlettered, hard-drinking men—outcasts from civil society, a breed apart. They were reviled by civilians and despised even by their own commanders. But those who knew them as individuals formed a different opinion of their character and worth. William Cobbett, before becoming a political journalist of high eminence in the United States and Britain, enlisted in the 54th Foot near the end of the American Revolution and served nine years as a common soldier. Afterwards he remembered his comrades with affection and respect. "I like soldiers as a class in life, better than any other description of men," he wrote. "Their conversation is more pleasing to me; they have generally seen more than other men; they have less vulgar prejudice about them."[6]

The British Regulars bonded closely with one another against a hostile world. They spoke their own distinctive dialect—a form of speech related to the "flash language" of the 18th-century underworld. Among themselves they kept a soldier's code of honesty, loyalty, and courage, and enforced it strictly upon one another in kangaroo courts that their officers knew nothing about. Cobbett recalled, "Amongst soldiers, less than amongst any other description of men, have I observed the vices of lying and hypocrisy."

These men were at their best on active service. But after a long winter in Boston garrison they were bored and restless. The supply of strong New England rum was cheap and abundant. "A man may get drunk for a copper or two," wrote Lieutenant Barker of the King's Own. In February, Major John Pitcairn of the British Marines told a friend, "We have lost seven by death, killed by drinking the cursed rum of this country. There are I believe several more [who] must die." By March, Major Pitcairn was so concerned about drunkenness in his battalion that he wrote directly to the First Lord of the Admiralty, "I have lived almost night and day amongst the men in their barracks for these five or six weeks past, to keep them from that pernicious rum. I would not have your Lordship think from this that we are worse than the other battalions here. The rum is so cheap that it debauches both navy and army, and kills many of them. Depend on it, my Lord, it will destroy more of us than the Yankies will."[7]

Several Regulars sold their muskets for drink. When a soldier in the King's Own was caught "disposing of his arms to the townspeople," he was trussed up like an animal on a tripod of sergeants' halberds and given 500 lashes on his bare back—enough to kill an ordinary man. The conscience of New England was deeply shocked by this cruelty—not only by its inhumanity as we would be, but also in another way. The biblical statutes of Massachusetts restricted whipping to thirty-nine strokes; anything more was thought to be unscriptural, and forbidden by God's express command. To the people of Boston, here was another Sign.[8]

In the British garrison, desertion rapidly increased. One of the best regiments, the Royal Welch Fusiliers, lost 27 men. Private Thomas Macfarlane of that unit enlisted on May 19, 1774, deserted on July 19, returned on October 6, and deserted again on December 2, 1774. A detachment of the 8th Foot arrived in Boston, on their way to join their regiment in Quebec. The most direct route would have been west through Massachusetts by the Boston Post Road. But Gage wrote, "If I had marched them thro' the country to Albany we should have lost half of them." He sent them by sea to New York.[9]

General Gage doubled his guards around the town, more to keep his own men in than the "country people" out. In desperation he began to execute his own men. When a young private tried to desert for the third time he was dressed in a white shroud of repentence, taken to Boston Common, and shot by a firing squad while the town watched in shock and horror. In New England, corporal punishment was lawful for the violation of God's Commandments, but not for the orders of General Gage.[10]

Another soldier in the 10th Regiment was shot on Christmas Eve, "the only thing done in remembrance of Christmas Day," Barker noted bitterly. In March Private Robert Vaughan of the 52nd Foot was caught in act of deserting, and sentenced to death. He was pardoned the night before his execution, and promptly disappeared into the countryside, with much help from the town. General Gage was informed by a Loyalist agent that the people of Boston had organized a secret escape route for British deserters, who were spirited away by boat across the Charles River. One soldier was given four dollars and a suit of clothes by a Boston merchant and taken to the town of Andover, Massachusetts. Another, Private John Clancey in the 47th Foot, was promised that he "should be made a gentleman" if he chose to desert. Whig leaders passed the word that they would give 300 acres in New Hampshire to any soldier who left his unit.[11]

Most of the Regulars refused these bribes, and stayed loyally with their comrades. They began to hate their commander in chief, who treated them as incipient felons, and punished them more severely then he did the Yankees. They equally despised the Bostonians who reviled them, and desperately wished for other duty. Even the officers of the garrison ran out of control. In late January, a party of subalterns viciously attacked the town watch. When the Dogberries defended themselves with their billhooks, the officers drew their swords. One watchman had his nose cut off; another lost his thumb.[12]

Other officers began to attack each other. Even senior officers joined in. At evening parade, Lieutenant-Colonel Walcott, commander of the 5th Foot, drew a sword on one of his junior officers, who was also his kinsman. General Gage ordered a court-martial for both men.[13]

The top commanders began to quarrel among themselves. General Gage and Admiral Graves were often at loggerheads. "It is a great misfortune to me," Marine Major John Pitcairn wrote, "that the General and Admiral are not as cordial as I could wish." In fact they hated and despised each other, and quarreled angrily over the Marine battalion that had been sent to reinforce the garrison. Graves refused to allow it to leave his ships unless he could continue to supply their rations, at a handsome profit. "The admiral can have no reason but to put money in the pursers' pocket," Major Pitcairn wrote.[14]

Both the army and the navy in Boston were at the end of a long logistical lifeline that functioned fitfully in the best of times. Major Pitcairn struggled incessantly with the Admiralty to supply his men with uniforms and equipment. They had been sent to New England in December without winter garments. Pitcairn had greatcoats, leggings and warm caps made in Boston for every man in his command. As Spring approached, he begged the Admiralty for campaigning equipment with little result. One letter sought swords for his grenadiers and drummers. Pitcairn wrote furiously, "the last have nothing to defend themselves but their drumsticks."[15]

Many junior officers turned their frustration against the people of New England. Major Pitcairn went over the heads of his superiors, and dispatched an angry letter directly to the First Lord of the Admiralty, urging hard measures against the colonists. "One active campaign, a smart action, and burning two or three of their towns, will set everything to rights," Pitcairn wrote, "Nothing now, I am afraid, but this will ever convince those foolish bad people that England is in earnest."

This hard-bitten Marine officer had formed a complete contempt for the Americans. "I assure you, " he wrote from a Boston coffee house to a fellow Marine in Britain, "I have so despicable an opinion of the people of this country that I would not hesitate to march with the Marines I have with me to any part of the country, and do whatever I was inclined. I am satisfied they will never attack Regular troops."[16]

On the other side, Bostonians were increasingly contemptuous of the British troops. The town itself became a tinderbox, and on March 6, 1775, a small spark nearly set it ablaze. That day a huge crowd squeezed into the Old South Meetinghouse to mark the fifth anniversary of the Boston Massacre. Paul Revere was probably there, along with John Hancock, the Adamses, the British spy Dr. Benjamin Church, and many others. Also in the audience were many bored and idle British officers who were looking for trouble. The meeting began with high solemnity. Dr. Joseph Warren rose into a pulpit that was hung with heavy black cloth, and delivered the major speech in a flowery provincial style that was much admired in Boston but little to the taste of English gentlemen. When he finished, Sam Adams rose to his feet in the pew where he was sitting with the Selectmen, and moved that "the thanks of the town should be presented to Dr. Warren for his elegant and spirited oration."

Several British officers in the crowd began to hiss. One shouted, "Oh! fie! Oh! fie!"

The people of Boston did not understand that elegant imprecation of the new Imperial elite. In the New England dialect with its lost postvocalic *r*'s, "Fie! Fie!" sounded like "Fire! Fire!"

Panic broke out. Shouting men and screaming women pushed toward the doors. Several people hurled themselves from the windows into the street. At that unlucky moment the fifes and drums of the 43rd Regiment marched past the meetinghouse with a great rattle and crash of military music. The frightened townfolk saw the marching troops, heard the drums of the 43rd, and thought they were under attack. Lieutenant Frederick Mackenzie, the cool-headed adjutant of the 23rd Royal Welch Fusiliers, observed that "almost every man had a short stick or bludgeon in his hand, and . . . many of them were privately armed." Any violent act, he believed, "would have been the signal for battle. Both sides were ripe for it, and a single blow would have occasioned the commencement of hostilities."[17]

Britons and Bostonians alike were shocked by what had nearly happened. Whig leaders struggled to calm their neighbors, while senior British officers worked to keep their men in check. The town was quiet for a few days.

Then, on March 9, a Yankee pedlar named Thomas Ditson got into the quarters of the 47th Regiment. With more enterprise than judgment, Ditson offered to buy the soldiers' uniforms, and even their weapons. Several were willing to sell, but others reported Ditson to their commander. The pedlar was seized by order of an officer, tarred and feathered "from head to foot" by the rank and file, and mounted in a chair on top of a cart, and paraded through the town to the Liberty Tree. A fife and drum played a raucous Rogues March, and the colonel of the regiment led the procession.

The parade passed directly under the window of the commander in chief, who heard the irregular beat of the drum, but thought (as he later explained) that the men were merely "drumming a Bad Woman through the streets." When he found out what had happened, General Gage was infuriated. He severely chastised the 47th for lowering itself to the level of a Boston mob, "below the character of a soldier."[18]

Other incidents followed. On March 16, Bostonians complained that a party of soldiers led by their officers had deliberately disrupted a solemn Fast Day called by the Congregational clergy.

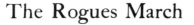

# The Rogues March

MUSIC Traditional
SOURCE Bland and Weller –
Entire New and Compleat Instructions for the Fife

"The Rogues March" is thought to have descended from a brutal Scottish drum-tune called "Cuckolds Come Dig," which was played when whores were flogged through the streets of Edinburgh. For three centuries it was heard in English-speaking armies when men were drummed out of their regiments. British Regulars made it into a drinking song:

> Fifty [lashes] I got for selling my coat
> Fifty for selling my blanket,
> If ever I 'list for a soldier again,
> The devil shall be my sergeant.

From Lewis Winstock, *Songs and Music of the Redcoats.*

On March 17, the many Irish Catholic soldiers in the garrison celebrated St. Patrick's Day with a Hibernian enthusiasm that appalled the Protestant town. Scarcely a day passed without an incident.

The Whigs of Boston added to the growing tension. General Gage, scrupulous as ever to protect the rule of law, had left New England's press free to publish without restraint. Polemics poured from Boston printshops, and added greatly to the pressures that were building in the town. Once again, Paul Revere played a prominent role. Between his many rides and various other activities, he found time in the Winter and early Spring of 1775 to engrave a series of hard-hitting political cartoons on Whiggish themes. Revere was no Hogarth; his engravings were crude and primitive. But they made their point, and summarized the complex ideology of the revolutionary movement in simple images that reached a larger public with greater force than John Adams's subtle briefs for liberty, or Sam Adams's solemn orations, or Joseph Warren's ornate phrases.[19]

Some of Paul Revere's cartoons in early 1775 were done at the request of his friends Isaiah Thomas and Joseph Greenleaf, for a new periodical called the *Royal American Magazine,* which despite its name had a strong Whig tone. In its January issue, Revere published a copper-plate engraving called "A Certain Cabinet Junto." It showed Lord North offering King George III a bill for the "Abolition of Civil and Religious Liberty in America." Behind the King lurked the sinister figure of the Earl of Bute, the King's Scottish mentor. In the center was the saturnine figure of Lord Justice Mansfield, giving his approval to the Act for the Better Administration of Justice, which Revere called by its Boston name, the Murder Act. On the far left sat the feminine figure of British America in deep distress. At her side was the shield that symbolized Britannia, and by her feet was the Indian bow and quiver that represented America. Tucked under her arm were a Phrygian cap and liberty pole that symbolized freedom in the iconography of 18th-century Whiggery.[20]

By our standards Paul Revere's engravings were very crude. He borrowed heavily from other prints, even to the point of what we would consider plagiarism. The four ministerial figures, the suffering figure of British America, and the liberty pole and cap were all staples of English caricature, copied line for line from the work of English artists.[21]

But even as Paul Revere borrowed freely from British Whig-

Paul Revere published this cartoon in January 1775. America appears as a lady in distress, surrounded by the symbols of liberty. Lord North hands George III a "Bill for the total abolition of civil and religious liberty in America," while Justice Mansfield offers an "act for murdering the Bostonians" and the Earl of Bute looks on approvingly. Revere copied the figures from an English print, and added a strong religious theme. (American Antiquarian Society)

gery, he added a strong spiritual theme that was his own invention, and uniquely a product of New England. Revere's feminine figure of British America looked to the heavens, and prayed (in italics), "Lord thou didst drive out the heathen before, our hope is in thee." From a heavy threatening thundercloud, she was answered (in boldface), "I have delivered and I WILL deliver."

Imperial officials were outraged by these publications. On March 10, 1775, the same 47th Regiment that had tarred and feathered the Yankee pedlar Thomas Ditson mustered in front of Isaiah Thomas's print shop. With their colonel at their head and the regimental band playing the Rogue's March, they warned the publisher that he would be next to wear a coat of tar and feathers.[22]

Paul Revere's engravings for the *Royal American Magazine* were models of restraint, compared with the abuse that streamed from other Yankee presses. General Gage himself became the favorite target. As early as 1775, American journalists had already

*The able Doctor. or America Swallowing the Bitter Draught.*

Lord North pours tea into a helpless America (wearing an Indian headdress and not much more), while Lord Mansfield pinions her arms, the Earl of Sandwich peeks under her skirts, and Britannia averts her eyes. Paul Revere copied this cartoon line for line from the London Magazine, adding only the word "Tea" to Lord North's kettle for anyone who missed the point. (American Antiquarian Society)

formed the habit of reducing complex public questions to personal attacks on prominent leaders. They accused General Gage of every imaginable vice from alcoholism to pederasty. In Newburyport's *Essex Journal,* for example, one journalist wrote:

> In truth, it's judg'd by men of thinking,
> That GAGE will kill himself a drinking.
> Nay, I'm informed by the inn keepers,
> He'll bung with shoe-boys, chimney sweepers.[23]

Worse, in New England eyes, he was accused of being a Papist, whose secret purpose was to convert all of America to Roman Catholicism by the sword. It was utterly without foundation, but had a powerful impact on American opinion.

This steady drumfire of personal abuse changed Boston's attitude toward General Gage. Up to this point, despite many differences, both sides had been careful to preserve the decencies. As late as January 1775, Samuel Adams believed that Gage was a virtuous victim of corrupt advisers who were "perpetually filling his ears with gross misrepresentations.[24] By March, Sam Adams was telling his friends that Thomas Gage was a man "void of a Spark of Humanity, who can deliberately be the instrument of depriving our Country of its Liberty, or the people of their lives in its defence."[25]

On the other side, these personal attacks also had an impact on the thinking of General Gage. He bitterly condemned the "flagitious prints" of New England, and accused them of spreading the "grossest forgeries, calumnies and absurdities that ever insulted human understanding."[26] His letters home to ministers in Britain betrayed increasing anger against the people of Massachusetts.

The letters that came back from London added to the tension in yet another way. Thomas Gage's superiors were losing patience with their man in America. For months they had been urging him to act, without result. On April 2, two ships from England arrived at Marblehead with unofficial reports that new orders were on their way to General Gage—firm instructions to move decisively against the rebellion and to arrest its leaders.

These rumors from London proved to be correct. As so often, they reached the people of Massachusetts before they got to the commander in chief. The news was sent by a galloper from Marblehead to Boston. Many leading Whigs astonished the British commander by instantly packing their bags and leaving town. By April 8, only two major Whig leaders, Joseph Warren and Paul Revere, remained behind.

The commander in chief caught wind that reports from London had arrived in Marblehead, but nobody on his staff could tell him what news they contained. He wrote home, "I can't learn whether she brought letters to any of the Faction here, but the news threw them into a consternation, and the most active left the Town before night."[27]

Finally on April 14, 1775, the dispatch ship HMS *Nautilus* reached Boston, with the secret orders that the Boston Whigs had already learned about. The documents were carried by Captain Oliver De Lancey, Mrs. Gage's American cousin and the son of the acting governor of New York. De Lancey came ashore, resplendent in a uniform of the 17th Light Dragoons. His crested cavalry helmet was adorned with his distinctive regimental badge, a huge grinning death's head and crossbones that made a fitting symbol for the grim tidings that were delivered by this harbinger of war.[28]

The most important dispatch was a confidential letter to Gage from the Earl of Dartmouth, dated January 27, 1775. It promised that more troops were on the way: another 700 Marines, three regiments of foot, and De Lancey's dragoons, which were thought to be specially effective in the suppression of civil disturbances. General Gage was bluntly informed that the King's ministers did not accept his estimate that the conquest of New England would require 20,000 men. He was told that if he needed more men, he should raise a corps of infantry from "friends of government in New England." He was also instructed in no uncertain terms that the time had come for decisive action against "proceedings that amount to actual revolt." The ministers insisted that nothing less than the sacred honor of the Empire and that of the King himself were at stake: "The King's dignity, and the honor and safety of the Empire, require, that, in such a situation, force should be repelled with force."

The ministers were aware of General Gage's scrupulous concern for the rule of law. They reminded him that "the charter of Massachusetts impowers the governor to use and exercise the law-martial in time of actual war, invasion, or rebellion." They were explicit about the specific steps that Gage should take. He should seize the ringleaders, and disarm the population. Dartmouth told him, "It is the opinion of the King's servants, in which His Majesty concurs, that the first and essential step to be taken towards re-establishing Government, would be to arrest and imprison the principal actors and abettors of the Provincial Congress whose proceedings appear in every light to be acts of treason and rebellion."[29]

The King's ministers were entirely optimistic about the outcome. They had suppressed many insurrections in Ireland, Scotland, the Colonies, and even England itself. In the absence of a professional police force, the Regular Army had been routinely assigned to do this work and had become highly skilled at it. Many of the regiments in Boston had recently seen service on similar missions in Britain itself. Just before coming to America, the Royal Welch Fusiliers had been used to "restore order" throughout Devon and Cornwall, and especially the towns of Penryn, Truro, and Falmouth. The 18th Foot had been called out to stop riots against Press Gangs in Whitehaven. The 43rd and eight other regiments had been assigned to put down agrarian risings that spread through twelve counties of the South Midlands and East Anglia in 1766. The 4th, and many other units, had been busy along the south coast of England, suppressing rings of highly organized tea-smugglers whose activities made the Boston Tea Party seem like an affair of amateur theatrics by comparison. The British Marines had been sent on a similar mission into Romney Marsh. Ireland had been in a state of insurrection in 1771 and 1772; several of General Gage's regiments had come directly from that realm of incessant strife. In England itself, between 1740 and 1775, there had been at least 159 major riots, and minor ones beyond counting. Many were put down by the army. To the King's ministers in London, the troubles in distant Boston seemed merely another routine disturbance that could be dealt with in the usual way.[30]

These men, who knew so little of America, assured General Gage that the "rebels" of Massachusetts were merely "a rude Rabble without plan, without concert, and without conduct." Gage was told that "a smaller force now, if put to the test, would be able to encounter them with greater probability of success than might be expected from a greater army." He was advised that "if the steps taken upon this occasion be accompanied with due precaution, and every means devised to keep the measure secret until the moment of execution, it can hardly fail of success, and will perhaps be accomplished without bloodshed."[31]

It all seemed so easy, three thousand miles away. Still, in the eternal manner of politicians everywhere, the ministers were careful to cover themselves. The Earl of Dartmouth added, "It must be understood, however, after all I have said, that this is a matter for discretion." In other words, if all went right the Government would claim the credit; if anything went wrong General Gage would bear the blame. Nevertheless, Gage's orders were clear enough. He was to move quickly and decisively with all the strength at his disposal. In the name of the King himself he was commanded to arrest the leaders of the rebellion, to disarm their followers, and to impose order on the Province of Massachusetts by "law-martial" if necessary.

With these instructions on his desk, General Gage studied the calendar. The snow had melted in New England. The ground was still soft, but the season for campaigning would soon begin. It was time to prepare.

# THE MISSION

## ❧ British Plans, American Preparations

> Keep the measure secret until the moment of execution, it can hardly fail of success. . . . Any efforts of the people, unprepared to encounter with a regular force, cannot be very formidable.
>
> —Earl of Dartmouth to General Gage,
> Jan. 27, 1775

> We may all be soon under the necessity of keeping Shooting Irons.
>
> —Samuel Adams to Stephen Collins,
> Jan. 31, 1775

IN HIS METHODICAL WAY, General Thomas Gage had already begun to make the necessary preparations, even before his new orders arrived from London. This time he vowed that the outcome would be different—not like the embarrassing fiasco at Portsmouth or the painful humiliation at Salem. The lessons of experience were very clear. He must strike at the heart of the rebel movement and cripple it with quick, clean blows before its large numbers could be mustered against his little army. If he wished to act without awakening the wrath of the continent against him, it was necessary to do these things without the shedding of blood, or at least with as little bloodshed as possible. Everything hinged on secrecy, surprise, and sound intelligence.

On the other side, Whig leaders in New England were preparing too. Forewarned by friends in London, they knew that the British army was about to move against them, but not precisely where or when. They were prepared to fight for their freedom, but they could not start the fight without forfeiting the moral advantage of their cause. These New England Whigs believed that if shots had to be fired, it was urgently important that a British soldier must be the one to fire first. Only then would America stand united. Samuel Adams was very clear about that. On March 21, 1775, this canny politician reminded his fellow Whigs, "Put your enemy in the wrong, and keep him so, is a wise maxim in politics, as well as in war."[1]

New England leaders resolved not to move until Gage committed his forces. Once he had done so, their intention was to react quickly, and muster their full strength against him with all the force at their command. Everything depended on careful preparation, timely warning, and rapid mobilization.

Each side recognized the critical importance of intelligence, and both went busily about that vital task. But they did so in different ways. The British system was created and controlled from the top down. It centered very much on General Gage himself. The gathering of information commonly began with questions from the commander in chief. The lines of inquiry reached outward like tentacles from his headquarters in Province House. This structure proved a source of strength in some respects, and weakness in others. The considerable resources of the Royal government could be concentrated on a single problem. But when the commander in chief asked all the questions, he was often told the answers that he wished to hear. Worse, the questions that he did not think to ask were never answered at all.

The American system of intelligence was organized in the opposite way, from the bottom up. Self-appointed groups such as Paul Revere's voluntary association of Boston mechanics gathered information on their own initiative. Other individuals in many towns did the same. These efforts were coordinated through an open, disorderly network of congresses and committees, but no central authority controlled this activity in Massachusetts—not the Provincial Congress or Committee of Safety, not the Boston Committee of Correspondence or any small junto of powerful leaders; not Sam Adams or John Hancock, not even the indefatigable Doctor Warren, and certainly not Paul Revere. The revolutionary movement in New England had many leaders, but no commander. Nobody was truly in charge. This was a source of weakness in some ways. The system was highly inefficient. Its efforts were scattered and diffuse. Individuals demanded a reason for acting, before they acted at all. They wrangled incessantly in congresses, conventions, committees and town meetings. But by those clumsy processes, many autonomous New England minds were enlisted in a common effort—a source of energy, initiative, and intellectual strength for this popular movement.

In the beginning, General Gage held the initiative. He organized a formal intelligence staff that consisted largely of his kinsmen—mostly relatives by marriage whom he felt that he could trust. His deputy adjutant-general for intelligence was his American brother-in-law, Major Stephen Kemble, an officer in the British army. His confidential secretary was Samuel Kemble, another brother-in-law. His aide-de-camp for confidential matters was his wife's cousin, Captain Oliver De Lancey.

Young Captain De Lancey was typical of the American Loyalists who joined this new transatlantic Imperial elite. He came from a rich and powerful New York family which owned a large part of Manhattan Island and Westchester County. His uncles included the acting governor of New York and the chief justice of that colony. De Lancey had been sent to school at Eton, and a commission had been bought for him in a crack British cavalry regiment. He joined Gage's headquarters in 1775.[2]

In the winter and spring of 1774–75, two months before Gage's secret orders arrived, his staff began to collect information about eastern Massachusetts. Every officer in the garrison with knowledge of the countryside was ordered to report to headquarters. Loyalist agents were actively recruited. They began to send a steady flow of information on provincial politics and military affairs.[3]

As General Gage studied the reports that came across his desk, his first thought was to revive an earlier plan, and strike at the shire town of Worcester, forty miles west of Boston. That village had become a major center of the revolutionary movement. Various provincial bodies had met there. A large supply of munitions was stored in its houses and barns, and the tools of war were manufactured in its mills. Agents reported that fifteen tons of gunpowder were on hand, and thirteen cannon were parked in front of the Congregational meetinghouse. For many months the inhabitants of Worcester had been outspoken in support of the Whig cause, and had spurned all compromise.[4] As early as the summer of 1774, Gage had written to Dartmouth, "In Worcester they keep no terms, openly threaten resistance by arms, have been purchasing arms, preparing them, casting ball, and providing powder, and threaten to attack any troops who dare to oppose them." He concluded: "I apprehend I shall soon be obliged to march a body of troops into that township."[5]

General Gage decided to postpone that plan after the Powder Alarm in September 1774; but through the fall and winter, Worcester continued to be on his mind. In the last week of February 1775, Gage summoned two enterprising young officers, Captain John Brown and Ensign Henry De Berniere of the 10th Foot. He asked them to go out on a confidential mission. They were to dress in plain country clothing and walk from Boston to Worcester, and to return with a sketch of the countryside and a report on the roads. In particular, they were to look for dangerous ambush sites along the way. The need for secrecy was strongly impressed upon them. If anyone asked their business, the British officers were to pretend to be surveyors.[6]

De Berniere and Brown were bored by garrison life and leaped at the assignment. The result was yet another bizarre cultural collision between Britain's Imperial elite and the folkways of New England. The mission began as low comedy, and nearly ended in calamity for the young British officers. They set off on foot, "disguised like countrymen, in brown cloaths and reddish handkerchiefs round our necks." They were delighted to discover that General Gage himself was unable to recognize them. But when they left town by the Charlestown ferry, a British sentry saluted briskly and nearly gave the game away.[7]

They walked west through Cambridge, and by mid-day reached a Whig tavern in Watertown, where they decided to stop for something to eat. The officers had insisted upon traveling with a batman whom they called "our man John."[8] When they entered the tavern, these young British gentlemen banished their servant to a separate table, and "called for dinner" in what seemed to them an ordinary tone of voice. To their surprise, they noticed that the black serving maid began to "eye us very attentively," as they wrote in their report.

"It is a fine country," the officers said in their most agreeable manner, forgetting that they were supposed to be countrymen themselves.

"So it is," answered the maid with a knowing look, "and we have got brave fellows to defend it, and if you go up any higher you will find it so."[9]

The officers were stunned by her reply. "This disconcerted us a good deal," they reported, "and we resolved not to sleep there that night." They called for the bill, and betrayed themselves again by trying to settle in British sterling an account that had been reckoned in the mysterious complexity of Massachusetts "Old Tenor" currency. While they struggled with the rate of exchange, the black waitress approached their batman again and delivered another gratuitous warning: "She said she knew our errand was to take a plan of the country," and "advised him to tell us not to go any higher, for if we did we should meet with very bad usage."

Brown and De Berniere held a quick "council," and decided that they could not return to Boston without dishonor, an act unthinkable for a British officer. They resolved to push on, but agreed that in deference to the customs of this strange country, their batman would be promoted to a condition of temporary equality with themselves—even at dinner. They wrote in their report, "We always treated him as our companion, since our adventure with the black woman." At least one human relationship was briefly transformed by the American Revolution, even as it had barely begun.

In wintry weather, the three men continued west on the Old Boston Post Road to the Golden Ball Tavern, which still stands today in the suburban town of Weston. This was a Tory inn. They were treated well, but warned once again not to go higher into the country. Still, they gamely insisted on pressing on. Their Tory host in Weston sent them to a Loyalist tavernkeeper in Marlborough, and from there to another Tory inn in Worcester which they reached on Saturday night. Here again they were treated courteously, and even offered the symbolic dish of tea that proclaimed the politics of the establishment.

The strict New England Sabbath began at sundown on Saturday. The British officers were warned that movement was impossible for them until sunset on Sunday. They explained to their superiors, "We could not think of travelling, as it is contrary to the custom of the country, nor dare we stir out until the evening because of meeting, and nobody is allowed to walk the streets during the divine service, without being taken up and examined."

When the Sabbath ended on Sunday evening, they left the Tory tavern and mapped the hills and roads around Worcester. Then they started back toward Boston, crisscrossing the country lanes of Middlesex County. They spent their nights in Tory taverns, and took their lunches in the woods, dining on a bit of bread and "a little snow to wash it down." Even so, their movements were quickly discovered and carefully observed. Groups of silent coun-

The Golden Ball Tavern still stands on the Old Boston Post Road in Weston, Massachusetts. It was one of a network of Tory safe houses used by General Gage's spies, Captain Brown and Ensign De Berniere, on their reconnaissance missions in 1775. Innkeeper Isaac Jones, a Loyalist "friend to government," guided them on part of their journey. This early photograph, circa 1868, shows the tavern in winter as it was seen by the British officers. (Courtesy Golden Ball Tavern)

tryfolk people gathered in the villages, watching ominously as they walked through. Horsemen rode up to them on the road, studied their appearance without saying a word, then wheeled and galloped away.

They were saved from further attentions by a late snowstorm that covered their tracks and kept the "country people" indoors. Increasingly fearful for their lives, the British officers pressed on through the storm, heading back toward Boston. In one horrific day they plodded thirty-two miles in ankle-deep snow, finally arriving exhausted and half frozen at the Golden Ball Tavern in Weston. The next morning, while parties of Whigs scoured the countryside, the landlord guided them through back roads to the safety of Boston.[10]

General Gage was pleased with the thoroughness of their report, but not happy at the thought of sending a force to Worcester. The distance was so great that surprise could not be assured. The roads were difficult, and a dangerous river crossing through the broad marshes at Sudbury could turn into a deadly trap. The commander in chief returned to his map of New England and searched for another target. His eyes fell on the half-shire town of Concord.[11] This village had also become an arsenal of revolution. The Provincial Congress had been meeting there. It was barely twenty miles from Boston—half as far as Worcester. With hard marching on dry roads, Gage reckoned that his troops could be there and back again in a long day.

In mid-March, he summoned Captain Brown and Lieutenant De Berniere to Province House, and asked them to go out again on another secret mission, this time to explore the roads to Concord. On March 20, they left Boston by way of Roxbury and Brookline, and walked through Weston on what was called the Concord Road, at that time the most direct route from Boston Neck to their destination. They found it very dangerous for a marching army, and reported that it was "woody in most places and commanded by hills," as it remains today.

When they reached Concord, the town appeared to them like an armed camp, with sentries posted at its approaches, and vast quantities of munitions on hand. The British officers met a woman in the road and asked directions to the house of Daniel Bliss, a Loyalist lawyer and one of Concord's leading citizens. She showed them the way. Bliss welcomed the two officers, and offered them dinner. A little later the woman suddenly returned, weeping with fear. She explained between her tears that several Whigs had stopped her and "swore they would tar and feather her for directing Tories."

A moment later a message arrived for lawyer Bliss himself, threatening death if he did not leave town. The British officers, who were carrying arms, gallantly offered to escort him back to Boston, and protect him with their lives. The three men set out for Boston. Bliss showed them another route that ran further to the north, through Lexington and the village of Menotomy (now Arlington). It was longer than the roads through Weston, but the countryside was more open, and ambuscades were less to be feared. The British officers returned to Boston and made their report, strongly recommending the northern route through Lexington as the best approach.[12]

Gage had found the target for his next mission, and a satisfactory way of getting there. It would be Concord, by the Lexington Road. Now his intelligence efforts began to center on the town itself. He had secret agents there, Loyalists who have never been identified, but lived in or near the town and were exceptionally well informed. One of them wrote regularly to Gage in bad French, describing in detail the munitions stored throughout the town, and the temper of the inhabitants.

Among these reports was a detailed inventory, house by house and barn by barn, of munitions stored throughout the entire community. One building alone was thought to hold seven tons of gunpowder.[13] General Gage ordered a map of Concord to be prepared, showing the location of every building known to harbor military stores. He was also told that John Hancock and Sam Adams were staying in the town of Lexington, a smaller community of scattered dairy farms five miles east of Concord center.

In early April, General Gage began to organize his marching force. In strictest secrecy he drafted its orders in his own hand. To command the expedition he selected Lieutenant Colonel Francis Smith of the 10th Foot. Smith was a senior officer, very near retirement. Another officer described him as a "heavy man," inactive, overweight, unfit for arduous service.[14] But he was known to be an officer of prudence, moderation, and maturity. His choice betrayed Gage's own caution and restraint. So also did his orders. Smith was instructed to march "with utmost expedition and secrecy to Concord, where you will seize and destroy all the Artillery, Ammunition, Provisions, Tents, Small Arms, and all Military stores whatever."

Nothing was mentioned in writing about the arrest of Whig leaders. Gage seems not to have been happy with that part of his instructions. He understood better than men in London the structure of the revolutionary movement. He knew that nobody was really in command of it. If one leader were arrested, ten more would be ready to take his place.

Further, Gage believed in the rule of law. Throughout these turbulent events, even when he was furiously angry with the Whig leaders, he rejected a policy of arbitrary arrest. His written orders for the expedition said nothing about seizing Whig leaders, despite explicit instructions from London for their apprehension. Colonel Smith was given strict orders to keep carefully within the law. "You will take care," Gage told him, "that the soldiers do not plunder the inhabitants, or hurt private property."[15]

Gage believed that the expedition might be resisted by armed force, and urged many precautions. Smith was ordered to march to Concord by the Lexington Road that offered the least danger of ambush, and he was told to secure the bridges of Concord "as soon as possible" when he reached the town.

With startling prescience, Gage understood the form that re-sistance would probably take. On March 4, 1775, he wrote to Dartmouth in London, "The most natural and eligible mode of attack on the part of the people is that of detached parties of bushmen who from their adroitness in the habitual use of the firelock suppose themselves sure of their mark at a distance of 200 rods [he surely meant yards]. Should hostilities unhappily com-mence, the first opposition would be irregular, impetuous, and incessant from the numerous bodies that would swarm to the place of action, and all actuated by an enthusiasm wild and ungovern-able."[16]

Even if the worst happened, Gage believed that a strong force of Regular troops under experienced professional officers had little to fear from these "bushmen." He wrote that he was "firmly persuaded that there is not a man amongst [them] capable of taking command or directing the motions of an army." It was his only error in a remarkably trenchant analysis—but one error would be more than enough. His mistake in judgment was not about the probability of resistance, or the motives, tactics, and fighting skills of the New England militia, but about the quality of leadership among them.[17]

In Boston, the British regiments were ordered to repair their tents, mend their camp kettles, and break out their field equip-ment. They were sent out on short marches through the country west of Boston, partly to toughen the men, partly to accustom the people of Massachusetts to their movements out of town. Two regiments, the 38th and 52nd Foot, were ordered to march as far as Watertown, and did not return until 5 o'clock at night. Mack-enzie noted, "As Watertown is farther than the Regiments have usually gone, and they remained out longer, the country was a good deal alarmed on the occasion."[18] No explanations were given, but Lieutenant Mackenzie surmised that "it is supposed the general has some object in view, and means to familiarize the people of the Country with the appearance of troops among them for a longer time than usual without creating an alarm."[19]

Some of these preparations could be made without raising suspicions. Others proved impossible to hide. On Wednesday, April 5, Gage asked the navy to prepare for a movement of troops by boat from Boston across the Back Bay to Cambridge. Admiral Graves, the senior naval officer present, was a difficult man: iras-cible, corrupt and stupid beyond belief. He did not like to do any soldier's bidding, and he particularly detested Thomas Gage. Unable to refuse the general's request, Admiral Graves acted with precipitate speed and no subtlety whatever. On the very next day, Thursday, April 6, he ordered his ships in the harbor to launch their longboats, and moor them under their sterns, ready for use. On Friday, April 7, that work was done in full view of the town.

The Whigs of Boston were quick to observe this flurry of activity in the harbor. They were also instantly informed that a party of British officers had been sent to examine the roads to Concord. Those two pieces of intelligence were put together, and it was concluded that General Gage was about to move against Concord. So active were the preparations in the harbor that on Saturday morning Whig leaders decided that the Regulars were ready to march, and guessed that these "godless myrmidons" would move on Sunday, April 9, striking on the Sabbath as they had done at Salem.

It was decided to send an urgent warning to Concord, and the job was given to Paul Revere. On Saturday, April 8, the day after Graves lowered his boats into the water, Revere mounted his horse and rode out of town. He reached Concord in the evening with a letter from Doctor Warren, addressed to the leaders of the town. The contents of the message were recorded by Concord's Jonathan Hosmer. "We daily expect a Tumult," he wrote to a friend, "There came up a post to Concord [on] Saturday night which informs them that the regulars are coming up to Concord the next day, and if they come I believe there will be bloody work."[20]

This first warning proved to be a false alarm. In their zeal Joseph Warren and Paul Revere had acted too quickly. General Gage was not yet ready to march. But Whig leaders were convinced that nothing was wrong in the warning except the date. The people of Concord began to move military supplies out of town, scattering them through the surrounding communities. The Provincial Congress, which had been meeting in Concord, suddenly agreed to adjourn on April 15 for a period of three weeks. Its members packed their bags, and hurried out of town.[21]

If the British garrison in Boston could keep nothing secret from the town, the same was true in reverse. Paul Revere's trip was quickly reported to General Gage. A secret agent in Concord sent a personal message to Province House: "last Saturday the 7th [actually the 8th] of April P:__ R:__ toward evening arrived at Concord, carrying a letter that was said to be from Mr. W[arre]n." Each side kept a wary eye upon the other.[22]

Through the week that followed, preparations continued in

the British garrison. On the evening of Saturday, April 15, Gage took another step that was impossible to hide. He ordered his regimental commanders to relieve their elite companies of grenadier and light infantry from "all duties till further orders." The official explanation, that the men were to learn "new evolutions," deceived nobody. "This I suppose is by way of a blind," Lieutenant Barker noted in his diary, "I dare say they have something for them to do." The orders were sent to eleven regiments, and instantly became common knowledge throughout the town. Bostonian John Andrews not only learned their content in a general way, but was able to repeat them verbatim in a letter to a friend.[23]

The next day was Sunday, April 16. Even though it was the New England Sabbath, Paul Revere made yet another ride. This time he went to Lexington, carrying news of the grenadiers and light infantry to John Hancock and Samuel Adams and other Whig leaders. He also met with Whigs in Cambridge and Charlestown and discussed with them the general problem of an early warning system. The Committee of Safety had already voted to establish a night watch in Roxbury, Cambridge and Charlestown to guard the exits from Boston. The Provincial Congress and its committees also organized an alarm system through New England, but this was a slow and cumbersome network of town committees.[24]

On April 16, Revere and his friends in Boston, Cambridge, Charlestown, and Lexington considered a more pressing problem: how to send an early warning of movements by the Regulars from Boston on short notice, in the middle of the night, and when exits from the town were closed by General Gage. They worked out what a later generation would call a fail-safe solution that was typical of Revere's planning: "expresses" of the usual sort if possible, special messengers by clandestine routes, and if all else failed a back-up system of lantern signals from Boston to Charlestown.[25]

This second trip by Paul Revere was also reported to General Gage. An alert British officer wrote that "the inhabitants conjectured that some secret expedition was on foot," and were "on the look-out." Once again it was abundantly clear to the British commander that he could scarcely make a move in Boston without Paul Revere's spreading the news through the countryside faster than his infantry could march. The Concord expedition was now seriously compromised. On Tuesday, April 18, one of Gage's Tory agents in Concord sent a report that most of the military stores had been removed from the town. But the spy added that large stocks of provisions were still there, along with several large 24-pounder cannon and a supply of powder.

Gage realized that unless the Whig express riders could be stopped, the Concord mission had no hope of success. He decided that special measures were necessary to maintain what remained of its secrecy, and specifically to keep Paul Revere from spreading the word. To that end, the British general and his aides planned an elaborate effort of what we would call counter-intelligence.

In the morning of April 18, General Gage sent out a mounted patrol of twenty men: ten officers and ten sergeants, commanded by Major Edward Mitchell of the 5th Foot. Their orders were to intercept American messengers and keep them from giving the alarm. Gage summarized their mission in a sentence to Colonel Smith, "A small party on horseback is ordered out to stop all advice of your march getting to Concord."[26]

The twenty British officers and sergeants left town across Boston Neck, and then fanned out, distributing themselves at chokepoints on the roads between Boston and Concord. Some covered the roads south and west of Roxbury and Brookline. At least two were sent north to Charlestown Neck. Others were posted near Watertown and the Great Bridge across the Charles River. Several patrolled the roads between Cambridge and Lexington. At least nine rode beyond Lexington to guard the approaches to Concord itself.[27]

Many people noticed them, and remarked upon their strange behavior. Often before, British officers had ridden into the countryside on various missions, or merely for exercise, but usually they returned to Boston before dark. This time they acted differently. The officers walked their horses slowly along the country roads, stopped for dinner in country taverns, and stayed out after sundown. Instead of the casual dishabille that British officers (then as now) often preferred to wear in the field, they were dressed in full uniform, with military cockades in their hats. The thick bulge of pistol-holsters and sword-pommels were clearly visible beneath their long dark blue riding coats. They conversed with travelers on the road, and asked many questions. In particular they inquired about the whereabouts of John Hancock and Samuel Adams.[28]

These roving British officers, whose assignment was to stop the New England alarm-riders, had the effect of alarming the countryside themselves. On the road that afternoon was Elijah Sanderson, a cabinetmaker. At about six o'clock in the evening, he "saw a party of officers pass up from Boston, all dressed in blue wrappers. The unusually late hour of their passing excited the attention of the citizens. I took my gun and cartridge box, and thinking that something must be going on more than common, walked up to John Buckman's tavern near the meeting house."

Solomon Brown, a Lexington lad of eighteen, was coming home from Boston market in late afternoon when he saw the British officers ambling slowly along the road. They seemed in no hurry to get where they were going, and appeared to be killing time. The evening was not very cold by New England standards, and yet Brown noticed that the officers were wearing heavy blue overcoats. Underneath he could make out the shape of their great horse pistols. Solomon Brown and the officers passed each other several times on the road. Then Brown rode away from them. When out of sight, he galloped to Lexington and told Sergeant William Munroe of the town militia what he had seen.[29]

In Menotomy the Provincial Committees of Safety and Supplies had been meeting through the day at Newell's Tavern. Late in the afternoon the members adjourned, and agreed to meet again the next day. Two of them, Richard Devens and Abraham Watson rode off in a chaise at sunset, heading east toward Charlestown. On the road they met a "great number of British officers and their servants on horseback, who had dined that day at Cambridge." The officers did not stop them but kept traveling slowly westward. Devens and Watson turned their chaise and rode back through the British officers to warn their fellow committeemen who were still in Menotomy—Elbridge Gerry, Charles Lee and Azor Orne—that British officers were abroad in the night. The warning was delivered, and Gerry instantly scribbled a note and sent it on to Adams and Hancock in Lexington.[30]

Gerry's report reached Lexington early in the evening, probably about 8 o'clock. Jonas Clarke, the town's minister, remembered that "on the evening of the 18th of April, 1775, we received two messages; the first verbal, the other by express in writing, from the Committee of Safety, who were then sitting in the westerly part of Cambridge, directed to the Honourable John Hancock, Esq; (who with the Honorable Samuel Adams, Esq; was then providentially with us) informing, 'that eight or nine officers of the King's troops were seen, just before night, passing the road towards Lexington, in a musing, contemplative posture; and it was suspected they were out upon some evil design. . . .' Mr. Hancock in particular, had been, more than once, personally insulted by some officers . . . it was not without some just grounds supposed, that under cover of darkness, sudden arrest, if not assassination, might be attempted."[31]

A squad of Lexington militia was asked to muster with their arms at the parsonage, and protect Adams and Hancock through the night against the British riders. Sergeant Munroe, on hearing that nine British officers were on the road, "selected eight men, armed, and placed them as a guard around the house of Mr. Clarke for the night and remained with them . . ." Another thirty Lexington militia gathered at the Buckman Tavern nearby. They were there by nine o'clock.[32]

Among the militia at the tavern were Sanderson, Brown, and Loring, who began to talk about the British officers whom they had seen on the road that day. In the manner of New England towns, these young men consulted their elders in the tavern as to what should be done. One venerable "old gentleman" advised the young men to "follow the officers and endeavor to ascertain their object." Elijah Sanderson announced, "If anyone would let me have a horse I would go in pursuit." Thaddeus Harrington said, "Take mine." Solomon Brown and Jonathan Loring also found horses. With Sergeant Munroe's consent, the three men volunteered to go out and watch the officers and report their movements.[33]

The three scouts started west from Lexington at about nine o'clock, Sanderson and Loring to observe the movements of the British patrol, and Brown to carry a warning to Concord. Half an hour later, they rode straight into a trap that the Regulars had laid across the highway. One of the Lexington men later wrote that they were "stopped by nine British officers just before we got to Brooks's in Lincoln. They detained us in that vicinity till a quarter past two o'clock at night. Sanderson recalled, "they put many questions which I evaded. They kept us separately and treated us very civilly." The officers particularly inquired after Hancock and Adams.[34]

Major Mitchell and his men continued to patrol the road to Concord. They passed the farmhouse of Josiah Nelson, who heard hoofbeats in the night and came half-dressed out of his house, to find out what was happening. Mistaking the British officers for countrymen in the dark, Nelson came up to them and said, "Have you heard anything about when the Regulars are coming out?"

Nelson startled the British officers. One of them, perhaps Major Mitchell himself, swung his sword, and slashed the American across the head, and took him prisoner. Bleeding profusely from his scalp, Nelson was released and warned that his house would be burned if he told anyone what had happened. He went back to his home, and his wife bandaged his bloody head. Then Josiah Nelson collected his weapons, saddled his horse, and rode off to warn his neighbors. The news began to spread across the countryside.[35]

# THE WARNING

∾ The Midnight Ride as a Collective Effort

> I told them what was acting, and went to git me a horse.
>
> —Paul Revere's account of the midnight ride, 1798

LATE IN THE AFTERNOON of April 18, 1775, a stable boy sprinted through the busy streets of Boston. He ran from Province House off Marlborough Street to the close-built neighborhood of the North End. When he reached Paul Revere's place he dashed through the door and announced his news—the Regulars were ready to march!

Catching his breath, the boy told Paul Revere what he knew. A friend was a hostler at a livery stable where the Regulars kept their horses. Earlier that day, several officers had gone there to work on their riding tack. As they tugged at their bridles and saddlery, they talked in low tones among themselves. From time to time, a voice rose high enough for the eavesdropping groom to hear a snatch of conversation—something about "hell to pay tomorrow!"[1]

Paul Revere listened as the boy told his story, and thanked him for coming. "You are the third person who has brought me the same information," he confided. All that day, Bostonians had noticed signs of activity in the British garrison. An "uncommon number of officers" were seen striding up and down Boston's Long Wharf, and talking earnestly among themselves on the far end of the pier that extended far into the waters of Massachusetts Bay. It was the only place in town that was safe from Yankee ears.[2]

At noon, people on the waterfront heard the high-pitched squeal of boatswains' pipes aboard British warships in the harbor, and the screech of heavy tackle. The townfolk could see crewmen bustling about the ships' longboats that were moored beneath the towering sterns of HMS *Somerset* and HMS *Boyne*.

In the early afternoon, several British seamen were sent ashore on various errands. In the immemorial way of sailors everywhere, some of them stopped for a quick pint at a waterfront tavern. Others may have found a moment to run upstairs with enterprising Yankee whores, who were renowned across the Seven Seas for the energy and speed of their transactions (the impact of the Puritan Ethic on the oldest profession was not precisely as the Founders had intended).[3]

Instantly, the navy's orders were known throughout the town. Boston was still a small community in 1775. In the manner of small towns, it soon learned every step that the Regulars were taking. Alert officers in the British garrison were equally quick to know that Boston knew. Frederick Mackenzie, the sharp-eyed adjutant of the Royal Welch Fusiliers, noted in his diary, "The town was a good deal agitated and alarmed at this movement, as it was pretty generally known by means of seamen who came on shore from their ships, about 2 o'clock, that the boats were ordered to be in readiness."[4]

Other signs of impending movement were also noticed by the people of Boston. Late in the afternoon, a British light infantry-man was seen in a shop "with his accoutrements on."[5] As evening fell, people watched from the waterfront as the navy's longboats began to move about the harbor, looking from a distance like small black beetles crawling across the surface of the water. The boats rowed toward HMS *Boyne,* and tied up together alongside her dirty, salt-stained hull.[6]

These movements were reported to Paul Revere and Joseph Warren. Only a few Whig leaders remained in Boston. Some were sitting with the Committees of Safety and Supplies in Cambridge. Others had fled in fear of arrest. John Hancock and Samuel Adams had left town several weeks earlier to attend the Provincial Congress in Concord, and had thought it prudent to remain in the country.

In their absence, Doctor Joseph Warren's office became a clearing house for information. In the highly charged atmosphere of Boston, scarcely an hour passed without some new rumor or alarm. Doctor Warren had become highly skilled at diagnosing these political symptoms. On the afternoon of April 18, as these reports suddenly multiplied, he began to suspect that the Regulars were at last about to make the major move that had long been expected.[7]

Doctor Warren was a careful man, and he decided to be sure. For emergencies he had special access to a confidential informer, someone well connected at the uppermost levels of the British command. The identity of this person was a secret so closely guarded that it was known to Warren alone, and he carried it faithfully to his grave.

Doctor Warren's confidential source was someone very near the heart of the British command, and so much at risk that he—or she—could be approached only in a moment of dire necessity. As evidence of British preparations began to mount, Warren decided that such a time had come. One who knew him wrote later that he "applied to the person who had been retained, and got intelligence of their whole design." The informer reported that the plan was "to seize Samuel Adams and John Hancock, who were known to be at Lexington, and burn the stores at Concord.[8]

Dr. Joseph Warren (1741–75), was a gentleman-revolutionary. Admired by his friends and respected even by his enemies, he contributed a quality of character to the Whig cause. This animated oil sketch by John Singleton Copley occupied the place of honor over the parlor fireplace in the Adams family home. Courtesy of the National Park Service, Adams National Historic Site, Quincy, Massachusetts.

We shall never know with certainty the name of Doctor Warren's informer, but circumstantial evidence strongly suggests that it was none other than Margaret Kemble Gage, the American wife of General Gage. This lady had long felt cruelly divided by the growing rift between Britain and America. Later she confided to a close friend that her feelings were those spoken by the lady Blanche in Shakespeare's *King John:*

> The Sun's o'ercast with blood; fair day, adieu!
> Which is the side that I must go withal?
> I am with both: each army hath a hand;
> And in their rage, I having hold of both,
> They whirl asunder and dismember me. . . .
> Whoever wins, on that side shall I lose.
> Assured loss, before the match be played.[9]

Margaret Gage made no secret of her deep distress. In 1775, she told a gentleman that "she hoped her husband would never be the instrument of sacrificing the lives of her countrymen."[10]

Her loyalty came to be suspected by both sides. The well-informed Roxbury clergyman William Gordon wrote that Dr. Warren's spy was "a daughter of liberty unequally yoked in the point of politics."[11] Many British officers, including Lord Percy and General Henry Clinton, believed that General Gage was "betrayed on this occasion" by someone very near to him. Some strongly suspected his wife.[12]

Even Gage himself appears to have formed his own suspicions. Earlier that same evening, he had summoned Lord Percy and told him that he was sending an expedition to Concord "to seize the stores." Percy was admonished tell nobody—the mission was to remain a "profound secret." As he left the meeting and walked toward his quarters, he saw a knot of eight or ten Boston men talking earnestly together on the Common. Percy approached them to learn what they were discussing. One man said:

"The British troops have marched, but will miss their aim."

"What aim?" Lord Percy demanded.

"Why, the cannon at Concord."

Percy was shocked. He hastened back to the general, and told him that the mission had been compromised. Gage cried out in anguish that "his confidence had been betrayed, for he had communicated his design to one person only," besides Percy himself.[13]

Before this fatal day, Gage had been devoted to his beautiful and caring wife. But after the Regulars returned from Concord, he ordered her away from him. Margaret was packed aboard a ship called *Charming Nancy* and sent to Britain, while the General remained in America for another long and painful year. An estrangement followed after Gage's return. All of this circumstantial evidence suggests that it is highly probable, though far from certain, that Doctor Warren's informer was indeed Margaret Kemble Gage—a lady of divided loyalties to both her husband and her native land.[14]

After hearing from his secret source, Dr. Warren sent an urgent message to Paul Revere, asking him to come at once. The time was between 9 and 10 o'clock when Paul Revere hurried across town. "Doctor Warren sent in great haste for me," Revere later recalled, "and begged that I would immediately set off for Lexington, where Messrs Hancock and Adams were, and acquaint them of the movement, and that it was thought they were the objects."[15]

Paul Revere's primary mission was not to alarm the countryside. His specific purpose was to warn Samuel Adams and John Hancock, who were thought to be the objects of the expedition. Concord and its military stores were also mentioned to Revere, but only in a secondary way.[16]

Warren appears to have known or suspected that British officers were patrolling the roads west of Boston. To be sure that the message got through, he told Revere that he was sending duplicate dispatches by different routes. One message had been entrusted to William Dawes, a Boston tanner. Dawes was not a leader as prominent as Revere, but he was a loyal Whig, whose business often took him through the British checkpoint on Boston Neck. As a consequence the guard knew him. He was already on his way when Revere reached Doctor Warren's surgery. Another copy of the same dispatch may have been carried by a third man.[17]

Dawes and Revere carried written messages, which Lexington's Congregational minister later copied into his records: "A large body of the King's troops (supposed to be a brigade of about 12, or 1500) were embarked in boats from Boston, and gone to land at Lechmere's point." Warren's estimate exaggerated the strength of the British expedition, but was accurate in every other detail.[18]

The messengers took different routes. William Dawes left town across Boston Neck—no small feat. He had to pass a narrow gate, closely guarded by British sentries who stopped all suspicious travelers. Dawes was remembered to have been "mounted on a slow-jogging horse, with saddle-bags behind him, and a large

William Dawes, Jr. (1745–99), was one of many Whig "expresses" who carried the Lexington Alarm. A Boston tanner of old Puritan and East Anglian stock, he was asked to be a courier on April 18, perhaps because his work often took him through the British "lines" on Boston Neck, and he knew many of the guard. (Evanston Historical Society)

flapped hat upon his head to resemble a countryman on a journey."[19]

Some say he attached himself to another party; others, that he knew the sergeant of the guard and managed to talk his way through. According to one account, a few moments after he passed the British sentries, orders arrived at the guardhouse, stopping all movement out of town. Once safely across the Neck, William Dawes eluded the British patrols in Roxbury, and rode west through Brookline to the Great Bridge that spanned the Charles River at Cambridge.[20]

Paul Revere made ready to leave in a different direction, by boat to Charlestown. His journey was not a solitary act. Many people in Boston helped him on his way—so many that Paul Revere's ride was truly a collective effort. He would be very much surprised by his modern image as the lone rider of the Revolution.

Revere had anticipated that the Regulars might try to stop all communications between Boston and the countryside. He would have remembered keenly his failure to warn the people of Salem in February, when Colonel Leslie's men held three of his fellow mechanics prisoner in Boston harbor until the expedition was on its way. The problem had been percolating in his mind for several weeks. Only the Sunday before, on his way home from Concord, Paul Revere had stopped at Charlestown and discussed the matter at length with Colonel William Conant and the Whig leaders of that town. Together they worked out a set of contingency plans for warning the country of any British expedition, even if no courier was able to leave town.[21]

Later Paul Revere recalled, "I agreed with a Colonel Conant and some other gentlemen, that if the British went out by water, we would shew two lanthorns in the North Church steeple, and if by land, one, as a signal, for we were apprehensive it would be difficult to cross the Charles River, or git over Boston neck."[22]

Revere called his signal lights "lanthorns," an archaic expression in England by 1775, but still widely used in Massachusetts, where translucent lantern-sides continued to be made in the old-fashioned way from paper-thin slices of cow-horn. These primitive devices emitted a dim, uncertain light. The problem was to make them visible from Boston to Charlestown, more than a quarter-mile distant across the water.[23]

Paul Revere and his friends agreed that the best place to display such a signal was in the steeple of Christ Church, commonly called the Old North Church. In 1775 it was Boston's tallest building. Its location in the North End made it clearly visible in Charlestown across the water.[24] But there was a problem. Christ Church was Anglican. Its rector was an outspoken Loyalist, so unpopular with his congregation that his salary had been stopped and the Church closed. As always, Paul Revere had several friends who could help. He was acquainted with a vestryman of Christ Church named Captain John Pulling, a staunch Whig and a member of the North End Caucus. Pulling agreed to help.[25]

Revere also knew the sexton of Christ Church, a young artisan named Robert Newman, who came from a prominent North End family that was down on its luck in 1775. Like many Boston families, the Newmans were a transatlantic cousinage, with branches in East Anglia and Massachusetts. Robert Newman's uncle was Sir Thomas Newman, Lord Mayor of Norwich. His father had been a prosperous Boston merchant, who built a big three-story brick house in the North End, with massive chimney stacks and a cupola that looked out upon his ships in the harbor. When Robert Newman was two years old, the family's fortunes were shattered by his father's death. His mother was forced to convert their handsome home into a boarding house, and Robert was apprenticed to a maker of leather breeches. Like many others in Boston, the Newman family was hard-pressed in 1775. They earned a few shillings by renting rooms to British officers, whom they disliked and resented. Robert Newman was unable to find work in his trade and could get employment only as a church sexton, a job that he despised. When Paul Revere asked him to help, he was happy to agree. Revere had chosen well. Robert Newman was known in the town as "a man of few words," but "prompt and active, capable of doing whatever Paul Revere wished to have done."[26]

On the afternoon of April 18, Revere alerted Newman and Pulling, and also another friend and neighbor, Thomas Bernard, and asked them to help with the lanterns. They were warned to be ready that night.[27]

It was about 10 o'clock in the evening when Paul Revere left Dr. Warren's surgery. He went quickly to the Newman house at the corner of Salem and Sheafe streets. As he approached the building, he peered through the windows and was startled to see a party of British officers who boarded with Mrs. Newman playing cards at a parlor table and laughing boisterously among themselves. Revere hesitated for a moment, then went round to the back of the house, and slipped through an iron gate into a dark garden, wondering what to do next.

Suddenly, Newman stepped out of the shadows. The young man explained that when the officers sat down to their cards, he pretended to go to bed early. The agile young sexton retired upstairs to his chamber, opened a window, climbed outside, and dropped as silently as a cat to the garden below. There he met Pulling and Bernard, and waited for Revere to arrive.[28]

Revere told his friends to go into the church and hang two lanterns in the steeple window on the north side facing Charlestown. He did not stay with them, but hurried away toward his own home. The men left him and walked across the street to the Old North Church. Robert Newman tugged his great sexton's key out of his pocket and unlocked the heavy door. He and Captain Pulling slipped inside, while Thomas Bernard stood guard.

Newman had found two square metal lanterns with clear glass lenses, so small that they could barely hold the stump of a small candle. Earlier that day he had carefully prepared the lanterns, and hidden them in a church closet. Newman took them from their hiding place. The men hung the lanterns round their necks by leather thongs, and stuffed flint and steel and tinder boxes into

At the Newman House, on the corner of Salem and Sheafe streets, Paul Revere met Robert Newman and John Pulling and asked them to hang the lanterns in the Old North Church. The building was a boarding house in 1775, occupied by British offficers. The storefront was a later addition. The building no longer stands. This old photograph by Wilfred French is in the Society for the Preservation of New England Antiquities.

their pockets. They climbed the creaking stairs, 154 of them, high into the church tower. At the top of the stairs they drew out their flints, and with a few practised strokes sent a stream of sparks into a nest of dry tinder. Gently they blew the glowing tinder into a flame, and lighted the candles.

Then they went to a narrow ladder above the stairs and climbed higher, rung after rung, past the open beams and great silent bells. At last they reached the topmost window in the steeple. They threw open the sash, and held the two lanterns out of the northwest window in the direction of Charlestown.[29]

The Old North Church from Hull Street, from an old photograph. To the left is Copp's Hill burying ground. To the right are houses that were occupied by British troops in 1775. The steeple window showing here faces north toward Charlestown. From it Newman and Pulling displayed two lanterns, one of which survives today in the Concord Museum. (Bostonian Society)

Across the river, the Charlestown Whigs were keeping careful watch on the steeple. In the night it appeared to them as a slim black spire, silhouetted against the starry southern sky. Suddenly they saw a flicker, and then a flash of light. They looked again, and two faint yellow lights were burning close together high in the tower of the church. It was the signal that Revere had promised to send if British troops were leaving Boston by boat across the Back Bay to Cambridge.

The lights were visible only for a moment. Then Newman and Pulling extinguished the candles, closed the window, descended the steeple stairs, and returned the lanterns to their closet. As they prepared to leave the church, they saw a detachment of troops in the street near the door. The two men ran back into the sanctuary of the church, searching for another way out. They climbed a bench near the altar, and escaped through a window, their mission completed.[30]

The men of Charlestown acted quickly on the signal. Some went down to the water's edge to look for Paul Revere. Others hastened to find him a horse. While waiting for his arrival they dispatched their own express rider to the Committee of Safety in Cambridge. One of them wrote later, "This messenger was also instructed to ride on to Messrs Hancock and Adams who I knew were at the Rev. Mr. [Clarke's ] at Lexington . . ."[31]

This anonymous Charlestown courier never reached his destination. Probably he was stopped by the British officers who lay in wait on the Lexington Road. General Gage's meticulous precautions were beginning to take effect. His roving patrols intercepted many travelers that night, and may have captured this first messenger who threatened to reveal his plans.

While the Charlestown Whigs were acting on the lantern signal, Paul Revere went to his own home in North Square, a few short blocks from the church. His family helped him to collect his heavy boots and long riding surtout. Perhaps he thought about taking his pistol, but decided to go unarmed, a decision that may have saved his life.

The time was about 10:15 when Revere left his house. Later he remembered, "I . . . went to the north part of the town, where I had kept a boat." Here again, Revere enlisted another group of friends to assist him. He sought the aid of two experienced Boston watermen to help him cross the Charles River. One was Joshua Bentley, a boat builder. The other was Thomas Richardson.[32]

Both men met Paul Revere by his boat, hidden beneath a wharf on the waterfront, in the North End. The folklore of old Boston cherishes many memories of that moment. It is said that Paul Revere absent-mindedly forgot his spurs and sent his faithful dog trotting home with a note pinned to his collar. A few minutes later the dog returned. The note was gone, and a pair of spurs was in its place. The reader may judge the truth of this legend.[33]

Another folktale has it that as Bentley and Richardson prepared to launch the boat, they discovered that they had forgotten a cloth to muffle their oars. The two men knocked softly at a nearby house. A woman came to an upper window, and they whispered an urgent request. There was a quick rustle of petticoats in the darkness, and a set of woolen underwear came floating down to the street. The lady's undergarments, still warm from the body that had worn them, were wrapped snugly round the oars.[34]

The three men balanced themselves in Paul Revere's little boat and pushed off into the harbor, rowing north from Boston toward Charlestown's ferry landing. Suddenly, another danger loomed in their path. The dark bulk of HMS *Somerset* was anchored squarely in their way. Four days earlier she had been moored between Boston and Charlestown to interrupt the nocturnal traffic between the towns. At 9 o'clock that night, the ferries that plied between the towns had been seized, and secured alongside the British ship, with all "boats, mud-scows, and canoes" in town. No crossings were allowed after that hour.[35]

Paul Revere looked up from his little rowboat at the great warship. She was a ship of the line, rated for 64 guns. He could expect the men of her watch to be alert, and armed sentries to be posted fore and aft. Probably he heard across the water the ship's bell chime twice in quick succession, then twice more, and once again as the midshipman of the watch marked the time at five bells in the evening watch, or 10:30 to a landsman.

Paul Revere sat quietly in the boat while his friends bent over their muffled oars. All his senses were alive, sharpened by the danger that surrounded him. Artist that he was, in that moment of mortal peril he noticed with special intensity the haunting beauty of the scene. Many years later the memory was still fresh in his mind. "It was then young flood, the ship was winding, and the moon was rising," he wrote in the haunting cadence of the old New England dialect. The great warship must have seemed a thing alive as she moved restlessly about her mooring, swinging slowly to the west on the incoming tide. In the fresh east wind, she pulled hard against her great hemp anchor cable that creaked and groaned like an animal in the night.

The moon was coming up behind Boston, a huge orb of light in the clear night sky. To Paul Revere it must have seemed impossible to pass the ship without detection. Then, miraculously, it was the moon that saved him. The moon was nearly full, a large pale yellow globe that was just beginning to rise in the southern sky.

Normally, Paul Revere's boat would have been caught in the bright reflection of the moonbeam on the water as he passed close by HMS *Somerset*. But there was something odd about the moon that night. Often it rose farther to the east, but that night it had a southern declination. A lunar anomaly caused it to remain well to the south on the evening of April 18, 1775, and to hang low on the horizon, partly hidden behind the buildings of Boston. The sky was very bright, and Paul Revere's boat was miraculously shrouded in a dark moonshadow that was all the more obscure because of the light that surrounded it. He passed safely "a little to the eastward" of the great ship's massive bowsprit that pointed downstream toward the incoming tide.[36]

Revere's skilled boatmen set him safely ashore at Charlestown's ferry landing. Another group of his many friends was waiting there. Later he remembered, "I met Colonel Conant, and several others; they said they had seen our signals. I told them what was acting."

Revere talked briefly with Richard Devens, the Charlestown Whig who was a member of the Committee of Supplies. As they walked from ferry landing into the town, Devens warned him to

This sinister cathead embellished an anchor-boom on the bow of HMS *Somerset*. Paul Revere's boat passed beneath it, as the great ship strained at her mooring against the incoming tide. In 1777, the cathead was salvaged from the wreck of the *Somerset* on Cape Cod, and survives today at the Pilgrim Monument and Province-town Museum.

take care on the road, and to stay alert for British officers who were patrolling the highway to Lexington. Devens added that he himself had met them earlier in the evening, "nine officers of the ministerial army, mounted on good horses, and armed, going towards Concord." Revere listened carefully. Then, he later wrote in his laconic Yankee way, "I went to git me a horse."[37]

The Charlestown Whigs had already given thought to the horse. One of the fleetest animals in town belonged to the family of John Larkin, a deacon of the Congregational church, who agreed to help. The Larkin horse was a fine great mare named Brown Beauty, according to family tradition. She was neither a racer nor a pulling animal, but an excellent specimen of a New England saddlehorse—big, strong, and very fast.[38]

Many years ago, equestrian historians concluded from their research that Brown Beauty was probably the collateral descendant of an East Anglian animal, distantly related to the modern draft horse known as the "Suffolk Punch." The horses of the Massachusetts Bay Colony, like the Puritans who rode them, came mainly from the east of England. In the new world these sturdy animals were bred with Spanish riding stock to create a distinctive American riding horse that can still be found in remote towns of rural Massachusetts. New England's saddle horses were bred for alertness and agility on Yankee ice and granite. At their best they were (and are) superb mounts—strong, big-boned, sure-footed, and responsive. Such an animal was Deacon Larkin's mare Brown Beauty, who was lent to Paul Revere that night.[39]

The horse was led out of the Larkin barn, and handed to Paul Revere by Richard Devens. The rider took the reins, put a booted foot into the stirrup, and sprang into the saddle. He said a last word to his friends, and urged the animal forward.

Brown Beauty proved a joy to ride. "I set off upon a very good horse," Paul Revere wrote later, "it was then about 11 o'clock, and very pleasant." The night was mild and clear. After a long New England winter, the first welcome signs of spring were in the air. The heavy musk of damp soil and the sweet scent of new growth rose around him in the soft night air.

Paul Revere headed north across Charlestown Neck, past the grim place where the rotting remains of the slave Mark still hung in rusty chains. Then he turned west on the road to Lexington, and kicked his horse into an easy canter on the moonlit road. He always savored that moment—a feeling that any horseman will understand. Psychologists of exercise tell us that there is a third

Paul Revere's leather saddlebags are in the collections of the Paul Revere Memorial Association, Boston.

stage of running, which brings euphoria in its train. There is also a third stage of riding, called the canter. After the tedium of the walk and the bone-jarring bounce of the trot, the animal surges forward in an easy rolling rhythm. Horse and rider become one being, more nearly so than in any other gait. The horse moves gracefully over the ground with fluent ease, and the rider experiences a feeling of completeness, serenity, and calm. Paul Revere's language tells us that such a feeling came to him as he cantered along the Lexington Road. Even at the vortex of violent events that were swirling dangerously around him, he experienced a sensation of quiet and inner peace.[40]

Suddenly the mood was shattered. It would have been the horse that noticed first, as horses often do. A rider as experienced as Paul Revere would instantly have seen the animal's head come up, and her ears prick forward, and her high-arched neck twist slightly from side to side as she came alert to danger. He would have felt a momentary break in the rhythm of the canter, a change in the tension of the reins, and a subtle shift of pressure beneath his seat.

Paul Revere searched the road ahead. Suddenly he saw two horsemen in the distance, almost invisible, waiting silent and motionless in the moonshadow of a great tree by the edge of the highway. As Revere rode closer, he made out the blur of military cockades on their hats, and the bulge of heavy holsters at their hips.

Regulars!

He pulled sharply on his reins, and Deacon Larkin's horse responded instantly. Even before she had stopped, Revere yanked her head around, and spurred her savagely in the opposite direction. The two officers gave chase. One tried to cut off Paul Revere by riding crosscountry, and galloped straight into an open claypit, miring his horse in the wet and heavy ground. The other kept to the road, but was soon left far behind by the long stride of Deacon Larkin's splendid mare.

As his pursuers disappeared in the darkness behind him, Paul Revere later recalled that he "rid upon full gallop for the Mistick road." His route took him to a small village north of Charlestown which is now the Boston suburb of Medford. It was commonly called Mystic in 1775, after the river of the same name. He had not planned to go that way. This road was a long detour for him, and added many northern miles to his westward journey. He must have cursed his luck. But as Prince Otto von Bismarck liked to observe, there is a special Providence for children, fools, drunkards—and the United States of America! Paul Revere's unwelcome detour took him safely around the roving British patrols that might have intercepted him.

Revere followed the Mystic Road over a wooden bridge, and clattered into the quiet village. From there he rode through north Cambridge to the little hamlet of Menotomy, now the town of Arlington. At the Cooper Tavern in Menotomy he met the King's Highway or Great Road, as it was variously called, and turned west toward Lexington. He continued along the road through rising hills to the town's meetinghouse at Lexington Common. There he came to the Buckman Tavern with its traditional bright red door. Perhaps still burning in the window was a small metal lantern with four candle stubs that signaled the availability of food, drink, lodging, and livery.[41]

At the Buckman Tavern, Paul Revere turned right into the Bedford Road. He traveled a few hundred yards past a fifty-acre tract of the minister's farmland to the parsonage that was the home of Lexington's clergyman, Jonas Clarke, his wife and many children.[42]

Inside the crowded house that night were at least ten Clarkes, and Sam Adams and John Hancock. With them were Hancock's "slight and sprightly" fiancée Dorothy Quincy, and his aged aunt Lydia Hancock. The Clarkes and Hancocks were kin. They were both old clerical families, deeply rooted in the extended cousinage of New England Congregationalism. John Hancock and his ladies had been there since April 7; Sam Adams since April 10.[43]

Everyone in the parsonage had retired for the night. Adams

and Hancock were sleeping in the downstairs parlor-bedroom. Aunt Lydia and Miss Dolly had the best chamber upstairs. Jonas Clarke and his wife were in another bedroom, and eight of their twelve children were in various trundle beds and backrooms. The old house was dark and silent. Outside, the faithful Sergeant William Munroe stood guard in the moonlight with ten or twelve Lexington militiamen.[44]

It was midnight when Paul Revere arrived, his horse probably flecked with foam and streaked with blood from the sharp rowels of his old-fashioned silver spurs. The scene that followed was not the heavy melodrama that one expects of great events, but a touch of low comedy that often incongruously happens in moments of high historical tension.

When Paul Revere came riding up to the parsonage, he met Sergeant William Munroe and called out to him in a loud voice. Sergeant Munroe did not know Paul Revere, and was not impressed by the appearance of this midnight messenger. In the eternal manner of sergeants in every army, he ordered Revere not to make so much noise—people were trying to sleep!

"Noise!" Paul Revere answered, "You'll have noise enough before long! The Regulars are coming out!"

The alert reader will note what Paul Revere did *not* say. He did not cry, "The British are coming." Many New England express riders that night would speak of Regulars, Redcoats, the King's men, and even the "Ministerial Troops," if they had been to college. But no messenger is known on good authority to have cried,

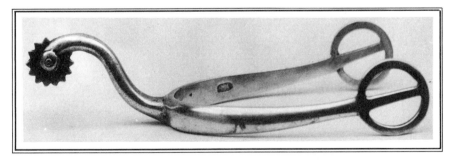

In American museums, Paul Revere spurs are as numerous as fragments of the True Cross. This one may be authentic. It is made of silver, bears the mark of Paul Revere, and is in the Metropolitan Museum of Art, New York. There is no evidence that Revere actually wore it, but he is known to have used spurs on his midnight ride, probably a pair of his own manufacture such as this one. Its sharp rowls would have left the flanks of his horse raw and bloody.

"The British are coming," until the grandfathers' tales began to be recorded long after American Independence. In 1775, the people of Massachusetts still thought that *they* were British. One of them, as we shall see, when asked why he was preparing to defend his house, explained, "An Englishman's home is his castle." The revolution in national identity was not yet complete.[45]

On the other side, the Regulars did not usually refer to the New England militia as Americans, but as "country people," "provincials," "Yankeys," "peasants," "rebels," or "villains" in the *Oxford English Dictionary*'s definition of "a low-born, base-minded rustic," or "boors" in the archaic sense of farmer (as Dutch *boer*).

As late as 1775, people on both sides in this great struggle still thought of themselves as of the same stock. They commonly spoke of their conflict not as the American Revolution, but as a "Civil War" or "Rebellion" that divided English-speaking people from one another. This was the way that Paul Revere was thinking on April 18, 1775, when he told Sergeant Munroe that the "Regulars are coming out."[46]

After exchanging a few choice words with the sergeant, Paul Revere went past him and banged heavily on the door of the parsonage. Up flew the sash of a bedroom window, and out popped the leonine head of the Reverend Jonas Clarke, perhaps wearing a long New England night cap. Other heads appeared from different windows—as many as ten Clarke heads in various assorted sizes. From yet another downstairs window emerged the heads of Sam Adams and John Hancock, who instantly recognized their midnight caller. "Come in, Revere," Hancock called in his irritating way, "we're not afraid of *you*."[47]

Paul Revere entered the Clarke house in his spurs and heavy riding boots, his long mud-spattered surtout swirling around him. He delivered his message to Hancock and Adams. The hour was a little past midnight. The men began to talk urgently among themselves. Revere asked if Dawes had arrived, and was concerned to hear that nobody had seen him. "I related the story of the two officers," Revere later recalled, "and supposed he must have been stopped, as he ought to have been there before me." Half an hour later, to everyone's relief, Dawes appeared with a duplicate of the message from Boston.

The two expresses remained in Lexington for another hour. "We refreshed ourselves," Revere wrote simply. Dorothy Quincy remembered later that John Hancock left the parsonage and walked down the Bedford Road to the tavern on the Common,

The Hancock-Clarke Parsonage was built in 1738 for Lexington's minister John Hancock. In 1775, it was occupied by his successor Jonas Clarke, whose silhouette still hangs in the house. Samuel Adams and John Hancock (grandson of the builder) were staying here when Paul Revere arrived with news that the "Regulars are out." The house was moved across the street in 1896, and returned to its original location in 1974.

where some of the Lexington militia had been staying the night. Sam Adams went along, as did the minister Jonas Clarke. Probably Revere and Dawes also went to the tavern to find "refreshment" for themselves, and their exhausted horses.

The men talked with members of Lexington's militia company. Jonas Clarke remembered that the conversation centered on the purpose of the British mission. They agreed on reflection that Doctor Joseph Warren must have been mistaken in thinking that the purpose of General Gage was the arrest of Hancock and Adams. It was true, as Jonas Clarke observed, that "these gentlemen had been frequently and publickly threatened." But the arrest of Hancock and Adams alone could not be the primary object of so large an expedition. "It was shrewdly suspected," Clarke later recalled, "that they were ordered to seize and destroy the stores belonging to the colony, then deposited at Concord."[48]

It was clear that Concord must be warned, and that the messengers from Boston were the men to do it. Once again, Paul Revere and William Dawes climbed into their saddles, probably a bit more slowly than before. They said farewell to Adams and Hancock, and turned the heads of their weary horses westward toward the Concord Road. Behind them, Lexington's town bell began to ring in the night.

# THE MARCH

❧ The Ordeal of the British Infantry

> This expedition . . . from beginning to end was as ill-planned and ill-executed as it was possible to be.
>
> —Lieutenant John Barker,
> 4th (King's Own) Foot,
> 1775

E ARLIER THAT EVENING, while Paul Revere and William Dawes were preparing to leave Boston, General Gage set his army in motion. Many precautions were taken to prevent discovery. The soldiers were awakened in their beds, "sergeants putting their hands on them, and whispering gently to them."[1] The men dressed quietly, strapped on their full cartridge boxes, and picked up their heavy muskets. They were ordered to leave their knapsacks behind, and to carry one day's provisions in their haversacks. One soldier remembered that he was told to bring 36 rounds of powder and ball.[2]

The British soldiers were "conducted by a back-way out of their barracks, without the knowledge of their comrades, and without the observation of the sentries." The men were ordered to move in small parties, so as not to alarm the town. They "walked through the street with the utmost silence. It being about 10 o'clock, no sound was heard but of their feet. A dog that happened to bark, was instantly killed with a bayonet."[3]

The Regulars made their way to a rendezvous chosen for its remoteness—an empty beach on the edge of the Back Bay, near

Boston's new powder house in "the most unfrequented part of town." When challenged by the sentries, they answered with the evening's countersign, "Patrole."[4]

First to arrive were the flank companies of the Royal Welch Fusiliers. Their regimental adjutant Frederick Mackenzie regarded punctuality as a point of honor. Next came the King's Own, who bivouacked near Boston Common, close by the beach. Other companies came in from Fort Hill, and some from Boston Neck, and a few from the Warehouse Barracks near Long Wharf. Several companies arrived from the North End after forming up near the North Church. They were the troops who had nearly intercepted Robert Newman and Captain Pulling. Altogether, the expedition numbered between 800 and 900 Regulars in twenty-one companies, plus a few volunteers and Loyalist guides.[5]

These were picked men, the flower of General Gage's army. In that era most regiments of British infantry had two elite units: a grenadier company and a light infantry company. The grenadiers were big men, chosen for size and strength. In the earlier 18th century their special task had been to hurl heavy hand grenades at the enemy, hence their name and stature. By 1775 they had lost that role and gained another, as shock troops whose mission was to lead the bloody assaults that shattered an enemy line, or captured a fortification by a *coup de main*.

The light infantry companies were a different elite—the most agile and active men, selected for fitness, energy and enterprise. They had been added to every British regiment in 1771 to serve as skirmishers and flank guards, partly at the urging of General Gage. In some regiments these men carried long-barreled muskets, which were more accurate at longer distances than the standard issue Tower musket. Some were equipped with hatchets modeled on American tomahawks.

In the French and Indian War, British commanders had sometimes collected their light infantry and grenadier companies into provisional units for special service. General Gage followed this common procedure. His Concord expedition consisted of eleven companies of grenadiers and ten of light infantry. That practice had the advantage of bringing together the best soldiers in the army. But it also had a major weakness. Officers and men of different regiments were not used to working with one another. They found themselves commanded by strangers, and compelled to fight alongside other units whom they did not know or trust. The regimental spirit that was carefully cultivated in the British army worked against the cohesion of ad hoc units. Further, the normal chain of command was broken above the company level, and the complex evolutions of 18th-century warfare sometimes dissolved in confusion.

That confusion began to appear in the first moments of the Concord expedition, when the companies came together on Boston's Back Bay. The 23rd's regimental adjutant, Frederick Mackenzie, was appalled by the disorder he met on the beach. He found no officer of high rank firmly in command of the embarkation, and separate companies straggling aimlessly. The junior officers had been told nothing about where they were going or what they were to do. Lieutenant Barker of the 4th (King's Own) wrote, "Few but the commanding officers knew what expedition we were going upon."[6]

The navy was there in good time, but Mackenzie counted only twenty ships' boats, not nearly enough to carry the entire force in a single crossing. Two trips were needed to move everyone across the water. Mackenzie peered across the dark river toward the opposite shore, and discovered still another problem that had not been anticipated. General Gage's staff had selected the crossing point mainly for secrecy. It ran from the most secluded spot in Boston across the Back Bay to a lonely beach on Lechmere Point in Cambridge, inhabited only by a single isolated farmstead known as the Phips farm.[7]

The bay was broad and shallow at that point. The boats' crews had to row more than a mile on a diagonal downstream course, against a rising Spring tide that was flowing up the Charles estuary. The Navy's longboats were clumsy, heavy craft, built for strength and stability in the open sea. They were ordered to be tied together, bow to stern, in strings of three or four. That precaution was thought necessary to keep coxswains from losing their way in the dark, but it made the crossing even slower when speed was vital to success.[8]

The soldiers were packed into the boats so tightly that there was no room to sit down. The vessels settled deep in the water until their gunwales were nearly awash. In the center of each boat the men stood quietly, their red coats nearly black in the moonlight and their long muskets slanting upward toward the bright sky. In the sternsheets beardless midshipmen whispered commands to weatherbeaten seamen while heavy ash oars creaked rhythmically against sturdy locust tholepins.

As the boats approached Lechmere Point, they went aground

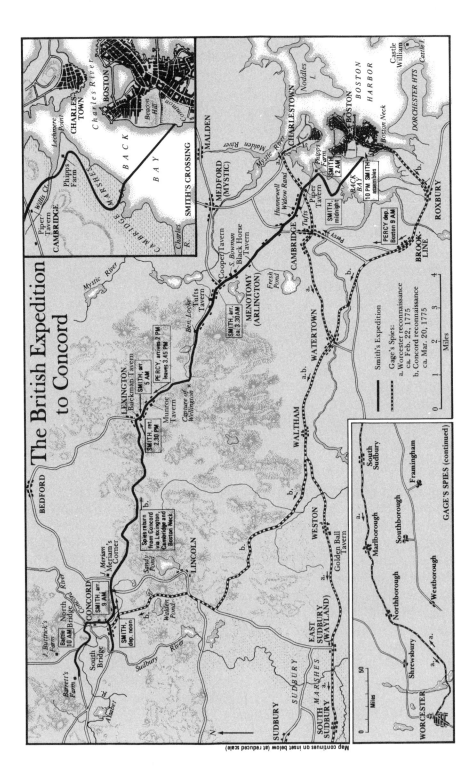

# The British Expedition to Concord

Map continues on inset below (at reduced scale)

Smith's Expedition

Gage's Spies:
a. Worcester reconnaissance ca. Feb. 22, 1775
b. Concord reconnaissance ca. Mar. 20, 1775

0   1   2   3   4
Miles

GAGE'S SPIES (continued)

0        50
Miles

SMITH'S CROSSING

in shallow water that was nearly knee deep. The soldiers climbed into the river and waded awkwardly ashore, muskets held at high port. Then the boats backed off, and returned for another load. It was slow and painful work. Not until midnight was every man landed. Two precious hours had been spent crossing the Charles River.

On the Cambridge shore there was another scene of confusion as officers and sergeants struggled to form their broken companies. The commander, Lieutenant Colonel Francis Smith, looked on with horror at the disorder that surrounded him. He was what another army in a later time would call a book soldier—methodical, cautious, and careful—an officer much to General Gage's liking. That night, when time was of the essence, Colonel Smith ordered each company to assemble in a predetermined order on the beach. First came the light infantry of his own 10th Foot, then the other companies of light infantry in order of their regimental number, and the heavy grenadiers in the same sequence. This tidy arrangement was not Colonel Smith's private obsession. It was a point of regimental pride in the British army. A regiment's number indicated its seniority. The 4th (King's Own) Foot had the lowest number that night, then the 5th, and others in numerical order. More time was lost as units jockeyed back and forth.[9]

At last every company was in its proper place, and the men were ordered to march. They advanced painfully in their soggy gaiters and square-toed shoes full of brackish river water. As they left the beach, the men discovered to their surprise that they had been landed squarely in the middle of the "marshes of Cambridge."[10] Their landing zone was sparsely inhabited because it was a swamp.

The men tried to move along the river's edge where the footing seemed more solid than in the swamp itself. But the slippery beach pebbles were treacherous underfoot, and the thick river mud sucked at their heavy shoes. The tide was still high. From time to time the column found itself plunging into the water again. One officer recalled that their route took them "at first through some swamps and slips of the sea," and "they were obliged to wade, halfway up their thighs, through two inlets." Lieutenant Barker was one of the lucky ones. He remembered that his company was wet merely "to our knees." Another officer recalled that his men were soaked "up to their middles."[11]

At last they came to a rough farm track that ran through the marsh. The road was soft and wet, but at least it resembled terra firma. Here Colonel Smith halted his men yet again, while he waited for the navy to deliver two days' provisions that had been prepared aboard ships in the harbor to avoid discovery. The Regulars stood quietly in the mud with the fatalism that is part of every soldier's life, while sergeants prowled restlessly through the ranks, making sure that every infantryman had 36 rounds and a full cartridge box. The men were increasingly miserable. It was not a cold night by New England standards, but the men were sopping wet and a chill wind was blowing. They began to tremble in their wet uniforms, which were uncomfortable enough, even when dry.

The uniform of the British soldier in 1775 might have been designed by some demonic tailor who had sworn sartorial vengeance upon the human frame. The grenadiers wore towering caps of bearskin (later coonskin for Fusiliers), adorned with white metal faceplates and colorful cords and tassels, and blazoned at the back with their regimental number on embossed metal disks. Their headgear was designed partly to allow muskets to be slung easily, but its major purpose was to magnify the height of the men who wore them. On active service the caps were awkward and top-heavy. They were also costly to replace, and had to be protected in the field with painted canvas covers—caps for caps, which were slung from a belt when not in use.

The light infantry wore tight helmets of black leather, adorned with feathers or horsehair crests, and constructed with whimsical peaks in front or behind, according to the fancy of the regimental commander. This headgear was less awkward than the bearskins of the grenadiers, but it offered little protection against the rain, and tended to crack in the sun. When wet the leather shrank painfully, gripping the head like a vise.

The ordinary rank and file were called "hat companies" after their standard-issue cocked hats. According to the prevailing fashion in 1775, they were worn too small to fit snugly around the crown, and merely perched on top of the head. To keep them from tumbling off, the hats had to be fastened to the hair by tapes, and hooks and eyes.

The hair itself was dressed according to the taste of each colonel. In some regiments it was powdered white; in others it was congealed with gleaming black grease. Mostly it was plaited or "clubbed" into a pigtail, doubled on itself, and tied neatly with ribbon. Bald men, and even those with thinning hair were required to

Lt. Col. Francis Smith of the 10th Foot commanded the British expedition to Concord. A veteran of 28 years' service, he joined in 1747 and saw much active duty. Some subordinates complained that he was fat, slow, stupid, and self-indulgent. Others including General Gage liked his prudence, caution, gravitas, and gentility. Both sets of qualities might be found in this painting, eleven years earlier. It is dated 1764, and hangs today in the British National Army Museum, Chelsea.

wear switches. The neck was swathed in tight stocks of horsehair or velvet that came nearly to the chin.

These men who stood in the muddy marshes of Cambridge wore snow white linen that had been changed only the day before. Every Wednesday and Sunday fresh linen was put on throughout the British army. They also were issued white or buff-colored waistcoats and breeches which were ordered to be kept immaculate on pain of a flogging. Later in the war, British soldiers were allowed to wear coveralls or loose "trowsers" on active service.

The most distinctive part of the uniform was the heavy red coat. For grenadiers and line companies this was a garment with long tails that descended nearly to the knee. The light infantry

This unidentified British subaltern wears the uniform of a flank company in the 4th (King's Own) Foot. The facings are royal blue. The epaulette, gorget, buttons, and sword-belt plate (with the regimental number clearly visible) are silver. The officer bids a sad farewell to a beloved foxhound as his ship prepares to sail in the background. The 4th Foot departed from the Isle of Wight for Boston on May 28, 1774. Many of its junior officers were casualties at Concord and Bunker Hill. One wonders if this melancholy portrait by Thomas Gainsborough, might have been a mortuary painting. National Gallery of Victoria, Melbourne.

wore short jackets that ended at the hip, and were much preferred on active service. Later in the Revolution, General John Burgoyne ordered all his men to cut down their coats into jackets. Contemporary illustrations commonly show that the red coats of 1775 were worn very tight, according to the 18th-century fashion. They were supposed to be preshrunk, but after exposure to rain they shrank again, sometimes so much that the men found it painful to move their arms.

Both coats and jackets were made of a coarse red woolen fabric that was strong and densely woven, and meant to stand hard service. After the battle, Dover militiaman Jabez Baker carried home one of these red coats as a souvenir. In the New England way, it was put to work as a scarecrow in the fields. So sturdy was its cloth that it was still in service as late as 1866, a tattered survivor of ninety New England winters and an impressive testament to the durability of its sturdy British cloth.[12]

The red coats were elaborately embellished with lace, wings, buttons, loops, knots, and incongruous heart-shaped badges on the coattails. Lapels and cuffs were turned to reveal contrasting "facings" of the regimental color. Royal regiments proudly wore facings of a rich dark blue—the original Royal blue. Men from three Royal regiments were standing in the Cambridge swamp this night—the King's Own, the Royal Irish, and the Royal Welch Fusiliers. Other regiments had facings of buff (the 52d), pale yellow (the 38th), or off-white (the 47th). Lord Percy's 5th Foot (soon to be the Northumberland Fusiliers) was elegant in facings of "gosling green." The 59th (later the East Lancashire Regiment) was resplendent in bright purple; the 10th (afterwards the Lincolnshire Regiment) was gaudy in an exceptionally vivid yellow; a few men on detached duty from the 64th (subsequently the Prince of Wales's North Staffordshire Regiment) wore facings of sinister black. The British Marines were made to wear snow-white facings which caused the men much trouble in the field. Their commander, Major Pitcairn, wrote home to a friend in the Admiralty, "I every day wish for any lapels but white . . . I wish his Lordship would give us blue, green, or black."[13]

Drummers and fifers, of whom thirty-nine were attached to the army units in the expedition, wore coats of the same color as the facings of their regiments (except in Royal regiments), and bright red breeches, linings, and vests. Their sleeves were heavily adorned with lace "as the Colonel shall think fit," often in thick white chevrons from wrist to shoulder, to make them highly visible on a field of battle, where they had a vital function in command and control.

In every regiment, equipment was suspended from white crossbelts: a broad belt over the left shoulder to support the cartridge box, a narrow belt over the right shoulder for a long sword, and a waistbelt for the bayonet and short sword. The belts were kept immaculate by frequent rubbing with pipeclay, a ritual for many generations in the British army. The light infantrymen wore tanned leather belts which were less visible and more practical.

The grenadiers on the Concord expedition were probably still wearing their winter gaiters of black heavy linen, which covered the legs from ankle to thigh and were secured below the knee with black garters so tight as to threaten the circulation. For durability the gaiters had hard leather tops that chafed the upper leg so severely that white linen knee-cuffs were added to cushion them. The light infantry wore short gaiters that offered more comfort, but less protection.

The most bizarre part of this infantry uniform was the footwear. In 1775, British regiments called "Foot" did not wear right and left shoes, but heavy interchangeable square-toed brogans that were reversed every day to keep them from "running crooked." The men of the Concord expedition would be asked to march forty miles in that unforgiving footgear.[14] Their special "marching socks" were made of linen, and soaked in oil to shed water. For this campaign, the historian of the King's Own notes that "for the first time we hear that the private soldiers wore underclothes, a pair of linen drawers being included in the list of necessaries."[15]

Officers's uniforms displayed many differences of social rank. Their coats were not red but scarlet, a distinction that continues today in the dress uniforms of some British regiments. The costly scarlet dye, prepared from the dried bodies of female cochineal insects, preserved its color long after the cheaper red coats of the rank and file had faded to a dusty rose. In the field, the brilliant scarlet tunics of the officers stood out at long distance from the brownish-pink of the rank and file—a dubious honor in America where unsporting Yankee marksmen went methodically about the business of killing the officers first.

Every article of dress became an emblem of rank. The men were given breeches of coarse white wool; officers on active service wore elegant "small clothes" of white leather. The uniform coats of the rank and file were embellished with lace of worsted woolen thread; their officers were adorned with lace of gilt or silver. Men wore a simple black stock around their necks; officers added a ceremonial gorget which was a vestigial relic of medieval armor—a crescent-shaped piece of metal, either silver or gilt to match the buttons of the regiment, embellished with the Royal arms, engraved with the regimental number, and suspended from a silk ribbon or a silver chain. Its highly polished surface sparkled in the light, and made a perfect aiming point just below the throat.

The men wore on their hips a gray canvas haversack prominently marked with the King's broad arrow, and in some regiments a small canteen. Old soldiers sometimes marched with two canteens—one for water, the other for Yankee rum, which may have been passed eagerly from mouth to mouth as they stood in the cold Cambridge marshes. Lord Percy himself carried a flask of fine French brandy.

The Regulars waited miserably in their wet uniforms for another hour, until at last their provisions were delivered by the navy. The army looked with disdain on naval rations, of which the staple was rock-hard ship's biscuit, often crawling with white maggots. An officer of the 23rd remembered that his Fusiliers threw away the navy food in disgust, having brought their own army rations with them.[16]

Finally, about two o'clock in the morning, a full four hours after leaving barracks in Boston, Colonel Smith ordered his column forward. To escape the marshes, it was necessary to double back nearly a mile to the east, on a farm road that curved around the northeastern side of a low hill.[17] Just as the men were beginning to dry out, they came to a little stream called Willis Creek that flowed into the Back Bay. A wooden bridge spanned the water, but Colonel Smith feared that the heavy tramp of army shoes would wake the sleeping countryside. He ordered his men off the road, and sent them sliding down a slippery mud embankment into a swirling stream that was frigid with melted snow. Lieutenant Barker vividly remembered the sensation of "wading through a very long ford up to our middles."[18]

The men were now shaking with cold. They formed up once again on the other side of the little stream and resumed the march. Steadily they advanced along the country roads past silent houses sleeping in the moonlight. Most of the soldiers still did not know where they were going or what they were asked to do. Even the company commanders had not been told the purpose of their mission. The men were wet, cold and numb. Few had slept since

This captain of light infantry in the 10th Foot is thought to be Thomas Hewitt, who joined the company in 1777, after every officer had been killed or wounded at Concord, Lexington, and Bunker Hill. His facings are yellow, and his regimental number (a Roman X) is visible on his gorget and swordbelt plate. Captain Hewitt survived the war, and left the army in 1785. The portrait is dated 1781, and signed by the artist William Tate. (British National Army Museum, Chelsea)

the night before. Many were hungry and thirsty, and had already drained their canteens. Some began to break ranks to drink from wells along the road. At least one soldier dropped out altogether, and went to the lonely farmhouse on Lechmere Point. The family took him in, learned about the expedition, and sent word into town.[19]

The Regulars continued on through Cambridge, following a road that curved around the north end of town. They passed Piper's Tavern in what is now Union Square, Somerville. An inhabitant saw them go by, and heard the soldiers repeat the name on the signboard, which they could read in the bright moonlight.

We think of our ancestors as early sleepers and early risers, but a remarkably large number were up and about in the small hours of that April night. In East Cambridge, the Widow Elizabeth Rand was wide awake. The day before, a hog had been butchered for her use. The carcass was hanging outside her house, and she worried that a thief might steal it in the night. About 2:30, she heard a strange noise and rushed outside in her nightgown to protect her property. To her amazement she saw 800 men marching silently toward her house. The Widow Rand dodged behind a rain barrel, and kept out of sight until the soldiers were gone. Then she tucked up her nightdress and sprinted to the home of her neighbor Samuel Tufts, who also was awake, hard at work with his slave, pouring lead into a bullet mold. Both men were so busy that they did not hear the Regulars go by. Tufts listened incredulously to the widow's story and refused to believe a word of it. She led him to the road, and with the aid of a lantern showed him the square shoeprints in the ground. Samuel Tufts was persuaded. He saddled his horse, and rode off to spread the word.[20]

The British Regulars continued west through Cambridge to the "great road" (now Massachusetts Avenue) that led to Lexington and Concord. As they turned onto the highway (at the present site of Porter Square), the British vanguard saw two countrymen coming toward them in a wagon. Thomas Robins and David Harrington of Lexington were taking a load of milk to market in Boston. They saw the British column at a distance, pulled off the road, and were working frantically to unhitch their horses when the Regulars were upon them. The two Lexington men were taken prisoner and made to march with the column. The horses were given to British officers.[21]

The column crossed a little stream (now called Alewife Brook) and entered the village of Menotomy. In a house by the road, a man opened his door and watched the column go by. A thirsty soldier left the ranks and asked for a drink of water. The householder, Lieutenant Solomon Bowman of the town's militia, asked the British Regular, "What are you out at this time of night for?" The soldier made no reply, and was sent on his way. Bowman went off to muster his company.[22]

In Menotomy the column passed the Black Horse Tavern where the Committee of Safety had been meeting that day. Three Whig leaders, Colonel Jeremiah Lee, Colonel Azor Orne, and Elbridge Gerry, were staying the night. The landlord saw a party of Regulars turn off the road toward the tavern and cried, "For God's sake, don't open the door!" As the soldiers approached the front of the inn, the Whig leaders dashed out the back door, and hid in the fields, lying flat on the wet ground behind a low stubble of last year's cornstalks. They were not discovered.[23]

Farther on, a party of young men were playing cards in a shop by the road; they heard the soldiers and went to warn others. At the Tufts Tavern in Menotomy, the innkeeper was awake and toiling at his endless chores. He looked out and saw several Regulars moving toward his barn where he kept a handsome white horse. The Yankee innkeeper ran to intercept them, and said to an officer, "You are taking an early ride, sir!" The Regular replied, "you had better get to bed and get your sleep while you can," and left, without the horse.[24]

At a place called Foot of Rocks (near today's Forest Street) the

Self-portrait of Captain William Glanville Evelyn, commander of No. 7 company, 4th (King's Own) Foot. Evelyn marched with Percy's Brigade to the relief of Smith's force, and was in the thick of the fighting from Lexington to Charlestown. He survived that day unscathed, but six weeks after inscribing this portrait to his mother he was mortally wounded at a small skirmish in Westchester County, New York. He was thirty-four years old. Evelyn left his estate to Peggie Wright, his servant who was with him in Boston. (Author's Collection)

British column passed a house where a light was burning. They knocked on the door, and were told by a woman that her "old man" was ill, and she was brewing him a pot of herb tea. In fact she and her husband (who was hale and hearty) had been busy melting their pewter dishes into bullets. The next house (now 21 Appleton Street, Arlington) belonged to Menotomy's militia captain Benjamin Locke. He also heard the column march past, and instantly set himself to rousing his neighbors.[25]

The leaders of the British expedition were increasingly concerned. They had been driving their men, hoping to make up the vital hours that had been lost in the Cambridge marshes. The column made remarkable time—a mile every sixteen minutes, a rapid clip for a night march in close order on a dark and muddy road. An officer noted that the pace was "hasty and fatiguing."[26]

But their commander was not pleased with their progress. Colonel Francis Smith was by nature a worrying sort of man. He worried about the late start and the early dawn that was now only a few hours away. Most of all, he worried about the bridges at Concord. What if the New England militia reached the bridges first? He might have to fight the "peasants" as he called them, or retreat as Colonel Leslie had done at Salem.

As the main body of the column moved into the village of Menotomy, Smith's worries got the better of him. He halted his command, gave the men a short rest, and summoned his second-in-command, Major John Pitcairn of the Royal Marines. Pitcairn was ordered to take the six leading companies of light infantry and advance at the quick march to Concord. There he was told to seize the bridges north and south of the town, and hold them until the grenadiers came up.

Pitcairn set off instantly, leading his six light companies at a rapid rate. To set the pace, he put one of his best men at the head of the column—Lieutenant Jesse Adair, a hard-charging young Marine who could be trusted to keep the column moving.[27]

With Adair in the van was a New England Tory named Daniel Murray, who had graduated from Harvard only three years before. He often tramped the roads between the college in Cambridge and his home in Worcester County, where his prominent family was much hated for their Loyalist sympathies; later his three brothers would take up arms for King and Empire. Also at the head of the column were several unattached officers: Lieutenant William Sutherland of the 38th Foot and Surgeon's Mate Simms of the 43rd Foot. Behind them came an advance party of eight light infantrymen, among them Private James Marr of the King's Own, a Scot whose speech carried a strong Aberdeen burr.

The hour was now near 4 a.m. Suddenly, the quiet of the night was broken by the heavy sound of hoofbeats from the west. In the vanguard of Pitcairn's advance force, Adair whispered to Lieutenant Sutherland and the Tory guide Daniel Murray, "Here are two fellows, galloping express to alarm the country!" As the horsemen approached, Sutherland leaped out of the shadows and seized the bridle of one horse while Murray grabbed the other. Both riders were turned out of their saddles, and their horses were taken by the officers. The captives were Asahel Porter and Josiah Richardson of Woburn. They were made to march with the column on pain of death.[28]

The Regulars became highly skilled at the art of snaring Yankees on the road. Two light infantrymen were posted well ahead in the shadows on either side of the highway. When a rider approached they allowed him to pass, then rose and closed upon him from the rear while others stopped him from the front. Two and a half miles east of Lexington the British vanguard captured an angry young man named Simon Winship. He was returning to his father's house, "peaceable and unarmed," and was ordered to dismount. At four o'clock in the morning he gave the Regulars a defiant lecture on liberty, demanding to know by what right they had stopped him in the public road. At gunpoint, he was pulled off his horse and put with the other prisoners.[29]

The column met more horsemen. It began to hear signal guns and alarm bells ahead and even behind. Colonel Smith halted the grenadiers, and ordered an aide to ride back to Boston with a message that surprise had been lost and reinforcements might be necessary. The British courier galloped away into the night. The column resumed its long march, moving deeper into the dark and hostile countryside.

# THE CAPTURE

~ A British Patrol Takes Paul Revere, and Is Taken by Him

> After they had taken Revere, they brought him within
> half a rod of me, and I heard him speak up with en-
> ergy to them."
>
> —Elijah Sanderson, Deposition,
> December 17, 1824

WHILE THE BRITISH COLUMN was beginning its march through Cambridge, Paul Revere and William Dawes traveled out of Lexington on their second mission of the night. As they headed west toward Concord, they were overtaken on the road by a handsome young country gentleman, splendidly mounted and elegantly dressed. He introduced himself as Doctor Samuel Prescott, a physician of Concord.

Young Doctor Prescott had other things on his mind than politics or war that night. He had been in Lexington courting Miss Lydia Mulliken, a young woman much celebrated in Middlesex County for her grace and beauty. Many a hopeful swain had beaten a path to the Mulliken door, but Miss Lydia had pledged herself to Doctor Prescott, and they had agreed to be married.

It was about one o'clock in the morning when Doctor Prescott said farewell to his fiancée and started home to Concord. He met Paul Revere and William Dawes, and rode along beside them. They found the congenial young doctor to be a "high son of liberty," and explained their mission to him. He instantly offered to help alarm the countryside.[1]

Paul Revere proposed a plan. As always he was thinking several steps ahead, and preparing for the worst case. He told Dawes and Prescott about the roving British patrols, and warned them that they might expect to be captured. "I told them of the ten officers that Mr. Devens met," he wrote later, "and that it was probable we might be stopped before we got to Concord . . . I likewise mentioned that we had better alarm all the inhabitants till we got to Concord."[2]

The others accepted his plan. Revere remembered that "the young doctor much approved of it, and said, he would stop with either of us, for the people between that [place] and Concord knew him, and would give the more credit to what we said." The three riders decided to alarm every house, taking turns from one farmstead to the next. Knowing that British patrols were abroad in the night, they urged others to help spread the warning. Working together, they made rapid progress through the western part of Lexington.

Two miles beyond Lexington Green, they entered the town of Lincoln, a new community that had been created only twenty years before. Paul Revere reckoned they had come "about half way from Lexington to Concord." Here the Great Road curved westward through open fields and pastures, interspersed with patches of swamp and woodland.[3] Very near the boundary between Lincoln and Lexington, the road ran past a little cluster of farmsteads, three or four of them, a few hundred feet apart. Each house was set only a few feet from the north edge of the highway, facing south toward the warmth of the sun, according to the Yankee custom. All were occupied by families called Nelson. This pattern of settlement was typical of old New England. It was the custom for sons to settle close to their fathers' land, while the daughters moved away. As a consequence, many town centers in Massachusetts were surrounded by small hamlets of households with the same surname.[4]

As the riders approached the Nelson farms, Dawes and Prescott left the road to awaken a family while Revere rode several hundred yards ahead, perhaps intending to stop at the next farm.[5] Suddenly in the bright moonlight he saw two horsemen lurking under a tree, "in nearly the same situation as those officers were, near Charlestown." Revere turned in his saddle and shouted a warning to his companions. They came riding up to him. Revere instantly proposed to attack, saying "There are two, and we will have them." Dr. Prescott turned the butt end of his riding whip and gamely prepared to give battle.[6]

As they advanced, the two horsemen suddenly multiplied into

four British Regulars in full regimentals, with swords and pistols in their hands. One shouted, "God damn you! Stop! If you go an inch further you are a dead man!"[7]

The New England men spurred their horses forward, trying to force a passage. "We attempted to git through them," Revere wrote, "but they kept before us." The ambush site had been chosen with cunning. Revere remembered that the shoulders of the narrow road "inclined each way," and left little room for maneuver. The armed British officers herded them at pistol-point toward a pasture north of the Great Road. The bars across the entrance to the pasture had been taken down. The officers "swore if we did not turn into that pasture they would blow our brains out."[8]

The New England men left the highway, with the British officers hovering about their flanks and rear. As they entered the pasture, Doctor Prescott saw an opportunity. He turned to Paul Revere who was riding beside him, and whispered urgently in the old Yankee dialect, "Put on!" Both men dug their heels into their horses' sides and galloped for their lives. Prescott turned left, jumped a low stone wall, and disappeared on a dark and narrow path that ran through woods and swamps. Several British officers gave chase, but Prescott knew the countryside, and his horse was strong and fresh. He vanished into the night.[9]

When Prescott turned left, Paul Revere headed to the right toward a tree line at the bottom of the pasture, hoping to escape into the woods. His splendid animal was very tired, but responded nobly to urgent command. Revere surged ahead of his captors. But just as he reached the trees, six more horsemen suddenly appeared. Now ten British Regulars surrounded him. They pointed their pistols at his heart, seized his bridle, tore his reins from his grasp, and held him firmly in their grasp.

In that moment of confusion, William Dawes got away. When the officers went after Revere and Prescott, Dawes turned back into the highway. He tried to confuse his captors by shouting "Halloo, my boys, I've got two of 'em!" As the officers went after Revere, Dawes galloped away in the opposite direction, to what appeared to be the safety of a nearby farm. As he approached the house in the darkness, his horse took fright and stopped so abruptly that Dawes pitched forward, out of his seat. He tumbled to the ground, losing his watch, his horse, and what remained of his composure. His frightened animal ran away, with empty stirrups banging crazily on the long leathers that were then in use.

The dark house that Dawes took to be a place of refuge turned out to be an abandoned building, perhaps inhabited by wild animals that had frightened his horse. Badly shaken, William Dawes decided that enough was enough. He went limping back toward Lexington in the moonlight, keeping in the shadows and out of sight.[10]

Meanwhile the British Regulars gathered around their prisoner. They were angry men. Ten of the King's officers had failed to snare two out of three suspicious countrymen who had ridden straight into their trap. They turned their hostility toward the one who remained in their hands. Revere was ordered to dismount. Some of the Regulars began to abuse him.

Suddenly another officer intervened. Paul Revere thought him "much of a gentleman." The officer addressed his captive as a gentleman too, with the elaborate courtesy of that distant age.

"Sir," the British officer said politely, "may I crave your name?"

"My name is Revere," the captive answered.

"What?" the officer exclaimed in surprise, "Paul Revere!"

"Yes," came the reply.[11]

Paul Revere was well known to these British officers. They began to talk among themselves with high excitement, then angrily turned back toward their captive. "The others abused me much," Paul Revere remembered, but their leader continued to treat him correctly. "He told me not to be afraid; they should not hurt me."[12]

Paul Revere began to look around him. He discovered that he was not the only prisoner. The officers had been stopping every suspicious rider who passed them on the road. They had caught Elijah Sanderson and Jonathan Loring, who had been sent from Lexington to watch them, and had also bagged Solomon Brown, a messenger who had been dispatched to Concord. Along the way, they also captured an innocent one-armed pedlar named Allen who had nothing to do with either side.[13] All of the prisoners had been interrogated at length. "They asked as many questions as a Yankee could," Sanderson later testified. He remembered that they "put many questions to us, which I evaded . . . they particularly inquired where Hancock and Adams were."[14]

The officers turned to Revere and began to question him in the same way. He answered truthfully. They demanded to know if he was an express, and were told yes. The other captives were too far away to hear all of the questions, but close enough to make out Paul Revere's replies. With six pistols pointed at him, Revere spoke with a spirit that the British officers found infuriating in a provincial prisoner, who seemed not to know his place, or to care about the danger he faced. One of the prisoners, Elijah Sanderson, listened at a distance and later remembered, "I heard him speak up with energy to them."[15]

"Gentlemen," Revere told them, "you've missed of your aim."

"What of our aim?" one answered in a "hard" tone. Another insisted that they were out after deserters, a frequent employment of British officers in America.

"I know better," Paul Revere boldly replied. "I know what you are after, and have alarmed the country all the way up."

Even as the British officers posed the questions, Paul Revere began to control the interrogation. Before the Regulars realized what had happened, the prisoner himself became the inquisitor. Paul Revere proceeded to tell his astonished captors more than they knew about their own mission. He informed them that Colonel Smith's expedition had left Boston by boat across the Back Bay, and that "their boats had catched aground" at Lechmere Point, and that the Regulars had come ashore in Cambridge.

He also told them what he had been doing that night, and warned that he had alarmed the militia at Lexington, and their lives would be at risk if they lingered near that town. "I should have 500 men there soon," he said, adding, "if I had not known people had been sent out to give information to the country, and time enough to get fifty miles, I would have ventured one shot from you, before I would have suffered you to have stopped me."[16]

As the conversation continued, the British officers grew more and more agitated. They were outraged by the effrontery of this infernal Yankee scoundrel who dared to threaten the King's officers even while their pistols were pointed at his breast. They were also increasingly disturbed by the unwelcome news that he brought them.

After Paul Revere had spoken, one of the Regulars rode off some distance to the highway, and came back at full gallop with his commander, Major Edward Mitchell of the 5th Foot. The major was an excitable man, and not in a happy frame of mind. He ordered that Revere be searched for weapons. None were found. Had he been carrying arms, the story of the midnight ride might have ended differently.

Then Major Mitchell himself came up to Paul Revere in a high temper. "He clapped [a] pistol to my head," Revere remembered, "and said he was agoing to ask me some questions, and if I did not tell the truth, he would blow my brains out."[17]

Paul Revere was angered by those words, and told the major that "he did not need a threat to make him speak the truth." He added contemptuously, "I call myself a man of truth, and you have stopped me on the highway, and made me a prisoner I knew not by what right. I will tell the truth, for I am not afraid."

That is precisely what Paul Revere proceeded to do. He told the truth without hesitation, while surrounded by armed and hostile horsemen in that dark pasture on the Concord Road. He spoke with a serene self-confidence, even to these armed and angry men who pointed their pistols at him, and were not happy to hear what he had to say.

Later, Paul Revere remembered that "the officer who led me said I was in a damned critical situation. I told him I was sensible of it." But even in this moment of mortal peril he spoke boldly to the British officers with the courage of an urgent purpose. Paul Revere had a particular object in mind. Everything, without exception, that he said and did to his captors was consistent with a single goal. He was trying to move these men away from Lexington— away from Hancock and Adams. Revere had reason to believe that the mission of the patrol was to arrest those two Whig leaders. He warned the British officers that if they remained in the vicinity of Lexington Green, they also would be in extreme danger, and he hinted that the expedition coming after them could start a war unless it was warned of the trouble that awaited them at Lexington center. In fact, trouble was gathering for them in many places that night, but Revere stressed only one place in particular—Lexington, where he had left Hancock and Adams.[18]

It was a remarkable performance. The soldiers listened carefully to Paul Revere, increasingly quiet and pensive. Then they withdrew a little way and began to talk among themselves. Suddenly they returned to Revere, and ordered him to mount. Another officer went to the captive Sanderson, who remembered that they "ordered me to untie my horse (which was tied to a little birch) and mount."

The party left the pasture, entered the road, and turned east toward Boston. "They kept us in the middle of the road, and rode on each side of us," Sanderson recalled. "They took all of us, Revere, Loring, Brown and myself." One of the officers took out his watch and looked at it. Sanderson asked him the time and was told it was a quarter past two.[19]

Paul Revere's words had worked brilliantly. The Regulars were increasingly tense and nervous. For many hours they had loitered on the road. Now they were in a hurry to ride east, and impatient of every delay. Sanderson was badly mounted on a slow horse. One officer struck the animal with the flat of his sword, and sent it skittering ahead.

The ten British Regulars and their four or five prisoners rode down toward Lexington. "When we got into the road," Revere remembered, "they formed a circle and ordered the prisoners in the centre, and to lead me in the front." The captives remembered that the pace was "prittie smart."[20]

With Paul Revere, the officers took special measures. He was made to mount with the others, but his reins were taken from him. Revere asked if he might hold the reins himself, and received a rude reply. The polished manners of these English gentlemen were beginning to wear thin. "God damn you, sir!" an officer said to him, "*you* are not to ride with reins, I assure you!"[21] Major Mitchell in particular was showing the strain. He told Paul Revere, "We are now going towards your friends and if you attempt to run or we are insulted, we will blow your brains out."

"You may do as you please," Revere answered.

Revere's reins were given to a sergeant who was ordered to draw his pistol, and use it to "execute the major's sentence" if the captive tried to bolt. The anger and frustration of the British Regulars were growing dangerously. Revere remembered that "I was often insulted by the officers, calling me damned Rebel &c. &c."

They were now about half a mile from Lexington Green. Suddenly they heard a gunshot. Major Mitchell turned in fury to his prisoner and demanded an explanation. Revere told him that it was a signal "to alarm the country." A few minutes later the riders were startled to hear the heavy crash of an entire volley of musketry, from the direction of Lexington's meeting house. Probably it came from a party of militiamen who were clearing their weapons before they entered the Buckman Tavern for a bit of cheer. The Regulars were appalled to hear it. Revere remembered that the volley "appeared to alarm them very much."[22]

At last the officers began to feel the full import of what Paul Revere had been telling them. His words of warning took on stronger meaning when punctuated by gunfire. The sound of a single shot had suggested to them that surprise was lost. The crash of a volley appeared evidence that the country was rising against them. As they came closer to the Common they began to hear

Lexington's town bell clanging rapidly. The captive Loring, picking up Revere's spirit, turned to the officers and said, "The bell's a'ringing! The town's alarmed, and you're all dead men!"[23]

The officers halted, rode apart from their captives, and once again talked urgently among themselves. They decided that they must gallop back to warn the commanders of the marching column. To travel faster, they resolved to release their captives.[24]

A young subaltern went over to Sanderson, ordered him to dismount, drew a sword, and said apologetically, "I must do you an injury." As the officer brandished his weapon, Sanderson wondered, what injury? The Regulars had already made him a prisoner, taken his property and threatened his life. What further injury remained? "I asked what he was going to do to me now?" Sanderson later wrote. The officer "made no reply, but with his hanger cut my bridle and girth, and then mounted." Sanderson, to his amazement, found himself a free man.[25]

Major Mitchell released the other prisoners. He ordered his men to cut their bridles and girths and drive the horses away. Then the major rode over to Paul Revere's guard, a sergeant of grenadiers, a big man on a little horse. The major asked if the sergeant's mount was fatigued, then gestured toward Revere and ordered, "Take that man's horse."[26] Paul Revere was told to dismount. Brown Beauty was given to the sergeant, who mounted quickly. Then the Regulars turned their horses and rode off to the east at what Sanderson called "a good smart trot."[27]

The liberated prisoners headed directly for Lexington Green. Paul Revere instantly began to think of capturing the men who had captured him. Sanderson remembered that they waded "through the swamp, through the mud and water, intending to arrive at the meetinghouse before they [the British officers] could pass, to give information to our people."[28]

But the Regulars were moving too fast to be caught. The former captives watched as they stopped briefly near the meetinghouse, talked among themselves, then started at full gallop toward Cambridge. "We saw no more of them," Sanderson remembered.[29]

It was also the last that Paul Revere saw of Brown Beauty. Deacon Larkin's splendid horse had served him nobly that night. He watched her disappear into the night with a sergeant of grenadiers bouncing on her back. The Larkin family were later told that she was driven until she dropped to her knees and died in the night. Whatever happened, Brown Beauty was never seen by her owners again.[30]

The released captives were exhausted by their ordeal. Sanderson headed straight for the beckoning lights of Buckman's Tavern on Lexington Green. "I went to the tavern," he recalled later, "the citizens were coming and going; some went down to find whether the British were coming; some came back, and said there was no truth in it. I went into the tavern, and, after a while, went to sleep in my chair by the fire."[31]

While Sanderson dozed in the warm tavern, Paul Revere remained outside, still on his feet. Suddenly he thought of one more urgent task that needed to be done. Revere turned away from the tavern lights, left the main road, and strode north across the countryside on yet another mission.

# THE ALARM

It must have been a preconcerted scheme in them.

—British Colonel Francis Smith
April 22, 1775

The men appointed to alarm the country on such occasions . . . took their different routes."

—American leader John Adams,
April 19, 1775

IN THE TIME THAT Paul Revere remained a prisoner, his message traveled rapidly across the countryside. To many Americans, the legend of the Lexington alarm conjures up the image of a solitary rider, galloping bravely in the darkness from one lonely farmstead to the next. This romantic idea is etched indelibly upon the national memory, but it is not what actually happened that night. Many other riders helped Paul Revere to carry the alarm. Their participation did not in any way diminish his role, but actually enlarged it. The more we learn about these messengers, the more interesting Paul Revere's part becomes—not merely as a solitary courier, but as an organizer and promoter of a common effort in the cause of freedom.

Earlier that evening, while Paul Revere was making ready for his own midnight ride, he and his Whig friends began the work of dispatching other couriers with news of the British march. While he was still in Charlestown, preparing to travel west to Lexington, arrangements were made for another "express" to gallop north with the news that he had brought from Boston. The identity of this other courier is not known. Many people heard him in the dark, but few actually saw him, and nobody recorded his name. He set out from Charlestown at about the same hour as Paul Revere himself. His route took him north, through the present towns of Medford, Winchester, Woburn, and Wilmington. So swiftly did he gallop on dark and dangerous roads that by two o'clock in the morning he was in the town of Tewksbury on the Merrimack River, twenty-five miles north of Boston.[1]

Whoever he may have been, this messenger knew exactly where he was going, and what he was to do. When he reached Tewksbury, he spurred his horse through the streets of the sleeping village, and rode directly to the farm of Captain John Trull on Stickney Hill, near the town's training field.

Captain Trull was the head of Tewksbury's militia, and a pivotal figure in the alarm system that Whig leaders had organized during the past few months. He was awakened by the courier who told him, "I have alarmed all the towns from Charlestown to here." Trull rose from his bed, and took up his musket. Still in his nightdress, he fired three times from his bedroom window. This was a signal previously arranged with the militia commander in the neighboring town of Dracut, north of Tewksbury on the New Hampshire border.[2]

The sharp report of Captain Trull's alarm gun carried across the Merrimack River, and the militia company of Dracut instantly began to muster. The hour was a little after two o'clock in the morning. At the moment when General Gage's Regulars were still in the marshes of the East Cambridge, the news of their secret mission had traveled thirty miles from Boston to the New Hampshire line. These were 18th-century distances. Thirty miles was normally a long day's journey in that era.[3]

The astonishing speed of this communication did not occur by accident. It was the result of careful preparation, and something else as well. Paul Revere and the other messengers did not spread the alarm merely by knocking on individual farmhouse doors. They also awakened the institutions of New England. The midnight riders went systematically about the task of engaging town leaders and military commanders of their region. They enlisted its churches and ministers, its physicians and lawyers, its family networks and voluntary associations. Paul Revere and his fellow Whigs of Massachusetts understood, more clearly than Americans of later generations, that political institutions are instruments of human will, and amplifiers of individual action. They knew from long experience that successful effort requires sustained planning and careful organization. The way they went about their work made a major difference that night.

While the Tewksbury rider was galloping north, Paul Revere himself was on the road, traveling northeast from Charlestown to Medford. As we have seen, he had not planned to go that way, but once in the village of Medford, he went quickly about the task of awakening that community with remarkable economy of effort. He rode directly to the house of Captain Isaac Hall, commander of Medford's minutemen, who instantly triggered the town's alarm system. A townsman remembered that "repeated gunshots, the beating of drums and the ringing of bells filled the air."[4]

From Medford, Paul Revere's friends started yet another express rider galloping to the northeast. He was Doctor Martin Herrick, a young Harvard graduate who studied in Medford and worked in the town of Lynnfield, fifteen miles to the north. Several Whig messengers that night were physicians. In that far-distant era when American physicians made house-calls, a country doctor was apt to own the best saddle horse in town, and be a highly experienced rider. He also tended to be a "high-toned son of liberty." So it was with Martin Herrick. He carried Paul Revere's message of alarm northeast from Medford to the village of Stoneham, then turned east toward Reading, where he roused the militia officers in the south precinct of that town. From Reading he rode to Lynn End, alarmed the militia company and later joined it as a volunteer on the march—a busy night for young Doctor Herrick.[5]

Within a few hours, Doctor Herrick awakened a large area on the North Shore of Massachusetts Bay. He also set other riders in motion. One "express" was in Lynn by "early morn."[6] Another galloped from Reading fifteen miles east to Danvers. A third rode fourteen miles north to Andover, where militiaman Thomas Boynton noted that "about the sun rising, the Town was alarmed with the News that the Regulars were on their March to Concord."[7] Another resident of Andover, slower to get the word, wrote in his diary, "About seven o'clock we had alarum that the Reegelers was gon to Conkord we gathered at the meting hous & then started for Concord."[8]

Along the North Shore of Massachusetts, church bells began to toll and the heavy beat of drums could be heard for many miles in the night air. Some towns responded to these warnings before a courier reached them. North Reading was awakened by alarm guns before sunrise. The first messenger appeared a little later.[9]

While the alarm was spreading rapidly to the north, Paul Revere and his fellow Whigs started yet another courier in a different direction—east from Medford to the town of Malden. This express rider delivered the alarm to a Whig leader who went to an outcropping called Bell Rock, and rang the town bell. That prearranged signal summoned the men of Malden with their weapons to a meeting place at Kettell's Tavern. From Malden, the alarm was carried east to Chelsea on the Atlantic coast.[10]

Meanwhile, Paul Revere himself was carrying the same message west from Medford to the village of Menotomy. There again he started other messengers in motion. This was the part of his journey of which he later wrote, "I alarmed almost every house, till I got to Lexington."[11] From some of those houses men rode north and northwest to the precincts above Cambridge and Menotomy. Captain Ebenezer Stedman, a prominent Whig leader, was awakened at an early hour. He sent an express rider to Captain Joshua Walker and Major Loammi Baldwin in Woburn, north of Menotomy. From Woburn village, Captain Walker sent a messenger riding west to Jonathan Proctor in the second parish, now the town of Burlington. The alarm was also carried to the northwest in the same way. All along Paul Revere's route, town leaders and militia commanders were systematically engaged—a fact of vital importance for the events that followed.[12]

Much of what happened that night was cloaked in secrecy, but repeated evidence indicates that Paul Revere played a unique role. From long association he was acquainted with leaders throughout the province. He knew who they were and where to find them, even in towns that he had not expected to visit. They knew him as well.

It is instructive in that regard to compare the conduct of Paul Revere and William Dawes, who went about their work in very different ways. Revere's ride to Lexington covered nearly thirteen miles in less than two hours. His circuit was a broad arc north and west of Boston. In every town along that route Paul Revere met with Whig leaders—Richard Devens in Charlestown, Isaac Hall in Medford, probably Ebenezer Stedman in Cambridge, Benjamin Locke and Solomon Bowman in Menotomy.[13]

William Dawes traveled a longer distance on a slower horse—nearly seventeen miles in about three hours. His route took him in a different direction, south across Boston Neck to Roxbury, then west and north through Brookline, Brighton, Cambridge, Menotomy, and Lexington. No evidence exists that he spoke with anyone before he reached the Clarke house in Lexington. It is difficult to believe that he did not talk with at least a few people on the road, but in many hundreds of accounts of the Lexington alarm, only one person remembered meeting him that night—Lexington's Sergeant Munroe, who was unable to recollect his name and called him "Mr. Lincoln."[14]

Along Paul Revere's northern route, the town leaders and company captains instantly triggered the alarm system. On the southerly circuit of William Dawes, that did not happen until later. In at least one town it did not happen at all. Dawes did not awaken the town fathers or militia commanders in the towns of Roxbury, Brookline, Watertown, or Waltham. Probably he did not know them. As we shall see, Roxbury and Brookline and Watertown would receive the alarm in other ways, long after Dawes had passed. Waltham never received it at all.

The town of Waltham lay just west of Watertown and south of Lexington. Its northern border was only two miles from Lexington Green, closer than any other community. But the alarm system was not triggered in Waltham until much later the next morning, too late for its militia companies to join the fighting. Only a few farmers in the neighborhood called Waltham Farms, at the north end of town, heard the alarm. Some of these men would see action, but no company of militia from Waltham fought that day. Several historians have suspected that the community was Tory in its sympathies—which certainly was not the case. Two days later, more than 200 Waltham men were in the field with the New England army. Many would fight bravely at Bunker Hill and on other fields. But on the 19th of April they mustered too late, through no fault of their own. Anyone with experience of military service will understand what happened. In the jargon of another war, Waltham was among the 10 percent who never got the word.[15]

The dogs that did not bark in Waltham and other southern towns were an important clue to the working of the alarm system, and to Paul Revere's role that night. In North Waltham we find evidence that a knock on a farmhouse door was not enough to set the process in motion. Scattered homes received the warning, but military officers and town fathers were not notified, and the militia failed to muster in time. Here was further proof that Paul Revere and his fellow riders on his northern route succeeded in spreading the alarm by engaging the institutions of these rural communities, in a way that William Dawes did not.

None of this is meant to deny William Dawes his role in the Lexington alarm. His ride was firmly documented, most of all by Paul Revere himself, who was always careful to give Dawes a share of the credit. On other occasions before and afterward, Dawes proved himself to be a brave and resourceful man who believed deeply in the Whig cause and served it faithfully. He carried his message to Lexington just as Doctor Warren had requested, in the face of many dangers. But Paul Revere did that, and more.[16]

When Dawes and Revere came together in Lexington, they began to work as a team. While they were at the Clarke house and the Buckman Tavern, other messengers were dispatched from Lexington center. Some rode east into parts of Cambridge that Revere had skirted on his detour to Medford. Lexington's minister remembered that between 12 and 1 o'clock "two persons were sent express to Cambridge."[17] The houses clustered around Harvard College received the news from the west at about two o'clock in the morning. Hannah Winthrop, who lived near Harvard yard, remembered that she was awakened by "beat of drum and ringing of bell," a few hours before dawn. These were the drums and bells that the British Regulars themselves had begun to hear with growing concern, as they hurried on their way.[18]

Two other Lexington men, Nathan Munroe and Benjamin Tidd, rode north from Lexington to warn the town of Bedford. They called at the house of Cornet Nathaniel Page, the color bearer of the Bedford militia, and shouted, "Get up, Nat Page, the Regulars are out!" Then they galloped west as far as Meriam's Corner in Concord, delivered their news, and trotted back to Lexington by side roads, while Page spread the alarm to his Bedford company.[19]

By that hour so many couriers were riding from Lexington Common across the countryside that Paul Revere and William Dawes were unable to find fresh horses for their trip to Concord. As they set out on their weary mounts, we have seen how they recruited Dr. Samuel Prescott to help them with his fresh animal. Here again, Revere and Dawes prepared carefully for contingencies, and worked out a plan in case they were captured. That act of individual foresight and collective effort made a vital difference.

Let us pick up Dr. Prescott's trail. He was well mounted, and master of the ground. When Dawes was stopped and Revere was captured, Prescott put heels to his horse, and disappeared into the countryside that he knew so well. Revere remembered that "the Doctor jumped his horse over a low stone wall" and got away. Prescott picked his way in the darkness through woods and swamps until he had eluded his English pursuers, then returned to the main road and galloped on alone. As he had promised, Prescott spread the word through Lincoln and Concord, making an effort to awaken ministers, militia officers, and the family networks of outlying hamlets. He also recruited other couriers, in the same way that Revere and Dawes had recruited him.

On the road in North Lincoln, Doctor Prescott came upon a young man named Nathaniel Baker, who like Prescott himself had been out courting his fiancée Elizabeth Taylor at her house near the present Lexington-Lincoln line. A good many travelers that Spring night were young men on errands of love. Nathaniel Baker "received the alarm" from Doctor Prescott, and carried it to his kinsman Amos Baker, who awakened his father, four brothers, and brother-in-law. They in turn went to warn others throughout the town of Lincoln.[20]

Still in Lincoln, Prescott also stopped at a blacksmith shop close to the road where one or two African slaves lay sleeping. The slaves carried the alarm to their mistress Mary Hartwell, who was in a nearby house with her newborn infant. So urgent did she think the news that she left her baby and ran across the fields to the home of militia captain William Smith and told him what she had heard. While Mary Hartwell hurried home to her baby, Captain Smith began to ring Lincoln's town bell and mustered his company. The time was about two o'clock in the morning.[21]

From Lincoln the news was also carried south to Weston. In that country town, Boston Whig leader Samuel Cooper had found refuge with the family of Samuel Savage near Daggett's Corner in the north part of Weston, near the Lincoln line. He was awakened with the alarm by Mrs. Savage at about 3 o'clock in the morning.[22]

While the warning was spreading to the south, Doctor Prescott galloped west into Concord center, and arrived there before two o'clock in the morning. He found someone to ring the Concord bell, then rode off to find the town's minister, William Emerson, and the militia leaders.[23] Emerson noted in his diary, "This morning between 1 and 2 o'clock we were alarmed by the ringing of the bell, and upon examination found that the troops to the number of 800, had stole their march from Boston in boats and barges . . . this intelligence was brought us at first by Samuel Prescott who narrowly escaped the guard that were sent before on horses, purposely to prevent all posts and messengers from giving us timely information. . . . He by the help of a very fleet horse crossing several walls and fences arrived at Concord at the time aforementioned."[24]

While the town of Concord was awakening, Prescott stopped at his own home where he lived with his father and brother—three physicians under one roof. In the town's tax list, they were assessed for four saddle horses, a greater number than any other household. Samuel Prescott asked his brother Abel to help spread the alarm. Abel quickly agreed, and went to saddle his horse—yet another physician who served as a courier that night.

Then, according to local memory, Dr. Samuel Prescott mounted his horse again and carried the alarm west from Concord into the town of Acton. He galloped to the house of militia captain Joseph Robbins. One of the children in that household remembered waking with a start, when the messenger "struck with a large heavy club . . . the corner of the house, never dismounting." While the wooden building reverberated from that blow, Doctor Prescott cried in haste, "Captain Robbins! Captain Robbins! Up! Up! The Regulars have come to Concord." Within minutes Captain Robbins mounted his "old mare" and carried the news to west Acton. He rode first to the house of Isaac Davis, captain of Acton's minutemen. Then he continued to the home of Deacon Simon Hunt who commanded Acton's "west company."[25]

Doctor Prescott galloped on, over a wooden bridge to the garrison house in South Acton where Major Francis Faulkner lived. In his nightshirt Faulkner fired his musket three times as fast as he could load—the prearranged signal for assembly in the town. Others repeated the signal. Major Faulkner's young son later remembered listening in fascination as the signal guns echoed in the distance.[26]

From Acton, a courier named Edward Bancroft took up the message and carried it northwest to the towns of Groton and Pepperell. Another messenger galloped north to the town of Billerica, where the militia were awakened between 3 and 4 o'clock. They mustered on the Common and at Pollard's Tavern. Yet a third express rider named Weatherbee galloped into Littleton in the early morning, and then continued across Beaver Brook Bridge to the towns beyond.[27]

A prearranged system of beacon fires and signal guns was used to muster the militia in what is now the town of Carlisle, north of Concord and Acton. An historian of the town writes that they "were wakened by the cannon and musket fire relay signal system, gathered up their muskets, powder and ball, and began to assemble at the First Parish Meeting House in Carlisle Center at about 7 a.m."[28]

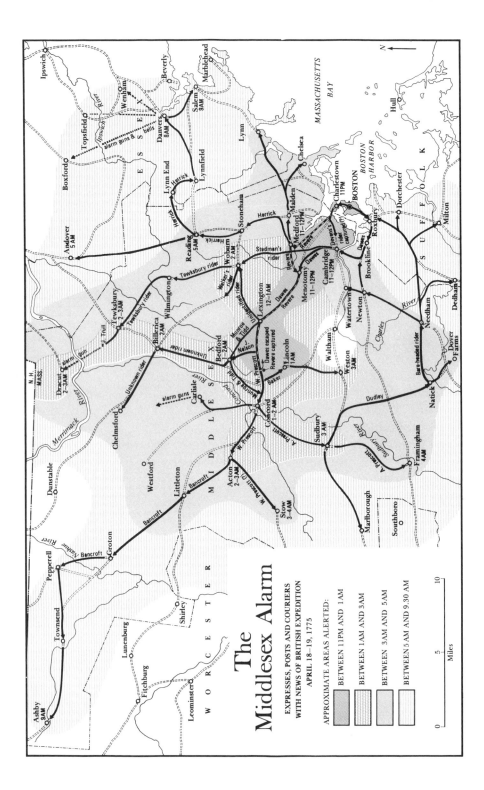

While Doctor Samuel Prescott was alarming the towns west of Concord his brother Abel Prescott traveled south to Sudbury and Framingham. He went to Thomas Plympton, the leading Whig in Sudbury, and the town's alarm bell began to ring about 3:30 or 4 o'clock in the morning. Warning guns were fired to summon militia companies on the west side of the Sudbury River and also in East Sudbury, now the green country town of Wayland. Within thirty-five minutes the entire town of Sudbury had been awakened.[29]

From Sudbury, Abel Prescott and other messengers continued south to Framingham and Natick, where the militia began to muster between 5 or 6 o'clock. The news was relayed from Framingham to Needham and Dover Farms by another "express" who was not known in those towns, but would be long remembered as the "bare-headed alarm rider." He "brought the news to Bullard's Tavern," where "Ephraim Bullard fired three musket shots from the hill behind his house, giving the agreed-upon signal to arouse the town." Distant parts of Needham were awakened by the trumpet of African slave Abel Benson.[30]

From Needham the alarm spread east to Newton, and from Dover Farms it raced south into what is now Norfolk County, circling back toward Boston whence it had begun.[31] The large town of Dedham, a few miles southwest of Boston, did not get the word until about 9 o'clock in the morning, when the alarm arrived by way of Needham and Dover, in a wide circuit of express riders from the west and north.[32] Roxbury, next to Boston, was not alerted until dawn. William Heath, the ranking military officer in that town, remembered that he was not "called from his bed" until daybreak. Here again, the news that had left Boston seven hours earlier arrived from the west in a long circuitous journey.[33]

In Watertown, the militia were not alarmed until word finally reached them indirectly from the northern towns that Paul Revere had alarmed, and from the western communities that had been awakened by the Prescotts. The alarm arrived in a manner that left the Whig leaders of Watertown in much uncertainty. While they debated what to do, Newton's militia companies marched into town on their way to Lexington. The men of Watertown promptly joined them.[34]

Thus the circle was complete. The alarm had passed from Paul Revere and William Dawes to Samuel Prescott, then to Abel Prescott, and on to other riders who spread the word to Natick, Framingham, Needham, Dover, Dedham, Roxbury, and Watertown, curving back to Boston in a great chain of alarm-riders.[35]

To study in detail the spread of the alarm, and to observe the towns from which the militia marched to Lexington and Concord, is to understand another layer of significance in Paul Revere's ride. In the flow of information one may discover the importance of the preparations he had made, the impact of his decisions along the way, and the role of his associations with other Whig leaders. Many of the links in that chain had been forged in advance. Others were improvised by Paul Revere and his friends who prudently prepared for the worst case.[36]

Had they acted otherwise, the outcome might well have been different. A few hours' delay in the alarm—perhaps less than that—might have been enough for General Gage's troops to have completed their mission and returned safely to Boston before an effective force could muster against them. The result would have been a small success for British arms, and an encouragement to the Imperial cause at a critical moment. On the other side, the revolutionary movement would have lost a moral advantage that had a major impact on events to come.

What made the difference was a complex sequence of contingencies, shaped by the interplay of individual choices and collective effort within a social frame. A major event happened that night in a way that was profoundly different from the popular image of solitary hero-figures, and also from the naive determinism of academic scholarship in the 20th century. Here was another part of Paul Revere's message for our time.

# THE MUSTER

❧ The Rising of the Militia

It seemed as if men came down from the clouds.

—A letter from Boston,
April 19, 1775

IMMEDIATELY after the alarm was received, the men of Massachusetts began to assemble in their towns. Lexington's Congregational minister Jonas Clarke remembered that within moments of Paul Revere's arrival "the militia of this town were alarmed, and ordered to meet on the usual place of parade." Everyone knew what to do. Literally within minutes, men throughout the town were dressing hastily and reaching for their muskets, while wives packed a few provisions in their shoulder bags, and small children sat up in their trundle beds and rubbed the sleep from their eyes.[1]

The commander of Lexington's militia, Captain John Parker, lived two miles from the Common in the southwest corner of the town. He had been elected by his fellow townsmen, and they had chosen well. John Parker was the sort of leader other men willingly follow in the face of danger. His grandson, the future minister Theodore Parker, remembered him as "a great tall man, with a large head and a high, wide brow." He was forty-six years old, and not in good health. Members of his family remembered that he had gone to bed ill the night before, and had slept only a few hours. Like many others in New England, John Parker suffered from pulmonary tuberculosis. Its ravages were far advanced in his lungs, and would have left their telltale signs in the burning intensity of his sunken eyes and the gauntness of his hollow cheeks.

Even so, he felt fit enough for military service, and his neighbors could think of no better man to lead them.

By occupation, John Parker was a Yankee farmer and mechanic. By long experience he was also an old soldier who had survived many a hard colonial campaign. He had been present at the siege of Louisbourg and the conquest of Quebec, and probably had done a tour of duty with Robert Rogers's American Rangers. Captain Parker had seen more of war than most of the British Regulars who were marching into his town. In the early hours of April 19, he gathered up his battered equipment that had seen many years of service, and set off to meet his company.[2]

The time was between 1 and 2 o'clock when Captain Parker's Lexington militia began to muster on the Common. Men drifted in for many hours. A fitful wind was blowing that April night, and played strange tricks with sound. Some householders at a far distance were awakened immediately by the alarm. Others close to the Common slept soundly in the arms of their wives until morning.[3]

The home of Captain John Parker was a typical Lexington farmstead—a simple wooden saltbox house which had been in the family since 1712. Parker's son and grandson Theodore Thaddeus Parker (1810–60) were born and raised in it.

As the Lexington militia gathered on the Common, Captain Parker exchanged a few words with each individual. He did so less as their commander than as their neighbor, kinsman, and friend. These sturdy yeomen did not expect to be told what to do by anyone. They were accustomed to judge for themselves. Many were hardworking dairy farmers in a community that was already known as a "milk town" for the Boston market. Their ages ranged from sixteen to sixty-six, but most were mature men in their thirties and forties. They were men of property and independence who served on juries, voted in town meetings, ran the Congregational church, managed their own affairs, and felt beholden to none but the Almighty.

The men of Lexington did not assemble to receive orders from Captain Parker, much as they respected him. They expected to participate in any major decisions that would be taken. Their minister wrote that the purpose of the muster was first and foremost to "*consult* what might be done."[4] They gathered round Captain Parker on the Common, and held an impromptu town meeting in the open air. The town minister Jonas Clarke was there, with John Hancock and Sam Adams. Possibly Paul Revere and William Dawes also attended briefly, before they left for Concord.[5]

The muster of the Lexington militia was the product of a long historical process in New England—a process that has been much misunderstood in popular histories of the event. The same legends that celebrate the myth of the solitary midnight rider tell us that the Middlesex farmers rose spontaneously in response to the alarm. This idea is very much mistaken. The muster of the minutemen in 1775 was the product of many years of institutional development. Like the alarm itself, it was also the result of careful planning and collective effort.

For six generations since the founding of the Massachusetts Bay Colony, every town had maintained its "training band." All able-bodied males of military age were required to serve except conscientious objectors, clergymen, college students, professors, and the mentally incompetent. The training bands were a response to hard necessity. Many times since its founding, Massachusetts had found itself at war. From 1689 to 1763, four major conflicts had broken out between the great European powers. All of them spread to New England.

The military institutions of Massachusetts became very active in time of danger. After every peace they lapsed into a state of suspended animation, until awakened by the next crisis. This rhythm repeated itself in the Fall of 1774, when the Provincial Congress of Massachusetts created a Committee of Safety, collected stocks of arms, and revived the old New England training bands in a new form. All men between the ages of sixteen and fifty were asked to "enlist" themselves in the militia. Older men from fifty to seventy were organized into another group called the alarm list, and ordered to be ready for service in dire emergency.[6]

The Provincial Congress recommended that one quarter of the militia should be organized in "minute companies," ready to march "at the shortest notice." Special groups of that sort had existed in New England since the mid 17th-century. In 1645, militia commanders throughout Massachusetts were ordered "to make choice of thirty soldiers of their companies in ye hundred, who shall be ready at half an hour's warning." On the eve of King Philip's War in 1675, the Suffolk and Middlesex regiments were required to "be ready to march on a moment's warning, to prevent such danger as may seem to threaten us." When the French wars began after 1689, and New England settlements were attacked by winter raiding parties, the Massachusetts legislature created special units of "snowshoe men," each to "provide himself with a good pair of snowshoes, one pair of moggisons and one hatchet," and to "hold themselves ready to march on the shortest warning." These were roving patrols of frontier guards. To support them other militia units were ordered in 1711 and 1743 to be "in readiness at a minute's warning." During the French and Indian War, militia companies that mustered for the Crown Point campaign of 1756, called themselves "minutemen." When the Provincial Congress advised the founding of minute companies, it was building on a long tradition.[7]

Late in 1774, the towns began to act, each in its own way. One of the first was Roxbury, which on December 26, 1774, created a company of "militia minutemen, so called," who were ordered to "hold themselves in readiness at a minute's warning, compleat in arms and ammunition; that is to say a good and sufficient firelock, bayonet, thirty rounds of powder and ball, pouch and knapsack." Roxbury's "militia minutemen" were required to exercise twice a week. They were paid one shilling "lawful money" for every day of service, and could also be fined a shilling for not appearing "at time and place as prefixt by the commanding officer."[8]

The arrangements varied from town to town, which responded to the Provincial Congress more as sovereign bodies than subordinate agencies. Some were very slow, but most moved quickly, with astonishing clarity of purpose. A case in point was the town of Lexington. In November 1774 the selectmen issued special warrants for a town meeting, "to see what method the Town will take to encourage Military Discipline, and to put themselves in a position of defence against their enemies." The town voted to tax itself forty pounds (no small sum for these poor farmers in 1775), "for the purpose of mounting the cannon, ammunition, for a pair of drums for the use of the Training Band in the town, and for carriage and harness for burying the dead." As early as November 1774 the people of Lexington knew what lay ahead for them. With astonishing prescience they prepared for the worst, even for burying the dead.[9]

Lexington's town meeting did not follow one suggestion of the Congress. It never raised a company of minutemen. It preferred to keep all of its militia in one exceptionally large company, which it continued to call by the 17th-century Puritan name of "the training band." Strictly speaking, there were no Lexington minutemen in 1775. It is inaccurate to call them so. The force that gathered on the Green was a traditional New England "training band."[10]

Other Massachusetts towns acted in the same spirit, building carefully on the folkways of their region. New companies of minutemen began by drawing up an old-fashioned "covenant" among themselves, in the same manner as a 17th century Puritan church or town. In the town of Methuen, for example, a muster roll in 1775 began with a formal "covenant," written in an uncertain hand, but with a firm grasp of regional traditions. "Whare Milartary Exercise hath ben much Nelciked," it stated, "We the Subscribers being the first Comptney in Methuen Do Covenant and Engage to form our Sevels into a Bodey in order to larn th manual Exercise to be suegat to such officers as Comptney shall Chuse by Voat in all Constutenel manner accorden to our Chattaers."[11]

These militia covenants differed in detail, but most were similar in fundamentals. All were voluntary associations, explicitly founded to defend a way of life. Most agreed to elect their own officers by majority vote, and to be bound by "equal laws" of their own making. In Dunstable, on March 1, 1775, twenty-eight men solemnly promised that they "do hereby voluntarily engage with each other in defence of our country, Priveledges and Libertys for the space of six months from this date; that we will submit ourselves to the Laws equally."[12] These rules were carefully observed. A Boston newspaper described a militia meeting in Roxbury, in which the "Reverend Mr. Adams opened the meeting with prayer, after which he was chosen moderator." Thereafter, the militia of Roxbury elected their captain, lieutenants, ensigns and sergeants.[13]

Many New England towns maintained a special "training field" where the militia assembled four times a year for military exercises. This also was an ancient custom. The author's town of Wayland (formerly East Sudbury) still has a "Training Field Road," which has existed since the mid 17th century. Professional soldiers smiled indulgently at the sight of the New England militia on its training days. They laughed contemptuously at the awkward drill, hooted at the clumsy marching, and howled with laughter at the bizarre Yankee custom of saluting an officer by discharging a blank-loaded musket at his feet. One British observer wrote, "It is a curious masquerade scene to see grave sober citizens, barbers and tailors who never looked fierce before, strutting about in their Sunday wigs with muskets on their shoulders . . . if ever you saw a goose assume an air of consequence, you may catch some faint idea." Major John Pitcairn of the Royal Marines bragged, "If I draw my sword but half out of my scabbard, the whole banditti of Massachusetts will run away."

But the Massachusetts training bands were far from being the military Yahoos they appeared to be. The citizen-soldiers of New England dressed in the country clothing of artisans and farmers, but they kept their weapons clean and knew how to use them. They neglected the manual of arms, but took pains to perfect their marksmanship and improve their rate of fire. They looked ridiculous in close-order drill, but Robert Rogers had taught them his methods of open-order skirmishing and trained them to use cover and to take advantage of the ground. The New England militia made a miserable appearance on parade, but they practiced mobilization with astonishing results. For all their ragtag appearance, many officers and sergeants were combat veterans who had seen hard service in the French and Indian War.

To European officers who had served with them in the last war, the behavior of the New England militia in combat had seemed erratic at best. Sometimes these citizen soldiers fought poorly; sometimes well. As a rule, they performed badly on foreign soil, and worse when under Regular officers who tried to bully them. They tended to be at their best when they fought on their own ground, under their own elected officers, in defense of their homes and their way of life.

The Regulars of the British army and the citizen soldiers of Massachusetts looked upon military affairs in very different ways. New England farmers did not think of war as a game, or a feudal ritual, or an instrument of state power, or a bloodsport for bored country gentlemen. They did not regard the pursuit of arms as a noble profession. In 1775, many men of Massachusetts had been to war. They knew its horrors from personal experience. With a few exceptions, they thought of fighting as a dirty business that had to be done from time to time if good men were to survive in a world of evil. The New England colonies were among the first states in the world to recognize the right of conscientous objection to military service, and among the few to respect that right even in moments of mortal peril. But most New Englanders were not pacifists themselves. Once committed to what they regarded as a just and necessary war, these sons of Puritans hardened their hearts and became the most implacable of foes. Their many enemies who lived by a warrior-ethic always underestimated them, as a long parade of Indian braves, French aristocrats, British Regulars, Southern planters, German fascists, Japanese militarists, Marxist ideologues, and Arab adventurers have invariably discovered to their heavy cost.

Before the citizen-soldiers of New England marched to war, they reflected at length on what they had to do, and how they meant to do it. When they believed that their homes and their way of life were at stake, they fought with courage and resolve—not for the sake of fighting, but for the sake of winning.

All of these things happened in Massachusetts on April 19, 1775. In the months before, the people of New England had come sadly to the conclusion that war was inevitable, and they had prepared for it with high seriousness. The town of Sudbury alone organized five militia companies, and required them to meet every week to practice mobilization and marksmanship. Others in the town busily collected supplies, and loaded them in wagons to follow the militia when they marched. When the alarm came to Sudbury, the town was ready to muster virtually all its men of military age, and to support them in the field.

Similar scenes were repeated throughout the towns of Middlesex County, with the same typically American combination of public organization and private effort. Acton's Captain Isaac Davis, a farmer and a gunsmith, built a firing range behind his house and shop. His company of minutemen practiced there twice a week from November to April, perfecting their marksmanship by shooting at targets. Captain Davis was a man of energy. He managed to make bayonets and cartridge boxes for his entire company—one of the few to be fully equipped.[14]

When the alarm came, the militia in these towns were ready to move quickly. In Concord, after the bell was rung and the alarm guns began to be fired, the town's soldiers mustered with astonishing speed. Private Thaddeus Blood remembered that he was called out of bed at two o'clock in the morning by his sergeant, within minutes of Dr. Prescott's arrival in the town. Blood joined his company, and went with them to the courthouse to draw ammunition. Amos Barrett, a private soldier in a Concord minute company remembered that "the bell rung at 3 o'clock for alarum as I was then a minute man I was soon in town."

Every town and household had its own story to tell. Some of these tales brought a laugh to later generations, and to the participants themselves in later years. In Lexington, sixteen-year-old Jonathan Harrington was a fifer in the town's militia company. Soon after Paul Revere reached town, he was awakened by his mother, who said to her teen-aged son, "Jonathan, get up! The Regulars are coming, and something must be done!"[15]

No two town stories were quite the same, but common threads appeared. It was common for New England towns to identify a common meeting place for their militia, and to mark it with something called an "alarm post." This was often a stout wooden pillar, with various public notices tacked to its sides. As the British troops marched through the Massachusetts countryside, one of them later wrote, "We vex the Americans very much, by cutting down their liberty poles and alarm posts."[16]

Sometimes the alarm post was a natural landmark. In Chelmsford, George Spaulding recalled that "we rallied at the alarm post, a boulder agreed upon by previous arrangement."[17] In other towns, the militia mustered at the meetinghouse. That was what happened in Andover, where one soldier recalled, "About seven o'clock we had alarum that the Reegelers was gon to Conkord we gathered at the meting hous & then started for Concord."[18]

Many towns tried to muster their full strength, and send its men together. Billerica's men arrived *en masse,* with those in neighboring hamlets, three or four hundred men together. Other towns sent their companies separately. In the sprawling town of Dedham, four companies "marched to the action by a different route."[19] A few towns never held a general muster; the men went running off in small groups, or even as individuals. This happened in Lynn, where many men "immediately set out, without waiting to be organized," much to their cost later in the day. In Chelmsford, one man remembered that "there was but little military order observed by us. We went off in squads as soon as convenient."[20]

Some towns mustered more quickly than others. A regimental commander had ordered the companies from Hollis and Prescott to assemble at Groton. Their historian writes, "So well prepared were they for such an emergency and so expeditious their rally, that they arrived at the Groton rendezvous, five miles distant, before the companies there were ready to march." Many did not follow the roads. The Brookline militia "marched towards Lexington across the fields, as a crow flies."[21]

The towns further west did not hear the alarm until after sunrise. In Pepperell, Abel Parker was plowing his fields three miles from Pepperell center. "He left the plow in the furrow, and without stopping to unyoke his oxen, ran to the house, and seizing his coat in one hand and his gun in the other, started on a run and did not stop until he overtook his comrades near the 'Ridges,' three miles below Groton." This was the ploughing season in Massachusetts. The folk image of the minuteman leaving his plough was literally the case in many towns that first heard the alarm after the sun was up.[22]

Wherever the alarm arrived after daybreak, the men were already hard at work. In Medfield, they mustered directly from their fields and shops. Captain Ephraim Cheney of that town was ploughing his field. He "unhitched his ox from the plough, left it where it was in the furrow, and started for the scene of the action at once." Silas Mason did the same. Hatter James Tisdale was "finishing a hat when the news reached him. He dropped the hat and brush, made himself ready, and started."[23]

When officers sometimes moved more slowly than their men, the major decisions were taken out of their hands. This happened in Salem, which did not get the word until eight or nine o'clock in the morning. One of its senior militia officers, Timothy Pickering, was very slow that day, perhaps because he was a conservative Whig and hoped to avoid hostilities. Pickering protested to his men that there was not time enough to march, that the Regulars would be back in Boston before his unit could reach the scene. His men forced him to mobilize and march. Still he delayed on the road, until a private soldier who happened to be one of Salem's richest merchants told him in no uncertain terms to get moving.

The men of Salem imposed their own judgment on their commander.[24]

Congregational ministers actively involved themselves in the muster, helping to awaken the men, leading the consultations, sometimes shouldering a weapon and joining the march themselves. Many companies gathered at their meetinghouses, and did not march until they had united in prayer. The militia from Dedham center heard a prayer from their clergyman as they stood in front of the meetinghouse. Then they all marched off together.[25] In Chelmsford, George Spaulding recalled, "Parson Bridge . . . wanted us to go into the meetinghouse and have prayers before we left town. Sergeant Ford replied to the good parson, that he had more urgent business on hand." But some sort of prayer was a common part of mobilization in New England.[26]

If the meetinghouses were part of the muster, so also were the families of New England. Some of the small towns in Middlesex County were 145 years old in 1775. For as many as six generations their families had interbred until they were extended cousinages, closely tied by blood and marriage. In Bedford's company, for example, it was said that "all 77 men with few exceptions were related." In Captain John Parker's Lexington's militia company, "over a quarter of those responding were his blood relatives or in-laws."[27]

Older men joined their sons and grandsons as volunteers. In Lexington, Moses Harrington was sixty-five years old. Robert Munroe was sixty-three. Sudbury's Deacon Josiah Haynes was eighty years old, but turned out with the militia and set a rapid pace on the road that left the young minutemen panting behind him. The militia were joined by large numbers of these "unenlisted volunteers" as they were called in Littleton. In Dedham, after the militia marched, "The gray-haired veterans of the French wars, whose blood was stirred anew by the sights and sound of war, resolved to follow their sons into battle." Many of these older men had much military experience. They would be among the most dangerous adversaries on the field that day.[28]

In many communities virtually the entire male population marched off to war. Dedham's minister remembered that the village was "almost literally without a male inhabitant below the age of seventy, and above that of sixteen."[29] Woburn's Major Loammi Baldwin wrote in his diary, "We mustered as fast as possible. The town turned out extraordinary, and proceeded toward Lexington."[30]

They dressed in ordinary working clothes. The men were clean-shaven, with long hair worn straight or pulled back in a queue, beneath large weatherbeaten hats with low round crowns and broad floppy brims. Among the younger men, earlocks were much in fashion, fastened with elegant pins on the side of the head. One eyewitness observed that "to a man they wore small-clothes, coming down and fastening just below the knee, and long stockings with cowhide shoes ornamented by large buckles."[31] Their shirts were linen and their stockings were heavy gray home-spun. As the night air was chill, many were wearing both coats and vests. An observer remarked that their "coats and waistcoats were loose and of huge dimensions, with colors as various as the barks of oak, sumac and other trees of our hills and swamps could make them." These were old New England's traditional "sadd colors."[32]

A few gentlemen of rank turned out in gaudy costumes. Brookline's Doctor William Aspinwall arrived at his town muster wearing an elegant and fashionable broadcloth coat of brilliant scarlet. His neighbors tactfully suggested that a coat of another color might be more suitable for the occasion. Dr Aspinwall hurried home and changed into an outfit that would not be mistaken for British regimentals.[33]

The firearms of these men were as various as their dress. The towns for many years had been required to keep their own supply of munitions. Some had maintained magazines in the Congregational meetinghouses. At Lexington barrels of gunpowder were stored as a "common stock" below the pulpit—a symbolic place in the minds of many Loyalists who had long complained against the explosive theology of the "black regiment" of the Congregational clergy. Littleton's company of 46 men marched off with 24 pounds of powder, and 38 pounds of bullets drawn from the "common stock."[34]

Most towns expected individual militiamen to supply their own weapons, and acted only to arm those who were unable to arm themselves. Newton's town meeting made special provision to arm its paupers at public expense: "Voted, that the Selectmen use their best discretion in providing fire-arms for the poor of the Town, who are unable to provide for themselves." Not many societies in the 18th century would have dared to distribute weapons to their proletariat. At the same time, the rich applied the New England habit of philanthropy to an unaccustomed cause. The town meeting in Newton also noted that "John Pigeon presented to the town

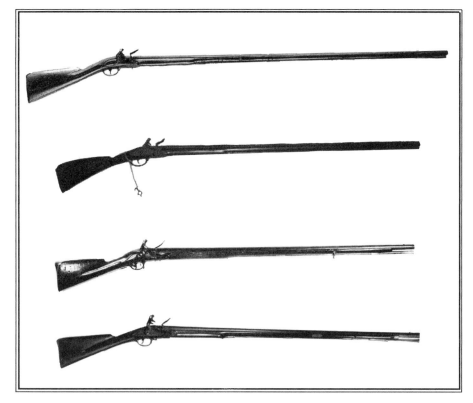

New England Fowler, Museum of Our National Heritage, Lexington
John Parker's Musket, Massachusetts State House
British Musket, Museum of Our National Heritage
British Officer's Fusil, Concord Museum

These were the most common types of firearms at Lexington and Concord. The long-barreled export fowler (top) was a hunting gun, carried on April 19 by Ezekiel Rice (1742–1835) of East Sudbury (now Wayland). It is owned by Peter A. Albee and exhibited at the Museum of Our National Heritage. The New England musket (2d from top) was carried by Captain John Parker on Lexington Green. It has no maker's marks, but appears to be of British or French manufacture with American replacement parts, and bears signs of heavy use, including extensive burnback from the pan. It is kept today in the Massachusetts Senate Chamber. The British Brown Bess was a long land pattern musket carried by many British units in Concord. This one is in the Museum of Our National Heritage. The short-barreled British Fusil was used by officers and sergeants in Grenadier companies. This example bears the markings of the 5th Foot and might have been carried by Lt. Thomas Baker, Sgt. George Kirk, or Sgt. Thomas Allen of the 5th Grenadiers, all of whom were wounded in the battle. Captured by an American militiaman, it is in the Concord Museum.

two field pieces, which were accepted, and the thanks of the town given him."[35]

Town stocks of munitions had been been growing in the winter and spring of 1775, despite the British embargo. But many militia and minute companies were still short of gunpowder and weapons on April 18. A few were not armed at all. Lincoln's Colonel Abijah Pierce carried nothing but a cane. His town had voted to furnish supplies a month earlier, but it was reported that only a "few were as yet well equipped." [36]

Many men armed themselves with weapons not designed for war. One man from Lynn carried a "long fowling piece, without a bayonet, a horn of powder, and a seal-skin pouch, filled with bullets and buckshot.[37] Some carried arms of great antiquity, whose origins told the history of the province. A witness wrote, "Here an old soldier carried a heavy Queen's arm with which he had done service at the conquest of Canada twenty years previous, while by his side walked a stripling boy with a Spanish fusee not half its weight or calibre, which his grandfather may have taken at the Havana, while not a few had old French pieces, that dated back to the reduction of Louisburg." None of these Massachusetts militia are known to have carried long rifles such as were becoming popular in Pennsylvania and the southern backcountry. Despite the urgings of the Congress, few had cartridge boxes or bayonets. Their few precious lead bullets were carefully wrapped in handkerchiefs and carried in pockets or under their hats. Gunpowder was carried in horns that had been passed down from father to son for many generations. Inscriptions carved onto these powder

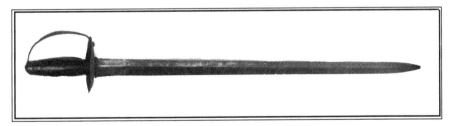

Among the variety of edged weapons carried by militia, one type often appeared in New England. It was a short rapier with a flattened diamond blade that had been made in Europe during the 17th century. At a later date, a New England blacksmith gave it a simple American grip. Many of these austere but efficient weapons have been found in Middlesex and Essex counties, where they had been in use since the mid-17th century—another material indicator of continuity in New England's culture. (Museum of Our National Heritage, Lexington)

horns told their history. Lexington's historical society cherishes a powder horn that descended from generation to generation in the Harrington family of that town. One of its owners carved his name into its side: "Jonathan Harrington His Horne, May the 4 AD 1747." It was later owned by the boy fifer Jonathan Harrington, the youngest soldier who mustered on Lexington Green on April 18, 1775. New England powder horns were elaborately decorated by professional carvers, in a manner much like scrimshaw. One ambivalent horn by Jacob Gay displayed the Royal arms of Britain on one side, and Paul Revere's print of the Boston Massacre on the other. Another made in Roxbury depicted "Tom Gage" as a diabolical figure, with a forked tail, sharp horns, and a serpent in his hand. Some showed idyllic scenes of town commons, and New England churches. Many were adorned with folk motifs, patriotic slogans, personal inscriptions, and snatches of homespun poetry that expressed the values of this culture. It is interesting to compare these objects with the artifacts of other American wars. The inspiring scenes and slogans carved into the powder horns of the American Revolution were profoundly different from the sentiments of alienation, anomie, self-pity, and profound despair inscribed on helmet covers and field equipment in Vietnam. In 1775, even young militia privates who were still in their teens, clearly understood what they were doing, and deeply believed in the cause that they were asked to defend.[38]

Officers and some private soldiers carried swords that were also material expressions of New England's culture and history. Their edged weapons were as various as firearms, but one distinctive type often appeared in eastern Massachusetts. It was short rapier with an antique steel blade that had been imported from continental Europe, and reset with a plain but functional grip by a Yankee blacksmith. This weapon was austere and very old-fashioned in its appearance, much like the short swords of Cromwell's New Model Army. In America the Middlesex sword was another cultural artifact, like the powder horns and firelocks and dress, that revealed the origins of the New England way, and the continuity that extended from the founding of the Puritan Colonies to the revolutionary movement of 1775.[39]

Some units carried flags of great antiquity, which had been passed down from the Puritan founders of New England. One of them survives today in the town of Bedford, Massachusetts. It was made in England sometime in the 17th century, and used as early as 1659 in Massachusetts. Against a crimson background, it shows

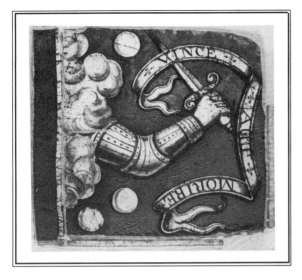

The Bedford Flag is thought to be the oldest surviving banner in English-speaking America. (Bedford Public Library)

the arm of God reaching down from the clouds, with a short sword in a mailed fist. A Latin motto reads, "Vince aut Morire" (Conquer or Die). According to the traditions of the town, this flag was carried on the morning of April 19, 1775, by Cornet Nathaniel Page of the Bedford militia.[40]

Like their Puritan ancestors whose banner they carried, these citizen-soldiers of Massachusetts were very clear about their purposes. They called to mind Oliver Cromwell's plain russet-coated captain, who knew what he fought for, and loved what he knew.

Many years later Captain Levi Preston of Danvers was asked why he went to war that day. At the age of ninety-one, his memory of the Lexington alarm was crystal clear, and his understanding was very different from academic interpretations of this event. An historian asked him, "Captain Preston, what made you go to the Concord Fight?"

"What did I go for?" the old man replied, subtly rephrasing the historian's question to drain away its determinism.

The interviewer tried again. ". . . Were you oppressed by the Stamp Act?" he asked.

"I never saw any stamps," Preston answered, "and I always understood that none were ever sold."

"Well, what about the tea tax?"

"Tea tax, I never drank a drop of the stuff, the boys threw it all overboard."

"But I suppose you have been reading Harrington, Sidney, and Locke about the eternal principle of liberty?"

"I never heard of these men. The only books we had were the Bible, the Catechism, Watts' psalms and hymns and the almanacs."

"Well, then, what was the matter?"

"Young man, what we meant in going for those Redcoats was this: we always had governed ourselves and we always meant to. They didn't mean we should."[41]

# THE GREAT FEAR

 A Rural Panic in New England

> Nor will old Time ever erase the horrors of the mid-
> night cry preceding the Bloody Massacre at Lex-
> ington.
>
> —Hannah Winthrop

AFTER THE MILITIA marched away, early in the morning of April 19, the mood was dark in the towns they left behind. Nearly everyone believed that this was no mere drill or demonstration. On both sides, there was a strange and fatal feeling that bloodshed was inevitable.

The people of New England did not wish for war. This was not a warrior culture. It did not seek glory on the field of valor, and showed none of the martial spirit that has appeared in so many other times and places. There were no cheers or celebrations when the militia departed—nothing like the wild exultation of the American South at the outbreak of the Civil War, or the bizarre bloodlust of the European middle classes in 1914.

The people of New England knew better than that. In 140 years they had gone to war at least once in every generation, and some of those conflicts had been cruel and bloody. Many of the men who mustered that morning were themselves veterans of savage fights against the French and Indians. They and their families knew what war could do. The mood in Massachusetts was heavy with foreboding.

In the town of Acton, Hannah Davis always remembered the terrible moment when her husband left her. He was about thirty years old, and the captain of Acton's minute company. She was

165

twenty-nine. Their children were very young, one of them a babe in arms. The season had been sickly in the Davis household. That morning all the children were ill, some with the dreaded symptoms of canker rash, a mortal disease that ravaged many a New England household. The Davis household had been awakened before dawn by an alarm rider. While Hannah comforted her crying children, the minutemen of Acton trooped into her kitchen, filling that small feminine space with the strong masculine presence of their muskets, bayonets, tomahawks, and powder horns.

Hannah remembered later that "my husband said but little that morning. He seemed serious and thoughtful; but never seemed to hesitate as to the course of his duty." As he left the house, Isaac Davis suddenly turned and faced his wife. She thought he wanted to tell her something, and her heart leaped in her breast. For a moment he stood silent, searching for words that never came. Then he said simply, "Take good care of the children," and disappeared into the darkness. Hannah was overwhelmed by an agony of emptiness and despair. By some mysterious power of intuition, she knew that she would never see him again.[1]

Other women shared that feeling as they watched their husbands march away. After the men were gone these individual emotions flowed into one another like little streams into a river of fear that flooded the rural towns of Massachusetts. On a smaller scale, it was not unlike the *grande peur* that swept across the French countryside in 1789, when ordinary people were suddenly consumed with a sense of desperate danger.[2]

The great fear in New England began with the first alarm that was spread by Paul Revere and the other midnight riders. We remember that moment as a harbinger of Independence. For us, it was an event bright with the promise of national destiny. But at the time it was perceived in a very different way—as a fatal calamity, full of danger, terror, and uncertainty. Many years afterward, Hannah Winthrop recorded her feelings of the moment, which were still very strong in her mind. "Nor will old Time ever erase," she wrote, "the horrors of the midnight cry preceding the Bloody Massacre at Lexington."[3]

Hannah Winthrop lived in Cambridge, where her husband John taught natural science at Harvard College. He was an elderly man, and not in good health. They lived near the Lexington Road, and felt themselves in harm's way. In company with many others, Hannah Winthrop's first impulse was to flee. She later wrote, "Not knowing what the event would be at Cambridge . . . it seemed necessary to retire to some place of safety till the calamity was passed. My partner had been a fortnight confined by illness. After dinner we set out not knowing whither we went, we were directed to a place called Fresh Pond about a mile from the town."

On the road they met a throng of fugitives who also sought safety in flight. When they reached Fresh Pond, the Winthrops stopped at a home by the road, and found it full of terrified refugees. "What a distressed house did we find there," Hannah wrote, "filled with women whose husbands were gone forth to meet the assailants, 70 or 80 of these, with numbers of infant children, crying and agonizing over the fate of their husbands."

The great fear had already taken possession of that teeming crowd. Hannah Winthrop and her invalid husband decided to flee again, this time to northern Massachusetts. "Thus," she wrote, "with some precipitancy were we driven to the town of Andover, following some of our acquaintances, five of us to be conveyed by one tired horse and chaise." The burden was too heavy for the horse, and the five refugees had to take turns in the chaise. "We began our passage alternately walking and riding," Hannah Winthrop later recalled, "the roads [were] filled with frightened women and children, some in carts with their tattered furniture, others on foot fleeing into the woods."[4]

The narrow country roads were jammed with traffic. Militiamen were advancing toward Lexington and Concord—some as individuals, others in small parties, many in entire companies marching behind a fife and drum. At the same time, women and children and noncombatant men were fleeing in the opposite direction. Carts and coaches were piled high with cherished possessions. Along the shoulders of the roads were forlorn groups of fugitives, the broken shards of shattered families who were traveling sadly they knew not where—anywhere that took them farther from the great fear that followed them.

While some people took to the roads, others hid themselves in the woods. In Lexington many families of the militia left their homes and disappeared into patches of forest. It was later remembered of Rebecca Harrington Munroe, whose male relatives made up a large part of Captain Parker's company, that this "worthy lady," with "other families in Lexington, fled on the 19th of April 1775, with their children to the woods, while their husbands were engaged with the enemy and their houses were sacked or involved in flames."[5]

Others ran to their neighbors and sought safety in the midst of others, sometimes in places very bizarre. In Charlestown on April 19, Jacob Rogers remembered, "I. . . put my children in a cart with others then driving out of town. . . . We proceeded with many others to the town's Pest House." This was a remote building where smallpox victims were confined. Others in Charlestown went to a building near the training field, "full of women and children in the greatest terror, afraid to go to their own habitations."[6]

Many hoped to find a place of sanctuary in the churches of New England. Lexington's meetinghouse was a large but fragile wooden building, sheathed in clapboards that could scarcely have stopped a pistol ball. It stood directly in the path of the approaching British Regulars, and very much in harm's way. Even so, the people found spiritual strength in their place of worship.[7]

Some of the clergy did what they could to help their frightened congregations. A craven few fled for their lives. In Weston after the militia left town, clergymen Samuel Cooper and Samuel Woodward became refugees themselves, fleeing first to Framingham ten miles west and then to Southborough, taking with them a cow and a skillet and a few provisions.[8] In Menotomy, Deacon Joseph Adams fled from his own house to the home of the minister Samuel Cooke, and buried himself in the hayloft of the minister's barn.[9] But most ministers stayed and tried to comfort members of their congregations who came for help. At Concord, on the morning of April 19, many terrified people hurried to the house of their minister, the Reverend William Emerson. Even as the fighting went on only a few yards away, an eyewitness remembered that "the lane in front of the house was nearly filled with people who came to the minister's house for protection." While soldiers marched and countermarched, William Emerson worked outside in the yard, moving among the women and children, and giving them bread and cheese and comfort.[10]

The minister's wife, Phebe Bliss Emerson, was deeply frightened. According to family tradition, Phebe was "delicate," a euphemism that commonly referred to a mental state rather than a physical condition. She had heard the alarm from her African slave Frank, who came running into her chamber with an axe in his hand, shouting that the Redcoats were coming. Phebe Emerson turned as white as a Concord coverlet and fainted away on the spot. When she revived, she looked around for her husband and saw him outside in the yard, helping people of the town who had gathered in front of the Old Manse. Phebe Emerson rapped sharply on the windowpane to get her husband's attention, and told him that "she thought she needed him as much as the others."[11]

Many people managed their fear by keeping very busy. In Watertown, tax collector Joseph Coolidge went off as a volunteer to show a militia company the road to Lexington. His wife busied herself by digging a hole, and burying the town's tax books for safekeeping.[12] Alice Stearns Abbott, then a child of eleven, later remembered that she and her sisters Rachel and Susanna awakened early. "We all heard the alarm," she recalled, "and were up and ready to help fit out father and brother, who made an early start for Concord. We were set to work making cartridges and assisting mother in cooking for the army. We sent off a large quantity of food for the soldiers, who had left home so early that they had but little breakfast. We were frightened by hearing the noise of the guns."[13]

Drinking men, of whom there were many in the rural towns of Massachusetts, dealt with their fears in a different way. In Menotomy two brothers-in-law named Jason Winship and Jabez Wyman took refuge in the Cooper Tavern. While confusion reigned around them, they ordered large mugs of flip, a potent drink much favored by tavern topers in the 18th century. They were sitting directly in the path of the British soldiers. Others warned them to flee for their lives. But as the alcohol warmed their spirits, they began to forget their fear. Jabez said to Jason, "Let us finish the mug, they won't come yet."[14]

The great fear was great because it was so general and all-encompassing. It became a broad undifferentiated emotion, feeding on anxieties that had nothing to do with the immediate cause. In the town of Framingham, ten miles southwest of Concord, a local inhabitant remembered that "soon after the men were gone, a strange panic seized the women and children living in the Edgell and Belknap district. Someone started the story that 'the negroes were coming to massacre them all!'" An historian of that town remembered that "nobody stopped to ask where the hostile negroes were coming from; for all our own colored people were patriots. It was probably a lingering memory of the earlier Indian alarms, which took this indefinite shape, aided by a feeling of terror awakened by their defenceless condition, and the uncertainty of the issue of the pending fight."[15]

Here was another parallel between this American great fear

and the *grande peur* in France in 1789. The same range of apprehensions appeared in different forms: French peasants worried
about "brigands," while Americans feared the rising of their slaves.

In both countries, strangers became suspect. The women of
Framingham prepared to defend themselves against they knew
not what. One townsman remembered that "the wife of Capt.
Edgell and other matrons brought the axes and pitchforks and
clubs into the house, and securely bolted the doors, and passed the
day and night in anxious suspense." Many accounts stress the effect of "anxious suspense" on the nerves of noncombatants. A
large part of the great fear arose from uncertainty.[16]

But others were clear enough about what should be done. A
case in point was the town of Pepperell, twenty miles northwest of
Concord. When the men of Pepperell marched away the women
came together and held their own town meeting. They organized
themselves into a military company, and elected as their captain
Prudence Cummings Wright, wife of a leading townsman, and
mother of seven children. "Prue" Wright, as she was called, was a
deeply religious woman who had joined the Congregational
church in 1770. Her family was divided in politics. Her brothers
were active Tories, but she and her husband were staunch Whigs.
They christened their infant son Liberty Wright.

Young Liberty Wright died in March 1775, and their daughter Mary had been buried only nine months earlier—a loss so
heavy that Prudence Wright left her own household for a time and
went home to her parents in New Hampshire. But by April 19,
1775, she was back again, and the women of Pepperell elected her
to lead them. She appointed Mrs. Job Shattuck as her lieutenant,
and organized the women into a company called "Mrs. David
Wright's Guard." They dressed themselves in their husbands'
clothing, armed themselves with guns and pitchforks, and began
to patrol the roads into the town.

These women of Pepperell kept patrolling even after dark.
They were guarding a bridge that night, when a rider suddenly
approached. The women stopped him at gunpoint and forced
him to dismount. He proved to be a Tory named Captain Leonard Whiting. They searched him, found incriminating papers,
marched him under guard to Solomon Rodger's tavern in the
town center and kept him a prisoner that night. The next morning
he was sent to Groton, and his papers were dispatched to the
Committee of Safety for study. The Pepperell town meeting later

reimbursed Mrs. Wright and the women of her company for their service. With a hint of condescension, the men voted "that Leonard Whiting's guard (so called) be paid seven pounds seventeen shillings and six pence by order of the Treasurer." But on the night of April 19, there was nothing of that attitude in Captain Leonard Whiting, when Prue Wright stopped him at gunpoint and threatened to kill him if he did not obey.[17]

Tories were arrested in many New England towns. At Scituate on the South Shore of Massachusetts, Paul Litchfield noted in his diary that "very early in the morning of April 20, the town "received news of the engagement between the king's troops and the Americans at Concord the day before, upon which our men were ordered to appear in arms immediately." Litchfield was sent to guard the coast, in fear of British attack from the sea, a feeling that was shared in many coastal communities. His company "about eight o'clock took two Tories as they were returning from Marshfield, who were kept under guard that night." The next day they arrested four Tories more, and confined them in the meeting-house.

The great fear continued for many days throughout New England. "Terrible news from Lexington, . . . rumor on rumor," John Tudor entered into his diary, "men and horses driving past, up and down the roads. . . . People were in great perplexity; women in distress for their husbands and friends who had marched. . . . All confusion, numbers of carts, etc. carrying off goods etc. as the rumour was that if the soldiers came out again they would burn, kill and destroy all as they marched."[18]

On the North Shore of Massachusetts, there was a special panic called the "Ipswich fright." A report spread through Essex County that British soldiers had come ashore in the Ipswich River and were murdering the population of that town. The rumor traveled at lightning speed up and down the coast. It was written that "all the horses and vehicles in the town were put in requisition: men, women, and children hurried as for life toward the north. Large numbers crossed the Merrimack, and spent the night in deserted houses of Salisbury, whose inhabitants, stricken by the strange terror, had fled into New Hampshire."[19]

The panic infected Salem, where John Jenks recorded in his diary on April 21, 1775, "A report was propagated that Troops was landed in Ipswich." Jenks heard the next day that "the report was false, no troops came there." But he and his fellow townsmen decided to take no chances. On the 23rd of April he wrote, "moved my goods up to my Uncle Preston in Danvers. A great number of teams was employed to carry provisions out of the town."[20]

In Newbury, a messenger appeared at an emergency town meeting, crying, "Turn out, for God's sake, or you will all be killed. The Regulars are marching on us; they are in Ipswich now, cutting and slashing all before them."[21] In the interior town of Haverhill, the Reverend Hezekiah Smith, pastor of the Baptist Church wrote in his diary, "a most gloomy time. . . . Repeated false alarms, and terrifying apprehensions." He held a day of fasting and prayer in his meetinghouse, as did many other ministers throughout New England.[22]

The same emotions spread to the interior of Massachusetts. They were felt at Sudbury, twenty miles inland, where Experience Wight Richardson kept a diary that was running record of her anxiety. She feared not for herself but for others: for her only son Josiah Richardson who went off to "fite" and for other men and families in her town. In particular, she feared for the people of Boston. "We are afraid that Boston people a great many will starve to death," she wrote. "O Lord! Appear for them I pray thee. O King Jesus help us I pray thee."[23]

The great fear reached as far as the town of Sutton, forty miles from the coast, and persisted there for many days. After April 19, the town's minister David Hall wrote, "That night there was several alarms. I was up most of the night and prayed with our minute companies a little before day." He comforted his congregation for many days. "A dark and melancholy week we had," he noted in his diary.[24]

The great fear also spread to Loyalists in Boston and even to the Regulars themselves. Admiral Samuel Graves later remembered that a wave of hysteria swept through the British troops, who were suddenly conscious that they were in "the neighbourhood of so enraged an host of people, breathing revenge for their slaughtered countrymen, and vowing to storm Boston, seize upon and demolish Castle William, fortify Point Alderton, burn all the men of war, and cut off every Tory." Graves recalled that "each of these reports through the fears of some and wickedness of others was industriously circulated, during the first week or two after the battle of Lexington, and some of them gained credit . . . such rumors spread abroad, could not but excite on our part the utmost attention."[25]

Among the American leaders, the great fear gave them yet

another task. At the same time that they worked to raise the alarm in Massachusetts, they also labored to quiet the anxieties of the people. The network of couriers continued to function for many days, keeping the towns informed about the course of events, but without laying their fears to rest. It was typical of this Calvinist culture that people interpreted this time of suffering as a divine judgment on their own depravity. For many Sundays afterward, the ministers of Massachusetts preached from the first verse of Lamentations: "The joy of our heart is ceased; our dance is turned into mourning. The crown is fallen from our head; woe unto us, that we have sinned."[26]

# THE RESCUE

~ Of John Hancock, Sam Adams, a Salmon, and a Trunk

> It is supposed their object there was to seize on Messrs.
> Hancock and Adams, two of our deputies to the General Congress. They were alarmed just in time to escape.
>
> —Letter from a Gentleman of Rank
> in New England, April 25, 1775

WHILE THE COUNTRYSIDE began to stir, the man who had set these events in motion hobbled back toward Lexington, painfully encumbered by his silver spurs and heavy riding boots. It was about 3 o'clock in the morning when Paul Revere regained his freedom. The night had turned cold and raw and darker than before—the damp Stygian darkness that so often comes before a New England dawn.

As Paul Revere passed the low swamps that lay west of Lexington Green, he would have felt the dampness in his weary bones. He made slow progress in his high-topped boots on the muddy road, but his mind was racing far ahead. He wondered what Samuel Adams and John Hancock had done since he left them. Had they ended their interminable debate? Were they still debating? Did they act wisely on their warning?

Knowing Hancock and Adams, Paul Revere decided that he had better be sure. Before he reached the center of the town, he turned off the road, plunged into a muddy swamp, and waded across the wetlands to Lexington's burying ground. In the darkness, he picked his way across the broken slates and canted stones that marked the last resting place of the town's founders.

As Paul Revere stumbled through a maze of burial mounds and sunken holes, perhaps he had a moment to think about the men and women whose mortal remains lay beneath him in the ground. Inconceivable as it may seem to their degenerate descendants, the Whig leaders of revolutionary America often had these periods of reflection. They took a long view of their temporal condition, in a way that Americans rarely do today. "Think of your forefathers!" John Quincy Adams urged his contemporaries, "Think of your posterity!"

Paul Revere and his fellow Whigs believed themselves to be the heirs of New England's founding vision, and the stewards of John Winthrop's City on a Hill. The moral example of their forebears haunted and inspired them. When Sam Adams signed his revolutionary writings with the pen-name "Puritan," and Paul Revere created his political engravings on godly themes, they expressed their strong sense of spiritual kinship with their ancestors.

For these men, the revolutionary movement was itself a new Puritanism—not precisely the same as the old, but similar in its long memories and large purposes. Like the old Puritans who had preceded them, these new Puritans were driven by an exalted sense of mission and high moral purpose in the world. They also believed that they were doing God's work in the world, and that no earthly force could overcome them. In the language of the first Puritans, they were both believers and seekers—absolutely certain of the rightness of their cause, and always searching restlessly for ways to serve it better. In that endless quest, the memory of distant ancestors who lay sleeping in the grave was a source of guidance and inspiration to them.

At the same time, they also thought of their posterity. These men were deeply conscious of their own mortality—more than we are apt to be today. They looked ahead to the time when they too would be lying beneath the broken slates of New England's burying grounds, and asked themselves if their acts would be worthy of generations yet unborn. Perhaps some of these thoughts (which have so little meaning to Americans today) may have occurred to Paul Revere, as he felt his way through the broken stones of Lexington's burying ground during the dark hours before the dawn of April 19, 1775.

At last Paul Revere emerged from the burying ground and turned north to the Bedford Road. He walked a few hundred yards to the Clarke parsonage, hoping to find that the men he had

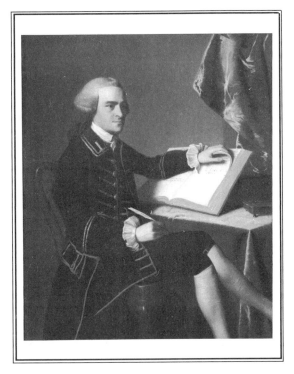

John Hancock, portrait by
John Singleton Copley,
1765. The sitter, at
twenty-eight had recently
inherited the largest fortune in New England. His
dress and furniture sug-
gest some of his great
wealth which made him
independent. But so
strong was the ethic of
work that he kept at his
calling even in his por-
trait, and sat for the artist
with his ledgers in hand.
(Museum of Fine Arts,
Boston)

come from Boston to warn were safely away. As he entered the door, Paul Revere was horrified to find that Sam Adams and John Hancock were precisely where he had met them three hours ago—still debating among themselves.

The household was an uproar. Elizabeth Clarke, then in her twelfth year, looked on wide-eyed at the scene of confusion that surrounded her. Crowded in the small house, beside Sam Adams and John Hancock, was Hancock's fiancée Dorothy Quincy, a young woman known to her friends as Miss Dolly, and celebrated throughout New England for her spirit and independence. Also present was John Hancock's fastidious aunt, the rich widow of the man who had made the largest fortune in New England, "as lady-like a woman as Boston ever bred," in Miss Dolly's measured phrase.

Young Elizabeth Clarke wrote many years later, "I . . . can see, in my mind, just as plain . . . the whole scene, how Aunt Hancock and Dolly Quincy, with their cloaks and bonnets on, Aunt crying and wringing her hands and helping mother dress the children, Dolly going round with Father to hide money, watches and anything down in the potatoes and up in the garret."[1]

Samuel Adams, portrait by John Singleton Copley, circa 1770–72. Adams wears a simple suit of dark crimson. In his right hand he holds the instructions of Boston Town Meeting. With his left, he points to the Massachusetts Charter. The portrait represents the personality of the man himself, and also the austerity of his Whig principles. (Museum of Fine Arts, Boston)

John Hancock sat at the Clarkes' table, busily sharpening the fragile blade of his fine dress sword, breathing fire and brimstone at the British Regulars, and debating furiously with Sam Adams all at the same time. Dorothy Quincy remembered that "Mr. H. was all the night cleaning his gun and sword, and putting his accoutrements in order, and was determined to go out to the plain by the meetinghouse, where the battle was, to fight."[2]

We think of John Hancock as a politician, but he regarded himself as a soldier, and in the small hours of the morning he talked bravely of joining the Lexington men on the Common, and facing the Regulars when they arrived. "If I had my musket," Hancock was heard to say, "I would never turn my back on these troops." He swore again and again that "it never should be said that he had turned his back" upon the Regulars.[3]

John Hancock punctuated these martial threats by shouting commands at his companions. At one stage Dorothy Quincy thought of her aged father in Boston, and said that she would return to him tomorrow. Hancock turned toward his fiancée and said in his imperious way, "No, madam, you shall not return as long as there is a British bayonet left in Boston." Miss Dolly answered firmly, "Recollect, Mr. Hancock, I am not under your control yet."[4]

Sam Adams tried in vain to persuade his fire-eating friend that he was more useful to the cause in other ways than by carrying a musket. Dorothy Quincy saw Adams clap John Hancock on the shoulder and say to him, "That is not our business. We belong to the cabinet."[5]

Paul Revere joined this conversation after he arrived. He added the weight of his recent experience to Adams's arguments, telling of his "treatment" at the hands of the British officers on the Concord Road. With great urgency Revere told Hancock and Adams that they must leave immediately. Dorothy Quincy remembered that "it was not till break of day that Mr. H. could be persuaded."[6]

The clinching argument was a report that one British officer had asked "where Clarke's Tavern was." There was no such tavern in Lexington; only the Clarke home where Adams and Hancock were staying. Tories were everywhere, and the location of the Revolutionary leaders could not long remain a secret. In the end, Hancock was "overcome by the entreaties of his friends, who con-

Dorothy Quincy was staying with her fiancé John Hancock in Lexington when Paul Revere arrived. She left a memorable account of the events that followed. Whig New England liked its women to be smart and strong. "Miss Dolly" was much celebrated for her beauty, brains, and spirit. The artist John Singleton Copley seems not to have been one of her admirers, and painted her in 1772 as something of a termagant. Her beauty is lost in this likeness, but her intellect and independence shine through. (Museum of Fine Arts, Boston)

vinced him that the enemy would indeed triumph, if they could get him and Mr. Adams in their power."[7]

As dawn approached, Hancock at last agreed to depart with Adams and Revere. Typically, he left his aunt and fiancée behind in the Clarke house, and insisted on traveling in high state. The fugitives set off in Hancock's heavy coach, making their way over muddy roads toward a parsonage in the second precinct of Woburn (now the town of Burlington), northwest of Lexington. There they were welcomed by the widow of the former minister, in the network of Congregational clergy that spanned the country-side of Massachusetts.

Soon after they arrived, John Hancock began to think about his dinner. In Lexington, an admirer had presented him with a fine great salmon, fresh caught in a New England river. The fish had been left behind at the Clarke house. Hancock sent back his coach with orders to return with Aunt Hancock, Miss Dolly, and the salmon. All arrived in good order. Hancock demanded the salmon straight away, and asked that it to be cleaned and cooked. His hostess went to work on it in the kitchen.

Adams, Hancock and their party were now alone with their host's family. Paul Revere was gone again. He had traveled with Hancock and Adams until he felt sure that they were out of danger. Then he decided to return to Lexington Green "to find out what was acting," as he liked to say. Back he went to the Clarke house, and rested for a few moments.

Suddenly another crisis burst upon him. A young Boston acquaintance named John Lowell appeared, and begged Revere to help him with an urgent task. Lowell was John Hancock's confidential clerk. He explained that when Hancock and Adams fled, they had left behind a large trunk stuffed with important papers. Lowell told Revere that the trunk had been left in an upper chamber at the Buckman Tavern on Lexington Common, a few hundred yards from where they were talking. It was very heavy—more than one man could carry. It contained the innermost secrets of the Whig cause, and written evidence that could incriminate many leaders.

Paul Revere rose quickly from his seat. With young Lowell, he walked down toward Lexington Common to rescue the trunk. The two men headed straight for the Buckman Tavern where they found a large crowd, many rumors, and much confusion. In the crowded taproom, they were astonished to be told that it was all a false alarm!

Lydia Henchman Hancock brought her husband Thomas Hancock the foundation of his fortune. He used it well, and made her the richest widow in New England. She was with her nephew John Hancock in Lexington on the night of April 18. When Paul Revere arrived, Aunt Lydia gave way to high hysterics. (National Portrait Gallery, Washington)

Revere quickly discovered what had happened. After he and Dawes had left for Concord, the men of Lexington had sounded the alarm. These prudent Yankee farmers decided to act on Revere's message, but also to confirm its accuracy by sending out their own "expresses" to the east. Two men of Lexington went riding off to Cambridge, with instructions to "gain intelligence of the motions of the troops, and what route their took." While they were gone, Captain Parker's men mustered on the Common.[8]

The two Lexington scouts traveled different roads and were away for several hours. One of them returned between 3 and 4 o'clock, and reported that Paul Revere's message was mistaken. He announced that "there was no appearance of the troops, on the roads for Cambridge or Charlestown, and that the movements of the army were but a feint to alarm the people."

On the strength of this report, Captain Parker dismissed his men, but ordered them to remain nearby, "within call of the drum" until the other scout came back. Many of the militia decided to stay at Buckman's tavern. Some had loaded their muskets. Before entering the taproom, they observed the time-honored American rule of no loaded weapons at the bar, and emptied their guns by firing them into the air. This was the "volley" that had so alarmed the British patrol. The militiamen were in the taproom, talking among themselves, when Paul Revere arrived.

Just then, the second Lexington express came racing up the Boston road at full gallop. He shouted that the Regulars were very near, and already past "the Rocks," a landmark barely half an hour east of Lexington Green. This other scout had found the marching column, but was trapped on the road behind them, unable to get past the troops and warn the town. Jonas Clarke remembered that "he was prevented [from returning sooner] by their silent and sudden arrival at the place where he was waiting for intelligence— so that, after all this precaution we had no notice of their approach till the brigade [*sic*] was actually in the town, and upon a quick march within about a mile and a quarter of the meetinghouse."9

Thus, despite its earlier warnings, the town of Lexington was taken by surprise. Captain Parker instantly mustered his company again. Alarm guns were fired, and the bell was rung once more. Parker summoned nineteen-year-old drummer William Diamond, a youngster who had just moved to Lexington from Boston, where he had been trained in the art of military drumming by a kindly British soldier. Diamond was ordered to beat the call to arms. The Lexington militia came running out of the tavern onto the Common.10

Lowell and Revere sprinted in the opposite direction, through the taproom, and climbed the stairs as fast as their weary legs could carry them. In a chamber on the second floor they found the trunk where John Hancock had left it. As they entered the room, Paul Revere turned and looked anxiously out of the tavern window toward the first streaks of light in the eastern sky.

In the soft gray dawn, he suddenly saw the British troops approaching—a long column winding inexorably up the Lexington Road, like a giant red centipede on its hundreds of white legs. Above the heads of the marching men, a steel fringe of bayonets was visible in the early morning light.

Paul Revere watched the Regulars for a moment. He thought they were "very near." Then, with renewed urgency, he returned to his task. On the floor was a stout wooden trunk, covered in leather and studded with nails, with a curved top and strong brass fastenings. It was indeed very large—four feet long, two feet wide, and about two and a half feet high. The trunk was full of papers, and immensely heavy.11

Revere and Lowell decided to carry it away from the tavern

John Hancock's trunk, filled with secret papers, was left behind in the Buckman Tavern. It survives today in the Worcester Historical Museum.

and hide it in the woods. They lifted the massive trunk, struggled down the narrow stairs with it, and staggered through the front door of the tavern. Outside, Captain John Parker was forming his militia on the Green. Revere and Lowell carried the trunk directly through the ranks of Parker's men, heading for a place of safety where the trunk and its contents could be hidden.

Meanwhile, in a Woburn parsonage, John Hancock was preparing at last to enjoy his salmon. Dorothy Quincy remembered later that he was just sitting down to a "tempting feast," when a man from Lexington came rushing in, shouting wildly, "The Regulars are coming! The Regulars are coming!" At the first appearance of the soldiers this messenger had left his family and hurried to warn the Patriot leaders. "My wife's in *eternity* now!" he cried hysterically in his Yankee twang, as everyone looked on in astonishment.

Once again, Hancock and Adams were warned that they were in danger. Their presence in Woburn was not easy to disguise if the Regulars should come that way. Hancock's large coach was parked prominently in front of the house, where all could see it. The household flew into action. The coach was driven into the trees, and hidden beneath a large pile of brush. Hancock and Adams abandoned their salmon once again, and ran into the woods of Woburn.

In fact, nobody was coming after them. When Tory Peter Oliver later heard the story of their hasty departure, he sneered that "their flight confirmed the observation made by Solomon, vizt the wicked fleeth when no man pursueth."[12]

A little later, when it was clear that the Regulars were not heading toward Woburn, Adams and Hancock were led out of the woods and taken deeper into the Middlesex countryside, to the modest house of Amos Wyman, "in an obscure corner of Bedford, Burlington and Billerica." Here they settled in and Hancock suddenly felt hungry again. One person recalled that he was "forced by the cravings of nature to call for food." Their new hosts had nothing in the house but a bit of cold boiled salt pork, brown bread, and potatoes. This was the ordinary fare of Middlesex farmers, but Dorothy Quincy observed that it was a "strange diet for these patriots, who were in the habit of having the best."[13]

While on their way to this new sanctuary, they began to hear the rattle of musketry in the distance. Sam Adams turned to his companion and said, "It is a fine day!"

"Very pleasant," John Hancock replied serenely, thinking that Adams was talking about the weather.

"I mean," Sam Adams explained, as if to a child, "this is a glorious day for America."[14]

# THE FIRST SHOT

∾ The Fight on Lexington Green

> I saw, and heard, a gun fired, which appeared to be a pistol. Then I could distinguish two guns, and then a continual roar of musketry."
>
> —Paul Revere, Deposition, 1775

WHILE Paul Revere escorted the Whig leaders to safety, General Gage's Regulars marched steadily toward Lexington. Five hours had passed since the British troops had left Boston, and still they did not know where they were going or what they were expected to do. Even the company commanders had not been told the purpose of the mission. But the men could feel the tension in the air, and they could see in the demeanor of Colonel Smith that things were not going according to plan. As they advanced rapidly through Cambridge, they began to hear gunshots in the distance. One officer looked at his pocket watch and noted that the time was about three o'clock. Another thought to himself, "a very unusual hour for firing."[1]

Suddenly they heard the hoofbeats of many horsemen galloping toward the column from the west. In the van, Marine Lieutenant Jesse Adair and Tory guide Daniel Murray anxiously searched the moonlit road ahead. In a moment, the riders were upon them, shouting General Gage's password, "Patrole! Patrole!"

It was the party of British officers who had been scouting the road to Concord—Major Edward Mitchell, Captain Charles Lumm, Captain Charles Cochrane, and seven others, fresh from their encounter with Paul Revere. The column halted to hear their news. In high excitement, Major Mitchell announced that "the whole country was alarmed" and that they had "galloped for their lives." He explained in a few breathless sentences what had happened on the Concord Road. "We have taken Paul Revierre," the major said, "but was obliged to let him go, after having cut his girths and stirrups."[2]

Mitchell repeated Paul Revere's warning that 500 New England men were mustering in Lexington. He told of the alarm bells and the signal guns, and the volley of musket-fire near the Green. The news raced back along the column. Lieutenant William Barker of the King's Own never forgot that moment, "about five miles on this side of a town called Lexington which lay in our road," when "we heard there were some hundreds of people collected together intending to oppose us and stop our going in."[3]

Others also remembered with vivid clarity this electrifying instant when they halted on the road, and Paul Revere's warning reached them through the mouth of his highly excited captor, Major Mitchell. The message struck the column with shattering force. For five hours they had been kept in the dark, in more senses than one. Most had left Boston with no idea of the mission's purpose, or whether it was a mission at all, or merely another training march.

They recognized the name of Paul Revere. Lieutenant William Sutherland of the 38th Foot made special mention in his report that it was Revere whom Major Mitchell intercepted on the road that night. Another wrote that the information had come from "the noted Paul Revere." The British soldiers knew this man. Some had heard that he was an "ambassador" from the Whig Committees of Massachusetts to the Continental Congress. Others were aware that he had frustrated their Portsmouth plans by galloping from Boston to New Hampshire. A few knew that he tried to do the same thing again to the Salem expedition, and that the 64th had caught his men and kept them prisoner at Castle William in Boston harbor.[4]

Now as they were marching deep into a dangerous country on a supposedly secret expedition, Paul Revere was ahead of them again—captured on a fast horse near Concord twenty miles west of Boston, while they were still slogging through Cambridge. They knew that this meddlesome Yankee meant trouble, and were horrified to learn from Major Mitchell that he knew more about their mission than they did. His presence was a sign that the people of New England were organizing against them. They would not be opposed merely by a milling mob of angry "peasants" with pitchforks in their hands.[5]

Suddenly they also knew what many had suspected from the start. This night march was no drill. They had not been sent on one of "Old Woman" Gage's hated training exercises, or another of his futile demonstrations to impress the country people of New England. They began to realize that they were marching deep into a hostile country, and might have to fight before the day was done. Few of these men had been in combat before. The thoughts of young soldiers on the eve of their first battle raced through their minds.

As if to punctuate the news that Major Mitchell brought them, the column heard more alarm guns, repeating in the distance. They listened as meeting bells begin to toll. The bells were not very loud—nothing like the carillons of ancient English churches they had known at home. These were small, solitary country bells, clanging faintly in the night, but the sounds came from every side—west, north, and even east behind the column.[6]

Ensign Jeremy Lister of the 10th Foot listened to the bells in the night. He searched the skyline, which now was faintly visible against the brightening sky. On distant hilltops he began to make out beacon fires burning brilliantly across the rolling landscape.[7]

The march resumed. Suddenly a Yankee rider came galloping out of a crossroad in front of the column, and was taken prisoner. Another horseman appeared, and vanished into the countryside. A small chaise of the sort that Yankees called a sulky came down the road toward them, driven by a "very genteel man" who warned the officers in the van that 600 men were waiting for them in Lexington. Lieutenant Adair responded by confiscating the sulky and riding in it himself for a time. The soldiers met a wagon coming toward them, full of cordwood for the Boston market. The teamsters solemnly assured them that 1000 men were in arms.[8]

It was now four o'clock in the morning, the hour when everything in New England appears cold and bleak and colorless. The countryside was beginning to grow visible in the first gray light of dawn. The men in the marching column looked about them. As their eyes adjusted slowly to the coming of the light, they noticed a figure in the distance moving parallel to their column. Then other figures came into sight. As the light improved they were shocked to discover that the distant fields were alive with armed men, half-walking, half-running to the west, faster than the column itself. In the vanguard, Lieutenant Sutherland could make out "a vast number of country militia going over the hill with their arms for Lexington." Further back in the column, a private soldier remembered that "about four o'clock in the morning . . . we could perceive inhabitants assembling in many parts."⁹

Lieutenant Sutherland suddenly collided with one of these inhabitants, a thirty-one-year-old Lexington militiaman named Benjamin Wellington, with his musket and bayonet in hand. Sutherland ordered the militiaman to give up his weapons, "which I believe he would not have done so easily," Sutherland wrote, "but for Mr. Adair's coming up." Outnumbered, Wellington surrendered. The British officers took his weapons and told him to go home, as if they were talking to an errant child. Wellington walked away in the direction whence he came. When out of sight he turned and ran toward Lexington center to warn his neighbors. Later he found another weapon and joined his company.¹⁰

A little after this encounter, a party of Yankee horsemen appeared in front of the column. They stopped at a distance from the British van and shouted a warning: "You had better turn back, for you shall not enter the town!" The riders wheeled and began to ride away. Then one of them turned back toward the Regulars. At the point of the column, Private James Marr of the 4th Foot watched the horseman raise his weapon and "offer to fire." In the half light, Marr swore he saw a flash of flame and puff of smoke. Others saw it too. It might have been an alarm gun, but the green British soldiers at the head of the column were sure that it was aimed at them.¹¹

The officers in the van called Major Pitcairn to the front, and reported that a "provincial" had fired on them. Instantly Pitcairn halted the column, and ordered the companies to load. The men reached into their cartridge boxes, withdrew a paper-covered round, ripped it open with their teeth, and poured powder and ball into the long barrels of their muskets, leaving a litter of torn cartridge papers in the road.¹²

The order to load was another moment of truth for the Regulars. Marine Captain William Soutar remembered, "We were surprised, not imagining in the least that we should be attacked or even molested on the march, for we had but that instant loaded and had marched all night without being loaded."¹³

The time was nearly 4:30 in the morning. It was almost light. Major Pitcairn studied with concern the rocky hills and granite outcroppings that were coming into view. He observed the strong stone "fences" as the Yankees called them: rude piles of granite boulders, topped with heavy logs. He ordered out flanking parties, and resumed the march. The Regulars were now very near to

Lexington center. In the distance they began to hear a military drum, beating a call to arms.[14]

A few minutes later the Regulars rounded a gentle turn in the road, and the village of Lexington came into view. The light was behind them, and the little hamlet lay half-shrouded in darkness. They could dimly make out a scattering of houses around a triangular village common. Directly ahead of them at the near corner of the triangle stood the large dark bulk of Lexington meetinghouse, three storeys high, with a large oak tree just beyond. To the left was the town's wooden bell tower, low and squat, still sounding the alarm. To the right was the Buckman Tavern, with its old fashioned gambrel roof and heavy chimney stacks.[15]

As the Regulars came closer they saw Captain Parker's militia near the northeast corner of the Common, hurrying into line to the long roll of William Diamond's drum. The Lexington men were forming up in two long ranks, partly hidden by the meetinghouse. To the left and right of the Common the British soldiers observed two other groups, mostly male, some of them armed.

Perhaps an observant Regular at the head of the column might have noticed two figures staggering across the Common with a heavy burden between them. One of these men was Paul Revere. With his gift for being at the center of events, he happened to be crossing Lexington Common just at the moment when the British troops arrived. Revere and John Lowell had emerged from the Buckman Tavern with John Hancock's trunk just as the Lexington militia were falling into formation. Their route took them directly through the long ranks of the soldiers. Paul Revere heard Captain John Parker speak to his company. "Let the troops pass by," Parker told his men. He added in the archaic dialect of old New England, "Don't molest them, without they being first."[16]

At the same moment the British officers were studying the militia on the Common in front of them. Paul Revere's warning of 500 men in arms echoed in their ears. As the officers peered through the dim gray light, the spectators to the right and left appeared to be militia too. Captain Parker's small handful of men multiplied in British eyes to hundreds of provincial soldiers.[17] Pitcairn thought that he faced "near 200 of the rebels;" Barker reckoned the number at "between two and three hundred."[18]

On the other side, the New England men also inflated the size of the Regular force, which was magnified by the length of its marching formation on the narrow road. As the militia studied the long files of red-coated soldiers, some reckoned the force at between 1200 and 1500 men. In fact there were only about 238 of all ranks in Pitcairn's six companies, plus the mounted men of Mitchell's patrol, and a few supernumeraries.[19]

The Lexington militia began to consult earnestly among themselves. Sylvanus Wood, a Woburn man who joined them, had made a quick count a few minutes earlier and found to his surprise that there were only thirty-eight militia in all. Others were falling into line, but altogether no more than sixty or seventy militia mustered on the Common, perhaps less. One turned to his captain and said, "There are so few of us it is folly to stand here."[20] But Parker had decided that the time for debate had ended. He turned to his men and told them, "The first man who offers to run shall be shot down." Some heard him say, "Stand your ground! Don't fire unless fired upon! But if they want to have a war let it begin here!"[21]

The Regulars came closer. To men on both sides, time itself seemed to stop—a temporal illusion that often occurs in moments of mortal danger. When the mind begins to move at lightning speed, the world itself seems to slow down. But in fact events were unfolding at a rapid rate. The Regulars came hurrying on at the quick march. Swarming around the head of the column was a cloud of mounted British officers—the same men who had captured Paul Revere and been told that they were in mortal danger. Many were highly excited. Prominent among them was the mercurial Major Mitchell.

In the British van was Marine lieutenant Jesse Adair, the hard-charging young Irishman who had been put at the head of the column by Major Pitcairn to keep it moving. Adair was a bold and aggressive officer—quick to act, but sometimes slow to understand.[22]

As he approached Lexington Common this young Marine had a momentous decision to make. The main road divided just before it reached the meetinghouse. Adair's Loyalist guide would have told him that the left fork led to Concord, running along the southwest edge of the Green. The right fork carried toward the northeast, past the Buckman Tavern to the Bedford Road.

Lieutenant Adair found himself in a dilemma. To bear left on the main road toward Concord would leave an armed and possibly hostile force on the open flank of his column. To take the right fork would carry the Regulars headlong toward the militia. The choice was his to make. His immediate superior, Major Pitcairn, was back in the column and could not help him. The commander of the expedition, Colonel Smith, was far in the rear with the grenadiers, and completely out of touch.

The young Marine did not hesitate. He made a snap decision of momentous consequence. Lieutenant Adair instantly turned to the right, and led the three forward companies directly toward the militia. "No sooner did they come in sight of our company," Lexington's minister later wrote, "but one of them, supposed to be an officer of rank, was heard to say to the troops, 'Damn them, we will have them!'"[23]

Back in the column Major Pitcairn saw what had happened, and kicked his horse into a canter, riding rapidly to the front. As he reached the fork, Pitcairn decided differently from Adair. He turned left instead of right, and the rest of the column followed him. It separated from the van and marched along the left fork that ran southwest of the meetinghouse. Beyond that building, Pitcairn halted them in the Concord Road. Somebody also stopped the last of Adair's three forward companies just beyond the meetinghouse, near the spreading oak tree.[24]

Two companies, light infantry of the 4th and 10th Foot, continued straight toward the Lexington militia. In this critical moment Pitcairn lost touch with those men. Adair led them onward at an accelerating pace. The quick march became a run that took the Regulars halfway across the Common in a few moments. About seventy yards from the militia, the two leading companies were ordered to deploy from a column into a line of battle. The men in the rear came sprinting forward. Sergeants and subalterns dropped back to take their places behind the line. The long files dissolved in a swirl of movement. The Regulars began to shout the deep-throated battle cry that was distinctive to British infantry—a loud "huzza! huzza! huzza!" Orders were difficult to hear above the cheering. One British officer remembered that he was deafened by the shouts of his own men.[25]

Pitcairn cantered across the Common toward the British line. Other mounted officers were already there. A Lexington militiaman, Elijah Sanderson, observed that "several mounted British officers were forward, I think five. The commander rode up, with his pistol in his hand, on a canter, the others following, to about five or six rods from the company, and ordered them to disperse. The words he used were harsh. I cannot remember them exactly."[26]

Many believed that this officer was Major Pitcairn, but others were unsure of his identity and uncertain of his words. Several

Major John Pitcairn (Royal Marines) was British commander in the skirmish on Lexington Green. Born in 1722, he was an officer of long experience, very near the end of his career. A strong Scottish Tory, he had no sympathy for the colonists; but American Whigs admired his character if not his principles. A New England clergyman described him as "a good man in a bad cause." (New England Historic and Genealogical Society)

men on both sides heard an officer shout, "Lay down your arms, you damned rebels!" In the front rank of the militia, John Robbins saw a party of three mounted British officers come directly toward him at "full gallop," and thought he heard the foremost officer say, "Throw down your arms, ye villains, ye rebels." Jonas Clarke thought that the officer said, "Ye villains, ye rebels, disperse, damn you, disperse!"[27]

Lexington's commander, Captain Parker, turned to his men and gave them new orders, different from before. He later testified, "I immediately ordered our militia to disperse and not to fire." Some began to scatter, moving backwards and to both sides. The town minister Jonas Clarke wrote, "Upon this, our men dispersed, but not so speedily as they might have done." In the confusion, some of the militia did not hear the order and stayed where they were. None of the militia laid down their arms.[28]

Behind the Lexington militia, Paul Revere and John Lowell were still struggling with their trunk. At last they reached the far end of the Common and crossed the road, heading toward a patch of woods beyond a house. Paul Revere glanced back over his shoulder and saw the red-coated Regulars approach the militia. As he returned to his task, suddenly he heard a shot ring out behind him. It sounded like a pistol, but he could not be sure, and he did not see where it came from or who fired it. He looked again and saw a cloud of white smoke in front of the Regulars. Revere could no longer see the American militia. He had passed beyond the houses on the edge of the Green, and a building blocked his sight. Later,

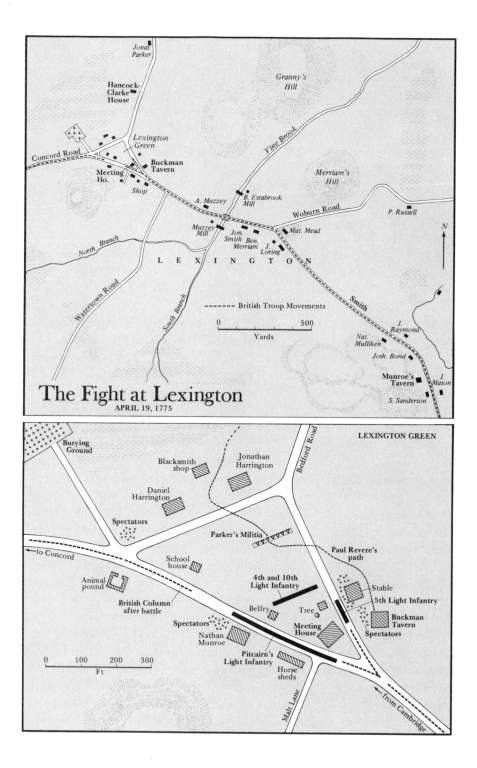

The Fight at Lexington
APRIL 19, 1775

Jonas Parker

Hancock-Clarke House

Granny's Hill

Lexington Green

Concord Road

Buckman Tavern

Meeting Ho.

Shop

A. Muzzey

B. Estabrook Mill

Vine Brook

Merriam's Hill

Woburn Road

P. Russell

Muzzey Mill

Jon. Smith Ben. Merriam

J. Loring

Mat. Mead

N

North Branch

L E X I N G T O N

Watertown Road

South Branch

– – – – – British Troop Movements

0                              500
Yards

Smith

J. Raymond

Nat. Mulliken

Josh. Bond

Munroe's Tavern

J. Mason

S. Sanderson

---

LEXINGTON GREEN

Burying Ground

Blacksmith shop

Jonathan Harrington

Bedford Road

Daniel Harrington

Spectators

Parker's Militia

Paul Revere's path

←to Concord

School house

4th and 10th Light Infantry

Stable

5th Light Infantry

Animal pound

British Column after battle

Belfry

Tree

Buckman Tavern

Spectators

Spectators

Nathan Munroe

Meeting House

0    100    200    300
Ft

Pitcairn's Light Infantry

Horse sheds

Malt Lane

←from Cambridge

his testimony indicated that he could not tell who fired first. With John Lowell he went back to his work, carrying the trunk to a place of safety.[29]

On the other side, Lieutenant Edward Gould was very near the center of the action. As an officer of light infantry in the King's Own, he was part of the force that Adair led directly toward the militia. As the two lines drew near, Gould heard the sharp report of a gun. Like Paul Revere he could not see where it came from, and was unable even to hear it clearly because his own men were cheering wildly. Lieutenant Gould, like Revere, was an honest man and a careful observer. He later testified, "Which party fired first I cannot exactly say, as our troops rushed on shouting and huzzaing."[30]

As the bitter smell of black powder began to spread across the Common, men on both sides searched quickly around them, looking for the source of the shot. On that field of confusion, one fact was clear enough. Nearly everyone, British and American, agreed that the first shot did not come from the ranks of Captain Parker's militia, or from the rank and file of the British infantry.[31]

Several British officers were convinced that they saw a "provincial" fire at them from behind a "hedge" or stone wall, some distance away from Parker's line. Lieutenant Sutherland of the 38th Foot wrote, "Some of the villains were got over the hedge, fired at us, and it was then and not before that the soldiers fired." Major Pitcairn to his dying day believed that "some of the Rebels who had jumped over the wall, fired 4 or 5 shott at the soldiers . . . upon this, without any order or regularity, the Light Infantry began a scattered fire."[32]

It might have been so, but other Regulars thought that the first shot came from "the corner of a large house to the right of the Church," which could only have been the Buckman Tavern. This also could have happened. Many armed men had been in the Buckman Tavern that night, and more than a few had partaken liberally of the landlord's hospitality. Firearms and alcohol made a highly explosive mixture.[33]

The Lexington men saw things differently. Most believed that the first shots were "a few guns which we took to be pistols, from some of the Regulars who were mounted on horses." As many as five or six mounted men were present with the forward companies. Most of the Lexington militia, only thirty yards from these men, clearly saw one of these British officers fire at them.[34]

Some thought that the first shot came from Major Pitcairn himself. One swore that he "heard the British commander cry,

'Fire!' and fired his own pistol and the other officers soon fired."
Pitcairn, an honorable man, absolutely denied that he did any such
thing, and insisted that he told his troops *not* to fire. His brother
officers strongly supported him. Lieutenant Sutherland wrote, "I
heard Major Pitcairn's voice call out, 'Soldiers, don't fire, keep
your ranks, and surround them.'"[35]

Other Americans believed that the first shot came from another British officer. Thomas Fessenden testified that as Pitcairn
rode to the front, a second officer "about two rods behind him,
fired a pistol." The minister Jonas Clarke also thought that "the
second of these officers fired a pistol towards the militia as they
were dispersing." It might have been the excitable Major Mitchell, or possibly Lieutenant Sutherland, an aggressive young volunteer who was armed with a pistol and mounted on a fractious horse
that he could not control.[36]

What probably happened was this: several shots were fired
close together—one by a mounted British officer, and another by
an American spectator. Men on both sides were sure that they
heard more than one weapon go off; men on each side were
watching only their opponents. If there were several shots at about
the same time then all spoke the truth as they saw it, but few were
able to see the entire field.[37]

It is possible that one of these first shots was fired deliberately,
either from an emotion of the moment, or a cold-blooded intention to create a incident. More likely, there was an accident. Firearms seemed to have a mind of their own in the 18th century. Only
a few years earlier, such an accident had happened at a military
review of the 71st Foot in Edinburgh, "some of the men's pieces
going off as they were presented." Many weapons at Lexington,
both British and American, were worn and defective. An accident
might well have occurred on either side. If so, it was an accident
that had been waiting to happen.[38]

We shall never know who fired first at Lexington, or why. But
everyone on the Common saw what happened next. The British
infantry heard the shots, and began to fire without orders. Their
officers could not control them. Lieut. John Barker of the 4th
Foot testified that "our men without any orders rushed in upon
them, fired, and put 'em to flight." Major Pitcairn reported that
"without any order or regularity, the light infantry began a scattered fire."

The British firing made at first a slow irregular popping
sound, which expanded into a sharp crackle. Then suddenly there

was a terrible ripping noise like the tearing of a sheet, as the British soldiers fired their first volley. That cruel sound was followed by what Paul Revere described as a "continual roar of musketry" along the British line.

Things were moving very quickly, but to the New England men who received this fire only a few yards away, events seemed to be happening in slow motion. Lexington militiaman Elijah Sanderson saw the Regulars shoot at him, but he was amazed that nobody seemed to fall, and thought that the Redcoats were firing blanks. Then one British soldier turned and fired toward a man behind a wall. "I saw the wall smoke with the bullets hitting it, Sanderson recalled, "I then knew they were firing balls."

John Munroe also believed that the Regulars were firing only powder, and said so to his kinsman Ebenezer Munroe who stood beside him. But on the second fire Ebenezer said that "they had fired something more than powder, for he had received a wound in his arm." He added, "I'll give them the guts of my gun," and fired back.[39]

The two lines, British and American, were very close—about sixty or seventy yards apart, John Robbins remembered. Others thought them even closer. Sanderson was amazed that the Regulars "did not take sight," but "loaded again as soon as possible." The British infantry were doing automatically what they had been taught. There was no command for "take aim" in the British manual of arms in 1775, only "present." The men were firing, reloading, presenting, and firing again with the incredible speed that made the British infantryman and his Brown Bess so formidable on a field of battle. One of the officers wrote that the firing "was continued by our troops as long as any of the Provincials were to be seen."[40]

With the crash of musketry, one of the British officers, Lieutenant Sutherland, lost control of his captured horse. The frightened animal bolted forward, straight through the New England militia to the far end of the Green. Sutherland managed to turn his terrified horse and galloped back again, as the militia and spectators scurried out of his way. Two New England men, Benjamin Tidd of Lexington and Joseph Abbott of Lincoln, were also looking on from horseback. After the volley from the Regulars they testified, "Our horses immediately started, and we rode off," not of their own volition.

The spectators fled for their lives. Timothy Smith of Lexington testified that after the Regulars fired, "I immediately ran,

Ralph Earl's sketch of the fight at Lexington Green was made shortly after the battle, on the basis of interviews with eyewitnesses. It is an important piece of evidence, very accurate in its location of British and American units, and in its rendering the Common itself. (New York Public Library)

and a volley was discharged at me, which put me in imminent danger. Thomas Fessenden, watching from near the meeting-house, said, "I ran off as fast as I could."[41] Heavy lead musket balls flew in all directions, making a low whizzing noise which sounded to some like a swarm of bees. Paul Revere, still struggling with John Hancock's trunk, found himself directly in the line of fire, about "half a gunshot" from the British troops. He later remembered that the balls were "flying thick around him." Revere and Lowell stayed bravely with the trunk as the British rounds passed close above their heads. They carried their precious burden into the woods beyond the Common, and remained there for about fifteen minutes.[42]

The Common was shrouded in dense clouds of dirty white smoke. One militiaman remembered, "All was smoke when the Foot fired." Another recalled that "the smoke prevented our seeing anything but the heads of some of their horses." The British infantry fired several ragged volleys, then charged forward without orders through the smoke, lunging with their long bayonets at anyone they found in their way.[43]

A few American militia managed to get off a shot or two. The youngsters ran, but several of the older men were determined to fight back. Many remembered seeing Captain John Parker's kinsman Jonas Parker "standing in the ranks, with his balls and flints in his hat, on the ground between his feet, and heard him declare, he would never run. He was shot down at the second fire . . . I saw him struggling on the ground, attempting to load his gun . . . As he lay on the ground, they run him through with the bayonet."[44]

John Munroe also fired back. "After I had fired the first time, I retreated about ten rods, and then loaded my gun a second time, with two balls . . . the strength of the charge took off about a foot of my gun barrel." Ebenezer Munroe stood and fought too. He wrote later, "The balls flew so thick, I thought there was no chance for escape, and that I might as well fire my gun as stand still and do nothing." He remembered trying to take aim, but the smoke kept him from seeing the Regulars, and he did not hear Captain Parker's orders to disperse.[45]

Most of the American militiamen did not return fire. Their minister Jonas Clarke wrote that "far from firing first upon the King's troops; upon the most careful enquiry, it appears that but very few of our people fired at all."[46] The British infantry suffered only one man wounded, Private Johnson of the 10th Foot, shot in the thigh. Major Pitcairn's horse was hit in two places, and Pitcairn himself was later seen nursing a bloody finger in Concord.[47]

On the other side, the toll was heavy. Two militiamen (only two) fell dead on the line where they had mustered—Jonas Parker and Robert Munroe. The rest were killed while trying to disperse, as they had been ordered. Jonathan Harrington was mortally wounded only a few yards from his home on the west side of the Common. His wife and son watched in horror as he fell in front of the house, and struggled to get up again, his life's blood coursing from a gaping chest wound. Jonathan Harrington rose to his knees and stretched out his hands to his family. Then he fell to the ground and crawled painfully toward his home, inch after inch, across the rough ground of the common. He died on his own doorstep.

Samuel Hadley and John Brown were also shot while running from the Common. Hadley's body was found near the edge of a nearby swamp. Asahel Porter, the Woburn man who had been taken prisoner, tried to run and was killed a few rods beyond the Common.[48]

Four Lexington militiamen were in the meetinghouse, which was also the town's powder magazine. They came out just as the shooting started. One of them, Caleb Harrington, was killed as he tried to flee. Another, Joseph Comee, was wounded in the arm as he ran for cover. A third, Joshua Simonds, ducked back into the meetinghouse with British soldiers in pursuit. He raced to the upper loft where the munitions were kept, sank to the floor, and thrust his loaded musket into a powder barrel, determined to explode the entire magazine if the Regulars entered. British soldiers moved toward the building; several began to enter it. Joshua Simonds heard their footsteps on the stair, and prepared to blow up the powder.[49]

At that moment Colonel Francis Smith suddenly arrived on the field, with the main body of his force. Smith was horrified by the scene that greeted him. The bodies of wounded and dead militiamen were scattered about the bloody ground. The British infantry, famous for their discipline in battle, were running wildly out of control. Their officers appeared helpless to restrain them. Small groups of Regulars were firing in different directions. Some

Tavernkeeper William Munroe was Lexington's orderly sergeant, who told Paul Revere not to make so much noise, as people were trying to sleep. Afterward he helped Adams and Hancock find a place of safety, and returned in time to muster with Captain Parker on Lexington Common. This portrait was painted by Ethan Allen Greenwood in 1813, when Munroe was seventy-one. (Lexington Historical Society)

were advancing on private houses. Others were moving toward the
Buckman Tavern. A few were inside the meetinghouse, and preparing to assault the upper story where Joshua Simonds awaited
them, with his musket plunged into a powder barrel and his finger
on the trigger.

Unlike his green junior officers, Colonel Smith knew from
long experience exactly what to do. He rode straight into the center of the scene, met Lieutenant Sutherland, and asked, "Do you
know where a drummer is?" A drummer was quickly found, and
ordered to beat to arms. The throb of the drum began to rever-
berate across the Common. The Regulars had been trained in
countless drills to respond automatically to its commands. The
British infantry heard the drum's call, steady and insistent even
above the rattle of musketry. Reluctantly, the men ceased firing
and turned toward their angry commander.[50]

Smith ordered them to form up. Some of the men responded
sullenly. Others did not respond at all. One officer remembered
"We then formed on the Common but the men were so wild they
could hear no orders." Another wrote, "We then formed on the
Common, but with some difficulty." Slowly the companies came
together, and sergeants prodded the men into ranks.[51]

Militiaman Amos Muzzey
mustered on Lexington
Green with Captain Parker's
company. This is one of the
few surviving paintings of an
American private who
fought on April 19. One sees
in this strong face the seriousness of purpose that contributed to the outcome of
that event. Fifty-three years
later, Muzzey was buried between his two wives in Lexington. His stone reads,
". . . reserved for Mr. Amos
Muzzey and wives, and no
other corpse to be laid
there." In death as in life,
Private Muzzey fiercely de-
fends his own turf. (Lex-
ington Historical Society)

Colonel Smith would have many detractors before this day was done, but one must respect his remarkable performance in recovering control of his men under fire on Lexington common. Many a life was saved by his intervention. He wrote later that "I was desirous of putting a stop to all further slaughter of those deluded people." To have succeeded in doing so was no small achievement.[52]

While the Regulars shuffled resentfully into line, Colonel Smith ordered his officers to gather round him. At long last he told them of their mission. For the first time they learned that Concord was their destination. The officers were appalled. The thought of marching farther into this hostile countryside with green and undisciplined troops, after the terrible accident that had just happened, filled them with horror. Several junior officers spoke out bravely at risk to their careers, urging Smith to "give up the idea of prosecuting his march." They reminded him about the "certainty of the country being alarmed and assembling." They asserted that the original purpose of the mission had become "impracticable," and recommended a speedy return to Boston. Colonel Smith listened politely and refused. He explained his reasons in terms that any soldier could understand, telling his officers simply that he "had his orders" and was "determined to obey them."[53]

While the officers met with their commander, the men stood in their ranks. One remembered that "we waited a considerable time there." At last the officers' call ended, and the order to march was given. Smith was concerned about the state of his troops. To revive their spirits and empty their weapons, he allowed them to fire a victory salute and give three cheers. A heavy volley of 800 muskets, and the soldiers' triumphant shouts echoed across the empty Common. Then the sergeants barked their harsh commands, and the column began to move toward Concord.

In the houses and woods along the road, the people of Lexington listened bitterly to the British cheers and began to count their dead. Seven Lexington men had been killed and also one of the Yankee prisoners taken on the road, the unlucky Woburn man who was shot while "trying to escape." Nine other Lexington men were wounded, some severely. The toll was heavy in that small town. Eight pairs of fathers and sons had mustered on the Common. Five of those eight were shattered by death. Most families in that small community suffered the loss of a kinsman—if not a father or son, then an uncle or cousin.

As the British troops disappeared into the west, the people of the town gathered on the Common. There was at first a sense of shock, a terrible numb and empty feeling of cruel and bitter loss. Then there was another raw emotion: deep, consuming, abiding anger. The people of Lexington asked themselves, who were these arrogant men in their proud red coats? By what right did they act as they did?

Other militiamen were now arriving from the far corners of the town. Those who had slept through the alarm began to appear, weapons in hand. Captain Parker mustered his company once again on the bloody ground. There were not sixty militia as before, but twice that number. The men were silent, grim and pensive. Most had lost friends and relatives only a few minutes before. Some wore bloody bandages. A few had faces and shirts blackened by powder stains. Their weapons were no better than before, but they replenished their ammunition from the dwindling store in the meetinghouse.

This time, there were no consultations or debates. With a few terse words of command, Captain Parker ordered his company to fall in. The men were no longer in doubt about what to do. They were ready to give battle again, but on different terms.

# THE BATTLE

❧ A Provincial Protest Becomes a World War

> We saw a large body of men drawn up with the great-
> est regularity. . . . with as much order as the best dis-
> ciplined troops."
>
> —British Ensign Jeremy Lister
> in Concord

> They began to march by divisions down upon us from
> their left in a very military manner.
>
> —British Lt. Wm. Sutherland,
> at the North Bridge

> Whoever dares to look upon them as an irregular
> mob, will find himself much mistaken. They have men
> amongst them who know very well what they are
> about.
>
> —Brigadier Lord Hugh Percy after
> returning from Lexington

AMERICANS HAVE A VIVID IMAGE of the fighting that began on the morning of April 19, 1775. In our mind's eye, we see a scattering of individual minutemen crouched behind low granite walls, banging away at a disciplined mass of British Regulars along the Battle Road. We celebrate the spontaneity of the event, and the autonomy of the Americans who took part in it. As a writer put it in the 19th century, "Every one appeared to be his own commander."[1]

That familiar folk-memory contains an important element of truth. One American militiaman testified that many times in the course of a long day "each one sought his own place and oppor-tunity to attack and annoy the enemy from behind trees, rocks, fences and buildings." But in more general terms, the idea that every minuteman fought his own private war against the British army is very much mistaken. It is wrong in the same way that the myth of the solitary midnight rider is inaccurate, and the legend of the spontaneous Middlesex rising is far off the mark. After close study of this event, the distinguished soldier and military historian John Galvin concludes that the clash at Lexington and Concord is "the least known of all American battles." Certainly it is one of the most misunderstood.[2]

The fighting on this day was not merely an open running skirmish along the Battle Road. It was also a series of controlled engagements, in which the Middlesex farmers fought as members of formal military units. Here again, America remembers the individual and forgets the common effort. It celebrates the spontaneous act, but shows little interest in its unique heritage of collective action in the cause of freedom. Let us look again at the events of this fateful day.

At Concord, the town fathers had been awakened by Dr. Samuel Prescott early in the morning of April 19. According to the custom in New England, they went to talk with their minister, William Emerson. In the cautious manner of these communities they decided to muster the militia immediately, and also to confirm the accuracy of the alarm by sending several gallopers to Lexington.

One of these "posts" was Reuben Brown, a Concord saddler who went riding down the Boston Road toward the first streaks of dawn in the eastern sky. Brown reached Lexington just before the Regulars arrived. He spoke briefly with Captain Parker on the Green, and was present when the firing began. Without waiting to see how it ended, Reuben Brown turned his horse, galloped home, and told Major John Buttrick what he had witnessed. Buttrick asked if the Regulars were firing ball. Brown answered, "I do not know, but think it probable."[3]

Concord's men of military age gathered together at the Wright Tavern. Like the Lexington militia, they held an impromptu town meeting among themselves. All agreed that the town should defend itself. The young men of the minute companies wished to march eastward and confront the Regulars outside the town. The men of middle age in the militia preferred to stand and fight in Concord. The town elders on the alarm list thought it wise to wait while their numbers continued to grow. After some discussion, it was decided in the consensual manner of a Massachusetts town that all of these things should be done.[4]

The minutemen marched off, spoiling for a fight. They went to the brow of a hill about a mile east of the town center, and looked out across the open countryside. Suddenly they caught their first sight of the advancing British force. It was a breathtaking spectacle: a long flowing ribbon of scarlet and white and sparkling steel that stretched a quarter mile along the road, and was moving relentlessly in their direction. Minuteman Thaddeus Blood, aged nineteen, wrote, "The sun was rising and shined on their arms, and they made a noble appearance in their red coats and glistening arms."[5]

The British commander saw the New England soldiers on the hill, and ordered his light infantry to deploy against them. The minutemen watched in fascination as the head of the long red formation suddenly opened outward to form a skirmish line. The young minutemen of Concord counted their own small numbers, and concluded that their elders had been right after all. They decided to withdraw into the town.[6]

The retreat was done in high style. Minuteman Amos Barrett recalled that the Concord men stayed on their hill until the British "got within 100 rods [1650 feet], then we was ordered to about face and marched before them." He remembered hearing "our drums and fifes a going, and also the B[ritish]. We had grand musick." The same ritual was repeated several times, as the minutemen retreated slowly before the advancing British troops.[7]

In Concord, the older men of the militia companies and the alarm lists were making ready to receive the Regulars in the village. They took a position on a high hill above the meetinghouse, near the town's tall liberty pole with its flag flying defiantly in the westerly breeze.[8] The hill was a strong position, with long views to the east. Here the Concord men consulted yet again. Their militant minister William Emerson told his fellow townsmen, "Let us stand our ground. If we die, let us die here!" One man remembered that many others "were for making a stand, notwithstanding the superiority in numbers."[9]

Some were of a different opinion. The debate continued on Meetinghouse Hill until suddenly the young men streamed back into town. Behind them the British column appeared in the distance, coming on at a quick march. The sun was rising higher in a bright blue sky, and the morning light reflected brilliantly on the burnished weapons of the advancing infantry. Emerson remembered the vivid spectacle of the Regulars "glittering in arms, advancing toward us with the greatest celerity."[10]

As the Regulars drew near, the throb of their drums began to be heard. William Emerson passed among the militia, speaking words of encouragement to the young soldiers. He came to Harry Gould, eighteen years old, who was "panic-struck at the first sound of the British drums." Emerson clapped him on the shoulder and said, "Stand your ground, Harry! Your cause is just and God will bless you!" Young Harry Gould took heart from William Emerson's words, and fought bravely through the rest of that long day. Others did the same, and long remembered the example of the man who had inspired them. After the battle a Concord soldier named his two sons "William" and "Emerson."[11]

On military questions, the men of Concord tended to defer to a small elite of elected officers who stood with them on the hill. The colonel of the Middlesex regiment was a Concord man, James Barrett, sixty-four years old, a prosperous miller who had held many offices of trust in the town. Concord's five company captains included Barrett's son-in-law Captain George Minot; his brother-in-law Captain Thomas Hubbard; and his nephew Captain Thomas Barrett. These leaders were respected in the town for their caution and prudence.[12]

But some of the younger men thought them a little too prudent. Their leader was Lieutenant Joseph Hosmer, thirty-nine years old, a prosperous farmer and furniture-maker. Hosmer was not trusted by the town's elders. His only jobs had been constable and hog-reeve, which went routinely to the newly married man. But in town meeting he was an eloquent and outspoken Whig, one of the few who could get the better of the polished Tory lawyer Daniel Bliss in political debate. In one of their exchanges, a Loyal-

William Emerson, the highly respected minister of Concord, was a militant Whig who stiffened the resolve of his town. This wax portrait is in the Concord Free Public Library

ist watched as lawyer Bliss "frowned, bit his lip, pounded with his boot-heel, and in a word showed marked discomposure."

"Who *is* this man?" the Loyalist asked imperiously.

"Hosmer, a mechanic," Bliss replied.

"Then how comes he to speak such pure English?"

"Because he has an old mother who sits in the chimney corner and reads English poetry all the day long, and I suppose it is 'like mother, like son.' He is the most dangerous man in Concord. His influence over the young men is wonderful, and where he leads they will be sure to follow."[13] On April 19, Lieutenant Hosmer and his radical young friends spoke out for strong measures. Colonel Barrett and his kin were voices of restraint.

The British drums were coming closer, but still the townsmen continued their debate. The men of Lincoln arrived, and joined in. One gestured toward the oncoming Regulars and said, "Let us go and meet them." Eleazer Brooks of Lincoln answered, "No, it will not do for us to begin the war."[14]

The drums were now very near. Once again the "more prudent" men repeated that it would be "best to retreat till our strength should be equal to the enemy's." Prudence prevailed. It was agreed to abandon the village to the advancing British force. The militia, still heavily outnumbered, retreated north to the next hill. To avoid an incident Colonel Barrett took them across the North Bridge, all the way to Punkatasset Hill, nearly a mile from the town center but overlooking it across the open country.[15]

Colonel Smith led his Regulars into an undefended village. No men of military age remained to oppose him—only women and children and old men. The people of the town had heard the news of Lexington (some of it at least), and they were angry. Two British officers described them as "sulky" and "surly." One infuriated elder attacked Major Pitcairn with his fists.

The British soldiers responded with restraint. Colonel Smith strictly enforced General Gage's orders that the people of Concord were to be treated correctly, and that private property was to be respected. Even so, there was a little looting. One soldier amazed the town by stealing a Bible from the meetinghouse. Another helped himself to a volume appropriately titled *Liberty of the Will*. Their officers permitted one act of political destruction: the town's liberty pole was cut down and burned. Otherwise, the troops remained on their best behavior.[16]

The Regulars went speedily about their business. General Gage's elaborate orders were followed to the letter. Both bridges into town were quickly secured. A single company of light infantry was thought sufficient to hold the South Bridge. A larger force, seven companies of light infantry, went to the North Bridge where the men of Concord had retreated. Four of those seven companies were sent on yet another long march, two miles beyond the North Bridge, to Colonel Barrett's house and mill, which Tories had reported to hold a great store of munitions. Two companies from the 4th and 10th Foot were ordered to hold the high ground along their route, and a company of the 43rd Foot guarded the bridge itself.[17]

The grenadiers remained in Concord center. Their assignment was to search the village, and to destroy any materials of war they found there. All morning they toiled at that thankless task. They worked systematically through the village, entering without warrant the houses that had been reported by General Gage's spies. No resistance was offered except at the tavern of Ephraim Jones, an innkeeper of outspoken Whig principles who doubled as the town's jailor. Major Pitcairn went directly to the inn and banged on the door. Jones defiantly refused to open it. A party of grenadiers broke it down. Pitcairn rushed inside, and hard words were exchanged. The angry Marine knocked the infuriated innkeeper to the ground, "clapped a pistol to his head," and threatened to use it unless information was forthcoming. At pistol-point, Jones led them to three large 24-pounder cannon, buried in his yard. Next door, a Tory was found languishing in the town jail, and speedily set free. Major Pitcairn then released his captive, and surprised him by offering to buy a breakfast for his men, and insisted on paying the bill.[18]

Aside from the three cannon, not much was turned up in the way of munitions. Paul Revere's repeated warnings had achieved their purpose. Many things of military value had been spirited away in the busy weeks since he had ridden to the town. The English Whig historian George Otto Trevelyan wrote contemptuously that the grenadiers "spoiled some flour, knocked the trunnions off three iron guns, burned a heap of wooden spoons and trenchers, and cut down a liberty pole."[19]

A cache of lead bullets was also uncovered and tossed into the millpond, from which it would be salvaged the next day. Some of the British Regulars made a pyre of wooden gun carriages, and set it ablaze. The fire spread quickly to the town house and threatened to destroy it. For a moment, in this strange semi-civil war, the soldiers and the townspeople forgot their differences and joined together in a bucket brigade to save the building. The gun carriages continued to burn, sending a cloud of smoke billowing high above the village.

Beyond the North Bridge, four companies of light Infantry marched to Colonel Barrett's house and mill, which only a few weeks earlier had indeed been an important arsenal. But since April 7, when Paul Revere carried his first warning to Concord, the town had been hard at work, moving military supplies to safety. Much material had been sent to Sudbury, Stow, and other places. What remained was hidden with high cunning. At the last minute, Colonel Barrett's sons plowed a field on his farm, planted weapons in the fresh furrows, and covered them over again. The British soldiers passed by without a second thought, little suspecting the crop that had been sown there. British Ensign De Berniere wrote in frustration "We did not find so much as we expected." In fact they found scarcely anything at all.[20]

The British troops took their time at Barrett's house. After the long night march they were tired and hungry, and several demanded breakfast from Mrs. Barrett. She gave them food and drink, saying coldly, "We are commanded to feed our enemy if he hunger." They offered to pay. When she refused, the soldiers tossed a few shillings into her lap. She told them, "This is the price of blood."[21]

At the North Bridge, the British companies awaited the return of their comrades, and guarded the line of their retreat. To the north, the men of Concord were gathering their strength on Punkatasset Hill as reinforcements came flowing in from surrounding towns. Hovering around them was a crowd of women, children, and dogs. Several soldiers led the noncombatants to a place of safety and tried in vain to shoo the dogs away, at some cost to military dignity.[22]

The militia consulted yet again, and decided to move closer. They marched south about 1000 yards from Punkatasset Hill to their muster field, a flat hilltop about 300 yards northwest of the bridge.[23] A company of British light infantry had occupied this high ground; but as the militia advanced, the Regulars retreated down the hill toward the bridge. The New England men and the British troops eyed each other warily, a few hundred yards apart.

Among the militia was an English immigrant named James Nichols, who had become a farmer in Lincoln. He was much liked by his American neighbors, who found him a "good droll fellow and a fine singer." Nichols was uneasy at the prospect of fighting the King's troops, more so than the Yankees who surrounded him. He stood quietly for a while, watching the Regulars, then turned to the men in his company and said, "If any of you will hold my gun, I will go down and talk to them." He walked down the hill, and chatted with the Regulars for a moment. Then he came back, retrieved his gun and announced that he was going home.[24]

While Nichols departed, many other men arrived from nearby towns. Parts of two New England regiments were now in the field. Concord's Major John Buttrick led the local regiment of Middlesex minutemen, of which five full companies were now assembled from Acton, Bedford, Lincoln, and two from Concord. Beside them stood Colonel James Barrett's regiment of Middlesex militia, five companies of older men from the same towns. Other men were streaming in from Carlisle, Chelmsford, Groton, Littleton, Stow, and Westford, west and north of Concord. Altogether, about 500 armed men were in the field.[25]

The senior officer present was Colonel Barrett, who took command of the entire force, supported by Major Buttrick. As a gesture of unity to the young men, Lieutenant Joseph Hosmer was invited to join them as adjutant. None of these officers was in uniform. Colonel Barrett was dressed in "an old coat, a flapped hat, and a leather apron." Hosmer commonly wore a homespun suit of butternut brown. These Concord leaders did not make an elegant appearance, but they understood their duty and had the confidence of their men.[26]

Colonel Barrett ordered the two regiments into a long line facing the bridge and the town, which was clearly in view across the open ground. The officers and men consulted together yet again. They were uncertain what to do. Then suddenly they began to notice smoke rising from the village. Young Lieutenant Joseph Hosmer turned to Colonel Barrett and asked boldly, "Will you let them burn the town down?"[27]

In any professional army, no lieutenant who valued his career would dare speak to his colonel that way. But this was the New England militia, and others joined in. Captain William Smith of Lincoln announced that he was prepared to drive the Regulars from the bridge. Captain Isaac Davis of Acton drew his sword and said, "I haven't a man who is afraid to go."[28]

Colonel Barrett ordered the men to load their weapons. Many had done so already; some deliberately double-shotted their muskets. In his prudent manner, Barrett walked the ranks, speaking words of caution to his men. Several remembered his "strict or-

Joseph Hosmer was the outspoken Concord artisan who challenged his commander Colonel James Barrett to advance on the Regulars at North Bridge. His portrait is in the Concord Free Public Library

ders" not to fire until the British fired first, but then "to fire as fast as we could."[29]

At Concord's North Bridge and Lexington Green, the actions of New England's military commanders were remarkably similar: to challenge the British force, but not to fire the first shot. It was agreed by these leaders that when the fighting began (most now believed it to be inevitable) the Regulars must start it. This strategy was adopted with surprising unanimity. Probably it was agreed in advance. Paul Revere's many rides to Concord and Lexington were not merely for the purpose of reporting British movements, but also of concerting the American response. Early that morning, Lexington's Captain Parker made sure that every private in his company understood this strategy. Concord's Colonel Barrett did the same thing at the North Bridge.

Then Colonel Barrett gave the order to advance. The men moved forward from their right in double file. This was not a combat formation. It was perhaps Barrett's hope to move across the bridge without engaging the Regulars, and to make a demonstration before the village.

Below them, the British soldiers were ordered to fall back across the bridge. Several began to pull up the wooden planking. At that sight, a wave of fury swept through the Concord ranks. Major John Buttrick shouted a warning to leave the bridge alone. This was *their* bridge! Buttrick's home was just behind him. Standing on his own land that had belonged to his family since 1638, he turned to his minutemen and said, "If we were all of his mind he would drive them away from the bridge, they should not tear that up." Amos Barrett remembered, "We all said we would go."[30] The New England men were thus consulted—not commanded—on the great question before them.[31]

The two New England regiments moved down the hill in a long column, led by young fifer Luther Blanchard of Acton, who had marched onto the field playing a spirited march called "The White Cockade," an old Jacobite song that was thought to be "intensely galling to the Hanoverians." Acton's minutemen were put in the van, because they were one of the few companies to be fully equipped with bayonets and cartridge boxes that allowed a greater rate of fire than powder horns. Behind the Acton company came the minutemen from other towns. The militia followed, and the alarm lists brought up the rear.[32]

The Regulars by the bridge turned and looked up the hill in amazement at the men coming toward them. They never imagined that these "country people" would dare to march against the King's troops in formation, and were astonished by their order and discipline. One British soldier wrote that the Yankee militia "advanced with the greatest regularity." Another noted that "they moved down upon me in a seeming regular manner." A third reported that "they began to march by divisions down upon us from their left in a very military manner." Slowly the British Regulars began to understand that this was no rural rabble confronting them.[33]

The senior British officer at the bridge was Captain Walter Laurie. With him were three light infantry companies from the

"The White Cockade" was a lively Jacobite tune that enjoyed wide popularity in 1775. It was played by Acton's fifer Luther Blanchard and drummer Francis Barker on the field at Concord's North Bridge. This rustic version was set down a few years later by a Yankee musician. It is in the collections of the New Haven Colony Historical Society.

4th, 10th and his own 43rd Foot, about 115 men in all.[34] Laurie
watched the New Englanders advance, and ordered his three companies to form for "street firing" behind the bridge. This was a
typically complex 18th-century maneuver, designed to dominate a
small space with overwhelming firepower. In one version, each
company was ordered to form in narrow ranks, one rank behind
the other. The men were trained to "lock" their formation—the
front rank kneeling, the second rank shifting half a step to one
side, and the third rank moving in the opposite direction, so that
three ranks could present their muskets and fire simultaneously.
After firing, the front ranks filed quickly to the rear and formed up
again. They reloaded while the next ranks stepped forward and
fired in their turn. The object was to present continuous volleys of
musketry in a constricted area.[35]

The Americans beyond the west bank of the river were in a
different formation. They came forward in double file, holding
their muskets at the trail in their left hands. The line of their long
formation curved down the hill to the southwest, then turned
eastward and followed a causeway that ran eastward beside the
river to the bridge.[36]

As the New England militia approached, the British soldiers
on the other side of the river struggled to form up in their street-
firing formation behind the bridge. They were caught in a tangle
of confusion. Two companies had hurried back across the bridge
and collided with a third. All became intermingled in a milling
crowd. In the rear, Lieutenant Sutherland of the 38th ordered the
light infantry of the 43rd to move out as flankers onto a field to the
south of the road. But he was not their commander, and only three
men obeyed him.[37]

Suddenly a shot rang out. Captain Laurie saw with horror that
one of his own Regulars had fired without orders. Then two other
British soldiers fired before he could stop them, and the front rank
of the British troops discharged a ragged volley with the same
indiscipline that they had shown at Lexington.[38]

The inexperienced British infantry fired high, as green troops
tend to do. Most of their volley passed harmlessly over the heads of
the militia. Thaddeus Blood remembered that "their balls whistled
well."[39] But several shots hit home. Acton's quiet Captain Isaac
Davis was killed instantly by a ball that pierced his heart; the arte-
rial blood spurted from his wound, and drenched the men beside
him. Private Abner Hosmer of the same company fell dead, shot
through the head. Fifer Luther Blanchard was wounded, and

Ralph Earl's sketch of the engagement at Concord Bridge was crude in its drawing but careful of its facts. Earl worked from interviews of survivors, and he represented accurately the positions of British and American troops at the first fire. His drawing also gives a good sense of the open terrain in 1775. The house in the distance (turned slightly on its axis) belonged to Major John Buttrick, who led the American advance on his own land. The field in the foreground was next to William Emerson's Old Manse. (New York Public Library)

three others were hit. A man from Lincoln received a strange narrow cut from a grazing shot, and wondered aloud if the British were "firing jack knives." Nearly all of the wounds were to the head and upper body.[40]

Still the Americans came on steadily, with a discipline that astonished their enemies. They were now very close, fifty yards from the bridge, well within the killing range of 18th-century muskets.[41] As men began to fall around him, Major Buttrick of Concord turned and cried, "Fire, fellow soldiers, for God's sake fire!" The men themselves took up the command. Private Blood remembered that "the cry of fire, fire was made from front to rear. The fire was almost simultaneous with the cry."[42]

The New England muskets rang out with deadly accuracy.

Recent hours of practice on the training field had made a difference. The Americans aimed carefully and fired low. Many appear
to have drawn a bead on the British officers, whose brilliant scarlet
uniforms stood out among the faded coats of their men. Two
months later at Bunker Hill the best American marksmen were
ordered "to fire at none but the reddest coats." Something similar
happened at Concord. Of eight British officers at the North
Bridge, four were hit in the first American fire. At least three
privates were killed, and altogether nine men were wounded.[43]

The Regulars found themselves caught in a trap. The New
England minutemen and militia were deployed in two long files
curving down the hill and along the causeway. Many men in that
formation had a clear shot. The British soldiers were packed in a
deep churning mass; only the front ranks could fire. The loss of
officers compounded the confusion. As the firing continued,
dense clouds of white smoke rose on both sides of the river.[44]

The New England men peered through the fog of battle, and
saw a strange shudder pass through the smoke-shrouded ranks of
the British soldiers. Then, to the amazement of American militia,
the Regulars suddenly turned and ran for their lives. It was rare
spectacle in military history. A picked force of British infantry,
famed for its indomitable courage on many a field of battle, was
broken by a band of American militia. British Ensign Lister wrote
candidly, "The weight of their fire was such that we was obliged to
give way, then run with the greatest precipitance."[45]

The British light infantry fled pell-mell back toward Concord
center, defying their officers and abandoning their wounded, who
were left to drag themselves painfully away. The American militia
watched, less in exhilaration than in what seems to have been a
kind of shock, as the Regulars disappeared in the distance, followed by wounded men "hobbling and a'running and looking back
to see if we was after them."

The New England formation was also disrupted by its own
success. It had no idea what to do with its victory. This was the
moment when one soldier, Thaddeus Blood, remembered that
"after the fire every one appeared to be his own commander."[46]
Some advanced; others retreated. Order and discipline disinte-
grated. A few of the Yankee militia had seen enough of soldiering,
and departed for the day. The wife of Captain Nathan Barrett saw
one of these men walking away from the bridge. She "called to him
and enquired of him where he was a going. He says I am a going
home. I am very sick. She says to him, you must not take your gun

with you. Yes, he says, I shall. No, stop, I must have it. But no, so off he went upon the run, and she after him, but he got away and she gave up the chase."[47]

The American dead were taken to the house of Major Buttrick near the muster field, where Captain Isaac Davis was laid out in the parlor. Colonel Barrett sent the wounded to his own home, to be looked after by his wife. As that lady was dressing a flesh wound she said, "Poor man, and a little more and you would have been in eternity." He answered sharply, "Yes, damn it, and a little more and the ball would not have touched me." When the bandage was complete, he returned to his company.[48]

As the British soldiers fled toward the village, a solitary American entered the road near the bridge, carrying a hatchet in his hand. He came upon a severely wounded Regular on the ground before him. The American raised his hatchet and brought it down on the head of the helpless soldier, crushing his skull and exposing his brains, but not killing him.[49]

Meanwhile in Concord center, Colonel Smith had been overseeing the search of the houses by his Regulars when a message arrived from Captain Laurie at the North Bridge, asking urgently for reinforcements. Suddenly Smith heard the crash of heavy firing. His experienced ear told him that this was no mere skirmish. He mustered two companies of grenadiers and led them himself toward the sound of the guns. On the road to the bridge, they met the broken remnants of the light infantry, retreating in disorder. Smith, marching at the head of the grenadiers, knew that four of his companies were still beyond the bridge at Colonel Barrett's house. The British commander was concerned to hold open their line of retreat.

The New England officers began to recover control of their scattered men—no small achievement with green militia after a battle. Colonel Barrett took a chance and divided his force. He held the older men of the militia and the alarm lists on the west side of the river, and sent them to their muster field. Buttrick's minutemen crossed the North Bridge, advanced a short distance toward Concord center, and took up a strong defensive position on a hill behind a stone wall. One of the men with Buttrick, Concord minuteman Amos Barrett, wrote later in his Yankee dialect, "We then saw the hull body acoming out of town we then was orded to lay behind a wall that run over a hill and when they got ny anuff mager buttrick said he would give the word fire but they did not come quite so near as he expected before tha halted. The commanding officers ordered the hull battalion to halt and officers to the frunt march and the officers then marched to the front thair we lay behind the wall about 200 of us with our guns cocked exspecting every minnit to have the word fire. Our orders was if we fired to fire 2 or 3 times and then retreat."[50]

The grenadiers saw the minutemen behind their wall on high ground, and halted while still out of range 200 yards away. The British officers came to the front, and studied the American force with a new respect. Amos Barrett wrote later, "If we had fird I be leave we could kild all most every officseer thair was in the front, but we had no orders to fire and their want a gun fird."[51]

Colonel Smith observed the strength of the American position, and the steadiness of the quiet men who held it. He wisely ordered the Grenadiers to fall back. "They stayed about 10 minutes and then marched back," Blood remembered.[52]

While the two forces confronted one another, a strangely surrealist scene ensued. A madman wandered unmolested through the center of the action. He was Elias Brown of Concord, a "crazy man" his minister called him. He had long been allowed to move freely in the town, doing odd jobs for his neighbors. That day he had been happily pouring hard cider for men on both sides. His Concord cider had fermented all winter and was twenty proof by April; Elias Brown did a brisk business that day. When the fighting began at the North Bridge he went among his New England townsmen and said that he "wondered what they killed them [the Regulars] for. They were the prettiest men he had ever seen and kept him drawing cider all the time." For a moment this "crazy man" may have been the sanest person in town.[53]

At last the four British companies came hurrying back from Colonel Barrett's mill on the far side of the North Bridge. When they saw what had happened, they began to run toward the bridge, in fear of being cut off. Their route took them directly under the muskets of Barrett's militia west of the river, and Buttrick's minutemen on the east side. To the surprise of the British officers, the New England men held their fire, still reluctant in this twilight zone between peace and war to attack the King's troops without cause. The British infantry were suddenly very careful not to provoke these dangerous and unpredictable men.

The four companies of light infantry crossed over the North Bridge and turned toward Concord. In the road they came upon the dying Regular who had been brained with an American hatchet, and appeared to have been scalped as well. Instantly the

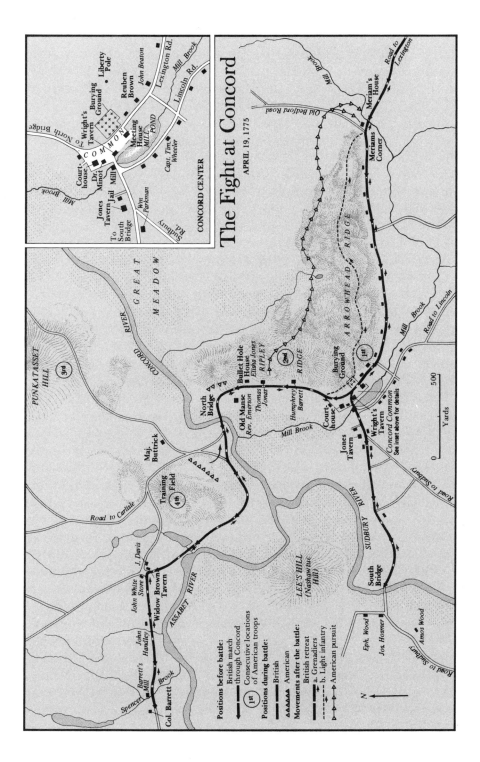

The Fight at Concord
APRIL 19, 1775

CONCORD CENTER

Positions before battle:
British march
through Concord
1st   Consecutive locations
of American troops

Positions during battle:
▲▲▲▲▲ British
▲▲▲▲▲ American

Movements after the battle:
British retreat
a. Grenadiers
b. Light Infantry
American pursuit

0      500
Yards

N

word spread among the Regulars that the Americans were murdering prisoners and torturing the wounded. The story flew from mouth to mouth, growing as it traveled. By the time it reached Ensign Lister he was told that "four men of the Fourth company [had been] killed and afterwards scalped, their eyes gouged, their noses and ears cut off."[54]

That report was false, but what had actually happened was bad enough. A wanton atrocity had been committed by a young Concord man, and witnessed by four companies of British troops. It instantly changed the tone of the engagement. Many British Regulars had long felt contempt for New England Yankees; now a spirit of hatred began to grow. The thin veneer of 18th-century civility was shattered by this one atrocity at the North Bridge. It would lead to many others by both sides before the day was out.

The morning hours were rapidly consumed by these events. It was half past eleven before all of the Regulars were back in Concord center. Still, for some unknown reason, Colonel Smith held his men in the town for another thirty minutes. Why he did so is unclear. The Americans, watching from the hills north of the town, observed what they took to be signs of fatal indecision. "For half an hour," Emerson wrote contemptuously, "the Enemy by their marches and countermarches discovered great fickleness and inconstancy of mind, sometimes advancing, sometimes returning to their former posts."[55]

North of the village, the Americans began to move east across the hills, threatening to cut off the road from Concord to Boston. Smith sent three companies to the high ground north of the highway, with orders to hold open his line of retreat. At the same time he reorganized his command, and formed it into a marching column. Men from broken units were seconded to other formations. The light infantry of the King's Own was so shattered by its losses at the North Bridge that it was attached to other companies. Horse-drawn chaises were taken from Concord stables to serve as ambulances. Wounded officers were tucked into the small vehicles, and were made as comfortable as possible on pillows and mattresses that had been stripped from Concord beds. Wounded soldiers of "other ranks" were left to shift for themselves. The walking wounded joined the column with bloody bandages around arms and heads, trying desperately to keep up in fear of American hatchets and scalping knives. Severely wounded private soldiers were left behind.[56]

At high noon the British column was at last ready to march.

Meriam's Corner and the Meriam farmhouse, in a 19th-century photograph. The season appears to be early Spring. The trees are still bare, as they were on April 19, 1775. The countryside was more open than today, when the forest has reclaimed the fields and rocky pastures. The ruts of light chaises are visible in the unpaved road. The ash in front of the house is still standing today. (Concord Free Public Library)

Colonel Smith lifted his heavy body into the saddle, and gave the order to move out. His command set off in a long column on the road to Boston, nearly twenty miles away. As he rode out, Smith studied the hills surrounding the town, and saw "vast numbers assembling in many parts." He noticed a high ridge that rose abruptly on the north side of the Boston road and ran alongside the highway from Concord center for nearly a mile. A large party was ordered to secure the ridge, and protect the flank of the column. Other flankers were sent into low open meadows south of the road. This tactic was successful. No fighting occurred as the Regulars marched the first mile from Concord.

Farther on, the long ridge ended at a place called Meriam's Corner, an important road junction where several country lanes came together and the highway crossed a small bridge over a stream.[57] Many militia and minutemen were arriving on those roads—parts of two regiments from Chelmsford, Reading, and

Billerica to the north. One of Billerica's minutemen had a special reason for being there. He was Private Thomas Ditson, the Yankee pedlar who had been tarred and feathered in Boston by the soldiers of the 47th Foot.[58]

The men from Tewksbury also reached Meriam's Corner about noon, having mustered and marched twenty miles since 2 o'clock that morning. Other companies were coming up from Sudbury and Framingham, as far as fifteen miles to the south, and joined forces with the companies that had fought at Concord Bridge. The American strength was now more than 1000, larger than Smith's force for the first time that day.[59]

At least six colonels of Massachusetts militia were in the field, and took a leading part at Meriam's Corner. Lieutenant-Colonel William Thompson, a veteran of two colonial wars, formed three companies from his hometown of Billerica into a line running east from the Meriam farmhouse. Colonel David Green brought five companies alongside Thompson. Tewksbury's Captain John Trull also led his company to the line, formed them up in close order and told them, "Stand trim boys, or the rascals will shoot your elbows off!"[60]

Other men took positions as skirmishers in the fields, or found cover in the farm buildings. Major John Brooks led his Reading minutemen into a strong position "covered by a barn and walls around it," about 100 yards from the bridge.[61]

As the Regulars approached Meriam's Corner, the British flank guard came down off the hill to cross the bridge. This time there were no fifes and drums, no "grand musick," and none of the pageantry of 18th-century war. Nothing was heard but the tramp of the weary infantry, and the mournful creak of the ambulance carriages. A Reading man, Edmund Foster, remembered that "silence reigned on both sides."

Suddenly the silence was broken by a musket shot. Probably an American militiaman fired first, and missed at extreme range. The Regulars turned, presented muskets, and discharged a volley. The balls buzzed above the heads of the militia. Once again, by accident or design, the British troops had fired high. No New England men were hit.[62]

The Americans returned fire with greater accuracy. At least two Regulars fell dead, and another officer was wounded, Lieutenant Lister of the 10th Foot. As many as half a dozen British soldiers may have been hit in rapid succession before the column moved

Major John Brooks was a country doctor who showed a high talent for command on April 19. On the road to Concord, he collected three or four militia companies and led them into action at Meriam's Corner, Lincoln Woods, Lincoln Plain, and Fiske Hill. Later he rose to the rank of brigadier general. This painting by Gilbert Stuart is in the Honolulu Academy of Art.

out of range. Amos Barrett followed the retreating Regulars into the road. He remembered, "When I got there, a great many lay dead and the road was bloody."[63]

The British column hurried on past Meriam's Corner, into a cultivated countryside of fields, orchards, meadows and pastures. The road and landscape were very different from their appearance today. Historian Allen French observes that "the present broad highway, with its few curves and easy grades, gives little idea of the one of 1775. The narrow road dropped at times into small ravines which were commanded by hillsides above. At least two large sections of the road bent to the northward, rejoining the modern road after a detour." Many of these ravines and hillocks were leveled in the 19th century, and sharp bends were taken out.[64]

The terrain was not as densely wooded as today, but more open along the road. Fields were lined with stone "fences," not the neat masonry walls of myth, but straggling piles of rough granite rocks, topped with heavy logs and split rails to a considerable height, and not easy for a man to cross. Much of the land by the side of the highway consisted of rock-studded pastures, open meadows, and arable fields, subdivided by complex systems of drainage ditches, and joined by nearly invisible lanes that threaded their way through swamps and soft ground from one holding to the next. The people who lived in the countryside could move easily through this terrain, but the ground was difficult for men unfamiliar with it.

The open land along the road was broken by patches of orchard and woodlots on rising and rocky ground. Well back from the road were large tracts of woodland, of such a size that the area was called "Lincoln Woods." Even the forested tracts tended to be comparatively open, with long views through the trees. The hardwoods were still leafless on April 19. Ensign De Berniere remembered seeing that "all the hills on each side of us were covered with rebels." Colonel Smith sent out his flanking parties again. A few militiamen fired at long range, but the flankers kept them at a distance from the fast moving column.[65]

A mile beyond Meriam's Corner the road entered a stretch of rising ground that was called Brooks Hill, after a tavern and several farms owned by several members of the Brooks family.[66] As the British column reached the hill, they observed a large force of American militia gathering in close formation on the high ground ahead. Sutherland remembered, "Here I saw upon a height to my right hand a vast number of armed men drawn out in Battalia order, I dare say near 1000 who on our coming nearer dispersed into the woods." By "battalia," he meant "line of battle."[67]

The American militia officers saw an opportunity here. As many as nine companies from Framingham and Sudbury, nearly 500 men, reached this part of the road before the Regulars. They were led by able and experienced officers—Lieutenant-Colonel Thomas Nixon, his older brother Captain John Nixon, and Captains Nathaniel Cudworth, Simon Edgell, Micajeh Gleason and Jesse Eames. Five of these six men were combat veterans who had served together in the French and Indian War. They were accustomed to working as a team, and used their experience to prepare an ambush in the woods south of the road.[68]

The trap was sprung too soon. The Americans were visible in the woods, still bare of foliage, and some militiamen may have fired prematurely. Smith's vanguard charged straight up the hill toward the Americans, with the gallantry for which British infantry were renowned. The Americans stood their ground, and the British force was hit by heavy volleys of plunging fire from the Framingham and Sudbury men on the slope above them.[69]

In Nixon's company of Sudbury minutemen, two men fought side by side at Brooks Hill. One was a tense and nervous youngster who had never been in action before. The other was a tough old soldier, a Scottish immigrant named John Weighton who had sur-

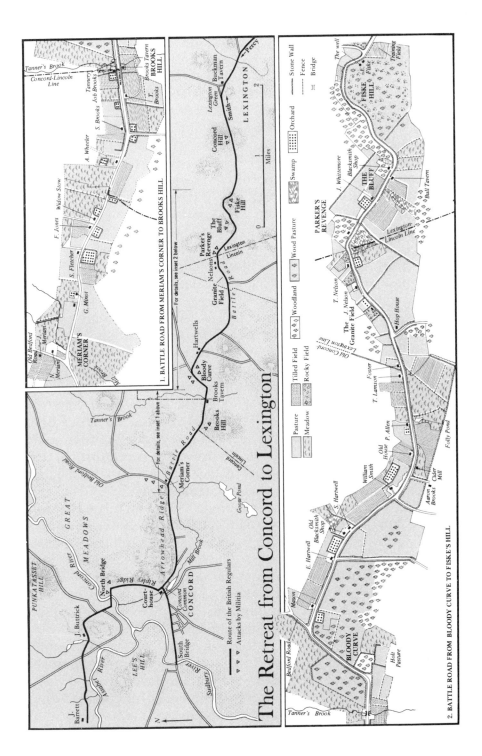

# The Retreat from Concord to Lexington

**Legend:**
— Route of the British Regulars
▽▽▽ Attacks by Militia

——— Stone Wall
——— Fence
⌡⌡ Bridge

Pasture
Meadow

Tilled Field
Rocky Field

Orchard
Swamp

Woodland
Wood Pasture

## Map 1 — Battle Road from Meriam's Corner to Brooks Hill

**Locations:** Tanner's Brook, Concord-Lincoln Line, Brooks Tavern, BROOKS HILL, S. Brooks, Job Brooks, T. Brooks, A. Wheeler, Widow Stow, F. Jones, S. Fletcher, G. Minot, Meriam, Old Bedford Road, MERIAM'S CORNER, Mill Brook

*1. BATTLE ROAD FROM MERIAM'S CORNER TO BROOKS HILL.*

## Map — Concord area

**Locations:** PUNKATASSET HILL, GREAT MEADOWS, Concord River (Assabet River), Old Bedford Road, J. Buttrick, North Bridge, Arrowhead Ridge, Ripley Ridge, Court-house, Concord Common, CONCORD, South Bridge, LEE'S HILL, J. Barrett, Sudbury, River, Mill Brook, Goose Pond, Meriam's Corner, Brooks Hill, Brooks Tavern, Tanner's Brook, Bloody Curve, Hartwells, Concord Lincoln

For details, see inset 1 above
For details, see inset 2 below

## Map — Lincoln to Lexington

**Locations:** Percy, Smith, LEXINGTON, Lexington Green, Buckman Tavern, Concord Hill, Fiske Hill, The Bluff, Parker's Revenge, Nelsons, Granite Field, Lexington Lincoln, Battle Road

Miles — 0, 1, 2

## Map 2 — Battle Road from Bloody Curve to Fiske's Hill

**Locations:** The well, Training Field, FISKE HILL, E. Fiske, J. Whittemore, Blacksmith Shop, THE BLUFF, Bull Tavern, PARKER'S REVENGE, Lexington Lincoln Line, T. Nelson, Hop House, The J. Nelson Granite Field, Old Concord Line, Foster, T. Lamson, Folly Pond, Old House, P. Allen, Cider Mill, William Smith, S. Hartwell, Old Blacksmith Shop, Aaron Brooks, E. Harwell, Mason, BLOODY CURVE, Holt Pasture, Tanner's Brook, Bedford Road

*2. BATTLE ROAD FROM BLOODY CURVE TO FISKE'S HILL.*

vived Braddock's defeat, and said that he "had been in seven battles, and this eight." The green young minuteman recalled that "after we had discharged our guns I observed to the Scot, who appeared very composed, I wished I felt as calm as he appeared to be." The old soldier answered, "It's a trade to be larnt." His young friend wrote later, "Before I served through one campaign, I found the Scot's remark a just one."[70]

The fighting grew heavier near the Brooks Tavern. Here a company from Bedford had cut across the the "great fields" at Meriam's Corner. They were in the "thickest of the fight near the Brooks Tavern." The Bedford men lost their captain there, killed in action, and others wounded.[71]

On the north side of the road, other men from Bedford, Chelmsford, Billerica, and Reading joined the battle, firing from rough pastures and treelines, and forming in little knots around grizzled veterans of colonial wars. The Chelmsford militia were led by Sergeant John Ford at Brooks Hill. A comrade remembered that Ford "was prominent on the hill. He was an old fighter of the French and Indians, and knew how to handle his musket to an advantage." Sergeant Ford's musket was seen to bring down five British soldiers that day. Even this veteran was shocked by the growing intensity of the fighting along the Battle Road. Later he and another old campaigner said that "the day was full of horror to them. The Patriots seemed maddened and beside themselves."[72]

Smith disengaged his force and drove it forward through the ambush. Beyond Brooks Hill the road descended into the valley of Tanner's Brook, then begin to climb steeply again to a higher hill. As it did so, it entered another patch of woods, and turned sharply to the north—dangerous terrain for the British column. Here, in a "young growth of wood" at the bend in the road, another ambush was organized by militia from a fresh New England regiment, who came running to the action from the north. These were Woburn men, 200 strong. Their commander was Major Loammi Baldwin, a leader of high ability. Later Baldwin wrote, "We proceeded down the road and could see behind us the regulars following. We came to Tanner Brook, at Lincoln bridge, and then concluded to scatter and make use of the trees and walls for to defend us, and attack them." With a good eye for the ground, he chose a position on a wooded rise near the bend on the south side of the road.[73]

Other Americans ran to take up positions in the woods on the north side of the highway. Reading militiaman Edmund Foster remembered, "We saw a wood at a distance, which appeared to lie

The Battle Road, looking east beyond Meriam's Corner. This glass-plate negative was made by Concord photographer Alfred Hosmer in the 19th century. The narrow highway ran between fields and pastures, with stone walls and fruit trees by the edge of the road. A few apples may be seen still on the trees in the upper left. (Concord Free Public Library)

on or near the road the enemy must pass. Many leaped over the wall and made for that wood. We arrived just in time to meet the enemy. There was then, on the opposite side of the road, a young growth of wood well filled with Americans."[74]

The Regulars approached rapidly. In the van was the light infantry of the 10th Foot. Its commander, Captain Parsons, was the only officer still unwounded in his company. Behind them came the light infantry of the 5th Foot, and what remained of the King's Own. The head of the British column reached the bend in the road.

As the British van began to turn the corner, Major Baldwin ordered his Woburn men to fire. From the other side of the road, the Reading men attacked as well. The Regulars were caught in a deadly crossfire and suffered grievously. Foster recalled that "the enemy was now completely between two fires, renewed and briskly kept up. They ordered out a flank guard on the left to dislodge the Americans from their posts behind large trees, but they only became a better mark to be shot at."[75]

Many Regulars were killed or wounded. Once again the Americans aimed at the officers. In the light Infantry of the 5th

The terrain north of the Battle Road appears in this artless 19th-century photograph by Alfred Hosmer. The camera faces west toward Concord, across an open landscape of rock-strewn pastures, high stone walls, tree lines, and farming hamlets. (Concord Free Public Library)

Foot, every officer but one was hit. Only one officer in the Fourth remained unscathed. The British sergeants took over their companies, rallied the men, and led them forward directly into the brush with the valor that these weary men displayed all day.

The Regulars drove through the ambush in savage fighting, only to meet another one 500 yards beyond, where the road came to another sharp bend at a large "woodpasture." Here another large force of militia arrived from the east and north, and joined other New England men who had run through a country lane north of the highway. The Americans used cover skillfully, and lost only four men. The British infantry fought with dogged courage in the open road, and lost thirty killed and wounded in this deadly stretch of road that came to be remembered as the Bloody Curve. [76]

While Loammi Baldwin's Woburn companies engaged the head of the British column from the right, and the men of Reading attacked from the left, another fresh American regiment from Westford, Stow, and Groton attacked the rear. At the same time, Colonel Barrett's Concord men and three other regiments fired into the column from the northwest.[77]

The British troops came through the Bloody Curve at a trot, faster than the Americans could make their way through the swamps and woods beside them. As the Regulars kept moving, the

Major Loammi Baldwin, thirty years old, was another field-grade officer who gave direction to the battle. He led three companies from Woburn, and organized the deadly ambush that gave the Bloody Curve its name. As the British column retreated in growing disarray, Baldwin led his men in pursuit, so close that he was nearly killed by Percy's cannon. (Hurd, *History of Middlesex County*)

American troops, now more than 2000 strong, converged behind them on the highway and became so entangled that control was lost. That disorder allowed the British column to get clear.[78]

East of the Bloody Curve, the road passed into open farmland. Colonel Smith got his flankers out again, and kept the American soldiers at bay, but not for long. The road curved to the south, past the farms of Ephraim and Samuel Hartwell. Here more militia companies from Bedford, Woburn and Billerica joined the fight and took cover behind barns and outbuildings close to the road. Their numbers were small, but they were aggressively led by Bedford's Captain Jonathan Wilson, who had little respect for his enemies and a great desire for close combat. Earlier that morning, when he and his men stopped on their march at the Fitch Tavern in Bedford, he was heard to boast, "We'll have every dog of them before night."[79]

Wilson placed his men behind a barn on the Hartwell farm, very close to the road. They waited until the long red column approached, then fired directly into the van with deadly effect. As the Americans reloaded, a flanking party of British grenadiers caught the militia from behind. Captain Wilson was killed, and Lieutenant Job Lane was severely wounded. With the Bedford men was Woburn militiaman Daniel Thompson, who fired into the column from the barn, then ducked back to reload. A grenadier came around the corner of the building, and shot him. Another Woburn man shot the grenadier, who fell dying in the Hartwell yard.[80]

Beyond the Hartwell farm the British force continued to lose men to long range fire and skirmishes around homes by the side of the road. The column was now approaching the boundary between Lincoln and Lexington. To the south, the terrain was low and wet. North of the road was a pasture studded with large granite boulders. Beyond it was a steep rocky hillside, part of a five-acre woodlot that belonged to the farm of Tabitha Nelson. The road headed directly toward the hill, then veered south around it.[81]

Waiting on the hill was a band of Yankee militia with a score to settle. They were Captain John Parker's Lexington company— many of the same farmers who had stood on their town green. Parker had rallied them after their shattering defeat and brought them back into combat—an extraordinary feat of leadership. He led his men westward to the Lexington-Lincoln line, and some of his company took positions in the granite-strewn pasture on the north side of the road just within the town of Lincoln. They found cover in drainage ditches and large stone outcroppings, alongside the Lincoln militia. As the British column approached, the New England men fought stubbornly from behind the great gray boulders. Lincoln's William Thorning, a crack shot, opened fire from a drainage ditch, retreated to the cover of a large rock, and fired

The Bloody Curve was a series of engagements at two sharp turnings in the highway on wooded ground. This 19th century photograph by Alfred Hosmer shows the intersection of the Bedford Road (left) and the portion of the highway that is now called Virginia Road. The militia were in the trees to the left and right. (Concord Free Public Library)

again, killing two Regulars. A British flanking party cleared the ground, but at a cost. More men were killed and wounded.[82]

Just ahead, Captain Parker and the rest of his Lexington company waited on the rocky hill where the road entered their town. Some of the men wore bloody bandages over stiffening wounds they had received that morning. Others were blackened by powder smoke. They knelt grimly on their steep wooded hillside behind large granite boulders as the Regulars approached.[83]

The Lexington men held their fire until the van of the British column came very close to their position. Then, as Colonel Smith himself rode up, Parker ordered them to fire. Smith tumbled out of the saddle, painfully wounded in the thigh. Captain Parsons, the last unwounded officer of the 10th Foot, was hit. So great was the shock of this attack that the British column stopped for a moment, compressing on the road. Major Pitcairn came galloping up, and sent the British infantry charging forward up the rocky hillside, driving Parker's militia away from the road. Now the Americans began to take casualties. Lexington's Jedidiah Munroe, wounded in the morning, was killed. The American ambush was cleared, but more Regulars were dead and wounded on a rocky hillside that is remembered as Parker's Revenge.[84]

A few hundred yards beyond, to the north of the road lay yet another wooded hill, so steep that it was called the Bluff. Major Pitcairn sent his own reserve of British Marines to clear it, which they did with high courage, in an action that explains why the Marines had the heaviest losses of all the British units engaged this day.[85]

The Marines took the hill, only to discover that one more wooded purgatory lay just beyond, at a place called Fiske's Hill. Here another New England regiment came into action from the east, led by a company from Cambridge under Captain Samuel Thatcher. The New England men waited patiently as the British column marched toward them. One watched in fascination as "an officer, mounted on an elegant horse, and with a drawn sword in his hand, was riding backwards and forwards, commanding and urging the British troops." The Americans held their fire until the Regulars were in range. Then, an eyewitness recalled, "A number of Americans behind a pile of rails, raised their guns and fired with deadly effect. The officer fell and the horse took fright, leaped the wall and ran directly towards those who had killed his rider."[86]

It was Major Pitcairn himself who had gone down, not killed as the American believed, but badly shaken in his fall. His horse bolted with Pitcairn's two elegant Scottish pistols secured to the saddle. The Marine officer struggled to his feet, bound up an injured arm, and returned to his command. At least five British Regulars were left dead or dying in the road.

The plight of the British force was growing desperate. Colonel Smith himself had been wounded and Pitcairn injured. Many company officers had been hit. A large proportion of the men had been wounded, and the rest were utterly exhausted. The entire force was nearly out of ammunition, and the Americans were up with them again, firing from every side.

Men on both sides were very tired, and consumed with thirst. Vicious fire-fights broke out by wells along the road. At the Fiske house, a British soldier ran to drink from the well at the same moment that James Hayward of the Acton company came limping up with the same idea in mind. The Regular raised his musket and cried, "You are a dead man." Hayward took aim and said, "So are you." Both fired at the same instant. The Regular was killed. Hayward was mortally wounded by splinters from his own powder horn. The two men fell side by side at the Fiske farm, while other soldiers drank quickly from the cooling waters of the well and returned to the fighting.[87]

At Fiske Hill the British column began to come apart. The officers lost control of their men. Some simply sat down by the side of the road and waited for the end. Noah Eaton of Framingham came upon a Regular with an empty musket. Eaton took aim and said, "Surrender or die." The British soldier surrendered—not knowing that Eaton's musket was also empty, or perhaps no longer caring.[88]

Lexington militiaman Joshua Simonds captured two British soldiers. The first was a straggler who had somehow become separated from his unit, and was walking alone on the Boston Road. Simonds later recalled that this soldier was Irish, and surrendered without a fight. Many of the Regulars had been recruited in Ireland. As the day wore on, they were beginning to think that this developing disaster was yet another "English war, and an Irish fight."

Later, Simonds captured a musician, a boy fifer whose coat was closely buttoned, and fife projecting from it. This English fifer was but a child, and begged Simonds not to kill him. The militiaman discovered that the coat had been buttoned to staunch a fatal wound. The child was taken to an American farmhouse, and died a few days later.[89]

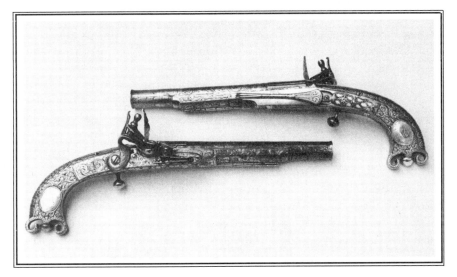

Major Pitcairn armed himself with this elegant brace of silver-mounted Scottish pistols. On the retreat from Concord he secured them to his saddle for safekeeping. Near Fiske Hill he was unhorsed and his mount was captured by an American militiaman, who sold the pistols. They were later given to the Lexington Historical Society, where they may be seen today.

The Regulars in the van began to run forward in a desperate effort to escape their tormenters. The wounded dropped behind, and British flanking parties were no longer able to keep up. De Berniere, one of the few officers still unwounded, remembered, "When we arrived within a mile of Lexington, our ammunition began to fail, and the light companies were so fatigued with flanking that they were scarce able to act, and a great number of wounded scarce able to get forward, made a great confusion; Col. Smith (our commanding officer) had received a wound through his leg, a number of officers were also wounded." De Berniere remembered that "we began to run rather than retreat in order. The whole behaved with amazing bravery but little order. We attempted to stop the men and form them two deep, but to no purpose, the confusion increased rather than lessened."[90]

The retreat continued across a swale of open land (now the roadbed of Route 128) to another elevation called Concord Hill. The few officers left in the vanguard formed a line across the road, facing backward toward the column, and tried desperately to force their men into ranks. De Berniere wrote, "At last after we got to Lexington the officers got to the front and presented their bayonets, and told the men if they advanced they should die. Upon this, they began to form under heavy fire."[91]

The end was very near for these brave men. Behind them were growing numbers of angry American militia. Ahead was Lexington Green, where they could expect no mercy. The van of the column came round a bend in the road, and Lexington's meetinghouse came into view in the distance. Some of the officers were thinking of surrender. "We must have laid down our arms, or been picked off by the rebels at their pleasure," said Lieutenant Barker, the only officer still unscathed in the first three companies.[92]

Suddenly Barker was amazed to hear a wild cheer from the the weary, bleeding, smoke-stained men at the head of the column. He ran forward, and in the distance he saw one of the happiest sights of his young life—a full brigade of British infantry drawn up in line of battle on the heights east of the Lexington Common, with artillery at the ready. Near the center of the British line, a cannon boomed. A small black roundshot went soaring through the air, crashed into Lexington's wooden meetinghouse, and came out the other side in a cloud of flying splinters.

Smith's shattered force of Regulars stumbled forward in disorder toward the guns of their rescuers, while American militia came after them. On the hill ahead, a panoply of scarlet officers studied the scene with amazement. Their commander, Brigadier the Right Honorable Hugh Earl Percy, wrote later to his father the Duke of Northumberland, "I had the happiness . . . of saving them from inevitable destruction."[93]

# A CIRCLE OF FIRE

&#126; Lord Percy's Long Retreat

> We retired for 15 miles under an incessant fire, which
> like a moving circle surrounded and followed us
> wherever we went.
>
> —Lord Percy, April 20, 1775

G ENERAL GAGE had begun to worry about the Concord
expedition even before it left Boston. On the night of its
departure, he took the precaution of alerting Lord Percy's
1st Brigade. These were some of his best troops—three crack regiments of British infantry, and a battalion of Royal Marines. He
ordered them to be under arms at four o'clock the next morning,
and ready to march if needed.[1]

What followed was a chapter of accidents, typical of the hierarchical and highly secretive system of communications in the
British command. As always, General Gage acted with obsessive
secrecy. His orders to Percy's brigade were prepared in a single
copy and sent in a sealed letter, personally addressed to the one
man who needed to know—the brigade major, Captain Thomas
Moncrieffe.[2]

That unlucky officer was not in his quarters when the order
arrived. The letter was left with a servant, who put it on a table and
forgot to tell his master. Captain Moncrieffe returned early in the
morning, perhaps less alert than usual, and tumbled into bed
without discovering the message. At four o'clock, the hour when
the troops had been ordered to assemble, he was blissfully asleep
and the brigade was still in barracks.[3]

A little past five o'clock, General Gage was rudely awakened by a galloper from Colonel Smith, bearing a message that the countryside was alarmed and reinforcements would be needed. The unfortunate Captain Moncrieffe was summoned from his slumbers, and at six o'clock the brigade was ordered to muster in marching order. The men came pouring out of their quarters, still only half awake, frantically buttoning their uniforms and tugging at their equipment. They formed up in the streets of Boston, shuffling into a long column that stretched halfway across the town.

It was seven o'clock by the time they assembled, and the people of Boston were going about their morning business. Young Harrison Gray Otis, then nine years old, was on his way to Boston Latin School. He turned a corner and was amazed to find the street filled with British soldiers. Many years later Otis remembered that "in the morning, about seven, Percy's brigade was drawn up, extending from Scollay's Building through Tremont Street nearly to the bottom of the Mall, preparing to take their march for Lexington. A corporal came up to me as I was going to school, and turned me off to pass down Court Street which I did, and came up School Street to the school-house. It may well be imagined that great agitation prevailed, the British line being drawn up only a few yards from the school-house door. As I entered the school, I heard the announcement of *deponite libros*, and ran home for fear of the Regulars."[4]

By 7:30, Percy's brigade was ready to march—all except the British Marines, who were unaccountably absent. An hour passed, while the army waited restlessly in its long ranks. Finally an aide was sent to find the missing battalion. He discovered that once again the British chain of communications had failed, in precisely the same way as before. General Gage's secret orders for the Marines had been sent in another sealed letter, personally addressed to the battalion commander. This officer was Major John Pitcairn, who at that moment was otherwise engaged on Lexington Green. The orders lay unopened in his room, awaiting his return. This double failure of communications in General Gage's command delayed the assembly of the brigade by nearly five hours—the difference between life and death for many a British soldier on the Lexington Road.[5]

While the Marines assembled in high haste, the brigade commander moved easily among his troops. Lord Hugh Percy was one of the most able officers in Gage's army. He was a figure of high importance in our story—both for what he did, and who he was, and how he personified the clash of cultures that culminated in the American Revolution.

Lord Percy was the eldest son of the Duke of Northumberland, and sole heir to one of the greatest estates in England. He held a social rank that has no equivalent in our contemporary world. In 1775, the English aristocracy was very small—fewer than 190 peers in a nation of five million people. But its material powers were great, and growing greater throughout the English speaking world. We sometimes think of 18th-century revolutions as a rising middle class against a declining aristocracy. But the American Revolution (like that in France) was a violent collision between two moving forces—an expansive set of colonial cultures, and an aggressive British aristocracy that was extending its reach throughout the Empire.[6]

This aristocracy laid claim to ancient pedigrees, but many of its members had shallow roots, and were consumed with ruthless ambition in pursuit of wealth and power. The Dukes of Northumberland were a classic case in point. Lord Hugh Percy did not receive his noble name and rank at birth. He had been christened plain Hugh Smithson junior. His father was a mere baronet—a rank below the lowest peer, invented by the Stuarts as a fundraising device. Hugh Smithson senior was bright, ambitious, and by reputation the handsomest man in England. He courted a lady who by a series of strange dynastic accidents had become heiress to the Percy estates. She agreed to marry him, much against her family's wishes. Later, through a complex line of descent, the elder Smithson succeeded to the title of Earl of Northumberland. By special act of Parliament he was permitted to take the name and arms of Percy, and by Royal favor he was raised from his earldom to the rank of first Duke of Northumberland (in the "third creation").

This armigerous Horatio Alger rebuilt the Percy family's ruined castles, revived its wasted fortunes, restored its vast estates, planted 20,000 trees in its handsome parks, and developed large deposits of coal on ducal lands into a major source of energy for the industrial revolution. (By the 19th century, the estates of the Duke of Northumberland would yield the fifth largest landed income in England.)[7]

All this was the patrimony of Brigadier Lord Hugh Percy, who was heir to one of the great fortunes in the Western world. At the same time, he was also a highly skilled professional soldier, with military experience far beyond his thirty-two years. Percy was

Lord Hugh Percy, thirty-two years old, was the eldest son of the Duke of North-umberland, and colonel of the 5th Foot (later named the Northumberland Fu-siliers). He commanded the brigade that marched to the relief of the British Concord expedition. (Author's Collection)

gazetted ensign at the age of sixteen, earned his spurs at the battles of Bergen and Minden, became a lieutenant-colonel at nineteen, and aide-de-camp to King George III at the age of twenty-three. Like his father he married advantageously—to the daughter of the King's mentor Lord Bute. When his father was given a dukedom, he gained the courtesy title of Earl Percy, and was also elected to a seat in the British House of Commons.

In 1774 Lord Percy came to Boston as colonel of his own regiment, the 5th Foot, later to be known as the Northumberland Fusiliers. He was not much to look at. Like many of his officers and men, Percy was in chronically poor health. He was a sickly, wasted figure with a thin and bony frame, hollow cheeks, a large protruding nose, receding forehead, and eyes so dim that he was unable to read by candlelight. His body was beginning to be racked by a hereditary gout.[8]

But in colonial Boston he cut a great swath. Lord Percy rented a large house that had once been the residence of the Royal Governor. He bought what he took to be the best riding horse in New England for the princely sum of £450, and imported a matched pair of carriage horses when none of the local stock pleased him. In his dining room he lavishly entertained his brother officers, and made many friends in the garrison and the town. "I always have a table of twelve covers set every day," he wrote home.[9]

Throughout the army he was immensely popular. In an age of deference, many Englishmen deemed it an honor to be commanded by the eldest son of a Duke—a gallant young gentleman who perfectly personified the virtues of his class. He was honorable and brave, candid and decent, impeccably mannered, and immensely generous with his wealth. When his regiment came to Boston, Lord Percy chartered a ship at his own expense to bring over the wives and children. On another campaign he gave every man in the regiment a new blanket and a golden guinea out of his own pocket. He detested corporal punishment. At a time when other commanders were resorting to floggings and firing squads on Boston Common, he led his regiment by precept and example. When his men went on long marches, Lord Percy left his horse behind and made a point of marching beside them, gout and all. His mother wrote him in 1770, "I admire you for marching with your regiment; I dare say you are the only man of your rank who performed such a journey on foot."[10]

Lord Percy came to America with a strong sense of sympathy for the colonists. Like many high aristocrats in 18th-century England, he was a staunch Whig. In Parliament he had voted against the Stamp Act, and regarded Lord North's American policy as a piece of consummate folly. He had no wish to fight Americans. "Nothing less than the total loss or conquest of the colonies must be the end of it," he wrote, "either, indeed is disagreeable."[11]

But once in Boston, Lord Percy began to change his mind. He was appalled by what he took to be the narrowness of New England ways, and genuinely shocked by the mobbings that he witnessed in Massachusetts. His outrage was not that of a modern liberal, but of an 18th-century gentleman who came to regard the people of Boston as a race of money-grubbing hypocritical bullies and cowards, utterly devoid of honor, candor, and courage.

"Like all other cowards," he wrote, "they are cruel and tyrannical."[12]

Percy came to believe that the inhabitants of New England
were "the most designing artful villains in the world." He thought
that they had "not the least idea of religion or morality."[13] In
particular he detested the Congregational clergy for denying their
churches to Loyalists, and despised the Yankee town meetings for
their interminable debates. "The people here," he wrote home,
"talk much and do little." He thought that the men of New England were incapable of action, and utterly contemptible as a military force. "I cannot but despise them completely," he wrote. On
the morning of April 19, 1775, the American education of Lord
Percy was about to begin.[14]

The 1st Brigade finally marched at about 8:45. It made a
brave sight as it left the little town with music playing and colors
flying. In the lead was its commander, Lord Percy himself, splendidly mounted on his handsome sorrel horse, and resplendent
in a uniform of scarlet and gosling green with trimmings of silver
lace.

Behind him came three regiments of British infantry. Pride of
place went to the 4th (King's Own) Foot, proudly bearing the
monarch's cipher on its colors, and the dark blue facings of a Royal
regiment on its faded red tunics. Nobody trifled with the King's
Own. Even their nickname in the army connoted high respect.
They were called the Lions after their badge, which was the lion
rampant of England. That emblem had been awarded for gallantry by William III and was proudly embroidered on all four
corners of their regimental colors. In 1773, an inspector described
the King's Own as "a very fine body of men, well dressed and fit."
As it marched from Boston, an expert observer would have noticed that it was also exceptionally well equipped. The 4th had
recently been rearmed with a new musket, two inches shorter and
two pounds lighter than the previous issue, and so closely bored to
the caliber of its ammunition that the regiment was among the first
in Gage's army to be issued steel ramrods.[15]

Next in Percy's brigade came the 47th Foot, unkindly
nicknamed the Cauliflowers for their uncommon off-white facings, but highly respected as a fighting regiment. The 47th had
brilliantly distinguished itself in the conquest of Quebec, and gloried in the name of "Wolfe's Own." The entire army sang a drinking song called "Hot Stuff," to the tune of "The Lilies of France,"
that celebrated its valor:

Come each death-doing dog who dares venture his neck,
Come, follow the hero that goes to Quebec . . .
And ye that love fighting shall soon have enough:
Wolfe commands us, my boys; we shall give them Hot Stuff . . .
When the forty-seventh regiment is dashing ashore,
While bullets are whistling and cannons do roar.[16]

Percy's brigade also included one of the most colorful regiments in the army, the 23rd Royal Welch Fusiliers,[17] renowned equally for its steady courage and strange customs. Every St. David's Day (March 1) its new subalterns were compelled to stand with one foot on a chair and the other on a mess table and swallow a raw leek without flinching, while the regimental drummers beat a solemn roll. On parade, these men marched proudly behind their mascot, a snow white goat with gilded horns from the Royal herd at Windsor, a custom described as "ancient" as early as 1775. The regiment gloried in its nickname of the Nanny Goats.[18] For all its quaint folkways, it was a highly professional unit that had served with distinction at Namur, Blenheim, Ramillies, Oudenarde, Malplaquet, Minden, and many other fields. At Dettingen in 1743 the regiment was commanded by George II, the last British king to lead an army into battle. For its courage the 23rd was allowed to wear the White Horse of Hanover on its colors.[19] When the Royal Welch Fusiliers arrived in America, General Haldimand sent a glowing report in his native French to General Gage: "Je dois en Justice informer votre Excellence que les Fusiliers se sont tres bien conduit ici. Ce corps est bien composé et très bien commandé." General Gage replied, "I dare say the Fusiliers will deserve the character you give of them. They were always esteemed a good corps and have gained reputation wherever they served."[20]

Also in the column was Lord Percy's largest unit, a reinforced battalion of British Marines, the seagoing policemen of the Royal Navy, in brilliant red and blue uniforms with snow-white facings of a distinctive nautical cut. The men of the Marine battalion tended to be smaller in stature than those in the army. Their commander, Major Pitcairn, wrote home to a friend, "I am mortified to find our Marines so much shorter than the marching regiments. I wish you could persuade Lord Sandwich to give an order not to enlist any man under five feet six." But these men had a fearsome reputation as fighters, in combat and out. They marched behind their drums with a distinctive rolling swagger that marked them as a breed apart from the army.[21]

Interspersed between the long red columns of British infantry were the dark blue tunics of the Royal Artillery. Their regimental motto was *Ubique*, the same as the Royal Engineers. The Gunners insisted that their *Ubique* meant "Everywhere," while the slogan of the Sappers should be translated "All over the Place." In any case, here they were again, marching beside two stout six-pounder field guns, with long trails and massive wooden wheels that rumbled ominously through the streets of Boston.[22]

Also traveling with the brigade were armed New England Loyalists in civilian dress, who have rarely been noticed in American histories of the battles. These American Tories were angry men, hungry for revenge against the "Rebels" who cruelly tormented them. Some were employed as mounted scouts. Prominent on horseback at the head of the column was a Boston Tory named George Leonard. Others marched behind the infantry as civilian auxiliaries. One of their number was a Tory barber named Warden, who hated the Whigs of New England so passionately that he shouldered a musket and joined the brigade as a volunteer.[23]

The British soldiers were in a merry mood as they left town. No serious trouble was expected from the "country people," or at least nothing that these proud regiments would not be able to handle. Their fifes and drums played a spirited version of "Yankee Doodle" as a taunt to the inhabitants—a musical joke that would long be remembered in Massachusetts. Afterward, a London wit suggested that a more suitable song might have been "The Ballad of Chevy Chase":

> To drive the deer with hound and horn
> Earl Percy took his way.
> The child may rue that is unborn
> The hunting of that day![24]

The brigade marched south across Boston Neck, then west through the villages of Roxbury and Brookline, and north at the present site of Brighton to the Great Bridge over the Charles River. The long red column crossed into Cambridge, and wound its way past the austere brick buildings of Harvard College.

The towns along the route were normally teeming with activity at that hour, but this morning they appeared to be deserted. "All of the houses were shut up," Percy wrote, "and there was not the appearance of a single inhabitant. I could get no intelligence concerning them [*sic*] till I had passed Menotomy."[25]

One of the few people he met was Isaac Smith, an absent-minded Harvard tutor who had the misfortune to emerge from the College just as the brigade was passing. Percy asked the way to Lexington. Without thinking, Smith told him. Those who knew Tutor Smith believed that he did not intend to aid the enemy, but was merely oblivious to the larger world. Even so, the people of Cambridge were not amused. They were so displeased that Isaac Smith "shortly afterwards left the country for a while."[26]

With the help of directions from the distracted Harvard tutor, Percy found the road to Lexington. Still he knew nothing of what had happened to Colonel Smith's force, or what lay ahead for his own brigade. Not until he reached Menotomy at about one o'clock in the afternoon did he learn of the fighting on Lexington Green. A little further, he met a chaise coming toward him in the road. In it was Lieutenant Edward Gould of the King's Own, who had been wounded in the foot at Concord Bridge. Gould told Lord Percy that the grenadiers and light infantry had been "attacked by the rebels about daybreak, and were retiring, having expended most of their ammunition."[27]

Percy sent the wounded officer on his way and began to study the countryside with growing concern. A casual tourist might have taken pleasure in its rolling woods and fields, dotted with granite outcroppings and lined with picturesque stone "fences." But to the trained eye of a professional soldier, the terrain took on a more sinister appearance. "The whole country we had to retire through," Percy wrote, "was covered with stone walls, and was besides a very hilly stony country." Many other officers were also looking nervously about them. Lieutenant Barker of the King's Own noted that "the country was an amazing strong one, full of hills, woods, stone walls, etc."[28]

Two miles beyond Menotomy, the marching men began to hear the rattle of musketry in the distance. As they approached the village of Lexington the sounds of battle suddenly increased. Percy ordered his brigade to deploy on high ground half a mile east of Lexington Green, near a tavern owned by Sergeant William Munroe. The 4th was sent to the northern side of the road, and the 23rd to the south. The brigade rapidly formed into a line of battle on the hills of Lexington, with commanding views of the country-side. The Royal Artillery unlimbered its two guns on high ground and emplaced them with long fields of plunging fire along the road to the west.

Suddenly, beyond the village, the red uniforms of Colonel Smith's men came into view. The men of the brigade were shocked by the scene that unfolded before their eyes. The grenadiers and light infantry were less a marching column than a running mob, pursued by a cloud of angry countrymen on their flanks and rear. A full regiment of New England militia appeared in close formation behind the Regulars. At extreme range, Percy ordered his artillery to open fire. The cannon balls screamed through the air and the militia instantly dispersed, running for cover from a weapon they had not faced before.

The grenadiers and light infantry of Smith's shattered force ran up to Percy's line, and dropped exhausted to the earth. Behind them, the New England men also went to ground and began sniping at the brigade from long range. Their fire did little damage, but goaded the Royal Welch Fusiliers on Percy's left to break ranks and charge forward without orders. A British officer wrote, "Revenge had so fully possessed the breasts of the soldiers that the battalions broke, regardless of every order, to pursue the affrighted runaways. They were, however, formed again, tho' with some difficulty." Percy regained control of his troops, but he was beginning to have the same problems of discipline that had dogged Smith and Pitcairn. He made a point of moving among his men with an air of calm and competence.[29]

To keep the New England militia at bay, the British commander sent forward a screen of his own skirmishers. He also ordered his men to set fire to three houses that offered cover to marksmen. As the buildings began to burn, a pall of dark smoke rose over the scene. The firing slackened, and then nearly ceased for half an hour, while the New England regiments rested on one side of the village, and the British brigade remained on the other. Behind the line of Percy's infantry, the Munroe Tavern became a hospital for the many British wounded. Surgeon's Mate Simms of the 43rd Foot worked among them, digging the soft lead musket balls from shattered bone and torn flesh.

Percy called his officers together in the Munroe Tavern and considered his position. He had no idea that so many men were in the field against him. Later he wrote to a friend that he was amazed to find "the rebels were in great numbers, the whole country having collected for twenty miles around." Not having known the magnitude of his task, Percy had left Boston with no reserves of ammunition for his infantry beyond the 36 cartridges that each man carried in his kit. The artillery had only a few rounds in side boxes on the guns. The senior gunner in the garrison had strongly advised the brigade to bring an ammunition wagon, but Percy thought that it would slow his progress, and said that "he did not imagine there would be any occasion for more than there was in the side boxes."[30]

After the brigade had marched, Gage himself intervened, and sent two ammunition wagons with an escort of one officer and thirteen men. This little convoy was intercepted on the road by a party of elderly New England men from the alarm lists, who were exempt from service with the militia by reason of their age. These gray-headed soldiers did not make a formidable appearance, but they were hardened veterans who made up in experience what they lacked in youth, and were brilliantly led by David Lamson, described as a "mulatto" in the records.

With patience and skill these men laid a cunning ambush for the British ammunition wagons, waited until they approached, and demanded their surrender. The British drivers were not impressed by these superannuated warriors, and responded by whipping their teams forward. The old men opened fire. With careful

Lord Percy's brigade marched with two of these six-pounder field guns. They fired a solid iron ball, approximately three inches in diameter. Their presence forced a change in American tactics during the afternoon. Percy refused to take an ammunition wagon with him; the gunners had only the rounds in the small side boxes that are visible between the wheel and barrel. (Museum of Our National Heritage, Lexington)

economy of effort, they systematically shot the lead horses in their traces, killed two sergeants, and wounded the officer in command.[31]

The surviving British soldiers took another look at these old men, and fled for their lives. They ran down the road, threw their weapons into a pond, and starting running again. They came upon an old woman named Mother Batherick, so impoverished that she was digging a few weeds from a vacant field for something green to eat. The panic-stricken British troops surrendered to her, and begged her protection. She led them to the house of militia captain Ephraim Frost.[32]

Mother Batherick may have been poor in material things, but she was rich in the spirit. As she delivered her captives to Captain Frost, she told them, "If you ever live to get back, you tell King George that an old woman took six of his grenadiers prisoner." Afterward, English critics of Lord North's ministry used this episode to teach a lesson in political arithmetic: "If one old Yankee woman can take six grenadiers, how many soldiers will it require to conquer America?"[33]

The loss of the ammunition wagons gave Lord Percy another problem of arithmetic. "We had 15 miles to retire, and only our 36 rounds," he wrote. Colonel Smith's detachment had almost no ammunition at all. The problem of supply was desperate.[34] Percy summoned an aide-de-camp, a dashing young lieutenant of the King's Own named Harry Rooke, and asked him to gallop back to Boston with an urgent message for the commander in chief. Rooke was ordered to report that Colonel Smith's command had been rescued, but that the brigade would have to fight its way home, and that further reinforcement might be necessary.

The gallant young officer set off on a hazardous journey across many miles of hostile territory. The saga of Rooke's ride might be compared with the midnight journey of Paul Revere. The British courier took the same route back to Boston that Revere had followed coming out—Lexington to Charlestown, and then the ferry to Boston. Along the way he dodged hostile patrols just as Revere had done, but by a different method. Rooke left the road, jumping walls and brooks in a wild cross-country gallop. Not knowing the ground, which was very soft in April, he took twice as long to cover the same distance as Revere had done, and did not reach Boston until 4 o'clock in the afternoon, too late to influence the course of events.[35]

Even if Rooke had arrived sooner, there was little that General

Gage could have done. Half of his effectives were already in the field. His other regiments were needed to hold Boston against its own inhabitants. Gage ordered his small garrison to remain under arms in barracks, ready for a rising of the population. He asked the navy to send two small armed vessels up the Charles River to cover the bridge at Cambridge. Otherwise, the commander in chief could only sit and wait in suspense for the outcome of events that he had set in motion.

While Gage waited in Boston, Percy was busily reorganizing his forces in Lexington for the long march home. He handled his command differently from Colonel Smith. A larger force was at his disposal, between 1800 and 1900 men, counting the survivors of the Concord expedition.[36] For the march back to Boston, Percy decided not to deploy his men in a single road-bound formation, but to distribute them in three columns, with a strong advanced party and a powerful rear guard. Together its interlocking units made something like a mobile British square. Later he wrote that "very strong flanking parties" were "absolutely necessary, as there was not a stone wall, though before in appearance evacuated, from whence the rebels did not fire upon us."[37]

Percy expected that the pressure would be comparatively weak against the front of his column, but strong on his flanks, and strongest at his rear. He arranged his forces on that assumption. At the front of the formation he placed a small vanguard of fifty men whose task was to clear the road ahead. Behind them came the surviving light infantry of Smith's command, then the grenadiers, a convoy of carriages bearing wounded officers, and ten or twelve prisoners "taken in arms," several of whom would be killed by "friendly fire" on the march.[38]

To protect his right flank, Percy ordered five companies of the King's Own to march overland on high ground south of the road. On his exposed left flank, he sent a strong force of the 47th to the north side of the road. For his rear guard he selected the Royal Welch Fusiliers. Supporting the Fusiliers was the artillery. The Marines were his reserve, in a position to reinforce any side of the formation that might be threatened. Percy was prepared to fight in any direction, and could move his guns to the front or rear as need be. His deployment gave him the tactical advantage of interior lines. He could shift his reserves from one side to another more speedily than the Americans could move around the outside of the formation.[39]

Percy also made a change in march discipline. Colonel Smith, despite his reputation for lethargy, had driven his column so rapidly from Concord to Lexington that the flankers could not keep up. Percy decided to march more deliberately, and carefully regulated his pace, so that his flanking parties could keep abreast of the central column as they picked their way over unfamiliar ground. He also gave his men a long rest in Lexington, and planned another stop at Cambridge, halfway home.[40]

The terrain posed special problems, but also gave him an opportunity. In Menotomy a rocky ridge ran three miles along the south shoulder of the road, rising as high as 100 feet. Percy's right flanking column was ordered to secure the ridge; if they could do so, the south side of the formation was protected. To the north of the road were open fields and pastures. Further east the country became more thickly settled, so much so that Lieutenant Evelyn called it "a continued village" from the Lexington line to Boston. The advance guard was ordered to clear the houses close by the highway. Percy's deliberate pace was designed to leave time for that work.

While Percy reorganized his force, the American commanders were busy with their own arrangements. The regiments that had fought Smith's column had reached Lexington in some disorder. One regiment had been broken by Percy's artillery. The others had become somewhat intermingled after the morning's long pursuit. More companies were arriving from every direction. So well had the midnight riders done their work that elements of twelve New England regiments were in the field by early afternoon. Four of them were the Middlesex regiments (commanded by Colonels Barrett, Bridge, Green, and Pierce) that had fought at Concord. These units were now at full strength, perhaps more than full strength, with their many volunteers. Four other regiments (Colonels Davis, Gardner, Greaton, and Prescott) were at half strength, but rapidly increasing as other companies appeared. Four more regiments were just beginning to arrive from Essex and Norfolk Counties (Colonels Fry, Johnson, Robinson, and Pickering). In addition to these twelve, another eight regiments were gathering in Worcester County to the west. Altogether, no fewer than forty-seven regiments would muster throughout New England that day, perhaps as many as fifty-five. So rapid was their mobilization that several British officers believed they must have assembled several days before.

At Lexington, a general of Massachusetts militia assumed command. He was Brigadier William Heath, a gentleman farmer from Roxbury, then a beautiful green country town next to Boston. General Heath did not make a martial appearance. He looked the image of the contented country squire that he was—thirty-eight years old, fat, bald, jolly, affable. Sometimes he could be a little pompous; in his autobiography he always referred to himself as "our general." But he was much beloved by those who knew him well.[41]

Most of Heath's soldiering had been done on militia training days with Boston's Ancient and Honorable Artillery Company. He had not been in battle before, and had never commanded a large force in the field. But behind his country manner was a Yankee brain of high acuity. As early as 1770, William Heath had become convinced that the people of New England might be forced to fight in defense of their ancestral ways. He began to write for the local gazettes, publishing essays signed "a military countryman," which urged his neighbors to prepare for the test that lay ahead.

In Boston, William Heath haunted Henry Knox's bookstore, with its large stock of works on military subjects. By day he studied the Regulars at their drill on the Common. By night he toiled over his books in his Roxbury farmhouse, and made a serious study of war as he thought it might develop in America.[42]

In particular, William Heath became deeply interested in the tactics of the skirmish—the use of highly mobile light infantry in open order, trained to make full use of the terrain against a stronger force that stood against them in close formation. He believed that skirmishing was a method of war best adapted to the conditions in New England. Many American historians have believed that the inspiration for these tactics came from the Indians and the American wilderness. So it did, in large part. But William Heath and other New England leaders also looked to the old world for their military models, and found them in the campaigns of European irregulars. One of them described the Yankee militia as an organization of "colonist hussars."[43]

William Heath's military scholarship was respected in New England—more so than it might have been in other cultures which believed that experience is the only teacher. In the American Revolution, New England produced a remarkable generation of self-taught military commanders who trained themselves by systematic study. They had virtually no military experience, but two of them, Nathaniel Greene and Henry Knox, would be among the most able generals on the American side. Another, the brilliant turncoat Benedict Arnold, would become arguably the most able general on

General William Heath (1737–1814) was a Roxbury gentleman-farmer who commanded the New England militia in the afternoon of April 19. He had little military experience, but much native ability, and was held in high esteem by his men. The Marquis de Chastellux, who knew him well, wrote, "His countenance is noble and open; and his bald head, as well as his corpulence give him a striking resemblance to Lord Granby. He writes well and with ease, has great sensibility of mind, and a frank and amiable character."

both sides. William Heath was another of these intelligent citizen-soldiers. Later in the war he would have his military troubles, but on the day of Lexington and Concord he fully justified the confidence that others had placed in him.

That morning, William Heath had been awakened at dawn in Roxbury. He dressed quickly and went to join the Massachusetts Committee of Safety, scheduled to meet at the Black Horse Tavern in Menotomy, directly on the British line of march. The committee adjourned to Watertown, and was meeting there by ten o'clock. On a crossroad in that town, General Heath ran into Doctor Joseph Warren, who had left Boston that morning. Together they found the Committee. Only a few members were present: Elbridge Gerry, Jeremiah Lee, and Azor Orne, who had spent part of the night hiding in a field from the British troops. Paul Revere's friend Joseph Palmer functioned as secretary.[44]

Paul Revere himself may have joined the committee sometime that day. No evidence has been found of his movements, after he and his friend John Lowell had carried Hancock's trunk to a place of safety. Revere was dismounted and unarmed. He had not been to bed since the night of the 17th. One imagines him dozing for a few moments in a chimney corner at the Clarke house, or perhaps resting by the fire in the taproom of the Buckman Tavern. But soon he would have been stirring again. Sometime during the day he headed east, and by evening he was in the vicinity of Cambridge and Watertown. The next day he was meeting with the Committee of Safety, helping to organize the American effort.⁴⁵

Heath and Warren sat with the committee through the morning, then left to join the troops at Lexington. They arrived about the same time as Percy's brigade, and met with militia officers in the field. These discussions were followed by a change in American tactics for the afternoon.

Through the morning, the Yankee militia had many times offered battle in large formations in a manner that was far removed from the American myth of individual embattled farmers. At Concord Bridge, two New England regiments had boldly attacked the Regulars in close order. Later in the morning, a regiment of Middlesex minutemen had made a stand on the high ground east of Concord Bridge. Shortly after noon, elements of three Middlesex regiments stood in close formation at Meriam's Corner. On both occasions Colonel Smith had wisely declined to engage, and hurried on his way to Boston. Beyond Meriam's Corner, the Militia formed up once more in the line of battle that Lieutenant Sutherland called "battalia" order. From Concord to Lexington Green, the New England men fought from fixed ambush positions in more than company strength at least four times: Hardy's Hill, the Bloody Curve, Pine Hill, and Fiske's Hill. As Smith's column retreated to Lexington Green, it was pursued by a body of militia in regimental order, until dispersed by Percy's artillery.

Altogether, from Concord Bridge to Lexington Green, the New England militia stood against the British force in large formations at least eight times. Six of these confrontations led to fighting, four at close quarters. Twice the British infantry was broken, at Concord Bridge and again west of Lexington Green. Altogether, it was an extraordinary display of courage, resolve, and discipline by citizen-soldiers against regular troops.

Something even more remarkable happened in the afternoon. Now the New England men faced a different situation. They confronted a reinforced brigade of British infantry, nearly two thousand men with supporting artillery. The terrain east of Lexington was different too, and the New England men had a new commander who had studied the tactics of the skirmish.

General Heath and his officers did not attempt to stand against Percy in close formation or to fight from fixed positions in regimental strength, as had happened earlier that day. But neither did they dissolve into the military anarchy of myth and legend.

Instead, the New England men sought to surround Percy's marching square with a moving ring of American skirmishers, *"dispersed* tho' *adhering,"* in the descriptive phrase of one participant. The object was to fight a deadly battle of attrition that Britain's "clever little army" could never hope to win. American officers minimized their own losses by using mobility and cover, and by open-order skirmishing at long range. The men who led the New England militia were experienced in this sort of war. Equally important, they were also practical politicians who understood that in an open society a bloody victory can be worse than a defeat.[46]

This idea of a circle of skirmishers was a tactical plan well matched to opportunity and circumstance. But it was not easy to execute. The first task was to forge the ring firmly around Percy's brigade, and to maintain some degree of command and control over these active and independent men. The second task, equally difficult, was to ensure that the New England militia and minutemen were at once "dispersed" and yet "adhering." This was not an easy balance to maintain, especially with green troops. Yet it was maintained through a long afternoon—an artifact of active leadership in which General Heath and other American commanders played a vital role.[47] In the words of soldier-historian John Galvin, the American general proved to be "a genius of the minor plan . . . walking about the battlefield, helping regimental commanders to pull their people together, advising company commanders on the best use of terrain, moving units down on the flanks of the British . . . and above all simply by being present."[48]

When Heath reached Lexington he began by rallying the regiment that had been broken by Percy's artillery, and helped to sort out the other units that had become intermingled in the pursuit from Concord. Heath also ordered some of his regimental officers to move against the flanks of Percy's brigade. Major Francis Faulkner of Colonel Barrett's 1st Middlesex Regiment remembered "organizing his regiment to work upon the flank of the enemy so soon as he should move again for Boston."[49]

Couriers were dispatched to units on the march from distant towns, informing them about the course of the battle, and redirecting them to points east of their original destination. A soldier in Fry's Essex Regiment, marching from Andover far to the north, remembered that three couriers reached his regiment while they were on the road, urging them to move rapidly and turning them to the east.[50]

There was also some resupply of the American militia in the field. The town of Malden dispatched small boys on horseback with saddlebags full of supplies. Other towns sent wagons filled with food and ammunition to support their companies.[51]

While Heath and other officers were attending to this business, Percy suddenly started to march. The time was 3:15. The cumbersome British columns took nearly half an hour to get on the road. Not until 3:45 by Adjutant Mackenzie's pocket watch did the rear guard finally move out.

The American militia hurried to surround the British force. At first the ring was incomplete. As Percy had foreseen, the pursuit was closest in the rear, where the central Middlesex regiments occupied a broad arc behind the British troops. They engaged the rear guard so closely that the Royal Welch Fusiliers were compelled to march backwards, eight companies fighting in turn and leap-frogging over one another.

As the American attack was pressed home, the Fusiliers began to take casualties. The New England militia shot the colonel of this proud regiment and hit at least thirty-six of its 218 men in the course of the day. So many Fusiliers fell in this fighting that Percy relieved them, and was forced to commit his reserve of Royal Marines as their replacement early in the retreat. The Marines also began to lose heavily—more than seventy men that day. Later the Marines also had to be replaced as rear guard by companies of the King's Own and the 47th Foot.

British officers were astounded by the volume of American fire, and by the persistence with which New England men attacked from the rear. Mackenzie later wrote, "In our rear they were most numerous and came on pretty close, frequently calling out, 'King Hancock forever'." Heath and Warren (who fought beside him as a volunteer) themselves joined the militia against Percy's rear, urging the men forward but also keeping them dispersed. Throughout the afternoon, the two leaders were to be found where the action was hottest. One suspects that the action was hottest partly because they were there, rallying the militia forward in open order.

After the rear was engaged, the two American commanders moved to the left flank of Percy's column, and led other militia regiments from Essex and Middlesex to attack from the north. Here again Heath was in the thick of the fighting. He wrote later,

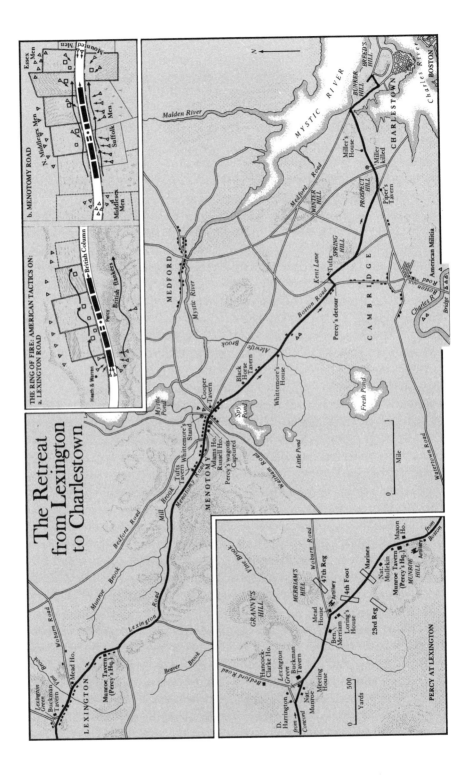

# The Retreat from Lexington to Charlestown

**b. MENOTOMY ROAD**

Essex Men
Mounted Men
N. Middlesex Men
Suffolk Men
Middlesex Men

**THE RING OF FIRE: AMERICAN TACTICS ON:**
**a. LEXINGTON ROAD**

British Column
British flankers
Heath & Warren

MYSTIC RIVER

Malden River

BREED'S HILL
BUNKER HILL
CHARLESTOWN
Charles River
BOSTON

Miller's House
Miller killed
PROSPECT HILL
Piper's Tavern

Medford Road
WINTER HILL
SPRING HILL
Kent Lane
Tufts

American Militia
Boston Road
Charles R.
Bridge

CAMBRIDGE

Percy's detour

Alewife Brook

Black Horse Tavern

Whittemore's House

Fresh Pond

Little Pond

Spy Pond

Waterville Road

Watertown Road

0 ___ Mile

MEDFORD

Mystic River

Mystic Pond

Cooper Tavern

Whittemore's Stand
Tufts Tavern
Adams Ho.
Russell Ho.
Percy's wagons Captured

MENOTOMY

Menotomy Road
Walham Road

Mill Brook

Bedford Road

Munroe Brook

Vine Brook

Woburn Road

GRANNY'S HILL

MERRIAM'S HILL
Mead House
Loring's House
Ben. Merriam

Woburn Road

47th Reg
Artillery
4th Foot
23rd Reg

Marines

Nat. Mullekin
Munroe Tavern (Percy's Hq.)
Mason Ho.
Artillery
MUNROE HILL
from Boston

**PERCY AT LEXINGTON**

Hancock-Clarke Ho.
Bedford Road
from Concord
D. Harrington
Lexington Green
Nat. Munroe
Meeting House
Buckman Tavern

0 ___ 500
Yards

Beaver Brook

LEXINGTON

Lexington Green
Buckman Tavern
Mead Ho.
Woburn Road
Munroe Tavern (Percy's Hq.)

N

"I was several times greatly exposed; in particular, at the high grounds at the upper end of Menotomy." Doctor Joseph Warren fought by his side, leading from the front with reckless courage. Heath remembered that Warren "kept constantly near me . . . a musket ball from the enemy came so near his head as to strike the pin out of the hair of his earlock [*sic*]."[52]

Percy's retreat had barely begun. And yet, while his column was still within the bounds of Lexington, the New England men were maintaining heavy pressure from the north as well as the west. Their fire drove Percy's northern flankers back toward the road. The Americans maneuvered in units as large as regimental formations, but attacked in smaller groups of company strength. One British officer observed that the New England men were very "much scattered, and not above fifty of them to be seen in any one place." Some complained that they rarely saw their enemies at all. Many Regulars expressed resentment and contempt of the Americans for fighting on their bellies and refusing to stand up.[53]

The American officers were prominent in the fighting, keeping their men dispersed but engaged. This was dangerous work. Many company officers were killed or severely wounded in the course of the day: Bedford's Captain Jonathan Wilson, Concord's Captain Nathan Barrett and Captain Charles Miles, Needham's Captain Eleazer Kingsbury and Lieutenant John Bacon, and others. Casualties also occurred among town elders who attached themselves as volunteers, and became battlefield leaders by reason of their social standing. Sudbury's Deacon Josiah Haynes was killed while leading his townsmen from the front. His example, and that of others like him, was remembered by men who fought that day.[54]

The British brigade was closely invested on both its rear and its left flank. On its right, Percy's large flanking column of the King's Own was able to keep the southern hills clear through the town of Lexington. But in Menotomy a new American force joined the battle. Heath later wrote that "the right flank of the British was exposed to the fire of a body of militia, which had come in from Roxbury, Brookline and Dorchester, etc." These were Heath's own neighbors and kin. Behind them came the first companies from Dedham and other towns in what is now Norfolk County, south of Boston. With their arrival the British column was in action on its rear and both flanks.[55]

Percy was astounded by the skill that American commanders showed in managing their forces on the field. Later he wrote,

"During the whole affair, the rebels attacked us in a very scattered, irregular manner, but with perseverance and resolution, nor did they ever dare to form into any regular body. Indeed they knew too well what was proper, to do so. Whoever looks upon them as an irregular mob, will find himself very much mistaken. They have men amongst them who know very well what they are about, having been employed as rangers against the Indians and Canadians, and this country being much covered with wood, and hilly, is very advantageous for their method of fighting."[56] Only a few days earlier, Percy himself had thought of these men as a mob. He told a friend when he got home, "For my part, I never believed, I confess, that they would have attacked the king's troops, or have had the perseverance I found in them yesterday."[57]

Soon the front of his column also began to be attacked, more heavily than Percy had anticipated. Some of the pressure on the van came from mounted militia. A few small units of New England cavalry were on the field that day. Individual militiamen also arrived on horseback—among them older men who were experienced hunters and veterans of earlier wars. They fought not in the traditional manner of the *arme blanche*, but rather as mounted infantry. They used their mobility with skill, riding ahead of the British column, dismounting, fighting on foot, then riding away to fight again.

British officers testified ruefully to the effectiveness of these men. "Numbers of them were mounted," Mackenzie remembered, "and when they had fastened their horses at some little distance from the road, they crept down near enough to have a shot; as soon as the column had passed, they mounted again, and rode round until they got ahead of the column, and found some convenient place from whence they might fire again. These fellows were generally good marksmen, and many of them used long guns made for duck-shooting."[58]

Many on both sides remembered a middle-aged militiaman named Hezekiah Wyman, from the outlying hamlet of Woburn that is now the town of Winchester. This day was his birthday. On the morning of April 19, 1775, Hezekiah Wyman turned fifty-five. His wife told him that he was too old to fight, but he saddled his "strong white mare" and galloped away. He collided with the British column on the Road east of Lexington, fired at an advancing Regular and brought him down. Hezekiah Wyman became highly visible on the battlefield—a "tall, gaunt" man with long gray locks, mounted on a white horse. The British infantry saw him many

times from Lexington to Charlestown, and grew to dread the sight
of him. Wyman was a crack shot. Again and again he rode within
range of the British vanguard, jumped off his horse, and laid the
long barrel of his musket across his saddle. As the Regulars approached he took careful aim, and squeezed off a shot with slow
deliberation. Then he remounted and rode ahead to a new
position—a grim, gray-headed messenger of mortality, mounted
on death's pale horse.[59]

When the mounted militia attacked from the front, Mackenzie remembered that "at the head of the column . . . the fire was
nearly as severe as in the rear." The ring of skirmishers was now
complete. Lord Percy himself wrote that his brigade was "under
incessant fire, which like a moving circle surrounded and followed
us wherever we went till we arrived at Charlestown."[60]

In the marching columns, the British soldiers suffered terribly
under this hail of fire, which they remembered as "incessant" and
"continual." Among them was Ensign Lister, who had been painfully wounded in Concord. Surgeon's Mate Simms had cut a Yankee bullet out of his elbow in the Munroe Tavern at Lexington,
while Lister nearly fainted from pain and loss of blood. He was
revived by a grenadier who brought him a hatful of dirty water
from a horse pond. Another soldier kindly shared a bit of bread
and beef with him. At Lexington, Lister was given a horse. He
climbed dizzily into the saddle, and rode among the wounded until
the firing became very heavy. Later he wrote, "When I had rode
about two miIes I found the balls whistled so smartly about my ears
I thought it more prudent to dismount, and as the balls came
thicker from one side or the other so I went from one side of the
horse to the other."[61]

Soon Lister found that the fire was coming from all sides. He
remembered that "a horse was shot dead close by me that had a
wounded man on his back and three hanging by his sides. They
immediately begged the assistance of my horse which I readily
granted, and soon after left him wholly in their care."[62]

Other wounded men rode on the guns of the Royal Artillery, clinging precariously to the long flat sideboxes that were
now nearly empty of ammunition. From time to time, when
larger formations of militia came in sight, Percy ordered the artillery to disperse them. As the field pieces were wheeled into
action, Ensign Martin Hunter of the 52nd Foot remembered
watching as the wounded men on the guns went tumbling to the
ground.[63]

The column now approached the village of Menotomy, and the fighting grew still more intense. Small parties of green American militia, newly arrived from northern Middlesex County and Essex County, took positions in houses and yards along the road, against the advice of experienced officers. They were joined by individual householders who fought stubbornly from their own doorsteps, even in the face of certain death as British flankers surrounded them.

One of these embattled householders was Jason Russell, fifty-eight years old and so lame that he could barely walk. Russell sent his family to safety, then made a breastwork from a pile of shingles at his front door. Friends urged him to flee. Russell answered simply, "An Englishman's home is his castle."[64] Others rallied with him, and a fierce fight took place in the dooryard of the Russell house. A party of grenadiers was sent to storm the building. Most of the Americans retreated inside or ran away, but Jason Russell was too lame to run. He stayed and fought, until a grenadier killed him in his own doorway. His wife and children returned to find his body pierced with many bayonet wounds. Altogether eleven Americans were found dead at the Russell house.

In Russell's orchard, a party of Danvers minutemen decided to organize an ambush before the British arrived. As they built a breastwork of stone and lumber, Captain Israel Hutchinson of another Danvers company passed by. A veteran of long experience, he warned them that they were too close to the road, and urged them to take cover on a distant hill. They ignored his advice, and a British flanking column surprised them. Seven Danvers men were slain, and four from Lynn were killed beside them.[65]

Some of these Americans were killed after surrendering. A Danvers man named Dennison Wallis was captured, and relieved of his watch and money. He watched as the British soldiers began to kill their prisoners, and ran for his life. The Regulars raised their muskets and fired a volley at him. Wallis was hit twelve times, and left for dead. But he survived to speak of what he had seen. The American atrocity at Concord's North Bridge was repaid many times over in Jason Russell's orchard.[66]

The fighting in Menotomy was bitter—house to house, room to room, and hand to hand. At close quarters, a Regular attacked Roxbury's Dr. Eliphalet Downer, and tried to kill him with a bayonet. Downer parried the blow, seized the soldier's musket, and impaled him on his own weapon. Menotomy's Lieutenant Solomon Bowman met another British soldier in single combat. Both men fired and missed; Bowman stunned his enemy with a musket butt and took him prisoner.[67]

Menotomy was the home of Samuel Whittemore, seventy-eight years old and badly crippled, but an old soldier and a strong Whig. When he heard that the Regulars were coming, Whittemore armed himself with a musket, two pistols and his old cavalry saber, and took a strong position behind a stone wall, 150 yards from the road. He waited patiently for the British column to approach. When it came in range, Whittemore got off five shots with such speed and accuracy that a large British detachment was sent to root him out. As the Regulars assaulted his position, Whittemore killed one soldier with his musket, and shot two more with his pistols. He was reaching for his saber when a British infantryman came up to him and shot away part of his face. Others thrust their bayonets into his body. After the battle he was found barely alive, bleeding from at least fourteen wounds. Friends carried him to Dr. Cotton Tufts of Medford, who shook his head sadly. But Samuel Whittemore confounded his physician. He lived another eighteen years to the ripe age of ninety-six, and populated a large part of Middlesex County with a progeny of Whittemores who are today as tough and independent as the sturdy old rebel who stood alone against a British brigade.[68]

The Regulars responded savagely to this resistance by individual householders. In defended buildings along the road, no quarter was given. Mackenzie wrote in his diary that "the soldiers were so enraged at suffering from an unseen enemy that they forced open many of the houses from which the fire proceeded, and put to death all those found in them." Lieutenant Barker, who was with the vanguard wrote candidly, "We were now obliged to force almost every house in the road, for the rebels had taken possession of them and galled us exceedingly, but they suffered for their temerity, for all that were found in the houses were put to death."[69]

In the Cooper Tavern at Menotomy, the Regulars found Benjamin and Rachel Cooper and their two steady customers, Jason Winship and Jabez Wyman, who had been fortifying themselves with mugs of flip. A British party broke in and did not stop to inquire what they were doing there. The two topers were later found "stabbed through in many places, their heads mauled, skulls broke and their brains out on the floor and walls of the house." More than 100 bullet holes were counted in the building. The fury of that attack was a measure of the growing rage and frustration that was felt by the British soldiers, some of whom were drinking heavily themselves from tavern stocks along the road.[70]

The fighting in Menotomy caused the heaviest casualties of the day. The Americans lost twenty-five men killed and only nine wounded, a suspicious ratio that tells much about the savagery of combat there. The British brigade suffered at least forty dead and eighty wounded in this town. Lord Percy himself was nearly killed there. A button on his waistcoat was shot away, but he escaped without a scratch. He wrote later of the "spirit of enthusiasm" which the inhabitants showed against his troops. "Many of them concealed themselves in houses," he wrote, "and advanced within ten yards to fire at me and other officers, though they were morally certain of being put to death themselves in an instant."

Inside the village Percy lost control of his men, who left their units to plunder the houses by the road. Lieutenant Barker of the 4th Foot noted in his diary, "The plundering was shameful; many hardly thought of anything else; what was worse they were encouraged by some officers." Lieutenant Mackenzie of the 23rd Foot added, "Many houses were plundered by the soldiers, notwithstanding the efforts of the officers to prevent it. I have no doubt this influenced the Rebels, and many of them followed us further than they would otherwise have done." Colonel Abercrombie of Gage's staff wrote, "I cannot commend the behaviour of our soldiers on their retreat. They began to plunder and paid no obedience to their officers."[71]

Here again, as at Lexington and Concord's North Bridge, the British troops defied officers who tried to stop them. Houses, taverns, and churches near the road were systematically stripped of their valuables. One Regular was shot as he ransacked a chest, and fell dead across the open drawers. Anything that could fit in a haversack was carried away. The British soldiers even stole the church's communion silver, and sold it in Boston, where it was later recovered. They smashed and destroyed much of what they could not carry, set fire to buildings, and killed livestock in a saturnalia of savagery. "We were much annoyed in a village called Anatomy," one Regular wrote.

At last the British troops got clear of Menotomy, crossed a small stream then known as the Menotomy River (today's Alewife Brook) and entered Cambridge. Here to their horror the fighting grew still more intense. Mackenzie remembered that "as the troops drew nearer to Cambridge, the number and fire of the rebels increased." In Cambridge, several fresh regiments of militia ap-

peared on the field in formation. Percy ordered his artillery to
disperse them. At a crossroads called Watson's Corner, the combat
was as close and bloody as in Menotomy, as newly arrived parties
of militia from Cambridge and Brookline were caught and killed
by British flanking parties before senior American officers were
able to disperse them.[72]

The British brigade was in trouble. The hour was late, and still
it had eight miles to go. Ammunition was running low. The artillery's side boxes were nearly empty. Fire discipline among Percy's
infantry was as poor as Smith's had been. Mackenzie noted that his
men returned fire "with too much eagerness, so that at first much
of it was thrown away for want of that coolness and steadiness
which distinguishes troops who have been inured to service. . . .
Most of them were young soldiers who had never been in action,
and had been taught that everything is to be effected by a quick
firing."[73]

The Charles River still lay between the British column and
safety, and the only bridge was just ahead in Cambridge. This was
the same span that Percy had used coming out. Commanders on
both sides had given much thought to the bridge. On the American side, one of General Heath's first acts was to send a detachment of Watertown militia with orders to remove the planking
from the bridge. This was done, but the thrifty Yankee soldiers
carefully piled the planks to the side for safekeeping. General
Gage sent a party of engineers under Captain Montresor, who
repaired the bridge and departed. The Americans came back, and
removed the planks once again, this time hurling them into the
Charles River.[74]

As Percy's brigade marched into Cambridge, Lieutenant
Barker in the vanguard looked ahead and observed that the bridge
was "broken down," and blocked by a large force of American
militia, with "a great number of men to line the road." The British
column was in grave danger of being cut off and pinned against
the riverbank.[75]

Instantly Percy made a bold decision. He abruptly turned his
column away from the bridge, and sent it eastward on a narrow
track called Kent Lane, toward another road that led to Charlestown. This sudden change of direction, and the brilliant use of an
obscure and unexpected road, took the New England men by
surprise. It broke the circle of fire around Percy's brigade. The
militia scrambled to get into position again. Another American
force moved quickly toward high ground called Prospect Hill,

which dominated the road to Charlestown. Percy advanced his cannon to the front of his column, and cleared the hill with a few well-placed rounds. It was the last of his ammunition for the artillery.[76]

The militia kept after him, and its numbers continued to grow. A large force from Salem and Marblehead at last arrived, and could have created a major problem for Lord Percy. But its commander, Colonel Timothy Pickering, was reluctant to engage. He had dallied earlier that day until urged forward by his men. Now he stopped at Winter Hill, north of Percy's route, and allowed the British brigade to pass. Pickering later fought bravely in the War of Independence. But he was conservative in his politics, and some have suggested that in 1775 he hoped for compromise, and wished to avoid total defeat for the British troops. Pickering later insisted that this was not the case, that he was halted on Heath's orders—which Heath strongly denied. Whatever the truth, Percy's brigade was allowed to pass by the last American force that could have stopped it.[77]

At the rear of the British formation, the New England men continued to fight stubbornly. A flurry of firing broke out in that quarter, and Percy turned once again to the British Marines. Major Pitcairn, the senior officer when the first shot was fired at Lexington, also commanded the rear guard in the last engagement of the day. While Pitcairn's Marines held the militia at bay, Percy's brigade at last reached Charlestown and safety.

# AFERMATH

## ❧ The Second Battle of Lexington and Concord

> I have now nothing to trouble your Lordship with, but
> an affair that happened on the 19th instant."
>
> —General Gage's report on Lexington
> and Concord, April 22, 1775

> All eyes are turned upon the tragical event of the
> 19th. . . . We are unanimous in the resolution, *to die,
> or be free.*"
>
> —A letter from a gentleman of rank
> in New England, April 25, 1775[1]

IT WAS NEARLY DARK when Lord Percy's men entered
Charlestown. Behind them the sun was setting on the ruins of
an empire. A great blood red disc of fire sank slowly into the
hills of Lexington, as the long column of British Regulars marched
doggedly down to the sea. The militia of New England followed
close at their heels. Fighting continued into the twilight, as fresh
regiments continued to arrive from distant towns. On Boston's
Beacon Hill, crowds of spectators could see the muzzle-flashes
twinkling like fireflies in the gathering darkness.[2]

Night had fallen when the last weary British troops crossed
over Charlestown Neck and took up a strong position on high
ground, supported by the heavy guns of HMS *Somerset*. American
General William Heath studied their deployment and decided that
"any further attempt upon the enemy, in that position, would have
been futile." He ordered the militia to "halt and give over the
pursuit," and called a conference of senior officers to make his
dispositions for the night. Fearing a British attack, General Heath
decided to withdraw the main body of the militia a few miles to the
rear. He ordered "centinels to be planted down the neck," and

"patrols to be vigilant in moving during the night." The rest of the New England troops were sent to Cambridge, and told to "lie on their arms."[3]

Attack was the last thing in British minds. As the rear guard of British Marines passed over Charlestown Neck, Lord Percy looked at his watch and noted that the hour was past seven o'clock. His men were utterly exhausted. The grenadiers and light infantry had not slept for two days. Some had marched forty miles in twenty-one hours. Most had been under hostile fire for eight hours. The soldiers sank gratefully to the soggy ground on the heights above Charlestown, and fell instantly asleep. One British officer, unconscious of the irony, noted that their refuge was a place called Bunker Hill.[4]

Later that night a cold rain began to fall, as it did so often after an American battle—as if heaven itself were weeping over the pain that mortal men inflicted on one another. Andover militia-man Thomas Boynton remembered that "there was a smart shower and very sharp lightning and thunder, the most of us wet to the skin."[5]

The many British casualties were ferried across the Charles River to Boston by seamen of HMS *Somerset*. Ensign De Berniere noted in his diary that "all her boats were employed first in getting over the wounded." Long rows of broken men with bloody bandages and smoke-stained faces lay quietly at Charlestown's landing, shivering from the shock of their wounds. One by one, seamen of the Royal Navy lowered them gently into longboats with the special tenderness that men of violence reserve for fallen comrades.[6] A spectator wrote that the boats were busy "till ten o'clock last night bringing over their wounded." So numerous were the British casualties that the navy needed three hours to ferry them across the river. Later that night, the remaining light infantry and grenadiers were also carried back to Boston. Fresh troops of General Gage's 2nd Brigade were sent to replace them on the hills of Charlestown.[7]

In the morning, the Regulars awoke to find themselves besieged by a vast militia army, which had marched from distant parts of New England. "The country is all in arms," wrote Lieutenant Evelyn of the King's Own on April 23rd, "and we are absolutely invested with many thousand men, some of them so daring as to come very near our outposts on the only entrance into town by land. They have cut off all supplies of provisions from the country."[8] Fresh food instantly disappeared from the beleaguered garrison. Ensign De Berniere wrote, "In the course of two days, from a plentiful town, we were reduced to the disagreeable necessity of living on salt provisions, and were fairly blocked up in Boston."[9]

British soldiers who strayed into American hands were now treated as enemies. One of Gage's officers reported that "the rebels shut up the [Boston] Neck, placed sentinels there, and took prisoner an officer of the 64th who was trying to return to his regiment."[10] Many of the British wounded had been taken captive, and remained in American hands. A private soldier's wife poured out her woes on paper. "My husband was wounded and taken prisoner," she wrote, "but they use him well and I am striving to get to him, as he is very dangerous; but it is almost impossible to get out or in. We are forced to live on salt provisions." She ended, "I hear my husband's leg is broke, and my heart is broke."[11]

Regulars of every rank felt the sharp sting of defeat, and many displayed a growing hatred of the "country people" who had humiliated them. A wounded survivor wrote home, "They did not fight us like a regular army, only like savages behind trees and stone walls, and out of the woods and houses, where in the latter we killed numbers of them."[12] Many repeated in their letters the story of the wounded Regular who had been killed with a hatchet. That atrocity made a great impression, and grew with every telling. One soldier wrote, "These people are very numerous, and as bad as the Indians for scalping and cutting the dead men's ears and noses off, and those they get alive, that are wounded, and cannot get off the ground."[13]

From General Gage to the humblest private, men of every rank had never imagined in their darkest dreams that such an event could happen to British infantry. Many searched for someone to blame. Lieutenant Barker of the King's Own held Colonel Francis Smith to be responsible. "Had we not idled away three hours on Cambridge marsh waiting for the provisions that were not wanted, we should have had no interruption at Lexington," he wrote in the privacy of his diary. Lt. Barker believed that Colonel Smith could also have prevented the fighting at Concord, if he had moved more quickly to the North Bridge when trouble threatened. "Being a very fat, heavy man," the angry young officer wrote, "he would not have reached the bridge itself in half an hour though it was not half a mile."[14]

Others blamed their much hated commander in chief. "The fact is," Lieutenant Mackenzie of the Welch Fusiliers confided to his diary, "General Gage . . . had no conception the Rebels would have opposed the King's troops in the manner they did."[15]

The senior officers themselves could not understand what had happened to disrupt their plans, and differed among themselves as to what should be done. Colonel Smith, in much pain from his wound, was still wondering what had hit him. He concluded that he was the victim of a deep-laid American conspiracy. "I can't think," he wrote, "but it must have been a preconcerted scheme in them, to attack the King's troops at the first favorable opportunity."[16]

Lord Percy, who alone emerged with credit from the affair, took a different view. He strongly advised a change of attitude, and warned his superiors they must not continue to underestimate their American opponents. "You may depend upon it," he wrote bluntly, "that as the Rebels have now had time to prepare, they are determined to go through with it, nor will the insurrection here turn out so despicable as it is perhaps imagined at home. For my part, I never believed, I confess, that they would have attacked the King's troops, or have had the perseverance I found in them yesterday."[17]

Gage later came to agree with Percy. He wrote to Dartmouth on June 25, "The Rebels are not the despicable rabble too many have supposed them to be, and I find it owing to a military spirit encouraged amongst them for a few years past, joined with an uncommon degree of zeal and enthusiasm that they are otherwise. . . . In all their wars against the French they never showed so much conduct, attention and perseverance as they do now."[18]

Admiral Samuel Graves, commanding the Royal Navy in Boston, responded in yet another way. Before the battle he had been outspoken in his contempt of Americans. Afterward, he gave way to alternate moods of rage and fear. He reported scathingly to the Admiralty, "The Rebels followed the Indian manner of fighting, concealing themselves behind hedges, trees and skulking in the woods and houses whereby they galled the soldiers exceedingly."[19]

In a moment of panic he ordered his captains to make elaborate preparations for his personal evacuation if the Americans should storm the town. He instructed them to "have your ship ready for action every Night, with Springs upon your cables, and in case the rebels should attempt to force the lines, you are to send a Boat armed with a Lieutenant and a Midshipman in her to what is commonly called the Admiral's Wharf or to Wheelwright's

Wharf, as the tide shall best serve. The Officer to come to me, the Boat to wait his return upon their oars."[20]

The next day Graves surrounded Boston with a ring of boats and ordered his men (much to their disgust) to stop every woman and child who tried to leave the town. His avowed object was to hold them hostage as a deterrent against attack. Afterward the admiral boasted that the decision "to keep the women and children in the town" helped to "prevent an attack upon Boston."[21] When the moment of immediate danger passed, the admiral's panic gave way to fury. He proposed to destroy the entire towns of Roxbury and Charlestown. His flag secretary later recalled that "it was indeed the Admiral's opinion that we ought to act hostile from this time forward by burning and laying waste to the entire country."[22]

General Gage stopped the admiral from executing his plan, and continued his search for a peaceful solution. He sent a plan of conciliation to Governor Trumbull of Connecticut and came close to negotiating a "cessation of hostilities" with two of Trumbull's emissaries, until Massachusetts Whigs learned what was happening and put a stop to it. In Boston, Gage refused to impose martial law immediately after the battle, though strongly urged to do so. To prevent bloodshed he persuaded the selectmen to arrange the surrender of all private weapons in the town, in return for a promise that all who wished to leave could do so. He kept his troops inside defensive lines and forbade them to attack the Americans, though many were itching to fight. "We want to get out of this cooped up situation," Lieutenant Barker wrote in frustration on May 1. "We could now do that I suppose but the General does not seem to want it. There is no guessing what he is at."[23]

While British commanders quarreled among themselves, the Americans went to work with a renewed sense of common purpose. Along the Battle Road they gathered up the wounded and buried the dead. Dedham's Dr. Nathaniel Ames went to the scene of the fighting. "Dead men and horses strewed along the road above Charlestown and Concord," he wrote in his diary. In the field, Dr. Ames dressed wounds and "extracted a ball from Israel Everett."[24]

In the town of Lincoln, Mary Hartwell watched with grief as the men of her family "hitched the oxen to the cart and went down below the house and gathered up the dead." Five British bodies were piled into the cart and carried to Lincoln's burying ground. She specially remembered "one in a brilliant uniform, whom I supposed to be an officer. His hair was tied up in a cue."[25]

At Menotomy, the dead militiamen from Danvers were heaped on an ox-sled and sent home to their town, while the children looked on. Many years later Joanna Mansfield of Lynn still vividly remembered the terrible image of the American dead piled high on the sled, their legs projecting stiffly over the side as they passed through her village. All of them, she recalled, were wearing heavy stockings of gray homespun.[26]

On Lexington Green, the minister's daughter, eleven-year-old Elizabeth Clarke, watched as the dead were gathered up and laid in plain pine boxes "made of four large boards nailed up." She wrote long afterward to her niece, "After Pa had prayed, they were put into two large horse carts and took into the graveyard where your grandfather and some of the neighbors had made a large trench as near the woods as possible, and there we followed the bodies of the *first slain*, father and mother, I and the baby. There I stood, and there I saw them let down into the ground. It was a little rainy, but we waited to see them covered up with the clods. And then for fear the British should find them, my father thought some of the men had best cut some pine or oak boughs and spread them on their place of burial so that it looked like a heap of brush."[27]

While these scenes were repeated along the Battle Road, the Whig leaders gathered in Cambridge and began to prepare for the struggle ahead. Once again, Paul Revere was at the center of events. On the morning after the battle he was at the Hastings House in Cambridge, which became the temporary seat of government in Massachusetts. There he was invited to meet with the Committee of Safety, the nearest thing to a functioning executive authority for the province.[28]

Rachel Revere remained in Boston, one of Admiral Graves's female hostages. She was less concerned about her own fate than about the safety of her husband. After the battle he managed to get a message to her, but Rachel continued to worry that he had nothing to live on but the charity of his many friends. She decided to smuggle money to him by Dr. Benjamin Church, who seemed able to pass through British lines with remarkable ease. Somewhere, perhaps from the cash box in the shop, she collected a substantial sum and sent it with a letter of love:

> My dear by Doctor Church I send a hundred and twenty-five pounds & beg you will take the best care of yourself & not attempt coming into this towne again & if I have an opportunity of coming or sending out anything or any

of the children I shall do it. Pray keep up your spirits & trust yourself & us in the hands of a good God who will take care of us. Tis all my dependence, for vain is the help of man. Adieu my love.
from your
Affectionate R. Revere

The message appears never to have reached its destination. The traitorous Doctor Church delivered even this testament of affection to General Gage, in whose papers it turned up two centuries later. One wonders what happened to the money.[29]

In Cambridge, Paul Revere had nothing but the clothes he had worn on his midnight ride. He wrote to Rachel, "I want some linen and stockings very much." Increasingly filthy and probably smelling more than a little ripe, he continued to attend meetings of the Committee of Safety at Hastings House.[30] At a session one day after the battle Doctor Warren, perhaps sitting downwind from Paul Revere, turned to him and asked if he might be willing to "do the out of doors business for that Committee." Revere agreed. For the next three weeks he traveled widely through New England in the service of the committee. Later he submitted an expense account for seventeen days' service from April 21 to May 7, at five shillings a day, plus "expenses for self and horse" and "keeping two colony horses."[31]

It was common practice in the American Revolution for leaders to be reimbursed for their expenses, and common also for lynx-eyed legislators to pare their accounts to the bone. George Washington himself served without salary during the Revolutionary War, on the understanding that he would be reimbursed only for his expenses. This was thought to be an act of sacrifice, until General Washington's expense account came in. Then there was much grumbling in Congress. The same thing happened to Paul Revere. A tight-fisted Yankee committee insisted on reducing his daily allowance from five shillings to four, before agreeing to settle his account.[32]

No evidence survives to indicate what exactly Paul Revere did for the Committee of Safety in the days after the battle. But in a general way, the activities of the committee are well known. It had much "outdoor work" to be done. The most urgent task was to raise an army. The committee resolved to enlist 8000 men for the siege of Boston, and sent a circular letter to town committees throughout the province.[33] A draft of this document survives, written in Doctor Warren's flowery style, and heavily revised by the

Paul Revere received no pay or reimbursement for his midnight ride, but like George Washington and many other leaders, he submitted an expense account "for self and horse," for extended service while "riding for the Committee of Safety" from April 21 to May 7, 1775. The account was approved, but only after his per diem expenses were reduced by one shilling a day, and the bill was signed by sixteen Whig leaders. (Massachusetts Archives)

Committee in the meetings that Revere attended. Its impassioned language tells us much about the state of mind among the Whig leaders after the battle:

> Gentlemen,—
>
> The barbarous murders committed on our innocent brethren, on Wednesday, the 19th instant, have made it absolutely necessary that we immediately raise an army to defend our wives and children from the butchering hands of the inhuman soldiery, who, incensed at the obstacles they met in their bloody progress, and enraged at being repulsed from the field of slaughter, will, without the least doubt, take the first opportunity in their power to ravage this devoted country with fire and sword. We conjure you, therefore, by all that is dear, by all that is sacred, that you give all assistance possible in forming an army. Our all is at stake. Death and devastation are the instant consequences of delay. Every moment is infinitely precious. An hour lost may deluge your country in blood, and entail perpetual slavery upon the few of your posterity who may survive the carnage. We beg and entreat, as you will answer to your country, to your own consciences, and above all, as you will answer to God himself, that you will hasten and encourage by all possible means the enlistment of men to form the army. . . .[34]

Paul Revere probably carried this document to meetings with town committees throughout the province. The men of New England responded with alacrity, turning out by the thousands to form new regiments which later became the beginning of the Continental Line.

The next "out of doors" job was to supply this army, the largest that New England had ever seen. Some "carcasses of beef and pork, prepared for the Boston market" were found in the hamlet called Little Cambridge. A supply of ship's biscuit, baked for the Royal Navy, was discovered in Roxbury. The kitchen of Harvard College was converted to a mess hall, and the militia were fed by a brilliantly improvised supply service. The army was successfully maintained in the field, but then another problem arose. Within weeks an epidemic (or polydemic) that was collectively called the Camp Fever broke out among the New England troops, and spread rapidly through the general population. The Camp Fever took a horrific toll. Rates of mortality surged to very high levels in many New England towns, spreading outward from the communities between Concord and Boston.[35]

The most important part of the committee's "out of doors work" was to rally popular support for the Whig cause, in the face of these many troubles. Within a few hours of the first shot, it began to fight the second battle of Lexington and Concord—a struggle for what that generation was the first to call "public opin-ion."[36] The Whig leaders in New England had none of our mod-ern ideas about image-mongering or public relations, and would have felt nothing but contempt for our dogmas about the relativity of truth. But long experience of provincial politics had given them a healthy respect for popular opinion, and they were absolutely certain that truth was on their side. With evangelical fervor they worked to spread what Doctor Warren called "an early, true and authentick account of this inhuman proceeding."[37]

The news of the battle was already racing through America as fast as galloping horses could carry it. A citizen of Lexington wrote that the report of the fighting "was spreading in every direction with the rapidity of a whirlwind." It was said that on April 19 Concord's Reuben Brown rode "more than 100 miles on horseback to spread the alarming news of the massacre at Lexington. This process of communication was not left to chance. From the start, the Committee of Safety worked actively to spread the news, and even to shape it according to their beliefs.[38]

As early as ten o'clock on the morning of April 19, when the Regulars had barely arrived in Concord, the committee sent out postriders with reports of the the first shots in Lexington. One of these hasty dispatches survives. It summarized what was known at that early hour, and was signed by Paul Revere's friend Joseph Palmer "for the committee." A postscript added that "the bearer Mr. Israel Bissel is charged to alarm the country quite to Connecti-cut & all persons are desired to furnish him with fresh horses as they may be needed."[39]

Israel Bissell, twenty-three years old, of East Windsor, Con-necticut, was a professional postrider who regularly traveled the roads between Boston and New York. On the morning of April 19, Bissell was in Watertown, ten miles west of Boston. The Commit-tee of Safety recruited him to carry an early report of the fighting at Lexington. He left about ten o'clock, and galloped west on the Boston Post Road, spreading his news to every town along the way. According to legend, Bissell reached Worcester about noon (more likely a little later), shouting, "To Arms! To Arms! The War has begun!" So hard had he ridden that as he approached Worcester's meetinghouse his horse fell dead of exhaustion. The men of Wor-cester remounted him and he galloped on, carrying his message "quite to Connecticut," as the committee had asked.[40]

Bissell made rapid progress on the road. He was in the Con-necticut town of Brooklyn by 11 o'clock on the morning of April

20, Norwich by 4 o'clock in the afternoon, and New London by 7 o'clock that evening. From New London, the news traveled west on Long Island Sound. It arrived in New Haven (150 miles from Boston) by noon on the 21st, and New York City (225 miles) by 4 p.m. on the 23rd. Another messenger continued through the night from New York to Philadelphia, and arrived at 9 o'clock in the morning of the 24th—ninety miles in seventeen hours. Baltimore heard the news by April 26, Williamsburg by the 28th, New Bern by May 3, and Charleston by May 9. In the second week of May, the first reports were carried across the mountains to the Ohio Valley. When news of the fighting reached a party of hunters in Kentucky, they called their campsite Lexington. It is now the city of the same name.[41]

These first reports of Lexington and Concord were received by Americans in a manner very different from our common way of thinking about great events—not merely as factual news of a secular happening, but as a sign of God's Redeeming Providence for America. A "gentleman of rank in New England" wrote to a friend on April 25, "I would only ask, if in all your reading of history, you have found an instance of irregular troops, hurried together at a moment's warning, with half the number at first, attacking and driving veterans, picked men, 17 miles, and continually firing the whole way, and not losing one third the number they killed? I view the hand of God in it, a remarkable interposition of Providence in our favour."[42]

This belief was shared by many Whig leaders in New England. They sought to propagate it, by private messages and the public press. Here again, careful preparations had been made. On the night of April 16, 1775, two days before the battle, Paul Revere's friend Isaiah Thomas, editor of the *Massachusetts Spy* in Boston, had packed up a press and printing types, and smuggled them across the Charles River with the help of the network that Paul Revere had established with the Whigs of Charlestown. After the battle, the Committee of Safety urged him to set up his press at Cambridge or Watertown, but Thomas preferred the safety of Worcester. The Provincial Congress found him a supply of paper, and his printing shop was soon back in operation, turning out the first newspaper to be published in an inland town of Massachusetts. Its motto was "Americans! Liberty or Death! Join or Die!"[43]

General Gage had respected freedom of the press, in the Blackstonian meaning of freedom from prior restraint. But Admi-

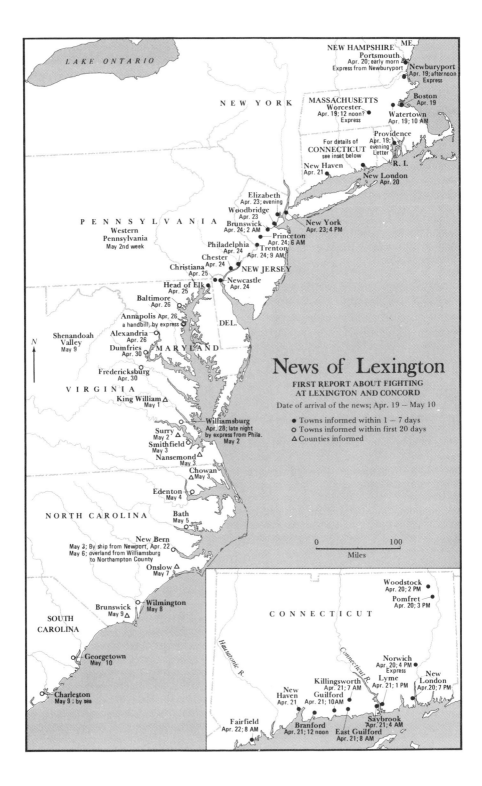

LAKE ONTARIO

NEW HAMPSHIRE ME.
Portsmouth
Apr. 20; early morn
Express from Newburyport Newburyport
Apr. 19; afternoon
Express

NEW YORK

MASSACHUSETTS
Worcester Boston
Apr. 19; 12 noon? Apr. 19
Express Watertown
Apr. 19; 10 AM

Providence
For details of Apr. 19;
CONNECTICUT evening
see inset below Letter

New Haven R. I.
Apr. 21 New London
Apr. 20

Elizabeth
Apr. 23; evening
Woodbridge
PENNSYLVANIA Apr. 23
Brunswick New York
Western Apr. 24; 2 AM Apr. 23; 4 PM
Pennsylvania Princeton
May 2nd week Apr. 24; 6 AM
Philadelphia Trenton
Apr. 24 Apr. 24; 9 AM
Chester
Apr. 24 NEW JERSEY
Christiana
Apr. 25 Newcastle
Head of Elk Apr. 24
Apr. 25
Baltimore DEL.
Apr. 26
Annapolis Apr. 26
a handbill, by express
Shenandoah Alexandria
Valley Apr. 26
May 9 Dumfries MARYLAND
Apr. 30
Fredericksburg
Apr. 30
VIRGINIA
King William
May 1

Williamsburg
Surry Apr. 28; late night
May 2 by express from Phila.
Smithfield May 2
May 3
Nansemond
May 3
Chowan
May 3
Edenton
May 4
NORTH CAROLINA Bath
May 5

New Bern
May 3; By ship from Newport, Apr. 22
May 6; overland from Williamsburg
to Northampton County
Onslow
May 7

SOUTH
CAROLINA Brunswick Wilmington
May 9 May 8

Georgetown
May 10

Charleston
May 9; by sea

# News of Lexington

FIRST REPORT ABOUT FIGHTING
AT LEXINGTON AND CONCORD

Date of arrival of the news; Apr. 19 — May 10

● Towns informed within 1 – 7 days
○ Towns informed within first 20 days
△ Counties informed

0               100
Miles

CONNECTICUT

Woodstock
Apr. 20; 2 PM
Pomfret
Apr. 20; 3 PM

Norwich
Apr. 20; 4 PM
Express New
London
Killingsworth Lyme Apr. 20; 7 PM
New Apr. 21; 7 AM Apr. 21; 1 PM
Haven Guilford
Apr. 21 Apr. 21; 10AM
Saybrook
Apr. 21; 4 AM
Fairfield Branford East Guilford
Apr. 22; 8 AM Apr. 21; 12 noon Apr. 21; 8 AM

N

ral Graves was not so scrupulous. He sent a party of seamen ashore with orders to arrest John Gill and Peter Edes of the *Boston Gazette* on a trumped-up charge of possessing firearms. They were imprisoned in Boston Gaol. Benjamin Edes got away, and with the support of the Committee of Safety began to issue his *Boston Gazette* from a battered press in Watertown.[44]

Other Whig printers were already hard at work. Ezekiel Russell's *Salem Gazette* printed an account of the battle as early as April 21. A few weeks later Russell issued a dramatic broadside, with forty small coffins across the top, and the headline, "Bloody Butchery by the British, or the Runaway Fight of the Regulars." The handbill was offered to New Englanders, "either to frame or glass, or otherwise preserve in their houses . . . as a perpetual memorial." It went through at least six printings. More coffins were added to subsequent editions, to represent New England men who died of wounds after the battle.[45]

The clergy were also recruited to preach from their pulpits. Before the battle, Concord's William Emerson delivered a sermon on II Chronicles 13:12: "And behold God himself is with us for our captain, and his priests with sounding trumpets to cry alarm." Afterward he was sent to Groton, where the minister had been "dismissed for Toryism," and delivered a sermon on the text, "It is better to put trust in the Lord than to put confidence in Princes." The Provincial Congress also recruited chaplains for the field, and ordered a series of anniversary sermons to commemorate the battle. The first would delivered in 1776 by Lexington's Jonas Clarke, and published with an eye-witness account of the event.[46]

While couriers, printers, and preachers were busy, the Committee of Safety tried to reach public opinion in yet another way. Within four days of the battle, it mobilized the justices of the peace, and systematically collected sworn testimony from eyewitnesses on the disputed question of the first shots at Lexington and Concord. Paul Revere was asked to testify, along with many others. Depositions were taken from most of the militiamen who had mustered on Lexington Common in the early morning. British prisoners in American hands were also asked to give evidence, and many did so. Other depositions were taken from men who had fought at Concord's North Bridge. These documents were edited and prepared for publication.[47]

On April 25, the Committee of Safety learned that General Gage was sending to London on that very day his own report of the battle. These official dispatches were entrusted to a British

The Coffin Broadside was a graphic illustration of American casualties on April 19. It was issued by Salem printer Ezekiel Russell in at least six editions. He carefully added more coffins in later printings, for Americans who died of wounds in the weeks after the battle. The broadside was part of a Whig campaign for public opinion, which succeeded brilliantly in both America and Europe. (American Antiquarian Society)

naval officer, Lieutenant Nunn, who was ordered to travel by the first available means, which turned out to be the brig *Sukey*, a slow sailing private vessel that belonged to Boston merchant John Rowe.

The Committee of Safety saw an opportunity, and acted with its usual dispatch. On April 26, it decided to send copies of nearly 100 depositions to London, together with a letter by Dr. Joseph Warren addressed to the "Inhabitants of Great Britain." The Whig leaders sought out Captain John Derby of Salem, owner of the very fast American schooner *Quero*. They also enlisted his sailing master, William Carleton, a skilled seaman with expert knowledge of winds and currents in the North Atlantic. Derby and Carleton were asked to carry the American depositions abroad as swiftly as possible. Confidential instructions from the Congress ordered them to make all speed to the coast in Ireland, then to cross the Irish Sea by stealth, and deliver the documents directly to the Lord Mayor of London, who was known to be sympathetic to the American cause. Captain Derby was told to keep his orders "a profound secret from every person on earth." Their crew was not to be told the purpose of the voyage until they cleared the Grand Banks and were safely in blue water.[48]

*Quero* sailed in ballast on April 29, four days after Gage's ship. So swift was her passage that she reached Southampton May 27, 1775, a full two weeks before *Sukey* straggled in. Captain Derby presented his documents to the Lord Mayor, and the American depositions were instantly published by the London press.[49]

The news caused a sensation. The British government, caught by surprise, was unable to confirm or deny the American accounts. The most powerful impression was made by a deposition from a mortally wounded British officer, who generally supported the American version of events and praised the humanity of his captors. A supporter of Lord North complained that "the Bostonians are now the favourites of all the people of good hearts and weak heads in the kingdom. . . . their saint-like account of the skirmish at Concord, has been read with avidity . . . [and] believed."[50]

Even Lord George Germain, no friend of the colonists, wrote on May 30, "The news from America occasioned a great stir among us yesterday . . . the Bostonians are in the right to make the King's troops the aggressors and claim a victory."[51]

When General Gage's dispatches at last arrived two weeks later, Lord North and his ministers drew the fatal conclusion that the failure in Massachusetts lay not with their own policies, but the man they sent to execute them. Lord Suffolk wrote to Germain, on June 15, "The town is full of private letters from America which contain much more particular accounts of the skirmish than are related by the general. They don't do much credit to the discipline of our troops, but do not impeach their readiness and intrepidity."

Germain wrote back, "I must lament that General Gage, with all his good qualities, finds himself in a situation of too great importance for his talents. . . . I doubt whether Mr. Gage will venture to take a single step beyond his instructions, or whether the troops have that opinion of him as to march with confidence of success."[52]

While the King's ministers in London judged General Gage to be weak and over-scrupulous, the Provincial Congress of Massachusetts condemned him in exactly the opposite way. On May 5, 1775, the Congress passed a sharply-worded resolution: "Whereas, his Excellency General Gage, since his arrival in this Colony, hath conducted as an instrument in the hands of an arbitrary Ministry to enslave this people. . . . Resolved, That the said General Gage hath, by these means, and many others utterly disqualified himself to serve this Colony as a Governor. . . . No obedience ought, in future, to be paid. . . ."[53]

British leaders tried their best to compete in this contest for popular opinion. General Gage himself took a leading role, both in England and America. While the Whig expresses were galloping across the countryside, the British commander in chief dispatched his own messengers with instructions to spread a "true account of all that has passed." These couriers were Loyalist "gentlemen," who were ordered to carry their dispatches directly to governors throughout the colonies.[54]

Altogether, General Gage became as active as the Whig leaders in trying to spread his version of events, but he went about that task in a different way. Where the New England leaders addressed themselves broadly to an entire people, the British commander sent his gentleman-couriers to senior officials. From long habit he preferred to work through a chain of command. He tended to trust others in proportion to their rank, and genuinely believed that the opinion of ruling elites was what really mattered in the world.

Further, Gage preserved his old habits of obsessive secrecy even when he was trying to communicate with others. This was not entirely by choice. Secrecy was forced upon him because the countryside was now strongly hostile, and his messages were intercepted. Gage warned Governor Colden that Whig leaders were "not suffering any letters to pass by the post, but those that would inflame the minds of the people."[55]

Gage's early efforts to make known his own account of the battle took the form of confidential communications to high officials, whom he expected to pull the levers of power in their provinces. Several tried to do so—Governor Trumbull in Connecticut and Governor Colden in New York with an eye to reconciliation; Lord Dunmore in Virginia with more militant purposes in mind. But they found themselves captives of public opinion that New England whigs had done so much to shape. Gage complained bitterly of the "inflammatory expresses from this province," and lamented their success. "They have had the effect the Faction here wished they should have," he wrote.[56]

Still, General Gage kept trying. When private couriers failed to make a difference, he also attempted to put his version of events into print. Once again he had very small success. While governor he had supported Loyalist printers. They failed him in his moment of need. On April 19, Boston had two newspapers that admitted Loyalist pieces. One of them, the *Massachusetts Gazette and Boston Post-Boy,* shut down immediately after the battle. The other waffled. At a time when Whigs were detailing the event in copious detail, the spineless Tory editor of the *Boston News-Letter* told his readers, "The reports concerning this unhappy affair, and the causes that concurred to bring on an Engagement, are so various, that we are not able to collect anything consistent or regular, and cannot therefore with certainty give our readers any further account of this shocking introduction to all the miseries of a Civil War."[57]

When Loyalist printers failed to get out the news, General Gage issued his own broadside, called "A Circumstantial Account of an Attack that happened on the 19th of April, 1775 on his Majesty's troops, by a Number of the People of the Province of Massachusetts Bay." Its argument was summarized in a sentence. "I have shewn them," Gage wrote, "that the people of this Province were the first aggressors, and that the conduct of the leaders here is the cause of all the misfortunes that have happened, or shall arise."[58]

The document was elegantly printed on good paper, and made a handsome appearance. But as an appeal to the public it was not a success. At a time when the Whig leaders were issuing

"The Yankey's Return from Camp" was also called "The Lexington March" after the battle. Like most 18th-century American songs, it borrowed a British tune and developed it in many different forms. This early version, published in 1775, has the same modal rhythm as the tune we know as "Yankee Doodle." American Antiquarian Society.

impassioned appeals to Heaven, Gage offered an arid factual statement—and one in which so many facts were mistaken that a week later this honorable man felt bound to issue his own correction. Worse, his argument was contradictory its substance, and stilted in its style. In describing the search of Concord, for example, Gage wrote, "Neither had any of the people the least occasion to complain, but they were sulky . . ." After thirty years of command, General Gage was not at his best in efforts of popular persuasion. The common touch consistently eluded him.[59]

This second battle of Lexington and Concord was waged not with bayonets but broadsides, not with muskets but depositions, newspapers and sermons. In strictly military terms, the fighting on April 19 was a minor reverse for British arms, and a small success for the New England militia. But the ensuing contest for popular opinion was an epic disaster for the British government, and a triumph for American Whigs. In every region of British America, attitudes were truly transformed by the news of this event.

Before the battle, John Adams had been toiling on a reasoned appeal to the rights of Englishmen, which he published under the significant pen name of *Novanglus*. Later he remembered that the news of Lexington put a sudden end to that project, and instantly "changed the instruments of War from the pen to the sword." John Adams was not a man of violence. He was genuinely shocked by news of the fighting, and deeply troubled by the question of how it began. Immediately after the battle, he saddled his horse and went off to find out for himself, traveling "along the scene of the action for many miles." He picked his way past burial parties and burned-out houses, through crowds of refugees with cartloads of household goods, and marching soldiers with their drums and guns. Everywhere he found "great confusion and distress." It was only a trip of a few miles from Braintree to Lexington, but John Adams later remembered it as one of the great intellectual journeys of his life. He wrote that he "enquired of the inhabitants the circumstances" of the fight, wanting to be sure about what had happened. Later he testified that his inquiries "convinced me that the Die was cast, the Rubicon crossed." John Adams returned from Lexington, went on to the second Continental Congress, and never looked back.[60]

In Pennsylvania, the news from Lexington had a similar effect on an English immigrant who had arrived only the year before. At the age of thirty-seven, Thomas Paine had lost everything in England: his home, two wives, and many jobs. He decided to start again in America, and with the help of a letter from Benjamin Franklin, he found employment in Philadelphia as editor of the *Pennsylvania Magazine*. Suddenly things began to go better for him. Circulation leaped from 600 to 1500 subscribers. Paine threw himself into his work and kept clear of politics. He wrote later that he regarded the Imperial dispute as merely "a kind of law-suit" which "the parties would find a way either to decide or settle." Then the news of Lexington arrived. Paine remembered that "the country into which I had just set my foot, was set on fire about my ears." Afterward he recalled, "No man was a warmer wisher for a reconciliation than myself, before the fatal nineteenth of April, 1775, but the moment the event of that day was known, I rejected the hardened, sullen-tempered Pharaoh of England forever."[61]

In Virginia, April was the planting time in the Potomac valley. The countryside was in bloom, and the air was soft with the scent of Spring. George Washington was working happily on his farm at Mount Vernon when the first report of Lexington arrived. Like many thousands of Americans, he left his fields and gathered up his weapons with a sadness that was widely shared in the colonies. To a close friend he wrote, "Unhappy it is, though, to reflect that a brother's sword has been sheathed in a brother's breast and that the once-happy and peaceful plains of America are either to be drenched with blood or inhabited by a race of slaves. Sad alternative! But can a virtuous man hesitate in his choice?"[62]

Many men, virtuous or not, faced that same choice throughout the colonies. The battles of Lexington and Concord posed it for them in a new way. Long afterward, the novelist Henry James visited the Old North Bridge, and looked back upon that moment of decision. He wrote, "The fight had been the hinge—so one saw it—on which the large revolving future was to turn."[63]

# EPILOGUE

## ❧ The Fate of the Participants

> It seemed as if the war not only required but created talents."
>
> —David Ramsay, 1793

T HE COST turned out to be very high—higher perhaps than our generation would be willing to pay. On both sides, many of the men who fought at Lexington and Concord died in the long and bitter war that followed. In the British infantry, few of the anonymous "other ranks" who marched to Concord survived the conflict unscathed. Many would be dead within two months.

At the battle of Bunker Hill on June 17, 1775, General Gage again used his ten senior companies of grenadiers and light infantry as a *corps d'elite*. They suffered grievously. The grenadier company of the Royal Welch Fusiliers went into that action with three officers, five noncoms, and thirty other ranks. It came out with one corporal and eleven privates. The light infantry company of the same regiment also lost most of its men—so many that it was said, "the Fusiliers had hardly men enough left to saddle their goat."[1]

Other regiments suffered even more severely. The grenadier company of the King's Own counted forty-three officers and men present before the battle of Lexington and Concord. Only twelve of that number were still listed as "effective" after Bunker Hill. Most of the flank companies in General Gage's army also experienced heavy losses.[2]

Altogether, seventy-four British officers had marched to Lex-

ington and Concord. Of that number, at least thirty-three were
killed or severely wounded between April and June in the fighting
around Boston. Others suffered minor wounds that were not
thought to be disabling.

Major John Pitcairn, the commander at Lexington, died of
wounds received at Bunker Hill. As he rallied his Marines for a
third assault on the American redoubt, he was shot in the head by
another veteran of April 19, an African-American militiaman
named Salem Prince. Major Pitcairn was carried off the field by his
own son, an officer in the same battalion, and died in Boston. His
death was mourned even by his enemies, who called him "a good
man in a bad cause." After the war his family asked that his remains should be returned for burial in London. According to an
old Boston tradition, the wrong body was sent by mistake, and
Major Pitcairn may still lie in the blue clay of Boston, or perhaps in
a vault beneath the Old North Church.[3]

Also at Bunker Hill was Lieutenant Jesse Adair, the hard-
charging young Irish Marine who had volunteered to lead the
British vanguard to Lexington, and sent it headlong into Parker's
militia. At Bunker Hill he volunteered again to lead the assault,
though he was not supposed to be there at all, and miraculously
survived. On the day the British army left Boston he volunteered
once more to command its rear guard. His orders were to slow the
American advance by scattering in its path a thick carpet of cal-
trops, or crow's feet, small iron devices shaped like a child's jack,
with needle-sharp spines that could cripple a man or horse. Lieutenant Adair behaved in his usual style, brave and brainless as
ever. An English officer remembered that "being an Irishman, he
began scattering the crow-feet about from the gate towards the
enemy, and of course had to walk over them on his return, which
detained him so long that he was nearly taken prisoner." Adair was
later promoted to captain, and rose to command Number 45 Company of the Royal Marines, in the Plymouth Division. He served
throughout the American war, but was not the sort of officer who
flourished in peace. In 1785 Captain Adair was "reduced," and
disappeared from the Marine List.[4]

Lieutenant-Colonel Francis Smith, who several junior British
officers held personally responsible for their troubles at Lexington
and Concord, was highly praised in dispatches by General Gage.
Afterward he was promoted to brigadier. At the siege of Boston,
Francis Smith's men brought him early notice of the American
occupation of Dorchester Heights. He is reported to have done

nothing, not even bothering to notify his commander of an event that made Boston untenable for the British garrison and forced them to evacuate the town. In the next campaign, at New York City, Smith commanded a brigade. At a critical moment Lieutenant Mackenzie, the able adjutant of the Royal Welch Fusiliers, showed him a way to cut off Washington's retreat. Mackenzie later wrote that the brigadier was not only "slow," but also seemed "more intent on looking out for quarters for himself than preventing the retreat." Afterwards he was promoted again, to the rank of major-general. Historian Allen French observes, perhaps a little harshly, that Francis Smith deserves more credit than he commonly receives, for singlehandedly "losing the American War."[5]

Lord Hugh Percy also fought at New York, with the same skill and courage that he had shown on the retreat from Lexington. He was instrumental in the capture of Fort Washington, the largest surrender of American troops up to that moment, and was promoted to Lieutenant General. But he grew so disgusted with the conduct of the war that he resigned his command and returned to Britain in 1777. Later he inherited the title of Duke of Northumberland. In his mature years he became one of the richest men in England, and also (it was said) one of the most irascible. His ill-temper was attributed to gout; perhaps his experiences in America also played a role. Percy died on July 10, 1817.

Several junior British officers who served at Concord survived the war and rose to high command. In 1775, George Harris was captain of grenadiers at Lexington and Concord. He was severely wounded in the head at Bunker Hill as he led the final assult on the American redoubt. Four of his grenadiers tried to carry him to safety, and three were shot. Harris cried out, "For God's sake let me die in peace." His men succeeded in rescuing him, and he was taken to Boston where a surgeon trepanned his skull while Harris stoically observed the operation by way of a mirror. He survived, returned to duty by 1776, fought in every major battle except Germantown, was severely wounded yet again, saw heavy campaigning in the West Indies, survived a major action at sea, was captured by a French privateer, and shipwrecked on his way to Ireland in 1780. When offered another command in America, he resigned his commission. Later he was persuaded to accept a command in India, where he played so large a part that he was raised to the peerage as Baron Harris of Seringapatam, Mysore, and Belmont in Kent. He died in 1829.

Captain Harris's able subaltern in the grenadiers of the 5th

Foot, Lord Francis Rawdon, survived Bunker Hill with two bullets through his cap. In later actions he rose rapidly to high command, with a record of brilliance and cruelty in the southern campaigns of the American War. In 1783 he was raised to the peerage, promoted to major-general ten years later, and succeeded his father as second Earl of Moira. In 1812 he became British commander in chief in India and governor-general of Bengal.

Another survivor was Ensign Martin Hunter of the 52nd Foot. He served with honor through the American war, commanded his regiment in India, rose to high rank in the Napoleonic wars, married a Scottish heiress, retired as General Sir Martin Hunter, and died full of honors in 1846, probably the last living British officer who had served at Lexington and Concord.[6]

In the Royal Navy, Admiral Samuel Graves continued to rage against the Americans with such undiscriminating fury that after the battles of Lexington and Concord he even had a fistfight with a Loyalist in the streets of Boston. Graves ordered his captains to burn every seaport north of Boston, and the town of Falmouth in Maine was actually destroyed in that way. The burning of Falmouth caused high outrage in America and Britain. Graves was relieved of command in January 1776 and ordered home. He was offered a face-saving assignment ashore, but refused it and died in retirement in 1787.

Several young officers who served under Admiral Graves at Boston went on to distinguished careers in the Royal Navy. Midshipman Cuthbert Collingwood, a "snotty" in Graves's flagship HMS *Preston*, served as a boat commander in the actions around Boston and was promoted for gallantry at Bunker Hill. He went on to become one of Nelson's "band of brothers," assumed command of the British fleet after the battle of Trafalgar, and was raised to the peerage as Lord Collingwood. He died in 1810.

HMS *Somerset*, the mighty warship that blocked Paul Revere's passage across the Charles River, came to a sad end. She was wrecked on the shoals of Cape Cod, and lost with many of her crew. From time to time, even today, the shifting sands of the Cape expose her shattered timbers of English oak, and then decently cover them again. Her heavy guns were salvaged and repaired by Paul Revere.[7]

On the American side, Dr. Joseph Warren was elected president of the Massachusetts Provincial Congress, and appointed general of Massachusetts troops. Shortly before his commission was to take effect, the battle of Bunker Hill occurred. Warren

The bones of HMS *Somerset* lie beneath the shifting sands of Cape Cod, where she was wrecked in a nor'easter on November 2, 1778. In a final irony, her guns were salvaged and repaired by Paul Revere, by then colonel of Massachusetts Artillery. In 1973, her timbers were briefly exposed by another storm, and photographed by Professor Nathaniel Champlin, who has kindly allowed this picture to be used here.

insisted on joining the fight as a private soldier. As on the day of Lexington and Concord, he deliberately sought the place of greatest danger, and during the final assault was killed in the American redoubt. He was buried by Captain Walter Laurie, the British commander at Concord's North Bridge, who later said that he "stuffed the scoundrel with another rebel into one hole, and there he and his seditious principles may remain." Many months later, two of Warren's brothers and the ubiquitous Paul Revere rowed over to Charlestown in search of his remains. They exhumed the body, and identified it by the artifical teeth that Revere had wired into Doctor Warren's jaw. His death was mourned as a national calamity. Paul Revere named his next-born son Joseph Warren Revere.

Captain John Parker, the able commander of Lexington's militia, was so gravely ill of consumption that he was unable to join his men at Bunker Hill. He died on September 17, 1775, at the age of forty-six. His musket passed to his grandson Theodore Parker, and is now an icon of American freedom in the Massachusetts State House.

Many of Parker's company of Lexington militia also died in the war. The Camp Fever took a heavy toll during the siege of Boston. Others died in combat. At the battle of Monmouth, Edmund Munroe and George Munroe were both killed by the same cannon ball, which also took off the leg of Joseph Cox of Lexington. Sergeant William Munroe, who met Revere at the end of the midnight ride, fought in the Saratoga campaign with many other Lexington men, and was present at the surrender of Burgoyne's army. Munroe rose from sergeant to the rank of colonel, then returned to his tavern, where he entertained George Washington at dinner in 1789. He held many high offices in Lexington and died in 1829.

Benjamin Wellington, the Lexington militiaman who was captured by the Regulars on the road to Lexington before the battle, also served at Saratoga. After the war he came home to his farm, and was twice elected selectman of Lexington, where he died in 1812. Lexington's African militiaman, Prince Estabrook, fought as a slave and was wounded on the Common. He won his freedom by his military service.

The last survivor of the Lexington company was the boy fifer Jonathan Harrington, who died in 1854 at the age of ninety-six. More American troops marched in his funeral than had fought at Lexington and Concord.[8]

Jonas Clarke returned to his pulpit and continued to serve his town as minister until his death in 1805. Five of his young daughters married ministers, and raised more ministers in their turn.

Dolly Quincy married John Hancock despite her misgivings, and her husband became president of the Continental Congress and governor of Massachusetts. He died in 1793 at the age of fifty-six, never having realized the promise of his early career. Two children were born of this union, an infant daughter who died in 1776 while John Hancock was presiding at the Congress, and a son named John George Washington Hancock, who was killed in an ice-skating accident at the age of eight. Dolly remarried, to James Scott, a ship's captain who had worked for her husband. She lived to a ripe age, became a great lady in Boston, and dined out on the story of Paul Revere and the salmon for half a century. She died in 1830 at the age of eighty-three.

In Concord, the Reverend William Emerson joined an expedition to Ticonderoga as chaplain to New England troops. He caught a "fever" and died at Rutland, Vermont, on October 20, 1776, at the age of thirty-three. Many years later, his grandson Ralph Waldo Emerson went searching for his grave but found no trace of it. A brick tomb was built for him in Concord, not far from the Old Manse and the North Bridge. It still lies empty today.[9]

Doctor Samuel Prescott, who carried Revere's message to Concord, became a surgeon in the Continental Army, and later joined the crew of a New England privateer. He was captured by the Royal Navy, and held prisoner in Halifax, where he died miserably in 1777, as did many thousands of American prisoners in British hands. His fiancée Lydia Mulliken had no word of him, and waited faithfully until peace came in 1783. Later she married another man, and raised a family in Haverhill, Massachusetts. Lydia's house, where Dr. Prescott had courted her on the night of April 18, was burned by retreating British soldiers. Her brother, Nathaniel Mulliken, joined the army besieging Boston, and in 1776 died of the dreaded Camp Fever that took off many more Yankee militia than British muskets ever did.[10]

Concord's young Doctor Abel Prescott Jr. who carried the alarm to Sudbury and Framingham, lived only a few months after the battle. As he rode home from Sudbury he ran into the British guard at Concord's South Bridge and was shot. The wound did not heal properly and he died in August 1775, of dysentery it was said.[11]

Ammi White, the Concord militiaman who disgraced his nation's cause by murdering a wounded British soldier at the North Bridge, survived the war and married Mary Minot in 1788. They lived in one end of her family's house, which is now the Concord Inn. Later he moved to Westmoreland, New Hampshire, where he died in 1820 at the age of sixty-six.[12]

William Dawes returned to the abandoned farmhouse where he had fallen off his horse, and found his missing watch. He appears to have taken no further part in the events at Lexington and Concord, but joined the army in the siege of Boston, fought at Bunker Hill, and won a commission as Commissary to the Continental Army. At the same time he went into the provisions business, and did well out of the war. But like many veterans he was never in good health after his military service and died at the age of fifty-three, on February 25, 1799. His body lies at King's Chapel in Boston.

Of the men who helped to display the lanterns at Old North Church, John Pulling was closely pursued by British soldiers but escaped by hiding in a wine cask at his mother's home, according to Boston folklore. Later Pulling fled the town disguised as a seaman.

Robert Newman was arrested by British troops at a funeral and imprisoned for a time. He had many troubles after the war, and died by his own hand in 1804.[13]

Doctor Benjamin Church, the spy who worked for both sides, was appointed director of the first American military hospital. He continued his espionage for General Gage until the summer of 1775 when one of his letters was intercepted. He was sentenced to imprisonment in Connecticut, but was permitted to leave America on condition that he should never return to his native land. He sailed for the West Indies on a ship that disappeared at sea. Doctor Church was never seen again. His death was as mysterious as his life.[14]

Four of the Americans who were at Lexington and Concord on April 19 went on to become governors of Massachusetts: John Hancock, Samuel Adams, Elbridge Gerry, and John Brooks. Gerry, who was nearly caught by the British troops the night before the battle at the Black Horse Tavern in Menotomy, later became an Anti-Federalist and Jeffersonian Democrat. He served as governor from 1810 to 1812, and was elected Vice President of the United States under James Madison. He died in 1814, on his way to a session of the Senate. John Brooks, the physician who led the Reading militia at Meriam's Corner, became a leader of the Federalist party, and was elected to six terms as governor from 1817 to 1822.

Woburn's Major Loammi Baldwin, who had shown a keen eye for the ground along the Battle Road, went on to become one of America's first professional topographical engineers. In 1794 he built the Middlesex Canal between the Charles and Merrimack rivers, the first important canal in America. On his farm in Woburn he also developed the Baldwin apple, which for many generations became the "standard winter apple of eastern America."[15]

Most of the Americans who fought at Lexington and Concord went back to the farms that their fathers had tilled before them. But things were never the same for them again. For the men who were there, the countryside was haunted by spirits of those who had fought and died. It was said of Concord's David Brown, who commanded the town's company of minutemen, that "the brave captain never crossed alone the causeway of the North

Bridge after dark on his way to and from the market, without singing at the top of his voice some good old psalm tune that would ring out in the night, and wake many a sleeper in the village, perhaps to lay the ghosts of the British soldiers buried there, perhaps as a requiem to their souls."[16]

The next generation, the children who heard the Lexington alarm but were too young to fight, grew up to be the statesmen of America's silver age. Their experience on the day of Lexington and Concord made a difference in their lives. At Braintree, Massachusetts, for example, a company of militia stopped at a farm on its way to the battle. The men were amused when an eight-year-old boy emerged from the house with a musket taller than himself, and performed the manual of arms before them. The child was John Quincy Adams. The nationalism that became central to his public career had its beginning in those early experiences. There were many others like him of the same age.[17]

Some of the most interesting careers were those of the third generation, who had no direct knowledge of the event. In the years just after war, they were raised on grandfathers' tales of Lexington and Concord, and went on to become great tale-tellers in their own right. The grandson of Paul Revere's friend Thomas Melville, who came home from the Boston Tea Party with his shoes full of tea, was the novelist Herman Melville. The grandson of Concord's minister William Emerson was Ralph Waldo Emerson. The grandson of Private John Thoreau, who served under Paul Revere's command later in the Revolution, was Henry David Thoreau. The grandson of Lexington's Captain John Parker was Theodore Parker. The grandson of Peleg Wadsworth, Revere's commander on the Penobscot Expedition, was Henry Wadsworth Longfellow. The grandson of a North Shore family named Hathorne who turned out for the Lexington alarm changed his name to Nathaniel Hawthorne and moved into the Old Manse next to the North Bridge. All the great literary figures of the American Renaissance except the New Yorker Walt Whitman and the southerner Edgar Allan Poe were grandchildren of men who served with Paul Revere or soldiered at Lexington and Concord.

There was also another group of Americans who took the opposite side in the War of Independence and experienced some of the worst sufferings of the war. Few of their countrymen felt much sympathy for them. William Brattle, whose letter to General Gage led to the Powder Alarm, was never able to return to his mansion in Cambridge. When the British army left Boston, Brattle went to Halifax, where he and other Loyalists "mess'd together in a little chamber over a grog shop." He died there in the Fall of 1776. In Cambridge his mansion still stands, and is now the Cambridge Center for Adult Education. Another Tory house, which had been besieged by 4000 angry men in the Powder Alarm, became the residence of Harvard's Dean of Faculty, and survived other sieges in the era of Vietnam and Watergate.

Daniel Bliss, the Tory lawyer in Concord who showed Ensign De Berniere and Captain Brown the route that the Regulars used to march upon his town, was never able to live in that community again. He fled to Boston, and later moved to New Brunswick in company with many other Loyalists, who had a major impact on Canada's history and politics. His estate was the only Tory property to be confiscated in Concord.

General Gage's American wife Margaret Kemble Gage was sent to England by her husband in the summer of 1775. She sailed in the transport *Charming Nancy*, with sixty widows and orphans and 170 severely wounded British soldiers who were bound for the Royal Hospital at Chelsea. It was a terrible voyage. When the ship put into the English port of Plymouth for a new mainmast, a correspondent in that town reported that "a few of the men came on shore, when never hardly were seen such objects! Some without legs, and others without arms; and their cloaths hanging on them like a loose morning gown, so much were they fallen away by sickness and want of proper nourishment. . . . the vessel itself, though very large, was almost intolerable, from the stench arising from the sick and wounded."[18]

General Gage remained in Boston for another catastrophic year. He was the British commander during the battle of the Bunker Hill, adding one more epic disaster to his long experience of defeat. Even that event did not end his career. He was reappointed to his command in August 1775, but in Boston his own officers refused to obey him. Finally, in October, he was recalled and sailed home from America, never to return. In Britain, he continued to hold the title of Royal Governor of Massachusetts even after American independence, and following Lord North's fall from power was promoted yet again to full general. After returning to London, he was estranged from his wife. In 1787 Thomas Gage died at his London home, and was buried at Firle Place, in his beloved Sussex countryside.

Paul Revere's life took a different path. In 1776 he joined the army with the rank of lieutenant-colonel, and was made commander of Castle William, with the urgent task of fortifying Boston against the expected British return. He desperately wanted a field command with the Continental Army and pulled every string to get one, but without result. In 1777 he complained to his old friend John Lamb, "I did expect before this to have been in the Continental Army, but do assure you I have never been taken notice of, by those whom I thought my friends, [and] am obliged to remain in this state's service."[19]

Twice during the war Paul Revere went on active service with state troops in New England. In 1778 he joined an abortive campaign against the British garrison on Rhode Island, as lieutenant-colonel of Massachusetts artillery. The following year he commanded the artillery in an ill-fated expedition by Massachusetts troops against a British fort at Penobscot Bay. The mission ended in disaster for the Americans, and led to an angry controversy in which he was deeply involved. Paul Revere's brief military career was the one great failure in his life.[20]

After the war Paul Revere returned to his ruined business. His silver shop expanded rapidly, shifting from custom work to standardized production. One scholar writes that Paul Revere "played an active role in not one, but two, revolutions: the War of Independence, and the nascent industrialization of American silversmithing."[21] Revere added other lines of business with mixed success. For a time he tried his hand at selling hardware, but found that business tedious and dull, and gave it up. More interesting to his restless and curious mind was the science of metallurgy, which he began to study after the war. He wrote for help to experts abroad, telling them candidly that he did not know much about "chemistree."[22]

While his son looked after the silver shop, Paul Revere taught himself to cast bell-metal, and opened a foundry in the North End for the manufacture of church bells in New England. He was just in time for a religious revival that historians call the second great awakening, and business boomed. The youngsters of the North End liked to visit Paul Revere in his bell foundry, gathering so close that he had to warn them away from the hammers and flames. Many years later, one of them remembered the old "founder," as he now called himself, prodding them cheerfully with his silver-headed cane and telling them with a laugh, "Take care, boys! If that hammer should hit your head, you'd ring louder than these bells do!"[23]

He also invented new alloys and amalgams, studied the latest

Paul Revere at the age of
seventy-seven in June
1813. His son Joseph
Warren Revere paid the
American artist Gilbert
Stuart $200 for these
paintings of his parents in
old age. Museum of Fine
Arts, Boston

European techniques, and became one of the first manufacturers
in America to roll copper sheets on a large scale. Paul Revere's
copper covered the top of the new Massachusetts Statehouse, and
the bottom of frigate *Constitution*. He made the boilerplate for
Robert Fulton's steamboats, and cannon for the forts and warships
of the new Federal government. Later he moved his business to
the rural town of Canton, where it expanded into the Revere Copper and Brass Company, one of New England's largest manufac-
turing enterprises.[24]

After the war Paul Revere also continued active in politics. He
was appalled by the disorders of the postwar period, and threw his
influence behind the framing of a Federal Constitution. When
John Hancock and Samuel Adams were reluctant to support its
ratification, Paul Revere organized the Boston mechanics into a
powerful political force, and worked behind the scenes with such
effect that he is commonly thought to have turned the narrow
balance in a critical state. Once again, he showed his genius for
being at the center of great events. His nation owes him another
debt for his role in the enactment of the new government.

During the early Republic, the Whig leaders of the American

Rachel Revere was sixty-seven years old when she sat for this painting. She died a few weeks later on June 26, 1813. (Museum of Fine Arts, Boston)

Revolution divided into two political parties. Revere's cousin Benjamin Hitchborn became a leader of the Jeffersonian Republicans in Massachusetts. Paul Revere himself was a Federalist of the old school, strongly opposed to the growth of Jeffersonian democracy. He wrote to an old comrade, "My friend, you know I always was a warm Republican. I always deprecated Democracy as much as I did Aristocracy."[25]

In old age, when young men began to wear pantaloons and top hats, Paul Revere continued to dress in knee britches and a cocked hat. In his last years he retired to a country estate next to his factory at Cantondale, surrounded by his large and growing family. More than fifty grandchildren had been born by the time of his death. Today his descendants are reckoned in thousands. When they return to visit the Revere House in Boston, the staff observes that many bear an uncanny resemblence to the portrait by John Singleton Copley.

Paul Revere died in the New England Spring, on May 10, 1818. His loss was mourned in Massachusetts as the passing of an age, but the myth and legend of his acts was only beginning its long career. Today, a long stretch of the road that he traveled on his midnight ride is a National Park. The anniversary of the ride and battle is still kept as a public holiday called Patriots' Day in Massachusetts and Maine. Every year since the battle itself, the event continues to be celebrated with what a 19th-century writer described as "new and old rehearsals of what occurred at the North Bridge at Concord, with the ringing of bells, the firing of salutes, the parade of military, orations, bonfires and general glorification."[26]

That custom of "general glorification" is still observed in the author's town of Wayland, the seat of the original Sudbury from which five companies of militia and minutemen marched to Concord. In some ways, the town itself has changed profoundly since 1775. Only a small minority of its inhabitants are of Yankee stock. A plurality of the church-going population is Roman Catholic, as in every county of New England. On the Boston Post Road where Ensign De Berniere stumbled through snowdrifts and the post-rider Israel Bissell carried his news of the battle, one finds today a gleaming Jewish synagogue on one side of the old highway, and a new Islamic mosque on the other.

Much has changed in this old New England town, but some things remain the same. On weekdays the people are still busy in their callings, and on Sundays the churches are as full as they were two centuries ago. The town meeting has moved to the high school

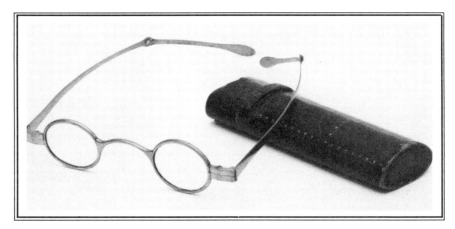

Near the end of his life, Paul Revere attended a meeting of a voluntary association in Boston, and absent-mindedly left his eyeglasses behind. They were picked up by someone else and found their way back to the Paul Revere House, where they may be seen today, as if he had dropped them only a moment ago. (Paul Revere Memorial Association)

gymnasium, but still operates very much as it did in 1774, when Parliament unwisely tried to curtail it. The common schools continue to be open to "the children of all," and the newspapers still exercise their ancestral right to rage against the government. The town has become a suburb of Boston, but it does not think of itself as subordinate to anything, and remembers its long history with fierce and stubborn pride.

Each year, that old memory is carefully renewed. On the 19th day of every April, at the same hour when the messenger of alarm arrived in 1775, the town's great bell is made to ring again in the night. The people of the town awaken suddenly in their beds, and listen, and remember. It is an ancient tradition in the town that the ringers should include the children, so that the rising generation will remember too. The bell itself was made by Paul Revere. Still it carries his message across the countryside.[27]

# APPENDIX A

### ✎ The Revere Family

Apollos Rivoire, the father of Paul Revere, was born in the parish of Sainte-Foy-la-Grande, France, Nov. 20, 1702, and died in Boston, July 22, 1754. On June 19, 1729, he married Deborah Hitchborn, who was born in Boston on Jan. 25, 1704, and died there on May 23, 1777. Twelve children were born of this marriage:

John Revere, born Jan. 10, 1730; died Dec. 1730.
Deborah Revere, born Feb. 21, 1732; died after 1763;
    she married Thomas Metcalf.
Paul Revere, born Dec. 21, 1734, baptized Dec. 22, 1735; died
    May 10, 1818.
Frances Revere, born June 11, 1736; died before March 1763;
    she married Edward Calleteau.
twin sons, born 1737?; both died "young."
Thomas Revere, baptized Aug. 27, 1738; died "young."
Thomas Revere, born Jan. 10, 1739/40; died in military
    service, *ca.* Oct. 1779; he married Mary [Churchill?].
John Revere, born Oct. 2, 1741, died July 8, 1808;
    he was a tailor; he married (1) Anna Clemens and (2) Silence Ingerfield.
Mary Revere, born July 10, 1743; died in Boston, Dec. 27, 1801;
    she married (1) Edward Rose and (2) Alexander Baker
Elizabeth Revere, born July 10, 1743; died July 20, 1743.
Elizabeth Revere, born Jan. 19, 1745; died Jan. 8, 1811;
    she married David Moseley.

Paul Revere married (1) Sarah Orne, Aug. 17, 1757. She was born in Boston on April 7, 1736, and died there on May 3, 1773, aged 37. They had eight children:

Deborah Revere, born April 8, 1758; died Jan. 8, 1797.
    She married Amos Lincoln, a carpenter and mason, and master workman in charge of construction for the Massachusetts State House. They had nine children.
Paul Revere, born Jan. 6, 1760; died Jan. 16, 1813.
    He became a silversmith and bell founder; he married Sally Edwards; they had twelve children.
Sarah Revere, born Jan. 3, 1762; died July 5, 1791.
    She married John Bradford.
Mary Revere, born March 31, 1764; died April 30 1765.
Frances Revere, born Feb. 19, 1766; died June 19, 1799.
    She married Thomas Stevens Eayres, a silversmith; they had five children.
Mary Revere, born March 19, 1768; died Aug. 12, 1853.
    She married Jedidiah Lincoln, a "wood-wharfinger" and "housewright"; they had seven children.
Elizabeth Revere, born Dec. 5, 1770; died April 1805.
    She married her brother-in-law Amos Lincoln, a carpenter and mason, after the death of her sister Deborah; they had five children.
Isanna Revere, born Dec. 15, 1772; died Sept. 19, 1773.

Paul Revere's second marriage, Oct. 10, 1773, was to Rachel Walker. She was born in Boston, Dec. 27, 1745, and died there June 26, 1813. They had eight children:

Joshua Revere, born Dec. 7, 1774; died Aug. 14, 1801.
    He was a "merchant," in business with his father.
John Revere, born June 13, 1776, died June 27, 1776.

Joseph Warren Revere, born April 30, 1777; died Oct. 12, 1868.

> He took over the copper business from his father in 1810, and married Mary Robbins; they had eight children.

Lucy Revere, born May 15, 1780; died July 9, 1780.

Harriet Revere, born July 20, 1782, died June 28, 1860.

> She never married, and lived with her brothers Joseph and John.

John Revere, born Dec. 25, 1783; died March 13, 1786.

Maria Revere, born July 14, 1785, died at Singapore, Aug. 22, 1847.

> She married Joseph Balestier, U.S. Consul in Singapore, and a planter in Malaya; they had one child.

John Revere, born March 27, 1787, died in New York April 29 or 30, 1847.

> He graduated from Harvard in 1807, studied medicine at Edinburgh, and became a professor of medicine at Jefferson Medical College and the University of the City of New York. He married Lydia Lebaron Goodwin; they had four children.

Paul Revere had at least 51 grandchildren (as enumerated above). Among them were John Revere, who became president of the Revere Copper Company; Grace Revere, who married in succession Dr. Samuel Gross and Sir William Osler, two of the leading surgeons in the Western world; Edward Hutchinson Revere, who joined the 20th Massachusetts Regiment in the Civil War and was killed at Antietam; Paul Joseph Revere, who also served in the 20th Massachusetts and died of wounds at Gettysburg; and Joseph Warren Revere, a brigadier general of Union troops.

SOURCE: Donald M. Nielsen, "The Revere Family," *NEHGR* 145 (1991): 291–316; Patrick M. Leehey, "Reconstructing Paul Revere: An Overview of His Life, Ancestry and Work," in Nina Zannieri, Patrick M. Leehey, *et al., Paul Revere—Artisan, Businessman, and Patriot; The Man Behind the Myth* (Boston, 1988), 15–39.

# APPENDIX B

### ❧ The Hitchborn Family

The first of this line in America was David Hitchborn, who migrated in 1641 from Boston, Lincolnshire, to Boston, Massachusetts, with his wife Catherine and infant son Thomas.

This son, Thomas Hitchborn I (b. 1640), was a man of humble but independent rank. He makes a fleeting appearance as "Hitchborn, Drummer" in the diary of Samuel Sewall (I, 138, April 25, 1687). He and his wife Ruth married before 1673, and had several children. Sewall recorded on June 22, 1691, that "Tom Hitchborn's son died this day" (I, 279).

A surviving son, Thomas Hitchborn II (1673–1731), was a joiner and boatbuilder. He prospered in his calling, became proprietor of Hitchborn's wharf, and was given a license for the sale of spiritous liquors. He married Frances Pattishall (1679–1749), who inherited the wharf and liquor license from her husband. They had at least six children:

> Thomas Hitchborn III (1703–77) became a boatbuilder and inherited the wharf. He married Isannah Fadree; they had at least ten children.
>
> Deborah Hitchborn (1704–77) married the goldsmith Apollos Rivoire and became the mother of the Patriot Paul Revere.
>
> Frances Hitchborn (born 1706) married Joseph Douglass.
>
> Nathaniel Hitchborn died "young."
>
> Richard Hitchborn died "young."

Mary Hitchborn (1713–1778) married Captain Phillip Marrett. They had at least one son, Phillip Marrett, who later served under Paul Revere's command in the War of Independence.

Thomas Hitchborn III (1703–77), the only surviving son of that union, and his wife Isannah Fadree had at least ten children, of whom nine lived past infancy. These were Paul Revere's Hitchborn cousins, with whom he played as a child:

Thomas Hitchborn IV (b. 1733) became a boatbuilder like his father, and proprietor of Hitchborn wharf.

Nathaniel Hitchborn (1734–96), also a boatbuilder, married Elizabeth King, prospered in his trade, and bought a three-story brick home in the North End, two doors from his cousin Paul Revere on North Square.

Frances Hitchborn (b. 1737) married (1) Thomas Fosdick, the hatter with whom Paul Revere had fisticuffs; and (2) John Glover, a rich merchant and Whig leader in Marblehead, who became the colonel of a famous fighting regiment of Marblehead mariners and later a general in the Continental army.

William Hitchborn (b. 1739), a hatter.

Robert Hitchborn (b. 1740), a sailmaker, who fell on hard times and borrowed money from Paul Revere for his children's schooling.

Mary Hitchborn (b. 1742) married a Captain Greeley.

Phillip Hitchborn (b. 1744) was apprenticed to a master tailor and died in his youth.

Benjamin Hitchborn (1746–1817) graduated from Harvard College in 1768, became an eminent lawyer, state senator and an associate of Paul Revere in many civic activities. He was the principal figure in a great Boston scandal. In 1779, Hitchborn was with his friend Benjamin Andrews. Hitchborn testified that he was handing Andrews a pistol to take on a trip when it went off, mortally wounding the latter. A year later Benjamin Hitchborn married Andrews' beautiful widow Hannah.

Samuel Hitchborn (b. 1752) was apprenticed to Paul Revere and became a prosperous silversmith. In 1817 President Monroe visited his home while in Boston.

Isannah Hitchborn (b. 1754), married Stephen Bruce.

NOTE: The family name was variously spelled Hitchbourn, Hichborn, Hitchbon, etc.

SOURCE: Patrick M. Leehey, "Reconstructing Paul Revere: An Overview of His Life, Ancestry and Work," in Nina Zannieri, Patrick M. Leehey, *et al.*, *Paul Revere—Artisan, Businessman, and Patriot; The Man Behind the Myth* (Boston, 1988), 15–39.

# APPENDIX C

### ❧ Paul Revere's Revolutionary Rides: Research by Michael Kalin

| Date | From | To | Duration | Purpose of trip |
| --- | --- | --- | --- | --- |
| 17 Dec.73 | Boston | New York & Phila. | 10 days | Explaining Tea Party |
| | Phila. | New York & Boston | | Concerting responses |
| 14 May 74 | Boston | New York & Phila. | | News of Intolerable Acts |
| | Phila. | New York, Hartford & Boston | | Response of Colonies |
| Summer 74 | Boston | New York | | Meetings with Whig leaders |
| | New York | Boston | | "for calling a Congress" |

| Date | From | To | Duration | Purpose of trip |
|------|------|-----|----------|-----------------|
| 11 Sep. 74 | Boston | Milton | 3 hours | Pick up Suffolk Resolves |
| 11 Sep. 74 | Milton | New York & Phila. | 6 days | Suffolk Resolves to Congress |
| 18 Sep. 74 | Phila. | Boston | 5 days | Congressional response |
| 29 Sep. 74 | Boston | Phila. | 6 days? | Response to British measures |
| 11 Oct. 74 | Phila. | Boston | 7 days? | Congressional resolves |
| 12 Dec. 74 | Boston | Portsmouth, N.H. | 1 day | Warning of British Attack |
| 13 Dec. 74 | Portsmouth | Boston | 1 day | |
| 26 Jan. 75 | Boston | Exeter, N.H. | 1 day? | Liaison with N.H.Congress |
| | Exeter | Boston | | |
| 7 Apr. 75 | Boston | Concord | 1 day | Warning to move stores |
| | Concord | Boston | | |
| 16 Apr. 75 | Boston | Lexington | 1 day | Meeting with town leaders |
| | Lexington | Charlestown | | |
| | Charlestown | Boston | | |
| 18 Apr. 75 | Boston | Lexington & Concord | 4 hours | Warning of British march captured in Lincoln |
| 20 Apr. 75 7 May 75 | Mass | Various places | 17 days | "Out of doors work" for the Committeee of Safety |
| 12 Nov. 75 | Boston | Philadelphia | 7 days | Studying methods for the |
| 24 Nov. 75 | Phila | Boston | 7 days | manufacture of munitions |

SOURCES: On Revere's ride after the Tea Party, Boston diarist John Boyle noted, "Mr. Paul Revere was immediately dispatched express to New-York and Philadelphia with the glorious intelligence," ("Boyle's Journal of Occurrences in Boston," Dec. 16, 1773, *NEHGR* 84 (1930): 371). He did not actually depart until Dec. 17. Ten days later, Boyle wrote, "Mr. Paul Revere returned from New-York and Philadelphia, performing his journey in a much shorter time than could be expected at this season of the year" (Dec. 27, 1773, *ibid.*, 372). Other documentation is in the diary of Thomas Newell, MHS; and the papers of Samuel Adams, NYPL.

The ride with news of the Boston Port Act is documented in Thomas Young to John Lamb, 1774, Lamb Papers, NYHS; Boston Committee of Correspondence to Philadelphia Committee, May 13, 1774, Cushing ed., *Writings of Samuel Adams,* II, 109–11; the *Essex Gazette,* May 30, 1774, noted Revere's return "on Saturday last [May 28]."Paul Revere's receipt for reimbursement, dated May 28, 1774, "for a journey to King's Bridge, New York, 234 miles," is in the Revere Family Papers, MHS.

The journey to New York in the Summer of 1774 "for calling a Congress is referred to in Paul Revere's letter to Jeremy Belknap, 1798. He appears to have traveled by sulky; see Paul Revere to John Lamb, Sept. 4, 1774, thanking "Capt. Sears, for his kind care of my horse and sulky," in Lamb Papers, NYHS.

The trip to the Continental Congress on Sept. 11, 1774, with the Suffolk Resolves is noted in Samuel Adams to Charles Chauncy, Sept. 19, 1774: "last Friday [Sept. 16] Mr. Revere brought us the spirited and patriotick resolves of your county of Suffolk." Cushing (ed.), *Writing of Samuel Adams,* III, 155. He left Philadelphia on Sept. 18, when Adams noted in his diary, "Wrote many letters to go by Mr. Revere." William Tudor in Boston noted that Revere was back in Boston "late on Friday evening [Sept. 23]. William Tudor to John Adams, Sept. 17, 26, 1774, Taylor (ed.), *Papers of John Adams,* II, 166, 174.

Revere departed again for Philadelphia on Sept. 29, 1774. John Adams wrote to his wife on Oct. 7, 1774, "Mr Revere will bring you the doings of the Congress, who are now all around me..." and to William Tudor, on the same day, "I have just time to thank you for your letters by Mr. Revere" (*ibid.,* 187). Revere left Philadelphia about Oct. 11, and was back in Boston before Oct. 19, with the resolves of the Congress (John Andrews to William Barrell, Oct. 19, 1774, Goss, *Revere,* I, 169).

On the ride to the New Hampshire Congress, see John Wentworth to T. W. Waldron, Jan. 27, 1775, *MHSC* IV (1891). The journey to Portsmouth, N.H., is documented on p. 381 below; the three trips to Concord and Lexington, on pp. 385 and 386, above.

The "out of doors work" for the Committee of Safety is documented in Revere's letter to Belknap (1798), and in a bill and receipt for expenses in the Massachusetts Archives, Boston. See also p. 268 above.

The munitions mission is in Robert Morris and John Dickinson to Oswell Eve, Nov. 21, 1775, Smith (ed.), *Letters of Delegates to Congress.* Revere's pass, signed by James Otis and dated November 12, 1775, is in the PRMA, and reproduced in Zannieri, Leehey, *et al., Paul Revere,* 178.

Appendix C Sources (*Cont.*)

Forbes mistakenly asserts (and Weisberger and others repeat after her) that Revere made his first ride on Nov. 30, 1773. "It was decided that neighboring seaports should be warned that the tea ships might try to unload at their wharves. Paul Revere and five other men were chosen to ride express (Forbes, *Revere*, 190). In this she is inaccurate. A meeting at Old South voted that six persons "who are used to horses be in readiness to give an alarm in the country towns, where necessary." They were William Rogers, Jeremiah Belknap, Stephen Hall, Nathaniel Cobbett and Thomas Gooding of Boston, and Benjamin Wood of Charlestown. See Drake, *Tea Leaves*, xlv.

Forbes also has Revere riding back to Boston after the battle of April 19, 1775. This too is unsupported by evidence.

# APPENDIX D

## ～ Paul Revere's Role in the Revolutionary Movement

The structure of Boston's revolutionary movement, and Paul Revere's place within it, were very different from recent secondary accounts. Many historians have suggested that this movement was a tightly organized, hierarchical organization, controlled by Samuel Adams and a few other dominant figures. These same interpretations commonly represent Revere as a minor figure who served his social superiors mainly as a messenger.

A very different pattern emerges from the following comparison of seven groups: the Masonic lodge that met at the Green Dragon Tavern; the Loyal Nine, which was the nucleus of the Sons of Liberty; the North Caucus that met at the Salutation Tavern; the Long Room Club in Dassett Alley; the Boston Commitee of Correspondence; the men who are known to have participated in the Boston Tea Party; and Whig leaders on a Tory Enemies List.

A total of 255 men were in one or more of these seven groups. Nobody appeared on all seven lists, or even as many as six. Two men, and only two, were in five groups; they were Joseph Warren and Paul Revere, who were unique in the breadth of their associations.

Other multiple memberships were as follows. Five men (2.0%) appeared in four groups each: Samuel Adams, Nathaniel Barber, Henry Bass, Thomas Chase, and Benjamin Church. Seven men (2.7%) turned up on three lists (James Condy, Moses Grant, Joseph Greenleaf, William Molineux, Edward Proctor, Thomas Urann, and Thomas Young). Twenty-seven individuals (10.6%) were on two lists (John Adams, Nathaniel Appleton, John Avery, Samuel Barrett, Richard Boynton, John Bradford, Ezekiel Cheever, Adam Collson, Samuel Cooper, Thomas Crafts, Caleb Davis, William Dennie, Joseph Eayrs, William Greenleaf, John Hancock, James Otis, Elias Parkman, Samuel Peck, William Powell, John Pulling, Josiah Quincy, Abiel Ruddock, Elisha Story, James Swan, Henry Welles, Oliver Wendell, and John Winthrop). The great majority, 211 of 255 (82.7%), appeared only on a single list. Altogether, 94.1% were in only one or two groups.

This evidence strongly indicates that the revolutionary movement in Boston was more open and pluralist than scholars have believed. It was not a unitary organization, but a loose alliance of many overlapping groups. That structure gave Paul Revere and Joseph Warren a special importance, which came from the multiplicity and range of their alliances.

None of this is meant to deny the preeminence of other men in different roles. Samuel Adams was specially important in managing the Town Meeting, and the machinery of local government, and was much in the public eye. Otis was among its most impassioned orators. John Adams was the penman of the Revolution. John Hancock was its "milch cow," as a Tory described him. But Revere and Warren moved in more circles than any others. This gave them their special roles as the linchpins of the revolutionary movement—its communicators, coordinators, and organizers of collective effort in the cause of freedom.

The following table does not include all the many associations in Boston that were part of the revolutionary movement. Another list (too long to be included here) survives of 355 Sons of Liberty who met at the Liberty Tree in Dorchester in 1769. Once again, Paul Revere appears on it. There were at least two other Masonic lodges in Boston at various periods before and during the Revolution; Paul Revere is known to have belonged to at least one of them. In addition to the North Caucus, there was also a South Caucus and a Middle Caucus. Paul Revere may or may not have belonged to them as well; some men joined more than one. No definitive lists of members have been found. But it is known that Revere was a member of a committee of five appointed "to wait on the South End caucus and the Caucus in the middle part of town," and that he met with them (Goss, *Revere*, II, 639). Several Boston taverns were also centers of Whig activity. Revere had connections with at least two of them—Cromwell's Head, and the Bunch of Grapes. The printing office of Benjamin Edes was another favorite rendezvous. In the most graphic description of a gathering there by John Adams, once again Paul Revere was recorded as being present.

In sum, the more we learn about the range and variety of political associations in Boston, the more open, complex and pluralist the revolutionary movement appears, and the more important (and significant) Paul Revere's role becomes. He was not *the* dominant or controlling figure. Nobody was in that position. The openness and diversity of the movement were the source of his importance.

| Name | St. Andrews Lodge 1762 | Loyal Nine 1766 | North Caucus 1771 | Long Room Club 1773 | Tea Party 1773 | Boston Committee of Correspondence 1774 | London Enemies List 1775 |
|---|---|---|---|---|---|---|---|
| Adams, John | | | X | X | | | |
| Adams, Samuel | | | X | X | | X | X |
| Allen, Dr. | | | X | | | | |
| Appleton, Nathaniel | | | X | | | X | |
| Ash, Capt. Gilbert | X | | | | | | |
| Austin, Benjamin | | | | | | | X |
| Austin, Samuel | | | | | | | X |
| Avery, John | | X | | | | | X |
| Baldwin, Cyrus | | | | | | | X |
| Ballard, John | | | X | | | | |
| Barber, Nathaniel | | | X | | X | X | X |
| Barnard, Samuel | | | | | X | | |
| Barrett, Samuel | X | | | | | | X |
| Bass, Henry | | X | X | | X | | X |
| Bell, Capt. William | X | | | | | | |
| Blake, Increase | X | | | | | | |
| Boit, John | | | | X | | | |
| Bolter, Thomas | | | | | X | | |
| Boyer, Peter | | | | | | | X |
| Boynton, Richard | | | | | | X | X |
| Brackett, Jos. | | | | | | | X |
| Bradford, John | | | | | | X | X |
| Bradlee, David | | | | | X | | |
| Bradlee, Josiah | | | | | X | | |
| Bradlee, Nathaniel | | | | | X | | |
| Bradlee, Thomas | | | | | X | | |
| Bray, George | X | | | | | | |

| Name | St. Andrews Lodge 1762 | Loyal Nine 1766 | North Caucus 1771 | Long Room Club 1773 | Tea Party 1773 | Boston Committee of Correspondence 1774 | London Enemies List 1775 |
|---|---|---|---|---|---|---|---|
| Breck, William | | | X | | | | |
| Brewer, James | | | | | X | | |
| Brimmer, Herman | | | | | | | X |
| Brimmer, Martin | | | | | | | X |
| Broomfield, Henry | | | | | | | X |
| Brown, Capt. Hugh | X | | | | | | |
| Brown, Enoch | | | | | | | X |
| Brown, John | | | | | | | X |
| Bruce, Stephen | | | | | X | | |
| Burbeck, Edward | X | | | | | | |
| Burbeck, William | X | | | | | | |
| Burt, Benjamin | | | X | | | | |
| Burton, Benjamin | | | | | X | | |
| Cailleteau, Capt. Edward | X | | | | | | |
| Callender, Elisha | X | | | | | | |
| Campbell, Nicholas | | | | | X | | |
| Cazneau, Capt. | | | X | | | | |
| Chadwell, Mr. | | | X | | | | |
| Champney, Caleb | | | X | | | | |
| Chase, Thomas | | X | X | | X | | X |
| Cheever, Ezekiel | | | X | | | | X |
| Chipman, Capt. Seth | X | | | | | | |
| Chrysty, Thomas | | | X | | | | |
| Church, Benjamin | | | X | X | | X | X |
| Clarke, Benjamin | | | | | X | | |
| Cleverly, Stephen | | X | | | | | |
| Cochran, John | | | | | X | | |
| Colesworthy, Gilbert | | | | | X | | |
| Collier, Gershom | | | | | X | | |
| Collins, Ezra | X | | | | | | |
| Collson, Adam | | | X | | X | | |
| Condy, James Foster | | | X | | X | | X |
| Cooper, Samuel | | | | X | X | | |
| Cooper, William | | | | X | | | |
| Crafts, Thomas | X | X | | | | | |
| Crane, John | | | | | X | | |
| Davis, Caleb | | | | | | X | X |
| Davis, Edward | | | | | | | X |
| Davis, Major Robert | | | | | X | | |
| Davis, William | | | | | | | X |
| Dawes, Thomas | | | | X | | | |
| Dennie, William | | | X | | | X | |
| Deshon, Moses | X | | | | | | |
| Dexter, Samuel | | | | X | | | |
| Dolbear, Edward | | | | | X | | |
| Doyle, Capt. Peter | X | | | | | | |
| Eaton, Capt. Joseph | | | | | X | | |
| Eayres, Joseph | | | | | X | | X |

| Name | St. Andrews Lodge 1762 | Loyal Nine 1766 | North Caucus 1771 | Long Room Club 1773 | Tea Party 1773 | Boston Committee of Correspondence 1774 | London Enemies List 1775 |
|---|---|---|---|---|---|---|---|
| Eckley, _____ | | | | | X | | |
| Edes, Benjamin | | X | X | | | | |
| Emmes, Samuel | | | X | | | | |
| Etheridge, William | | | | | X | | |
| Fenno, Samuel | | | | | X | | |
| Ferrell, Capt. Ambrose | X | | | | | | |
| Field, Capt. Joseph | | X | | | | | |
| Flagg, Josiah | X | | | | | | |
| Fleet, Thomas | | | | X | | | |
| Foster, Bos. | | | | | | | X |
| Foster, Capt. Samuel | | | | | X | | |
| Frothingham, Nathaniel | | | | | X | | |
| Gammell, John | | | | | X | | |
| Gill, Moses | | | | | | | X |
| Gore, Samuel | | | | | X | | |
| Gould, William | X | | | | | | |
| Graham, James | X | | | | | | |
| Grant, Moses | | | X | | X | | X |
| Gray, Capt. Wait | X | | | | | | |
| Greene, Nathaniel | | | | | X | | |
| Greenleaf, Joseph | | | X | | | X | X |
| Greenleaf, William | | | | | | X | X |
| Greenough, Newn | | | | | | | X |
| Ham, William | X | | | | | | |
| Hammond, Samuel | | | | | X | | |
| Hancock, Eben. | | | | | | | X |
| Hancock, John | | | | X | | | X |
| Hendley, William | | | | | X | | |
| Hewes, George R.T. | | | | | X | | |
| Hickling, William | | | X | | | | |
| Hicks, John | | | | | X | | |
| Hill, Alexander | | | | | | X | |
| Hitchborn, Nathaniel | X | | | | | | |
| Hitchborn, Thomas | | | X | | | | |
| Hobbs, Samuel | | | | | X | | |
| Hoffins, John | X | | | | | | |
| Holmes, Nathaniel | | | X | | | | |
| Hooton, John | | | | | X | | |
| Hopkins, Caleb | | | | | | | X |
| Hoskins, William | | | X | | | | |
| Howard, Samuel | | | | | X | | |
| Howe, Edward C. | | | | | X | | |
| Hunnewell, Jonathan | | | | | X | | |
| Hunnewell, Richard | | | | | X | | |
| Hunstable, Thomas | | | | | X | | |
| Hunt, Col. Abraham | | | | | X | | |
| Ingersoll, Daniel | | | | | X | | |
| Inglish, Capt. Alexander | X | | | | | | |

| Name | St. Andrews Lodge 1762 | Loyal Nine 1766 | North Caucus 1771 | Long Room Club 1773 | Tea Party 1773 | Boston Committee of Correspondence 1774 | London Enemies List 1775 |
|---|---|---|---|---|---|---|---|
| Isaac Peirce | | | | | | | X |
| Ivers, James | | | | | | | X |
| Jarvis, Capt. Edward | X | | | | | | |
| Jarvis, Charles | | | | | | | X |
| Jefferds | X | | | | | | |
| Jenkins, John | X | | | | | | |
| Johnston, Eben | | | | | | | X |
| Johonnott, Gabriel | | | X | | | | |
| Kent, Benjamin | | | X | | | | |
| Kerr, Capt. Walter | X | | | | | | |
| Kimball, Thomas | | | X | | | | |
| Kinnison, David | | | | | X | | |
| Lambert, John | | | X | | | | |
| Lee, Joseph | | | | | X | | |
| Lewis, Phillip | X | | | | | | |
| Lincoln, Amos | | | | | X | | |
| Loring, Matthew | | | | | X | | |
| Lowell, John | | | X | | | | |
| Machin, Thomas | | | | | X | | |
| Mackay, William | | | | | | X | |
| MacKintosh, Capt. | | | | | X | | |
| MacNeil, Archibald | | | | | X | | |
| Marett, Capt. Phillip | X | | | | | | |
| Marlton, John | X | | | | | | |
| Marshall, Thomas | | | | | | | X |
| Marston, John | | | | | | | X |
| Mason, Jonathan | | | | | | | X |
| Matchett, John | | | X | | | | |
| May, Col. John | | | | | X | | |
| McAlpine, William | X | | | | | | |
| Melville, Maj. Thomas | | | | | X | | |
| Merrit, John | | | X | | | | |
| Milliken, Thomas | X | | | | | | |
| Molineux, William | | | X | | X | X | |
| Moody, Samuel | X | | | | | | |
| Moore, Thomas | | | | | X | | |
| Morse, Anthony | | | | | X | | |
| Morton, Perez | | | X | | | | |
| Mountford, Joseph | | | | | X | | |
| Newell, Eliphelet | | | | | X | | |
| Nicholls | X | | | | | | |
| Noyces, Nat. | | | | | | | X |
| Obear, Capt. Israel | X | | | | | | |
| Otis, James | | | | X | | X | |
| Palfrey, William | X | | | | | | |
| Palmer, Joseph P. | | | | | X | | |
| Palms, Richard | | | X | | | | |
| Parker, Jonathan | | | | | X | | |

| Name | St. Andrews Lodge 1762 | Loyal Nine 1766 | North Caucus 1771 | Long Room Club 1773 | Tea Party 1773 | Boston Committee of Correspondence 1774 | London Enemies List 1775 |
|---|---|---|---|---|---|---|---|
| Parkman, Elias | | | X | | | | X |
| Patridge, Sam | | | | | | | X |
| Payson, Joseph | | | | | X | | |
| Pearce, Isaac Jun. | | | X | | | | |
| Pearce, Isaac | | | X | | | | |
| Peck, Samuel | X | | | | X | | |
| Peck, Thomas H. | | | X | | | | |
| Peters, John | | | | | X | | |
| Phillips, Capt. John | X | | | | | | |
| Phillips, Samuel | | | | X | | | |
| Phillips, William | | | | | | | X |
| Pierce, William | | | | | X | | |
| Pierpont, Robert | | | | | | X | |
| Pitts, John | | | | | | | X |
| Pitts, Lendall | | | | | X | | |
| Pitts, Samuel | | | | | | | X |
| Porter, Thomas | | | | | X | | |
| Potter, Edward | X | | | | | | |
| Powell, William | | | | | | X | X |
| Prentiss Capt. Henry | | | | | X | | |
| Prince, Dr. John | | | | | X | | |
| Prince, Job | | | | | | | X |
| Proctor, Edward | | | X | | X | | X |
| Pulling, Capt. John | | | X | | | | X |
| Pulling, Richard | X | | | | | | |
| Purkitt, Henry | | | | | X | | |
| Quincy, Josiah | | | | X | | X | |
| Randall, John | | | | | X | | |
| Revere, Paul | X | | X | X | X | | X |
| Roby, Joseph | | | | | X | | |
| Roylston, Thomas | | | | | | | X |
| Ruddock, Capt. Abiel | | | X | | | | X |
| Russell, John | | | | | X | | |
| Russell, William | | | | | X | | |
| Sessions, Robert | | | | | X | | |
| Seward, James | X | | | | | | |
| Sharp, Gibbens | | | X | | | | |
| Shed, Joseph | | | | | X | | |
| Sigourney, John R. | | | X | | | | |
| Simpson, Benjamin | | | | | X | | |
| Slater, Capt. Peter | | | | | X | | |
| Sloper, Ambrose | X | | | | | | |
| Smith, John | | X | | | | | |
| Spear, Thomas | | | | | X | | |
| Sprague, Samuel | | | | | X | | |
| Spurr, Col. John | | | | | X | | |
| Stanbridge, Henry | X | | | | | | |
| Starr, James | | | | | X | | |

| Name | St. Andrews Lodge 1762 | Loyal Nine 1766 | North Caucus 1771 | Long Room Club 1773 | Tea Party 1773 | Boston Committee of Correspondence 1774 | London Enemies List 1775 |
|---|---|---|---|---|---|---|---|
| Stearns, Capt. Phineas | | | | | X | | |
| Stevens, Gen. Ebenezer | | | | | X | | |
| Stoddard, Asa | | | X | | | | |
| Stoddard, Jonathan | | | X | | | | |
| Story, Dr. Elisha | | | X | | X | | |
| Swan, Col. James | | | X | | X | | |
| Sweetser, John | | | | | | X | |
| Symmes, Eben | | | X | | | | |
| Symmes, John | | | X | | | | |
| Tabor, Capt. Philip | X | | | | | | |
| Tileston, Thomas | | | X | | | | |
| Trott, George | | X | | | | | |
| Tyler, Royall | | | | X | | | |
| Urann, Thomas | X | | X | | X | | |
| Vernon, Fortesque | | | | | | | X |
| Waldo, Benjamin | | | | | | | X |
| Warren, Dr. Joseph | X | | X | X | | X | X |
| Webb, Joseph, Jr. | X | | | | | | |
| Webster, Capt. Thomas | X | | | | | | |
| Welles, Henry | X | X | | | | | |
| Wendell, Oliver | | | | | | X | X |
| Wheeler, Capt. Josiah | | | | | X | | |
| White, Samuel | | | X | | | | |
| Whitten, John | X | | | | | | |
| Whitwell, Samuel | | | | | | | X |
| Whitwell, William | | | | | | | X |
| Williams, Jeremiah | | | | | X | | |
| Williams, Jonathan | | | | | | | X |
| Williams, Thomas | | | | | X | | |
| Willis, Nathaniel | | | | | X | | |
| Wingfield, Capt. William | X | | | | | | |
| Winslow, John | | | | X | | | |
| Winthrop, John | | | X | | | | X |
| Wyeth, Joshua | | | | | X | | |
| Young, Dr. Thomas | | | X | | X | X | |

SOURCES: London List: "As the True Born Sons of Liberty in Boston . . . ," London, April 18, 1775, ms. MHS; Long Room Club: see below, p. 376; Tea Party: Francis S. Drake, *Tea Leaves: Being a Collection of Letters and Documents Relating to the Shipment of Tea to the American Colonies . . .* (Boston, 1884), 95–171; St. Andrews Lodge: Edith Steblecki, *Paul Revere and Freemasonry* (Boston, 1985), 100–01; Boston Committee of Correspondence: Richard D. Brown, *Revolutionary Politics in Massachusetts: The Boston Committee of Correspondence to the Towns, 1772–1774* (Cambridge, 1970), 59; The Loyal Nine: Pauline Maier, *From Resistance to Revolution; Colonial Radicals and the Development of American Opposition to Britain, 1765–1776* (New York, 1972), 307. Spellings follow original lists.

# APPENDIX E

## ❧ The British Army in Boston: Order of Battle, April 18, 1775

*Commander in Chief and Staff*
Lieutenant General the Hon. Thomas Gage (Colonel, 22nd Foot), commander in chief
Major General Frederic Haldimand (Colonel commandant, 2nd Battalion, 60th, or Royal
    American Regiment), second in command
    Col. James Robertson, Barrack Master General
    Major Stephen Kemble, Deputy Adjutant General
    Major William Shirreff, Deputy Quartermaster General
    Lieut. Harry Rooke, 4th foot, Aide de Camp
    Capt. Brehm, Aide de Camp
    Capt. Oliver De Lancey, 17th Light Dragoons, Aide de Camp
    Samuel Kemble, Esqr., Confidential Secretary

*1st Brigade*
Brigadier: the Rt. Hon. Hugh, Earl Percy (Colonel, 5th Foot)
Brigade Major: Captain Thomas Moncrieffe (59th Foot)
    4th Regiment of Foot, or the King's Own (Lt. Col. George Maddison)
    23rd Regiment of Foot, or the Royal Welch Fusiliers (Lt. Col. Benjamin Bernard)
    47th Regiment of Foot (Lt. Col. William Nesbitt)
    1st Battalion, British Marines (Major John Pitcairn)

*2nd Brigade*
Brigadier: Robert Pigot (Lt. Col., 38th Foot)
Brigade Major: Captain John Small (21st Foot)
    5th Regiment of Foot (Col. the Hon. Hugh Earl Percy)
    38th Regiment of Foot (Lt. Col. Robert Pigot)
    52nd Regiment of Foot (Lt. Col. Valentine Jones)

*3rd Brigade*
Brigadier: Valentine Jones (Lt. Col., 52nd Foot)
Brigade Major: Captain Francis Hutchinson (60th, or Royal American Regiment)
    10th Regiment of Foot (Lt. Col. Francis Smith)
    43rd Regiment of Foot (Lt. Col. George Clerk)
    59th Regiment of Foot (Lt. Col. Ortho Hamilton)
    18th Regiment of Foot, 3 companies (Capt. John Shea)
    65th Regiment of Foot, 2 companies (senior officer unknown)

*Troops not brigaded*
    64th Regiment of Foot (Lt. Col. the Hon. Alexander Leslie)
        in garrison, Castle William, Boston harbor
    4th Battalion, Royal Regiment of Artillery (Col. Samuel Cleveland)
        35 Battery (Capt. William Martin)
        38 Battery (Capt. Lt. W. Orcher Huddlestone)
        39 Battery (Capt. Anthony Farrington)
        42 Battery (Capt. Lt. Robert Fenwick)
    British Marines, shipboard detachments (Adm. Samuel Graves)
    Royal Engineers (Capt. John Montresor)

SOURCES: Thomas Gage, Distribution of His Majesty's Forces in America," July 19, 1775, *Gage Correspondence*, II, 690; Gage to Richard Rigby, July 8, 1775, with enclosure, "List of General and Staff Officers on the Establishment in North America, from 25th December 1774 to 24th June, 1775," *ibid.*, II, 687–89; Vincent J.-R. Kehoe, "We Were There!" April 19, 1775 (mimeographed typescript, 1974), vol. I,

11–27; Barker, *British in Boston*, 9, 11; Mackenzie, *Diary*, I, 8; Regimental Rosters, Muster Books and Pay Lists, WO12/2194–7377, PRO.

# APPENDIX F

### ❧ The British Army in Boston: Returns of Strength, 1775

These returns do not include commissioned officers, sergeants and musicians. The normal complement for an infantry regiment was 1 lieutenant colonel, 1 major, 8 captains, 20 lieutenants, 1 adjutant, 1 quartermaster, 1 surgeon, 1 surgeon's mate, 1 chaplain (4th and 10th regiment only), 20 sergeants, and 12 fifes and drums. Only corporals and privates were counted in these estimates of "rank and file." The normal complement of corporals was three to a company at full strength.

| Regiment | January 1, 1775 | | | April 1, 1775 | | | July 21, 1775 | | |
|---|---|---|---|---|---|---|---|---|---|
| | fit | unfit | wanting | fit | unfit | wanting | fit | unfit | wanting |
| 17th Light Dragoons | | | | | | | 161 | 60 | 1 |
| 4th Foot | 357 | 23 | 10 | 357 | 18 | 23 | 277 | 84 | 27 |
| 5th Foot | 354 | 21 | 15 | 351 | 18 | 21 | 192 | 148 | 50 |
| 10th Foot | 299 | 56 | 35 | 307 | 34 | 49 | 294 | 63 | 33 |
| 18th Foot | 295 | 19 | 76 | 295 | 5 | 90 | 157 | 33 | 103 |
| 22nd Foot | | | | | | | 355 | 29 | 1 |
| 23rd Foot | 317 | 39 | 34 | 313 | 27 | 50 | 294 | 58 | 36 |
| 35th Foot | | | | | | | 277 | 87 | 18 |
| 38th Foot | 359 | 10 | 21 | 336 | 25 | 29 | 239 | 111 | 40 |
| 40th Foot | | | | | | | 342 | 31 | 10 |
| 43rd Foot | 308 | 29 | 53 | 313 | 31 | 42 | 253 | 88 | 48 |
| 44th Foot | | | | | | | 344 | 34 | 3 |
| 45th Foot | | | | | | | 377 | 3 | 1 |
| 47th Foot | 300 | 29 | 61 | 285 | 48 | 57 | 274 | 64 | 39 |
| 49th Foot | | | | | | | 327 | 54 | 0 |
| 52nd Foot | 316 | 23 | 51 | 299 | 30 | 61 | 277 | 79 | 34 |
| 59th Foot | 259 | 16 | 115 | 250 | 16 | 124 | 278 | 63 | 47 |
| 63rd Foot | | | | | | | 299 | 76 | 15 |
| 64th Foot | 335 | 9 | 46 | 334 | 7 | 48 | n.a. | n.a. | n.a. |
| 65th Foot | 362 | 8 | 20 | 346 | 8 | 36 | 169 | 52 | 13 |
| 1st Marines | 382 | 5 | n.a. | n.a. | n.a. | n.a. | 346 | 116 | 18 |
| 2nd Marines | n.a. | n.a. | n.a. | n.a. | n.a. | n.a. | 357 | 104 | n.a. |

NOTE: In the period from January 1 to April 1, 1775, twelve regiments in Boston reported a net loss of 75 men, or 1.9% of effective strength. Gross attrition was higher, but replacements and transfers held the net wastage to this level. The reporting date for the 18th Foot (8 companies only) was Dec. 1, 1774 and March 1, 1775. Returns for the 65th Foot include six companies only. Contingency men are not included here.

SOURCES: Returns of His Majesty's Forces, April 1775 [strength reports for Jan. 1, 1775], add. ms. 29259I, BL; Returns of His Majesty's Forces, July 1775 [strength reports for April 1, 1775], add. ms., 29259K, BL; Present State of His Majesty's Forces at Boston, July 21, 1775, Haldimand Papers, add. ms. 21687, BL.

# APPENDIX G

## ✎ The Royal Navy in America, January 1, 1775

Admiral Samuel Graves's "List of the North American Squadron, on the 1st of January 1775"

| Vessels | Guns | Men | Commander | Location |
|---|---|---|---|---|
| Preston | 50 | 300 | Capt. John Robinson | Boston |
| Somerset | 68 | 520 | Capt. Edward Le Gras | Boston |
| Boyne | 70 | 520 | Capt. Broderick Hartwell | Boston |
| Asia | 64 | 480 | Capt. George Vanderput | Boston |
| Mercury | 20 | 130 | Capt. John Macartney | Boston |
| Glasgow | 20 | 130 | Capt. William Maltby | Boston |
| Diana schooner | 6 | 30 | Lt. Thomas Graves | Boston |
| Rose | 20 | 130 | Capt. James Wallace | Rhode Island |
| Swan, sloop | 16 | 100 | Capt. James Ayscough | Rhode Island |
| Hope, schooner | 6 | 30 | Lt. George Dawson | Rhode Island |
| Kingfisher, sloop | 16 | 100 | Capt. James Montague | New York |
| Magdalen, schooner | 6 | 30 | Lt. Henry Cotins | Philadelphia |
| Fowey | 20 | 130 | Capt. George Montague | Virginia |
| Cruizer, sloop | 8 | 60 | Lt. Tyr Howe | North Carolina |
| Tamer, sloop | 14 | 100 | Lt.? Edward Thornborough | South Carolina |
| Savage, sloop | 8 | 60 | Lt.? Edward Bromedge | Florida & Bahamas |
| St. John, schooner | 6 | 30 | Lt. William Grant | Florida & Bahamas |
| Lively | 20 | 130 | Capt. Thomas Bishop | Salem, Marblehead |
| Scarborough | 20 | 130 | Capt. Andrew Barkley | New Hampshire |
| Canceaux | 8 | 45 | Lt. Henry Mowat | New Hampshire |
| Gaspee, brig | 6 | 30 | Lt. William Hunter | Casco Bay |
| Halifax, schooner | 6 | 30 | Lt. Joseph Nunn | Casco Bay |
| Diligent, schooner | 6 | 30 | Lt. John Knight | Bay of Fundy |
| Tartar | 28 | 160 | Capt. Edward Meadows | Halifax |

SOURCE: Graves Papers, Gay Transcripts, MHS.

# APPENDIX H

## ✎ Weather Patterns, April 17-20, 1775

The weather on the day of the battle has been described by historians in contradictory ways. Hudson writes, "All accounts agree that the day was unusually warm for that season of the year" (*Lexington*, 197). Murdock disagrees. "Contrary to general belief," he writes, "the 19th of April seems to have been a cold, windy day, with a bright sun . . . evidently the wind was east" (*The Nineteenth of April, 1775*, 55). Both of these statements are incorrect.

The New England weather was typically volatile in this period. The 18th of April was wet through the day, followed by rapid clearing at night. Winds were variable, veering from the northeast to the south. The following diary entries were recorded for this day:

"rain" by Nathaniel Ames, Dedham; a "fine rain" by Jonas Clarke in Lexington; "rainy most of the day" by Joseph Andrews; "rain a.m. fair towards night by Ebenezer Gay of Suffield, Conn. An anonymous Concord weather diary records "rain" in the morning and "showers" in the afternoon, with a south wind. Jeremy Belknap in Dover, N.H., described the 17th of April as "fair" and "warm," with small showers in the afternoon and rain with a north-easterly wind at night, and the 18th as "warm rain pm cloudy."

In the evening and night of April 18 (when the British expedition set off for Concord, and Paul Revere made his midnight ride) clearing followed rapidly. Revere remembered in his letter to Jeremy Belknap that the night was "very pleasant." Sanderson described it as "a pleasant evening" (Phinney, *Lexington* 23).

For the 19th of April, the primary evidence of twelve diaries is highly consistent. In Cambridge, Harvard professor John Winthrop took two readings of his thermometer that day. At six o'clock in the morning, he noted that the temperature was 46 degrees, the barometer 29.56 inches and rising, the sky fair, and light winds from the west. At one o'clock in the afternoon, the temperature had risen to 52 degrees, the sky was fair with clouds, and the west wind had freshened. At that point he noted, "battle of Concord will put a stop to observing." He and his wife Hannah fled for their lives.

Other diarists described the weather that day in the same way. Lexington's minister Jonas Clarke found a moment to note that the day was "clear." In Boston, Dr. John Jeffries wrote, "clear and fair, fresh wind at W." The Rev. William Marrett in Burlington thought the day was "fair, windy and cold." Paul Litchfield of Scituate described it as "somewhat blustery and cool." Elizabeth Stiles in Newport, R. I., recorded a temperature of 53 degrees at 11 am, fair skies and the wind from west. Jeremy Belknap, in Dover, N. H., called it "fair, windy, cool, w[est wind]." Ebenezer Gay, in Suffield, Conn., thought the day was "fair, cold." Dr. Nathaniel Ames, in Dedham described it as "clear." William Clark in the same town described the day as "fair" with a "strong chilly west wind." An anonymous weather diary, now in the Concord Free Public Library, described the 19th as "fair with a westerly wind."

The best secondary account is David Ludlum, "The Weather of Independence," in *The Country Journal New England Weather Book* (Boston, 1976), 126-28. Ludlum, editor of the American Meteorological Society's journal *Weatherwise,* concludes that "these records indicate that a cold front passed through eastern Massachusetts about noon on April 18, bringing an end to the showery conditions, a shift of wind to the west, a rising barometer, and a rather rapid postfrontal clearing. Visibility was good late in the evening when the signal lamps were hung." This is by far the most accurate judgment, but requires amendment in one detail. Some diaries reported showers persisting into the late afternoon of the 18th. After two days of rain, the ground, normally wet in mid-April, was very soft—as one of Paul Revere's pursuers discovered by experience. The streams were high, as Smith's British infantry learned the hard way. By all accounts, the day of the battle was crisp, cool, and fair, with a rising westerly wind and fluffy cumulus clouds scudding across bright blue skies.

Late in the day, another storm system moved rapidly through the area, with a red sunset, and later a cold rain that made a miserable night for both the American militia who were "lying on their arms" at Cambridge, and the British Regulars who were sleeping in the open on Bunker Hill.

SOURCES: The Nathaniel Ames Diary and William Clark Diary, Dedham Historical Society; an anonymous weather diary, CFPL; the Winthrop weather diary, Harvard Archives; Jonas Clarke Diary, MHS; diaries of Jeremy Belknap, Ebenezer Gay, Joseph Andrews, and Paul Litchfield, all in MHS. The Marrett Diary is quoted in Frothingham, *Siege of Boston,* 59, 84n; the Stiles Diary and Jeffries Diary, in Ludlum, *The Country Journal New England Weather Book,* 127.

# APPENDIX I

### ❧ The Moon, April 18-19, 1775

Many participants remembered that the moon was nearly full on the night of April 18-19, 1775. "The moon shone bright," Paul Revere wrote in his deposition. His fellow captive Sanderson wrote independently, "It was a bright moon-light after the rising of the moon, and a pleasant evening" (Phinney, *Lexington,* 31).

These memories have been confirmed by two American astronomers, Donald W. Olson and Russell L. Doescher, who studied this subject in detail, and found that the nearest full moon occurred on April 15, 1775, and the last quarter on April 22. On the night of the midnight ride, they calculate that "there was indeed a bright waning-gibbous moon, 87 percent sunlit, in Boston on the night of April 18, 1775." They estimate that the moon rose over Boston at approximately 9:53 p.m., local apparent solar time (approximately 25 minutes later than our modern Eastern Standard Time).

On that night Olson and Doescher reckon that the moon had a strong southern declination of -18 degrees. If Revere's friends were rowing him across the Charles River at approximately 45 minutes after moonrise, the moon would have been very low in the southern sky—6 degrees above the horizon, on a true bearing of 121 degrees.

Revere's course from the North End of Boston to Charlestown's ferry landing was approximately 330 degrees. The moon was almost directly behind him, and as it was only 6 degrees above the horizon, his boat would have been shrouded in the dark moonshadow of the town's skyline, and very difficult to see from the deck of HMS *Somerset,* or even from British guardboats that were patrolling the river that night.

The transit of the moon occurred at 2:42 a.m. according to the computations of two other astronomers, Jacques Vialle and Darrel Hoff. The marker in the Minute Man National Historical Park that refers to a third quarter moon is not correct.

See Donald W. Olson and Russell L. Doescher, "Astronomical Computing: Paul Revere's Midnight Ride," *Sky and Telescope,* April 1992, pp. 437–40; also Jacques Vialle and Darrel Hoff, "The Astronomy of Paul Revere's Ride," *Astronomy* 20 (1992): 13–18.


# APPENDIX J

### ❧ Tidal Movements, the British March, and the Midnight Ride, April 18–19, 1775

Shakespeare observes that "there is a tide in the affairs of men; which, taken at the flood, leads on to fortune" (*Julius Caesar, IV, iii, 217*). So it was for Paul Revere, but General Gage would have been luckier at the ebb.

Tidal movements in the Charles River and Boston's Back Bay had an important impact on these events. Paul Revere remembered that when he crossed the Charles River at approximately 10:30 to 11:00 p.m., "It was then young flood." The strong Boston tide was flowing into the harbor and running westward up the estuary of the Charles River.

At that same hour, the British troops were moving across the Charles River to Lechmere Point in Cambridge. Lt. William Sutherland wrote that when they marched along the river at 2 a.m., "the tide being in we were up to our middles." Mackenzie remembered that the men were "obliged to wade, halfway up to their thighs, through two inlets, the tide being by that time up."

Modern computations confirm the accuracy of these accounts. Professors Olson and Doescher, using a method of harmonic analysis, estimate that on the afternoon of April 18, 1775, high tide in Boston harbor occurred at 1:14 p.m. local apparent solar time. Low water followed that evening at 7:19 p.m. and high tide again at 1:26 a.m. in the morning. These results confirm that the tide was rising when Revere and the British soldiers were crossing the river.

Early American almanacs were even closer to the descriptions of the participants. Three colonial almanacs variously estimated the time of high tide on the morning of April 19 at approximately 2:34 (Low) 2:36 (Isaiah Thomas), and 2:39 (Bickerstaff).

All this was an advantage for Paul Revere, and a problem for the British expedition. At the point where Revere crossed, the river flowed west around a bend. His course to Charlestown took him upstream. The Regulars crossed further west where the river was flowing southwest. Their course to Cambridge was downstream. Revere's passage was comparatively short, and as his route took him diagonally upstream he was moving with the tide. The British troops were moving diagonally downstream against the tide over a longer distance. Revere was traveling in a small rowboat with two experienced Boston watermen. The British troops were in heavy, overloaded longboats. The tide gave Revere an important advantage, and was a factor in speeding him on his way, while retarding the progress of the British troops.

See Donald W. Olson and Russell L. Doescher, "Astronomical Computing: Paul Revere's Midnight Ride," *Sky and Telescope,* April 1992, pp. 437-40.


# APPENDIX K

 ~ The British Concord Expedition: The Problem of Numbers


No official count of troop strength has been found for this mission. Estimates by participants and eyewitnesses ranged between 600 and 900 men. Barker thought it numbered "about 600 men"; an officer of the 59th Foot, "600 men including officers"; Evelyn, "near 700"; an anonymous light infantryman, precisely 756; and Richard Pope, "nearly 800 men." One observer, Boston printer John Boyle, counted "about 900 Regular troops, but his estimate has been rejected by all historians of the battle as too high. Cf. John Boyle, "Boyles Journal of Occurrences in Boston, 1759-1778," *NEHGR* 85 (1931) 8.

The estimates of historians have tended to vary according to their politics. In general, the more Whiggish the scholar, the larger his estimate of British numbers; the more Tory or Anglophile, the smaller the force becomes. The Whig historian Gordon reckoned the force at "800 men or better." Bancroft, Coburn, Frothingham, Hale, Hudson, Lossing, and Shattuck were content with 800. Robert Gross preferred "seven to eight hundred." French, Tourtellot, and Galvin reckoned "in the neighborhood of 700." The American Anglophile Harold Murdock extrapolated from average company strength of the 23rd Foot (28.2 men) to a controlled guess of 588 rank and file.

These estimates derive mainly from impressions of contemporaries, and the conventional judgments of other scholars, and in the case of Murdock from a strength report for a single regiment, drawn from the diary of Frederick Mackenzie.

Monthly strength reports for all units engaged at Lexington and Concord are missing in the Public Record Office, but another source helps to settle the question. Regimental rosters and paylists are available for the 1774–75. Each regiment submitted twice a year a roster, sworn before a magistrate and witnesses. These documents were meticulously compiled in elaborate detail. A separate folio sheet was prepared for each company, listing by name and rank every man who had served in the unit since the last report, with dates of duty, promotions, transfers, leaves, desertions, discharges, detached duty, etc. The Boston regiments in general submitted reports in the winter of 1774–75, and again in the summer of 1775. These documents were not snapshots, but moving pictures. They are imperfect in some details. Men who were relieved from duty for sickness or wounds or special assignments were listed only for the end of the reporting period, but not for other dates. Other movements are noted throughout the reporting period. These records reported an extraordinarily high rate of turnover. Men were frequently transferred in and out of individual companies, commonly from other units in the same regiment. Recruits and replacements arrived throughout the period.

No rosters were found for the British Marines before 1777. By the beginning of that year, the "American battalion" that had served at Boston had moved to Halifax. Its grenadier company had a strength of 3 officers and 29 men. Its light infantry company (the same that marched to Concord) was very much larger, with 117 other ranks; but it is not clear that the company was of similar size in April, 1775. Another method of estimation was used here to avoid an overcount. The total strength of the British Marine battalion in Boston was reported by its commander Major Percy at 387 effectives, 22 percent larger than the mean effective strength of the army regiments in Boston on April 1, 1775. An estimate for the Marine grenadiers and light infantry companies was added here in the same ratio, as 122% of mean strength in other companies. If the earliest pay rosters are an accurate indicator, the true strength was not 43 but 73 rank and file. The smaller number is used here, as a lower-bound estimate. Contingency men are not included.

These lists indicate the following numbers of "effectives" as of April 18, in the companies that marched to Lexington and Concord:

| Regiment | Company | Officers | Other Ranks | Total |
|---|---|---|---|---|
| 4th Foot | Grenadiers | 3 | 39 | 42 |
| | Light infantry | 3 | 34 | 37 |
| 5th Foot | Grenadiers | 3 | 38 | 41 |
| | Light Infantry | 2 | 42 | 44 |
| 10th Foot | Grenadiers | 3 | 32 | 35 |
| | Light Infantry | 3 | 34 | 37 |
| 18th Foot | Grenadiers | 3 | 37 | 40 |
| 23rd Foot | Grenadiers | 3 | 29 | 32 |
| | Light Infantry | 3 | 35 | 38 |
| 38th Foot | Grenadiers | 3 | 42 | 45 |
| | Light Infantry | 3 | 38 | 41 |
| 43rd Foot | Grenadiers | 3 | 37 | 40 |
| | Light Infantry | 3 | 38 | 41 |
| 47th Foot | Grenadiers | 3 | 41 | 44 |
| | Light Infantry | 3 | 34 | 37 |
| 52nd Foot | Grenadiers | 2 | 41 | 43 |
| | Light Infantry | 2 | 35 | 37 |
| 59th Foot | Grenadiers | 3 | 29 | 32 |
| | Light Infantry | 3 | 36 | 39 |
| British Marines | Grenadiers | 3 | 43 | 46 |
| | Light Infantry | 3 | 43 | 46 |
| Supernumeraries | | 6 | | |
| Mitchell's party | | 8 + | | |
| Total | | 74 | 777 | 841 |

There may have been as many as seven additional members of Mitchell's party, and perhaps another 60 Marines, if the 1777 rosters are correct, and Loyalist volunteers, minus one straggler at the Phips farm. The size of the Concord expedition might therefore have been as large as 909 officers and men. If so, the rejected estimate of John Boyle proves to be the most nearly accurate.

Are the muster rolls a trustworthy source? For the 23rd Royal Welch Fusiliers they can be tested against the diary of Frederick Mackenzie, who reported that the number of rank and file under arms on April 19 was precisely the same to the man as the estimate that emerges from the rosters. Gage and Haldimond established elaborate procedures to ensure accurate and honest reports, and were successful.

There is only one possible source of error. These estimates assume that the proportion of men who were ill, absent, on detached duty or otherwise "ineffective" was the same on April 19 as at the date of the preceding roster (*circa* Jan. 30, 1775). There was some attrition in Gage's army during the entire period. From January to June, net attrition other than losses in combat totalled only 1.9% for the rank and file in all companies of every marching regiment. A special effort was made to keep up the strength of grenadier and light infantry companies by transfering men from the line companies (Barker, *British in Boston,* 58–59). Even the mean attrition rate of the garrison as a whole would reduce these estimates by only 15 men. For flank companies, the wastage was smaller, and the net change may actually have been in the opposite direction, as men on detached duty returned to their units when they went on active service.

The sources for these estimates are Regimental Rosters in WO12, PRO. Cf. Barker, *British in Boston,* 31; W. G. Evelyn to his father, April 23, 1775, Scull, *Evelyn,* 53; an anonymous light infantryman in *Letters on the American Revolution,* 187–200; Pope, *Late News,* entry for April 18, 1775; French, *Day of Concord and Lexington,* 73; Murdock, *The Nineteenth of April,* 47; Tourtellot, *Lexington and Concord,* 104; Gross, *Minutemen and Their World,* 115.

# APPENDIX L

### ᴖ A Chronology of the British March, April 18–19, 1775

Many contemporary estimates are available for the chronology of the British expedition. With allowances for a range of variation in individual timepieces, they roughly agree. But several historians have rejected them. The first to do so was Frank W. Coburn, who in general revised the estimates of participants, assigning earlier times for the British march to Concord, and later times for the return. Allen French followed Coburn, but sometimes blurred individual events where discrepancies were specially apparent. Arthur Tourtellot was erratic, but tended to split the difference between Coburn's estimates and those in primary sources. These historians, who shared the general opinion that Smith was "very slow," could not believe that the British march was as rapid as contemporary estimates indicated.

This inquiry finds that the estimates of eyewitnesses were generally consistent, and the speed of the march was compatible with their descriptions of it. Further, a comparison of solar times with their estimates of the relationship of sunrise and sunset to events of the march confirms the accuracy of participant-observations. Coburn, French, and Tourtellot all followed one another into error on this question.

In the following variant estimates, primary sources are given in roman type; secondary estimates in italics.

| Time | Source |
|---|---|
| *British troops leave Boston* | |
| 10 p.m. | Mackenzie |
| "about 10 o'clock" | Gage |
| "between 10 and 11" | Barker |
| "the whole was not assembled 'till near 11." | Mackenzie |
| *arrive Phips Farm, Cambridge* | |
| 12 midnight | Mackenzie |
| "about 12 o'clock" | Basset |
| *leave Phips Farm* | |
| 12 midnight | De Berniere [error] |
| "about 2 o'clock" | Sutherland |
| "at two o'clock" | Barker |
| 2 a.m. | Pope |
| 1 a.m. | *French, 101* |
| 1 a.m. | *Coburn, 47* |
| 2 a.m. | *Tourtellot, 107* |
| *arrive Newell Tavern, Menotomy* | |
| between 2 and 3 a.m. | *Coburn, 114* |
| 3 a.m. | *Tourtellot, 108* |
| *meeting with Mitchell's patrol* | |
| "about three o'clock" | Gage |
| "between 3 and 4 in the morning" | Sutherland |
| *light infantry ordered to load* | |
| "about four o'clock" | Lister |
| 4:30 a.m. | Lexington depositions |
| *arrive Lexington* | |
| 5:00 a.m. | Pitcairn |
| "five o'clock" | Barker, 32 |
| 4:30 a.m. | *Coburn, 47n* |
| just at sunrise | *French, 105* |
| *arrive Concord* | |
| "2 hours after sunrise" | Barrett & 15 deponents 74 |
| 9–10 a.m. | De Berniere |
| "about 9 o'clock" | Gage |
| "between 7 & 8 o'clock | *Coburn, 74* |
| "before 8 a.m. | *French, 161* |
| "about 8 o'clock" | *Tourtellot, 153* |
| *action at North Bridge* | |
| 10 o'clock | *Coburn, 82,* |
| "between 9 & 10 o'clock | Adams, 32, |
| | David Brown Journal |
| *leave Concord* | |
| "about noon" | *Coburn, 95* |
| "noon" | *Tourtellot, 175* |
| *Percy's Brigade Assembles* | |
| "at half past seven" | Mackenzie |
| *Percy's March from Boston* | |
| 9 a.m. | Percy |

| Time | Source |
|------|--------|
| "a quarter before nine." | Mackenzie |
| *Smith arrives Lexington Common* | |
| "half after two" | Mackenzie |
| *Percy arrives at Lexington* | |
| "about two o'clock" | Percy |
| "about two o'clock" | Mackenzie |
| *leave Lexington Common* | |
| "about 1/4 past 3" | Mackenzie |
| 3:30–4 p.m. | *Coburn,* 129 |
| *arrive Cambridge* | |
| 5–6 p.m. | *Coburn,* 145 |
| *leave Cambridge* | |
| 6:30 pm | *Coburn,* 150 |
| *arrive Charlestown Neck* | |
| sunset | *Coburn* |
| "near six o'clock" | Basset [error] |
| "about seven o'clock" | De Berniere |
| "about 7 o'clock" | Mackenzie |
| "between 7 and 8" | Barker |
| "between 7 & 8" | Percy to Gage |
| "at 8 in the evening" | Percy to Harvey |
| "about 8 o'clock" | Percy to Northumberland |
| *wounded return to Boston* | |
| "about 9 o'clock" | Lister |
| *others return to Boston* | |
| "past 12 at night" | Mackenzie |

# APPENDIX M

### ❧ The British March: Time, Distance, Velocity

| March | Time | Distance | Period | Miles per hour | Minutes per mile |
|-------|------|----------|--------|----------------|------------------|
| Lechmere Pt. to Lexington | 2–5.20 a.m. | 11 miles | 3.20 hrs. | 3.44 | 18.8 |
| Lexington to Concord | 7–9 a.m. | 6.25 mi. | 2 hrs. | 3.12 | 19.2 |
| Concord to Lexington | noon–2.30 p.m. | 6.25 mi. | 2.5 hrs | 2.50 | 24.0 |
| Lexington to Charlestown | 3.15–7 p.m. | 11 miles | 3.75 hrs | 2.93 | 20.5 |

Source: Computed from Appendix L above.

# APPENDIX N

~ Methods of Timekeeping in 1775

Where clock time was given, it differed from the temporal conventions we keep today. Since 1883, Boston has run on Eastern Standard Time, which was invented to synchronize railroad timetables. In 1775, watches and clocks were commonly set by sunlines at high noon, or by what is called today local apparent solar time.

All estimates in this work should be understood as an approximation of local apparent solar time, not Eastern Standard Time. To convert from local apparent solar time to Eastern Standard Time in the longitude of Boston, one must subtract 25 minutes. If Paul Revere left Charlestown at 11:00 p.m. local apparent solar time, the equivalent would be 10:35 p.m. Eastern Standard Time, or 11:35 p.m. Eastern Daylight Time.

American clock-time in many accounts referred merely to the nearest hour. Some American clocks in 1775 had no minute hand. American narratives marked the time not by hours but natural events—sunrise and sunset, or the rising of the moon. One event was recorded as happening between first light and sunrise.

British officers tended to observe clock time and often used fractions of hours and even minutes. Elijah Sanderson, the Lexington man who was captured by the British patrol later testified, "They detained us in that vicinity till a quarter past two o'clock at night. An officer, who took out his watch, informed me what the time was" (Phinney, *Lexington*, 31).

Neither side appears to have synchronized watches, a practice that appears to have begun among Union armies in the west during the Civil War. In other wars during the 20th century, opposing sides set their clocks differently. This was not the case at Lexington and Concord. In some instances, British estimates of times tended to be later than those of the Americans. But the difference was small and inconstant.

One test of the accuracy of temporal estimates can be made by comparing hours of sunrise and sunset with primary estimates of the chronology of events. Many eyewitnesses on both sides wrote that the Regulars arrived at Lexington Green just at sunrise. They also agreed that the battle ended when Percy's brigade crossed Charlestown Neck at sunset. These events may be used to assess time-keeping by participants and historians. In general they confirm the accuracy of estimates by participants, and contradict the revisions that were introduced in the literature by Coburn, French, and in some cases by Tourtellot. On April 19, 1993, the hours of sunrise and sunset were as follows:

|                           | Sunrise   | Sunset    |
|---------------------------|-----------|-----------|
| Eastern Standard Time     | 4:57 a.m. | 6:30 p.m. |
| Eastern Daylight Time     | 5:57 a.m. | 7:30 p.m. |
| Apparent Local Solar Time | 5:22 a.m. | 6:55 p.m. |
| Low's Boston Almanack     | 5:19 a.m. | n.a.      |

This suggests that estimates of time by British officers were in general roughly accurate when understood as local apparent solar time. Secondary accounts by Coburn and French deliberately altered these times for the march from Cambridge to Concord, to conform with their understanding of events. They all believed that Col. Smith was "slow," and could not square that assumption with primary estimates of the rapidity of the British march. Rather than rethinking their assumption, they revised the evidence. A comparison of solar times with contemporary estimates shows that these revisions were erroneous. The student of the battle should in general trust the preponderance of primary temporal estimates, and reject those in secondary accounts by Coburn and French. These secondary works remain very valuable in other respects, but not on questions of chronology.

SOURCE: Nathaniel Low, *An Astronomical Diary; Or, Almanack for the Year of Christian Era, 1775* (Boston, 1775); solar tables, 1993.

# APPENDIX O

## ✎ The Lexington Militia: Quantitative Research by Jeremy Stern for this volume

*Strength*: The muster rolls of the Lexington Company, and lists compiled by Charles Hudson for his history of Lexington identify 141 men of all ranks. Of this number as many as 75 have been identified as present on Lexington Green when the first shot was fired. The total number of male polls in 1771 was 185; in 1775, 208; in 1785, 196; in 1790, 205. The number of males aged 16 and older in the census of 1790 was 251. The total population of the town was enumerated at 755 in 1770 and 941 in 1790.

| | |
|---|---|
| Captain: | John Parker, age 45, |
| Lieutenant: | William Tidd, 38 |
| Ensign | Robert Munroe, 62 |
| Ensign | Joseph Simonds, 35 |
| Clerk: | Daniel Harrington, 35 |
| Orderly Sergeant | William Munroe, 32 |
| Sergeant | Francis Brown, 37 ? |
| Sergeant | Ebenezer White, 28? |
| Corporal | Joel Viles |
| Corporal | Samuel Sanderson |
| Corporal | John Munroe, 43 |
| Corporal | Ebenezer Munroe, 22 |
| Fifer | Jonathan Harrington, 16 |
| Drummer | William Diamond, age unknown |
| Private Soldiers | 127 |
| | |
| *Total Strength* | 141 |

*Age*: The youngest militiaman was 16; the oldest, 66. Of those whose ages are known, 16.4% were under the age of 20; 25.5% were 20–29; 36.5% were 30–39; 13.6% were 40–49; and 8.2% were 50 and older. A total of 58.3% were 30 and older. Mean and median ages were in the range of 31.8 to 32.8. The Lexington militia were older than the Concord minutemen, as estimated by Robert Gross. In general, minutemen in many towns appear to have been younger than the militia, and much younger than men on the alarm lists, and not representative of the men who mustered and fought that day.

| Age | Present | Absent | Total |
|---|---|---|---|
| 16–19 | 8 | 10 | 18 |
| 20–29 | 17 | 11 | 28 |
| 30–39 | 21 | 19 | 40 |
| 40–49 | 9 | 6 | 15 |
| 50–59 | 3 | 0 | 3 |
| 60–69 | 1 | 5 | 6 |
| | | | |
| subtotal | 59 | 51 | 110 |
| unknown | 16 | 15 | 31 |
| total | 75 | 66 | 141 |
| | | | |
| mean age | 31.8 | 32.8 | 32.3 |
| median age | 31 | 32 | 31 |

*Prior Military Service*: From incomplete records, Charles Hudson estimated that a minimum of 28 to 33 men in Lexington, *ca.* 1775, who had seen active service in the French and Indian War. Probably the true number was much higher. The age of veterans in Captain Parker's company ranged from 62-year-old Ensign Robert Munroe to Amos Locke, aged 32.

*Wealth*: A linkage of various 1775 muster lists with the 1771 tax list shows that nearly all of these men were small landowners, neither rich nor poor. Of 141 men, 78 could not be located on the tax list of 1771, in almost all cases because they were under 21, or had not moved into the town, or could not be conclusively identified. Of 63 militiamen who could be identified, 58 were landowners in the town. Only 5 owned no land. The largest holding was assessed at 19 pounds annual worth, a comfortable but modest estate. Captain Parker was assessed at 11 pounds. Of the ten richest men on the list, eight were privates.

*Kinship*: The muster lists of the Lexington company included 16 Munroes, 13 Harringtons, 11 Smiths, 8 Reeds, 4 Browns, 4 Hadleys, 4 Muzzys, 4 Hastings, 4 Tidds, 3 Simonds, 3 Wellingtons, 3 Winships, and many pairs. Only 27 men of 141 did not share a name with another member of the company. The great majority belonged to one extended cousinage.

# APPENDIX P

❧ American Casualties, April 19, 1775, by town:

*Acton:* killed (3) Isaac Davis, James Hayward, Abner Hosmer; wounded (1) Luther Blanchard.
*Bedford*: killed (1) Capt. Jonathan Wilson; wounded (1) Job Lane.
*Beverly*: killed (1) Reuben Kenyme; wounded (3) Nathaniel Cleves, William Dodge III, Samuel Woodbury.
*Billerica*: wounded (2) Timothy Blanchard, John Nichols.
*Brookline*: killed (1) Isaac Gardner.
*Cambridge*: killed (6) John Hicks, William Marcy (noncombatant?), Moses Richardson, Jason Russell, Jason Winship (noncombatant), Jabez Wyman (noncombatant); wounded (1), Samuel Whittemore; missing (2) Samuel Frost, Seth Russell.
*Charlestown*: killed (2) Edward Barber (a 14-year-old noncombatant), James Miller.
*Chelmsford*: wounded (2) Oliver Barron, Aaron Chamberlain.
*Concord*: killed (none); wounded (5) Nathan Barrett, Jonas Brown, Charles Miles, George Minot, Abel Prescott, Jr.
*Danvers*: killed (7) Samuel Cook, Benjamin Deland, Ebenezer Golwait, Henry Jacobs, Perley Putnam, George Southwick, Jothan Webb; wounded (2) Nathan Putnam, Dennis Wallace; missing (1) Joseph Bell.
*Dedham*: killed (1) Elias Haven; wounded (1) Israel Everett.
*Framingham*: wounded (1) Daniel Hemminway.
*Lexington*: killed (10) John Brown, Samuel Hadley, Caleb Harrington, Jonathan Harrington, Jr., Jonas Parker, Jedidiah Munroe, Robert Munroe, Isaac Muzzy, John Raymond, Nathaniel Wyman; wounded (10) Francis Brown, Joseph Comee, Prince Estabrook, Nathaniel Farmer, Ebenezer Munroe Jr., Jedidiah Munroe, Solomon Pierce, John Robbins, John Tidd, Thomas Winship.
*Lynn*: killed (4) William Flint, Thomas Hadley, Abednego Ramsdell, Daniel Townsend; wounded (2) Joseph Felt, Timothy Monroe; missing (1) Josiah Breed.

*Medford:* killed (2) Henry Putnam, William Holly.

*Needham:* killed (5) John Bacon, Nathaniel Chamberlain, Amos Mills, Elisha Mills, Jonathan Parker; wounded (2) Eleazer Kingsbury, Tolman.

*Newton:* wounded (1) Noah Wiswell.

*Roxbury:* missing (1) Elijah Seaver.

*Salem:* killed (1) Benjamin Pierce.

*Stow:* wounded (1) Daniel Conant.

*Sudbury:* killed (2) Deacon Josiah Haynes (aet. 80), Asahael Reed; died of wounds (1), Thomas Bent (1); wounded (1) Joshua Haynes, Jr.

*Watertown:* killed (1) Joseph Coolidge.

*Woburn:* killed (2) Daniel Thompson, Asahel Porter; wounded (3), Jacob Bacon, Johnson, George Reed.

TOTAL: killed and died of wounds, 50; wounded, 39; missing, 5; total casualties, 94; towns with casualties: 23

SOURCES: Elias Phinney, *History of the Battle at Lexington...* (Boston, 1825), 27-30; John Farmer in *MHSC*, XVIII; Frothingham, *History of the Siege of Boston*, 80-81.

# APPENDIX Q

~ British Casualties, April 19, 1775

### Official Returns by General Gage, WO1/2/175, PRO

|                 | killed | wounded | missing |
|-----------------|--------|---------|---------|
| officers        | 1      | 15      | 1       |
| sergeants       | 1      | 7       | 2       |
| fifes and drums | 1      | 1       |         |
| rank and file   | 62     | 157     | 24      |
|                 |        |         |         |
| Total           | 65     | 180     | 27      |
| All Casualties  | 272    |         |         |

### Unofficial Estimate by Ensign De Berniere

|                | killed     | wounded | missing |
|----------------|------------|---------|---------|
| officers       | 2          | 13      | 3       |
| sergeants      | 2          | 7       | 1       |
| drummer        | 1          |         |         |
| rank and file  | 68         | 154     | 21      |
|                |            |         |         |
| Total          | 73         | 174     | 25      |
| All Casualties | 273 [*sic*] |         |         |

Estimate by Stephen Kemble, Gage's Intelligence [!] Officer: "We lost about 25 killed and about 150 wounded." Kemble Journals, N-YHS, 42–43.

Estimate by John Pope, a British soldier: 90 killed, 181 wounded, total 271

Estimate by an anonymous British soldier: "might have amounted to 500 killed and wounded" (Kehoe, "We Were There!" I, 174).

*Estimates of casualties by regiment*:

   *4th Foot:* "Our regiment had about four or five men killed, and about 25 wounded" (Evelyn); Gage reported 8 killed, 25 wounded, 8 missing.

   *5th Foot*: Of the grenadiers, "half the company and Lt. Baker were killed or wounded." For the entire regiment, Gage reported 5 killed, 18 wounded, 1 missing.

   *10th Foot*: Of the light infantry, "A sergeant of the company came to me and inform'd me he had but 12 men and could not find any other officer [Kelly, Parsons and Lister all were casualties]." (Lister). For the entire regiment, Gage reported 1 killed, 17 wounded, 1 missing.

   *18th Foot*: Of the grenadier company, the only unit engaged, 2 killed, 4 wounded (Gretton, *Regimental History*). Gage reported 1 killed 4 wounded, 1 missing.

   *23rd Foot*: "our regt had 5 killed and 31 wounded." (Mackenzie; aa4, 440); Gage reported 4 killed, 27 wounded and 6 missing.

   *38th Foot*: Gage reported 4 killed, 12 wounded.

   *43rd Foot*: Gage reported 4 killed, 6 wounded, 2 missing.

   *47th Foot*: Gage reported 5 killed, 23 wounded.

   *52nd Foot*: Gage reported 3 killed, 2 wounded, 1 missing.

   *59th Foot*: Gage reported 3 killed, 3 wounded.

   *British Marines*: Gage reported 27 killed, 40 wounded, 7 missing.

# APPENDIX R

## ❧ Casualties among British Officers on the Concord Mission, April 19 to June 17, 1775.

*Commanders*
   Lt. Col. Francis Smith, 10th Foot, wounded in retreat from Concord
   Major John Pitcairn, British Marines; injured in retreat from Concord, mortally wounded at Bunker Hill
*4th Foot, Light Infantry Company*
   Capt. Nesbit Balfour, wounded at Bunker Hill
   Lt. Edward Gould, wounded and captured on the Concord expedition
   Lt. John Barker
*4th Foot, Grenadier Company*
   Captain John West, wounded at Bunker Hill
   Lt. Edward Barron, wounded at Bunker Hill
   Lt. Leonard Brown, wounded at Bunker Hill
*5th Foot, Light Infantry Company*
   Capt. John Battier
   Lt. Thomas Hawkshaw, wounded on Concord expedition
   Lt. Thomas Cox, wounded on Concord expedition

*5th Foot, Grenadier Company*
    Capt. George Harris, wounded at Bunker Hill
    Lt. Thomas Baker, wounded on Concord Expedition
*10th Foot, Light Infantry*
    Capt. Lawrence Parsons, wounded at Concord, and again at Bunker Hill
    Lt. Waldron Kelly, wounded on Concord expedition
    Ensign Jeremy Lister, volunteer, wounded on Concord expedition
*10th Foot, Grenadier Company*
    Capt. Edward Fitzgerald, wounded at Bunker Hill
    Lt. James Pettigrew, wounded at Bunker Hill
    Lt. Thomas Verner, died of wounds at Bunker Hill
*18th Foot, Grenadier Company*
    Capt. John Shee
    Lt. George Bruere
    Lt. William Blackwood
*23rd Foot, Light Infantry Company*
    Capt. Robert Donkin
    Lt. Thomas Walsh
    Lt. Onslow Beckwith, wounded at Bunker Hill
*23rd Foot Grenadier Company*
    Capt. William Blakeney, wounded at Bunker Hill
    Lt. Thomas Gibbings
    Lt. John Lenthall, wounded at Bunker Hill
*38th Foot, Light Infantry Company*
    Capt. St. Lawrence Boyd, wounded at Bunker Hill
    Lt. William Wade
    Lt. Francis Johnstone
*38th Foot, Grenadier Company*
    Capt. William Crosbie
    Lt. John Howe
    Lt. Robert Christie, wounded at Bunker Hill
*43rd Foot, Light Infantry Company*
    Capt. Walter S. Laurie
    Lt. Edward Hull, mortally wounded on the Concord Expedition
    Lt. Alexander Robertson, wounded at Bunker Hill
*43rd Foot, Grenadier Company*
    Capt. John Hatfield
    Lt. Charles McLean
    Lt. William Gubbins
*47th Foot, Light Infantry Company*
    Capt. Thomas Henry Craig, wounded at Bunker hill
    Lt. John McKinnon
    Lt. Thomas Storey
*47th Foot, Grenadier Company*
    Capt. Richard England, wounded at Bunker Hill
    Lt. Christ. Hilliard, died of wounds at Bunker Hill
    Lt. Pook England, wounded at Bunker Hill
*52nd Foot, Light Infantry Company*
    Capt. William Browne
    Lt. George Hamilton
    Lt. Eward Collier
*52nd Foot, Grenadier Company*
    Capt. William Davison, killed at Bunker Hill
    Lt. John Thompson, wounded at Bunker Hill

*Lt. William Gordon*
*59th Foot, Light Infantry Company*
    *Capt. Narcissus Huson*
    *Lt. Ambrose Simpson*
    *Lt. George Cumine*
*59th Foot, Grenadier Company*
    *Capt. George Gray*
    *Lt. Melton Woodward*
    *Lt. Andrew Despard*
*British Marines, Light Infantry Company*
    *Capt William Souter,* wounded on retreat from Concord
    *Lt. William Pitcairn*
    *Lt. Philip Howe*
*British Marines, Grenadier Company*
    *Capt Thomas Averne,* wounded at Bunker Hill
    *Lt. William Finney,* killed at Bunker Hill
    *Lt. George Vevers*
*Advance Patrol, Volunteers and Officers on Special Assignments*
    *Major Edward Mitchell,* 5th Foot commanding
    *Capt. Charles Cochrane,* 4th Foot
    *Capt. Charles Lumm,* 38th Foot
    *Lt. William Grant,* Royal Artillery
    *Lt. F. P. Thorne,* 4th Foot
    *Lt. William Sutherland,* 38th Foot, wounded on Concord expedition
    *Lt. Jesse Adair,* British Marines
    *Lt. Hamilton,* 64th Foot, captured on Concord expedition
    *Surgeon's Mate Simms,* 43rd Foot

SOURCE: Muster Rolls and Pay Lists, WO12, PRO

# APPENDIX S

❧ Spread of the News of the First Shots at Lexington

| Day | Hour | Place | Means |
|-----|------|-------|-------|
| April 19 | 10 a.m. | Watertown, Mass. | |
| | | Boston, Mass. | |
| | 12 noon? | Worcester, Mass. | express |
| | afternoon | Newburyport, Mass. | express |
| | evening | Providence, R.I. | letter |
| April 20 | early morn | Portsmouth, N.H. | express from Newburyport |
| | 11 a.m. | Brooklyn, Conn | express |
| | 2 p.m. | Woodstock, Conn. | |
| | 3 p.m. | Pomfret, Conn. | |
| | 4 p.m. | Norwich, Conn. | express |
| | 7 p.m. | New London, Conn. | |

| Day | Hour | Place | Means |
|---|---|---|---|
| April 21 | 1 p.m. | Lyme, Conn. | |
| | 4 a.m. | Saybrook, Conn. | |
| | 7 a.m. | Killingsworth, Conn. | |
| | 8 a.m. | East Guilford, Conn. | |
| | 10 a.m. | Guilford, Conn. | |
| | 12 noon | Branford, Conn. | |
| | | New Haven, Conn. | |
| April 22 | 8 a.m. | Fairfield, Conn. | |
| April 23 | 4 p.m. | New York, New York | |
| | evening | Elizabeth, N.J. | |
| | | Woodbridge, N.J. | |
| April 24 | 2 a.m. | Brunswick, N.J. | |
| | 6 a.m. | Princeton, N.J. | |
| | 9 a.m. | Trenton, N.J. | |
| | | Philadelphia, Pa. | |
| | | Chester, Pa. | |
| | | Newcastle, Delaware | |
| April 25 | | Christiana, Delaware | |
| | | Head of Elk, Md. | |
| April 26 | | Baltimore, Md. | |
| | | Annapolis, Md. | a handbill, by express. |
| | | Alexandria, Va. | |
| April 28 | late night | Williamsburg, Va. | by express from Phila. |
| April 30 | | Dumfries, Va. | |
| | | Fredericksburg, Va. | |
| May 1 | | King William, Va. | |
| May 2 | | Williamsburg, Va. | |
| | | Surry, Va. | |
| May 3 | | Smithfield, Va. | |
| | | Nansemond, Va. | |
| | | Chowan, N.C. | |
| | | New Bern N.C. | by ship from Newport April 22 |
| May 4 | | Edenton, N.C. | |
| May 5 | | Bath, N.C. | |
| May 6 | | New Bern, N.C. | overland from Williamsburg to Northampton County. |
| May 7 | | Onslow, N.C. | |
| May 8 | | Wilmington, N.C. | |
| May 9 | | Brunswick, N.C. | |
| | | Charleston, S.C. | by sea |
| May 10 | | Georgetown, S.C. | |

Interior Settlements:

| | | | |
|---|---|---|---|
| May 9 | | Shenandoah Valley, Va. | |
| May, 2d week | | western Pennsylvania | |

*SOURCES*: John H. Scheide, "The Lexington Alarm, AAS *Proceedings* 50 (1940): 49–79; Peter Force (ed.), *AA4*, II, 363–69; Edward McCrady, *The History of South Carolina Under the Royal Government, 1719–1776* (New York, 1899), 789; Lester Cappon *et al.*, *Atlas of American History*, 42, contains many inaccuracies.

# HISTORIOGRAPHY

## ∾ Myths After the Midnight Ride

> Seldom has fact supported legend, seldom has nature imitated art so
> successfully.
>
> —Edmund S. Morgan

Even as the event was still happening, the legend began to grow. Long before Paul Revere reached home again, rumors of the midnight ride began to fly across the countryside. Returning British soldiers reported their encounter with "the noted Paul Revere" on the Concord Road. A newspaper in the city of New York informed its readers that Paul Revere was "missing and supposed to be waylaid and slain."[1] In Boston, the story of the signals from the Old North Church made too good a story for Whig leaders to keep secret very long. Within days, a Tory refugee named Ann Hulton wrote to an English friend, "The people in the country . . . had a signal, it is supposed, by a light from one of the steeples in town, upon the troops embarking."[2]

By early June, the first report of Paul Revere's ride appeared in print. Its author was William Gordon, Roxbury's English-born Congregationalist minister, who appointed himself the first historian of the American Revolution. After the battle, Gordon rode to Concord and interviewed many participants, including Paul Revere himself. In the first week of June, he published an account of the battle which mentioned Revere by name, and briefly described the midnight ride, the capture, the rescue of John Hancock's trunk, and Revere's presence at the battle of Lexington. Gordon's essay was very short, but remarkably full and accurate. Yet even as he wrote, the first of many myths was beginning to take form around the subject. Its inventors were the participants themselves.[3]

## ∾ Participant Historians: The Myth of Injured Innocence

While Gordon was publishing the first account, the Whig leaders themselves kept silent. Many had sworn a vow of secrecy about their activities, and were guarded even in conversation with one another. One of their sons remembered that as late as the early 19th century, the story of the signal lamps and the midnight ride was "common talk at my father's, where they often met, although I can call to mind they were careful of calling names, having some fear of liability."[4]

Fear of liability was not the only factor. The silence of the Whigs also had another cause. The elaborate preparations that lay behind the midnight ride did not fit well with the Whig image of Lexington and Concord as an unprovoked attack upon an unresisting people. Here was the first of many myths that came to encrust the subject—the myth of injured American innocence, which the Whigs themselves actively propagated as an instrument of their cause.

To maintain that interpretation, the earliest written account of the midnight ride by Paul Revere himself appears to have been suppressed by Whig leaders. In the aftermath of the battles Revere and many other eyewitnesses were asked to draft a deposition about the first shot at Lexington. He produced a document that was doubly displeasing to those who requested it. Revere refused to testify unequivocally that the Regulars had fired first at Lexington Common. He also added an account of the midnight ride that suggested something of the American preparations that preceded the event.

Other depositions were rushed into print by the Massachusetts Provincial Congress, and circulated widely in Britain and America, but Revere's testimony was not among them. It did not support the American claim that the Regulars had started the fighting, and revealed more about the revolutionary movement than Whig leaders wished to be known.

Paul Revere's deposition was returned to him. It remained among his private papers, unpublished until 1891.[5]

The myth of wounded innocence was given wide currency by Whig leaders. It dominated the first American accounts of the battles of Lexington and Concord—and most graphically appeared in drawings that were commissioned by Whig leaders themselves. Two weeks after the battles, the artist Ralph Earl was relieved of duty as a Connecticut militiaman, and asked to make a set of sketches of the events at Lexington and Concord. Earl walked the ground, interviewed survivors, and met with Whig leaders. He prepared a series of four drawings. The first and most important represented the fighting at Lexington as a slaughter of American innocents, who appeared mainly to be trying to get out of the way. Earl showed a disciplined formation of Regulars firing a deliberate volley on command into the backs of the militia, who were dispersing peaceably and making no effort to resist.[6]

This myth of American innocence became an instrument of high importance in the events that it purported to describe. It strengthened the moral foundations of the American side, and weakened the ethical underpinnings of the Imperial cause. There was little room in this interpretation for the careful preparation that lay behind the American alarm system, and even less for the elaborate efforts that set the machine in motion. Among Whig leaders, a conspiracy of silence surrounded the midnight ride for many years after the event.

### ❧ Children of the Founders: The Myth of the Patriot Fathers

Despite the reticence of Whig leaders, oral reports of Paul Revere's ride continued to spread through New England, and passed rapidly into the realm of regional folklore. A child of the Revolution remembered that "we needed no fairy tales in our youth. The real experiences of our own people were more fascinating than all the novels ever written."[7] In that spirit, the children of Boston learned the story of the signal lanterns and the midnight ride as it passed from one person to another. "I have heard it told over many times, and never doubted," recalled Joshua Fowle of his Boston boyhood, "I knew in my young days many of the prominent men who took an active part in the doings of those days. Paul Revere lived near me. . . . It was common talk."[8]

That common talk made Paul Revere a local hero throughout New England. After the Revolution was over, his exploits began to be set down on paper, sometimes in highly inflated ways. The growth of his reputation as a regional folk-hero was evident as early as 1795. To mark the twentieth anniversary of the event, a Yankee bard who signed himself Eb. Stiles composed an epic poem about the midnight ride that endowed the hero and his horse with more than mortal powers:

> He raced his steed through field and wood
> Nor turned to ford the river,
> But faced his horse to the foaming flood
> They swam across together.
>
> He madly dashed o'er mountain and moor,
> Never slackened spur nor rein
> Until with shout he stood by the door
> Of the Church on Concord green.

Never mind that the actual ride of Paul Revere ended short of Concord, or that the nearest equivalent to a foaming flood was a sluggish stream called the Mystick River, which he crossed without getting his feet wet. It was in the nature of a mythic hero to transcend the limits of mundane fact. So it was with Eb. Stiles's poetic image of Paul Revere.[9]

As the mythmaking grew more extravagant, the newly organized Massachusetts Historical Society decided to issue a documentary record of the event. Jeremy Belknap, corresponding secretary of the society, approached Paul Revere and asked him to contribute a history of the midnight ride for publication in its *Proceedings*. Revere's account, which finally arrived in 1798, twenty-three years after the event, was brief, understated, and self-effacing. It also strongly supported the Whig interpretation. Before it went into print, Revere carefully deleted from his first draft an incautious phrase that described his attempt to attack the British patrol when he first sighted it—an aggressive impulse that was not consistent with the myth of American innocence. Revere intended his account to be anonymous. He signed it "A Son of Liberty in 1775," and requested Belknap, "Do not print my name." Belknap ignored the request, and identified Revere as the author without permission.

Through Paul Revere's lifetime, the reticence of the revolutionary generation continued. It appeared even in his obituary, which abundantly praised his private life and public service, but made no mention of the midnight ride or any of his clandestine activities before the Revolution. The conspiracy of silence continued.[10]

In the years after Revere's death in 1818, however, attitudes began to change. Published accounts of the midnight ride began to multiply. Some came from surviving eyewitnesses who confirmed the factual accuracy of Paul Revere's letter to Belknap, and added colorful details to his laconic interpretation of the event.

Several of these narratives emerged from a bizarre dispute between the towns of Lexington and Concord over the question of who fired the first shot. Immediately after the battles, as we have seen, Whig leaders had been at pains to demonstrate that the Regulars had fired first. Fifty years later, their descendants battled furiously over the question of which town deserved the honor of being first to fire back. Concord lawyer Samuel Hoar started the controversy in 1824. In a speech of welcome to the Marquis de Lafayette, Hoar claimed that his town was the scene of "the first forcible resistance" to British arms.

Outraged citizens of Lexington responded by collecting depositions from surviving militiamen in their town, who now testified that the first American shots were fired not at Concord's North Bridge but on Lexington's village green, after the Regulars had fired at them. The citizens of Acton joined in, with impassioned testimony that their forebears had fired the first American shots and suffered the first losses at the North Bridge after the militia of Concord had cravenly refused to take the lead. The inhabitants of West Cambridge (later the town of Arlington, earlier the hamlet called Menotomy) offered further evidence that the heaviest fighting of the day occurred neither in Concord or Lexington, but in their village.[11]

These polemics generated much fresh evidence about the battles, and also produced some new material on Paul Revere's ride. They also helped to transform the prevailing interpretation of those events. The men who actually did the fighting in 1775 had cultivated an image of themselves as innocent and even passive victims of British aggression. The next generation remembered them in a very different way—as bold, active, and defiant defenders of home and hearth.

The new interpretation most vividly appeared in the changing iconography of the fight at Lexington. The earliest prints of the battle, which had represented it as a slaughter of the innocents, gave way to new images that showed increasing ardor on the American side. In 1830 a lithograph showed some of the militia firing back at the British. By 1855 an engraving by Hammatt Billings for Charles Hudson's *History of Lexington* had most of the Americans actively in the fight. In 1886, a painting by Henry Sandham for Lexington's town hall represented all of the militia standing firm and fighting bravely in heroic postures of defiance.[12]

A parallel transformation also occurred in the image of Paul Revere. Even his own deposition of 1775 (which Whig leaders had thought too candid for publication) represented his own role as that of a peaceable citizen, innocently deprived of his liberty by a party of violent and blasphemous British officers who "stopped me on the highway, and made me a prisoner I knew not by what right."[13]

In the 19th century, newly published eyewitness accounts portrayed him in a different

The Monument at Concord's North Bridge, a pastoral painting by Fitzhugh Lane. (Concord Free Public Library)

light as an active and aggressive leader, boldly organizing resistance in Boston, concerting military preparations, shouting his alarm to Sergeant Munroe, and actively hurling defiance at his British captors.[14] This new image of Paul Revere appeared in depositions by Elijah Sanderson and William Munroe, in anniversary orations, and in a book called *History of the Siege of Boston, and of the Battles of Lexington, Concord, and Bunker Hill* (1849). Its author, Richard Frothingham, was an antiquarian historian of Charlestown. He published fresh material from the papers of Richard Devens, the Whig leader who helped Paul Revere on his way, and was one of the first scholars to recognize in print the range and importance of Paul Revere's activity in the revolutionary movement. He wrote, "Paul Revere, an ingenious goldsmith, as ready to engrave a lampoon as to rally a caucus, was the great confidential messenger of the patriots and the great leader of the mechanics."[15]

As this interpretation took hold, the first biographical sketches of Paul Revere began to be published. Chief among them was a long essay published anonymously by Boston editor Joseph Buckingham in his *New England Magazine* (1832). Buckingham himself had not been born until 1779, but he knew Paul Revere, interviewed his friends, and acquired some of his manuscripts. Informants told him that Revere was "one of the persons who planned and executed one of the most daring projects which characterized the times—the destruction of tea." Buckingham represented Paul Revere as a major Whig leader, and described his many Revolutionary activities, several for the first time. He also reprinted Revere's letter to Jeremy Belknap about the midnight ride, commenting that it "contains incident enough to supply a novelist with the basis of a romance." The figure that emerged from Buckingham's sketch was a strong and active leader in the forefront of the Revolution.[16]

Ten years later, Alden Bradford included a life of Paul Revere in a volume on distinguished men in New England. These writings began to celebrate Paul Revere not only for what he did but who he was. Daniel Webster described him as "a man of sense and character, and of high public spirit, whom the mechanics of Boston ought never to forget."

Webster himself could not quite remember what Paul Revere did for a living, but he was very clear about the large meaning of his life.[17]

In the mid-19th century, cities and towns throughout Massachusetts began to commemorate Paul Revere in their place names. Boston's May Street became Revere Street in 1855. Other Revere streets appeared in the towns of Arlington, Cambridge, Chelsea, Everett, Hudson, Hull, Lexington, Malden, Medford, Milton, Quincy, Sudbury, Weymouth, Winthrop, and Woburn. In 1871, the entire Boston suburb of North Chelsea took the name of Revere. Many other places were so named in New England, but few in the nation at large. Paul Revere was still mainly a regional hero.[18]

## ⮯ The Union in Crisis: Longfellow's Myth of the Lone Rider

In the year 1861, Revere's reputation suddenly expanded beyond his native New England. As the nation moved toward Civil War, many northern writers contributed their pens to the Union cause. Among them was New England's poet laureate, Henry Wadsworth Longfellow, who searched for a way to awaken opinion in the North. On April 5, 1860, Longfellow suddenly found what he was looking for. He and his friend George Sumner went walking in the North End, past Copp's Hill Burying Ground and the Old North Church, while Sumner told him the story of the midnight ride. The next day, April 6, 1860, Longfellow wrote in his diary, "Paul Revere's Ride begun this day." Two weeks later he was still hard at work: "April 19, I wrote a few lines in 'Paul Revere's Ride.' this being the day of his achievement." Perhaps on that anniversary day he found his opening stanza, which so many American pupils would learn by heart:

> Listen my children, and you shall hear,
> Of the midnight ride of Paul Revere,
> On the eighteenth of April, in Seventy-five;
> Hardly a man is now alive
> Who remembers that famous day and year.

Not so well remembered were the lines near the end, that summarized the larger purposes of the poem:

> For, borne on the night-wind of the past,
> Through all our history to the last,
> In the hour of darkness and peril and need,
> The people will waken and listen to hear,
> The hurrying hoof-beats of that steed,
> And the midnight message of Paul Revere.

The poem was first published by *The Atlantic* in January 1861. It had an extraordinary impact. The insistent beat of Longfellow's meter reverberated through the North like a drum roll. It instantly captured the imagination of the reading public. This was a call to arms for a new American generation, in another moment of peril. It was also an argument from Paul Revere's example that one man alone could make a difference, by his service to a great and noble cause.

From an historiographical perspective, Longfellow's poem contained a curious irony. He appealed to the evidence of history as a source of patriotic inspiration, but was utterly without scruple in his manipulation of historical fact. As an historical description of Paul Revere's ride, the poem was grossly, systematically, and deliberately inaccurate. Its many errors were not merely careless mistakes. Longfellow did some research on his subject. He consulted amateur scholars such as Sumner, probably knew Frothingham's *Siege of Boston* and George Bancroft's *History of the United States,* which had sold very briskly only a few years before, and appears to have been familiar with Paul Revere's account, which had been in print for sixty years. To enlarge his stock of poetic imagery, Longfellow climbed the steeple of the North Church, scattering the pigeons from their roosts in his search for color and detail. Even the pigeons went into the poem for a touch of verisimilitude.[19]

Having done all that, Longfellow proceeded to change the history of Paul Revere's ride as radically as his poetic predecessor Eb. Stiles had transformed its geography. His most important revision was not merely in specific details that he so freely altered, but in a new interpretation that had a powerful resonance in American culture.

For his own interpretative purposes, Longfellow invented an image of Paul Revere as a solitary hero who acted alone in history. He allowed his mythical midnight rider only a single henchman, an anonymous Boston "friend" who appeared in the poem as a Yankee Sancho Panza for this New England knight-errant. Otherwise, Longfellow's Paul Revere needed no help from anyone. He rowed himself across the Charles River, waited alone for a signal from the Old North Church, made a solitary ride all the way to Concord, and awakened every Middlesex village and farm along the way.

As a work of history, that interpretation was wildly inaccurate in all its major parts. But as an exercise of poetic imagination it succeeded brilliantly. Longfellow's verse instantly transformed a regional folk-hero into a national figure of high prominence. Paul Revere entered the pantheon of patriot heroes as an historical loner of the sort that Americans love to celebrate.

From Captain John Smith to Colonel Charles Lindbergh, many American heroes have been remembered in that way, as solitary actors against the world. This was not entirely an American phenomenon. It was an attitude that belonged to a time as well as a place. Many Romantic writers in the late 19th century—Emerson, Carlyle, Nietzsche—celebrated world-historical leaders as heroic individuals who faced their fate alone. That idea had powerful appeal in a world that was becoming more ordered, and more institution-bound. The genius of Longfellow's poem was to link this powerful theme to a patriotic purpose. It stamped its image of Paul Revere as an historical loner indelibly upon the national memory.

New England antiquarians responded to Longfellow's poem with expressions of high indignation for its gross inaccuracy. Charles Hudson, town historian of Lexington, Massachusetts, wrote angrily in 1868, "We have heard of poetic license, but have always understood that this sort of latitude was to be confined to modes of expression and to the regions of the imagination, and should not extend to historic facts . . . when poets pervert plain matters of history, to give speed to their *Pegasus,* they should be restrained, as Revere was in his midnight ride."[20]

For many years historians in New England labored to correct Longfellow's errors. They demonstrated exhaustively that Paul Revere did not receive the lantern signals from the Old North Church, but helped to send them. They documented abundantly the fact that he did not row alone across the Charles River, but was transported by others. They proved conclusively that Paul Revere did not reach Concord, and that another messenger succeeded where he failed. Other midnight riders were much discussed: notably Dr. Samuel Prescott, and William Dawes, who began to receive more attention than Paul Revere himself.

But the scholars never managed to catch up with Longfellow's galloping hero. Generations of American schoolchildren were required to memorize Longfellow's poem. Even today many older Americans are still able to recite stanzas they learned in their youth, long after their memory of more recent events has faded. Whatever the failings of the poem as an historical account, it gave new life and symbolic meaning to its subject. It also elevated Paul Revere into figure of high national prominence, and made the midnight ride an important event in American history.

Longfellow's interpretation of Paul Revere was taken up by many popular writers who came after him. Several generations of American artists also borrowed Longfellow's theme of the lone rider. Howard Laskey in 1891 did a drawing called "The Ride," in which Paul Revere and his galloping horse appeared entirely alone, floating in an empty space with nothing in sight but their own shadow.[21] Grant Wood in 1931 did a striking painting of "The Midnight Ride of Paul Revere," (1931), which gave the same interpretation a different

Grant Wood, *Paul Revere's Ride,* 1931. The painter gives us a new version of Longfellow's myth with a 20th-century twist. Paul Revere appears as a lone midnight rider, galloping across a sterile, soulless Anerican landscape. (Courtesy, Metropolitan Museum of Art and VAGA, Inc.)

twist. The midnight rider appeared as a dark, faceless, solitary figure, galloping alone through an eery New England townscape that appeared sterile and lifeless in the brilliant moonlight.

Longfellow's interpretation was given a new form in 1914 by Thomas Edison, who made a silent film called "The Midnight Ride of Paul Revere." Like many autodidacts, Edison was deeply contemptuous of schools and scholars. "I should say," he wrote, "that on the average we only get about two percent efficiency out of school books as they are written today. The education of the future as I see it, will be conducted through the medium of the motion picture, a visualized education, where it should be possible to obtain a one hundred percent efficiency." To that end, Edison made a film of Paul Revere's ride as a way of teaching American history through the camera. His interpretation closely followed Longfellow's poem in substance and detail—myths, legends, errors, pigeons and all.[22]

### ❧ Myths for Imperial America: Colonel Revere as a Man on Horseback

Thanks largely to Longfellow's poem, Paul Revere's stature increased steadily during the late 19th century, and spread throughout the United States. Towns were named after him not merely in New England, but also in Pennsylvania, Minnesota, and Missouri.

The centennial celebrations of the American Revolution that began in 1875 also inspired much popular interest in his life and work. Many celebrations were held in that year, when President Ulysses Grant himself came to Lexington and Concord. The Old North Church began to keep the custom of its annual "lantern ceremony."

The Paul Revere of the late 19th century began to be given a new persona, that was thought to be more meaningful in a different era of American history. During this period he was commonly called Colonel Revere, the military title that came to him later in the War of Independence. Increasingly he became a militant symbol of American strength, power and martial courage.

In 1885 the city of Boston decided that this man on horseback needed an appropriate equestrian monument. It sponsored a prize competition that was won by an unknown young artist named Cyrus Dallin, an American sculptor who later came to be widely known for his muscular Puritans, melancholy Indians, heroic pioneers, and courageous soldiers of the Civil War. Dallin's monumental Paul Revere was the proverbial man on horseback, a militant figure standing straight up in his long stirrup leathers, in a costume that was cut to resemble a Continental uniform. The midnight rider appeared as a strident symbol of American power, with bulging muscles, a military appearance, and a murderous expression. To complete the effect, even the horse was transformed. Deacon Larkin's mare Brown Beauty suffered the indignity of being changed into a stallion, and given the head of a Greek war horse, and the body of a Renaissance military charger.

There was an interpretative problem in the first design of Dallin's sculpture. It was called "Waiting for the Light," and showed Paul Revere in Charlestown, looking back toward the Old North Church for the lantern signal." The committee liked the conception, and awarded its prize to Dallin. But critics forcefully pointed out that the interpretation was an error borrowed from Henry Wadsworth Longfellow. Dallin was sent back to his studio, and produced another version of Paul Revere, as militant as before, but without Longfellow's errors. The ensuing controversy, however, destroyed the momentum for the project, and the money could not be found to construct a full-scale bronze statue. Dallin's sculpture remained a plaster model for many years, which he redesigned at least seven times. But even in its unfinished state, it captured the spirit of yet another myth of the midnight rider. In this latest incarnation, Paul Revere became less a man than a military monument. He was made to personify the new union of power and freedom in a Great Republic that was beginning to flex its muscles throughout the world.[23]

The interpretative mood in this era was also captured by a piece of music titled "Paul Revere's Ride; a March-Two Step," published in 1905 by E. T. Paull, a prolific composer of popular music. This musical version of the midnight ride began with the faint hoofbeats of a galloping horse. It advanced through movements that the composer called the "The Cry of Alarm," "The Patriots Aroused," "The Call to Arms" (double fortissimo), the Battle of Lexington and Concord (triple fortissimo), and "The Enemy Routed" (quadruple fortissimo). The piece was advertised as "one of E. T. Paull's greatest marches," no modest claim for the composer of "The Burning of Rome" and "Napoleon's Last Charge." His rendition of the midnight ride was "respectfully inscribed to the Daughters of the American Revolution."[24]

In Boston, the Daughters of the American Revolution actively promoted the reputation of Paul Revere. They took an active part in the rescue and preservation of Paul Revere's home, which had become a rundown tenement in Boston's North End. To preserve it, a voluntary society was founded with the name of the Paul Revere Memorial Association. It acquired title to the house, restored it with high enthusiasm, and opened it to the public in 1908 as a shrine of the Revolution. Today, the Paul Revere House is the only 17th-century building that survives in what was Old Boston.[25]

In 1891, the first full-length biography of Paul Revere was published by Elbridge Henry Goss, a Boston antiquarian. It was a classic specimen of a two-volume Victorian "Life and Letters" biography, mainly a compendium of primary materials in two thick volumes, handsomely embellished with many illustrations and facsimiles. Goss was mostly interested in his subject as Colonel Revere, a political and military figure. Nearly 100 pages (of 622 in

The Filiopietists in Full Cry. This musical version of the militant Paul Revere had a grand crescendo scored quadruple fortissimo. (Brandeis University Library)

the two volumes together) were devoted to the Penobscot Expedition alone. Very little attention was given to Revere's private life.

The major contribution of the work was to assemble and reprint primary evidence of Revere's public life. Goss was given access to Revere manuscripts by the family. He published for the first time many letters and documents, including Revere's deposition on the midnight ride, and also collected much colorful testimony from Boston families who preserved the folklore of the event. Every subsequent student of Revere's life is heavily in Goss's debt for the materials that he collected. Wherever possible, the author allowed Paul Revere to speak for himself. His chapter on the midnight ride consisted entirely of a transcription of Revere's fullest account, with explanatory footnotes.[26]

The larger purpose of the book was to celebrate Paul Revere's qualities of character, as one of Boston's "truest, most noble and patriotic sons." In 1891, Elbridge Goss expressed a complete confidence that Revere's reputation would continue to grow. "As time goes on," he wrote, "such lives as his will be studied, honored, cherished and remembered with still greater reverence."[27]

## ❧ U.S. v. The Spirit of '76: Paul Revere and the American Anglophiles

Goss's prediction proved to be right in one way, but wrong in another. Revere continued to be studied, but not always with "greater reverence." In the 20th century, strong
countervailing tendencies also began to appear. One of them was a new sympathy in the
United States for the British side of the American Revolution. The late 19th century was a
moment of Anglo-American rapprochement, when writers on both sides of the Atlantic
suddenly discovered a sense of solidarity among the "Anglo-Saxon" nations. One result in
academic scholarship was the "imperial school" of George Louis Beer and Charles Maclean
Andrews, who rewrote early American history from the perspective of London and the
Empire. Another was a circle of antiquarians who included Elizabeth Ellery Dana, Charles
Knowles Bolton, and especially William Clements (1861–1934), a wealthy Michigan indus-
trialist, and Harold Murdock (1862–1934), a prominent Boston banker.

This circle of American Anglophiles studied the outbreak of the Revolution as an
Anglo-Saxon Civil War. They searched British homes and archives and unearthed many
new primary sources on the Revolution, which they purchased from their impoverished
owners and carried home in triumph to the United States. At the same time they also
contributed many secondary studies, laboring to explode the patriot myths of American
innocence on the one hand and British oppression on the other.[28]

They showed no animus against the more conservative American revolutionaries, who
were regarded as Anglo-Saxons too (even one who was half Huguenot), but they were
strongly hostile to America's Revolutionary myths. Paul Revere continued to be celebrated
by these authors, but more for his character than his cause. One called him a "man of solid
substance," who was "quite unconscious of the heroic figure which he was to make in
history." At the same time Longfellow's legend of the midnight ride was derided, and the
patriot myths were furiously attacked. Behind this work lay a dream of Anglo-Saxon solidarity that was as romantic in its own way as Longfellow's myth of the lone rider.[29]

The American Anglophiles produced a large crop of monographs on the battles of
Lexington and Concord. Among them was Frank Coburn's study, *The Battle of April 19,
1775*, privately published in 1912. Coburn reconstructed the details of the battle with great
care, and traced on his bicycle the routes of the midnight riders and the marching armies,
calculating distances on his bicycle speedometer, calibrated in eighty-eighths of a statute
mile. The result was an interpretation that mediated not only between Britain and the
United States, but also between Lexington and Concord, and even between the partisans of
Paul Revere and William Dawes. Coburn summarized his theme in a sentence: "I am glad to
add," he wrote, "that the bitterness and hatred, so much in evidence on that long ago battle
day, no longer exist between children of the great British nation."[30]

Anglophile interpretations acquired a new urgency during the First World War. In
1917, an American film about Paul Revere's ride was ordered to be seized under the Espionage Act, on the ground that it promoted discord between the United States and Britain.
The case was heard in the Federal District Court of Southern California, and called *United
States v. The Spirit of Seventy Six*.[31]

## ❧ An Age of Disbelief: The Myths of the American Debunkers

At the same time, another line of interpretation was also developing—a school of
historical skepticism that was hostile to the myth of the midnight ride for different reasons.
Early expressions of this attitude appeared in an unexpected place—the writings of the
Adams family. They had a score to settle with Paul Revere. In the early republic Revere had
become a high Federalist, in company with many merchants and manufacturers in New
England who had little liking for the presidency of John Adams, and even less for what
Boston regarded as the "apostasy" of John Quincy Adams. That hostility was reciprocated
by the Adams family toward Boston in general, State Street in particular, and Paul Revere

among the rest. The Adamses expressed strong resentment against what they regarded as the absurd inflation of Paul Revere's reputation. In 1909, Charles Francis Adams, Jr., expressed his outrage "in the matter of Mr. Longfellow, and the strange perversion he has given to historical facts as respects Paul Revere and his famous ride." Adams wrote that the duty of the historian was to "exorcise, so to speak, a popularly accepted legend." Adams's strongest resentment was against Longfellow, but there was no love lost for Paul Revere.[32]

Others were happy to take up this task of historical "exorcism." As early as 1896, Helen More contributed a sarcastic scrap of light verse called "What's in a Name?" which suggested that William Dawes did the work and Paul Revere got the credit.

> Tis all very well for the children to hear
> Of the midnight ride of Paul Revere;
> But why should my name be quite forgot
> Who rode as boldly and well, God wot?
> Why, should I ask? The reason is clear—
> My name was Dawes and his Revere.[33]

The prominence of William Dawes increased when his descendant Charles Dawes became Vice President of the United States under Calvin Coolidge. Several accounts asserted (with as much inaccuracy as Stiles and Longfellow) that Dawes had succeeded in reaching Concord when Paul Revere was arrested. There was no truth in this idea, but it was widely repeated.

In the popular press, Paul Revere became increasingly an object of good-humored derision. The *Boston Globe* on April 19, 1914, marked the anniversary of the midnight ride by publishing an irreverent satire called "The Ride of the Ghost of Paul Revere, by Two Long Fellows."

> It was two by the village clock
> When his inner tube gave a hiss.
> He felt the car come down with a shock,
> He jacked, and pried, and pumped, and said,
> "I wish I'd come on a horse instead."

This mood grew stronger in the era that followed the First World War, when patriotic symbols everywhere came to be regarded with increasing suspicion. The word "debunk" was first recorded in 1923 to describe this new school of historical criticism. The legend of Paul Revere's ride instantly became a favorite target. There was little anger or hostility in this literature, but much good-natured contempt, and sophomoric humor that rings strangely in the ear of another generation.[34]

Even Paul Revere's horse was debunked. Patriotic engravers in the 19th century had represented Brown Beauty as a fine-boned thoroughbred. Debunkers in the 20th century took pleasure in proclaiming that Paul Revere was actually mounted on a plodding plough horse. That revision was as mistaken as the image it was meant to correct, but it came to be widely repeated in the 1920s, and has crept into the historical literature.

In 1923, one exceptionally bold debunker went so far as to assert that the midnight ride never happened at all. At that point, the President of the United States felt compelled to intervene. "Only a few days ago," Warren Harding declared with high indignation, "an iconoclastic American said there never was a ride by Paul Revere." The President was shaky in his facts, but rock-solid in support of Paul Revere. "Somebody made the ride," he reasoned, "and stirred the minutemen in the colonies to fight the battle of Lexington, which was the beginning of independence in the new Republic in America. I love the story of Paul Revere, whether he rode or not."[35]

Through the 1920s, debunkers were strongly resisted by filiopietists who defended the patriot myths with high enthusiasm, sometimes in surprising ways. In 1922, Captain E. B. Lyon of the U.S. Army followed the path of Paul Revere's midnight ride in a military aircraft, dropping "patriotic pamphlets" along the way.[36]

The debunkers were undeterred by flying filiopietists and presidential reprimands. With the growing antiwar movement of the 1930s they also turned their attentions to the myth of the minutemen, who were increasingly represented as cowardly country bumpkins, and bad shots to boot.[37] In the late 1930s an army officer was detailed to make a study of the battles of Lexington and Concord. He concluded that there was nothing of professional interest to be learned from the event.[38]

On the midnight ride, both debunkers and filiopietists continued to be very active through the 1930s, much to the bewilderment of the reading public. H. L. Mencken's irreverent magazine *The American Mercury* was publishing iconoclastic attacks on the legend of Paul Revere as late as 1938.[39] When Esther Forbes brought out her biography of Paul Revere in 1942, she reported in amazement, "Since I have begun on this book I have been asked several times if it is true that Paul Revere never took that ride at all."[40]

## ❧ Crusade for Democracy: The Myth of the Common Man

The age of the debunker ended abruptly with the outbreak of World War II. As fascist and communist dictatorships gained strength throughout the world, and free institutions were increasingly under violent attack, Americans began to think again about their national heritage of liberal values and democratic purposes.

Once again the reputation of Paul Revere was a sensitive indicator of cultural change. The reputation of the midnight rider began to be refurbished to meet the changing needs of a new generation. In 1940, the city of Boston finally got around to erecting Cyrus Dallin's equestrian statue of Paul Revere as a symbol of resistance to tyranny and aggression.

One might have expected that the militant Paul Revere of Dallin's monument would have returned to fashion in a world at war. But something else happened. Paul Revere was suddenly given a new image, different from all that came before, and yet perfectly matched to the needs of a democratic crusade against fascism and militarism.

The architect of this new interpretation was Esther Forbes, a New England novelist who turned her hand to the writing of history with high success. It was one of the more improbable pairings of subject and author—a masculine figure whose life had been absorbed in the hurly-burly of politics, war and business; and a New England spinster who worked beside her aged mother in a quiet alcove of the American Antiquarian Society.

In that setting, Esther Forbes wrote a book called *Paul Revere and the World He Lived In*. It was published in 1942, the year of Corregidor and Midway, and gave the midnight rider a new identity suitable to the nation's great crusade for freedom and democracy. Esther Forbes interpreted her hero as an ordinary American, a peace-loving common man who rose to the challenge of great events. In a letter to her editor, she summarized her idea of Paul Revere in two sentences. "He represents a typical and important type of man about which very little is written," she wrote; "I mean the simple artizan [sic]."[41]

To make her case for Paul Revere as a "simple artizan," Forbes gave much attention to his commmunity, and especially to his domestic life. She had little interest in the details of politics, or military career, or business affairs, beyond an evocation of Revere's colonial silver shop and intimate vignettes of his bell foundry. Her idea of the American Revolution was a hierarchical movement in which Sam Adams appeared as the "mastermind" and Paul Revere as a "lone horseman" who acted as "courier" for his social superiors. The midnight ride was given merely twelve pages out of five hundred in the book, and interpreted as an event of minor consequence, except for its status as a myth and symbol. Most of the book was about the social world of a "simple artizan" in colonial Boston.

Esther Forbes celebrated the everyday life of an ordinary man with grace, verve, deep feeling for her democratic theme, and high good humor. She was less enthusiastic about Paul Revere himself, whose personality tended to disappear into the social background. The organizing idea of Paul Revere as a "simple artizan" was very far off the mark—as romantic and inaccurate in its own way as Longfellow's solitary rider.[42]

Academic historians have also tended to criticize the scholarship of the work in another way, complaining that it "lacks citations" and "uses significant literary license."[43] This criticism is unfair. It is true that the book is not well documented, and it has been corrected in detail by subsequent research. But Forbes made excellent use of the materials assembled by Goss and also of the Revere Family Papers. The book is beautifully crafted as a work of popular biography and still very fresh and lively. Its sustained interest in social history was far in advance of academic scholarship. For its timely expression of the new national mood, *Paul Revere and the World He Lived In* won the Pulitzer Prize in 1943.[44]

Esther Forbes's interpretation of Paul Revere as a "simple artizan" was taken up by many other American writers in the mid-20th century. It lent itself perfectly to a new generation of children's books by Dorothy Canfield Fisher, Jean Fritz, and especially Robert Lawson's *Mr. Revere and I* (Boston, 1953), a charming fable told by Paul Revere's horse, whom the author renamed Scheherazade. Lawson's witty drawings showed Paul Revere as an ordinary American who reluctantly left his domestic hearth and rose heroically to keep his rendezvous with destiny—an interpretation very close to that of Esther Forbes. [45]

## ❧ The Cold War: The Myth of the Capitalist Democrat

In 1949, a symbolic event occurred in Boston. Paul Revere's "patriotic bowl," commissioned by the Sons of Liberty in 1768 to commemorate the courage of ninety-two members of the Massachusetts legislature, was returned to the Commonwealth with high ceremony. The bowl had passed into the hands of private collector, Mrs. Marsden Perry. It was purchased from her estate for $56,000, raised partly from schoolchildren in Boston, in a campaign sponsored by Yankee social leaders, Jewish businessmen, and Irish politicians led by Thomas P. O'Neill, Jr., then speaker of the Massachusetts House of Representatives. Paul Revere's bowl with its libertarian inscriptions was placed in the Museum of Fine Arts as an icon of American freedom, and a symbol of a new society which was open to people of diverse origins.

With the beginning of the Cold War, Paul Revere began to appear as a personification of the linkage between capitalism and democracy, and the symbol of an open pluralist society in the "free world." On the anniversary of the ride in 1950, the *Boston Herald* warned that "tyranny of Red Coats takes a new form—Communism. In saluting the patriots of Concord and Lexington we sound the alarm once again. The enemy is now in our midst."[46]

Much popular writing in this era stressed the connection between Paul Revere's activities as a Son of Liberty and his career as a "businessman" and an archetype of "free enterprise." The image of Paul Revere became increasingly prominent in commercial advertising. The Paul Revere Insurance Company reached its public with the slogan, "Revere, a name you can trust." The Revere Sugar Corporation used the silhouette of the midnight rider as its advertising logo. The Revere Copper and Brass Company, which had grown from Paul Revere's business, stamped a profile of its founder's head on the bottom of each of its copper-clad saucepans, which it sold by the millions to American housewives.

The most widely read work in this period was a lively piece of popular history by Arthur B. Tourtellot, first published in 1959 as *William Diamond's Drum* and reissued as *Lexington and Concord: The Beginning of the War of the American Revolution* (1963). Tourtellot was a specialist in public relations for Time, Inc., and director of its television productions from 1950 to 1952. He drew heavily on the British materials found by American Anglophiles to celebrate the minutemen and the midnight riders as defenders of a free society.

Another expression of this interpretative mood was an important and highly original work by John R. Galvin, a graduate of West Point in the class of 1954, who served in Latin America, Vietnam, and ended a distinguished career as Commanding General of NATO. Galvin was also a trained historian of high ability, with a master's degree in history from Columbia University. During the early 1960s, while a junior officer stationed at Fort Devens, Massachusetts, he wrote a book, later published under the misleading title of *The*

*Minute Men: A Compact History of the Defenders of the American Colonies, 1645–1775.* Of the twenty-nine chapters in this work, twenty-three were devoted to events of 1774 and 1775, seventeen of them to the battles of Lexington and Concord.

Galvin's interpretation was conceived in the context of the new military thinking about "unconventional warfare" that developed in the early 1960s. He found the battles of Lexington and Concord deeply interesting in that respect. At the same time, he studied the minutemen and the midnight riders as products of a deeply rooted American tradition, and in general celebrated their conduct on April 19 as a model of military preparedness and unconventional warfare, from which soldiers and civilians in the 20th century had much to learn. In the process, Galvin offered a revisionist account of the fighting, that corrected many myths. The book also gave new meaning to Paul Revere's role as an active and highly effective leader who had a major impact on events, including the fighting itself.[47]

The books of Tourtellot and Galvin were serious and able works of scholarship. At the same time, popular writers during the 1950s and early 1960s began to celebrate the midnight riders and the minutemen with unrestrained enthusiasm. One example was a children's book of this period, William De Witt's *History's Hundred Greatest Events* (New York, 1954). It elevated Paul Revere's ride to equal rank with the crucifixion of Christ, the discovery of penicillin, and the struggle against Communism in Korea.

## The Age of Vietnam: The Myth of the Evil Americans

As the celebrations became more exaggerated, the midnight messenger was riding for a fall. A reversal of his reputation came with a vengeance, during the late 1960s and 1970s. The American mood changed more abruptly and radically in that period than in any other era of the nation's history. Once again the reputation of Paul Revere was a highly sensitive cultural barometer.

The deeply troubled generation of Vietnam and Watergate returned to a mood of iconoclasm that was very different from the light-hearted debunking of the early 20th century. The first generation of American debunkers had often come from the right. From the Adamses to Henry Ford and H. L. Mencken, they were deeply uncomfortable with the principles of American liberalism and democracy. The iconoclasts of the 1960s and 70s came mostly from the left, and complained of collusion between capitalism and democracy. The tone was different too. The old debunkers had cultivated a light touch. The new iconoclasts were bitter, cynical, cruel and angry. They turned furiously against the culture of the nation they called Amerika, and published scathing attacks on its patriotic symbols. A favorite target was Paul Revere.

One iconoclast of this new school was Richard Bissell, a dramatist whose credits included the popular broadway shows *The Pajama Game* and *Say, Darling.* In 1975 Bissell tried his hand at history. For the bicentennial celebration of the American Revolution he contributed a little book loosely modeled on *1066 and All That,* called *New Light on 1776 and All That.* One of its chapters demolished the myth of Paul Revere and the battles of Lexington and Concord. Earlier iconoclasts had been content to accuse Paul Revere of failing to complete his ride, and stealing the glory from William Dawes and Samuel Prescott. Richard Bissell went further. He informed his readers that Paul Revere was a coward and traitor who "sang like a canary" to his British captors, and betrayed his friends to save his own skin. This interpretation was illustrated with a bizarre cartoon of Paul Revere as a canary, chirping away in his cage. Bissell's account was grossly inaccurate, the very opposite of what actually happened; but it was what some Americans wanted to hear about their heroes.[48]

A similar interpretation was repeated by a writer named John Train who in 1980 told a reporter for the *Washington Post* that Paul Revere "set out with two other guys for money . . . he was quite a despicable . . . he was arrested en route by the British. He turned stool pigeon and betrayed his two companions." In fact Revere was not paid for his midnight ride, and in no way betrayed anyone. There was no truth whatever in these

The iconoclasm that followed the Vietnam War was very different from the good-natured debunking of the 1920s. Several writers in the 1970s casually invented an accusation that Paul Revere's Ride ended not merely in failure but in treason to his cause. One asserted that he "sang like a canary" to his British captors. As evidence, one iconoclast published this bizarre illustratiom to make his case. It was the opposite of what actually happened, but Americans in that unhappy era wanted desperately to disbelieve. (Little, Brown and Company)

interpretations, which combined credulity and cynicism in equal measure. But in the turbulent wake of Watergate and Vietnam, some Americans wanted desperately to disbelieve.[49]

In 1968, the editors of the *Boston Globe* joined in. That paper published an editorial on Patriots' Day which roundly asserted as fact (with absolutely no evidence whatever) that early in the midnight ride Medford's Captain Isaac Hall "gave Paul a little something to warm his bones," and that it was "a little rum poured on top of patriotic fervor that caused Paul to sound his cry of alarm." The only possible foundation for this idea was the fact that Captain Hall happened to own a distillery. There was nothing else in the record to support it, and much to the contrary about Revere as a man of temperate habits. But this schoolboy humor by the editors of the *Globe* was widely read and believed. Revere scholar Jayne Triber concludes that became "one source for the recent cynical belief that 'Revere was drunk when he made the ride.'"[50]

Iconoclasm became something of an industry in this period. A professional iconoclast named Richard Shenkman was regularly employed by newspapers and television networks to explode the patriot myths of American history. In 1989 he captured the national mood in a book called *Legends, Lies and Cherished Myths of American History,* which included Paul Revere among its many targets. The author minimized the importance of the midnight ride, assuring its readers that Revere's "role in warning of approaching redcoats has been exaggerated." This work was followed by another volume called *"I Love Paul Revere, Whether He Rode or Not."* The title, a garbled quotation from Warren Harding, hinted that maybe the midnight ride never actually happened at all. That innuendo was corrected inside the book, but once again bewildered students began to ask their teachers if it was true that Paul Revere never made his ride at all. From the work of the new iconoclasts, one could not be sure.[51]

Filiopietists fought back. On April 19, 1775, in a bicentennial celebration of the American Revolution, the two parties confronted one another at Concord's North Bridge. On one side was the official Revolutionary Bicentennial Commission led by President Gerald Ford, which celebrated Paul Revere and the minutemen as symbols of free enterprise and democracy On the other side was the People's Bicentennial Commission, with Pete Seeger and Arlo Guthrie, who read (very selectively) from James Otis, Thomas Paine and Abigail Adams, and converted the occasion into an impassioned attack on American capitalism and multinational corporations. Altogether 100,000 people attended the event. The only damage was to the environment, from 822 tons of litter left by filiopietists and iconoclasts alike.[52]

Something of the searing impact of the Vietnam War on historical memory in the United States appeared in an essay called "Ambush," published by novelist and Vietnam veteran Tim O'Brien in 1993. The piece consisted of a series of passages on the fighting of April 19, 1775, alternating with the author's highly personal memories of Vietnam. "The parallels," O'Brien wrote, "struck me as both obvious and telling. A civil war. A powerful world-class army blundering through unfamiliar terrain. A myth of invincibility. Immense resources of wealth and firepower that somehow never produced definitive results. A sense of bewilderment and dislocation."

This American identified mainly with the British Regulars, the grunts of an earlier war. "Down inside," he added, "in some deeply human way, I had more in common with those long-dead redcoats than with the living men and women all around me. I felt a member of a mysterious old brotherhood: shared knowledge and shared terror. I could hear 700 pairs of boots on the road; I could smell the sweat and fear. Somewhere inside me, Vietnam and Battle Road seemed to merge into a single ghostly blur across history."

What was most extraordinary in this work was its idea of history itself. "History was not made by plan or policy," O'Brien asserted, "but by the biological forces of fatigue and fear and adrenaline." He appeared to reject any idea of progress or purpose in human history. "What happens is this," he insisted, "time puts on a fresh new uniform, revs up the firepower, calls itself progress."

The author claimed a kinship with soldiers who came before him, but his essay was profoundly different from writings by veterans of earlier wars, including the men of Lexington and Concord whom he claimed as brothers in misfortune. The difference appeared not merely in the self-pity and despair of the Vietnam veteran, but in his profound rejection of any sort of teleology in history.[53]


## ❧ Academic History, Political Correctness, and Paul Revere

Parallel trends also appeared in changing patterns of professional scholarship. In the early 20th century, Paul Revere's place in college textbooks had seemed secure. The academic historiography of that era centered on narrative sequences of political events. Paul Revere's ride was given an important role as a device that connected one event to another. A case in point was Morison and Commager's *Growth of the American Republic,* which represented Paul Revere's ride as a major event that linked the coming of American revolution to the War of Independence. In an interpretation carefully balanced between Paul Revere and William Dawes, both figures appeared as heroic men on horseback who "aroused the whole countryside." For any slow-witted sophomore who may have missed the point, both rides were dramatically plotted on a full-page map, with romantic silhouettes of galloping horses racing across the countryside.[54]

After the generation of Morison and Commager, the dominant school of American historiography turned its attention from narratives of public events to analyses of intellectual systems and material structures—a change that reduced happenings such as Paul Revere's ride to trivial incidents of no significance. Two of the leading college textbooks in this era, *The National Experience* (1962) and *The Great Republic* (1977), made no mention of Paul Revere's ride whatever. The only published essay on the midnight ride in an historical journal during this period pronounced it to be a happening of "minor importance."[55] A popular historian, Virginius Dabney, published a biographical history of the Revolution in which Paul Revere was deliberately omitted, and the midnight ride was dismissed as an event "of little or no importance."[56]

With the rise of the new social history, Paul Revere returned to the textbooks, but as a different character. The midnight rider was dismounted, and converted into a more pedestrian figure of one sort or another. Social historians variously represented him according to their politics, as a Boston artisan, a bourgeois businessman, a leader of Boston's "mechanic interest," an active joiner of voluntary associations, or a producer of revolutionary propaganda. He became a figure of more complexity but less autonomy—not really an actor, but an exemplar of class movements and the organization of the means of production. There was no sense of contingency in these interpretations, and little recognition of individual agency. They rested on assumptions that individual actors in history are significant mainly as instruments of large processes over which they have little control. For the generation of Vietnam and Watergate, those organizing ideas became very strong in American universities.[57]

## ❧ Crosscurrents

Today attitudes are changing yet again, and interpretations of Paul Revere reflect the new mood. Levels of interest in various aspects of his career are stronger than ever before, and more diverse than in any earlier period. Many schools of interpretation compete with one another. Filiopietists are still out in force; celebrations of Patriots' Day in Massachusetts are larger and more enthusiastic than ever before. More than a million tourists a year visit the North Bridge at Concord, and flock in growing numbers to Boston's Freedom Trail. British travel writer Jack Crossley wrote after a visit to Boston, "You can also take a delightful hop-on-off trolley ride round the major attractions. The guide's patter on these trips is a hoot. 'You'll hear a lot about Paul Revere on this ride. In fact you'll get sick to death of his name, believe me.' History is around every corner, and indeed Paul Revere is on most of them."[58]

At the same time, iconoclasts also continue to be very active, seeking to expose the underside of the American past. Many seem to be guides on Boston's Freedom Trail, where they titillate the tourists by inventing new scandals about the midnight rider. The highly professional staff of the Paul Revere House was recently asked by a group of visitors if it was true, as their guide had told them, that Paul Revere had an affair with Mother Goose!

Many scholars are now busily at work, pursuing different lines of research on various aspects of Paul Revere's life. A major study of Boston artisans is under way by Professor Alfred Young. A dissertation by Jayne Triber of Brown University is examining Revere's republican principles. Specialists in material culture at the Winterthur Program and elsewhere have done much research on Revere's silver, and on his business career. A catalogue by Morrison Heckscher and Leslie Bowman for an important exhibition at the Metropolitan

Museum of Art studies him as a highly inventive artist within the design tradition that they call American Rococo. Patrick Leehey, head of research at the Paul Revere House, is looking carefully into the Penobscot Expedition, the darkest episode in Revere's life. Edith Steblecki has published an enlightening monograph on Revere and Freemasonry, a subject of growing interest to cultural historians. At the center of this activity is the Paul Revere Memorial Association, a flourishing organization that runs educational programs, awards fellowships to students, sponsors exhibitions, conducts an active publication program, serves as a clearing house for ongoing research, and welcomes more than 200,000 visitors each year to the Revere House in downtown Boston.[59]

New interpretations of Paul Revere are as diverse as the topics and problems that are being studied. In general, Paul Revere is approached today as a figure of high complexity who is interesting both for what he was and what he did. One new theme is beginning to emerge. In new work on the design of his silver, on his business career, on his civic activities, and in this monograph on his midnight ride, Paul Revere is increasingly interpreted as a man who made a difference in the world. At a time when we are witnessing the rebirth of free institutions in many nations, it is interesting to observe that this ever-changing historical figure is perceived in terms of choice, contingency, and agency.

For our subject, the new trends inevitably mean another turn of the interpretative wheel. Through two centuries, the myth of the midnight ride has been continuously reinvented by Americans in response to changing circumstances. In every generation we have been given a new Paul Revere—the injured innocent of Whig propaganda, the ardent patriot of the new republic, the historic loner of Longfellow's romantic poem, the man on horseback of the late 19th century, the "man of solid substance" of the American Anglophiles; the colonial clown of the debunkers; the "simple artizan" of Esther Forbes, the capitalist-democrat of the Cold Warriors, the patriot-villain of the post-Vietnam iconoclasts, and in a new age of global democracy a leader of collective effort in the cause of freedom.

To the passing generations, Paul Revere has been all of these things and more—a man and a myth that has grown with the nation that he helped to found. Like the reflective surfaces of Copley's portrait, each of the many reconstructions of his life reflects the circumstances of their creators. But nearly all of them have added to our understanding of a complex figure. Every generation does not merely rewrite the history books. It also revises them, and refines our knowledge of the past. Through that long process, Paul Revere is not only a creature of changing fashion. He is also an enduring symbol of an historical truth that by changing grows deeper and yet more true. That may be his most important message for our time.

# BIBLIOGRAPHY
### ~ Selected Primary Sources

> Amid all the terrors of battle I was so busily engaged in Harvard
> Library that I never even heard of . . . [it] until it was completed."
>
> —a scholar on the battle of Bunker Hill,
> June 17, 1775[1]

No other happening in early American history has left such an abundance of evidence as did the events of April 19, 1775. This selected survey is limited to primary materials (and the means of access to them). Secondary and tertiary works are included only if they contain primary materials. The survey is organized in the following parts:

Bibliographical sources
Primary sources
    Depositions
        Depositions taken from American militia
        Depositions taken from British troops
        Pension applications
        Claims for damages
    Personal papers and accounts
        Papers of Paul Revere
        Papers of Thomas Gage
        Personal records of other American participants
        Personal records of other British participants
    Official records
        American government documents
            Provincial and State Records
            Town Records
        British government documents
            Colonial Office
            War Office
            Admiralty
    Other primary sources
        Published collections of primary documents
        Newspaper accounts
        Anniversary sermons and orations
        Material artifacts
        Terrain studies
Secondary works that contain primary materials
    Biographical studies
        Paul Revere
        Thomas Gage
        Other participants
    Local histories
        Town studies
        County histories
    Histories of military units
        The British army
        The American militia
        Naval history
        Weapons and equipment

## ❧ Bibliographies

The most comprehensive general bibliography of the American Revolution is Ronald Gephart, *Revolutionary America, 1763-1789: A Bibliography*. 2 vols. (Washington, D.C., 1984). Dwight L. Smith and Terry A. Simmerman, *Era of the American Revolution: A Bibliography* (Santa Barbara, 1975), is a helpful compilation of 1400 abstracts from *America, History and Life*. A remarkably comprehensive work is Lawrence H. Gipson, *A Bibliographical Guide to the History of the British Empire, 1748-1776*, published as Volume 14 in his *History of the British Empire Before the American Revolution* (New York, 1968).

W. J. Koenig and S. L. Mayer, *European Manuscript Sources of the American Revolution* (London and New York, 1974), surveys primary materials in foreign archives.

On the coming of the Revolution: a helpful work is Thomas R. Adams, *American Independence, The Growth of an Idea: A Bibliographical Study of the American Political Pamphlets Printed Between 1764 and 1776 Dealing with the Dispute Between Great Britain and Her Colonies* (Providence, 1965); and *idem, The American Controversy: A Bibliographical Study of the British Pamphlets About the American Disputes, 1764-1783*. 2 vols. (Providence, R.I., 1980).

J. Todd White and Charles H. Lesser (eds.), *Fighters for Independence: A Guide to Sources of Biographical Information on Soldiers and Sailors of the American Revolution* (Chicago, 1977), lists 538 narratives, diaries, journals, and autobiographies by men and a few women who fought for American independence. Many of these works refer to events at Lexington and Concord.

In 1959 Arthur Tourtellot printed privately *A Bibliography of the Battles of Lexington and Concord* (New York, 1959). A much abridged version was appended to his own popular history of these events, first published as *William Diamond's Drum* (New York, 1959) and then reissued as *Lexington and Concord; The Beginning of the War of the American Revolution* (New York, 1963).

The Paul Revere Memorial Association maintains an unpublished bibliography, "Research Papers on File in the PRMA Library" (revised to Sept, 1992), which lists the studies of Paul Revere in its holdings at the Revere House in Boston.

## ❧ Depositions: American Militia and Minutemen

Among the richest source material for this inquiry are American depositions taken a few days after the fighting on April 19, 1775. They were recorded for the specific purpose of proving that British soldiers fired the first shots at Lexington Green and Concord's North Bridge. Depositions that supported this case were published as *A Narrative of the Excursion and Ravages of the King's Troops* (Worcester, 1775). This pamphlet has often been reissued: in print by Peter Force (ed.), *American Archives*, 4th ser., II, 487-501; on microprint in the Readex microprint edition of *Early American Imprints*, Evans 14269; and on microfiche in Kinvin Wroth *et al.* (eds.), *Province in Rebellion*, document 591, pp. 1804-29. Depositions not clearly supportive of the American position were revised before publication, or not published at all.

The manuscript depositions themselves are scattered through several repositories. Many are at the University of Virginia and Harvard University. John Parker's deposition is in the Lexington Historical Society. Paul Revere's depositions (not published by the Provincial Congress) are in the Revere Family Papers, in the Massachusetts Historical Society. Early transcripts of Lexington depositions are in WCL.

American signers from Lexington include: James Adams, Joseph Abbott, Ebenezer Bowman, John Bridge, Jr., James Brown, Solomon Brown, John Chandler, John Chandler, Jr., Isaac Durant, Thomas Fessenden, Isaac Green, William Grimer, Micah Hagar, Daniel Harrington, John Harrington, Levi Harrington, Moses Harrington, Moses Harrington III, Thaddeus Harrington, Thomas Harrington, Isaac Hastings, Samuel Hastings, Thomas Headley, Jr., John Hosmer, Benjamin Lock, Reuben Lock, Jonathan Loring, Abner Mead, Levi Mead, John Monroe, Jr., William Munroe, William Munroe III, Nathaniel Mullekin, John Muzzy, Ebenezer Parker, John Parker, Jonas Parker, Nathaniel Parkhurst, Solomon Pierce, Joshua Reed, Joshua Reed, Jr., Nathan Reed, John Robbins, Philip Russel, Elijah Sanderson (2 documents), Samuel Sanderson, Joseph Simonds, John Smith, Phineas Smith, Timothy Smith, Simon Snow, Phineas Stearns, Jonas Stone, Jr., Benjamin Tidd, Samuel Tidd, William Tidd, Joel Viles, Thomas Price Willard, Enoch Willington, John Winship, Simon Winship, Thomas Winship, and James Wyman.

From the town of Lincoln: John Adams, Abraham Garfield, John Hoar, William Hosmer, Benjamin Munroe, Isaac Parks, Gregory Stone, John Whitehead.

From the town of Concord: Thaddeus Bancroft, James Barrett, John Barrett, Nathaniel Barrett, Samuel Barrett, John Brown, Joseph Butler, Nathaniel Buttrick, Joseph Chandler, Jonathan Farrer, Stephen Hosmer, Jr., Thomas Jones, Ephraim Melvin, Timothy Minot Jr., Nathan Peirce, Edward Richardson, Bradbury Robinson, Samuel Spring, Silas Walker, Francis Wheeler, and Peter Wheeler.

From other towns: Paul Revere (2 drafts).

More depositions were collected through the next half-century for other purposes, mainly by local historians in various controversies that arose among the towns. These materials were recorded long after the event, and are sometimes inaccurate in matters of detail, but they tend to be more full and comprehensive than the earlier depositions.

Elias Phinney, *History of the Battle at Lexington* (Boston, 1825), printed depositions by Abijah Harrington, Amos Lock, Ebenezer Munroe, John Munroe, Nathan Munroe, William Munroe, James Reed, Elijah Sanderson, William Tidd, and Joseph Underwood.

Ezra Ripley, *History of the Fight at Concord* (Concord, 1827, 2nd ed., 1832), a reply to Phinney, included four new depositions from five participants: Robert Douglass (May 3, 1827), John Harwell (July 19, 1827), John Richardson (June 25, 1827), Joseph Thaxter (Feb. 24, 1825), and Sylvanus Wood (June 17, 1826).

Josiah Adams, *Centennial Address on Acton* (Boston, 1835), and *Letter to Lemuel Shattuck, Esq., of Boston . . . in Vindication of the Claims of Capt. Isaac Davis, of Acton . . .* (Boston, 1850), published eight new depositions from six participants: Charles Handley, Hannah Davis Leighton, Solomon Smith (2 depositions), Thomas Thorp (2 depositions), all sworn in 1835; plus Bradley Stone (sworn Aug. 16, 1845) and Amos Baker (sworn April 22, 1850).

For another history of Concord, Lemuel Shattuck interviewed eyewitnesses including Mrs. Peter Barrett (Nov. 3, 1831); Abel Conant (Nov. 8, 1832), Reuben Brown, and others. His manuscript notes are in the New England Historic and Genealogical Society, Boston.

A deposition by Tilly Buttrick, at the age of 78, is in Letterfile 7, B6, CFPL.

The last deposition from a participant was recorded seventy-five years after the battle. It was taken from Amos Baker of Lincoln in 1850, when he was ninety-four years old and was thought to be the last survivor of the American militia at the North Bridge. The document was sworn as an affadvit before three witnesses. Baker's memory misled him in a few details, but was still crystal clear and can be confirmed by other accounts. It was published in Robert Rantoul, Jr., *Oration and Account of the Union Celebration at Concord, Nineteenth of April, 1850* (Boston, 1850), 133–35.

## ❧ Depositions of British Troops

Nothing as full as the systematic collection of sworn testimony from the American side is available from British participants. But there are several bodies of depositional materials that have yet to be used extensively by historians. Among them are depositions by British soldiers stationed in Boston during 1769-70. They were taken with particular attention to the Boston Massacre, and also contained much information about conditions of British troops in Boston and the repeated violence of the inhabitants toward them, all of which help to explain hostile attitudes of British regulars toward Americans in general and New Englanders in particular. These documents were not used in the Massacre trial, and have not been published in any study or compilation. They are in manuscript in the Public Record Office (CO 5/88). Transcripts are in the author's possession.

They include depositions from Lt. Alexander Ross, Capt. Charles Fordyce, Sgt. John Phillips, Cpl. Samuel Heale, Pvt. Jonathan Stevenson, Ens. John Ness, Sgt. Samuel Hickman, Pvt. William Fowler, Pvt. John Kirk, Lt. Daniel Mather, Ens. Cornelius Smelt, Cpl. Thomas McFarland, Pvt. Samuel Bish, Pvt. Stephen Cheslett, Sgt. Thomas Light, Pvt. Samuel Unwin, Pvt. Jessey Lindley, Pvt. John Park, Pvt. Thomas Sherwood, Pvt. Robert Holbrook, Pvt. William Morburn, Pvt. Richard Ratcliff, Pvt. John Woolhouse, Cpl. William Lake, Sgt. Thomas Hood, Drummer John Gregory (2 depositions), Pvt. Thomas Smith, Sgt. Hardress Gray, Pvt. Roger McMullen, Sgt. John Norfolk, Pvt. William McCracken, Pvt. William Browne, Pvt. Joseph Whitehorse, Cpl. Robert Balfour, Pvt. David Young, Pvt. William Banks, Cpl. William Halam, Pvt. Thomas Lodger, Pvt. Richard Henley, Cpl. John Arnold, Pvt. John Shelley, Pvt. Dennis Towers, Pvt. Jacob Brown, Sgt. Thomas Thornby, Cpl. John Shelton, Pvt. James Botham, Pvt. William Mabbot, Pvt. William Wilson, Pvt. William Barker, Pvt. Gavin Thompson, Sgt. John Ridings, Sgt. John Eyley, Pvt. George Smith, Pvt. John Care, Sgt. William Henderson, Pvt. William Leeming, Pvt. Eustace Manyweather, Pvt. Edward Osbaldistan, Pvt. Jacob Moor, and Pvt. George Barnet all of the 14th Foot.

Also Ens. Alexander Mall, Pvt. William Godson, Pvt. Henry Malone, Pvt. William Normanton, Pvt. Cornelius Murphy, Sgt. Thomas Smilie, Cpl. Alexander McCartney, Pvt. Patrick Donally, Pvt. John Rodgers, Sgt. Hugh Broughton, Pvt. John Dumphy, Pvt. James McKaan, Pvt. John Croker, Cpl. John Fitzpatrick, Cpl. Hugh McCann, Pvt. James Corkrin, Cpl. Thomas Burgess, Pvt. Joshua Williams, Sgt. William James, Sgt. Richard Pearsall, Pvt. John Timmons, Cpl. Henry Cullin, Pvt. Patrick Walker, Cpl. William Murray, Pvt. Richard Johnson, Pvt. Robert Ward, Pvt. John Addicott, Pvt. George Irwin, Surgeon's Mate Henry Dougan, Ens. Gilbert Carter, Capt. Jeremiah French, Cpl. John Eustace, and Drummer Thomas Walker of the 29th Foot.

Depositions were also taken after the fighting at Lexington and Concord from British troops who bore witness to the American atrocity committed on a wounded British soldier near Concord's North Bridge. Deponents included Cpl. Gordon, Pvt. Thomas Lugg, Pvt. William Lewis, Pvt. Charles Carrier, and Pvt. Richard Grimshaw of the 5th Foot; all sworn on April 20, 1775, and witnessed by Capt. John G. Battier, 5th Foot. They are published in part by Allen French in *General Gage's Informers*, 111.


## ❧ Pension Applications

A large body of sworn testimony by veterans of the War of Independence also appears in records of Federal pension applications submitted under U.S. pension acts of 1818 and 1832. These acts required veterans to submit a narrative of Revolutionary service, sworn in a court of law, and supported by two character witnesses, one of whom had to be a clergyman. Pension agents played an active role in this process. Many accounts were dictated to court stenographers, sometimes in front of a large crowds. John Dann writes, "The pension application process was one of the largest oral history projects ever undertaken." Altogether, under all the pension acts, as many as 80,000 narratives were processed. They are available on microfilm from the National Archives, in a collection of 898 reels. The author used the set at the New England Regional Center of the National Archives, in Waltham, Mass. The records are indexed by name (not, unhappily, by subject, date, or place of service), in *Index of Revolutionary War Pension Applications in the National Archives* (Washington, D.C., 1976). These materials must be used with caution. Problems of evidence are complex, but not more or less than for other historical sources. Among the narratives used for this study were those of Jonathan Brigham (Marlborough, Mass.), Richard Durfee (Tiverton, R.I.), Nathan Fisk (Northfield, Mass.), Robert Fisk, Abel Haynes (Barre, Mass.), Robert Nimblet (Marblehead, Mass.), John Nixon (Sudbury, Mass.), Abel Prescott (Westfield, Mass.), Jesse Prescott (Kensington, N.H.), Richard Vining (East Windsor, Conn.), Ammi White (Concord, Mass.), Cuff Whittemore, Sylvanus Wood (Woburn, now Burlington, Mass., 1830), and Hannah Davis Leighton, the widow of Captain Isaac Davis (Acton, Mass.).

## ❧ Claims for Damages, April 18–19, 1775

Many householders who lived along the Battle Road submitted claims for losses. These records also document some of the events of the day. They are in the Massachusetts Archives, Columbia Point, Boston. Some are published in the *Journals of the Provincial Congress of Massachusetts:* Joseph Loring, Jonathan Harrington, Lydia Winship, John Mason, Matthew Mead, Benjamin Merriam, Nathaniel Farmer, Thomas Fessenden, Benjamin Fiske, Jeremiah Harrington, Robert Harrington, Joshua Bond, Benjamin Brown, Hepzibah Davis, Benjamin Estabrook, Samuel Bemis, Nathan Blodget, Elizabeth Samson, Jonathan Smith Jr., John Williams, John Winship, Margaret Winship, Marrett Monroe, William Munroe, Amos Muzzy, Lydia Mulliken.

Another file of damage claims by Concord residents, including Ezekiel Brown, Reuben Brown, William Emerson, Abel Fisk, Timothy Minot, and others, is in the 1775 Folder, Concord Archives, CFPL

## ❧ Personal Records: The Papers of Paul Revere

The Revere Family Papers in the Massachusetts Historical Society include a large quantity of business records, but less in the way of materials of a personal or political nature. They are stronger for Revere's life after the American Revolution than for the period before 1776. The collection is available on microfilm, with a calendar. Many scholars since Elbridge Goss have worked through the Revere Papers, but much remains to be gleaned from them. Of particular value are Paul Revere's letters to and from his relatives abroad, and his correspondence with public figures in the early republic. This collection also includes some business records before 1776, and Paul Revere's three accounts of the midnight ride, which have been published many times. The standard edition is Edmund S. Morgan (ed.), *Paul Revere's Three Accounts of His Famous Ride* (Boston: Massachusetts Historical Society, 1968). Serious students should read these works in manuscript (or in the facsimiles published by Morgan), for Revere deleted important passages that do not appear in printed texts.

Many other American repositories have a few Revere manuscripts in autograph collections and vertical files. Scattered items are also to be found in the Massachusetts Archives, which has bills and receipts by Paul Revere for courier service, 1774-75. The Paul Revere Memorial Association holds a pass signed by James Otis for Revere to ride express to the Continental Congress, November 12, 1775.

Much Revere material also appears in the papers of other American Whig leaders. The manuscripts that survive in these collections were carefully pruned by American leaders.

Benjamin Edes kept the records of the Boston Tea Party under lock and key for many years, and deliberately destroyed them before he died. In Samuel Adams's house it was said that "trunks and boxes were filled, and shelves around the walls of the garret piled high with letters and documents" (William Wells, *Samuel Adams.* 3 vols. [Boston, 1865], I, xi). Many were destroyed by Adams himself, who was observed by others in his late years reading through his papers and throwing them one by one onto the fire. After his death, an "ignorant servant" was discovered using much of what survived for kindling. The remnant found its way to the New York Public Library, and includes correspondence to and from Paul Revere, with many references to his activities.

Also in the New York Public Library (among the papers of the historian George Bancroft) are the records of the Boston Committee of Correspondence, which were specially helpful to this inquiry for letters from other towns, and for material on the Powder Alarm. A small but very important set of letters to and from Revere and about him is in the John Lamb Papers at the New-York Historical Society.

Other relevant materials are in the Sparks Papers and the Palfrey Family Papers in the Houghton Library at Harvard University. Also useful are the papers of William Heath, John Thomas, Henry Knox, Thomas Young, and various members of the Warren family in the Massachusetts Historical Society, and the papers of John Hancock and Isaiah Thomas at the American Antiquarian Society.

## ❧ Personal Records: Thomas Gage

One of the best documented public careers in the old British Empire was that of General Thomas Gage. Every year during his tenure as commander in chief he sent home a large wooden chest full of papers—twelve chests altogether. That collection was bought by American collector William L. Clements and moved to the United States, where it was sumptuously bound in leather folios, and housed in the William L. Clements Library on the campus of the University of Michigan, Ann Arbor.

Gage's official correspondence is at the Public Record Office in Kew, outside London. Much (but not all) of his correspondence with the Secretaries of State, the War Office, and the Treasury has been published in a generally accurate but idiosyncratic work by Clarence E. Carter (ed.), *The Correspondence of General Thomas Gage.* 2 vols. (New Haven, 1933; rpt. 1969). Unofficial documents in the Gage Papers relevant to Paul Revere, and to the battles of Lexington and Concord, have also been published in whole or part in Allen French, *General Gage's Informers: New Material Upon Lexington and Concord . . .* (Ann Arbor, 1932).

Gage himself also published his own short account of Lexington and Concord as "A Circumstantial Account of an Attack that happened on the 19th of April, 1775." A copy of the first edition, with Joseph Warren's pungent marginalia, is in the Massachusetts Historical Society. Reprints have appeared in Peter Force (ed.), *American Archives*, 4th ser., II, 435; and *MHSC* II, 224. Also of much interest are Gage's "Replies to Queries by Historian George Chalmers," MHSC, 4th ser., 4 (1858): 369-70, and his letters on the battle to colonial governors: Trumbull of Connecticut, Colden of New York, and Dunmore of Virginia, also in *AA4*, II, 434-37, 482-83, and in *Letters and Papers of Cadwallader Colden*, vol. VIII, *N-YHS Collections* 66 (1923): 283-87. Many other letters from Gage are published in the Colden Papers. Others appear in Sylvester Stevens *et al., The Papers of Col. Henry Bouquet* (Harrisburg, 1940-42), and James Sullivan *et al., The Papers of Sir William Johnson* (Albany, 1921). Gage's papers concerning the Boston Massacre have been published in Randolph G. Adams (ed.), *New Light on the Boston Massacre* (Worcester, 1938).

Less abundant are materials on Gage's private life. One of his biographers complains that the Gage Papers "contain almost nothing of a personal nature, and after all my research I felt that I knew Gage the military bureaucrat but not Gage the man" (John Shy, *A People Numerous and Armed* (New York, 1976), 73). It is also important to remember that

Gage's papers document in a meticulous way what he wanted us to know. They must be cross-examined for the truths that they betray.

Other unpublished Gage manuscripts are in the Haldimand Papers (British Library, London), which reveal more of Gage's personality than any other source, especially in letters written during Gage's leave in England. Other items are in the Amherst Papers at the Public Record Office, but this collection holds very little on the events of 1774–75.

### ✎ Personal Records of American Participants

Particularly helpful to this inquiry were the many diaries kept in New England. A new computer data base at the Massachusetts Historical Society was used to identify systematically all diaries in that repository within the period Sept. 1, 1774 to May 17, 1775. Other materials are in the form of correspondence, memoirs, and narratives, as follows:

John Adams: *Diary and Autobiography*. 4 vols. Ed Lyman Butterfield (Boston, 1961; rpt. 1964); *Papers of John Adams*. 3 vols. Ed. Robert J. Taylor *et al.* (Cambridge, 1977).

John Quincy Adams: *Memoirs*. 12 vols. Ed. Charles F. Adams (Philadelphia, 1874–77).

Samuel Adams: *Writings*. 4 vols. Ed. Harry A. Cushing (New York, 1904).

Hannah Adams: Memoir, May 17, 1775, published in S. A. Smith, *West Cambridge on the 19th of April 1775* (Boston, 1864), and Kehoe, "We Were There!" I, 128.

Nathaniel Ames: Diary, 1756–1821, ms., Dedham Historical Society, one of the great American diaries, an extraordinary record of events in a New England town by its physician, who also describes his trip to the battlefield after the fighting.

Mrs. John Amory: Diary, published as *The Journal of Mrs. John Amory with Letters from Her Father Rufus Greene*, ed. Martha Codman (Boston, 1923). Katherine Green Amory: Diary, 1775, MHS.

John Andrews: "The Andrews Letters, 1772–76," ms., MHS, pub. in *MHSP* 8 (1865): 316–412; very rich for life in Boston.

Joseph Andrews: Diary, 1752–81, MHS, events in Hingham, Mass.

James Baker: Diary, 1775, MHS.

Loammi Baldwin: Diary, 1775, Harvard

Amos Barrett (var. Barret) Concord militiaman: Narrative published in Henry True, *Journal and Letters* (Marion, Ohio, 1906), copy in CFPL; a major document on the battle.

Jeremy Belknap: Journal, published as "Journal of my tour to the camp . . . ," *MHSP* 4 (1858): 77–86; includes interviews with Bostonians on events of April 18 and the beginning of Paul Revere's ride; Diary, 1774–75, MHS.

Joshua Bentley: Reminiscence, communicated by his grandson, Charles Wooley, to Elbridge Goss, May 1886, published in Goss, *Revere*, I, 189n; one of the men who rowed Revere across the Charles River.

William Bentley: *The Diary of William Bentley, D.D. Pastor of the East Church, Salem, Mass.* 4 vols. (Salem, 1905–14); the son of Joshua Bentley. The published edition is incomplete and inaccurate; for any serious purpose the original manuscripts should be consulted at the American Antiquarian Society.

Samuel Bixby, a militiaman from Sutton, Mass.: Diary, 1775, *MHSP* 14 (1875–76), 285.

Thaddeus Blood, Concord militiaman: Narrative, ms. CFPL; published in the (Boston) *Daily Advertiser*, April 20. 1886; especially valuable for the North Bridge and Meriam's Corner.

Benjamin Boardman: Diary, 1775, *MHSP* 7 (1891–92): 400–413.

John Boyle: "Journal of Occurrences in Boston, 1759–1778," *NEHGR* 84 (1930): 142–71, 248–72, 357–82; 85 (1931): 5–28, 117–33; a very full account of events in Boston, with details of Paul Revere's earlier rides.

James Boynton: Diary, 1775, MHS.

Thomas Boynton: Journal, April 19, 1775, *MHSP* 15 (1877): 254–55.

Chelmsford Bridge: Diary, April 19–21, 1775, published in Brown, *Beside Old Hearthstones*, 253–54.

John Buttrick, Lincoln, Mass.: Deposition, Nov. 1776, published in Frothingham, *History of the Siege of Boston*, 68, and Hurd, *Middlesex County*, II, 619.

John Checkley: Diary, published as *Diary of Reverend Samuel Checkley*, ed. Henry Winchester (n.p., n.d.).

William Cheever: Diary, MHS.

William Clark: Diary, 1775–1812, ms. transcript, Dedham Historical Society.

Elizabeth Clarke, "Extracts from Letter of Miss Betty Clarke, Daughter of Rev. Jonas Clarke," *Lexington Historical Society Proceedings* 4 (1905–10): 91–93.

Jonas Clarke, minister in Lexington: Almanac Diary, 1774–75, LHS and MHS; "Narrative of events on April 19," ms., LHS; published in Hudson, *History of Lexington*, I, 1–7, "The Fate of the Bloodthirsty Oppressors," Sermon, 1776 (Lexington, LHS, 1901), includes the narrative of events as an appendix; *Opening of the War of the Revolution, 19th of April, 1775, A Brief Narrative of the Principal Transactions of That Day* (Lexington, n.d.), a participant history.

Benjamin Cooper: Memoir, May 19, 1775, in S. A. Smith, *West Cambridge on the 19th of April 1775* (Boston, 1864); Kehoe, "We Were There!" I, 128.

Rachel Cooper: Memoir, May 19, 1775, in Kehoe, "We Were There!" I, 128.

Samuel Cooper, a refugee in Weston: Diary, 1775–76, MHS, published by Frederick Tuckerman (ed.), *AHR* 6 (1901): 301–41.

Richard Devens: Memorandum, n.d., published in Frothingham, *History of the Siege of Boston*, 57–58. Devens was an important Whig leader in Charlestown who helped Revere to "git" his horse.

Ebenezer Dorr: Account Book, 1766–1776, MHS.

William Dorr: Diary, 1775, MHS.

Eliphalet Downer, Recollections, ms., NEHGS.

Peter Edes: Diary kept in Boston Gaol, June 19–Oct. 3, 1775, ms., MHS; harrowing account of his arrest and confinement.

Andrew Eliot: Diary, 1740–84, MHS.

John Eliot: Diary, 1775, MHS.

William Emerson: Diary, 1775, published in *Proceedings of the Centennial Celebration of Concord Fight* (Concord, 1876), and Amelia Forbes Emerson (ed.), *Diaries and Letters of William Emerson, 1743–1776, Minister of the Church in Concord, Chaplain in the Revolutionary Army* (Boston, 1972). A leading source for events in Concord.

Joseph Fairbank, militia captain in Harvard, Mass.: Papers, 1775, in Castle *et al.* (eds.), *The Minute Men*, 123, includes records of the "Alarm Men," who are not in the town's militia and minute companies.

Amos Farnsworth: Diary, 1775–79, published in S.A. Greene (ed.), "Three Military Diaries," *MHSP* 12 (1873): 74.

Elijah Fisher: *Journal, 1775–1784* (Augusta, 1880).

John Fitch: Diary, *MHSP* 2 9 (1894–95): 41–91.

Edmund Foster: letter to Col. Daniel Shattuck, March 10, 1825; Coburn, *Battle of April 19, 1775*, 34; Kehoe, "We Were There!" I, 253–56.

Joshua B. Fowle: Letters to Samuel H. Newman, July 28, 1875, and August 1876, on the signal lanterns; Wheildon, *Paul Revere's Signal Lanterns*, 34–36. The Rev. Caleb Gannett: Diary, Houghton Library, Harvard University.

John Gates: Diary, April 1775, MHS.

Ebenezer Gay, Suffield, Conn.: Diary, 1738–94, MHS.

William Gordon, minister in Roxbury: Narrative published as "An Account of the Commencement of Hostilities Between Great Britain and America, in the Province of Massachusetts Bay," May 17, 1775," *AA4*, II, 625–31.

Joshua Greene: Diary, 1775, extracts, MHS.

The Rev. Cyrus Hamblin: *My Grandfather, Colonel Francis Faulkner* (Boston, 1887); valuable for the Lexington alarm west of Concord.

Samuel Hawes: Diary, in *The Military Journal of Two Private Soldiers, 1758–1775*, ed. Abraham Tomlinson (Poughkeepsie, 1875), the alarm in Wrentham, Mass.

William Heath, militia general: Memoir, published as *Memoirs* (Boston, 1798); manuscripts in the Massachusetts Historical Society are available on microfilm and are published in part in *MHSC*5 4 (1878): 1–288); *MHSC*7 4 (1904): 1–354; 5 (1905): 1–419.

George R. T. Hewes: *A Retrospect of the Boston Tea Party, with a Memoir of George R. T. Hewes, by a Citizen of New York* (New York, 1834), an important source for life in Boston, and the revolutionary movement.

Robert Honyman: *Colonial Panorama, 1775; Dr. Robert Honyman's Journal* (San Marino, Calif., 1939).

Jonathan Hosmer: Letter to Oliver Stevens or Joseph Standley, April 10, 1775, privately owned; excerpts published in a dealer's catalogue, Joseph Rubenfine, *The American Revolution, List 114* (West Palm Beach, Fla., n.d), n.p.; a copy is in the Concord Antiquarian Museum.

Thomas Hutchinson: *The Diary and Letters of His Excellency Thomas Hutchinson, Esq.* 2 vols. (Boston, 1884), helpful on the impact in Britain of the news of the battle; Hutchinson's manuscripts include correspondence from Massachusetts, on the events of 1774–75. They are in the British Library, Egerton ms. 2659, 1670–73

Phineas Ingalls, minuteman from Andover, Mass.: Diary, 1775, transcript, MHS.

Edward Jarvis, "Traditions and Reminiscences of Concord, Massachusetts; or a Contribution to the Social and Domestic History of the Town, 1779 to 1878," ms., CFPL.

John Jenks, Salem, Mass.: Diary, 1775, MHS.

John Jones, Jr., captain of minutemen, Princeton, Mass.: Letter on the alarm, muster, and aftermath, published in Frank Smith, *History of Dover, Mass.* (Dover, 1897), 93.

John Kettell: Diary, 1775, MHS, a Charlestown source, good for the siege of Boston.

John Leach: "Journal Kept . . . During his Confinement by the British in Boston Gaol, in 1775," *NEHGR* 19 (1865): 255.

Paul Litchfield: Diary, ms., MHS, published in part in *MHSP* 19 (1882): 377–79; the alarm in Scituate, Mass.

Israel Litchfield: "Diary," *NEHGR* 129 (1975): 152.

Jeremiah Loring: Letter, n.d. [Oct. 1876], on the signal lanterns; Wheildon, *Paul Revere's Signal Lanterns*, 34–36.

Benjamin Lynde: Diary, 1775, MHS; events in Salem.

David McClure: Diary, *MHSP* 16 (1878): 155–61, includes an interview after the battles with British Lieutenant Edward Hull.

Isaac Mansfield, Jr.: Thanksgiving Sermon in Camp at Roxbury, Nov. 23, 1775, in J. W. Thornton (ed.), *Pulpit of the American Revolution* (Boston, 1860), 236; includes material on the battles of Lexington and Concord.

John Marrett, minister in Woburn: Interleaved almanac diary entries from Jan. 1, 1775, to Dec. 31, 1776, published in part in Samuel Dunster (ed.), *Henry Dunster and His Descendants* (Central Falls, 1876). Extracts are also printed in Hurd, *Middlesex County*, 674–80. The entry for April 19 was omitted by Hurd, as it had been published previously in Samuel Sewall's *History of Woburn*, 363, 78, 573.

Thompson Maxwell, a Medford teamster: Narrative published in Drake, *History of Middlesex County* I, 244–45; on the Boston Road, April 18, 1775.

Joseph Merriam, militiaman: Diary, 1775, BPL.

Timothy Merriam: Narrative of the Battles of Lexington and Concord, 1830, MHS.

Martha Moulton, Concord: Petition to General Court, Feb. 4, 1776, published in Frothingham, *History of the Siege of Boston*, 369–70.

Thomas Newell: Diary, 1773–74, MHS.

Timothy Newell: Diary, 1775–78, published as "A Journal During the Time Yt Boston

Was Shut Up in 1775–76," *MHSC4* 1 (1852): 260–76; an important source on Boston affairs.

Peter Oliver: *Origin and Progress of the American Revolution* (Palo Alto, 1961); a Tory polemic. Its story of the "remarkable heroine" who fired at a "house door" and was killed by British troops on the Battle Road," is often reprinted as fact (e.g., *Boston Globe,* April 19, 1993), but appears to have no foundation. Oliver's account is more useful for its insight into the mind of an American Loyalist. The manuscript of the work, and the Oliver Letter Book, are in the British Library, Egerton ms. 2670.

Harrison Gray Otis, a Boston schoolboy: Memoir of April 19, 1775, *Boston Advertiser,* April 19, 1858; it was reprinted in Edward Everett Hale, *One Hundred Years Ago* (Boston, 1875), 156–57.

Robert Treat Paine: Papers, *ca.* 1743–1814, MHS; include material on Whig activities at the beginning of the American Revolution.

James Parker: Diary, published as "Extracts from the Diary of James Parker of Shirley, Mass.," *NEHGR* 69 (1915): 117–27.

Henry Pelham: Family Correspondence, a large body of materials especially strong on events in Boston and Newton, Mass., is in "Intercepted Copley-Pelham letters," PRO, C05/39.

Timothy Pickering: Papers, MHS. In 1775, Pickering was a colonel of militia whose reluctance to march or engage allowed Percy to escape. His papers include two letters describing events of April 19; published in part in French, *Day of Concord and Lexington,* 261.

Robert Pierpont: Record of interview with General Gage, March 20, 1775, Adams Mss, NYPL.

Levi Preston: Interview by Mellen Chamberlain, published as "Why Captain Preston Fought," *Danvers Historical Collections* 8 (1920): 68–70.

Dorothy Quincy, John Hancock's fiancée: Narrative to William H. Sumner, 1825, published as "Reminiscences by Gen. William H. Sumner," *NEHGR* 8 (1854): 188–91; colorful details of the Clarke parsonage and the rescue of Hancock and Adams.

Experience Wight Richardson, Sudbury: Diary, 1775, microfilm, MHS; useful for the alarm and Great Fear.

Jacob Rogers: Petition, Oct 10, 1775, MA.

John Rowe, Boston merchant: Diary, ms., MHS; published in part as *Diary of John Rowe* (Cambridge, 1895); and Anne Rowe Cunningham (ed.), *Letters and Diary of John Rowe, Boston Merchant* (Boston, 1903). Published editions are incomplete; the manuscript should be consulted for any serious purpose.

Samuel P. Savage II: Papers, MHS; include 3 letters and a memorandum on April 19, 1775.

Hezekiah Smith, Haverhill, Mass.: Diary, 1773–74, MHS.

Luke Smith, son of Acton militiaman Solomon Smith: *Boston Globe,* April 18, 1893; Kehoe, "We Were There!" I, 308–9.

William Smith: Petition and Account, MA, vol. 182, 199–300, published in Hudson, *History of Lexington,* 189; pagination varies in other editions.

James Stevens: Journal, April 19, 1775; published as "Journal of James Stevens," *EIHC* 48 (1912): 41.

Nathan Stow: Journal, 1776–80, Stow Family Papers, CFPL; "Sergeant Nathan Stow's Orderly Book," *Putnam's Monthly Magazine* 1 (1892–93): 307–8. William Tay, Woburn: Petition Sept. 20, 1775, published in Frothingham, *History of the Siege of Boston,* 368–69.

Joseph Thaxter: Letter dated Nov. 30, 1824, *Historical Magazine* 15 (2nd ser. V: 206–7); also in *United States Literary Gazette* 1 (1825): 264.

John Tudor: Diary, typescript, MHS, on the alarm in Cambridge; published as William Tudor, *Deacon Tudor's Diary* (Boston, 1896).

Mary Palmer Tyler: *Grandmother Tyler's Book; The Recollections of Mary Tyler [Mrs.*

*Royall Tyler]*, ed. Frederick Tupper and Helen Tyler Brown (New York, 1925). She was the daughter of Revere's friend Joseph Palmer.

Artemas Ward: Papers, MHS. The general who wasn't there, but his manuscripts hold much material about the Massachusetts militia.

Dr. John Warren: Diary, April 19, 1775–May 11, 1776, reported in private hands many years ago; not found.

Samuel Weld, Roxbury: Diary, 1773–76, Rhode Island Historical Society.

John Whiting: Diary, 1743-84, ms., Dedham Historical Society.

Stephen Williams, minister in Longmeadow, Mass.: Diary, 1775, in Castle *et al.* (eds.), *The Minute Men*, 147.

Hannah Winthrop: Letter (n.d.) to Mercy Warren, *MHSP* 14 (1875): 29–31; a good source on the Great Fear.

Anna Green Winslow: ed., *Diary of Anna Green Winslow: A Boston School Girl of 1771*. ed. George Francis Dow (Cambridge, Mass., 1894).

## ❧ Personal Records of British Participants

Many British soldiers who marched to Concord left written accounts of their experiences. Some were published immediately after the event. Others were found in British archives by American Anglophiles; a remarkable number are still coming to light. Among the most useful are the following (in alphabetical order):

Anonymous officer in the 5th Regiment: Letter of July 5, 1775, published in Frothingham, *History of the Siege of Boston*, 75.

Anonymous officer of the 59th Regiment: Undated letter in Ezra Stiles, *Literary Diary*, II, 575 (June 22, 1775).

Anonymous officer who marched to Concord: Letter dated April 20, 1775, *Farley's Bristol Journal*, June 17, 1775; Willard (ed.), American *Letters on the Revolution*, 76–77; Kehoe, "We Were There!" I, 165.

Anonymous officer: Diary 1775–77, reported sold Jan. 10, 1921, by the Anderson Auction Co. to a private collector; said to include an account of the capture of Paul Revere (Forbes, *New England Diaries*, 334). Not found.

Anonymous seaman? on board a British ship in Boston harbor: Letter dated April 21, 1775, *Letters of the American Revolution*, 77–79; Kehoe, "We Were There!" I, 184.

Anonymous soldier, 23rd Foot (Welch Fusiliers): Letter, April 30, 1775, published in *Essex Gazette*, May 12, 1775; rpt. *AA4*, II, 440–41.

Anonymous soldiers (3?), units unknown: Intercepted letters, *AA4*, II, 439–40.

Anonymous soldier's wife: Letters, *AA4*, II, 439–40.

Lt. Col. James Abercrombie, 22nd Foot: Letter to Colden, May 2, 1775, *MHSP* 2,11 (1897): 306.

Lt. John Barker, 4th (King's Own) Foot: Diary, published in part as "A British Officer in Boston," *Atlantic Monthly* 39 (1877): 389–401, 544–54; a more complete transcription appears in Harold Murdock and Elizabeth E. Dana (eds.), *The British in Boston* (Boston, 1924); a most important first-hand account of the Concord expedition.

Major William Basset, 10th Foot?: Letter April 23, 1775, published with Lister, narrative; a few helpful vignettes.

Pvt. John Bateman, 52nd Foot: Deposition after capture, April 23, 1775, *AA4*, II, 496.

Lt. William Carter, 40th Foot: Letters dated 1775–76, published as *Genuine Detail . . .* (London, 1784), copy in Houghton Library, Harvard University.

Col. Samuel Cleveland, Royal Artillery: Narrative; Kehoe, "We Were There!" II, 179, citing MSS Royal Artillery Record Office.

Gen. Sir Henry Clinton: William B. Willcox (ed.), *The American Rebellion* (New Haven, 1954). Clinton did not arrive in America until after the battles, but had interesting comments on Gage's performance.

J[ohn?] [Crozier?], master of British transport *Empress of Russia*: Letters dated April 23, 1775, *et seq.*, in Rockingham Mss., City Library, Sheffield, published as "An Account of Lexington in the Rockingham Mss. at Sheffield," ed. J. E. Tyler, *WMQ3* 10 (1953): 99-107.

Ens. Henry De Berniere, 10th Foot: Narrative, published as *Narrative of Occurrences, 1775* (Boston, 1779), rpt. in *MHSC2*, 4 (1816): 204–15; *idem, General Gage's Instructions* (Boston, 1779), a very full account of the reconnaissance missions and the Concord expedition.

Major Robert Donkin: *Military Collections and Remarks* (New York, 1777).

Capt. W. Glanville Evelyn, 4th Foot: Letter, April 23, 1775, published in *Memoir and Letters of Captain W. Glanville Evelyn, of the 4th Regiment ("King's Own") from North America, 1774–1776*, ed. G.D. Scull (Oxford, 1879), 53-55; valuable for the life of a junior officer in Boston.

Lt. Edward Thoroton Gould, 4th (King's Own) Foot: Deposition after capture, April 25, 1775, published in *AA4*, II, 500–501.

Vice Admiral Samuel Graves, Royal Navy, commanding at Boston: "The Conduct of Vice Admiral Samuel Graves in North America in 1774, 1775 and January 1776," a defense of his acts, with copious extracts from his papers by his flag secretary, George Gefferina, dated Dec. 11, 1776, and signed Dec. 1, 1777; two ms. vols., British Library, add. m. 14038–39; transcripts in MHS; published in part in *NDAR*, I, 193, 206; his official correspondence is in the Public Record office, ADM1/485.

Frederick Haldimand: Papers, British Library, add. ms., 21665–97; Gage's second in command, an exceptionally full and revealing correspondence, Haldimand writing in French, Gage in English. See also Allen French, "General Haldimand in Boston," *MHSP* 66 (1942): 91.

Capt. George Harris, 5th Foot: Stephen R. Lushington, *The Life and Services of General Lord Harris, GCB* (London, 1840), colorful details.

John Howe, alleged British spy: Journal, published as *The Journal Kept by John Howe, as a British Spy* (Concord, N.H., 1827). The authenticity of this source is very doubtful. No use of it has been made in this inquiry.

Ens. Martin Hunter, 52d Foot: *The Journal of General Sir Martin Hunter* (Edinburgh, 1894), vignettes.

Lt. Edward Hull, 43rd Foot: Narrative, *MHSP* 16 (1878): 155–58.

Lt.-Col. Stephen Kemble: Deputy Adjutant General to Gage, Journals, published in *The Kemble Papers*, N-YHS *Collections for the Year 1883* (New York, 1884), offers many insights into the operation of Gage's staff.

Capt. Walter S. Laurie, 43rd Foot: Letter to Gage, April 26, 1775, published in *General Gage's Informers* (Ann Arbor, 1932), 95–98; another letter, dated April 21, in *Manuscripts of the Earl of Dartmouth*, III, *American Papers* (London, 1887–96), 292; Historical Manuscripts Commission, Fourteenth Report, Appendix, part 10; a letter about his living arrangements in Boston is in the Copley-Pelham Papers, PRO.

George Leonard: Loyalist volunteer with Percy's brigade: Deposition, May 4, 1775, *General Gage's Informers*, 57.

William Lewis: see Gordon.

Ens. Jeremy Lister, 10th Foot: Narrative, 1782, published as *Concord Fight*, ed. Harold Murdock (Cambridge, 1931), rpt. Spartanburg, S.C., 1969; rpt. in *The Nineteenth of April, 1775*, ed. Clement Sawtell (Lincoln, Mass., 1968), a major narrative of the expedition by an officer in the lead company. His account of the battles of Lexington and Concord and other letters are in the Lister Family Papers, Shibden Hall Folk Museum of West Yorkshire, Halifax.

Lt. Frederick Mackenzie, 23rd Foot, or Royal Welch Fusiliers: Diary, in Regimental Museum, Royal Welch Fusiliers, Caernarfon Castle, Wales, published as *A British Fusilier in Revolutionary Boston*, ed. Allen French (Cambridge, 1926), the most meticulous of British accounts. The Regimental Museum also has a portrait of Mackenzie, painted on his retirement as lieutenant-colonel.

Pvt. James Marr, 4th Regiment: Deposition after capture April 23, 1775, published in *AA4*, II, 500.

Capt. John Montresor, Corps of Engineers: *The Montresor Journals*, ed. G. D. Scull, N-YHS *Collections for the Year 1881* (New York, 1882).

Col. Hugh Percy, 5th Foot, commander relief expedition: *Letters*, ed. C. K. Bolton (Boston, 1902); his report on the battle is in the Public Record Office, London, CO5/92-93; other correspondence is in the Haldimand Papers, BL.

Major John Pitcairn, Royal Marines: Letters and reports to Admiralty, published in *Sandwich Papers*, Navy Records Society; report to Gage, published in *General Gage's Informers*, 55; correspondence with Col. John Mackenzie in Mackenzie Papers, vol. IV, add. ms. 39190, BL.

Richard Pope: Narrative, Huntington Library, California, photostat, NYPL. Published as *Late News of the Excursion and Ravages of the King's Troops on the 19th of April 1775* (Boston, 1927). The author of this document has not been conclusively identified. French thought him a private or noncommissioned officer, 47th Regiment. Tourtellot believed that he was a Boston Loyalist who marched with the Regulars as a volunteer (*Bibliography*, 19).

Lord Rawdon, subaltern in the 5th Foot: Papers in the British Library, London.

Richard Reever: Letters from America, 1775–77, in the Buckinghamshire Record Office, Aylesbury.

Earl of Sandwich: *The Private Papers of John, Earl of Sandwich.* 3 vols. (London, Navy Records Society, 1932–38), the correspondence of the First Lord of the Admiralty.

Lt.-Col. Francis Smith, 10th Foot: Report to General Gage, April 22, 1775, PRO, CO5/92; printed in *MHSP* 14 (1876): 350–51; letter to Major R. Donkin, Oct. 8, 1775, Gage Papers, WCL, published in part in *General Gage's Informers*, 61.

Capt. William Soutar, Royal Marines: Narrative, published in part without citations in Hargreaves, *Bloodybacks*, 219–22.

Charles Stedman: *History of the Origin, Progress, and Termination of the American War.* 2 vols. (London and Dublin, 1794). The author was a serving British officer in the American War of Independence. He knew and interviewed many participants; primary materials on Lexington and Concord (I, 116–20). For a critique, see R. Kent Newmeyer, "Charles Stedman's History of the American War," *AHR* 63 (1957–58): 924–34.

Lt. William Sutherland, 38th Foot: Narrative letter to Kemble, April 27, 1775, Gage Papers, WCL, published in Wroth *et al.* (eds.), *Province in Rebellion* (Cambridge, 1975), doc. 721, pp. 2024–29; narrative letter to General Clinton, April 26, 1775, published in *Late News of the Excursion and Ravages of the King's Troops on the Nineteenth of April, 1775*, ed. Harold Murdock (Boston, 1927).

Maj. James Wemyss: "Character Sketches of Gage, Percy and Others," Sparks Papers, Harvard University, xxii, 214.

Lt. Richard Williams, Royal Welch Fusiliers: Jane van Arsdale (ed.), *Discord and Civil Wars; Being a Portion of a Journal Kept by Lieutenant Williams of His Majesty's Twenty-Third Regiment While Stationed in British North America During the Time of the Revolution* (Buffalo, 1954). Williams arrived after the battles; graphic accounts of Boston, but troubling questions of authenticity.

## ✒ American Government Documents

Among province and colony records, an important source for this inquiry are the records of the Provincial Congress in William Lincoln (ed.), *The Journals of Each Provincial Congress of Massachusetts (Colony) in 1774 and 1775, and of the Committee of Safety, with an Appendix* (Boston, 1838). A more generous selection of materials pertaining mainly to the Provincial Congresses has been issued in microfiche as L. Kinvin Wroth *et al.* (eds.), *Province in Rebellion; A Documentary History of the Founding of the Commonwealth of Massachusetts, 1774–1775* (Cambridge, Mass., 1975).

Other sources include "Letters and Doings of the Council," manuscript notebook covering period April 9, 1774–April 21, 1776, Massachusetts Archives. The Massachusetts Tax List for 1771 is in the Massachusetts Archives, Columbia Point, and has been published in summary form by Bettye Hobbs Pruitt.

The Town Records of Boston have been published as Boston Record Commissioners Report, 39 vols. (Boston, 1876–1909). Specially helpful are vol. 1, *Boston Tax Lists, 1674–1675*; vol. 18, *Boston Town Records, 1770 Through 1777*; vol. 24, *Boston Births, 1700–1800*; vol. 28, *Boston Marriages, 1700–1751*; vol. 30, *Boston Marriages, 1752–1800*; and vol. 22, *The Direct Tax of 1798*.

Other town records are included with local history, below

## ❧ British Government Documents

In the new Public Record Office, Kew, official materials relevant to this inquiry are mainly to be found in three broad record-groups: the Colonial Office, War Office, and the Admiralty.

Colonial Office records on military affairs in CO5/92-93 are especially rich on events of 1774–75, and include the official reports on the battles from Smith, Percy, and Gage. Also helpful are Colonial Office records on admiralty matters in CO5/120-21. Orders in Council are in CO5/29-30, and letters to the secretary of state from Massachusetts are in Co5/769. Instructions to Provincial Governors of Massachusetts, 1631–1775, available to American readers in eight volumes of transcripts at the MHS.

Military records in the Public Record Office include Secretary at War, In-Letters Wo1; Out-Letters, Wo4; Commander in Chief, WO3; Marching Orders, Wo5; Headquarters Papers, WO28, and Troop Movements, WO379. The Amherst Papers, WO34, contain much on America, but little about Lexington and Concord. Service records of officers and printed Army Lists are in WO 65, are on open shelves in the Public Record Office; they include officers of the Royal Marines for this period. American Rebellion Entry books, WO 36, include orders for the Boston garrison from June 10, 1773, to Jan. 10, 1776, Gage's orderbook from July 10, 1774, to Dec. 9, 1774, is in N-YHS. His orderbook from Dec. 10, 1774, to June 6, 1775, is at BPL. For individual regiments, the surviving Monthly Returns, Wo17, hold much material before 1773 and after 1783, but very little in between.

Another record-group in the Public Record Office of special importance for the battles of Lexington and Concord is a large collection of regimental rosters, muster books, and paylists (WO12). They are nearly complete for the British regiments in Boston during the period Nov. 1774–Oct. 1775. These are huge red-bound elephant folios with separate sheets for each company in every regiment. They identify by name, rank, and record of service for this period virtually all British troops who served in Boston and fought at Lexington and Concord. The important materials are in Wo 12/2194 (4th Foot); 2289 (5th Foot); 2750 (10th Foot); 3501 (18th Foot); 3960 (23rd Foot); 5171 (38th Foot); 5561 (43rd Foot); 5871 (47th Foot); 6240 (52nd Foot); 6786 (59th Foot); 7313 (64th Foot); and 7377 (65th Foot).

Some official British military records have found their way into other archives. Summaries of monthly returns by regiment for January and April 1775 are to be found (filed under later dates) in the British Library, add. ms., 29259/I-L. The records of the 52nd Foot, later the Oxfordshire Light Infantry, for the period 1775–1822, are in the Bodleian Library. Orderly Books of the 10th and 23rd Foot are in WCL.

Douglas Sabin, historian of the Minuteman National Historical Park, with the endorsement of the British Military Attaché in Washington, wrote to every regimental association and museum for units present at Lexington and Concord. Virtually no manuscript material was turned up by this inquiry, but a generous file of photocopies from published regimental histories was forthcoming. The material is in the Library of the Minuteman National Historical Park, Concord, Massachusetts.

Admiralty Records in the Public Record Office include Admirals Dispatches, North America, ADM 1/484-90. Among the more important ships' logs for these events are those of HMS *Canceaux*, ADM 51/4136; HMS *Kingfisher*, ADM 51/506; HMS *Preston*, ADM 51/720; HMS *Scarborough*, ADM 51/867; and HMS *Somerset*, ADM 51/906. Fragmentary records of the Royal Marine battalions serving with the army are in Muster Books and Pay Lists, ADM 96/153. Records of individual Marine officers appear in ADM 157, 159, 192/2, 196/1, and 196/68.

## ❧ Documentary Collections

Peter Force (ed.), *American Archives*, 4th series., 6 vols., March 7, 1774, to Aug. 21, 1776, and 5th series, 3 vols., May 3, 1776, to Dec. 31, 1776 (Washington, D.C., 1837-53), a vast compilation in nine large folio volumes of primary materials, many of which are relevant to this inquiry, and some of which have been lost since Force published them.

Vincent J. R. Kehoe (ed.), "We Were There!" 2 vols. (mimeographed typescript, Chelmsford, 1975). This is a full collection of primary materials on the fighting at Lexington and Concord, April 19, 1775, compiled with great care and attention to detail. One volume is devoted to "The American Rebels" and another to "British Accounts." Complete sets are nonexistent in academic libraries, and very rare in other institutions, but may be found at the Watertown Public Library, the Arlington Public Library, and the Library of Minuteman National Historical Park.

Benson J. Lossing, *Hours with Living Men and Women of the Revolution* (New York, 1889). Frank Moore (ed.), *The Diary of the American Revolution*. 2 vols. (New York, 1858, rpt. 1967), consists mostly of extracts from newspapers. Margaret Wheeler Willard (ed.), *Letters on the American Revolution, 1774–1776* (Boston, 1925), includes many relevant epistolary materials.

## ❧ Newspaper Accounts

Boston newspapers of general interest in the period 1774-75 include Isaiah Thomas's *Massachusetts Spy* and Benjamin Edes's and John Gill's *Boston Gazette,* both strongly Whig; the *Massachusetts Gazette and Boston News-Letter,* a moderate Tory paper; the *Massachusetts Gazette and Boston Post Boy,* a strong Tory paper; and the *Boston Evening Post,* which tried to remain neutral.

Specially helpful were the *Salem Gazette,* April 21, 1775; Salem's *Essex Gazette,* April 25, 1775; (Worcester) *Massachusetts Spy,* May 3, 1775; (Portsmouth) *New Hampshire Gazette,* April 21, 28, 1775; *New York Journal,* May 25, 1775; *New York Gazetteer,* April 27, 1775; *New York Weekly Gazette and Mercury,* April 1775.

## ❧ Anniversary Sermons and Orations

Every year on the day of the battle, the Massachusetts Provincial Congress sponsored sermons to mark the event. Some were delivered by eyewitnesses, and included primary material. Those published during the War of Independence included: Jonas Clarke of Lexington, *The Fate of Blood-thirsty Oppressors and God's Tender Care of His Distressed People* (Boston, 1776); Samuel Cooke of Cambridge, *The Violent Destroyed and Oppressed Delivered* (Boston, 1777); Jacob Cushing of Waltham, *Divine Judgments* (Boston, 1778); Samuel Woodward of Weston, *The Help of the Lord, in Signal Deliverances and Special Salvation, to be Acknowledged and Remembered* (Boston, 1779); Isaac Morrell of Wilmington, *Faith in Divine Providence* (Boston, 1780); Henry Cummings of Billerica, *A Sermon Preached in Lexington, on the 19th of April, 1781* (Boston, 1781); Phillips Payson of Chelsea, *A Memorial of Lexington*

*Battle and of Some Signal Interpositions of Providence in the American Revolution* (Boston, 1782); Zabdiel Adams of Lunenberg, *The Evil Designs of Men Made Subservient by God to the Public Good, particularly illustrated in the Rise, Progress and Conclusion of the American War* (Boston, 1783).

## ∾ Military Manuals

These works are indispensable for a study of formations and tactics used by both sides on April 19, 1775. Some of the relevant works are as follows: *Gentleman's Compleat Military Dictionary* (18th ed., Boston, 1759); *The Manual Exercise, as Ordered by His Majesty in 1764* (Boston, n.d. [late 1774 or early 1775?]); William Windham, *Plan of Discipline Composed for the Use of the Militia of the County of Norfolk* (London, 1759); Humphrey Bland, *A Treatise of Military Discipline* (7th ed., London, 1753); William Brattle, *Sundry Rules and Directions for Drawing Up a Regiment, Posting the Officers, etc.* (Boston, 1773); Richard Draper, *"A Plan of Exercise for the Militia of the Province of Massachusetts-Bay," Extracted from the Plan of Discipline for the Norfolk Militia* (Boston, 1772); Phineas Lyman, *General Orders of 1757*, ed. William S. Webb (New York, 1899); Timothy Pickering, Jr., *Easy Plan of Discipline for a Militia* (Salem, 1775); Thomas Simes, *The Military Guide for Young Officers* (3rd ed., London, 1781).

## ∾ Material Artifacts

Any student of Paul Revere's life has much to learn from his silver, and that of his father. The major public collections are in the Boston Museum of Fine Arts, the Worcester Art Museum, the Metropolitan Museum of Art, and at Yale University. Their work contains many clues to character and personality, as well to the culture within which they lived. There is today much fashionable interest in the study of "material culture," but scholars have so far had little success in moving beyond an academic antiquarianism and linking material culture to large historiographical questions. With imagination and creativity, important work can be done, but here is an interpretative problem that remains to be solved. Paul Revere offers many possibilities.

The Revere House itself is a primary source, much altered through the years, but still the building speaks to us of Paul Revere's world; as also do Old North Church, Fanueil Hall, the Old Boston State House, Copp's Hill Burying Ground, and the streets of the North End. Of the wooden buildings that stood along the Battle Road in 1775, a remarkable number survive, some still bearing the scars of the conflict more than two centuries later. The Lexington Historical Society maintains the Hancock-Clarke house (with a very strong collection of original furnishings), the Buckman Tavern and the Munroe Tavern, and welcomes many thousands of visitors each year.

For the battles of Lexington and Concord, many material artifacts have survived. With others of the period, they may be studied in the British National Army Museum, and in regimental museums, as well as in the Concord Museum and the Museum of Our National Heritage (Lexington, Mass.).

## ∾ Terrain Studies

The historian of any battle must attend carefully to the ground. The scene of the events of April 18 and April 19, is today much changed. All of it lies within metropolitan Boston, and most of the Battle Road is today a busy suburban highway. I was fortunate to be able to tour the road with Douglas Sabin, historian of the Minuteman National Historical Park, who himself has written a detailed history of the battles. It is still possible today to observe major terrain features at the North Bridge, Ripley's Ridge, Revolutionary Ridge, Meriam's Corner, Brooks Hill, the Bloody Curve, Nelson Road, and Parker's Hill, Fiske Hill, and Concord Hill. A not entirely successful attempt was made some years ago to restore the Nelson Road area to something like its appearance in 1775

A pioneering terrain study is Joyce Lee Malcolm, *The Scene of the Battle, 1775, Historic Grounds Report* (Boston, 1985), a published examination of land use along the Battle Road, mainly from an investigation of deeds and other records. Another general project is presently under way by Brian Donahue, Brandeis University, linking deeds to topographical surveys, soil maps, and other sources in computer-generated maps of the area.

The staff of the Minuteman National Historical Park has sponsored many specialized studies in the form of National Park Service Reports. All can be consulted at the library at the Park. Among the most useful for this project are: L. J. Abel and Cordelia T. Snow, "The Excavation of Sites 22 and 23, Minuteman National Historical Park, Massachusetts" (Concord, 1966), a study of the area where Paul Revere is thought to have been captured; Cynthia E. Kryston, "The Muster Field: Historical Data" (Concord, 1972), on the field near the Buttrick house; John F. Luzader, "Elisha Jones or 'Bullet Hole House'" (1968), on Monument Street in Concord; *idem*, "Samuel Hartwell House and Ephraim Hartwell Tavern" (1968), on the Battle Road in Lincoln; David H. Snow, "Archeological Research Report, Excavation at Site 264" (1973), on the Thomas Nelson house near the Lincoln-Lexington line; Clifford A. Kaye, *The Geology and Early History of the Boston Area of Massachusetts, a Bicentennial Approach* U. S. Geological Survey Bulletin 1476 (Washington, D.C., 1976); Ricardo Torres-Reyes, Captain Brown's House: Research Report (Washington, D.C., 1969).

## ❧ Biographical Works on Paul Revere

This list is confined to works that contain primary material not available elsewhere. For secondary and tertiary interpretations of Paul Revere, see Historiography, pp. XX, above.

[Joseph Buckingham], "Paul Revere," *New England Magazine* 3 (1832): 304-14, was an early biography by an author who knew him well, and included some primary material that has not appeared in any subsequent biography before the present volume. Elbridge Henry Goss, *The Life of Colonel Paul Revere.* 2 vols. (Boston, 1891), is a documentary history, still very useful for the materials that it includes. Charles F. Gettemy, *True Story of Paul Revere* (Boston, 1905), has somewhat of a debunking flavor. Harriet E. O'Brien, *Paul Revere's Own Story; An Account of His Ride as Told in a Letter to a Friend, Together with a Brief Sketch of His Versatile Career* (Boston, privately printed, 1929), is especially valuable for its rich trove of illustrative materials. Esther Forbes, *Paul Revere and the World He Lived In* (1942, rpt. Boston, 1969), is a lively modern biography by a New England novelist, weak on the ride and political and military events but very strong on the details of domestic life. In general, it was carefully done, but it must be approached with caution in matters of fact. Walter S. Hayward, "Paul Revere and the American Revolution, 1765-1783," is an unpublished Harvard dissertation, 1933. Nina Zannieri, Patrick Leehey, *et al.*, *Paul Revere—Artisan, Businessman, and Patriot* (Boston, Paul Revere Memorial Association, n.d. [1988]), is an important collection of scholarly essays on various aspects of Paul Revere's career, and also the catalogue of an exhibition, sponsored by the PRMA. A review of the exhibition itself by Alfred Young appears in *Journal of American History* 76 (1989): 852–57. The volume includes Patrick M. Leehey, "Reconstructing Paul Revere; An Overview of His Ancestry, Life and Work," pp. 15–40, a meticulous work by an able and very careful scholar who is head of research at the Paul Revere House.

## ❧ Paul Revere's Family

Elizabeth Grundy and Jayne Triber, "Paul Revere's Children: Coming of Age in the New Nation," unpublished essay, in the Paul Revere Memorial Association, adds biographies of Paul Revere, Jr., Joseph Warren Revere, Harriet Revere, and Maria Revere Balestier. Donald M. Nielsen, "The Revere Family," *NEHGR* 145 (1991): 291–316, corrects earlier studies.

## ❧ Paul Revere: The Copley Portrait

Robert Dubuque, "The Painter and the Patriot: John Singleton Copley's Portrait of Paul Revere," *Revere House Gazette* 17 (1989): 1–5. Paulette Marie Kaskinen, "Artists, Craftsmen and Patriots: Social Pretensions and Propaganda in John Singleton Copley's Portraiture," unpub. master's thesis, Univ. of Virginia, 1992.

## ❧ Paul Revere: Huguenot Origins

Charles W. Baird, *History of the Huguenot Emigration to America,* 2 vols. (New York, 1885; rpt. Baltimore, 1966); Jon Butler, *The Huguenots in America: A Refugee People in New World Society* (Cambridge, Mass., 1983); Patrick M. Leehey, "The Huguenot Communities in New England: Boston, New Oxford, Narragansett and Dresden, Maine," unpublished ms., 1988, Paul Revere Memorial Association.

## ❧ Paul Revere's Business Activities

*A Brief Sketch of the Business Life of Paul Revere* (Taunton, 1928); Mark Bortman, "Paul Revere and Son and Their Jewish Correspondents," *Publications of the American Jewish Historical Society* 43 (1953–54): 199–229; Clarence S. Brigham, *Paul Revere's Engravings* (Worcester, 1954); Kathryn C. Buhler, "The Ledgers of Paul Revere," *Museum of Fine Arts Bulletin,* June 1936, pp. 38–45; Renee Ernay, "The Revere Furnace, 1787–1800," unpub. master's thesis, University of Delaware, 1989; Ruth L. Friedman, "Artisan to Entrepreneur: The Business Life of Paul Revere," unpublished research paper, Paul Revere Memorial Association Library, 1978; John J. Kebabian, "Paul Revere and His Water Dam," *CEAIA* 30 (1977): 12–13; Maurer, Maurer, "Copper Bottoms for the United States Navy, 1794–1803," *The United States Naval Institute Proceedings* 17 (June 1945); Edward Moreno, "Patriotism and Profit: The Copper Mills at Canton," Zannieri. Leehey, *et al., Paul Revere—Artisan, Businessman, and Patriot,* 95–116; James A. Mulholland, *A History of Metals in Colonial America* (Birmingham, 1981); Arthur H. Nichols, "The Early Bells of Paul Revere," *NEHGR* 48 (April 1904): 151–57; Arthur H. Nichols, "The Bells of Paul and Joseph W. Revere," *EIHC* 47 (Oct. 1911): 293–316; Jane Ross, "Paul Revere—Patriot Engraver," *Early American Life* 6 (April 1975): 36–37; Edward Stickney and Evelyn Stickney. *The Bells of Paul Revere, His Sons and Grandsons* (Bedford, Mass., 1976).

## ❧ Paul Revere's Silver

A leading authority is Kathryn C. Buhler, who has given us *American Silver* (Cleveland, 1950); *American Silver, 1655–1825, in the Museum of Fine Arts.* 2 vols. (Boston, 1972); *American Silver from the Colonial Period Through the Early Republic in the Worcester Art Museum* (Worcester, 1979); "Master and Apprentice: Some Relationships in New England Silversmithing," *Antiques* 68 (1955): 456–60; "Paul Revere, Patriot and Silversmith," *Discov-*

*ering Antiques* 57 (1971): 1350–54; and *Paul Revere, Goldsmith 1735–1818* (Boston, n.d.). Louisa Dresser, "American and English Silver Given in Memory of Frederick William Paine, 1866–1935," *Worcester Art Museum Annual* 2 (1936–37): 89–98; Deborah A. Federhen, "From Artisan to Entrepreneur: Paul Revere's Silver Shop in Operation," in Zannieri, Leehey, *et al.*, *Paul Revere—Artisan, Businessman and Patriot*, 65–93; Morrison H. Heckscher and Leslie Greene Bowman, *American Rococo: Elegance in Ornament* (New York, 1992); Janine E. Skerry, "The Revolutionary Revere: A Critical Assessment of the Silver of Paul Revere," Zannieri, Leehey, *et al.*, *Paul Revere—Artisan, Businessman and Patriot*, 41–63.

## ❧ Paul Revere's Military Service

Two accounts of the Penobscot Expedition are Russell Bourne, "The Penobscot Fiasco." *American Heritage*, Oct. 1974, pp. 28–33, 100–101; William M. Fowler, Jr., "Disaster in Penobscot Bay," *Harvard Magazine*, July–Aug. 1979, pp. 26–31. Chester B. Kevitt, *General Solomon Lovell and the Penobscot Expedition, 1779* (Weymouth, 1976), reproduces many relevant documents. James S. Leamon, *Revolution Downeast: The War for American Independence in Maine* (Amherst, Mass., 1993), includes an excellent bibliography. Linda Webster, "The Penobscot Expedition: A Study in Military Organization," is an unpublished senior thesis, Bates College, 1983; a copy is in the Paul Revere Memorial Association.

## ❧ Paul Revere's Masonic Activities

Edith J. Steblecki, *Paul Revere and Freemasonry* (Boston, 1985), is the best study of its subject, with much valuable data in its appendices and a good bibliography; the same author also has published "Fraternity, Philanthropy and Revolution: Paul Revere and Freemasonry," in Zannieri, Leehey, *et al.*, *Paul Revere—Artisan, Businessman and Patriot*, 117–47. Other works in a large literature include: Harry Carr, *Six Hundred Years of Craft Ritual* (Grand Lodge of Missouri, 1977); and *The Constitutions of the Ancient and Honorable Fraternity of Free and Accepted Masons Containing Their History, Charges, Addresses and Collected and Digested from Their Old Records, Faithful Traditions and Lodge Books. For the Use of Masons to Which Are Added the History of Masonry in the Commonwealth of Massachusetts, and the Constitution, Laws and Regulations of Their Grand Lodge Together with a Large Collection of Songs, Epilogues, etc.* (Worcester, 1792).

## ❧ Paul Revere's Horse

William Ensign Lincoln, *Some Descendants of Stephen Lincoln, Edward Larkin, Thomas Oliver, Michael Pearce, Robert Wheaton, George Burrill, John Porter, John Ayer* (New York, 1930), is the nearest thing to a primary source. Also helpful is Patrick M. Leehey, "What *was* the Name of Paul Revere's Horse?" *Revere House Gazette* 16 (1965): 5; and *idem*, "A Few More Words on 'Paul Revere's Horse,'" *ibid.* 17 (1989): 6.

## ❧ Biographies of Thomas Gage

By comparison with the vast outpouring of scholarship on Paul Revere, remarkably little has been published on General Gage. The standard biography is John R. Alden, *General Gage in America* (Baton Rouge, 1948), now much in need of revision. A short study by a leading historian of the British army in the Revolution is John Shy, "Thomas Gage: Weak Link of Empire," in George A. Billias (ed.), *George Washington's Opponents: British*

*Generals and Admirals in the American Revolution* (New York, 1969), 3–38. An important study of Gage's career is Frederick Bernays Wiener, *Civilians Under Military Justice; The British Practice since 1689, Especially in British North America* (Chicago, 1967). The author was a Washington lawyer with much practical experience in related fields.

### ᴥ Biographies (Alphabetical by Subject)

Some of these works belong more to the realm of memory than history. They are filiopietistic in tone and substance, and enter exaggerated claims for the acts of ancestors. But they also contain many memoirs, family stories, and personal documents. When used with care and caution they greatly enrich our knowledge of the event.

On Samuel Adams: Ralph Volney Harlow, *Samuel Adams, Promoter of the American Revolution: A Study of Psychology and Politics* (New York, 1923), is occasionally useful, despite its Freudian bias; John C. Miller, *Sam Adams, Pioneer in Propaganda* (Boston, 1936), is still the standard work, stressing his Puritan roots. Clifford Shipton, "Samuel Adams," *Sibley's Harvard Graduates*, is a serious work of scholarship, but colored by a strong Tory bias.

Other biographical material on April 19 appears in: Robert L. Volz, *Governor Bowdoin and His Family* (Brunswick, Me., 1969); George Tolman, *John Jack, the Slave, and Daniel Bliss, the Tory* (Concord, Mass., 1902); G. W. Brown, "Sketch of the Life of Solomon Brown," Proceedings, LHS II (1890): 124; Charles F. Carter, "The Rev. Jonas Clarke, Minister and Patriot," *Lexington Historical Society Proceedings* IV (1905–10): 82–90. Jules David Prown, *John Singleton Copley*. 2 vols. (Cambridge, 1966); Henry W. Holland, *William Dawes and His Ride with Paul Revere* (Boston, 1878); Cyrus Hamlin, *My Grandfather, Colonel Francis Faulkner* (Boston, 1887); George Billias, *Elbridge Gerry* (New York, 1976); idem, *General John Glover and His Marblehead Mariners* (New York, 1960); Hall Gleason, "Captain Isaac Hall," *Medford Historical Register* 8 (1905): 100–103.

On John Hancock: A large but thin literature includes: James Truslow Adams, "Portrait of an Empty Barrel," *Harper's Magazine* 161 (1930): 425–34; Oliver M. Dickinson, "John Hancock, Notorious Smuggler or Near Victim of British Revenue Racketeers?" *MVHR* 32 (1945–46): 517–40; Herbert Allen, *John Hancock: Patriot in Purple* (New York, 1948).

Also, Josephine Hosmer, "Memoir of Joseph Hosmer," *The Centennial of the Concord Social Circle* (Cambridge, Mass., 1882), 116–17; and the larger ms., "Memoir of Joseph Hosmer," Concord Antiquarian Society Papers, CFPL; Bernard Bailyn, *The Ordeal of Thomas Hutchinson* (Cambridge, Mass., 1974); Joseph Grafton Minot, *A Genealogical Record of the Minot Family in America and England* (Boston, 1897); Robert Newman Sheets, *Robert Newman; His Life and Letters in Celebration of the Bicentennial of His Showing of Two Lanterns in Christ Church, Boston, April 18, 1775* (Denver: Newman Family Society, 1975); Andrew Oliver, comp., *Faces of a Family* (Boston: privately printed, 1960).

Much has been written on James Otis: William Tudor, *Life of James Otis* (Boston, 1823), is still the best biography, despite its age; Alice Vering, "James Otis," is a dissertation at the University of Nebraska, 1954; Ellen Brennan, "James Otis, Recreant and Patriot," *NEQ* XII (1939): 691–725, centers on his early writings; John J. Waters, Jr., *The Otis Family In Provincial and Revolutionary Massachusetts* (1968; New York, 1975), is an excellent social history of the family.

Other biographical materials include Elizabeth S. Parker, "Captain John Parker," LHS *Proceedings* 1 (1866–89): 43; Theodore Parker, letter of Feb. 16, 1858, published in Lexington *Townsman*, April 21, 1932, copy in LHS; Denison Rogers Slade, "Henry Pelham, the Half-Brother of John Singleton Copley," *Transactions of the Colonial Society of Massachusetts* 5 (1897–98): 193–211; Usher Parson, *The Life of Sir William Pepperrell, Bart.* (Boston, 1855); Henry Winchester Cunningham, *Christian Remick: An Early Boston Artist* (Boston, 1904).

On Joseph Warren: There are many studies, and still a need for a comprehensive modern biography; still useful are: Alexander Everett, *Joseph Warren*, in Jared Sparks (ed.),

*Library of American Biography* (Boston, 1838), 1st series, X, 91–183; A Bostonian [Samuel Adams Wells], *Biographical Sketch of General Joseph Warren* (Boston 1857); Richard Frothingham, Jr., *The Life and Times of Joseph Warren* (Boston, 1866); John Cary, *Joseph Warren, Physician, Politician, Patriot* (Urbana, 1961).

## Local Histories: Boston

General works include: Justin Winsor (ed.), *The Memorial History of Boston*. 4 vols. (Boston, 1880–81); Gerald B. Warden, *Boston, 1689–1776* (Boston, 1970); Annie Haven Thwing, *The Crooked and Narrow Streets of the Town of Boston, 1630-1822* (Boston, 1920); Samuel Adams Drake, *Old Landmarks and Historical Personages of Boston* (1872; rev. ed., Boston, 1906; rpt. 1971, 1986).

On topography and terrain: Samuel Barber, *Boston Common: A Diary of Notable Events, Incidents and Neighboring Occurrences* (Boston, 1916); Walter M. Whitehill, *Boston: A Topographical History* (Cambridge, 1959; 2nd ed., 1968, 1975); *idem*, "Paul Revere's Boston, 1775–1818," *Harvard Magazine* 77 (1975): 28–36; Wendy A. Cooper, "Paul Revere's Boston," *Antiques* 108 (July 1975): 80–93.

On demographic history: John B. Blake, *Public Health in the Town of Boston, 1630–1822* (Cambridge, 1959).

On social and economic structure: Boston Board of Assessors. "Assessors 'Taking Books' of the Town of Boston, 1780." *The Bostonian Society Publications* 9 (1912): 9–59; James Henretta, "Economic Development and Social Structure in Colonial Boston," *William and Mary Quarterly* 22 (1965): 75–92.

On politics and the Boston town meeting: *A Report of the Record Commissioners of the City of Boston, Containing the Boston Town Records, 1770–1777* (Boston, 1887).

On the military occupation: Oliver M. Dickerson, *Boston Under Military Rule, 1768–1769* (1936; rpt. Westport, Conn., 1971), is a compendium of materials culled mostly from newspapers.

On neighborhoods: William Sumner, *The History of East Boston* (Boston, 1858), has primary material on April 19, 1775; Carol Ely, "North Square: A Boston Neighborhood in the Revolutionary Era," unpublished paper, Brandeis University, 1983, PRMA, applies the methods of New England town histories to the study of Paul Revere's urban neighborhood.

On patterns of association: Allan Forbes, *Taverns and Stagecoaches of New England*. 2 vols. (Boston, 1954), 18-27; Walter K. Watkins, *Old Boston Taverns and Tavern Clubs* (Boston, 1917); and Samuel Adams Drake, *Historic Fields and Mansions of Middlesex* (Boston, 1873), with a quantitative appendix drawn from 18th-century tax lists.

## Massachusetts Town Histories and Town Records

Secondary works of this genre must be approached with caution; the same local pride that inspired them often colored the substantive result. But they include much primary material that is no longer available. Specially valuable for primary materials on the events of April 19 are the works listed below by Josiah Adams on Acton; Ripley, Shattuck, and Wheeler on Concord; Charles Hudson and Elias Phinney on Lexington, Alfred Hudson on Sudbury, Wayland, and Marlborough, and Smith and Cutler for Arlington.

Many town histories published in the late 19th century also included genealogical appendices which are useful for the identification of participants. The genealogical data are also useful checks for the accuracy of historical materials. Some of the more helpful works used in this inquiry are:

Acton: Josiah Adams, *Acton Centennial Address* (Boston, 1835); *idem, Letter to Lemuel Shattuck, Esq.* (Boston, 1850); Harold R. Phalen, *History of Acton* (1954).

Andover: Sarah L. Bailey, *Historical Sketches of Andover, Massachusetts* (Boston, 1880).

Arlington, formerly called West Cambridge and Menotomy: Benjamin & William Cutler, *The History of the Town of Arlington* (Boston, 1880); Samuel A. Smith, *West Cambridge on the Nineteenth of April, 1775* (Boston, 1864).

Attleborough: John Daggett, *A Sketch of the History of Attleborough* (Boston, 1894).

Bedford: Abram English Brown, *The History of the Town of Bedford* (Bedford, 1891).

Beverly: Charles F. Smith, *Proceedings of the Beverly Historical Society of Massachusetts on the Occasion of the Presentation of a Tablet Commemorating the Minute-Men of Beverly*, lst Ser., no. 1 (New York, 1896); E. M. Stone, *The History of Beverly* (Boston, 1843); Thomas A. and Jean M. Askew, *Beverly, Massachusetts, and the American Revolution* (Beverly, 1525).

Billerica: John Farmer, *Historical Memoir of Billerica* (n.p., n.d.); Henry A. Hagen, *History of Billerica* (Boston, 1883).

Braintree: Samuel A. Bates (ed.), *Records of the Town of Braintree, 1640–1793* (Randolph, Mass., 1886). Charles F. Adams, *History of Braintree, the North Precinct of Braintree, and the Town of Quincy* (1891).

Brookline: *Muddy River and Brookline Records, 1634–1839* (Brookline, 1875). Charles Knowles Bolton, *Brookline, the History of a Favored Town* (Brookline, 1897); John W. Curtis *History of the Town of Brookline, Massachusetts* (Boston, 1933). David Hackett Fischer (ed.), *Brookline: The Social History of a Suburban Town, 1705–1850* (Waltham, 1986).

Cambridge, *Town Records of Cambridge, 1630–1703* (Cambridge, 1896). J. W. Freese, *Historic Houses and Spots in Cambridge, Massachusetts, and Near-by Towns* (Boston, 1897); Lucius Paige, *History of Cambridge, 1630-1877* (Boston, 1877).

Carlisle: Sidney, *History of Carlisle* (Cambridge, 1920).

Charlestown: Richard Frothingham, Jr., *The History of Charlestown, Massachusetts* (Boston, 1845). James F. Hunnewell, *A Century of Town Life: Charlestown, Massachusetts, 1775–1887*. 2 vols. (Boston, 1888).

Chelsea: *A Documentary History of Chelsea*. 2 vols. Ed. Mellon Chamberlain (Boston, 1908).

Concord: David Hackett Fischer, *Concord: The Social History of a New England Town, 1750–1850* (Waltham, 1983); Robert Gross, *The Minutemen and Their World* (New York, 1976); Lemuel Shattuck, *History of the Town of Concord to 1832* (Concord, 1835); Ruth Wheeler, *Concord, Climate for Freedom* (Concord, 1967); Ezra Ripley, *History of the Fight at Concord* (Concord, 1827; 2nd ed., 1832); Alfred S. Hudson, *History of Concord* (Concord, 1904); *Social Circle Memoirs*, vols. I, II.

Danvers: Daniel P. King, *Address Commemorative of Seven Young Men of Danvers Who Were Slain in the Battle of Lexington* (Salem, 1835). J. W. Hanson, *History of the Town of Danvers* (Danvers, 1848).

Dedham: Robert Brand Hanson, *Dedham, Massachusetts 1635–1890* (Dedham, 1976); Erastus Worthington, *The History of Dedham* (Boston, 1827); Erastus Worthington II, *Proceedings at the 250th Anniversary . . . of the Town of Dedham* (Cambridge, 1887).

Deerfield: George Sheldon, *A History of Deerfield, Massachusetts*. 2 vols. (Deerfield, 1896).

Dover: Frank Smith, *A History of Dover, Massachusetts* (Dover, 1897).

Dudley: *Town Records of Dudley, 1732–1754* (Pawtucket, 1893).

Duxbury: *The Records of Duxbury, 1642–1770* (Plymouth, 1893).

Framingham: William Barry, *History of Framingham* (Boston, 1847); Josiah Temple, *The History of Framingham* (Framingham, 1887).

Fitchburg: James F. D. Garfield, "Fitchburg's Response to the Lexington Alarm," *Fitchburg Historical Society Proceedings* 1 (1892–94): 113–122. *idem*, "Fitchburg's Soldiers of the Revolution," *ibid.* 4 (1908): 172–232.

Groton: Caleb Butler, *The History of the Town of Groton* (Boston, 1848); Samuel Abbot Green, *Groton During the Revolution*; *Groton Historical Series* (4 vols., 1887–99).

Harvard: H. S. Nourse, *History of Harvard, Massachusetts, 1732–1893* (Harvard, 1984).

Ipswich: Joseph B. Felt, *History of Ipswich, Essex and Hamilton* (1834); Arlin Ira

Ginsberg, "Ipswich, Massachusetts, during the American Revolution," diss., University of California, Riverside).

Lexington: Elias Phinney, *History of the Battle of Lexington* . . . (Boston; 1825, rpt. 1875). Charles S. Hudson, *History of the Town of Lexington, Mass.* . . . (Boston, 1868; 2 vols., 1913).

Lincoln: Paul Brooks, *Trial by Fire: Lincoln, Massachusetts, and the War of Independence* (Lincoln, 1975); John C. Maclean, *A Rich Harvest; The History, Buildings, and People of Lincoln, Massachusetts* (Lincoln, 1987).

Lynn: Alonzo Lewis and James R. Newhall, *History of Lynn, Essex County, Massachusetts* . . . (Boston, 1865; Lynn, 1890, 1897); Howard K. Sanderson, *Lynn in the Revolution*. . . . 2 vols. (Boston, 1919).

Lynnfield: Thomas B. Wellman, *History of the Town of Lynnfield, Massachusetts, 1635–1895* (Boston, 1895).

Medford: Charles Brooks and James M. Usher, *History of Medford* (Boston, 1886); Helen Tilden Wild, *Medford in the Revolution; Military History of Medford, Massachusetts, 1765–1783* (Medford, 1903); Richard B. Coolidge, "Medford and Her Minute Men," *Medford Historical Society Register* 28 (1927): 40–51; Jason L. Tiner, "The Role of Medford, Massachusetts, in the Revolutionary War," paper, Brandeis University, May 7, 1992, includes a quantitative study of Medford men serving in the War of Independence.

Melrose: Elbridge H. Goss, *The History of Melrose* (Melrose, 1902).

Natick: Oliver Bacon, *History of Natick from Its First Settlement in 1651* (Boston, 1856).

Needham: George K. Clarke, *History of Needham, Massachusetts, 1711–1911* (Cambridge, 1912).

Newton: S. F. Smith, *The History of Newton* (Boston, 1880); Francis Jackson, *A History of the Early Settlement of Newton* (Boston, 1854).

Roxbury: Francis S. Drake, *The Town of Roxbury* (Boston, 1905); *idem, The Town of Roxbury; Its Memorable Persons and Places* (Roxbury, 1878).

Salem: Sidney Perley, *History of Salem*. 2 vols. (1924–26); James Duncan Phillips, *Salem in the Eighteenth Century* (Boston, 1937).

Sudbury: Alfred Sereno Hudson, *The History of Sudbury, Massachusetts, 1638–1889* (Sudbury, 1889); *Idem, The Annals of Sudbury, Wayland and Maynard* (n. p., 1891); *The War Years in the Town of Sudbury, Massachusetts, 1765–1781* (Sudbury, 1975), extracts from military records.

Waltham: David Hackett Fischer (ed.), *Waltham: A Social History* (Waltham, 1994); Charles A. Nelson *Waltham, Past and Present* . . . (Cambridge, 1882); Edmund L. Sanderson, *Waltham as a Precinct of Watertown and as a Town, 1630–1884* (Waltham, 1936).

Watertown: *Watertown Records, Fifth Book, 1745–1769*; and *Sixth Book, 1769–1702*, ed. William McGuire (Newton, 1928). G. Frederick Robinson and Ruth Robinson Wheeler, *Great Little Watertown; A Tercentenary History* (Watertown, 1930); *Watertown's Military History: Authorized by a Vote of the Inhabitants of the Town of Watertown, Massachusetts* (Boston, 1907).

Weston: *Weston Town Records, 1754–1803* (Boston, 1893); Brenton H. Dickson and Homer C. Lucas, *One Town in the American Revolution; Weston, Massachusetts* (Weston, 1976).

Westford: Rev. Edwin Hodgman, *History of the Town of Westfield, 1659–1883* (Lowell, 1883).

Henry S. Chapman, *History of Winchester, Massachusetts* (Winchester, 1936).

Woburn: Samuel Sewall, *The History of Woburn, 1640–1860* (Boston, 1868).

## ❧ Town Histories: New Hampshire

Many people who participated in the events of April 19 later moved to New Hampshire. Local histories with primary materials include: William Willes Hayward, *The History of Hancock, New Hampshire, 1764–1889.* 2 vols. (Lowell, Mass., 1889); Charles Henry Chandler, *The History of New Ipswich, New Hampshire* (Fitchburg, Mass., 1914); Henry Ames Blood, *The History of Temple, New Hampshire* (Boston, 1860).

## ᕗ County Histories

By comparison with the wealth of town histories, and the abundance of county studies in other parts of the United States, county histories in New England tend to be impoverished. But there are important exceptions. Two works of Duane Hamilton Hurd, *History of Essex County, Massachusetts* (Philadelphia, 1888) and *History of Middlesex County, Massachusetts.* 3 vols. (Philadelphia, 1890), are careful, informed, and accurate. They reproduce much reprinted primary material that can be found nowhere else—for example, the diary of Loammi Baldwin, a leading source for the fighting at the Bloody Curve. Hurd is specially valuable for the spread of the Lexington alarm, which he followed with more attention than any other work. Also useful in a heuristic way is Samuel A. Drake, *Historic Fields and Mansions of Middlesex* (Boston, 1873), also published as *Old Landmarks and Historic Fields of Middlesex* Drake scooped up vast quantities of material and published them in his many antiquarian volumes. Used with caution, his writings are still valuable as a source of leads and possibilities. Also very helpful is Ronald N. Tagney, *The World Turned Upside Down; Essex County During America's Turbulent Years, 1763–1790* (West Newbury, Mass., 1989).

## ᕗ Political History of the Revolution

In a very large literature, the following monographs were specially helpful for this inquiry: David Ammerman, *In the Common Cause: American Response to the Coercive Acts of 1774* (Charlottesville, 1974); Bernard Bailyn, *Ideological Origins of the American Revolution* (Cambridge, 1967); idem, *Faces of Revolution* (New York, 1990); Richard D. Brown, *Revolutionary Politics in Massachusetts: The Boston Committee of Correspondence and the Towns, 1772–1774* (Cambridge, 1970); Oliver M. Dickerson, *The Navigation Acts and the American Revolution* (Philadelphia, 1951); Francis S. Drake, *Tea Leaves: Being a Collection of Letters and Documents . . .* (Boston, 1884); Bernhard Knollenberg, *Origin of the American Revolution, 1759–1766* (rev. ed., New York, 1961); Benjamin Labaree, *The Boston Tea Party* (New York, 1964); Pauline Maier, *From Resistance to Revolution* (New York, 1972, 1974); Edmund S. and Helen M. Morgan, *The Stamp Act Crisis; Prologue to Revolution* (Chapel Hill, 1953); Arthur M. Schlesinger, *The Colonial Merchants and the American Revolution* (New York, 1957); Hiller B. Zobel, *The Boston Massacre* (New York, 1970).

## ᕗ The Powder Alarms

On the Charlestown Alarm: Robert P. Richmond, *Powder Alarm, 1774* (Princeton, 1971), is the fullest account, with a bibliography.

On the Portsmouth Alarm: Charles L. Parsons, "The Capture of Fort William and Mary, December 14 and 15, 1774," *New Hampshire Historical Society Proceedings* 4 (1899–1905): 18–47; Ballard Smith, "Gunpowder for Bunker Hill," *Harper's Monthly Magazine* 73 (1886): 236–43; Elwin L. Page, "The King's Powder, 1774," *NEQ* 18 (1945): 83–92.

On the Marblehead and Salem Alarm: William Gavett, Samuel Gray, Samuel Holman, Abijah Northey, Joseph Story, *EIP* 1 (1859): 120–35; John Pedrick, "Narrative," *EIHC* 17 (1880): 190–92; Susan Smith, "Memoir," (Boston) *Columbian Centinel*, Sept. 19, 1794; anonymous account, *EIHC* 38 (1901): 321–52; *Essex Gazette*, Feb. 28, Mar. 7, 1775; Charles M. Endicott, "Leslie's Retreat," *EIP* 1 (1859): 89–120; James Duncan Phillips, "Why Colonel

Leslie Came to Salem," *EIHC* 90 (1953): 313; *Essex Journal* Mar. 1, 1775; *Salem Gazette*, Feb. 28, Mar. 3, 1775.

### ❧ The Midnight Ride, and Signals from Old North Church

Remarkably little has been published in a scholarly way on the midnight ride. The few recent works are written mainly as popular history: e.g., Bernard A. Weisberger, "Paul Revere, the Man, the Myth, and the Midnight Ride," *American Heritage* 28 (1977): 24–37; Richard W. O'Donnell, "On the Eighteenth of April, in Seventy-five . . . 'Longfellow didn't know the half of it,'" *Smithsonian* 4 (1973): 72–77; and Thomas J. Fleming, "Paul Revere— He Went Thataway," *Yankee* 39 (1975): 94, 98–103, 112–14, 116. Gwen Ellen Brown, "A Study of Paul Revere's Ride," is an unpublished essay, at the Paul Revere House.

On the signal lanterns, there are: Richard Frothingham, *The Alarm on the Night of April 18, 1775* (Boston, 1876); John Lee Watson, "Revere's Signal," *MHSP* 15 (1876): 163–77; idem, *Paul Revere's Signal* (Boston, 1876), (Cambridge, 1877) also *MHSP1* 15, 163; William W. Wheildon, *History of Paul Revere's Signal Lanterns* (Boston, 1878); and Charles K. Bolton, *Christ Church, A Guide* (Boston, 1941).

### ❧ The Battles of Lexington and Concord

Richard Frothingham, Jr., *History of the Siege of Boston, and of the Battles of Lexington, Concord, and Bunker Hill* (Boston, 1851), publishes primary materials no longer available elsewhere.

Works published for the centennial include: Frederic Hudson, "The Concord Fight," *Harper's Monthly Magazine* 50 (1875), a monograph on the battle with much useful material; and the Rev. Artemas B. Muzzey, "The Battle of Lexington, with Personal Recollections of Men Engaged in It" (Boston, 1877), reprints material that appeared in *NEHGR*, 31 (1877): 377; and Grindall Reynolds, *Concord Fight, April 19, 1775* (Boston, 1875).

Frank Warren Coburn, *The Battle of April 19th, 1775* (Lexington, 1912; rev. ed., 1922), is specially helpful on the march out, and on the fighting in Menotomy and Cambridge. The second edition publishes many, but not all muster rolls; also Frank Warren Coburn, *Truth and Fiction About the Battle on Lexington Common* (Lexington, 1918).

Harold Murdock, *The Nineteenth of April, 1775* (Boston, 1923), is a collection of essays by an American Anglophile; an intelligent and suggestive work, but with a strong bias.

Ellen Chase, *The Beginnings of the American Revolution.* 3 vols. (New York: Baker & Taylor, 1910), is a remarkable work which gleaned much valuable material from antiquarian sources; very carefully done, with excellent citations and many good leads.

Allen French published many important monographs, including *The Day of Concord and Lexington: The Nineteenth of April, 1775* (Boston, 1925); *General Gage's Informers: New Material Upon Lexington and Concord. Benjamin Thompson as Loyalist & the Treachery of Benjamin Church, Jr.* (Ann Arbor, 1932); and *The First Year of the American Revolution* (Boston, 1934).

Douglas P. Sabin, "April 19, 1775: A Historiographical Study" (Concord, 1987), is a major study, historical as well as historiographical, of the battles by the historian at Minuteman National Historical Park. For many aspects of its subject, this is the most full and careful investigation. It is an indispensable work for serious students of the battles and deserves to be published by the National Park Service.

Many works center on the role of militia from individual towns. Ezra Ripley, *History of the Fight at Concord, on the 19th of April 1775* (Concord, 1827; 2nd ed., 1832), stresses the role of Concord men; William W. Wheildon, *New Chapter in the History of the Concord Fight* (Boston, 1885), centers on the Groton minutemen. Abram English Brown, *Beneath Old Roof Trees* (Boston, 1896); idem, *Beside Old Hearthstones* (Boston, 1897), two volumes of stories and legends by a historian of Bedford. Frederick Brooks Noyes, *The Tell-tale Tomb* (n.p., n.d.), stresses "Acton aspects of the Concord fight."

Specialized studies include John R. Alden, "Why the March to Concord," *AHR* 49 (1943-44): 446-54, on Gage's secret orders of Jan. 27, 1775; George Lincoln Goodale, *British and Colonial Army Surgeons on the 19th of April, 1775* (Cambridge, 1899).

W. E. Griswold, *The Night the Revolution Began* (Brattleboro, Vt., 1972), and Frank Wilson Cheney Hersey, *Heroes of Battle Road* (Boston, 1930).

### ❧ Military and Naval Histories: The British Army

Richard Cannon, *Historical Records of the British Army* (London, 1850–70). Edward E. Curtis, *The Organization of the British Army in the American Revolution* (New Haven, 1926). Sir John Fortescue, *History of the British Army*. 13 vols. in 20 (London, 1899–1930), a monument of military historiography, with an extreme Tory bias, not at its best on the American Revolution, but the maps are excellent. Sylvia Frey, *The British Soldier in America* (Austin, 1981). J. F. C. Fuller, *British Light Infantry in the Eighteenth Century* (London, n.d.). Charles Hamilton (ed.), *Braddock's Defeat* (Norman, Okla., 1959). Reginald Hargreaves, *The Bloodybacks; The British Serviceman in North America and the Caribbean, 1655–1783* (New York, 1968), anecdotal. J. A. Houlding, *Fit for Service: The Training of the British Army, 1715–1795* (Oxford, 1981). Robin May, *The British Army in North America, 1775–1783* (London, 1974), is helpful on uniforms and equipment. Stanley Pargellis, "Braddock's Defeat," *AHR* 41 (1936): 253–69. John Shy, *Toward Lexington: The Role of the British Army in the Coming of the American Revolution* (Princeton, 1965).

### ❧ British Unit Histories

4th Foot (King's Own): L. I. Cowper, *The King's Own: The Story of a Royal Regiment* (Oxford, 1939), one of the best of the British regimental histories.

5th Foot (Northumberland Fusiliers): Lt.-Col. R. M. Pratt, *The Royal Northumberland Fusiliers* (Alnick, 1981); H. M. Walker, *A History of the Northumberland Fusiliers, 1674–1919* (London, 1919); Walter Wood, *The Northumberland Fusiliers* (London, n.d.).

10th Foot: Albert Lee, *History of the Tenth Foot (The Lincolnshire Regiment)* (London, 1911); Col. Vincent J.-R. Kehoe, *A Military Guide: The Tenth Regiment of Foot of 1775*, 2d edition enlarged, 4 vols. (Somis, Calif., 1993).

18th Foot: G. E. Boyle, "The 18th Regiment of Foot in North America," *Journal of the Society of Army Historical Research* 2 (1923): 65.

23rd Foot; or Royal Welch Fusiliers: A. D. L. Cary and Stouppe McCance (eds.), *Regimental Records of the Royal Welch Fusiliers (Late the 23rd Foot)*, Vol. I, 1689–1815 (London, 1921); also *The Regimental Museum of the Royal Welch Fusiliers, 23rd Foot* (n.p., n.d.).

43rd Foot: Sir Richard G. A. Levinge, *Historical Records of the Forty-Third Regiment, Monmouthshire Light Infantry* (London, 1868).

47th Foot: H.G. Purdon, *An Historical Sketch of the 47th (Lancashire) Regiment and the Campaigns Through Which They Passed* (London, 1907); Col. H. C. Wylie, *The Loyal North Lancashire Regiment*. 2 vols. (London, 1933).

59th Foot: Anonymous, "Notes for a History of the 59th Foot," *ca.* 1920, Regimental Headquarters, Queen's Lancashire Regiment, Fulwood Barracks, Preston, Lancashire; photocopies in the library of the Minuteman National Historical Park, Concord.

64th Foot: H. G. Purdon, *Memoirs of the Services of the 64th Regiment (Second Staffordshire) 1758 to 1881* (London, n.d.).

Royal Regiment of Artillery: Francis Duncan, *History of the Royal Regiment of Artillery*. 2 vols. (London, 1872). Royal Marines: Col. C. Field, *Britain's Sea Soldiers*. 2 vols. (Liverpool, 1924); Capt. Alexander Gillespie, *Historical Review of the Royal Marine Corps* (Birmingham,

1803); J. L. Moulton, *Royal Marines* (London, 1972); Lt. P. H. Nicolas, *Historical Records of the Royal Marine Forces.* 2 vols. (London, 1845).

### Naval and Maritime History

William Bell Clark, *NDAR,* Vol. I, *American Theatre: Dec. 1, 1774–Sept. 2, 1775 . . .* (Washington, D.C., 1964), a very full collection of documents. Marjorie Hubbell Gibson, *H. M. S. Somerset, 1746–1778: The Life and Times of an Eighteenth Century British Man-o-War and Her Impact on North America* (Cotuit, Mass., 1992).

### The New England Militia

General studies include: Fred Anderson, *A People's Army, Massachusetts Soldiers and Society in the Seven Years' War* (Chapel Hill, 1984), an academic monograph, strong on the social history of its subject. John R. Galvin, *The Minute Men: A Compact History of the Defenders of the American Colonies, 1645–1775* (New York, 1967), an important and useful work by an experienced infantry officer and onetime commanding general of NATO. Two of the most valuable works are unpublished dissertations: Archibald Hanna, Jr., "New England Military Institutions, 1693–1750," unpub. diss., Yale, 1951; John Murrin, "Anglicizing an American Colony: The Transformation of Provincial Massachusetts," unpub. diss., Yale, 1966. Norman Castle *et al.* (eds.), *The Minute Men, 1775–1975* (Southborough, Mass., 1777), is a collection of fifty essays on minutemen in individual towns, with much material not available elsewhere.

### ❧ Weapons and Equipment

In this highly specialized field, some of the leading works include: Anthony D. Darling, *Red Coat and Brown Bess* (Ottawa, 1970); Lindsay Merrill, *The New England Gun* (New Haven, 1975); Howard Blackmore, *British Military Firearms, 1650-1850* (New York, 1968); Warren Moore, *Weapons of the American Revolution . . . and Accoutrements* (New York, 1967); George C. Neumann, *History of the Weapons of the American Revolution* (New York, 1967); George C. Neumann and Frank J. Kravic, *Collectors' Illustrated Encyclopaedia of the American Revolution* (Harrisburg, 1975).

Charles ffoulkes and E. C. Hopkinson, *Sword, Lance and Bayonet* (London, 1938); George C. Neumann, *Swords and Blades of the American Revolution* (Harrisburg, 1973); R. J. Wilkinson-Latham, *British Military Bayonets, from 1700 to 1845* (New York, 1969); Graham T. Priest, *The Brown Bess Bayonet, 1720–1860* (Wiltshire, 1968); R. D. C. Evans and F. J. Stephens, *The Bayonet: An Evolution and History* (London, 1985); Robert M. Reilly, *American Socket Bayonets and Scabbards* (Lincoln, R. I., 1990), with a bibliography of the journal literature.

Madison Grant, *Powder Horns and Their Architecture* (York, Pa., 1987); Nathan L. Swayze, *Engraved Powder Horns of the French and Indian War and Revolutionary War Era* (Yazoo City, Miss., 1978); William H. Guthman, *Drums A'beating, Trumpets Sounding; Artistically Carved Powder Horns in the Provincial Manner, 1746–1781* (Hartford, Conn., 1993), with an excellent bibliography of the large journal literature.

Frank E. Schermerhorn, *American and French Flags of the Revolution, 1775–1783* (Philadelphia, 1948); anonymous, "The Bedford Flag," *MHSP* (1885): 166, 199; *NEHGR* 25 (1871): 138–39.

### ~ The Aftermath

Richard D. Brown, *"Knowledge is Power": The Diffusion of Information in Early America, 1700–1865* (New York, 1989); Philip Davidson, *Propaganda and the American Revolution, 1763–1783* (Chapel Hill, 1941); Fred J. Hinkhouse, *The Preliminaries of the American Revolution as Seen in the English Press, 1763–1775* (New York, 1926; rpt. 1969); Frank L. Mott, "The Newspaper Coverage of Lexington and Concord," *NEQ* 17 (1944): 489–505; Ian M. G. Quimby, "The Doolittle Engravings of the Battle of Lexington and Concord," *Winterthur Portfolio Four* (Charlottesville, 1968), 83–108; Robert S. Rantoul, "The Cruise of the 'Quero': How We Carried the News to the King," *EIHC* 36 (1900): 5–13; J.H. Scheide, "The Lexington Alarm," *AAS Proceedings* 50 (1940): 49–79; Arthur M. Schlesinger, *Prelude to Independence: The Newspaper War on Britain, 1764–1776* (New York, 1958).

### ~ The Myth of the Midnight Ride

General studies include: Sidney George Fisher, "The Legendary and Mythmaking Process in Histories of the American Revolution," *APS Proceedings* 51 (1912): 53–76; Dixon Wecter, *The Hero in America: A Chronicle of Hero Worship* (New York, 1941), chap. 5, "The Embattled Farmers"; Wesley Frank Craven, *The Legend of the Founding Fathers* (New York, 1956); Jayne Triber, *The Midnight Ride of Paul Revere: From History to Folklore* (Boston. n.d.); and an unpublished research report for the Paul Revere Memorial Association; Michael Kammen, *The Mystic Chords of Memory* (New York, 1991), a major work; Susan Wilson, "North Bridge: Span of History," *Boston Globe*, April 15, 1993, an excellent and informative essay; Arthur Bestor, "Concord Summons the Poets," *NEQ* 6 (1934) 602–13; Josephine L. Swayne (ed.), *The Story of Concord, Told by Concord Writers* (Boston, 1905); George L. Varney, *The Story of Patriots' Day . . .* (Boston, 1895).

# ABBREVIATIONS

## ❧ And Methods of Transcription

| | |
|---|---|
| *AA4* | Peter Force (ed.), *American Archives*, 4th series., 6 vols., March 7, 1774, |
| *AA5* | to Aug. 21, 1776, and 5th series, 3 vols., May 3, 1776, to Dec. 31, 1776 (Washington, D.C., 1837–53), |
| AAS | American Antiquarian Society |
| *AHR* | *American Historical Review* |
| APS | American Philosophical Society |
| BL | British Library |
| BPL | Boston Public Library |
| CAM | Concord Antiquarian Museum |
| CFPL | Concord Free Public Library |
| *EIP* | *Essex Institute Proceedings* |
| *EIHC* | *Essex Institute Historical Collections* |
| LC | Library of Congress |
| LHS | Lexington Historical Society |
| MA | Massachusetts Archives |
| MHS | Massachusetts Historical Society |
| *MHSC* | *Massachusetts Historical Society Collections* |
| *MHSP* | *Massachusetts Historical Society Proceedings* |
| NANE | National Archives, New England Regional Center |
| *NDAR* | William Bell Clark (ed.), *Naval Documents of the American Revolution*, vol. I (Washington, D.C., 1964) |
| *NEHGR* | *New England Historic and Genealogical Register* |
| NEHGS | New England Historic and Genealogical Society |
| *NEQ* | *New England Quarterly* |
| N-YHS | New-York Historical Society |
| NYPL | New York Public Library |
| PRMA | Paul Revere Memorial Association |
| PRO | Public Record Office, Kew |
| WCL | William L. Clements Library, Ann Arbor, Michigan |

Note: In direct quotations, spelling and punctuation have been modernized where necessary to make the meaning clear to a modern reader. The method of transcription in these cases, as in *Albion's Seed* (New York, 1989), 906, follows Samuel Eliot Morison's "modern" (*not* modernized) text. The rule is to "spell out all contractions and abbreviations in the manuscript, to adopt modern usage as to capitalization, punctuation and spelling," but scrupulously to respect . . . language." The method is explained at greater length in *Harvard Guide to American History* (Cambridge, Mass., 1954), 94–99.

# NOTES

## ❧ Introduction

1. David Gergen on Senator Paul Tsongas, MacNeil-Lehrer News Hour, October 1992.
2. See below, pp. 327–44, for a more extended discussion of historiography.
3. Allen French, *The Day of Lexington and Concord* (1925; rpt. Boston, 1975), 1.

4. Such an approach to narrative history differs fundamentally from two others that have recently appeared in the academic literature. Social historians in the past generation called for a "revival of narrative" in which individual actors appear mainly as the captives of large deterministic processes. That approach to story-telling failed completely, for narrative without contingency lacks the vital tension that holds a story together.

More recently, several popular writers, and even some professional historians of a relativist bent have suggested that historians should solve the problem of narrative by adopting the methods of fiction, and (within various limits) openly fabricating their stories, their characters, and even their sources. This also will not do. An historian cannot manufacture his materials without ceasing to write history. Further, the remodeled relativism that has been offered as a rationalization for this practice is itself a fallacy.

Any true revival of serious narrative history must rest on two firm premises: first, no narrative without contingency; second, no history without a rigorous respect for fact.

5. None of this is meant to assert his priority over other leaders. Many volumes might be written about figures of equal or greater importance. But this is a book about Paul Revere.

6. There were at least four ideas of liberty in early America: the ordered freedom that was carried from East Anglia to Puritan New England in the great migration of 1629–40; the hegemonic freedom that went from the south and west of England to Cavalier Virginia, *ca.* 1640–80; the reciprocal freedom that was brought by Quakers from the North Midlands of England and Wales to the Delaware Valley; and the natural freedom that traveled from the borderlands of North Britain and northern Ireland to the American backcountry. All were challenged in 1775 by a fifth idea of a free society in Britain's Imperial elite. For extended discussion see D. H. Fischer, *Albion's Seed* (New York, 1989).

### ❧ 1. Paul Revere's America

1. Covenant of the Methuen Militia in *EIHC* 7 (1870): 243; Benjamin Bangs Diary, Sept. 10, 1747, MHS; Amos Barrett, Narrative, in *Journal and Letters of Henry True* (Marion, Ohio, 1906); Thomas Boynton, Journal, April 19, 23, 1775, MHS; published in *MHSP* 15 (1877): 254–55.

2. His master was John Coney (1655–1722); the inventory of his estate, in the records of Suffolk County, included an appraisal of "Paul Rivoires time about three years and half as per. indenture, [L]30-O-O" and a note, "cash recd for Paul Rivoire's Time, more than it was prized at . . . £10." John Coney Inventory, Suffolk Probate Records, file 4641.

3. For the growth in his reputation in the past fifty years, compare John M. Phillips, "The Huguenot Heritage in American Silver," *Legion of Honor Magazine* 11 (1940): 70, and Esther Forbes, *Paul Revere and the World He Lived In* (Boston, 1942), 10; Janine Skerry, "The Revolutionary Revere: A Critical Assessment of the Silver of Paul Revere," in Nina Zannieri, Patrick Leehey, *et al.*, *Paul Revere—Artisan, Businessman and Patriot: The Man Behind the Myth* (Boston, 1988), 44–46. Skerry writes, of the sleeve buttons in particular, "The engraved border on these sleeve buttons of overlapping leaves surrounding a stylized flower is a common decorative motif on New England silver in this period . . . the basic shape of these buttons, however, is unusual . . . the shape of Revere's round sleeve buttons is not only distinctive but challenging to fabricate as well." One might add that the aesthetics of these small pieces also show a refinement that is not merely a matter of technique. Something similar appears also in Apollos Rivoire's larger silver pieces.

4. Three proceedings for debt against Apollos Rivoire are in the Suffolk County Court files, 42893 (1736); 46500 (1738), and 47232 (1738); Donald M. Nielsen, "The Revere Family," *NEHGR* 145 (1991): 293.

5. On variant spellings, see Elbridge Henry Goss, *The Life of Colonel Paul Revere,* 2 vols. (New York, 1891), I, 10; "Rwoire" is in the Coney inventory; on the "bumpkins," John Rivoire to Paul Revere, Jan. 12, 1775, RFP, MHS.

6. Milton Halsey Thomas (ed.), *The Diary of Samuel Sewall,* 2 vols. (New York, 1973), I, 406 (Jan. 4, 1699).

7. Of Huguenot marriages in Boston, 1700–1749, only 31 of 266 (11.7%) were endogamous; Jon Butler, *The Huguenots in America; A Refugee People in New World Society* (Cambridge, Mass., 1983), 82.

8. Patrick M. Leehey, "Reconstructing Paul Revere: An Overview of His Life, Ancestry and Work," in Zannieri, Leehey, *et al., Paul Revere,* 36n.

9. See Appendix A for genealogical data, drawn mainly from Nielsen, "The Revere Family," 291–316; and Patrick Leehey, "Reconstructing Paul Revere," in Zannieri, Leehey, *et al., Paul Revere,* 15–39; both correcting many errors in Forbes, *Revere,* 469, and other works.

10. Paul Revere to John Rivoire, May 19, 1786, RFP, MHS.

11. Robert F. Seybolt, *The Public Schools of Colonial Boston, 1635–1775* (Cambridge, Mass., 1935), 23–25; D. C. Colesworthy, *John Tileston's School* (Boston, 1887).

12. Paul Revere, Engraving for North Battery Certificate, n.d., *ca.* 1762, reproduced in Clarence S. Brigham, *Paul Revere's Engravings* (Worcester, Mass., 1954), 12; Forbes, *Revere,* 29.

13. Calvinist churches included 8 Congregationalist, 1 Anabaptist, 1 Presbyterian, and 1 French Reformed. Others were two Anglican churches and one Quaker meeting. A third Anglican church, Trinity, was founded in 1733 but its building was not open until Aug. 15, 1735; cf. Walter M. Whitehill, *Boston: A Topographical History* (2nd ed., Cambridge, Mass., 1968). For the location of Boston's churches, see John Bonner and William Price, "A New Plan of the Great Town of Boston in New England" (n.p., 1733, 1743, 1769).

14. John Tucker Prince, "Boston in 1813," *Bostonian Society Publications* 3 (1906): 86.

15. Lt. Richard Williams, in Jane Van Arsdale (ed.), *Discord and Civil Wars, Being a Portion of a Journal Kept by Lieutenant Williams of His Majesty's Twenty-Third Regiment While Stationed in British North America During the Time of the Revolution* (Buffalo, 1954), 5 (June 12, 1775).

16. For a reconstruction of kinship in the North End, see the excellent study by Carol Ely, "North Square: A Boston Neighborhood in the Revolutionary Era," unpublished paper, Brandeis University, 1983 (copy on file at the Paul Revere House, Boston); for the street cry, see Dirk Hoerder, *Crowd Action in Revolutionary Massachusetts, 1765–1780* (New York, 1977), 226.

17. Ron Johnston, Graham Allsopp, John Baldwin, and Helen Turner, *An Atlas of Bells* (Oxford, 1990), 178.

18. John Dyer, Paul Revere, Josiah Flagg, Bartholemew Flagg, Jonathan Law, Jonathan Brown junior, and Joseph Snelling, Bell Ringing Agreement, n.d., *ca.* 1750; Old North Church; facsimile in Zannieri, Leehey, *et al., Paul Revere,* 149.

19. The business appears to have remained in his mother's name until Paul Revere reached his majority; conversation with Patrick M. Leehey, Coordinator of Research, PRMA.

20. "Mrs. Deborah Revere, Dr. To 12 Months Board from December 12, 1761 to December 12 1762 at 6/8 per week. . . . 18.16.8." Paul Revere Waste Book, RFP, MHS.

21. These were the teeth of animals, secured by metal wires. Revere claimed in his advertisements that he had set "hundreds" of false teeth; see *Boston Gazette,* Sept. 19, 1768.

22. Peter Jenkins, Oct. 9, 1763, Paul Revere Waste Book, RFP, MHS.

23. Paul Revere Ledgers, Jan. 3, 1761, May 6, 1786, Aug. 24, 1794, RFP, MHS.

24. Paul Revere Waste Book, Sept. 27, 1774, RFP, MHS.

25. After many years of unqualified admiration, another generation of experts has studied Revere's silver with a more critical eye. See Skerry, "The Revolutionary Revere," in Zannieri, Leehey, *et al., Paul Revere,* 41–64.

26. Appendix A, below; Daniel Scott Smith, "The Long Cycle in American Illegitimacy and Prenuptial Pregnancy," Peter Laslett, *et al.* (eds.), *Bastardy and Its Comparative History* (Cambridge, Eng., 1980), 362–78.

27. Forbes is mistaken in thinking that the grave marker for Sarah Revere was "a type of stone at the moment in high fashion." More recent work shows that Revere preferred the older New England customs to the new fashions of the age. Cf. James Deetz, *In Small Things Forgotten; The Archaeology of Early American Life* (New York, 1977), 70.

28. It is reproduced in facsimile in Goss, *Revere*, I, 110; for the children born of this union, see Appendix A. When a French cousin asked in 1786 about the number of his children, Paul Revere answered carefully that he had fifteen "born in wedlock." Could this mean that there were others? Cf. Paul Revere to John Rivoire, May 19, 1786, RFP, MHS.

29. Paul Revere to Rachel Revere, Aug. 1778, RFP, MHS.

30. Rachel Revere to Paul Revere, undated, Gage Papers, WLC; published in Allen French, *General Gage's Informers* (Ann Arbor, 1932), 170–71.

31. For further discussion, see David Hackett Fischer, *Albion's Seed* (New York, 1989).

32. Rowland Ellis to E. H. Goss, July 19, 1888, Goss, *Revere*, I, 30n, II, 611.

33. For Revere and the street lamps, *Boston Town Records, 1770–1777*, May 11, 1773, p. 136; for his service as coroner, some of the records are in the Revere Family Papers, MHS; for his tenure on the Board of Health after a yellow fever epidemic in 1799–1800, see John B. Blake, *Public Health in the Town of Boston* (Cambridge, 1959), 166; on the Charitable Mechanic Association, (Boston) *Columbian Centinel*, Dec. 31, 1794; and Joseph T. Buckingham, *Annals of the Massachusetts Charitable Mechanic Association*; on his jury service in 1806, see Justin Winsor, *Memorial History of Boston*, 4 vols. (Boston, 1880-81), IV, 588.

34. Notably Esther Forbes; see below, p. 338.

35. Some scholars have speculated that the decision to represent Paul Revere in the dress of an artisan was made by the painter, not the subject. No primary evidence bears explicitly on this point; I think the motif was more likely to be the result of mutual agreement. It is in any case a point of no relevance here.

36. The British officer spoke very differently to humble farmers and tradesmen. See also William Shirley, Commission to "Paul Revere, gentleman," Feb. 18, 1755/56, RFP, MHS; and *Boston Town Records, 1770–1777*, July 19, 1774, p. 182.

37. Paul Revere to Supply Belcher, April 9, 1810, RFP, MHS.

38. Paul Revere to John Rivoire, May 19, 1786, RFP, MHS.

39. Ownership appears in bills and receipts for "my horse" during his rides before 1775; evidence of a mare being sent for grazing to Groton appears, without citation, in Forbes, *Revere*, 161–69.

40. The record of the case, before Judge Richard Dana, is reprinted in Goss, *Revere*, Appendix H, II, 667–68.

41. Paul Revere summarized his service record in a certificate dated April 27, 1816, reprinted in Goss, *Revere*, I, 22.

42. Edith J. Steblecki, "Fraternity, Philanthropy and Revolution: Paul Revere and Freemasonry," in Zannieri, Leehey, *et al.*, *Paul Revere*, 117–47; Steblecki, *Paul Revere and Freemasonry* (Boston, 1985), 11–12. For a description of the Green Dragon as "the greatest celebrity among all the old Boston hostelries," see Samuel Adams Drake, *Old Landmarks and Historic Personages of Boston* (1872, 1906; rpt. Rutland, Vt., 1971), 148.

43. A list of sixty members of the North Caucus who attended a meeting on March 23, 1772, appears in Goss, *Revere*, II, 635–44. Its leaders were an inner group of eleven men who served on executive committees: Gibbens Sharp, Nathaniel Barber, Thomas Hichborn [*sic*], Captain John Pulling, Henry Bass, Paul Revere, John Ballard, Dr. Thomas Young, Thomas Kimball, Abiel Ruddock, and John Lowell, names that will reappear many times in our story. Other members included Samuel Adams, William Molinaux, Dr. Joseph Warren, and Dr. Benjamin Church.

44. Its members included John Hancock and James Otis, John and Samuel Adams, Dr. Joseph Warren and Dr. Benjamin Church, Samuel and William Cooper, Josiah Quincy and Samuel Phillips, Thomas Dawes and Samuel Dexter, Thomas Fleet, John Winslow, Royall Tyler, and Thomas Melville.

45. John Adams, Diary, Oct. 27, 1772, *Diary and Autobiography of John Adams,* 4 vols., ed. Lyman H. Butterfield (New York, 1964), II, 64–65.

46. On Cromwell's Head, kept by Joshua Brackett in School Street, see Clarence S. Brigham, *Paul Revere's Engravings* (Worcester, 1954), 116–17; Alice Morse Earle, *State Coach and Tavern Days* (New York, 1900), 86; Drake, *Old Landmarks and Historic Personages of Boston,* 61–62.

47. This group began as the Secret Nine or Loyal Nine, Boston artisans and shop-keepers. See Edmund S. and Helen M. Morgan, *Stamp Act Crisis; Prologue to Revolution* (Chapel Hill, 1953), 121–22; George P. Anderson, "A Note on Ebenezer MacKintosh," *CSM* 26 (1927): 348–61; the leading study is Pauline Maier, *From Resistance to Revolution: Colonial Radicals and the Development of American Opposition to Britain, 1765–1776* (New York, 1972).

48. Paul Revere, "View of the Obelisk erected under the Liberty-Tree in Boston on the Rejoicings for the Repeal of the—Stamp Act, 1766," Brigham, *Paul Revere's Engravings,* 21–25; Goss notes, "It was designed by Revere, and he had prepared and issued a descriptive plate before the celebration took place." Cf. Goss, *Revere,* I, 39.

49. Dennis Dooley *et al.,* *The Glorious Ninety-Two . . . Published under the Authority of the Committees on Rules of the Two Branches of the General Court to Commemorate the Return to Massachusetts of the Paul Revere Liberty Bowl* (Boston, 1949).

50. John Rowe, Diary, May 27 1773, MHS; published in part as *Letters and Diary of John Rowe* (Boston, 1903), 245.

51. Brigham, *Paul Revere's Engravings,* 58–60.

52. Many attacks on British soldiers in Boston before the Boston Massacre are documented in depositions collected from the troops themselves, in the summer of 1770. They have never been published in America, and are to be found CO 5/88, 179–262, PRO.

53. The Massacre print was drawn and engraved by Henry Pelham, and re-engraved at least three times by Paul Revere. In turn, Revere's work was copied by Jonathan Mulliken and others. On March 29, 1770, Pelham drafted an angry letter to Paul Revere, accusing him of bringing out an edition of the print without permission, and depriving Pelham of his "advantage . . . as truly as if you had plundered me on the public highway." Revere and Pelham resolved their differences and were soon doing business together again. Brigham, *Paul Revere's Engravings,* 41–46; Cf. Zobel, *Boston Massacre* (New York, 1970), 197–98. Scholars sympathetic to Revere have suggested that Pelham's letter survives only in draft and was never actually sent. Evidence internal to the draft strongly indicates that the letter was actually delivered. The original document survives as Henry Pelham to Paul Revere, March 29, 1770, Intercepted Copley-Pelham Letters, CO5/39, PRO.

54. "To the Freeholders and Inhabitants of the Town of Boston in Town Meeting," Jan. 29, 1771; Intercepted Copley-Pelham letters, CO5/39, PRO.

55. Var. Snider, Snyder.

56. *Boston Gazette,* March 11, 1771.

57. *A Retrospect of the Boston Tea Party, with a Memoir of George R. T. Hewes* (New York, 1834), 40; another interesting account of the origin of the Tea Party by a seaman who joined the North End mobs and was later pressed on board HMS *Captain,* appears in a Deposition of Samuel Dyer, July 30 1774, in the papers of Admiral Montagu under the date of Aug. 10, 1774, ADM1/484, PRO, Kew.

58. Francis S. Drake, *Tea Leaves: Being a Collectrion of Letters and Documents Relating to the Shipment of Tea to the American Colonies in the Year 1773 . . .* (Boston, 1884). lxvii, lxxxix, xcii, clxxvi.

59. Goss, *Revere,* I, 150.

60. Revere was reimbursed for his expenses by the town of Boston. See Paul Revere to David Wood, May 28, 1774; his bill read: "to a journey of my horse to King's Bridge, New York, 234 miles." RFP, MHS. For Revere's appointment by town meeting, see Newell Diary, May 13, 1774; and Samuel Adams (Boston) to Paul Revere (Philadelphia), May 18, 1774,

RFP, MHS; *Boston Town Records,* May 18, 1774, p. 175. For further details and for sources, see below, Appendix D.

61. See Appendix D for a chronology of all known rides, and sources. His expenses were paid for these trips (but not the midnight ride) by the town of Boston, and later by the provincial government. Various bills and receipts are in Revere Family Papers at the Massachusetts Historical Society, the Massachusetts Archives, and the Paul Revere House; some are reproduced in facsimile in Goss, *Revere,* I, 144.

62. John Wentworth to T. W. Waldron, Jan. 27, 1775, *6MHSC* 4 (1891): 73–74.

63. "As the True Born Sons of Liberty in Boston . . ." April 18, 1775, oversize ms., MHS.

64. Tory writers commonly misunderstood the American Revolution as an authoritarian movement, rigidly controlled by "Sam Adams and his myrmidons," as one of them described it. This is a common error in revolutionary conflicts, too often perpetuated by historians. Cf. Andrew Oliver Letterbook, 1767–74, Egerton ms. 2670, BL.

65. The seven lists were: the Masonic lodge that met at the Green Dragon, the Loyal Nine (1766); the North Caucus (1771); the Long Room Club (1773); the Tea Party participants (1773); the Boston Committee of Correspondence (1774); and a London Enemies List on April 18, 1775. See Appendix E for rosters, comparisons, computations, other leaders, and discussions of these groups in relation to others in the Whig movement.

66. Thomas Young to John Lamb, Lamb Papers, N-YHS.

67. Paul Revere to John Lamb, Sept. 4, 1774, Lamb Papers, N-YHS.

68. Boston Town Meeting, May 13, 1774, *Boston Town Records, 1770–1777,* 174.

69. Nathaniel Ames, *Almanack for 1762* (Boston, 1761); Sam. Briggs (ed.), *The Essays, Humor and Poems of Nathaniel Ames, Father and Son, of Dedham, Massachusetts, from Their Almanacks, 1726–1775* (Cleveland, 1891), 327. Illustrations for the Ameses' diaries were engraved by Paul Revere. See Brigham, *Paul Revere's Engravings,* 133-36; Goss, *Revere,* I, 113.

70. Milan Kundera, *The Book of Laughter and Forgetting* (New York, 1980), 3.


### ❧ 2. General Gage's Dilemma

1. Major William Sheriff to General Frederick Haldimand, Sept. 12 1774, Haldimand Papers, add. ms. 21665, BL.

2. Gage to Dartmouth, Aug. 27, 1774, and Gage to Barrington, Aug. 27, 1774, Clarence E. Carter (ed.), *The Correspondence of General Thomas Gage,* 2 vols. (New Haven, 1931; rpt. New York, 1969), I, 365; II, 651. For Gage's bodyguard, see Percy to General Harvey, Aug. 21, 1774, Charles Knowles Bolton (ed.), *Letters of Hugh Earl Percy from Boston and New York, 1775–1776* (Boston, 1902), 36; for the warning by his aides, see "The Journals of Captain John Montresor," N-YHS *Collections* (1881), 123.

3. Gage to Barrington, June 25, 1775, *Gage Correspondence,* I, 687.

4. Gage to Barrington, private, Nov. 12, 1770, *ibid.,* II, 564.

5. Percy to Duke of Northumberland, Aug 8, 1774, *Letters of Percy,* 31.

6. Intelligence Report from Concord to Gage, April 14, 1775, John R. Alden, *General Gage in America* (Baton Rouge, 1948), 227.

7. The standard biography is still Alden, *General Gage in America;* a more recent work is John Shy, "Thomas Gage: Weak Link of Empire," George Billias (ed.), *George Washington's Opponents: British Generals and Admirals in the American Revolution* (New York, 1969), 3–38; reprinted with a new preface in John Shy, *A People Numerous and Armed* (New York, 1976), 73–108.

8. This was Sir John Gage of Firle, who was said to have treated England's future Queen with cruel "severity." His death before she came to the throne may have saved the family from disaster.

9. Alden, *Gage,* 1–3.

10. *Ibid.,* 5.

11. Romney Sedgwick (ed)., *Some Materials Towards Memoirs of the Reign of King George II by John, Lord Hervey,* 3 vols. (London, 1931), I, 265.

12. The history of Thomas Gage's dialect remains to be written, perhaps because it is often thought to be proper English, and not perceived as dialect. But see A. S. C. Ross, "Linguistic Class-Indicators in Present-day English," *Neuphilologische Mitteilungen* 55 (1954); J. and L. Milroy, *Authority in Language* (London, 1985); Tony V. Crowley, *The Politics of Discourse* (London, 1989), and *idem* (ed.), *Proper English? Readings in Language, History and Cultural Identity* (London and New York, 1991). For Revere's speech, see David Hackett Fischer, *Albion's Seed* (New York, 1989), 57–62.

13. For other versions, see J. W. Fortescue, *A History of the British Army,* 12 vols. (London, 1935), II, 115–16.

14. Of Braddock's 1,459 officers and men, 977 (67%) were killed or wounded. Some historians have held Gage responsible for Braddock's defeat, for it was the collapse of Gage's van that began the disaster. But Gage's comrades on that field did not condemn him, and several including Washington praised his courage and efficiency in restoring discipline among his men on the retreat. Cf. Lawrence H. Gipson, *The Great War for Empire; Years of Defeat, 1754–1757* (New York, 1968), VII, 94, who is severe on Gage; and Stanley M. Pargellis, "Braddock's Defeat," *AHR* 41 (1936): 251–59, who holds Braddock responsible.

15. Francis Parkman, *Montcalm and Wolfe,* 2 vols. (Cambridge, 1898), II, 259; Gipson, *The Great War for Empire,* VII, 219–33; Alden, *Gage,* 45.

16. Captain John Small wrote to Copley, "Your picture of the General is universally acknowledged to be a very masterly performance, elegantly finish'd, and a most striking likeness." "Letters and Papers of John Singleton Copley and Henry Pelham," *MHSC* 71 (1914): 77.

17. Alden, *Gage,* 72.

18. *Ibid.,* 284.

19. *Ibid.,* 14.

20. James Johnson to Haldimand, Sept. 15, 1774, Haldimand Papers, add. ms. 21665, BL.

21. Gage to Hillsborough, July 31, 1768, Aug. 17, 1768, July 7, 1770, *Gage Correspondence,* I, 205, 184, 263; to Shelburne, Oct. 19, 1767, *ibid.,* I, 154.

22. Gage to Hillsborough, Aug. 17, 1768, *ibid.,* I, 183–86.

23. He continued: "No laws can be put in force, for those who should execute the laws, excite the people to break them, and defend them in it. Nothing can avail in so total an anarchy but a very considerable force, and that force empower'd to act." Gage to Barrington, July 6, 1770, *ibid.,* II, 544–47.

24. Burke,"On Conciliation with America," March 22, 1775, *Speeches and Letters on American Affairs* (London, 1956), 102.

25. Gage to Conway, Jan. 16, 1765, *Gage Correspondence,* I, 80–81.

26. Gage to Conway, Dec 21, 1765, *ibid.,* I, 79.

27. Gage to Hillsborough, Sept. 7, 1768, *ibid.,* I, 191.

28. Alden, *Gage,* 177.

29. Gage to Barrington, private, Nov. 12, 1770, *Gage Correspondence,* II, 563–64.

30. Gage to Barrington, Aug. 5, 1772, *ibid.,* II, 615–16.

31. Gage to Hillsborough, Nov. 10, 1770, *ibid.,* I, 277.

32. Gage to Hillsborough, Oct. 31, 1768, *ibid.,* I, 205.

33. Gage to Hillsborough, Oct. 31, 1768, *ibid.,* I, 204.

34. Gage to Dartmouth, Oct. 30, 1774, *ibid.,* I 382.

35. Gage to Dartmouth, Sept. 12, 1774, *ibid.,* I, 373–74; Gage to Hillsborough, Nov. 10, 1770, *ibid.,* I, 277.

36. Gage to Barrington, private, Sept. 8, 1770, Alden, *Gage,* 188.

37. Gage to Haldimand, Aug. 4, 1774, Haldimand Papers, add. ms. 21665, BL.

38. George III to Lord North, Sir John Fortescue (ed.), *The Correspondence of George the Third from 1760 to December, 1783,* 6 vols. (London, 1927–28), III, 59.

39. Gage's commission and instructions, and materials concerning his arrival as governor are reproduced in L. Kinvin Wroth *et al.* (eds.), *Province in Rebellion; A Documentary History of the Founding of the Commonwealth of Massachusetts, 1774–1775* (microfiche edition and guide, Cambridge, 1975), documents 1–11, pp. 1–63. A large part of this vast and very useful collection, drawn mainly from the Massachusetts Archives but also from many other sources, deals with the developing conflict between Gage and the legislature and towns of Massachusetts (documents 12–333, pp. 64–1068).

40. Gage to Haldimand, May 15, 1774, Haldimand Papers, add. ms. 21665, BL.

41. John R. Galvin, *The Minute Men: A Compact History of the Defenders of the American Colonies 1645–1775* (New York, 1967), 90.

42. Andrew Oliver Letterbook, 1767–1774, Egerton ms 2670, BL; *Gage Correspondence,* I, 1365–66.

43. The Dyer affair has been misunderstood as an arrest by Gage himself under the new Coercive Acts (Alden, *Gage,* 209). This incident happened in a different way. The true facts are laid out in a secret letter from Gage to Dartmouth, Oct. 30, 1774, CO5/92, PRO.

44. [J. T. Buckingham], "Paul Revere," *New England Magazine* 3 (1832): 304–14.

45. Gage to Dartmouth, May 30, 1774, *Gage Correspondence,* I, 356.

46. Gage to Dartmouth, Sept. 2, 1774, *ibid.,* I, 371.

47. Gage to Dartmouth, Oct. 30, 1774, *ibid.,* I, 382.

48. Gage to Dartmouth, Aug. 27, 1774, *ibid.,* I, 367; Alden, *Gage,* 212.

49. He called it a "phrensy" and added his hope that "it's only a fit of rage that will cool," and his belief that all the trouble "has taken its rise from the old source at Boston" (*Gage Correspondence,* I, 367, Aug. 27, 1774). In an amiable letter to Peyton Randolph of Virginia, Gage expressed a wish that "decency and moderation here would create the same disposition at home." He looked forward to a moment when "these asperities between the Mother Country and the Colonies have terminated like the quarrels of lovers and increased the affection they ought to bear to each other" (Gage to Peyton Randolph, Oct. 20, 1774, CO5/92, PRO).

50. Gage to Dartmouth, Aug. 27, 1774, *Gage Correspondence,* I, 365.

## ❧ 3. First Strokes

1. Gage to Dartmouth, Sept. 2, 1774, *Gage Correspondence,* I, 369.

2. Brattle to Gage, Aug. 26, 1774, Peter Force (ed.), *American Archives,* 9 vols. (Washington, D.C., 1837–53), 4th series, I, 739.

3. The site is now a park at Powder House Square, Somerville, Mass.

4. "[Account of Col. Maddison's Expedition]," Sept. 5, 1774, *AA4,* I, 762; *Massachusetts Gazette and Boston News-Letter,* Sept. 5, 1774; Ezra Stiles, *Literary Diary,* ed. F. B. Dexter, 3 vols. (New York, 1901), II, 479 (Sept. 25, 1774).

5. Robert P. Richmond, *Powder Alarm, 1774* (Princeton, 1971), 1–31.

6. Stiles, *Literary Diary,* II, 479 (Sept. 25, 1774).

7. *Ibid.*; Benjamin Church to Samuel Adams, Sept. 4, 1774, Samuel Adams Papers, NYPL.

8. Joseph Warren to Samuel Adams, n.d. [*ca.* Sept. 4, 1774], Samuel Adams Papers, NYPL.

9. Thomas Oliver, statement dated Sept. 2, 1774, *AA4,* I, 763; John Rowe, Diary, Sept. 1–3, 1774, MHS; published in part in *Letters and Diary,* 283–84.

10. One of these papers survives in ADM 1/485, PRO; for the "hot, dry" weather on Sept. 1 and 2, 1774, see Jonas Clarke Diary, LHS.

11. Revere introduced his messenger as John Marston, "a gentleman of my acquaintance, a high son of Liberty, and one that can give you a particular detail of our affairs, much better than I can write them. You will introduce him to your friends as such." He also

thanked Isaac Sears for "his kind care of my horse and sulky." Paul Revere to John Lamb, Sept. 4, 1774, Lamb Papers N-YHS; rpt. Goss, *Revere*, I, 150–53.

12. Rowe, Diary, Sept. 3, 1774, MHS; published in part in *Letters and Diary*, 284.

13. Gage to Dartmouth, Oct. 30, 1774, *Gage Correspondence*, I, 383.

14. Gage to Dartmouth, Sept. 25, 1774, and Gage to Hillsborough, Sept. 25, 1774, *Gage Correspondence*, I, 377; II, 654.

15. David Ammerman, *In the Common Cause; American Response to the Coercive Acts of 1774* (New York, 1975), 129.

16. Gage was one of the first to conclude that "foreign troops must be hired, for to begin with small numbers will encourage resistance." Gage to Barrington, Nov. 2, 1774, *Gage Correspondence*, II, 659; and various dispatches in Co5/92/1.

17. Piers Mackesy, *The War for America, 1775–1783* (Cambridge, Eng., 1964), 524.

18. Dartmouth to Gage, Jan. 27, 1775, *Gage Correspondence*, II, 181; the Marine battalion, commanded by Major John Pitcairn, began to arrive on Dec. 5, 1774, in HMS *Asia;* Barker, *Diary*, 10.

19. Revere to Jeremy Belknap [*ca.* 1798], Edmund Morgan (ed.), *Paul Revere's Three Accounts* (Boston, 1961), n.p.

20. *Ibid.;* in Puritan Boston, Bible-swearing had been condemned as idolatry; a century later, attitudes had changed. Morgan (ed.), *Paul Revere's Three Accounts*, introduction.

21. *Ibid.*

22. *Ibid.;* in the manuscript Revere identified their place of meeting as the Masonic hall, then crossed it out and wrote in the name of the Green Dragon Tavern.

23. The decision to warn Portsmouth appears to have been made by Revere and a rump of the committee. A "gentleman of Boston" wrote to Rivington in New York, Dec. 20, 1774, "On Monday, the 12th inst. our worthy citizen, Mr. Paul Revere, was sent express from only two or three of the Committee of Correspondence at Boston, as I am creditably informed (of whom no number under seven are empowered to act) to a like committee at Portsmouth." *AA4*, I, 1054.

24. Captain's Log, HMS *Somerset,* Dec. 11–14, 1774, ADM51/906, part 6, PRO.

25. Allen French, *The First Year of the American Revolution* (Boston, 1934), 650.

26. For the weather in New Hampshire, see Lois K. Stabler (ed.), *Very Poor and of a Lo Make; The Journal of Abner Sanger* (published for the Historical Society of Cheshire County, Portsmouth, N. H., 1986), 15–17.

27. *New York Journal,* Dec. 29, 1774; "A Letter from a Gentleman in New Hampshire to a Gentleman in New York," Dec. 17, 1774, Nathaniel Bouton *et al.* (eds.), *Documents and Records Relating to the Province of New Hampshire*, 40 vols. (Concord, N.H., 1867–1943), VII, 423; the major documents are collected in Charles L. Parsons, "The Capture of Fort William and Mary, December 14 and 15, 1774," New Hampshire Historical Society *Proceedings* 4 (1890–1905): 18–47. The mansion of Samuel Cutts stood on Market Street, next to what is today called the Ladd House, directly across from his wharf on the Piscataqua River. The house burned in 1802. See Cecil Hampden Cutts Howard, *Genealogy of the Cutts Family in America* (Albany, 1892), 518–19.

28. Capt. John Cochran to Gov. John Wentworth, Dec. 14, 1774, *AA4*, I, 1042; also William Bell Clark (ed.), *Naval Documents of the American Revolution* (Washington, D.C., 1964+), I, 18–19.

29. Capt. John Cochran to Gov. John Wentworth, Dec. 14, 1774, *AA4*, I, 1042; also *NDAR*, I, 18–19; Parsons, "Capture of Fort William and Mary," 22.

30. Capt. John Cochran to Governor John Wentworth, Dec. 14, 1774, ADM1/485; *AA4*, I, 1042. Capt. Andrew Barkley, R.N., to Vice Adm. Samuel Graves, Dec. 20, 1774, *NDAR*, I, 38; Parsons, "Capture of Fort William and Mary," 19–23. Lord Percy wrote home, "What is most extraordinary in this event is, that notwithstanding the Captain fired at them, both with some field pieces and small arms, nobody was either killed or wounded," Percy to Grey Cooper, after Dec. 13, 1774, *Percy Letters*, 46–47. Percy was mistaken. Cochran and at least one other soldier were wounded.

31. Wentworth to Gage, Dec. 16, 1774, *AA4*, I, 1042; Parsons, "Capture of Fort William and Mary," 23–25.

32. *New York Journal*, Dec. 29, 1774.

33. Captain's Log of HMS *Scarborough*, Dec. 15–19, 1774, PRO Admiralty 51/867; Captain's Log of HMS *Canceaux*, Dec. 15–18, 1774, ADM 51/4136; Capt. Andrew Barkley to Vice Adm. Graves, Dec. 20, 1774, ADM1/485, published in part in *NDAR*, I, 35, 38.

34. *Providence Gazette*, Dec. 23, 1774.

35. Wentworth to Graves, Dec. 14, 1774; Graves Papers, Gay Transcripts, MHS. Percy to Grey Cooper, post Dec. 13, 1774, *Percy Letters*, 46.

36. Percy to Grey Cooper, after Dec. 13, 1774, *ibid.*

37. Percy to Duke of Northumberland, Sept. 12, 1774, *ibid.*, 38.

38. Gage to Dartmouth, March 4, 1775, *Gage Correspondence*, I, 393–94.

39. Thomas Hutchinson, Jr., to Elisha Hutchinson, March 4, 1775, Hutchinson Papers, Egerton ms. 2659, BL; Ann Hulton to Mrs. Adam Lightbody, Nov. 25, 1773, Harold Murdock *et al.* (eds.), *Letters of a Loyalist Lady* (Cambridge, Mass., 1927), 63.

40. The 64th Foot knew Salem well; two of its companies had been assigned there to guard General Gage during his sojourn at the nearby Hooper mansion in Danvers.

41. Forbes, *Revere*, 235–38, makes this inference. I have found no primary evidence to confirm it, but it seems a reasonable supposition. Flucker had been a conduit for other information; see Revere to Belknap, 1798; and French, *General Gage's Informers*, 164; for Gage's suspicion of Henry Knox, and Knox's association with Paul Revere in intelligence activities, see North Callahan, *Henry Knox; General Washington's General* (New York, 1958), 30.

42. The source is a letter to the Sons of Liberty in New York signed by Joshua Brackett, keeper of the Cromwell Head; Paul Revere, Benjamin Edes, printer; Joseph Ward, distiller; Thomas Crafts, painter; and Thomas Chase, distiller:

"Boston 1st March 1775

"Sir, Agreeable to what Mr. Revere wrote you by the last Monday's Post, the subscribers have this day met and have determined to send you weekly the Earliest and most authentic intelligence of what may be transacted in this Metropolis and Province, relating to the public affairs and general concerns of America; that you may have it in your power to contradict the many infamous lies which are propagated by the Enemies of our Country. And we beg it as a particular favor that you would appoint or agree with a number of gentlemen for the above purpose in your city that we may have early information from you of whatever transpires in your city and province of a public nature. At this critical period we conceive it to be very important to our Common Cause to have weekly or frequent communications.

We are Sir, Your most obedient and most humble servants, [signed] Joshua Brackett, Paul Revere, Benj. Edes, Joseph Ward, Tho. Crafts Junr., and Thomas Chase"

"P.S. Enclosed you have an account of the late Expedition which terminated to the honour of Americans. In addition to the secrecy with which the maneuvre to Salem was conducted, we inform you that *three* [italics added] persons were occasionally at the castle on Saturday afternoon and were detained there till 10 o'clock on Monday lest we should send an Express to our brethren at Marblehead and Salem."

The original letter is in the Lamb Papers, N-YHS; the transcript in Goss is inaccurate, substituting "these" for the italicized "three" in the postscript. Forbes (pp. 236–37) built an entire new interpretation on this misreading. She took "these" to refer to all of the signers of the letter and concluded mistakenly that Paul Revere himself had been imprisoned. There is no evidence that this is the case.

43. William Gavett, "Account of the Affair at North Bridge," *EIP* 1 (1859): 126–28; Joseph Story, "Account Dictated," *ibid.*, 134–35; Charles M. Endicott, "Leslie's Retreat or the Resistance to British Arms at the North Bridge in Salem, etc.," *ibid.*, 120; James Duncan Phillips, "Why Colonel Leslie Came to Salem," *EIHC* 90 (1953): 313; "Leslie's Retreat," *EIHC* 17 (1880): 190–92.

44. An excellent account appears in James Duncan Phillips, *Salem in the Eighteenth Century* (Boston, 1937), 350–60, 464–65.

45. "Leslie's Retreat," *EIHC* 17 (1880): 190–92. This source, described as a "Narrative found in the Family Papers of Major John Pedrick," was written long after the event, apparently by one of Major Pedrick's descendants. It contains many inaccuracies.

46. George A. Billias, *General John Glover and His Marblehead Mariners* (New York, 1960), 64.

47. *Ibid.*

48. Salem still remembers that event as "the first blood of the American Revolution."

49. Gavett, "Account of the Affair at North Bridge," I, 126-28; Joseph Story, "Account Dictated," *EIP* 1 (1859): 134-35; Charles M. Endicott, "Leslie's Retreat," *ibid.*, 120 Essex *Gazette*, Feb. 28, March 7, 1775; (Boston) *Massachusetts Spy*, March 2, 1775.

50. *AA4*, I, 1267–68; Thomas Hutchinson, Jr., to Elisha Hutchinson, March 4, 1775, Egerton ms. 2659, BL; "The regulars attempt to seize cannon at Salem, but are frustrated," Jonas Clarke Diary, Feb. 26, 1775, ms., LHS. Galvin, *Minute Men*, 95, writes that from the moment when the Regulars reached the North River Bridge "the story of Leslie's march really becomes two very different tales," one more or less as told here, the other as related by Loyalists, who asserted that Leslie marched to the town as ordered, found that the guns did not exist except for some "harmless old ships' cannons," and returned to Boston. Galvin argues that "the British were convinced they had achieved a minor victory, and this is important, because it increased Gage's reliance on these short marches as a way to control the province" (p. 97). Other evidence, such as that of Hutchinson above, suggests that in this instance the Whig version of events was credited by Loyalists as well, and confirmed by evidence from both sides.

51. Gage to Dartmouth, March 4, 1775, *Gage Correspondence*, I, 393–94.

## ᴄ 4. Mounting Tensions

1. Percy to the Rev. Thomas Percy, April 8, 1775, *Percy Letters*, 48–49.

2. *Ibid.*

3. John Barker, Diary, published as, *The British in Boston, Being the Diary of Lieutenant John Barker of the King's Own Regiment from November 15, 1774 to May 31, 1776 . . .* , ed. Elizabeth Ellery Dana (Cambridge, Mass., 1924), 5.

4. *Ibid.*, 12.

5. Samuel Adams to Arthur Lee, March 4, 1775, Cushing (ed.), *Writings of Samuel Adams*, III, 197; Barker, *The British in Boston*, 11; John Andrews, Letters, *MHSP* 8 (1865): 405 (Dec. 16, 1774).

6. Robin May, *The British Army in North America, 1775–1783* (London, 1974), 11.

7. Barker, *British in Boston*, 11; Pitcairn to Col. John Mackenzie, Feb. 16, 1775, Mackenzie Papers, add. ms., 39190, BL; Pitcairn to Lord Sandwich, March 4, 1775, *The Private Papers of John, Earl of Sandwich, First Lord of the Admiralty, 1771–1782*, ed. G. R. Barnes and J. H. Owens, 4 vols. (London, 1932–38), I, 59–62.

8. *Diary of Frederick Mackenzie*, 2 vols. (Cambridge, Mass., 1930), I, 7 (Feb. 1–4, 1775); Dirk Hoerder, *Crowd Action in Revolutionary Massachusetts* (New York, 1977), 191.

9. Regimental Rosters, 23rd Foot, W12/3960, PRO; Gage to Haldimand, July 3, 1774, Haldimand Papers, add ms. 21665, BL.

10. Rowe, Diary, Sept. 9, 1774, MHS; for the doubling of guards, Sept. 9, 1774.

11. Barker, *British in Boston*, 14 (Dec. 24, 1774); Mackenzie, *Diary*, I, 9 (March 4–9, 1775); Deposition of Samuel Marett, July 1774, Papers of Admiral John Montagu, ADM1/484, PRO; deposition of Pvt. John Clancey, Gage Papers, WCL; in Wroth *et al.* (eds.), *Province in Rebellion*, doc. 717, p. 2015.

12. Barker, *British in Boston*, 21–22 (Jan. 21, 1775); Mackenzie, *Diary*, I, 4; Andrews, Letters; "Proceedings of a Court of Enquiry held at Boston the 23rd January 1775," Gage

Papers, WCL; printed in Wroth *et al.* (eds.), *Province in Rebellion*, document 420, pp. 1353–73. American accounts and the testimony of British officers involved were directly contradictory. John Andrews reported that "last evening a number of drunken officers attacked the town house watch between eleven and twelve o'clock when the assistance of the New Boston watch was called, and a general battle ensued; some wounded on both sides." The British officers insisted that they were innocent victims. It appears even from their testimony that after an exchange of insults ("Tory Rascal!" "The General is a Rascal!" "The King is a rascal!") a British officer attacked a citizen, and he and his friends were soon involved in a fight with the watch. The private diaries of two British officers, Barker and Mackenzie, both contradict the public testimony of the Regulars involved, and support the American version of events. But it should also be noted that the Regulars were subject to constant verbal abuse from Bostonians, and to sporadic acts of physical violence as well.

13. Mackenzie, *Diary*, I, 13 (March 27, 1775); Barker, *British in Boston*, 27 (March 23, 1775).

14. Major John Pitcairn to Col. John Mackenzie, Dec. 10, 1774, Mackenzie Papers, add. ms. 39190, BL.

15. Pitcairn to Col. John Mackenzie, Feb. 16, 1775, Mackenzie Papers, add. ms. 39190, BL.

16. Pitcairn to Sandwich, March 4, 1775, *Sandwich Papers*, I, 59–62; reprinted in Clark (ed.), *NDAR*, I, 124–26; Pitcairn to Col. John Mackenzie, Dec. 10, 1774, Mackenzie Papers, add. ms. 39190, BL.

17. Mackenzie, *Diary*, I, 10 (March 6, 1775).

18. John Rowe, *Diary*, March 9, 1775, MHS; Sam Adams to Richard H. Lee, March 21, 1775, *Writings*, IV, 205-9; Gage to Dartmouth, March 28, 1775, *Gage Correspondence*, I, 394; Depositions of Thomas Ditson, March 9, 1775, and Private John Clancey, March 14, 1775, Gage Papers, WCL; published on microfiche in Wroth *et al.* (eds.), *Province in Rebellion*, docs. 716–17, pp. 2013–18.

19. Brigham, *Paul Revere's Engravings*, 79–92.

20. Paul Revere, "A Certain Cabinet Junto," *Royal American Magazine* 2 (1775), plate I; reproduced with British sources in Brigham, *Paul Revere's Engravings*, 92.

21. Authors and artists borrowed freely from one another in that way during Paul Revere's era. This was a world without our highly developed sense of individual creativity, and therefore without a strong imperative against plagiarism. It was an ethos with a stronger sense of collective belonging, and weaker ideas of individuality than in our own thinking. In all of this there was an important parallel to ideas of "publick liberty" which pervaded Revere's revolutionary consciousness; that is, liberty as a collective possession, rather than a purely personal freedom.

22. Isaiah Thomas, *The History of Printing in America* (1810; rpt. New York, 1970), 272n.

23. (Newburyport) *Essex Journal*, Feb. 22, 1775.

24. Samuel Adams to Arthur Lee, Jan. 29, 1775, *Writings of Samuel Adams*, III, 169.

25. Gage to Arthur Lee, March 4, 1775, *ibid.*, III, 195.

26. (Worcester) *Massachusetts Spy*, June 12, 1775, Arthur M. Schlesinger, *Prelude to Independence; The Newspaper War on Britain, 1764–1776* (New York, 1958), 234.

27. Gage to Dartmouth, April 22, 1775, *Gage Correspondence*, I, 396.

28. The 17th Light Dragoons adopted its death's head badge in 1759 to mourn the death of General James Wolfe. Later they added the motto "Or Glory," and acquired the nickname "Death or Glory Boys." They were at Bunker Hill in 1775, and they led the charge of the Light Brigade at Balaclava. In World War I they were the escort of Field Marshal Haig.

29. The "principal actors" were not identified by name.

30. A. D. L. Cary and Stouppe McCance, *Regimental Records of the Royal Welch Fusiliers (Late the 23rd Foot)* (London, 1921), I, 151; J. A. Houlding, *Fit for Service: The Training of the British Army, 1715–1795* (Oxford, 1981), 46–96; W. A. Smith, "Anglo-Colonial Society and the Mob, 1740-1775," unpublished dissertation, Claremont, 1965, 29.

31. Dartmouth to Gage, Jan. 27, 1775, *Gage Correspondence*, I, 179–83; for a discussion of this dispatch, see John R. Alden, "Why the March to Concord?" *AHR* 49 (1944): 446–54.

## ❧ 5. The Mission

1. Sam Adams to Jonathan Augustine Washington, March 23, 1775, Cushing (ed.), *Writings of Samuel Adams*, III, 211.

2. "List of General and Staff Officers on the Establishment in North America," Gage to Richard Rigby, July 8, 1775, *Gage Correspondence*, II, 687–88.

3. Some of these intelligence reports survive in the Gage Papers, WCL, and have been published in part in French, *General Gage's Informers*, 3–33; Wroth *et al.* (eds.), *Province in Rebellion*, docs. 670–95, pp. 1967–94.

4. French, *General Gage's Informers*, 15.

5. Gage to Dartmouth, Aug. 27, 1774, *Gage Correspondence*, I, 366.

6. Gage to Captain John Brown and Ensign Henry De Berniere, Feb. 22, 1775, *AA4*, I, 1263.

7. Ensign Henry De Berniere, Report to Gage, n.d., *ca.* March 1, 1775, *AA4*, I, 1263–68.

8. A batman was (and is) a private soldier assigned as an officer's personal servant. A large proportion of Gage's army were detailed as officers' servants.

9. De Berniere, Report to Gage, n.d., *ca.* March 1, 1775, *AA4*, I, 1263.

10. *Ibid.*

11. A shire town was the county seat. A half shire town was a community in which the county courts also met.

12. De Berniere, Report to Gage, *AA4*, I, 1268.

13. French, *General Gage's Informers*, 13. These letters were actually written from Boston, but the writer of them was exceptionally well informed about Concord, Worcester, and other country towns.

14. Mackenzie, *Diary*, I, 24, 29 (April 18–20, 1775).

15. French, *General Gage's Informers*, 29–30.

16. Gage to Dartmouth, March 4, 1775, Bancroft Collection, NYPL; French, *Day of Concord and Lexington*, 57–58; this document is not included in the *Gage Correspondence*.

17. *Ibid.*

18. Earlier, the 4th Foot and other "off duty" regiments had "marched into the Country to give the men a little exercise." A British officer commented that "as they marched with knapsacks and colours the People of the Country were allarm'd." Barker, *British in Boston*, 11 (Dec. 16, 1774).

19. Mackenzie, *Diary*, I, 14–15 (April 7, 1775).

20. Jonathan Hosmer to Oliver Stevens or Joseph Standley, April 10, 1775, privately owned; excerpts published in a dealer's catalogue, Joseph Rubenfine, *The American Revolution, List 114* (West Palm Beach, Fla., n.d.), n.p.; a copy is in the Concord Antiquarian Museum. I am grateful to David Wood for calling this document to my attention.

21. Amelia Forbes Emerson (ed.), *Diary and Letters of William Emerson, 1743–1776* (Boston, 1972), 71 (April 15, 1775).

22. Alden, *General Gage in America*, 227.

23. Barker, *British in Boston*, 64.

24. William Lincoln (ed.), *The Journals of Each Provincial Congress of Massachusetts (Colony) in 1774 and 1775, and of the Committe of Safety, with an Appendix* (Boston, 1838), 513, Wroth *et al.* (eds.), *Province in Rebellion*, doc. 592, pp. 1830–88.

25. Revere to Belknap, *ca.* 1798, RFP, microfilm edition, MHS.

26. French, *General Gage's Informers*, 32.

27. Galvin, *Minute Men*, 123.

28. Six of these men can be identified. The patrol included Major Edward Mitchell (5th Foot), commanding; Capt. Charles Cochrane (4th Foot), Capt. Charles Lumm (38th Foot),

Lt. Peregrine Thorne (4th Foot), Lt. Thomas Baker (4th Foot), and Lt. Hamilton (64th Foot). Some were noncommissioned officers, and others were described by Americans who observed them as servants.

29. William Munroe, Deposition, in Elias Phinney, *History of the Battle of Lexington, on the Morning of the 19th April, 1775* (Boston, 1925), 33–35; Solomon Brown, Deposition, in Lemuel Shattuck, *History of Concord* (Concord, 1835), 341.

30. Richard Devens, Memorandum, in Richard Frothingham, Jr., *History of the Siege of Boston, and of the Battles of Lexington, Concord, and Bunker Hill* (Boston, 1849), 57.

31. Hancock's reply to Elbridge Gerry is reproduced in Frothingham, *History of the Siege of Boston*, 57:

Lexington April 18, 1775

Dear Sir:

I am much obliged for your notice. It is said the officers are gone to Concord, and I will send word thither. I am full with you that we ought to be serious, and I hope your decision will be effectual. I intend doing myself the pleasure of being with you to-morrow. My respects to the Committee.

I am your real friend,

John Hancock

32. Munroe, Deposition, Phinney, *Lexington*, 33–35.

33. Eljah Sanderson, Depositions, Phinney, *Lexington*, 31–33; Solomon Brown, Jonathan Loring, and Elijah Sanderson, Depositions, April 25, 1775, *AA4*, II, 490.

34. Sanderson, Deposition, Phinney, *Lexington*, 31–33.

35. John C. Maclean, *A Rich Harvest: The History, Buildings and People of Lincoln, Mass.* (Lincoln, 1907), 264–65; citing Abram E. Brown, *Beneath Old Roof Trees* (Boston, 1896); Hurd, *Middlesex County*, II, 619.

## ✎ 6. The Warning

1. Some versions of this event report that the stable boy ran to William Dawes, who carried the news to Revere. In other accounts, the stable boy ran directly to Revere himself. Cf. Forbes, *Revere*, 252; Holland, *Dawes*, 9; Ellen Chase, *The Beginnings of the American Revolution*, 3 vols. (New York, 1910), II, 342.

2. Jeremy Belknap, "Journal of my tour to the camp and the observations I made there," Oct. 25, 1775, *MHSP* 4 (1860): 77–86.

3. Jane Van Arsdale (ed.), *Discord and Civil Wars, Being a Portion of a Journal Kept by Lieutenant Williams of His Majesty's Twenty-Third Regiment While Stationed in British North America During the Time of the Revolution* (Buffalo, 1954), 5 (June 12, 1775).

4. Mackenzie, *Diary*, I, 18 (April 18, 1775).

5. Jeremy Belknap, "Journal of my tour to the camp . . . ," 77–86; Samuel A. Drake, *Historic Fields and Mansions of Middlesex* (Boston, 1873), 354; French, *Day of Concord and Lexington*, 76; Winsor, *Memorial History of Boston*, III, 68.

6. "The Boats of the Squadron, by desire of the General, were ordered to assemble alongside the Boyne by 8 o'clock in the evening, and their officers were instructed to follow Lt. Bourmaster's direction." See "The Conduct of Admiral Graves," British Museum, add. ms., 14038, 81; French, *General Gage's Informers*, 36; E. E. Hale, in Winsor, *Memorial History of Boston*, III, 68n; Alden, *Gage*, 244, 249, uses this story in attempting to prove that Margaret Gage could not have been the informer, but it is certainly false. Alden has no other evidence to support him on this question. It should be remembered that "evening" was used to indicate afternoon in 18th-century speech.

7. John Cary, *Joseph Warren, Physician, Politician, Patriot* (Urbana, Ill., 1961), 182–83.

8. Jeremy Belknap, "Journal of my tour to the camp . . . ," 77–86.

9. Richard A. Roberts (ed.), *Calendar of Home Office Papers of the Reign of George III, 1773–1775* (London, 1899), 479; Alden, *Gage*, 249; Shakespeare, *King John*, III, i, 326. In

an earlier speech, Blanche says to her husband: "Upon my knees, I beg, go not to arms." III, i, 308.

10. Hutchinson, *Diary and Letters of Thomas Hutchinson*, I, 497–98.

11. William Gordon, *History of the Independence of the United States*, 4 vols. (London, 1788), I, 321; quoted in Alden, *Gage*, 247.

12. Henry Clinton, note, n.d., Clinton Papers, WCL; quoted in Alden, *Gage*, 244.

13. Charles Stedman, *History of the Origin, Progress, and Termination of the American War*, 2 vols. (London and Dublin, 1794), I, 119; Frothingham, *Warren*, 456.

14. Hutchinson, *Diary and Letters of Thomas Hutchinson*, I, 476; Alden, *Gage*, 249–50. Historians have divided on this question. Alden, Gage's biographer, asserts that "only the strongest evidence should lead us to suspect that the wife betrayed her husband." But he does not hesitate to convict the spouse of a private soldier of having conveyed the same information! As we shall see, Gage's soldiers had no secrets to betray. Even company and field-grade officers were kept ignorant of the mission's purpose and destination until they reached Lexington Common.

Others have argued that the source was an agent who worked for money. The only evidence is a passage in Jeremy Belknap's diary that Dr. Warren's informer was "a person kept in pay for that purpose." But this was merely a rumor he heard in the American camp six months later. Cf. Belknap, "Journal of my tour to the camp . . . ," 77–86.

On the other side there is no direct proof, but much circumstantial evidence in Gage's cry to Percy that he had confided to one person only; testimony of Gordon, Clinton, Stedman, and Wemyss; Margaret Gage's own statement of divided loyalties, her husband's decision to send her away from him after the battles, and the failure of their marriage.

15. Revere's Draft Deposition, *ca.* April 24, 1775, RFP, MHS, was more specific: "I was sent for by Doctor Joseph Warren about 10 o'clock that evening, and desired, 'to go to Lexington and inform Mr. Samuel Adams and the Hon. John Hancock Esqr. that there was a number of Soldiers composed of Light troops and Grenadiers marching to the bottom of the Common, where was a number of boats to receive them, and it was supposed, that they were going to Lexington, by the way of Watertown to take them, Mess. Adams and Hancock or to Concord.'" Probably, Revere went to Doctor Warren a little before 10, given the chronology of events that followed; hence the estimate in the text of 9 to 10.

16. Revere's three accounts differed in detail on this question. In his first draft of a deposition, recorded immediately after the ride, he wrote: "I was sent for by Doctor Joseph Warren about 10 O'Clock that evening, and desired, 'to go to Lexington and inform Mr. Samuel Adams, and the Hon. John Hancock Esqr. that there was a number of Soldiers composed of the Light troops and Grenadiers marching to the bottom of the Common, where was a number of boats to receive them, and it was supposed, that they were going to Lexington, by the way of Watertown to take them, Mess. Adams and Hancock, or to Concord."

The revised deposition was modified in the last sentence to read, "that they were going to Lexington, by way of the Cambridge River, to take *them*, or go to Concord, to distroy the Colony Stores."

In 1798, Revere wrote Belknap. "Dr. Warren sent in great haste for me, and begged that I would immediately set off for Lexington, where Messrs Hancock and Adams were, and acquaint them of the Movement, and that it was thought they were the objects." Cf. Revere, Draft Deposition, *ca.* April 24, 1775; Deposition, *ca.* April 24, 1775; Revere to Belknap, *ca.* 1798, all in Revere Family Papers, microfilm edition, MHS.

17. Most historians believe that Warren sent only two messengers: Revere and Dawes. But Jeremy Belknap found evidence of a third who has never been identified. He wrote, "Two expresses were immediately dispatched thither, who passed by the guards on the Neck just before a sergeant arrived with orders to stop passengers. Another messenger went over Charlestown ferry." See Belknap, "Journal of my tour to the camp . . . ," 77–86. For Dorr's role, see C[atherine] C[urtis], *NEHGR* 10 (1853): 139; W. H. Holland, *William Dawes and His Ride with Paul Revere* (Boston, 1878). Long after the event, several historians

suggested that the third messenger was Ebenezer Dorr, a leading citizen of Roxbury, and a Whig committeeman in that town. But this is an error that arose in the late 19th century, when a Boston journalist mistakenly wrote "Dorr" for "Dawes."

18. Sanderson, Deposition; Jonas Clarke, "Narrative of the Events of April 19," ms., LHS.

19. The same source reports that Col. Josiah Waters of Boston "followed on foot on the sidewalk at a short distance behind him until he saw him safely through the sentinels." Francis S. Drake, *The Town of Roxbury: Its Memorable Persons and Places* (Roxbury, 1878), 74.

20. *Ibid.*

21. Revere to Belknap, *ca.* 1798, RFP, microfilm edition, MHS.

22. *Ibid.*

23. For 18th-century distances, see Lt. [Thomas Hyde] Page, *A Plan of the Town of Boston with the Intrenchments, &c. of His Majesty's Forces in 1775* (London, 1777); reproduced with other contemporary maps of less accuracy in Kenneth Nebenzahl (ed.), *Rand McNally Atlas of the American Revolution* (New York, 1974), 42.

24. In the late 19th century, the identity of the church was called into question. Revere called it the "North Church." But there were several steeples in the North End. One was the present Old North Church, an opulent structure then also known as Christ Church, or the Seven Bell Church after the carillon that Paul Revere had rung as a child. Another was a Congregational meetinghouse in North Square, often called the North Meeting, or Old North Meeting. This building no longer stands; it was pulled down for firewood by British troops during the siege of Boston. Richard Frothingham argued in *The Alarm on the Night of April 18, 1775* that the lanterns were displayed from this building, and not the Old North Church. Frothingham was mistaken. An old inhabitant of Boston, Joshua Fowle, remembered long after the event, "There is no dispute, or ought not to be, in regard to the display of lights at the North Church by your father. The Seven Bell Church was always called by that name; the others were always called meeting houses, old Puritanic names, and by no other." Joshua B. Fowle to Samuel H. Newman, July 28, 1875; Aug. 1876; also Jeremiah Loring to Wheildon?, Oct. 1876, William W. Wheildon, *History of Paul Revere's Signal Lanterns* (Boston, 1878), 34–36.

Further, the North Meeting at North Square had a low steeple on the south side of the North End, and could barely be seen from Charlestown.

Moreover, the identity of the men who displayed the lanterns was known in Boston soon after the event. Both were associated with North Church, not North Meeting. For all of these reasons, we may safely conclude that that the lanterns were displayed from Christ Church, now known as Old North Church.

The prominence of the Old North Church in the city's skyline may be seen in Paul Revere's "A View of Part of the Town of Boston in New England and British Ships of War Landing their Troops, 1768" (Boston, 1770), in Brigham, *Paul Revere's Engravings*, 60.

25. Wheildon, *Paul Revere's Signal Lanterns*; John L. Watson, *Paul Revere's Signal* (Cambridge, 1877); Goss, *Revere*, I, 247–58.

26. Robert Newman Sheets, *Robert Newman; His Life and Letters in Celebration of the Bicentennial of His Showing of Two Lanterns in Christ Church, Boston, April 18, 1775* (Denver; Newman Family Society, 1975).

27. Jeremiah Loring to Wheildon?, Oct. 1876, Wheildon, *Paul Revere's Signal Lanterns*, 34–36.

28. Sheets, *Robert Newman; His Life and Letters . . .* , 3.

29. Watson, *Paul Revere's Signal*, argued that Capt. John Pulling displayed the lights from the tower. Wheildon (*Paul Revere's Signal Lanterns*) responded that the work was done by Newman, an interpretation repeated by Goss, Forbes, and Sheets. There is good evidence that both men were involved, and Bernard as well. Given the intrinsic difficulty of carrying two lanterns to the top of the tower, lighting them with flint and steel, and displaying them simultaneously by hand out of the window, I think it probable that Newman and Pulling worked together in the tower, while Bernard kept watch below.

No source survives to establish the sequence of events in the tower. It would have been dangerous to light the lanterns on the ground floor of the church, with British soldiers passing in the street, and impossible to light them at the top of a narrow ladder.

30. Revere's account was confirmed by Richard Devens, who wrote, "I soon received intelligence from Boston that the enemy were all in motion, and were certainly preparing to come out into the country. Soon afterwards, the signal agreed upon was given; this was a lanthorn hung out in the upper window of the tower of N. Ch towards Charlestown." Richard Devens, Narrative, published in Frothingham, *History of the Siege of Boston,* 57.

31. Devens, Memorandum; Frothingham, *Siege of Boston,* 58–59.

32. Goss, *Revere,* I, 188–89, based upon letters of John Revere to Goss, Oct. 11, 1876, and Charles Wooley to Goss, May 1886.

33. Revere wrote that he kept his boat in "the north part of the town." The story of the spurs descended in the Revere family from Paul Revere's daughter Mary Revere Lincoln to her son William O. Lincoln, who recorded it for Goss, *Revere,* I, 189–90.

34. The Boston lady who donated her underwear to the boatmen was an ancestor of John R. Adan; John Revere to Goss, Oct. 11, 1876, Goss, *Revere,* I, 190.

35. W. W. Wheildon, *Curiosities of History,* 36; Goss, *Revere,* I, 188.

36. Donald W. Olson and Russell L. Doescher, "Astronomical Computing: Paul Revere's Midnight Ride," *Sky and Telescope* 83 (1992): 437–40; Jacques Vialle and Darrel Hoff, "The Astronomy of Paul Revere's Ride," *Astronomy* 20 (1992): 13–18; *Boston Globe,* April 19, 1992.

37. The horse was presumably "got" by the combined efforts of Deacon Larkin, Devens, and Revere. Devens later recalled, "I kept watch at the ferry to watch for boats till about eleven o'clock, when Paul Revere came over and informed that the Troops were actually in their boats. I then took a horse from Mr. Larkin's barn and sent off P. Revere to give the intelligence at Menotomy and Lexington." Devens, Memorandum, in *History of Charlestown,* 315–16; Frothingham, *History of the Siege of Boston,* 57–58; Revere also left an account of this conversation in his third account of the ride.

38. William Ensign Lincoln, genealogist of the Larkin family, recorded in 1930 a family tradition that the horse was a mare named Brown Beauty, which belonged to Samuel Larkin, chairmaker and fisherman of Charlestown (1701–84). Lincoln writes, "The mare was borrowed at the request of Samuel's son, Deacon John Larkin, and was never returned to the owner."

John Larkin (1735–1807) was a merchant and deacon of the First Congregational Church in Charlestown. His estate was probated for $86,581.00, an exceptionally large holding. See William Ensign Lincoln, *Some Descendants of Stephen Lincoln, Edward Larkin, Thomas Oliver, Michael Pearce, Robert Wheaton, George Burrill, John Porter, John Ayer* (New York, 1930), 119, 123. Also very helpful on this question is Patrick M. Leehey, "What *was* the Name of Paul Revere's Horse?" *Revere House Gazette* 16 (1965): 5.

Other secondary accounts are erroneous in various details. Richard O'Donnell mistakenly describes the animal as a "little brown mare," but Revere's own accounts indicate that she was a large horse, and after his capture she was taken by a sergeant of grenadiers to replace his own small mount. Cf. O'Donnell, "'On the Eighteenth of April, in Seventy-five . . .' Longfellow didn't know the half of it," *Smithsonian* 4 (1973): 72–77.

Various names have been suggested in the literature on Paul Revere's ride. Galvin (*Minute Men,* 123–24) calls her Thunderer (without supplying a source). Popular writers have inventively named her Meg, Scherazade, Dobbin, and Sparky (after "the spark struck out by the steed that night").

39. Not even Paul Revere's horse has been spared the attentions of the revisionists. Filiopietists have represented Paul Revere's horse as a fine-boned thoroughbred, with a long gait and an elegant Arabian head. Iconoclasts have insisted, on the other hand, that she was a heavy, plodding "ploughhorse." Both interpretations are mistaken, and the truth was not "in between."

40. Revere to Belknap, *ca.* 1798, RFP, microfilm edition, MHS.

41. The red door and four-stub lantern may still be found in the Buckman Tavern, which

since 1913 has been owned by the town of Lexington. It is now operated by the Lexington Historical Society. See also Willard D. Brown, *The Story of Buckman Tavern* (rev. ed., Lexington, 1989).

42. The parsonage still stands today. It has been moved twice, and is back close to its original site. See S. Lawrence Whipple, *The Hancock-Clarke House, Parsonage and Home* (Lexington, 1984).

43. Jonas Clarke Diary, April 7, 10, 1775, MHS.

44. Whipple, *The Hancock-Clarke House, Parsonage and Home,* 13–16; for the size of the guard, see Jonas Clarke, "Narrative of the Events of April 19."

45. Richard L. Merritt, *Symbols of American Community* (New Haven, 1966).

46. Louise K. Brown, *A Revolutionary Town* (Canaan, N.H., 1975), 16.

47. Phinney, *History of the Battle at Lexington,* 17.

48. Jonas Clarke, "Narrative of the Events of April 19."


### ❧ 7. The March

1. Jeremy Belknap, "Journal of my tour to the camp . . . ," Oct. 25, 1775, MHS; pub. in *MHSP* 4 (1860): 77–86.

2. Letter from a "Private Soldier in the Light Infantry," Aug. 20, 1775, Margaret Wheeler Willard (ed.), *Letters on the American Revolution* (Boston, 1925), 187–200.

3. Belknap, "Journal of my tour to the camp . . . ," 77–80 (Oct. 25, 1775); Mackenzie, *Diary,* I, 18 (April 18, 1775).

4. Sutherland to Clinton, April 26, 1775, published in Harold Murdock (ed.), *Late News of the Excursion and Ravages of the King's Troops on the Nineteenth of April, 1775* (Boston, 1927); Mackenzie, *Diary,* I, 18 (April 18, 1775).

5. Barker, *British in Boston,* 31; Capt. W. G. Evelyn to Rev. William Evelyn, April 23, 1775, *Memoir and Letters of Captain W. Glanville Evelyn, of the 4th Regiment ("King's Own,") from North America, 1774–1776,* ed. G. D. Scull (Oxford, 1879), 53–55; anonymous light infantryman in Willard (ed.), *Letters on the American Revolution,* 187–200; Pope, *Late News,* entry for April 18, 1775; French, *Day of Concord and Lexington,* 73; Murdock, *The Nineteenth of April,* 47; Tourtellot, *Lexington and Concord,* 104; Gross, *Minutemen and Their World,* 115; Sabin, "April 19, 1775," I, 9.

6. Barker, *The British in Boston,* 31.

7. French, *General Gage's Informers,* 35.

8. Donald W. Olson and Russell L. Doescher, "Astronomical Computing: Paul Revere's Midnight Ride," *Sky and Telescope,* April 1992, pp. 437–40; also Jacques Vialle and Darrel Hoff, "The Astronomy of Paul Revere's Ride," *Astronomy* 20 (1992): 13–18; see Appendix J below.

9. Lister, *Narrative*; Galvin, *Minute Men,* 125. There was a curious irony here; the system of regimental seniority had been established only in 1751—an example of what has been called the modernity of tradition. See J. A. Houlding, *Fit for Service: The Training of the British Army, 1715–1795* (Oxford, 1981), 8, passim.

10. Lt. Edward Thoroton Gould, Deposition, April 25, 1775; *AA4,* II, 500.

11. Mackenzie, *Diary,* I, 19; French, *General Gage's Informers,* 40.

12. Frank Smith, *A History of Dover, Massachusetts* (Dover, 1897), 93–94.

13. Maj. John Pitcairn to Col. John Mackenzie, Feb. 16, 1775, Mackenzie Papers, add. ms., 39190, BL.

14. Robin May, *The British Army in North America* (London, 1974), 33. May reproduces the Royal Warrant of 1768 for Infantry Clothing, 29–31.

15. L. I. Cowper, *The King's Own: The Story of a Royal Regiment* (Oxford, 1939), 228.

16. Mackenzie, *Diary,* I, 18.

17. The route was reconstructed in 1912 by Frank Warren Coburn, in *The Battle of April 19, 1775* (1912; new ed., Philadelphia, 1988).

18. Barker, *The British in Boston*, 32.

19. Coburn, *Battle of April 19, 1775*, 48.

20. Drake, *Middlesex County*, II, 311–12.

21. Galvin, *Minute Men*, 126.

22. Samuel Abbott Smith, *West Cambridge on the Nineteenth of April, 1775* (Boston, 1864), 18.

23. Coburn, *Battle of April 19, 1775*, 55; details of this incident must be read with caution. It was used as an electioneering weapon against Gerry when he ran as a Jeffersonian candidate for governor.

24. *Ibid.*, 55.

25. *Ibid.*, 56.

26. Mackenzie, *Diary*, I, 18.

27. Sutherland to Clinton, April 25, 1775; on Adair, see below, Epilogue.

28. Coburn, *Battle of April 19, 1775*, 54–56.

29. Simon Winship, Deposition, April 25, 1775, *AA4*, II, 490; *Narrative of the Excursion and Ravages of the King's Troops* (Worcester, 1775), 664. This pamphlet has often been reissued: on microprint in the Readex microprint edition of *Early American Imprints*, Evans 14269; on microfiche in Wroth *et al.* (eds.), *Province in Rebellion*, document 591, pp. 1804–29; and *AA4*, II, 489–501, 673–74.

## 8. The Capture

1. Paul Revere to Belknap, n.d. *ca.* 1798, RFP, microfilm edition, MHS; Arthur B. Tourtellot, *Lexington and Concord* (New York, 1959), 100.

2. Goss, *Revere*, I, 202.

3. Paul Revere, Draft Deposition, n.d., *ca.* April 24, 1775, RFP, MHS.

4. Joyce Lee Malcolm, *The Scene of the Battle, 1775; Historic Grounds Report; Minuteman National Historical Park*, Cultural Resources Management Study No. 15 (Boston, 1985), 27–35.

5. Revere, Draft Deposition, *ca.* April 24, 1775; Revere to Belknap, n.d., *ca.* 1798; in one account Revere estimated that he was 200 yards ahead of the others, in another he estimated the distance at 100 rods, or 550 yards. In 1775 many British and New England narrators reckoned middle distances in rods of 16.5 feet.

6. Revere to Belknap, *ca.* 1798; this passage was deleted from the published text but appears in the ms. draft in the MHS archives, MHS; *idem*, Draft Deposition.

7. Goss, *Revere*, I, 185.

8. Revere to Belknap, *ca.* 1798; Revere Draft Deposition, ca. April 24, 1775; Sabin, "April 19, 1775," I, 20.

9. A tablet presently marks the supposed spot of Revere's capture. If it is in the right place, the pasture was part of a farm owned by William Dodge and occupied by a tenant farmer named Jacob Foster in 1775. The stone wall that Prescott jumped would have been the old boundary between Concord and Lexington, before the division of the town of Lincoln. A wood is shown north of the pasture, as Revere remembered, in a map drawn in 1902 by George A. Nelson. This location also squares with Revere's estimate that they were halfway between Lexington and Concord.

Sanderson's account, however, suggests another location. He remembered that he was stopped "just before we got to Brooks's in Lincoln," and led off the road to what he suggested was the same "field" where Paul Revere was later captured. The farms of the Brooks family were 9000 feet west of Foster's pasture, on the Concord-Lincoln line.

If Sanderson was correct, Revere traveled nearly two miles farther. But this was in a deposition taken fifty years after the battle. It is controverted not only by Revere's account but also by independent evidence of the identity of Lincoln residents who were awakened by Dr. Prescott after his escape and Revere's capture. Their homes lay to the east of the

Brooks farms, and some were just to the west of the place that is identified today as the site of the capture. Taken together, these sources strongly indicate that the place where Paul Revere was captured must have been west of the Josiah Nelson house and east of Samuel Hartwell's farm. The site of the modern monument (much debated by the staff of the National Park) appears to be roughly in the right place, if not precisely correct.

A nagging doubt arises from the facts that the present line of the road, and its inclination, do not match Revere's description, and the shoulders do not incline each way as Revere remembered. But the terrain along the highway has been much altered in the past two centuries by road construction and changes in land use. Cf. Malcolm, *The Scene of the Battles, 1775*, 41, 51–53; David H. Snow, "The Thomas Nelson, Sr., Farm," National Park Service, 1969, pp. 21–23; Leland J. Abel and Cordelia Thomas Snow, "The Excavation of Sites 22 and 23, Minuteman National Historical Park," Concord, Massachusetts, National Park Service, 1966; Sabin, "April 19, 1775," I, 18–19.

10. Henry W. Holland, *William Dawes and His Ride with Paul Revere* (Boston, 1878); the site of the house where Dawes's ride ended was identified by National Park archaeologists in 1964 as a shallow depression approximately 100 yards west of the Josiah Nelson house, of which nothing remains but a ruined chimney. See Abel and Snow, "The Excavation of Sites 22 and 23 . . ."; Sabin, "April 19, 1775," I, 18–19.

11. Revere, Draft Deposition, *ca.* April 24, 1775.

12. *Ibid.*

13. Sanderson remembered that "they detained us in that vicinity till a quarter past two o'clock at night. An officer, who took out his watch, informed me what the time was. It was a bright moon-light." The testimony of Revere and that of Sanderson closely coincide; cf. Elijah Sanderson, Deposition, Dec. 17, 1824, in Elias Phinney, *History of the Battle of Lexington, on the Morning of the 19th April, 1775* (Boston, 1825).

14. *Ibid.*

15. *Ibid.*

16. Revere, Draft Deposition, *ca.* April 24, 1775; Sanderson, Deposition, 32; Sanderson's version of this conversation is generally consistent with Revere's deposition, but more detailed and dramatic. Here as elsewhere, Paul Revere's three accounts err on the side of understatement.

17. Revere, Draft Deposition, *ca.* April 24, 1775.

18. No secondary study has got this episode right. Most authors, even those sympathetic to Revere, represent him as merely responding more or less passively to his British captors. Iconoclasts and debunkers (p. 340, above) have accused him of betraying the American cause. They fail to take account of Sanderson's deposition, and of a passage in Revere's manuscript draft of his letter to Belknap that was excised from the published text. Forbes missed this passage altogether, relying as she did on published texts; Goss worked from the manuscript and knew about it, but missed its significance. These primary sources are evidence of a response by Revere that is very different from what appears in the secondary literature—not at all passive, but active and very aggressive.

Secondary accounts also fail to notice a deeper pattern in Revere's behavior while a prisoner—the fact that all of his words and acts were consistent with the single purpose of trying to move the British patrol away from Lexington, and to protect Hancock and Adams, which was the primary purpose of Revere's mission that night. Far from betraying the American cause, as the debunkers have suggested, Revere was serving it with skill and courage. Only Galvin (*Minute Men,* 124) saw a larger significance in his behavior while a prisoner, mainly in its impact on the fighting that followed.

19. Sanderson, Deposition, 31–33.

20. *Ibid.;* Revere, Draft Deposition, *ca.* April 24, 1775.

21. Revere, Draft Deposition, *ca.* April 24, 1775; Revere to Belknap, *ca.* 1798.

22. Revere, Draft Deposition, *ca.* April 24, 1775; Sanderson, Deposition, 31–33.

23. Sanderson, Deposition, 32.

24. For the number of captives, see Revere, Draft Deposition, *ca.* April 24, 1775; other accounts vary in detail.

25. Sanderson, Deposition, 32.

26. Revere to Belknap, *ca.* 1798.

27. Sanderson, Deposition, 31–32.

28. *Ibid.*

29. *Ibid.*

30. Goss, *Revere*, I, 205.

31. Sanderson, Deposition, 31–33.

## ❧ 9. The Alarm

1. Duane Hamilton Hurd, *History of Middlesex County, Massachusetts*, 3 vols. (Philadelphia, 1890), II, 257, 294.

2. Samuel Adams Drake, *History of Middlesex County* (Boston, 1880), II, 376; Chase, *The Beginnings of the American Revolution*, II, 63–64.

3. Coburn, *The Battle of April 19, 1775*, 41.

4. Hall Gleason, "Captain Isaac Hall," *Medford Historical Society Publications* 8 (1905): 100–103; Helen Tilden Wild, *Medford in the Revolution; Military History of Medford, Massachusetts, 1765–1783* (Medford, 1903), 8; Charles Brooks, *History of the Town of Medford* (Boston, 1886).

5. Galvin, *Minute Men*, 124; Chase, *The Beginnings of the American Revolution*, II, 333; Dr. Martin Herrick was born *ca.* 1746, and died July 10, 1820, in Lynnfield, aged 74. *Vital Records of Lynnfield, Massachusetts, to the End of 1849* (Salem, 1907), 85; much relevant material appears in T. B. Wellman, *History of the Town of Lynnfield, Mass., 1635–1895* (Boston, 1895).

6. Galvin, *Minute Men*, 124; Coburn, *The Battle of April 19, 1775*, 32; Alonzo Lewis and James R. Newhall *History of Lynn, Essex County, Massachusetts . . .* (Boston, 1865), 33.

7. Thomas Boynton Journal, April 19–26, 1775, MHS; printed in *MHSP* 15 (1877): 254.

8. "Journal of James Stevens," *EIHC* 48 (1912): 41 (April 19, 1775); Richard D. Brown, *"Knowledge is Power": The Diffusion of Information in Early America, 1700–1865* (New York, 1989), 250.

9. Coburn, *The Battle of April 19, 1775*, 34.

10. Wild, *Medford in the Revolution*, 8; "Medford and Her Minutemen," *Medford Historical Society Publications* 28 (Sept. 1925): 44–45; Mellen Chamberlain, *A Documentary History of Chelsea*, 2 vols. (Boston, 1908), II, 425–31.

11. Revere to Belknap *ca.* 1798, RFP, microfilm edition, MHS.

12. "This morning a little before break of day, we were alarmed by Mr. Stedman's Express from Cambridge." Loammi Baldwin, Diary, April 19, 1775, in Hurd, *Middlesex County*, I, 447. The Committee of Safety had held its first meeting in Stedman's house, Nov. 2, 1774; Coburn, *Battle of April 19, 1775*, 11, 33. For the messenger from Captain Joshua Walker to Jonathan Proctor in what is now Burlington, see Castle et al. (eds.), *The Minute Men, 1775–1975* (Southborough, 1977), 314; a copy of this rare work is in the library of the Minuteman National Historical Park, Concord.

13. Coburn reckoned Revere's ride to the Clarke house at 12.98 miles, and Dawes's to the same point as 16.83 miles. Several modern attempts to reconstruct these routes have yielded similar estimates of distances traveled. See Coburn, *Battle of April 19, 1775*, 25.

14. William Munroe, Deposition, March 7, 1825, Elias Phinney, *History of the Battle at Lexington, on the Morning of the 19th April, 1775* (Boston, 1825), 33–35.

15. Hurd, *Middlesex County*, II, 712; cf. Edmund L. Sanderson, *Waltham as a Precinct of Watertown and as a Town* (Waltham, 1936), 56; Charles A. Nelson, *Waltham, Past and Present . . .* (Cambridge, 1882), 101–02. A Waltham company in Gardner's Regiment submitted a muster roll for service "on Alarm in Defense of the Liberties of America under the

command of Abraham Pierce Captain to Concord and Lexington Fite!" (April 19, 1775, MA). But there is no evidence that it arrived in time to join the battle, and independent scholars conclude that it was not in combat. Most of the companies submitting muster rolls under the Lexington Alarm did not actually see action that day.

16. Partisans of Dawes have asserted his equality with Revere, and even his priority. These claims continue to be made in print by his descendants, and have been taken up by iconoclasts who use them as a way of disparaging Paul Revere and the event itself. The correct interpretation is a mediating judgment that respects Dawes's role, but also recognizes the important qualitative difference between his actions and those of Paul Revere.

17. Clarke, "Narrative of Events of April 19."

18. Hannah Winthrop to Mercy Otis Warren, n.d., *MHSP* 14 (1875): 29–31.

19. Nathan Munroe testified in 1824, "In the evening of the 18th of April . . . I with Benjamin Tidd, at the request of my captain [John Parker] went to Bedford in the evening, and notified the inhabitants through the town, to the great road at Merriam's Corner, so called, in Concord, then returned to Lexington." In Bedford the alarm was given by ringing the bell in the bell tower on the common lands. Louise K. Brown, *A Revolutionary Town* (Canaan, N.H., 1975), 116; Hurd, *Middlesex County*, II, 830; Nathan Munroe, Deposition, Dec. 22, 1824, Phinney, *History of the Battle at Lexington*, 38.

20. Nathaniel Baker and Elizabeth Taylor married in 1776. See Amos Baker, Deposition; John C. Maclean, *A Rich Harvest: The History, Buildings and People of Lincoln, Mass.* (Lincoln, 1907).

21. William Smith was the brother of Abigail Smith Adams, the wife of future President John Adams. See MacLean, *A Rich Harvest . . .* , 264–69; for a critique of local legends; also very valuable is Douglas Sabin, "April 19, 1775," II, 22–24; Frank W. C. Hersey, *Heroes of the Battle Road* (Boston, 1930), 21–22; and Abram English Brown, *Beneath Old Roof Trees* (Boston, 1896), 320.

22. Samuel Cooper, "Diary, 1775-6," *AHR* 6 (1901): 301–41; Brenton H. Dickson and Homer C. Lucas, *One Town in the American Revolution: Weston, Massachusetts* (Weston, 1976), 85.

23. William Emerson's independent account entirely confirms the accuracy of Paul Revere's testimony. "This morning between 1 & 2 o'clock we were alarmed by the ringing of the bell, and upon examination found that ye Troops, to ye number of 800, had stole their march from Boston in boats and barges from ye bottom of ye Common over to a point in Cambridge, near to Inman's farm. . . . This intelligence was brought us at first by Samuel Prescott who narrowly escaped the guard that were sent before on horses, purposely to prevent all posts and messengers from giving us timely information. He by the help of a very fleet horse crossing several walls and fences arrived at Concord at the time above mentioned." Diary, April 19, 1775, Amelia Forbes Emerson (ed.), *Diaries and Letters of William Emerson, 1743–1776* (Boston, 1972), 71.

24. *Ibid.*

25. *Ibid.*

26. Hurd, *Middlesex County*, II, 253.

27. *Ibid.* II, 872; Castle *et al.* (eds.), *The Minute Men*, 144.

28. Castle *et al.* (eds.), *The Minute Men*, 81.

29. A "Revolutionary soldier" in Sudbury later remembered that "an express from Concord to Thomas Plympton Esquire who was then a member of the Provincial Congress [reported] that the British were on their way to Concord. In 35 minutes between 4 and 5 o'clock in the morning the sexton was immediately called on, the bell ringing and the discharge of musket which was to give the alarm. By sunrise the greatest part of the inhabitants were notified. The morning was remarkable fine and the inhabitants of Sudbury never can make such an important appearance probably again." Hudson, *Sudbury*, 364.

30. Castle *et al.* (eds.), *The Minute Men*, 208.

31. Francis Jackson, *A History of the Early Settlement of Newton, County of Middlesex, Massachusetts, from 1639 to 1800* (Boston, 1854), 184–85.

32. Robert B. Hanson, *Dedham, Massachusetts, 1635–1890* (Dedham, 1976), 152; *History and Directory of Dedham, Mass., for 1889* (Boston, 1889), 22–23.

33. William Heath, *Memoirs,* 5.

34. According to tradition in Watertown, the word reached town "through the messenger Paul Revere," Hurd, *Middlesex County,* II, 385; see also *Watertown's Military History* (Boston, 1907), 77.

35. Samuel F. Haven, *Historical Address, Dedham, September 21, 1836* (Dedham, 1836), 46; Coburn, *Battle of April 19, 1775,* 45.

36. The only accurate secondary account of Revere's role in the alarm system is Galvin, *Minute Men,* 124.

## 10. The Muster

1. Jonas Clarke, "Narrative of Events of April 19."

2. John Parker, Deposition, April 25, 1775, *AA4,* II, 491; Elizabeth S. Parker, "John Parker," in LHS *Proceedings* 1 (1866–89) 47.

3. Thomas Fessenden and William Draper, Depositions, April 23-25, 1775, *AA4,* II, 496.

4. Clarke, "Narrative of Events of April 19."

5. This is an undocumented hour in Paul Revere's activities, between midnight (or a little later) when he arrived in Lexington and one o'clock or (or a little after) when he and Dawes left for Concord. Revere wrote only that they refreshed themselves. If that happened at the Buckman Tavern, it is probable that he and Dawes might have joined Captain Parker in some of the early discussions.

6. These customs gave rise to the American expression "enlisted men," still commonly used in the United States, but not in the United Kingdom, where enlisted men are called "other ranks." These terms express two profoundly different systems of military stratification in the English-speaking world.

7. Galvin, *Minute Men,* 17–46; The earliest recorded use of the word "minuteman" found by Galvin was in the payroll of Abadiah Cooley's Brookfield company and was endorsed "Minute Men on the Crown Point Expedition, 1756" (p. 41).

A large literature on the New England militia includes: John Shy, "A New Look at the Colonial Militia," *A People Numerous and Armed* (New York, 1976), 22–33; Timothy Breen, "The Covenanted Militia of Massachusetts: English Background and New World Development," *Puritans and Adventurers* (New York, 1980), 24-45; Fred Anderson, *A People's Army; Massachusetts Soldiers and Society in the Seven Years' War* (Chapel Hill, 1984).

Much recent work studies the militia as a social institution, an approach very different from Galvin's, who considers them as functioning military organizations from the perspective of a professional military officer. A major opportunity exists for a cultural historian who might wish to combine these two approaches.

8. Francis S. Drake, *The Town of Roxbury* (Roxbury, 1878), 30. Heath in a letter to Harrison Gray Otis, April 21, 1798, claimed that the first company of minutemen was raised in Roxbury.

9. Lexington Town Records, Nov. 10–Dec. 27, 1774, Lexington Town Hall.

10. "Training Band" is the word that appears in the Lexington Town Records, Nov. 28, 1774. Captain Parker himself, and other members of the Lexington company always described themselves as militia, not minutemen. They were part of Gardner's Regiment of Militia, not of the various regiments of minutemen. In 1774 the town agreed to support both its "training band" and its "alarm list," but no mention was made of "minutemen." The town records of Lexington were reported "lost" long ago for the period from January 1 to April 19, 1775. Someone, many years ago, ripped out four pages. Their absence allowed the

myth of the Lexington minutemen to flourish. Cf. Galvin, *Minute Men*, 262, and Hudson, *Lexington*, 162, 177.

11. Galvin, *Minute Men*, 72.

12. Edward Butterfield, March 1, 1775, in Hurd, *Middlesex County*, II, 751.

13. *Boston Gazette*, Nov. 28, 1774.

14. Castle *et al.* (eds.), *The Minute Men*, 28.

15. Amos Barrett in the letters of the Rev. Henry True (1900); Jonathan Harrington in Hudson, *Lexington*, 94.

16. *AA4*, II, 441.

17. Abram English Brown, *Beside Old Hearthstones* (Boston, 1897), 249–50.

18. Richard D. Brown, *"Knowledge is Power": The Diffusion of Information in Early America, 1700–1865* (New York, 1989), 250; "Journal of James Stevens," *EIHC* 48 (1912): 41 (April 19, 1775).

19. *Boston Daily Advertiser*, April 20, 1886; *History and Directory of Dedham, Massachusetts* (Boston, 1889), 23.

20. Alonzo Lewis and James R. Newhall, *History of Lynn, Essex County, Massachusetts . . .* (Boston, 1865), 338; Brown, *Beside Old Hearthstones*, 249–50.

21. *Ibid.;* Hudson, *Lexington*, 208.

22. Hurd, *Middlesex County*, II, 231.

23. W. S. Tilden, "Medfield Soldiers in the Revolution," *Dedham Historical Register* 8 (1897): 70–76.

24. *Memoirs of Major-General William Heath by Himself*, ed. William Abbott (1798; New York, 1901), 72.

25. George O. Trevelyan, *American Revolution*, 4 vols. (London, 1909–12), I, 287.

26. Brown, *Beside Old Hearthstones*, 249–50.

27. Garry Wills, *Inventing America: Jefferson's Declaration of Independence* (New York, 1978), 36.

28. Erastus Worthington II, *Proceedings at the 250th Anniversary . . . of the Town of Dedham* (Cambridge, 1887), 78; Hurd, *Middlesex County*, II, 872.

29. Trevelyan, *American Revolution*, I, 287.

30. Loammi Baldwin, "Diary," April 19, 1775, in Hurd, *Middlesex County*, I, 447; Trevelyan, *American Revolution*, I, 286.

31. Frederic Kidder, *The History of New Ipswich* (Boston, 1852), 95; Christopher Ward, *The War of the Revolution*, 2 vols. (New York, 1952), I, 78.

32. *Ibid.*

33. "Reminiscence of Col. Aspinwall," Hudson, *Lexington*, 208.

34. Hurd, *Middlesex County*, II, 872.

35. Newton Town Records, Jan. 2, 1775; Francis Jackson, *A History of the Early Settlement of Newton, County of Middlesex, Massachusetts, from 1639 to 1800* (Boston, 1854), 183.

36. Kidder, *New Ipswich*, 95; Amos Baker, Affidavit, April 22, 1850, Robert Rantoul, Jr., *Oration* (Boston, 1850), 133-35; John C. Maclean, *A Rich Harvest: The History, Buildings and People of Lincoln, Mass.* (Lincoln, 1907).

37. Lewis and Newhall, *History of Lynn*, 338.

38. William H. Guthman, *Drums A'Beating, Trumpets Sounding; Artistically Carved Powder Horns in the Provincial Manner, 1746–1781* (Hartford, 1993), 159, 162, 167. An account of the Harrington horn is in Brown, *Buckman Tavern*, 22. The assertion that it was earlier owned by Henry Dunster is probably incorrect. Another horn in the same collection has three inscriptions. The first reads, "Zapnin Sythe, His Horne, April ye 17, 1774." Later the owner added a snake and a turtle, with the words, "Horne we will strife together ZS 1776." The following year he carved, "Noe boots or bread Dec. ye 11th 1777 Valley Forge," *ibid.*, 22. I am grateful to David Wood for his advice and suggestions.

39. Examples of this short rapier may be seen in the Museum of Our National Heritage, Lexington. I am much endebted to John Hamilton, curator of the museum, for sharing his expertise on edged weapons in New England.

40. The flag survives today in the Bedford Library. Several iconoclasts have challenged its authenticity, but the provenance is well established and supporting documentation exists in 17th-century British sources.

41. Mellen Chamberlain (1821–1900) was a jurist and antiquarian of high probity; the interview took place *ca.* 1843, when Chamberlain was twenty-one and Preston was ninety-one. Several different versions of this interview have crept into the literature. One of them ends differently, "We always had been free and we meant to be free always!" Cf. "Why Captain Levi Preston Fought: An Interview with One of the Survivors of the Revolution by Hon. Mellen Chamberlain of Chelsea," *Danvers Historical Collections* 8 (1920): 68–70; and John S. Pancake, *1777, the Year of the Hangman* (University, Ala., 1977), 7.

### ❧ 11. The Great Fear

1. Solomon Smith, Deposition, July 10, 1835; Hannah Davis Leighton, Deposition, Aug. 14, 1835; Josiah Adams, *Centennial Address on the Founding of Acton* (Boston, 1835), 16, 19; *idem, Letter to Lemuel Shattuck, Esq.* (Boston, 1850), Allen French, *Day of Concord and Lexington* (Boston, 1925), 183–84.

2. Georges Lefebvre, *La Grande Peur de 1789* (Paris, 1932, 1970); translated by Joan White as *The Great Fear of 1789; Rural Panic in Revolutionary France* (1973, Princeton, 1982); Henri Dinet, *La Grande Peur dans la généralité de Poitiers: juillet-août 1789* (Paris, 1951); *idem,* "Les peurs du Beauvaisis et du Valois, juilliet, 1789," *Paris et Ile-de-France: Mémoires* 23–24: (1972–74): 199–392, a major work with many documents; and other works by the same author cited therein; Michel Vovelle, *De la cave au grenier: un itinéraire en Provence au XVIIIe siècle* (Quebec, 1980), 221–62; Clay Ramsay, *The Ideology of the Great Fear: The Soissonnais in 1789* (Baltimore, 1992). A similar phenomenon in yet another revolutionary setting is explored in G. Chiselle, "Une panique normande en 1848," review in *La Pensure,* April 1912.

3. Hannah Winthrop to Mercy Warren, n.d., *MHSP* 14 (1875): 29–31.

4. *Ibid.*

5. Obituary of Rebecca Harrington Munroe, (Boston) *Daily Advertiser,* April 11, 1834.

6. Extract from a Petition of Jacob Rogers, Oct. 10, 1775, Frothingham, *History of the Siege of Boston,* 371–72.

7. Elijah Sanderson, Deposition, Dec. 17, 1824, Elias Phinney, *History of the Battle at Lexington, on the Morning of the 19th April 1775* (Boston, 1825), 31–33.

8. Samuel Cooper Diary, April 19, 1775; Brenton H. Dickson and Homer C. Lucas, *One Town in the American Revolution: Weston, Massachusetts* (Weston, 1976), 86.

9. Arthur B. Tourtellot, *Lexington and Concord* (New York, 1959), 199; Experience Wight Richardson Diary, April 1775, MHS.

10. French, *Day of Concord and Lexington,* 204–5.

11. Amelia Forbes Emerson (ed.), *Diaries and Letters of William Emerson, 1743-1776* (Boston, 1972), 73.

12. G. Frederick Robinson and Ruth Robinson Wheeler, *Great Little Watertown: A Tercentenary History* (Watertown, 1930), 63.

13. Vincent J. R. Kehoe, "We Were There!" mimeographed typescript, 2 vols., (n.p., n.d.), I, 271.

14. Harold Murdock, *The Nineteenth of April, 1775* (Boston, 1925), 128.

15. Josiah Temple, *The History of Framingham* (Framingham, 1887), 275.

16. Hurd, *History of Middlesex County,* II, 624.

17. A history of this episode was published by the Daughters of the American Revolution, *Prudence Wright and the Women Who Guarded the Bridge* (n.p., 1899; rpt. 1979). A modern investigation is Francine A. Stracuzzi, "Prudence Wright: A Heroine of the American Revolution," unpublished paper, History 151a, Brandeis University, Spring 1992. According to legend, Capt. Whiting approached the bridge in company with another Loyalist, who

was none other than Prudence Wright's Tory brother Thomas Cumming. He took one look at his determined sister, and galloped the other way. A local poet Annie Cuthbertson commemorated that encounter in a verse:

> One who rode with Whiting cried
> "Tis my sister Prue! Alas,
> She would never let me pass
> Save when her dead body fell!
> I turn back from Pepperell."

For other sources, see Hurd, *Middlesex County*, II, 231. A memorial to Prudence Wright and her company was erected in 1889.

18. John Tudor Diary, April 19–20, 1775, MHS.

19. John Greenleaf Whittier, *Prose Works* (Boston, 1866), II, 116.

20. John Jenks Diary, April 20–23, 1775, Pickering Family Papers, MHS.

21. Thomas F. Waters, *Ipswich in the Massachusetts Bay Colony* (Ipswich, 1905-17), II, 320; Christopher Jedrey, *The World of John Cleaveland* (New York, 1979), 137; Arlin I. Ginsberg, "Ipswich, Massachusetts, During the American Revolution," dissertation, Univ. of California at Riverside, 1972, pp. 112–13.

22. Hezekiah Smith, Diary, April 19, 1775, MHS; I owe this source to the kindness of Brenda Lawson.

23. Experience Wight Richardson, Diary, April 19–24, 1775, microfilm, MHS.

24. David Hall, Diary, April 30, 1775, MHS.

25. "The Conduct of Vice Admiral Graves in North America, in 1774, 1775 and 1776," Dec. 11, 1776, signed G. G[efferina], Graves's flag secretary], BL; copy in Graves Papers, Gay Transcripts, MHS.

26. Mr. Grosvenor preached from the first verse of Lamentations: "How doth the city sit solitary that was full of people! how is she become as a widow! she that was great among the nations, and princess among the provinces, how is she become tributary!" Paul Litchfield, Diary, May 11, 1775, MHS; published in part in *MHSP* 19 (1882): 377.

## ✎ 12. The Rescue

1. Elizabeth Clarke to Lucy Ware Allen, April 19, 1841, LHS *Proceedings* 4 (1905–10): 91–93; Tourtellot, *Lexington and Concord*, 141–42; Vincent J. R. Kehoe (ed.), "We Were There!" mimeographed typescript, 2 vols. (n.p., n.d.), I, 274–75. Watertown Public Library.

2. Dorothy Quincy Hancock Scott, conversation with William H. Sumner, "Reminiscences by General William H. Sumner," *NEHGR* 8 (1854): 187.

3. William Munroe, Deposition, March 7, 1825, Elias Phinney, *History of the Battle at Lexington, on the Morning of the 19th April, 1775* (Boston, 1825), 17, 34.

4. Dorothy Quincy Hancock Scott, conversation, 187; Tourtellot, *Lexington and Concord*, 140–41.

5. Dorothy Quincy Hancock Scott, conversation, 187.

6. Revere to Belknap, *ca.* 1798, RFP, microfilm edition, MHS; Dorothy Quincy Hancock Scott, conversation, 187.

7. *Ibid.*

8. Jonas Clarke, "Narrative of the Events of April 19, 1775."

9. *Ibid.*

10. On William Diamond, see manuscript notes and materials in the Worthen-Diamond Correspondence, LHS.

11. Long afterward Dorothy Quincy Hancock gave the trunk to the American Antiquarian Society, and that Society in turn deposited it in the Worcester Historical Museum, where it rests today.

12. Peter Oliver, "American Rebellion," Hutchinson Papers, BL.

13. Much later, John Hancock sent his Spartan hostess a cow as a gift of thanks for her Yankee hospitality. The source is a narrative by Samuel Sewall, in Kehoe (ed.), "We Were There!" I, 272-73.

14. William Gordon, *The History of the Rise, Progress and Establishment of the Independence of the United States of America* . . . , 4 vols. (London, 1788), I, 479; Richard Frothingham, *Life and Times of Joseph Warren* (Boston, 1865), 459. Gordon based his account of this event on personal interviews immediately after the battle. The authenticity of this conversation is supported by evidence in John C. Miller, *Sam Adams, Pioneer in Propaganda* (Boston, 1936), 332.

## ҩ 13. The First Shot

1. Sutherland to Kemble, April 27, 1775, Gage Papers, WCL, pub. in Wroth *et al.* (eds.), *Province in Rebellion*, doc. 721, pp. 2024–29; for other editions of this letter, which is often identified as written to General Gage, see Bibliography.

2. *Ibid.*

3. Barker, *The British in Boston*, 32.

4. Richard Pope testified of Major Mitchell's party, "They took three prisoners, one, the noted Paul Revere, who assured them that the country was alarmed, and that he saw the embarkation, which was then publick. This information was soon after confirmed by the Firing of Alarm guns; the bells rang, and drums beat to arms in Concord."
The identity of Pope is in doubt. From internal evidence, he was not in Smith's column, but marched with Percy's brigade. Harold Murdock identified him as a private or noncommissioned officer in the 47th Foot, but no soldier named Pope appears on the muster roll of that regiment. Richard Pope's Book, April 18, 1775, Huntington Library, San Marino, Calif.; published in Murdock, *Late News from New England* (Boston, 1927).

5. *Ibid.*

6. The immigrant Congregational minister from East Anglia, William Gordon, noted that these were "only small-sized bells (one in a parish), just sufficient to notify to the people the time for attending worship." Gordon, "An Account of the Commencement of Hostilities Between Great Britain and America, in the Province of Massachusetts Bay," May 17, 1775, *AA4*, II, 625.

7. "We got into the road leading to Lexington. Soon after the country people begun to fire their alarm guns, and light their beacons, to raise the country." Ensign Jeremy Lister, Narrative, published as *Concord Fight* (Cambridge, 1931), 63–67.

8. Sutherland to Kemble, April 27, 1775. Pitcairn wrote: "Near Three in the morning, when we were advanced within about Two miles of Lexington, Intelligence was received, that about 500 Men in arms were assembled, determined to oppose the King's troops and retard them in their March." Pitcairn to Gage, April 25, 1775, Gage Papers, WCL; also in Military Dispatches, CO5/92-93, PRO; printed in French, *General Gage's Informers*, 52–54.

9. Sutherland to Kemble, April 27, 1775; letter from a "private soldier at Boston to his relatives," Aug. 20, 1775, Willard, *Letters on the American Revolution*, 187–200.

10. He cut across the country to the meetinghouse and arrived soon after Bowman; see Phinney, *Battle at Lexington*, 19; for a brief sketch, see Hudson, *Lexington*, 255.

11. James Marr, Recollection, as recorded in Gordon, "Account"; also Pitcairn to Gage, April 25, 1775; Smith to Gage, April 22, 1775; and Gage, "Circumstantial Account." The British commanders later made much of this episode as evidence that they did not fire the first shot.

12. Ensign Jeremy Lister wrote that, "about 4 o'clock, the five front companies were ordered to load, which we did" (Lister, Narrative, *Concord Fight*, 64–67). The American militiaman William Munroe later went to the place where the British were "when they first heard our drum beat, which was about 100 rods [1650 feet] below the meeting-house, and saw the ends of a large number, I should judge 200, of cartridges, which they had dropped,

when they charged their pieces." Munroe, Deposition, March 7, 1825, in Phinney, *Battle at Lexington,* 34.

13. Major W. Soutar, as quoted in Reginald Hargreaves, *The Bloodybacks; The British Serviceman in North America and the Caribbean 1655–1783* (New York, 1968), 219.

14. Galvin, *Minute Men,* 129; on drummer William Diamond, see Coburn, *Battle of April 19, 1775,* 61n; *Boston Globe,* Sept. 23, 1903.

15. For a physical description of Lexington Common in 1775, see Charles Harrington, "Memoir of Levi Harrington, an eyewitness" (1846), LHS. The Common was bigger in 1775 than it is today, when modern roads have reduced its dimensions. The meetinghouse appears to have stood a little to the east of the present marker stone, perhaps in what is now an asphalt intersection of two busy suburban roads. The terrain is much changed as well. In 1775, it was rough and broken ground. Since the mid-19th century, the Common has been graded at least three times. Harrington remembered there was a large oak stump near the meeting house and a growth of brush on the south side. The place itself was called interchangeably a "Common" or "Green," with the former term predominating in the 18th century (when the Common was not very green), and the latter increasing in the 19th century (when the Green was not very common). Elias Phinney, for example, referred to it as the "triangular green or common" in his *History of the Battle at Lexington* (Boston, 1825), 10.

16. Revere, Deposition, *ca.* April 24, 1775, RFP, MHS.

17. Sutherland thought he saw three companies of militia; Sutherland to Kemble, April 27, 1775.

18. Barker, *British in Boston,* 32; Pitcairn to Gage, April 25, 1775; De Berniere estimated the number at "about 150." Another British officer, Edward Gould, got the number right: "a body of provincial troops armed, to the number of about 60 or 70 men." But this estimate was reported after he was captured and had talked with men on the other side; cf. De Berniere, *Narrative of Occurrences, 1775* (Boston, 1779); rpt. *2MHSC* 4(1816): 204–15; Gould, Deposition, April 25, 1775, *AA4,* II, 500–501.

19. "1200 or 1500 was the number we then supposed the Brigade [*sic*] to consist of." Jonas Clarke, "Narrative of the Events of April 19," an estimate of true strength is computed from data in Appendix K below.

20. Phinney, *Battle at Lexington,* 19; Sylvanus Wood, Deposition, June 17, 1826, Ripley, *Battle of Concord,* 53–54; Paul Revere thought that the militia numbered "fifty or sixty"; Tourtellot (*Lexington and Concord,* 128–29) estimated that 70 militia and 100 spectators were present—altogether nearly 25 percent of the town's population; French reckoned the number of spectators at "not more than forty" (*Day of Concord and Lexington,* 108–9).

21. "Them are the very words that Captain Parker said," swore William Munroe in 1822 (*Report of the Committee on Historical Monuments and Tablets* [n.p., 1884]). Parker's threat to shoot men who ran was heard by two men, Robert Douglass and Joseph Underwood, and separately reported in their depositions; Phinney, *History of the Battle at Lexington,* 39; Ripley, *History of the Fight at Concord*; Coburn, *The Battle of April 19, 1775,* 63n.

This raises a question of conduct and motive in Captain Parker. Why did he muster his company on the Green? The sequence of events compounds the question. Parker mustered his men, consulted with them, dismissed them, mustered them again, ordered them not to fire unless fired upon, warned them that he himself would shoot them if they ran, and then ordered them to disperse when the Regulars formed a line of battle. Six hypotheses come to mind.

    (1.) He might have wished to provoke an incident in which the Regulars appeared as the aggressors.

    (2.) He did not wish to start a fight, but was unwilling to run away from one: "If they want to have a war let it begin here!"

    (3.) He may have intended to make a demonstration of symbolic resistance, to vindicate the honor of his town, but only to the point of actual fighting, and not beyond, and lost control of the event.

(4.) Not knowing if Hancock and Adams had left the parsonage, and thinking that their arrest was one of the objects of the expedition, he mustered his men at the north corner of the Green, very near the Bedford Road, either to block the British troops or to turn them in another direction.

(5.) He changed his purposes with changing circumstances.

(6.) He was severely ill, very tired, deeply confused, and not thinking coherently. The sixth hypothesis is clearly mistaken. It is true that Parker was terminally ill, and according to one member of his family had not slept the night before, but there is not the slightest hint of confusion in many narratives and depositions. The fifth begs the question. The first goes too far, in my judgment, and the third not far enough. This leaves the second and fourth, which in combination are the most plausible explanations.

22. See below, p. 282.

23. Clarke, "Narrative of the Events of April 19." Captain Parker also observed that "immediately said troops made their appearance and rushed furiously." See John Parker, Deposition; also William Draper, Deposition.

24. Galvin writes, "Pitcairn let his column go to the right and galloped around to the left of the meetinghouse, thus momentarily separating himself from his men. He was never able to regain full control of them" (Galvin, *Minute Men,* 135). Ralph Earl's drawing of the fight at Lexington, based on interviews with survivors soon after the event, clearly shows this division, with three companies moving to the right (north) of the meetinghouse, and the rest of the column marching to the left.

25. William Draper: "The regular troops made an huzza, and ran towards Captain Parker's company"; Thomas Rice Willard: "The officers made an huzza, and the private soldiers succeeded them"; Thomas Fessenden: "The Regulars kept huzzaing"; Depositions, April 23, 25, 1775, *AA4,* II, 490–501.

26. The distance between British troops and the American militia was variously estimated at "five or six" or "eight to ten" rods, that is, between 82.5 and 165 feet. The dimensions of the Common, and the judgment of Jonas Clarke, recorded shortly afterward, support the smaller estimates. The words used by the British officers were also remembered differently. One of them was heard to say, "Damn you, why don't you lay down your arms?" Clarke, "Narrative of the Events of April 19."

27. John Robbins, Deposition, April 24, 1775, *AA4,* II, 491.

28. Clarke, "Narrative of of the Events of April 19"; 62 depositions collected from American eyewitnesses all testified that Parker's militia was dispersing before it was fired upon.

29. Revere's three accounts of the battle add different details. All are combined here.

30. One of the most careful British accounts was by Lt. Frederick Mackenzie of the 23rd Welch Fusiliers. He was not present at Lexington in the morning, but marched there with Percy later in the day. Mackenzie spoke with "an officer of one of the Flank companies," who told him that "shots were immediately fired; but from which side could not be ascertained, each party imputing it to the other. Our troops immediately rushed forward, and the Rebels were dispersed, 8 of them killed, and several wounded. One Soldier was wounded, and Major Pitcairn's horse was wounded." Mackenzie, *Diary,* I, 24.

31. On that field of confusion, two facts are clear enough. It was almost universally agreed that the first shot did not come from Captain Parker's militia or the British infantry. Parker himself testified that the British troops "fired upon and killed eight of our party, without receiving any provocation." In another deposition, thirty-three Lexington militiamen testified that "not a gun was fired by any person in our Company on the Regulars, to our knowledge, before they fired on us." Altogether, fifty surviving members of the Lexington company swore under oath that none of their company fired first. By general (if not universal) agreement on both sides, it is also clear that the first shot did not come from the rank and file of the British Regulars. Two eyewitnesses, Benjamin Tidd and Joseph Abbott, testifed in their depositions that the first shots were "a few guns which we took to be pistols, from some of the regulars who were mounted on horses." Many honorable British soldiers insisted that none of the light infantry companies fired first.

32. Barker, *British at Boston,* 32; Pitcairn to Gage, April 25, 1775. American eyewitnesses agreed on some of these facts, but not upon the sequence. Lexington militiaman Nathan Munroe willingly testified that he himself "got over the wall into Buckman's land, about six rods from the British, and then turned and fired at them," but he insisted that this happened after the Regulars had fired at him. Nathan Munroe, Deposition, Dec. 22, 1824, Phinney, *Battle at Lexington,* 38; Sabin, "April 19, 1775," II, 7.

33. At least one American, Sergeant William Munroe, also saw somebody (later identified as Lexington man Solomon Brown) fire from the back door of the Buckman Tavern, then reload and fire again from the front. Munroe testified many years later, that this happened after the first shots had been fired. According to a Lexington legend, the man who fired at the Regulars from the Tavern was Solomon Brown. The story is told that innkeeper John Buckman drove Brown out of the tavern, in fear that the Regulars would burn it to the ground, but not before the Regulars returned fire, leaving a bullet hole in the front door that still may be seen today. If this happened at all, it must have been after the first shot. William Munroe, Deposition March 7, 1825; Phinney, *Lexington,* 34; Sabin, "April 19, 1775," II, 7; Willard D. Brown, *The Story of Buckman Tavern,* 14–15. The authenticity of the bullet hole is also very doubtful.

34. Sutherland wrote after the action, "Major Pitcairn, Major Mitchell, Capts. Lumm, Cochrane, Mr. Thorne of the 4th Regiment, Mr. Adair of the Marines, Captain Parsons of the 10th and Lieutenant Gould and Barker of the 4th I believe will pretty nearly agree in most particulars of the above." This may be taken as a list of British officers who were engaged on Lexington Green. Three were on foot with the light infantry of the 4th and the 10th Foot when they deployed in front of Parker's line: Gould, Barker, of the Fourth; and Parsons of the 10th. Four others were mostly members of Mitchell's patrol: Mitchell himself, Lumm, Cochrane, and Thorne. Pitcairn commanded the advanced column, and Adair had been put in the van. Also with the two companies were Captain Nesbit Balfour of the 4th, Lieutenant Waldron Kelly, and Ensign Jeremy Lister of the 10th (a volunteer replacing Lt. Hamilton at the last minute).

35. Sanderson, Deposition, Dec. 17, 1824, Phinney, *Battle at Lexington,* 31–33; Sutherland to Kemble, April 27, 1775.

36. Fessenden, Deposition, April 23, 1775, *AA4,* II, 495–96; Barker, *British in Boston,* 32. On Sutherland, see the next chapter, below. Sutherland is an interesting character. He tells us that he joined the expedition as a volunteer, and appears to have been hungry for action. His accounts of the battle are exceptionally full and descriptive, but also differ from those of other officers. He tended to be more hostile to the Americans, more strongly assertive that the militia fired the first shots at Lexington, and also Concord where no other British officer concurred with him, more manipulative of facts, more defensive about the British conduct, and more self-serving. Sutherland appears to have been one of the few junior officers who was ordered by Gage's staff to make a report of his actions; one wonders if Gage had his own suspicions. A distinct possibility is that Sutherland was the man who fired the first shot, perhaps by inadvertence when he was having trouble with his horse. It is the author's experience that riders who have the most trouble controlling their horses are those least able to control themselves. This is merely a hypothesis, but the reader will note Sutherland's behavior at Concord's North Bridge.

37. This hypothesis of several "first shots," nearly simultaneous, has not been suggested or supported by any other major published history of the event, but it makes a maximum fit with virtually all of the evidence.

38. J. A. Houlding, *Fit for Service: The Training of the British Army, 1715–1795* (Oxford, 1981), 141.

39. John Munroe, Deposition, Dec. 28, 1824, Phinney, *Battle at Lexington,* 36–37.

40. The British muskets had no rear sights; only a bayonet lug near the muzzle, which disappeared when bayonets were mounted. British infantry were trained to fire with their heads erect, not bent along the musket. One officer observed in 1757, "Any commander that desires his men to hold up their heads when they fire . . . was never a marksman

himself; and in such case, you may set Blind men a Firing as a man that can see." George Grant, *The New Highland Military Discipline* (1757; rpt. Ottawa, 1967); quoted in Houlding, *Fit for Service,* 279–80.

41. Timothy Smith, Deposition, April 23, 1775; Thomas Fessenden, Deposition, April 25, 1775; *AA4,* II, 494, 496.

42. William Gordon, "An Account of the Commencement of Hostilities Between Great Britain and America," May 17, 1775, *AA4,* II, 40.

43. hn Munroe, Deposition, Dec. 28, 1824, Phinney, *Battle at Lexington,* 35.

44. *Ibid.*

45. *Ibid.;* Ebenezer Munroe, Deposition, April 2, 1825, Phinney, *Battle at Lexington,* 37; the remains of John Munroe's shortened musket may be seen today in the Munroe Tavern, Lexington.

46. Kehoe, "We Were There!" typescript, I, 134–41,Watertown Public Library.

47. Sabin, "April 19, 1775," II, 15, 18; Lister wrote, "We had but one man wounded of our company in the leg his name was Johnson." No soldier of this name was on the muster roll of the light infantry company as of April 19, 1775, but Private Thomas Johnston was listed as transferring from another company in the 10th Foot to the light infantry company, effective April 24. One wonders if, like Lister, Private Johnston marched as a volunteer replacement. If so, he was a hard-luck soldier, the only man hit at Lexington, and mortally wounded at Bunker Hill. He died on June 23, 1775. Cf. Lister, Narrative; Muster Roll, 10th Foot, WO12/2750, PRO.

48. William Munroe, Deposition, March 7, 1825.

49. Ebenezer Munroe, Deposition, April 2, 1825, Phinney, *Battle of Lexington,* 37.

50. The drum call was not the tattoo, as some secondary accounts surmise.

51. Gould, Deposition; Sutherland to Kemble, April 27, 1775; Barker, *The British in Boston,* 32.

52. Lt. Col. Francis Smith to Major Robert Donkin, Oct. 8, 1775, Gage Papers, WCL, published in part in French, *General Gage's Informers,* 61; Sabin, "April 19, 1775," II, 12–13.

53. Mackenzie, *Diary,* I, 32.


∾ 14. The Battle

1. Thaddeus Blood, "Statement on the Battle of April 19, 1775," *Boston Daily Advertiser,* April 20, 1886; ms., CFPL.

2. Galvin, *Minute Men,* 258.

3. Emerson, *Diaries and Letters,* 71; Shattuck, *History of Concord,* 8.

4. Emerson, *Diaries and Letters,* 71–72.

5. Thaddeus Blood, "Statement on the Battle of April 19." The location of this hill is not clear in primary sources. Some scholars have assumed it to be the eastern end of Revolutionary Ridge, the long hill that runs parallel to the Concord-Lexington Road from Concord center to Meriam's Corner. It could also have been Hardy's Hill, a mile to the east. Statements about the view to the east support the first interpretation; implications of distances marched suggest the second. On balance, the first interpretation is more probable.

6. Gould, Deposition, April 25, 1775, *AA4,* II, 500–501.

7. Barrett, Deposition, April 23, 1775, *AA4,* II, 500.

8. What flag was flying from the liberty pole? Some scholars believe that it was the "pine tree flag" of New England, a red flag with a pine tree on a white canton. Another New England flag had a red cross of St. George on a white canton above a red field. Also in use were white flags with a green liberty tree, and the motto "An Appeal to Heaven." The Sons of Liberty in Massachusetts flew a flag with vertical red and white stripes. Cf. Ruth R. Wheeler, *Concord: Climate for Freedom* (Concord, 1967), 116–17.

9. Abel Conant, interview, Nov. 8, 1832; Shattuck's Historical Notes, NEHGS; Shattuck, *History of Concord,* 105–6.

10. Emerson, Diary, April 19, 1775, *Diaries and Letters of William Emerson,* 71. The pronoun "us" is interpolated here.

11. The story of Harry Gould was told by the militiaman himself to James D. Butler. See James D. Butler, Jr., to Edward W. Emerson, April 25, 1888, in Emerson, *Diaries and Letters of William Emerson,* 133–34; for the naming of the sons, see Gross, *Minutemen and Their World,* 118; and family reconstitution sheets compiled by the Brandeis Concord Group and Robert Gross, Brandeis University.

12. Brandeis Concord Group, Family Reconstitution Sheets; Gross, *The Minutemen and Their World,* 158; French, *Day of Concord and Lexington,* 158.

13. Shattuck, *History of Concord*; Josephine Hosmer, "Memoir of Joseph Hosmer," *The Centennial of the Concord Social Circle* (Cambridge, Mass., 1882), 116–17; Gross, *Minutemen and Their World,* 64–65; Sabin, "April 19, 1775," III, 29.

14. Even Concord's fiery young minister William Emerson wrote, "We were the more careful to prevent a rupture with the King's troops, as we were uncertain what had happened at Lexington, and knew not they had begun the quarrel." It was urgently important to these New England men that they should not strike the first blow. See *Diaries and Letters of William Emerson,* 72.

15. *Ibid.,* 71–72; Ripley, *Fight at Concord,* 16.

16. Gross, *Minutemen and Their World,* 122; accounts of Reuben Brown, William Emerson, Abel Fisk, Dr. Timothy Minot, and Ezekiel Brown, 1775 Folder, Concord Archives, CFPL. Much of the property listed as missing was not looted but taken by order of Colonel Smith for carrying the wounded to Boston.

17. British strength and dispositions at the North Bridge were variously reported in three eyewitness accounts. Lister thought that five companies were sent to North Bridge; Barker counted six; Laurie reported six were originally sent, and later reinforced by a seventh. Laurie, the senior officer present, appears to have been correct. From various sources seven companies of light infantry can be identified by regimental number as present there: the 4th, 5th, 10th, 38th, 43rd, 52nd, later reinforced by the 23rd. The 43rd remained at the North Bridge, as did the 5th for a time. Captain Parsons led the 38th and the 52nd to Barrett's, where they were joined by the 5th, and according to Lister the 23rd as well. The 4th and 10th occupied the high ground along their route. See Smith to Gage, April 22, 1775; Lister, Narrative; Barker, *British in Boston,* 33-34; Sutherland to Kemble, April 27, 1775; Sutherland to Clinton, April 26, 1775; Laurie to Gage, April 26, 1775; French, *General Gage's Informers,* 98.

18. Interview with Ephraim Jones by Marquis de Chastelleux, Nov. 7, 1782, in Howard Rice (ed.), *Travels in North America in the Years 1780, 1781, and 1782,* 2 vols. (Chapel Hill, 1963), II, 481–82.

19. Trevelyan, *American Revolution,* I, 286; Shattuck supplies a more exact inventory: 60 barrels of flour of which nearly half was later preserved; 3 cannon damaged by smashing of their trunnions; 16 gun carriage wheels burned, a few barrels of wooden trenchers, and spoons burned, and 500 pounds of ball thrown into the millpond, and later rescued.

20. De Berniere, Narrative.

21. Shattuck, *History of Concord,* 107–9.

22. Sutherland observed that "part of them formed in a meadow and the rest went still further off with the women and the children, and formed in another meadow on a rising ground. I saw more men in arms on a height that rose above the last mentioned party, which were none of those that passed the bridge sometime before." Sutherland to Kemble, April 27, 1775; Sutherland to Clinton, April 26, 1775.

23. The present site of the muster field lies to the west of the 20th-century Buttrick Mansion, now a visitor center in the National Park. Beside it is the old house of Major Buttrick himself.

24. Josiah Adams, *Letter to Lemuel Shattuck, Esq.* (Boston, 1850), 20–21; Amos Baker, Affadavit; Rantoul, *Oration,* 134.

25. A Hunt family tradition, recorded by French, *Day of Concord and Lexington,* 182n.

26. Interview with Mrs. Peter Barrett, Nov. 3, 1831, Shattuck's Historical Notes, NEHGS; Shattuck, *History of Concord*, 109; Gross, *Minutemen and Their World*, 123.

27. Shattuck, *History of Concord*, 111; Josephine Hosmer, "Memoir of Joseph Hosmer"; Gross, *Minutemen and Their World*, 220.

28. Frothingham, "Statement of Major John Buttrick," 52; Adams, *Letter to Lemuel Shattuck*, 45.

29. Amos Barrett, Narrative.

30. *Ibid.*

31. The sequence of events was reported differently by participants on both sides. Eight Lincoln men testified, "We then seeing several fires in the town, thought that the houses in Concord were in danger, and marched towards the said bridge, and the troops who were stationed there, observing our approach, marched back over the bridge, and then took up some planks." The same words were exactly repeated in a deposition signed by sixteen Concord men.

Colonel Barrett, on the other hand, testified, "I ordered them to march to the North Bridge, so called, which they had passed, and were taking up. I ordered said Militia to march to said bridge and pass the same, but not to fire on the king's troops, unless they were first fired upon." Bradbury Robinson and two others deposed that the Regulars "were taking up said bridge, when about three hundred of our militia were advancing towards said bridge."

Lieutenant Barker recalled, "The rebels marched into the Road and were coming down upon us when Captain Laurie made his men retire to this side of the bridge, which by the by he ought to have done at first, and then he would have had time to make a good disposition." Cf. Depositions of John Hoar *et al.*, Nathan Barrett *et al.*, and James Barrett, all dated April 23, 1775, published as *A Narrative of the Excursion and Ravages of the King's Troops Under the Command of General Gage* (Worcester, 1775); rpt. in Lincoln, *Journals of Each Provincial Congress*, 661–74; also in Wroth *et al.* (eds.), *Province in Rebellion*, doc. 769, pp. 2083–87; and *AA4*, II, 489–502; Barker, *British in Boston*, 34.

32. George Tolman, *Events of April 19, 1775* (Concord, n.d.), 29; Sabin, "April 19, 1775," II, 38; on the shortage of bayonets, see Amos Baker, Affadavit. Some historians also place Lt.-Col. John Robinson of Westford at the head of the column with Major Buttrick. According to tradition he was invited to take command, but Robinson deferred to Buttrick as his own men were not yet there, and marched as a volunteer. See Edwin R. Hodgman, *History of the Town of Westford* (Lowell, Mass., 1883), 106.

33. Sutherland to Kemble, April 27, 1775; Lister, Narrative; Laurie to Gage, April 26, 1775; American accounts were similar. Blood recalled "our men marching in very good order along the road," in "Statement on the Battle of April 19," CFPL.

34. For the effective strength of these units, see Appendix K, below.

35. Lister wrote, "Our companies was drawn up in order to form for Street firing." The best discussion of this part of the battle is in French, *Lexington and Concord*, 195.

36. Hodgman, *History of the Town of Westford*, 106.

37. The confusion was compounded by another problem. The drill for street firing was not familiar to all the units at the bridge. It had not been included in the 18 evolutions required in the King's Regulations of 1765. Laurie's regiment appears to have practiced it, but not the 4th, where it was "not even understood by the officers who thought that by some mistake the companies had got one behind the other." L. I. Cowper, *The King's Own; The Story of a Royal Regiment* (Oxford, 1939), 239; Barker, *The British in Boston*, 34.

38. Testimony was mixed, but Captain Laurie himself deposed that "I imagine myself that a man of my company (afterwards killed) did first fire his piece." Most historians have accepted Laurie's testimony. Blood recalled that "at that time an officer rode up and a gun was fired. I saw where the ball threw up the water about the middle of the river, then a second and a third shot." Some have surmised that the first shot may have been fired as a warning; a more likely explanation is an accidental discharge. Cf. Laurie to Gage, April 26, 1775; Blood, "Statement on the Battle of April 19," CFPL.

39. *Ibid.;* Baker, Deposition; French, *Concord and Lexington,* 198.

40. The bodies of Davis and Hosmer were exhumed in 1851 for reburial at a monument on Acton Common, and opened for anyone to view the remains. People were able to see where the ball entered Hosmer's cheek below the left eye and exited at the back of the neck. The remains of Captain Isaac Davis were "remarkably well preserved." Castle *et al.* (eds.), *The Minute Men,* 30

41. Amos Barrett recalled in his idiosyncratic spelling which is not altered here, "We marched two deep it was a long being round by the river. Captain Davis had got I be leave within 15 rods of the B[ridge] when they fired three guns one after the other. I see the balls strike in the river to the right of me." Blood's memory was generally the same, but differed in one respect: "An officer rode up and a gun was fired. I saw where the ball threw up the water, about the middle of the river, then a second and a third shot." One wonders if this officer might have been Sutherland, the only one at the North Bridge who was known to be mounted. Sutherland was also in that position on Lexington Green. By comparison with his brother officers, Sutherland's letters were exceptionally aggressive and hostile to the Americans, and much more insistent that they fired first, even at Concord, where many other witnesses on both sides contradicted him. One wonders if he might have been an instigator on both fields. There is, however, no firm evidence beyond this suspicious pattern. Cf. Amos Barrett, Narrative, in *Journal of Letters of Henry True,* 11–14; Blood, "Statement on the Battle of April 19," CFPL.

42. Some accounts suggest that every American had a clear shot. Many did, but not all. Blood wrote, "We then was all ordered to fire that could fire and not kill our own men."

43. This estimate of casualties follows the report from Captain Walter Laurie, the senior British officer at the bridge: killed, three privates; wounded, four officers, a sergeant and four other ranks. Several scholars have suggested that the toll might have been smaller, but I see no reason to doubt the accuracy of Laurie's report (allowing that one of his killed may have been mortally wounded. If anything the toll was more likely to have been higher, as British units in the 18th century did not normally report minor wounds but only those that were incapacitating. See Captain Walter Laurie to Gage, April 26, 1775, Gage Papers, WCL; published in French, *General Gage's Informers,* 95–98; also Wroth *et al.* (eds.), *Province in Rebellion,* doc. 721, pp. 2023–24; on the scarlet coats at Bunker Hill, Richard M. Ketchum, *Decisive Day: The Battle for Bunker Hill* (1962, new edition, New York, 1974, 1991), 191.

44. Visual evidence appears in Ralph Earl's sketch of the action, which he carefully drew after interviewing participants in the weeks immediately following the battle. Earl showed most of the New England men firing simultaneously, nearly all of them with clear shots at the British troops across the bridge. Only the front ranks of the Regulars could fire back. In terms of naval tactics, the American militia had "crossed the T," a rare event in land warfare.

45. Lister, Narrative, in French (ed.), *Concord Fight.*

46. Blood, "Statement on the Battle of April 19," CFPL.

47. Nathan Barrett III, Reminiscences, ms., CFPL.

48. *Ibid.;* this version is closest to the event; the same story has also been told of Jonas Brown and his mother, of Luther Blanchard and Mrs. Humphrey Barrett, and of Luther Blanchard and Mrs. Nathan Barrett; cf. Castle *et al.* (eds.), *The Minute Men,* 221; Gross, *The Minutemen and Their World,* 221; Shattuck, *History of Concord,* 114.

49. For many years the town of Concord threw a shroud of silence round this event. Nathaniel Hawthorne, an outsider, suggested that the atrocity was committed by a "loutish boy" who was hired as a wood-chopper by William Emerson; the Emersons insisted that no such person existed. Others have suggested that the deed was done by the Emersons' African slave Frank, but the Emersons insisted that Frank was with them, and could not possibly have done it.

Many people in Concord believed that the perpetrator was Ammi White, aged 20 or 21, a private in Captain Brown's militia company. Ruth Wheeler reported this tradition in print, and it is accepted by many historians. It is the most probable identity.

Nearly sixty years later, Mrs. Peter Barrett attempted to justify the act, telling an interviewer that the wounded soldier was "lying in a puddle of water in so much distress that he was trying to drown himself and begged someone to kill him." There is no evidence to support her, and nobody at the time offered this justification. See Emerson, *Diaries and Letters,* 74; Shattuck, Historical Notes, NEHGS; Gross, *Minutemen,* 127; Wheeler, *Concord, Climate for Freedom,* 228; Hawthorne, *Mosses from an Old Manse,* preface; Sabin, "April 19, 1775," III, 58.

50. Barrett, Narrative.

51. *Ibid.*

52. Blood, "Statement."

53. Emerson, *Diaries and Letters,* 75 (April 19, 1775).

54. "Corpl Gordon, Thos Lugg, Wm. Lewis, Charles Carrier and Richd Grimshaw in the presence of Captn Battier of the 5th light company do solemnly declare, when they were returning to Join the grenadiers they saw a man belonging to the Light Company of the 4th regiment with the Skin over his Eye's cut and also the top part of his ears cut off. This declaration made in the presence of me, John G. Battier, Capt. LI 5th foot."

55. Emerson, *Diaries and Letters,* 72. Smith is often condemned for being fatally slow. Trevelyan (I, 286) wrote that he "delayed till noon; and those two hours were his ruin." But he was waiting for his four companies to return from Colonel Barrett's mill, which he had explicit orders to search.

56. The chaises were taken from John Beaton and Reuben Brown.

57. Two streams along the Battle Road bore the same name of Elm Brook. The first was this one, a few yards east of Meriam's Corner. The second was at the Concord-Lincoln line, by the houses of Joshua Brooks and Job Brooks, and in 1775 also called Tanner's Brook, after a slaughterhouse and tanning mill that stood beside it. Cf. Malcolm, *The Scene of the Battle, 1775,* map III.

58. Private Thomas Ditson appears on the muster roll of Captain Jonathan Stickney's company of minutemen; Coburn, *Battle of April 19, 1775,* expanded edition, appendix, p. 16.

59. The best account of the engagement at Meriam's Corner is Sabin, "April 19, 1775," IV, 1–13. For units engaging, see Coburn, *Battle . . . ,* 97, an incomplete list which omits the Tewksbury companies and others; their presence is documented in Chase, *Beginnings of the American Revolution,* II, 64.

60. This version of Captain Trull's remark follows Chase, *Beginnings of the American Revolution,* II, 63; a different version, four generations removed, is in Hurd, *Middlesex County,* II, 294. The presence of regimental officers at Meriam's Corner was missed by Coburn, French, Tourtellot, and most other historians who stressed the spontaneity and individuality of the American response. Though the role of these commanders was documented in primary evidence, and in town histories, it was omitted from most general accounts until Galvin, *Minute Men,* 171.

61. Many cinematic versions of the battle, and some written accounts as well, represent the American militia as fighting behind stone walls directly beside the road. Thomas Edison's first film of the battle showed the muzzles of American muskets projecting halfway across the highway. A Hollywood version of Howard Fast's novel *April Morning* (1988) was similar, with Americans kneeling at the edge of the road behind massive walls that appeared to have been constructed from Tennessee limestone by Italian masons, or lurking behind roadside trees which miraculously had sprouted their Summer foliage in early Spring.

This common image of the battle is not correct. At Meriam's Corner, and throughout the day, experienced American officers deliberately held their units well back from the road at maximum effective musket range, approximately 100 yards. A British officer observed that "a soldier's musket, if not exceedingly ill-bored (as many of them are), will strike the figure of a man at eighty yards; it may even at 100, but a soldier must be very unfortunate who shall be wounded by a common musket at 150 yards, provided his antagonist aims at him;

and as to firing at a man at 200 yards with a common musket, you may just as well fire at the moon" (quoted in Galvin, *Minute Men,* 77).

Sometimes, as we shall see, green troops and a few inexperienced but highly aggressive American officers tried to fight at shorter range. When they did so, the British Regulars closed quickly or attacked with flanking parties, with results that were frequently fatal to the Americans.

At greater distances, the New England militia took a steady toll of the British column, and suffered few casualties in return. Several historians (French, Murdock, and others) have noted the very high ratio of ammunition fired to men hit as evidence of American incompetence. The opposite was the case—heavy expenditure of shot and powder at long range was part of a highly effective solution to the difficult tactical problem of fighting Regular infantry with militia. Murdock and French also failed to note that the ratio of rounds fired to men hit was even higher on the British side than the American.

62. At Meriam's Corner once again the first shot is a subject of controversy. The balance of testimony by Lister, Sutherland, and also by the American Major Brooks indicates that New England men fired first. Edmund Foster, a reliable witness, thought that the first shot came from the Regulars. But the weight of evidence is on the other side.

63. Individual accounts varied. Blood remembered that "there was a heavy fire but the distance was so great, that little injury was done on either side; at least, I saw but one killed. Number wounded I know not" (Blood, "Statement"). Lister wrote that the "rebels begun a brisk fire but at so great a distance it was without effect, but as they kept marching nearer when the Grenadiers found them they returned their fire. Just about that time I received a shot through my right elbow joint which effectually disabled my arm" (Lister, Narrative, *Concord Fight,* 29).

Brooks recalled that nine British soldiers were left "hors de combat" near the bridge. Sutherland believed that two Americans were killed, but they have not been identified. The interpretative balance lies between Blood and Lister on one side, and Brooks and Barrett on the other.

64. French, *Day of Concord and Lexington,* 8–9, 152–55, 219.

65. For "Lincoln Woods," see Temple, *Framingham,* 274.

66. Brooks Hill came to be called Hardy's Hill in the 19th century and Smith's Hill in the 20th. Galvin, and the staff of the Minute Man National Historical Park inaccurately refer to it by its 19th-century name. The U.S. Geological Survey identifies it on topographical maps by its early 20th-century name.

67. "Battalia" in the 18th-century English military usage did not mean a unit of battalion strength, as modern students of the battle have mistakenly believed. It was used to indicate "a large body of men in battle array." Sutherland was reporting that here again, as at Meetinghouse Hill, Punkatasset Hill, North Bridge, the ridge east of the bridge, and Meriam's Corner, the American militia formed up in close order, in regimental strength. Cf. *Oxford English Dictionary,* "battalia," 1,2. Sutherland to Clinton, April 26, 1775; Allen French believed that Sutherland was describing Meriam's Corner in this passage, but Douglas Sabin observes that it is "more appropriate to Hardy's Hill." French is mistaken; Sabin is correct. Cf. Sabin, "April 19, 1775," V, 3.

68. Galvin, *Minute Men,* 176–77.

69. At Brooks Hill in 1775, the south of the road (from west to east) included a 10 acre tract (A) described as woodland, tillage, and pasture in 1769, then a tract of pasture and orchard (B), and then just east of Brooks Road another tract for which no data exist (C). Woodland lay behind these tracts on high ground about 500 yards from the highway. North of the highway were three close-built houses and houselots, probably with small patches of orchard and tillage close by; then two small tracts of poor land called "upland" in the deeds (D), and a large 20 acre "houselot" that was probably mixed pasture and tillage (E).

The fight on Brooks Hill was probably begun by Americans in woodland south of the road on tract A and in the woods behind it. This was sharply rising ground, with good cover and excellent fields of fire. The fighting probably continued through Tracts B and C. North of the road, were the upland tracts and the 20-acre houselot, the west end of which may have been wood pasture with mature trees in the pasture land, and tree lines at field boundaries, where the Chelmsford men fought. There are strong traditions that the Chelmsford men were heavily engaged at Hardy's Hill and Sergeant Ford's gallantry was specially noted in the same place. (Sabin, "April 19, 1775," V, 3; Frederic Hudson, "The Concord Fight," *Harper's New Monthly Magazine* 50 (1875): 801). The large formation of 1000 men that Sutherland saw was, I believe, the militia from Framingham and Sudbury. Here again there is a strong town tradition that Captain Nathaniel Cudworth's Sudbury Company were heavily engaged on Brooks Hill (Hudson, *Sudbury*, 380). Sabin concludes that "it is also possible that other units from Sudbury's six companies joined the ambush at Hardy's [i.e., Brooks] Hill," and that "the Sudbury forces enjoyed the support of men from Framingham's three companies at Hardy's Hill" (V, 1, 4). These nine companies included 500 men. Others from adjacent Middlesex towns could easily have made Sutherland's 1000.

70. Hudson, *Sudbury*, 365; citing Stearns Collection, [Sudbury Papers], MHS, now lost.

71. Hurd, *History of Middlesex County*, II, 830; other accounts differ in detail on the place of Captain Wilson's death.

72. Samuel Adams Drake, *History of Middlesex County* (Boston, 1880), I, 375; Sabin, "April 19, 1775," V, 3; Chase, *Beginnings of the American Revolution*, II, 64.

73. Baldwin's reference to Tanner's Brook places his ambush position at the first bend, where the highway turned sharply north into what was called the Old Bedford Road. His men were in a "young growth of wood" on land that is now in the roadbed of modern Route 2A. A conflict of evidence appears here, between the early terrain studies and the eyewitness accounts of the battle. In this case, the latter may help us to refine the former. Terrain studies identified this tract as orchard, but this is from a deed that describes it as "young orchard" in 1791. In 1775 it must have been something else, probably an abandoned field or pasture that had gone to second growth timber, hence Foster's description as a "young growth of wood" on the south side of the road. The land on the northwest side was called "pasture" in 1791, but much 18th-century pasture was rough ground, interspersed with mature trees that had been browsed up to a height of four or six feet, the "large trees" of Foster's narrative. The terrain rises steeply from Tanner's Brook to Baldwin's "young growth" of wood. It would have been a perfect ambush site, with cover, elevation, and an enfilade position. Extracts from Loammi Baldwin's diary are published in Hurd, *Middlesex County*, II, 445–47.

74. Edmund Foster to Col. Daniel Shattuck, March 10, 1825, Kehoe, "We Were There!" I, 253–54. Most historians believe that this passage in Foster's letter refers to the Bloody Curve (Sabin, "April 19, 1775," V, 7). Galvin places it on Hardy's [Brooks] Hill, but recent research tends to support Sabin's reading (cf. Galvin, *Minute Men*, 178).

75. The Rev. Edmund Foster to Lemuel Shattuck, March 10, 1825; Galvin, *Minute Men*, 176, and Coburn, *Battle . . .* , 101, are correct; French's account (in *Concord and Lexington*, 220–21) is inaccurate in regard to American movements. Malcolm, maps III and IV, also appears to be mistaken in her identification of the terrain, missing the "young growth" of wood that Foster described, and woodlands that appear in other accounts. Sabin cautions that "the historical record concerning the action on Hardy's Hill [Brooks Hill] is clouded." Particular problems appear in estimates of casualties. Cf. Sabin, "April 19, 1775," V, 4.

76. This is not correctly called the Bloody Angle, an error term introduced after the Civil War that is both inaccurate and anachronistic. It has been used uncritically by many historians of the battle and is perpetuated by the National Park Service. The name was borrowed from another war to which it properly belongs; it also does not describe the terrain, which consisted of a series of bends along the curving road—not merely one. Changes in modern road construction have compounded the confusion here. The older and more correct name of Bloody Curve was recorded in Wheeler, *Concord: Climate of Freedom*, 127. The second ambush was near the intersection of the Woburn Road, the Old Bedford Road, and the Virginia Road. The peach orchard identified here in some terrain studies appears to have

been planted later. The "woodpasture" lay to the south, with a "parcel" to the west that may have been a combination of rough pasture and woodland.

77. Again the best accounts are Galvin, Coburn, Hurd, and Sabin.

78. This was the place where Foster wrote, fifty years afterward, that there was "little or no discipline or order, on the part of the Americans during the remainder of that day. Each sought his own place and opportunity to attack and annoy the enemy from behind trees, rocks, fences and buildings, as seemed most convenient." This memory appears to be correct in what happened after the engagement began at the Bloody Curve, but it is certainly incorrect for the "rest of the day." As we shall see, attacks were mounted in company and even regimental strength later in the morning, and Percy noted that the British column was closely pursued by a large body of American troops in close formation.

79. Sabin, "April 19, 1775," V, 17.

80. The best account of the fighting at the Hartwell farms is in Sabin, "April 19, 1775," V, 18.

81. The town line ran through the rock-strewn pasture. The wooded slope to the north-east, sometimes called Pine Hill, lay just inside Lexington. Today it is just east of Airport Road, and the National Park Visitor Center. The terrain and foliage today on Parker's Hill are very similar to what existed at the time of the battle, except that the undergrowth has been browsed by deer, which are more abundant two centuries later than in 1775. When the author and park historian Douglas Sabin climbed this hill on April 16, 1993, deer droppings were abundant on top of the rocky hill.

82. Several antiquarian accounts have identified a rock only thirty feet from the road as the place where Thorning (still a local hero) made his stand. This "Minuteman Rock" is another myth. No evidence survives to document the place, and a position only ten yards from the highway would have been suicidal. Another factor is that the ground close to the road is very soft in the Spring; on April 16, 1993, there was much standing water on both sides of the old road. Cf. Hersey, *Heroes of Battle Road*, 27–29; and the correction by Sabin, "April 19, 1775," V, 25.

83. Historians and eyewitnesses disagree as to the location of the Lexington ambush. Coburn (p. 104) places it in Lincoln, "not far from the Nelson and Hastings homes." French (p. 223) puts it further east, "within the bounds of Lexington." Hudson (p. 195) believed that it happened "in Lincoln" with Parker's company "taking a position in the fields." Ezra Ripley, *A History of the Fight at Concord*, 31, placed Parker's men in the woods within the boundary of Lexington south of the road. Malcolm, in her Grounds report, finds no woodland south of the road, but a large woodlot to the north. Galvin, with his eye for terrain, thinks that Parker "selected the hill east of Nelson's bridge as his ambush position . . . the first hill inside the Lexington line" (p. 190). One of Parker's militia, Nathan Munroe, remembered, "We met the enemy within the bounds of Lincoln," but fought them in Lexington. Archaeological evidence of fighting was found in 1895 on the high ground north of the road (Coburn, *Battle* . . . , 106). These various materials can be reconciled with the interpretation presented in the text.

84. On the death of Jedidiah Munroe see Galvin, *Minute Men*, 193; Hudson, *Lexington*, 154; Coburn, *Battle* . . . , 130. Munroe was killed on Pine Hill in Lexington. Here is another indication that Parker put his men on both sides of the road, in the field and on the wooded hill.

Historians have differed on the place where Colonel Smith was wounded. Coburn (p. 107) believes that it happened on Fiske Hill. Sabin suggests that the site was Concord Hill further east (VI, 7); Galvin (p. 192) favors Pine Hill and the Parker ambush site. The best primary source on the British side is De Berniere's Report to Gage, which states that Smith had already been wounded before the column was "within a mile" of Lexington. Fiske Hill was about 1.5 miles from Lexington Common; Parker's ambush was about 1.9 miles. Another clue may be found in Pitcairn's conduct, which suggests that he had assumed active command of the column before Fiske's Hill, but that Smith was still in that role before crossing the Lincoln line. This suggests that Parker's men shot him from their ambush near the town line.

85. Fiske Hill is today at the eastern end of the National Park, just west of Route 128.

86. Foster, "Narrative"; Galvin, *Minute Men*, 193–94; Coburn, *Battle . . .* , 108–10.

87. Hayward had lost his toes in a chopping accident and was exempt from service, but he mustered anyway. See Coburn, *Battle . . .* , 108; Fletcher, *Acton*; Adams, *Address Delivered at Acton*, 48. A well is still there at approximately the same spot, and was full of water in April 1993 when last visited by the author and Douglas Sabin.

88. Galvin, *Minute Men*, 194.

89. Simonds, "The Affair in the Lexington Meetinghouse."

90. De Berniere, Report to Gage; the terrain in this stretch of road has been radically altered by the construction of Route 128 (Interstate 95), the broad modern beltway around Boston that passes between Fiske's Hill and Concord Hill.

91. *Ibid.*

92. Barker, *The British in Boston*, 35, 37.

93. Percy to the Duke of Northumberland, April 20, 1775, *Percy Letters*, 54.

## 15. A Circle of Fire

1. Gage had earlier prepared the 1st Brigade for its mission this day. On March 29, 1775, he ordered "the first brigade to be under arms tomorrow morning at six o'clock with their knapsacks on. The brigade will assemble on the Grand parade, with four companies of light infantry, and four companies of Grenadiers, to the right of the whole." The next day Barker noted in his diary, "The 1st Brigade marched into the country at 6 o'clock in the morning; it alarmed the people a good deal. Expresses were sent off to every town near: at Watertown about 9 miles off, they got two pieces of cannon to the bridge and loaded 'em but nobody would stay to fire them; at Cambridge, they were so alarmed that they pulled up the bridge." Extracts of Orders given to the British Army in America," n.d. [March 29, 1775?], WO 36/1, PRO; Barker, *British in Boston*, 27 (March 30, 1775).

2. On Captain Moncrieffe's career, see *Gage Correspondence*, II, 74, 300, 383, 409, 430–32, 461–62, 486, 610, 630, 667, 688.

3. Letter from an officer in the 5th Foot, July 5, 1775; printed in *Detail and Conduct of the American War* (3rd ed., London, 1780), 10; and Frothingham, *History of the Siege of Boston*, 75.

4. Samuel Eliot Morison, *The Life and Letters of Harrison Gray Otis, Federalist, 1765–1818*, 2 vols. (Boston, 1913), I, 13.

5. Frothingham, *Siege of Boston*, 75; Mackenzie, *Diary*, I, 19.

6. John Cannon, *Aristocratic Century; The Peerage of Eighteenth-Century England* (Cambridge, 1984, 1987), solidly documents the growing power of the English aristocracy in this period. To his trenchant analysis a chapter might be added on the aristocracy in the Empire, and the American colonies in particular.

7. David Carradine, *The Decline and Fall of the British Aristocracy* (New Haven, 1990), 710. An illegitimate son of the first Duke, James Smithson, was raised as James Macie by his mother. Later in life he changed his name to Smithson, developed republican leanings, and left a large fortune to the United States to found the Smithsonian Institution, in hopes that his name would "live in the memory of man when the titles of the Northumberlands and the Percies are extinct and forgotten." The founder of the Smithsonian was a half-brother of our Lord Percy.

8. Percy to Northumberland, July 27, 1774, Bolton (ed.), *Percy Letters*, 30.

9. His hospitality has inspired a delightful piece of historical whimsy by Harold Murdock, *Earl Percy's Dinner-Table* (Boston, 1907).

10. *Percy Letters*, 21.

11. Percy to the Rev. Thomas Percy, Oct. 27, 1774, *ibid.*, 40.

12. Percy to Northumberland, July 27, 1774; to Henry Reveley, Aug. 8, 1774, *ibid.*, 31.

13. Percy to the Rev. Thomas Percy, Nov 25, 1774, *ibid.*, 44.

14. Percy to Northumberland, July 27, 1774, *ibid.*, 27.

15. L. I. Cowper, *The King's Own: The Story of a Royal Regiment* (Oxford, 1939), 226.

16. Murdock, *Earl Percy's Dinner-Table*, 69.

17. The regiment's defiant spelling of Welch led to a two hundred years' war with higher authority. The War Office capitulated in 1920.

18. For an account of the regiment's celebration of St. David's Day in Boston, March 1, 1775, see Mackenzie, *Diary*, I, 8. According to another account by Lt. Richard Williams, the goat got loose at the dinner and escaped into Boston, hotly pursued by the regiment and its guests.

19. The regiment has been awarded 144 battle honors in many wars, but none for the American War of Independence, the only major war in modern British history for which no honors were given (at least for fighting in British North America itself). This was said to be at the command of George III, on the grounds that the American Revolution was only a domestic insurrection.

20. Haldimand to Gage, July 28, 1774; Gage to Haldimand, Aug. 7, 1774, Haldimand Papers, add. ms. 21665, BL.

21. Major John Pitcairn to Col. John Mackenzie, Feb. 16, 1775, Mackenzie Papers, add. ms. 39190, BL; for the order of march, see Mackenzie, *Diary*, I, 19.

22. Antony Beevor, *Inside the British Army* (London, 1990, 1991), 368.

23. Statement by George Leonard, May 4, 1775, French, *General Gage's Informers*, 57.

24. French, *Day of Concord and Lexington*, 229n, citing Horace Walpole to Sir Horace Mann, June 5, 1775; also Gordon, "Letter," *AA4*, II, 438; and *History*, I, 312. The oft-repeated error that Percy's men marched to the ballad "Chevy Chase" is a misreading of this source.

25. Percy to Gage, April 20, 1775, *Percy Letters*, 50.

26. Coburn, *Battle* . . . , 117; Edward Everett Hale in *Memorial History of Boston*, III, xxx.

27. Percy to Gage, April 20, 1775, draft, *Percy Letters*, 51n.

28. Percy to General Harvey, April 20, 1775, *ibid.*, 52; Barker, *British in Boston*, 35.

29. Mackenzie, *Diary*, I, 20; Sutherland to Kemble, April 27, 1775; Galvin, *Minute Men*, 207.

30. Col. R. A. Cleveland to master of ordnance, n.d., in W. G. Evelyn, *Memoir and Letters of Captain W. Glanville Evelyn of the 4th Regiment ("King's Own"), from North America, 1774–1776*, ed. G. D. Scull (Oxford, 1879), 98–99. Colonel Cleveland reported that the side boxes held 24 rounds for each gun. But Ensign Lister believed that they had only 7 rounds.

31. Many legends surround this event. The most detailed account in Smith, *West Cambridge in 1775*, 31-32, identifies David Lamson as the leader and names as participants Jason and Joe Belknap, James Budge, Israel Mead, and Ammi Cutter, and others to the number twelve. Another account by Joseph Thaxter asserts that the leader was a clergyman, Edward Brooks of Medford; a third version names a Chelsea minister, Payson, as the leader (cf. French, *Day of Concord and Lexington*, 230).

32. American Anglophile historians heaped scorn on this episode and the "anniversary oratory" that it inspired; cf. Murdock, *Nineteenth of April*, 100; but much evidence exists; David McClure, *Diary*, April 19, 1775, ed. F. B. Dexter (1899), 161; Joseph Thaxter, Narrative, Nov. 30, 1824, *United States Literary Gazette* I (1825): 264; Coburn, *Battle of April 19*, 119–20; Smith, *West Cambridge in 1775*, 27–30; French, *Day of Concord and Lexington*, 230.

33. Smith, *West Cambridge in 1775*, 30.

34. Percy to Gage, April 20, 1775, *Percy Letters*, 50.

35. Mackenzie, *Diary*, I, 23.

36. The total effective strength of the three marching regiments and Marine battalion in Percy's brigade on April 1 was 1,363. Of that number, 322 had marched with Smith's force, which also included 519 others. If we assume that half of the killed and missing had been lost on the return to Lexington, and add 50 men for Mitchell's patrol, the Royal Artillery,

and others on special assignment, then Percy's force numbered 1,886 men when it left Lexington.

37. Percy to Gage, April 20, 1775, CO5/92, PRO.

38. The grenadiers and light infantry appear to have alternated in the lead. Sutherland reported that at the beginning of the march the light infantry came first. A different order appears in Galvin, *Minute Men*, 218.

39. A different interpretation appears in Galvin (*ibid.*, 219), who believes that "the order of march was Percy's only major mistake this day." But given Percy's choices, it is difficult to fault his dispositions.

40. For the speed of the march, see Appendix M, below.

41. *Memoirs of Major-General William Heath by Himself*, ed. William Abbott (1798; New York, 1901), 5ff.

42. *Ibid.*, 3.

43. Stiles, *Literary Diary*, I, 551–52; (May 12, 1775).

44. Letter of John R. Adan, n.d., in Frothingham, *Warren*, 457.

45. Forbes has Revere make a dramatic return to Boston on April 19, 1775, but there is no evidence that he did so, and the inferences from later correspondence to his wife suggest that he remained in the country. There is positive evidence that he was meeting with the Committee of Safety in Cambridge by early morning on April 20, and with others in Watertown on the same day. He must have been close to that town on the night of April 19–20. Beyond these facts the sources are silent.

46. Ezra Stiles, *Literary Diary*, I, 551–52.

47. One of the few historians to recognize the importance of Heath's leadership is the soldier-scholar, John Galvin, himself an infantry officer of long experience. Galvin observes that "Heath's firm grasp of the tactics of the skirmish line and his tendency to see any battle as a series of isolated little fights was just what the provincials needed." Galvin, *Minute Men*, 215.

48. *Ibid.*; a similar judgment is in Coburn, *Battle* . . . , 132, 135ff; different interpretations appear in Tourtellot, *Lexington and Concord*, 192, and French, *Day of Concord and Lexington*, 242.

49. Cyrus Hamblin, *My Grandfather, Colonel Francis Faulkner* (Boston, 1887), 6; Galvin, *Minute Men*, 213.

50. Thomas Boynton, "Journal," April 19, 1775, *MHSP* 15 (1877): 254–55; Sarah L. Bailey, *Historical Sketches of Andover* (Boston, 1880), 308.

51. Galvin, *Minute Men*, 212.

52. Warren, like many other men that day, wore his hair in fashionable "earlocks," secured by pins on each side of his head. Cf. Frothingham, *Warren*, 461; Heath, *Memoirs*, 8.

53. Tourtellot, *Lexington and Concord*, 196; Galvin, *Minute Men*, 207.

54. Heath, *Memoirs*, 5.

55. *Ibid.*, 8.

56. Percy to General Harvey, April 20, 1775, *Percy Letters*, 52.

57. *Ibid.*

58. Mackenzie, *Diary*, I, 26–27. The early iconography of Lexington and Concord sometimes showed the minutemen carrying long-barreled weapons. A later generation of historians inferred that these weapons were long rifles. Revisionists such as Harold Murdock, Christopher Ward, and Allen French pointed out that this idea was mistaken—the long rifle was an artifact of another regional culture in British America, that the New England militia were armed with muskets and were poor shots. Elements of truth and error are combined in these revisionist interpretations. On the day of Lexington and Concord many experienced hunters carried long-barreled muskets and fowling pieces, and used them with deadly accuracy. These men were specially feared by the British soldiers. The musketry of the militia at the North Bridge was also very accurate.

59. Henry S. Chapman, *History of Winchester* (Winchester, 1936), 104–5; the "white mare" appears again in Hezekiah Wyman's will, four years after the battle. Other mounted

militia who appear in the incomplete records included William Polly of Medford, who was mortally wounded while fighting on horseback. Entire cavalry troops mustered that day in Sudbury, Groton, and Ipswich. Many officers also were mounted. See Galvin, *Minute Men*, 220; Hudson, *Sudbury*.

60. Mackenzie, *Diary*, I, 21.

61. Lister, "Narrative."

62. *Ibid.*

63. Martin Hunter, *The Journal of General Sir Martin Hunter* (Edinburgh, 1894), 161.

64. The quotation was commonly used by American writers with "English" excised!

65. Daniel P. King, *Address Commemorative of Seven Young Men at Danvers . . .* (Salem, 1835); J. W. Hanson, *History of the Town of Danvers* (Danvers, 1848), 108.

66. Galvin, *Minute Men*, 229.

67. Heath, *Memoirs*, 8; Smith, *West Cambridge in 1775*, 47; Coburn, *Battle . . .* , 146.

68. Smith, *West Cambridge in 1775*, 39-43; Coburn, *Battle . . .* , 142; Tourtellot, *Lexington and Concord*, 198; (Boston) *Columbian Centinel*, Feb. 6, 1793.

69. Mackenzie, *Diary*, I, 19–22; Barker, *British in Boston*, 36; an attempt by Anglophile historian Harold Murdock to deny British atrocities in Menotomy fails in the face of repeated testimony by British officers; just as do attempts by other scholars to gloss over the American atrocity at the North Bridge; cf. Murdock, *Nineteenth of April*, 83–134.

70. Benjamin and Rachel Cooper, Depositions, *Journals of the Provincial Congress*, ed. Lincoln, 678.

71. French, *Day of Concord and Lexington*, 250.

72. Coburn, *Battle . . .* , 147; Lucius Paige, *History of Cambridge, 1630–1877* (Boston, 1877), 414.

73. Mackenzie, *Diary*, I, 26.

74. On the bridge, see Coburn, *Battle . . .* , 116, citing Isaac Mansfield, Jr., Thanksgiving Sermon in Camp at Roxbury, Nov. 23, 1775, in J. W. Thornton (ed.), *Pulpit of the American Revolution* (Boston, 1860), 236; Heath, *Memoirs*, 7; Montresor.

75. Barker, *British in Boston*, 36.

76. The Kent Lane route, which has been missed by historians of the battle, appears in a manuscript sketch map from Percy's papers, reproduced in *The American War of Independence, 1775–1783; A Commemorative Exhibition Organized by the Map Library and the Department of Manuscripts of the British Library Reference Division* (London, 1975), 44.

77. A controversy surrounds Pickering's actions. He later asserted that he had stopped on Heath's orders. Heath contradicted him. Cf. Galvin, *Minute Men*, 225, 237–38; Octavius Pickering, *Timothy Pickering*, 4 vols. (Boston, 1867), I, 74–77; Heath, *Memoirs*, 8-9; Coburn, *Battle . . .* , 155; French, *Day of Concord and Lexington*, 262–64.

## ❧ 16. Aftermath

1. Gage to Barrington, April 22, 1775, Gage *Correspondence*, II, 673; (London) *Lloyd's Evening Post and British Chronicle*, June 17–21, 1775.

2. John Andrews, Letters, *MHSP* 8 (1865): 405.

3. William Heath, *Memoirs*, ed. Wiliam Abbatt (1798, New York, 1901), 8–9.

4. Coburn, after a careful reconstruction of estimates of routes and distances marched by British soldiers, reckoned that Smith's main body went 35 miles; the detachment to the Concord's South Bridge, 37 miles, the guard at North Bridge, 36 miles; the companies dispatched to the Barrett farm, 40 miles; Percy's brigade, 26 miles. Coburn, *The Battle . . .* , 161.

5. Thomas Boynton, *Journal*, Aug. 19–26, 1775, MHS, published in part in *MHSP* 15 (1877): 254. So often did rain follow the major battles of the American Civil War that meteorologists believed the concussion of combat was the cause. Theologians had another explanation.

6. De Berniere to Gage, n.d. [*ca.* April 20, 1775?]; *MHSC2*, 4 (1816): 215–19; Gage to Barrington, April 22, 1775, *Gage Correspondence*, I, 673–74.

7. Andrews, Letters, 405.

8. Capt. W. G. Evelyn to the Rev. Wm. Evelyn, *Memoir and Letters of W. G. Evelyn* (Oxford, 1879), 54–55.

9. De Berniere, 319.

10. *Ibid.*

11. "Intercepted Letter of a Soldier's Wife," May 2, 1775, *AA4*, II, 441.

12. "Intercepted Letters of the Soldiery in Boston," April 28, 1775, *AA4*, II, 439-40.

13. *Ibid.*

14. Barker, *British in Boston,* 37, 34.

15. Mackenzie, *Diary,* I, 29 (April 21, 1775).

16. Smith to Gage, April 22, 1775.

17. Percy to Harvey, April 20, 1775, Bolton (ed.), *Percy Letters,* 52–53.

18. Gage to Dartmouth, June 25, 1775, CO5/92, PRO, Kew.

19. Graves to Philip Stephens, April 22, 1775, ADM1/485, PRO, Kew.

20. "The Conduct of Vice Admiral Graves in North America, in 1774, 1775 and 1776," Dec. 11, 1776 [postscript dated Dec. 1, 1777] signed G. G[efferina]. The author was Graves's flag secretary in Boston. Graves Papers, Gay Transcripts, MHS.

21. *Ibid.*

22. *Ibid.*

23. Barker, *British in Boston,* 40.

24. Nathaniel Ames, Diary, April 19, 1775, and April 19, 1815; Dedham Historical Society. I owe these references with thanks to Robert B. Hanson, who observes that the bullet was not all that Dr. Ames extracted from his patient. The physician's account book contains an entry: "To extracting a Bullet from the Cubitus of Israel Everett, jr which he received in the battle of Lexington the first of the War with Great Britain, 3s; To sundry visits and dressings of the wound, 12 shilling." Nathaniel Ames Account Book, April 19, 1775; see also Robert B. Hanson, *Dedham, 1635–1890* (Dedham, 1976), 154.

25. Abram E. Brown, *Beneath Old Roof Trees* (Boston, 1896), 226.

26. Sabin, "April 19, 1775," VII, 19; Chase, *The Beginnings of the American Revolution,* 156–57.

27. Elizabeth Clarke, "Extracts," LHS *Proceedings* IV (1905–10): 91–93.

28. Revere to Belknap, *ca.* 1798, RFP, microfilm edition, MHS.

29. Rachel Revere to Paul Revere, n.d., Gage Papers, WCL; printed in French, *General Gage's Informers,* 170–71.

30. Paul Revere to Rachel Revere, n.d., Goss, *Revere,* I, 263.

31. Revere to Belknap, *ca.* 1798; drafts of Committee Circulars in Massachusetts Archives; Frothingham, *Warren,* 466; Cary, *Warren,* 188; Paul Revere, "To the Colony of Massachusetts Bay . . . ," Aug. 22, 1775, MA; a facsimile is published in Harriet O'Brien (ed.), *Paul Revere's Own Story* (Boston, 1929), 37.

32. There is no evidence that Revere received money for the midnight ride, but he was reimbursed for his expenses on earlier and later occasions. The spirit of bureaucracy appeared at this early date. An authorization to pay Paul Revere ten pounds four shillings had to be passed as a resolution by the entire Massachusetts House of Representatives and countersigned by sixteen men, including James Warren, Samuel Adams, and John Adams. House Resolution, Aug. 22, 1775, "Resolved that Mr. Paul Revere be allowed and paid . . . ," MA; facsimile in O'Brien (ed.), *Paul Revere's Own Story,* 36.

33. Proceedings of the Committee of Safety, *AA4,* II, 744, 765.

34. Warren, Circular Letter, n.d., April 20. 1775, published in Frothingham, *Warren,* 466.

35. Heath, *Memoirs,* 10.

36. The earliest recorded use of the phrase "public opinion" appeared in Edward Gibbon's *Decline and Fall of the Roman Empire,* the first volume of which appeared in 1776. The

expression occurs in chapter xxxi, III, 257 (1781). The first recorded American use is by Thomas Jefferson.

37. Josiah Warren, "Address to the Inhabitants of Great Britain," April 26, 1775, Wroth *et al.* (eds.), *Province in Rebellion,* doc. 509, pp. 1730–31.

38. Phinney, *Battle at Lexington,* 23; *Memoirs of the Concord Social Circle,* 1st series, 97.

39. Its progress was recorded in endorsements by each successive committee.

40. This folktale cannot be correct in its estimate of elapsed time; Bissell would have had to maintain a speed of 18 miles an hour. His next stop was in Brooklyn, Connecticut, at 11 o'clock the next morning, a distance of 45 miles. Thereafter the news traveled through the northeast at about five miles an hour—an exceptionally rapid rate of sustained long distance travel in that era. But the other details may be true. Cf. John H. Scheide, "The Lexington Alarm," AAS *Proceedings* 50 (1940): 63.

41. The chronology of the news of Lexington and Concord is grossly inaccurate in Lester Cappon *et al., Atlas of Early American History* (Princeton, 1976). A more accurate source is Scheide, "The Lexington Alarm," 49–79; the story of the Kentucky hunters is in George Bancroft, *History of the United States from the Discovery of the American Continent* (Boston, 1858), VII, 312.

42. "A Letter from a Gentleman of Rank in New England April 25, 1775," (London) *Lloyd's Evening Post and British Chronicle,* June 17–21, 1775.

43. Isaiah Thomas, *The History of Printing in America,* 2 vols. (1810, 1874; New York, 1970), x, I, 168–69; Arthur Schlesinger, Jr., *Prelude to Independence: The Newspaper War on Britain 1764–1776* (New York, 1958), 236–37.

44. Peter Edes, "Diary Kept in Boston Gaol," June 19, 1775, MHS.

45. Frank Luther Mott, "The Newspaper Coverage of Lexington and Concord," *NEQ* (1944), 489–504.

46. Emerson, *Diaries and Letters,* 61, 76.

47. On April 24, 1775, Jonas Clarke wrote in his Lexington diary, "committee taking depositions concerning the fatal action at Lexington," Jonas Clarke Diary, MHS.

48. Robert S. Rantoul, "The Cruise of the 'Quero': How We Carried the News to the King," *EIHC* 36 (1900): 5–13; Cary, *Joseph Warren,* 191.

49. Gage's courier Lieutenant Nunn did his best. He left *Sukey* twelve leagues at sea, boarded a faster vessel, landed at Portland, and raced to London, but the damage had been done. Gage was sharply reprimanded and instructed not to use a merchant ship for his dispatches, but one of the "light vessels" of the Royal Navy. See Dartmouth to Gage, June 10, 1775, CO5/92, PRO Kew; for the impact of the news in London, see Fred J. Hinkhouse, *The Preliminaries of the American Revolution as Seen in the English Press, 1763–1775* (1926, New York, 1969), 183–97.

50. Hutchinson, *Diary,* I, 454–63; *London Packet,* June 7, 1775; Hinkhouse, *Preliminaries of the American Revolution,* 188. Some accounts have represented British opinion as hostile to the American cause. This was true of Parliament, the Universities, the Church of England, and fashionable London, but not of the nation at large.

51. Lord George Germain to John Irwin, May 30, 1775, add ms. 42666, BL.

52. Suffolk to Germain, June 15, 1775; Germain to Suffolk, June 15, 1775, add. ms. 42266, BL.

53. *AA4,* II, 786; copies of this resolution were quickly sent to London; see ADM1/293, PRO, Kew.

54. Gage to Dartmouth, May 13, 1775, *Gage Correspondence,* I, 398.

55. Gage to Colden, May 4, 1775, *Colden Papers, 1765-1775,* VII, 291.

56. *Ibid.*

57. *Boston News-Letter,* April 20, 1775; Mott, "The Newspaper Coverage of Lexington and Concord," 493–94; Schlesinger, *Prelude to Independence,* 233.

58. Gage to Dartmouth, May 13, 1775, *Gage Correspondence,* I, 398.

59. Thomas Gage to Cadwallader Colden, April 29, May 4, 1775, *Colden Papers,* VII, 283–91.

60. John Adams, *Diary and Autobiography,* ed. Lyman Butterfield, 4 vols. (1961; New York, 1964), III, 314.

61. David Freeman Hawke, *Paine* (New York, 1974), 20, 29, 32, 35; Thomas Paine, *Common Sense* ed. Nelson F. Adkins (1776; New York, 1953), 27.

62. Washington to George William Fairfax, May 31, 1775, Fitzpatrick (ed.), *Writings of George Washington,* III, 291–92.

63. Wheeler, *Concord,* 131.

### ❧ 17. Epilogue

1. "Return of Officers, Noncommissioned Officers and Privates killed and wounded of His Majesty's Troops at the Attack of the Redoubts and Entrenchments on the Heights of Charlestown, June 17, 1775," WO1/2/241–42; Muster Rolls of the 23rd Foot or Royal Welch Fusiliers, Jan. 24, 1775, Sept. 24, 1775, WO 12/3960.

These data correct estimates in Harold Murdock, "The Myth of the Royal Welch Fusiliers," in *Bunker Hill; Notes and Queries on a Famous Battle* (Boston, 1927), 142–43; and Ralph Ketchum, *Decisive Day, the Battle for Bunker Hill* (New York, 1962; rpt. 1974), 190. In general, pay lists and muster rolls understate casualties in these battles as many wounded men continued to be listed as "effectives" and others returned to active duty before the next roster was compiled in September. Most seriously wounded men were described as "sick," and officers were recorded as on "King's leave."

2. "Return of Officers, Noncommissioned Officers and Privates killed and wounded of His Majesty's Troops at the Attack of the Redoubts and Entrenchments on the Heights of Charlestown, June 17, 1775," WO1/2/241–42; Muster Rolls of the 4th Foot, Jan. 15, 1775, Sept. 14, 1775; WO12/2194, PRO.

For the use of the "ten eldest compys" of grenadiers and light infantry, that is, the ten regiments with the lowest numbers on the army list, see Barker, *British in Boston,* 60. The attrition of these units may be observed in Muster Rolls of W012/ 2194, 2289, 2750, 3960, 5171, 5561, 5871, 6240, 6786, PRO, Kew; also "Present State of His Majesty's Forces at Boston," July 21, 1775, Haldimand Papers, add. ms 21687, BL.

3. Harold Murdock, *The Nineteenth of April, 1775* (Boston, 1925), 30, 35–38; Ezra Stiles, *Literary Diary,* I, 604; Samuel Adams Drake, *Old Landmarks and Historic Personages of Boston* (1872; rev. ed., 1906, rpt. Rutland, Vt., 1971), 217.

4. General Sir Martin Hunter, *Journal* (Edinburgh, 1894), 15; Frothingham, *Siege of Boston,* 310; French, *First Year of the American Revolution,* 670; *A List of the Officers of His Majesty's Marine Forces . . .* (London, 1777), PRO; ADM 192/2; *Army List* (London, 1775), 180; (1781), 292; (1782), 292; (1783), appendix, 15; (1784), appendix, 12; (1785), 361.

5. Mackenzie, *Diary,* I, 49; French, *First Year of the American Revolution,* 660; Ketchum, *Bunker Hill,* 217.

6. General Sir Martin Hunter, *Journal* (Edinburgh, 1894).

7. Marjorie Hubbell Gibson, *H.M.S. Somerset, 1746–1778; The Life and Times of an Eighteenth Century Man-o-War and Her Impact on North America* (Cotuit, Mass., 1992).

8. Hudson, *Lexington,* 94–96.

9. Wheeler, *Concord,* 135.

10. *Ibid.,* 113; Hudson, *Lexington,* 142–43.

11. Wheeler, *Concord.* 115.

12. *Ibid.,* 228.

13. Robert Newman Sheets, *Robert Newman; His Life and Letters in Celebration of the Bicentennial of His Showing of Two Lanterns in Christ Church, Boston, April 18, 1775* (Denver: Newman Family Society, 1975), 13.

14. Church's intercepted letter is in the George Washington Papers, LC.

15. Ulysses P. Hedrick, *Cyclopedia of Hardy Fruits* (New York, 1922), 17.

16. *Memoirs of the Social Circle in Concord,* second series, 78.

17. Samuel Flagg Bemis, *John Quincy Adams and the Foundations of American Foreign Policy* (New York, 1965), 6.

18. *Annual Register* (1775), 157; French, *First Year of the American Revolution*, 324.

19. Revere to Lamb, April 5, 1777, Goss, *Revere*, I, 279–81.

20. The Penobscot Expedition was the low point of his career. The American commanders were unable to act decisively, and unwilling to withdraw. Revere urged repeatedly that the mission be abandoned. Overruled, he decided to take his men home, and was accused of insubordination and cowardice. A court-martial (convened at his request) cleared his name in 1782. Many of the of relevant documents are reprinted in C. B. Kevitt, *General Solomon Lovell and the Penobscot Expedition* (Weymouth, Mass., 1976), and Goss, *Revere*, II, 317–97.

21. Skerry, "The Revolutionary Revere," 58.

22. Revere to Dr. Lettsom, Dec. 3, 1791, RFP, MHS.

23. Forbes, *Revere*, 388.

24. Renee L. Ernay, "The Revere Furnace, 1787–1800," unpublished M.A. thesis, University of Delaware, 1989.

25. Paul Revere to Thomas Ramsden, Aug. 4, 1804, RFP, MHS.

26. Hurd, *Middlesex County*, II, 283.

27. Wayland's bell appears in Edward and Evelyn Stickney, *The Bells of Paul Revere* (Bedford, 1976), 18. There can be no doubt about its authenticity. The original bill and receipt, dated Oct. 24, 1814, is in the Wayland Historical Society: "bo't of Paul Revere and Son a Church Bell $509.50; credit by the old bell, $43.75; $465.75 received payment Paul Revere and son." I owe this document to the kindness of Elizabeth Garside Goeselt, curator of the Wayland Historical Society.


## Historiography

1. (New York) *Weekly Gazette and Mercury*, May 1775.

2. Ann Hulton to Mrs. Adam Lightbody, n.d. [April 1775]; Harold Murdock *et al.* (eds.), *Letters of a Loyalist Lady* (Cambridge, Mass., 1927), 77. The letter is undated, but from internal evidence ("the 18th inst") was written before the end of April.

3. William Gordon, "An Account of the Commencement of Hostilities Between Great Britain and America, in the Province of Massachusetts-Bay. By the Reverend Mr. William Gordon of Roxbury, in a letter to a Gentleman in England, dated May 17, 1775." This essay was published in the (Philadelphia) *Pennsylvania Gazette*, June 1775; and reprinted in *AA4*, II, 626–31. Gordon later published *The History of the Rise, Progress, and Establishment of the Independence of the United States of America*, 4 vols. (London, 1788). The first American edition of this work was issued in three volumes at New York in 1789. Gordon mentioned Revere by name, and referred specifically to having interviewed him.

4. Joshua B. Fowle to Samuel H. Newman, July 28, 1875, in Wheildon, *Paul Revere's Signal Lanterns*, 34–35.

5. The second draft of the deposition was reproduced in facsimile by E. H. Goss in his *The Life of Colonel Paul Revere*, 2 vols. (Boston, 1891), I, 214–20. Members of the Revere family donated the second draft to the Massachusetts Historical Society in 1956, and added the rough draft in 1960. They were published with Revere's letter to Belknap by the MHS in Edmund S. Morgan (ed.), *Paul Revere's Three Accounts of His Famous Ride* (Boston, 1961).

6. Ralph Earl, "Four Different Views of the Battle of Lexington, Concord, etc.," engraved by Amos Doolittle (New Haven, 1775), and advertised for sale in the *Connecticut Journal*, Dec. 13, 1775. A similar interpretation appears in another drawing for John W. Barber's *History of New Haven*. This pattern was first observed by Harold Murdock in *The Nineteenth of April, 1775* (Boston, 1925), 3–9; at least one early illustration does not fit this frame, but in general Murdock's interpretation appears correct. A facsimile edition,

"Famous Doolittle Prints of Concord and Lexington, April 19, 1775" (Concord, Minute Man Printing Corporation, n.d.), is available at Minute Man National Historical Park, Concord.

7. Pamela Brown Fiske, narrative, in Kehoe, "We Were There!" I, 270. Pamela Fiske's grandfather, Francis Brown, mustered on the morning of April 19, fought through the day, and was severely wounded during the afternoon in the granite field at the Lincoln line by a British musket ball that entered his cheek and lodged in the back of his neck. The bullet was removed in 1776 and he succeeded Parker as captain of the Lexington militia.

Pamela Fiske, at the age of ninety-four, recalled that as a little girl she was taught to trace the history of the Revolution with her fingertip, on the wound scars that her grandfather wore as proudly as a decoration. "I used to put my finger on these scars as he told me just how the ball went," she remembered, *ca.* 1894. The memory is so vivid, and told with such sincerity, that one thinks it must have been true. I was very sorry to discover in the genealogical records that Francis Brown died April 21, 1800, and Pamela was born on July 29 of the same year—a caution to uncritical users of grandfathers' tales. Cf. Hudson, *Lexington,* genealogical appendix, 29.

8. Wheildon, *History of Paul Revere's Signal Lanterns.*

9. A manuscript copy of the poem is in the Collections of the Massachusetts Historical Society. Much poetry was inspired by the ride. John Pierpont composed a six-page epic for the dedication of Acton's revolutionary monument:

> . . . the foremost Paul Revere
> At Warren's bidding, has the gauntlet run,
> Unscathed, and dashing into Lexington,
> While midnight wraps him in her mantle dark
> Halts at the house of Reverent Mr. Clark.

10. *Boston Intelligencer and Weekly Gazette,* May 10, 1818.

11. Elias Phinney, *History of the Battle at Lexington* (Boston, 1825, rpt. 1875); Ezra Ripley, *History of the Fight at Concord* (Concord, 1827; 2nd ed., 1832); Josiah Adams, *Acton Centennial Address* (Boston, 1835).

12. Murdock, *The Nineteenth of April, 1775,* 4–13.

13. Paul Revere, Draft Deposition, *ca.* April 24, 1775, Morgan (ed.), *Paul Revere's Three Accounts,* [21].

14. Depositions of Elijah Sanderson, Dec. 17, 1824; and William Munroe, March 7, 1825, in Phinney, *History of the Battle at Lexington,* 31–35.

15. Richard Frothingham, Jr., *History of the Siege of Boston, and of the Battles of Lexington, Concord, and Bunker Hill; also, an Account of the Bunker Hill Monument* (Boston, 1849), 23, 58, 60, 366.

16. [J. T. Buckingham,], "Paul Revere," *New England Magazine* 3 (1832): 304–14.

17. *Ibid.,* 307–14; Alden Bradford, *Biographical Sketches of Distinguished Men in New England* (Boston, 1842), 349–51; Daniel Webster, Speech at Pittsburgh, July 8, 1833, quoted in Jayne Triber, "The Midnight Ride of Paul Revere: From History to Folklore" (Boston: Paul Revere Memorial Association, n.d.), 3.

18. Frederic W. Cook, *Historical Data Relating to Counties, Cities and Towns in Massachusetts* (Boston, 1948).

19. Longfellow, Journals, April 5, 1860. George Bancroft's accurate account appears in *History of the United States from the Discovery of the American Continent,* VII (Boston, 1858), 288–96.

20. Hudson, *Lexington,* 171.

21. Howard G. Laskey, "The Ride," in Goss, *Revere,* I, 197. The caption read, "Shouting at every house he reaches, startling the affrighted inmates from their slumbers with his wild halloo, this strange herald of danger thunders on."

22. Maury Botton, "Thomas Edison's 'Midnight Ride of Paul Revere'—A Silent Film,"

*Revere House Gazette* 25 (1991): 1–7; a copy of the film is owned by the Paul Revere Memorial Association. I am grateful to Patrick Leehey for the loan of it.

23. The original model is reproduced in Harriet E. O'Brien, *Paul Revere's Own Story* (Boston, 1929), facsimile 1; see also Wayne Craven, "Cyrus Edwin Dallin," in *Dictionary of American Biography*, ed. Allen Johnson, 20 vols. (New York, 1927–81), supplement III, 210–11; *New York Times*, Nov. 15, 1944; Kammen, *Mystic Chords of Memory*, 504; John C. Ewers, "Cyrus E. Dallin: Master Sculptor of the Plains Indian," *Montana* 18 (1968): 35–38.

24. E. T. Paull, "Paul Revere's Ride; March-Two Step" (New York: E.T. Paull Music Company, 1905); also "Paul Revere; A Musical Comedy in Three Acts. Book, Lyrics and Music by May Hewes Dodge and John Wilson Dodge," Piano-Vocal Score (Cincinnati, 1919), NYPL.

25. Another surviving 17th-century structure within the present limits of Boston is the Blake House, but this was originally part of the town of Dorchester. No other 17th-century building survives today in Boston, New York, Philadelphia, or Baltimore.

26. Goss, *Life of Colonel Paul Revere*, II, 622.

27. *Ibid.*

28. Murdock, *The Nineteenth of April 1775*, 84, 133.

29. French, *Day of Concord and Lexington*, 52, 77–80.

30. Frank Warren Coburn, *The Battle of April 19, 1775, in Lexington, Concord, Lincoln, Arlington, Cambridge, Somerville, and Charlestown, Massachusetts* (Lexington, 1912), vii.

31. Zechariah Chafee, "Freedom of Speech in Wartime," *Harvard Law Review* 32 (1918–19): 939–40; I owe this reference to the kindness of Morton Keller.

32. In the same letter, Charles Francis Adams, Jr., raged against a recent account that Thomas Jefferson had ridden to his inauguration on horseback instead of by carriage, and in an egalitarian gesture had tied his horse to a fence outside the Capitol. Michael Kammen observes that "Adams preferred truth to fairy tales, especially if the tales were intended to exemplify an egalitarian ethos. Truth is particularly preferable to fiction when the fiction sustains a value system that one finds unwarranted." Kammen, *Mystic Chords of Memory*, 84.

33. "What's in a Name?" *Century Illustrated Monthly Magazine* 51 (Feb. 1896): 36; Dixon Wecter, *The Hero in America* (New York, 1941).

34. A good example of this dated humor is Robert Benchley, "Paul Revere's Ride: How a Modest Go-Getter Did His Bit for the Juno Acid Bath Corporation," *Inside Robert Benchley* (New York, 1942), 195–201.

35. Richard Shenkman, *"I Love Paul Revere, Whether He Rode or Not"* (New York, 1991), vii.

36. Jayne Triber, "Paul Revere's Ride: From History to Folklore," ms., PRMA.

37. A leading critic of American marksmanship was Allen French, *The Day of Lexington and Concord*, 27–36, 255–58, who reckoned from the arithmetic of British casualties and New England muster rolls that "not one American in ten made his mark upon the enemy" (p. 258). This statement was seized upon by debunkers in the 1930s and 1970s as evidence that the heroes of the American Revolution were military incompetents who "could not shoot straight" (e.g., Richard Shenkman, *Legends, Lies, and Cherished Myths of American History*, [N.Y., 1988], 79–80). Echoes of this interpretation continued in the academic scholarship of the Vietnam generation.

It is mistaken—a compounding of many errors. British casualty reports included only deaths and very serious wounds. Even so, the ratio of hits to rounds fired was higher on the American than the British side, and much higher than in other wars. Fighting with 18th-century weapons, and being deliberately held at long range by their commanders, the fire of the New England militia was in fact remarkably accurate. The strongest evidence comes from Regular British officers who were on the receiving end. Carter, Percy, Lister, Barker, and Mackenzie testified that the American fire was in Carter's words "heavy and well-directed."

38. "There is little tactical benefit from a study of these operations," Fred M. Green, "Lexington and Concord," *Infantry Journal*, April–May, 1935, pp. 109–16.

39. Nathan Schachner, "Do School-Books Tell the Truth? *American Mercury,* Dec. 1938, p. 416.

40. Forbes, *Revere,* 475n.

41. Kammen, *Mystic Chords of Memory,* 504; quoting Forbes to R. N. Lincott, July 24, 1940, Forbes Papers, Houghton Library, Harvard University.

42. Forbes, *Revere,* 23, 319.

43. Donald M. Nielsen, "The Revere Family," *NEHGR* 145 (1991): 291.

44. Forbes, *Revere,* 475; for complaints of "literary license," see Neilsen, "The Revere Family," 291.

45. Robert Lawson, *Mr. Revere and I* (Boston, 1953); Jean Fritz, *And What Then Happened, Paul Revere* (New York, 1973).

46. *Boston Herald,* April 18, 1950.

47. Galvin, *Minute Men.*

48. Richard Bissell, *New Light on 1776 and All That* (Boston, 1975), 34–40.

49. Quoted in Triber, "The Midnight Ride," [7].

50. *Ibid.,* [6–7].

51. Richard Shenkman, *Legends, Lies and Cherished Myths of American History* (New York, 1989), 23–24, 82, 154.

52. Susan Wilson, "North Bridge: Span of History," *Boston Globe,* April 15, 1993.

53. Tim O'Brien, "Ambush!" *Boston Magazine,* April 1993, pp. 62–67, 101–06.

54. Samuel Eliot Morison and Henry Steele Commager, *The Growth of the American Republic,* 2 vols. (New York, 1930).

55. Bernard Bailyn *et al., The Great Republic: A History of the American People* (1977), 277; John M. Blum *et al., The National Experience* (New York, 1962); Bernard Weisburger, "Paul Revere, the Man, the Myth, and the Midnight Ride," *American Heritage* 28 (1977): 25–37.

56. Virginus Dabney, *The Patriots* (1976), v, vi.

57. Mary Beth Norton *et al., A People and a Nation; A History of the United States.* 2 vols. (Boston, 1986), I, 136.

58. (London) *Times,* Feb. 25, 1993.

59. A history appears in *Handbook of the Paul Revere Memorial Association* (Boston, 1950); and its current activities are summarized in, Nina Zannieri, director, *Paul Revere Memorial Association, Annual Report, 1991/1992* (Boston, 1992).

## ❧ Bibliography

1. Louis Shores, *Origins of the American College Library 1638–1800* (Nashville, 1934), 215; quoted in Frederick Rudolph, *The American College & University: A History* (Athens, Ga., 1990), 287.

# ACKNOWLEDGMENTS

This project began in the Spring of 1992, with an invitation from Len Tucker to present a paper to the Massachusetts Historical Society. I am grateful to the members and staff of the Society for their encouragement and support.

In the following year that paper grew into this book. A critical stage in its conceptual development came in an unexpected place during the summer of 1992, when James McPherson and I were refighting the western campaigns of the Civil War for a floating alumni college on board the steamboat *Delta Queen*. We had occasion to talk about our mutual interest in contingency and choice in history. One night, while making an advance visit to the battlefields, we made a mistaken choice of our own, and tried to get too close to the site of Fort Henry (now underwater). Our car sank deep into the mud of the Tennessee River. As we walked many miles through a dark night while bolts of lightning flashed on the horizon, the idea of contingency struck home with special force! I have a major debt to Jim for his pathbreaking work on this problem.

Another large debt is due to Bertram Wyatt-Brown, who read a rough draft and offered many helpful suggestions for the narrative construction of the work. As always I have learned much from his depth of insight into historical problems.

In Boston, many scholars shared their expertise on various aspects of the midnight ride. A large debt is due to Nina Zannieri, director of the Paul Revere Memorial Association, and to Patrick Leehey, head of research at Paul Revere House. Both Nina and Pat found time in their busy schedules to read the manuscript in several drafts. They gave it the most careful, rigorous, and constructive criticism I have ever received on any project. In subsequent conversations they and Edith Steblecki and other members of the staff at the Paul Revere House helped on many questions of substance, detail, bibliography, and illustrations.

On the fighting at Lexington and Concord, I have learned much from Douglas Sabin, chief historian at Minute Man National Historic Park, the leading authority on the battle. Doug generously shared his own unpublished research, walked the Battle Road with me, and closely criticized several drafts of this manuscript. Three historians of Lexington and Concord also read the manuscript: Robert Gross of the College of William and Mary, Joseph Fairbanks of Whittier College, and David Wood at the Concord Museum. All made helpful suggestions, and shared unpublished materials. Other scholars helped with specific problems in the course of the research: Marjorie Hubbell Gibson and Nathaniel Champlin on HMS *Somerset*, and Thomas Boaz on Major Pitcairn and the Royal Marines, Thomas Smith on Loammi Baldwin, the Reverend Robert W. Golledge of Old North Church, and S. Lawrence Whipple on Lexington Common. Colonel Vincent Kehoe sent the results of his latest research on the 10th Foot.

At the American Antiquarian Society, Georgia Barnhill was as always a model of high efficiency. With her unrivaled expertise on early American imprints, she also helped to locate materials at other institutions. Also helpful in other ways were Judith McAllister Curtis at the Adams National Historic Site, Braintree; Christine MacKenzie and Diane Broadley at Anderson Photo, Inc.; Meredith McCulloch at the Bedford Public Library, Philip Bergen of the Bostonian Society, Laura Monti at Boston Public Library, the staff at the British Library and the British Public Record Office, Susan Danforth of the John Carter Brown Library, Charles Sullivan at the Cambridge Historical Commission, John Dann and Arlene Shy at the William L. Clements Library, Mrs. William H. Moss and Joyce Woodman at the Concord Free Public Library, Carol Haines at the Concord Museum, Robert Hanson at the Dedham Historical Society, Nancy Heywood and William La Moy at the Essex Institute, Mark Burnette at the Evanston Historical Society, Ed Olsen and Susan Cifaldi of the Fifers and Drummers Museum, Sanna Deutsch at the Honolulu Academy of Arts, Sarah Brophey and Anne Ireland at Lexington Historical Society, Jane Eastman at the Lexington Library, Bernice H. Fallick, Town Clerk of Lexington, Louis Plummer of Photoassist, Inc.

who helped with the Library of Congress, Bobbie Robinson and Frank Sorrentino at Massachusetts Archives, Peter Drummey, Virginia Smith, Catherine Craven and Brenda Lawson at Massachusetts Historical Society, Susan Greendyke Lachever of the Massachusetts Art Commission, Eileen Sullivan at Metropolitan Museum of Art, Karen Otis of Boston's Museum of Fine Arts, John Hamilton and Maureen Harper at the Museum of Our National Heritage, Lexington, Claire Wright and Emma Armstrong at the British National Army Museum, Philip Jago at the National Gallery of Victoria in Melbourne, Liza Verity at the National Maritime Center, George Price of the National Park Service, Ralph Crandall and Linda Skinner at the New England Historic and Genealogical Society; Jim Campbell and Vicki Chirco at the New Haven Colony Historical Society, Roberta Waddell at the New York Public Library, Roxana Adams and Peggy Pritchard at the Provincetown Museum, Jane Porter of the Portsmouth Athenaeum; Lorna Condon at the Society for Preservation of New England Antiquities, Nancy Petersen at the Timken Museum of Art, Robert Panzer of VAGA, Inc., Elizabeth Garside Goeselt of the Wayland Historical Society, W. N. Stelzer of Winterthur Museum, Bill Wallace at Worcester Historical Museum, Suzanne Warner at the Yale University Art Gallery, and Timothy Goodhue at Yale Center for British Art.

My excellent Brandeis colleagues in American history helped in various ways. Morton Keller read and criticized the manuscript. Sam Bass Warner called my attention to materials I would otherwise have missed. Jacqueline Jones tested several chapters on two young critics in her household, and gave the project her warm encouragement. James Kloppenberg had a helpful thought on an interpretative problem. Ina Malaguti and Judy Brown helped with many logistical problems, as did the staff of the Brandeis Library System.

Through the years, three graduate students completed independent research papers on Paul Revere and taught their teacher in the process: Ruth Friedman on Paul Revere's business career, Carol Ely on the community of the North End, and Ellen Shea on Paul Revere's other rides. Five Brandeis undergraduates also worked as paid research assistants on this project: Elizabeth Arnold, Keri Fisher, Michael Kalin, David Lawrence, and Jeremy Stern.

At the Oxford University Press, my editor and friend Sheldon Meyer read the manuscript and made many substantive suggestions for its improvement. Leona Capeless gave the book the benefit of her peerless copyediting, and Karen Wolny guided the book through the labyrinth of the Oxford University Press, refining it in many ways.

Andrew Mudryk did the maps with high skill and creativity. Once again it was a great pleasure to work with him, and to share his love of cartography as an art-form. Michael Farny of the Lincoln Guide Service loaned us a rare topographical survey of the Battle Road. Brian Donahue generously supplied materials from his own research on landholdings along the battle road. I am also endebted to Joyce Malcolm for her published studies of the land use in Concord, Lincoln, and Lexington.

Special mention is due to my riding teachers Mary Cressy and Lee Cressy, and to a spirited New England saddle horse named Quentin, who through the years taught the author many hard lessons on equestrian aspects of the midnight ride. Laura Goeselt also helped with questions of horsemanship, and reprogrammed a recalcitrant computer at a critical moment.

As always, my family pitched in. My wife Judith helped in many ways. John Henry Fischer read an early draft and gave me the benefit of his wise counsel. Norma Fischer contributed helpful advice and support. Miles Pennington Fischer criticized the chapters on the battle from the perspective of his own military service. Kate Fischer, Anne Fischer, Frederick Turner, John Anderson Fischer and William Pennington Fischer had words of encouragement in the early stages of the project. Specially helpful in this project was my daughter Susanna Fischer. Her candid and rigorous criticism of the manuscript improved it in many ways, and she found time in her busy career to help track down British materials. The book is dedicated to Susie, with much love.

*Wayland, Massachusetts*                                                          D. H. F.
*21 December 1993*

# INDEX

19, 1775, they stood against Thomas Gage's Regular Infantry in fixed positions and close formations at least six times. Twice the Regulars were broken. In the afternoon, the American leaders changed their tactics. Now facing a larger enemy and artillery, they forged a moving "circle of fire" around the the British force and maintained it for many hours—an extraordinary feat of combat leadership with citizen soldiers.

After the fighting was over, many of these same men, including Paul Revere and Thomas Gage, fought the second battle of Lexington and Concord. This was a contest for what their generation was the first to call popular opinion, and even more decisive than the battle itself. Yankee leaders were victorious in spreading their version of events through the colonies. George Washington, Thomas Jefferson, John Adams, and Thomas Paine all testified that the news of Lexington was, in Adams's phrase, their revolutionary Rubicon.

The true story of Paul Revere's ride is very different from the popular myth of the lone rider of the Revolution. It is also far removed from the heavy determinism of academic historiography. This is a tale of contingency, with great events hanging in the narrow balance. It is the story of free people, making hard choices. Most of all, it is about America's half-remembered heritage of collective action in the cause of freedom. When Paul Revere and his many friends alarmed the Middlesex countryside, they were carrying that message for us.

Mt. Desert Island, Maine, 1992

David Hackett Fischer was born at Baltimore in 1935, took his degrees at Princeton and Johns Hopkins, and is presently Warren Professor of History at Brandeis. He has also taught at Harvard, the University of Washington, and in 1985 was elected Harmsworth Professor of American History at Oxford, and Fellow of Queens College. He has won many awards for scholarship and teaching, and in 1991 he received the Carnegie Prize as Massachusetts Teacher of the Year. His books include the highly acclaimed *Albion's Seed* and *Growing Old in America*.